PSYCHOANALYTIC TREATMENT OF SCHIZOPHRENIC, BORDERLINE, AND CHARACTEROLOGICAL DISORDERS

PSYCHOANALYTIC TREATMENT OF SCHIZOPHRENIC, BORDERLINE, AND CHARACTEROLOGICAL DISORDERS

Second Edition
Revised and Expanded

by
L. Bryce Boyer, M.D.
and
Peter L. Giovacchini, M.D.

NEW YORK • JASON ARONSON • LONDON

ISBN: 0-87668-408-8

Library of Congress Catalog Number: 80 – 66352

Contents

Preface to the Second Edition

The treatment of patients suffering from severe emotional illness has to be the concern of all mental health professionals, because these are the patients we most commonly encounter. There are many approaches to these patients, but for the most part clinicians have placed little value on a purely psychological approach and have directed their attention to behavioral and somatic therapies. The two editions of this book emphasize another viewpoint.

THE CLASSICAL ATTITUDE

Prior to the publication of the first edition in 1967, most analysts strongly believed that psychoanalysis was a form of treatment reserved for mild to moderately neurotic patients. The suggestion that schizophrenic and borderline patients might be amenable to psychoanalytic treatment often provoked vehement objections. In fact, even raising questions about clinical areas other than that of the oedipal neuroses might jeopardize the student and cause him to be labeled a rebel or considered a person who because of personal resistances was not really interested in psychoanalysis.

In large measure these ad hominem attacks and out-of-hand rejection of possible innovations was the outcome of an overidentification with Freud. Freud believed that patients suffering from narcissistic neuroses, patients who today would be considered either schizophrenics or character disorders, could not be analyzed because they did not form transferences. Potential patients therefore had to be carefully screened to determine whether they were analyzable and properly motivated.

Analysts who still adhere to rigid classical standards of selection continue to turn away patients who come to them specifically for analysis. We have seen innumerable patients desperately seeking analysis who have consulted several analysts and who have been faced with suspicion and sometimes simple rudeness. Apparently these analysts behave as if they are conducting stress interviews to uncover the patient's true motivations. These interactions often have a paranoid tinge—that is, the analyst's provocative questions do—and as though these patients have not already had enough stress throughout their lives, the so-called therapeutic situation appears to provide more.

THE PSYCHOANALYTIC SETTING AND PRIMITIVE MENTAL STATES

The authors of this volume first met in 1962 at a meeting of the American Psychoanalytic Association and were delighted to discover that they had been developing similar ideas about the treatment of patients suffering from primitive mental states. The outcome of our friendship and innumerable discussions with a small but growing cadre of colleagues, many of them from the West Coast, was the publication of the first edition of this book in 1967.

Within the analytic framework, we have shifted our focus from a unilateral transference attachment to a neutral analyst to the intricacies of the transference-countertransference relationship. In addition, as we dealt with primitive mental states, we found that the conflict-defense model was not conceptually useful. We learned that the clinical material we encountered involved the projection of parts of the self, as well as states of primitive agitation indicating an inability to maintain the stimulus barrier and organize percepts. We have become preoccupied with different ways of looking at what we believe to be, in essence, the same data. Different viewpoints, however, can have momentous impact affecting diagnosis and attitudes regarding treatability.

In the first edition we questioned the dicta of the inapplicability of the psychoanalytic method that Freud insisted upon and that are still taught at many psychoanalytic institutes. Some analysts were receptive and enthusiastic, but others were not. In 1965, at the fall meeting of the American Psychoanalytic Association in New York, Giovacchini presented a paper on the psychoanalytic treatment of character disorders, now published as chapter 6 of this book. The paper was vigorously questioned. The discussant criticized underlying concepts, technique, and indeed even the data. What was noteworthy was the intensity of the discussion rather than its rationality or logic.

Fortunately, the ideas that were denigrated at that meeting over a decade ago have now become commonplace. Several years later, at a meeting of the Chicago Psychoanalytic Society, a presenter mentioned in passing that psychoanalysis was the treatment of choice for character disorders. On this occasion, the statement met no resistance whatsoever.

Our attitudes have changed considerably, and we have become much less rigid about the limitations of the psychoanalytic method. This means that today we are more confident and less defensive about psychoanalysis. Our attitudes are more flexible, and we no longer consider ourselves the practitioners of a method that can be used only with an exclusive group of patients. Freud provided us a beginning, but when clinical necessity dictates, we must be prepared to extend his concepts. Many of us no longer view ourselves as members of an esoteric cult, an elitist attitude that had justifiably antagonized our colleagues and infantilized our students. We are clinicians who want to treat patients by a method that aids us in realizing our ideal of fostering autonomy. This requires openness and self-examination rather than seclusion and smugness.

Thus, within our ranks, we can no longer unquestionably accept what the master has taught us. True, Freud was a genius who discovered a system of concepts and therapy which, in the history of the world, remains unparalleled. Freud has to be read over and over to be truly appreciated. Still, he would have been the first to encourage his followers to go beyond him, that is, to cause the young science to grow. The treatment of primitive mental states represents the direction of that growth.

Only through such growth and development can we maintain our professional identities as psychoanalysts and clinicians. Many analysts, sympathetic to the viewpoints of this book, *know* that some patients suffering from schizophrenia or character disorders can be treated psychoanalytically. We know this because we have conducted such treatment with effective results. This is empirical fact and can not be disputed. All that can be argued is whether we are really using the psychoanalytic method. We believe that we are, and we can integrate our technique with our psychoanalytic ego-ideal. Inasmuch as the latter is based upon our therapeutic frame of reference, we can support it by being active clinicians. This means we have to treat patients, and the patients that come to us happen to be suffering from characterological problems.

THE CONTEMPORARY CLINICAL SETTING

The analysis of some schizophrenic patients and character disorders can be a gratifying experience. Since the first edition of this book has been published, there have been many papers and books concentrating upon patients with structural defects. The discussion of the borderline patient has become an extremely popular subject. We believe this interest is the outcome of necessity. If we are to continue functioning as analysts, we have to learn as much as possible about this large group of potential patients. It is they, not the classical psychoneurotics Freud thought he was describing, who represent the majority who seek our help.

The problem, however, has been confusing. Even though we may all be examining the same elephant, like the proverbial blind men, we are simultaneously examining different aspects and presenting conflicting viewpoints. For example, what Kernberg (1975a) diagnoses as borderline is considered a character neurosis by Giovacchini (1979). Masterson (1976) places the fixation point for borderline patients at the separation-individuation phase, whereas Giovacchini locates it much earlier, at the symbiotic phase and containing presymbiotic elements.

These differences, however, are the natural outcome of explorations of new clinical areas or, at least, of different viewpoints on what are essentially the same data. We believe that we have now progressed to the point that we can begin to define our terms. We can conduct a rational discourse in which we do not have to become involved in controversy. This means that we have reached a stage of scientific development at which we can classify our data. For the moment this would take the form of nosological distinctions, the establishment of diagnostic categories. Diagnosis, however, is not necessarily related to the question of treatability.

In this book we have for the most part discarded the psychoeconomic hypothesis. The psychodynamic approach, while not abandoned, has not proven especially useful in understanding the majority of patients entering our consultation rooms. Conflicting forces and defenses were inadequate to explain the problems our patients presented. They seemed to manifest defective psychic structure, and oedipal conflicts, if at all visible, were on the distant horizon. Oedipus was replaced by Narcissus. We discovered that we were dealing with a lack of cohesion of the identity sense and the transference regression focused upon symbiotic fusion. Our perspective gradually shifted from id to ego psychology, the latter dealing specifically with defects in the self-representation and with fixation on the symbiotic phase. Without such a theoretical perspective we could not treat our patients within a psychoanalytic context.

Since the first edition of this volume, other clinicians have viewed patients from a similar perspective. Kernberg has constructed an ego-psychological frame of reference based heavily on Hartmann's concepts. Interestingly enough, he has been able to integrate within this conceptual scheme many of Melanie Klein's formulations. Kohut is another psychologist whose ideas have blossomed since our first edition. They were comprehensively expressed in *The Analysis of the Self*, which appeared in 1971.

These writers have had considerable influence in directing the attention of clinicians to areas this book has emphasized. In many ways, they have helped reorient the thinking of psychotherapists along the lines we have suggested. Still, the reader of this revised edition will note how the writers who followed us have, in many instances, echoed and paraphrased what we had formulated in 1967.

For example, the term *self-object* has been attributed to Kohut. Though it is acknowledged that many writers, beginning with Freud, had a firm grasp of the conceptual implication of the term (another expression for secondary narcissism), the term itself has been considered Kohut's and supposedly represents a significant advance in our understanding of the structural defects of patients fixated at early stages of emotional development. On page 269 of the first edition (p. 000 of this edition) we used the term *self-object* in exactly the same way as Kohut and his followers. This is not in itself important, but it is noteworthy because to know where we stand conceptually the truly innovative must be distinguished from what is already part of our theoretical edifice.

As we become more comfortable in dealing with schizophrenic and borderline patients, it is natural that we experience some confusion. The maintenance of an historical perspective will help us achieve stabilization. We believe that emphasizing the ideas presented in our first edition and then studying what followed, as either extensions or digressions, will anchor our thinking and help us in dealing with our patients. Noting the connections between past and present will perhaps provide us a glimpse of the future.

THE FUTURE

Our purpose has been to update certain sections of our initial volume. Boyer, in his revised first chapter, emphasizes the rapid and sweeping changes in our concepts about genetic and biochemical aspects of psychotic disorders. Considerable progress has been made in our understanding of the organic substrata of severe characterological disorders, but there are as yet no conclusions sufficiently definite to provide us any guidance in instituting rational and effective treatment approaches. Perhaps, as some psychopharmacologists eagerly assert, we will someday find some drug that will reconstruct malformed character.

But until that day, we need not lose our professional identities. We will continue treating patients and documenting our findings, as Boyer has done in his new chapter 5. There he illustrates how a very sick patient, one who in the past would have been summarily rejected for analytic treatment (and would be rejected today, even by some analysts congenial to our viewpoint), can be successfully treated. He is, indeed, dealing with a primitive mental state.

As we learn more about primitive psychic structure, we find ourselves once again in a quandary. Our earlier understanding, reflected in the first edition, proves inadequate when we are presented with certain types of patients. We began by thinking we understood them, but felt uneasy about our formulations. Our problem was that we kept trying to fit our data into a new but by now fairly familiar conceptual scheme. To our minds, this is the repetition of that first occurrence, in our earlier edition, when we tried to use id psychology to conceptualize data from patients suffering from ego defects.

As we learn more about psychic structure, we find that our patients are introducing us to earlier and earlier developmental phases. The first edition of this book did not contain descriptions of ego states earlier than those characterized by symbiotic fusion. It did not because we knew very little about presymbiotic elements and their contribution to psychopathology. In this second edition, chapter 9 deals with clinical issues that require knowledge of this earliest prementational stage of psychic development.

This is a new and exciting area. Recognizing the manifestations of regression to the presymbiotic stage, as well as its role in producing states of disruptive agitation, enables us to deal analytically with patients fixated in very primitive mental states. Of course, these patients also have higher psychic structures, which permit them to function in the external world and to maintain some object relationships. However, their adjustment may be minimal; in some instances they may require hospitalization. Our psychoanalytic insights will be crucial in the hospital setting if we are to create a milieu directed toward the patient's needs rather than those of the staff.

Twelve years ago we introduced a point of view which at that time was foreign to psychoanalytic thinking. Since then, many of these ideas have become accepted by a large number of psychoanalysts, who have, however, not significantly extended or elaborated them. Consequently, this book is still very much current. Furthermore, the presymbiotic phase and its developmental antecedents remain an area that has received practically no attention from modern clinicians. Just as in the first edition we presented a viewpoint that allowed psychoanalysts to understand and treat patients whose psychic orientations are more primitive than the classical psychoneuroses, we now tentatively bring into focus the therapeutic interaction with patients whose ego states are based upon presymbiotic fixations. This in our minds represents a further extension of what has been considered analytically treatable.

Our first edition was followed by an era in which certain types of psychopathology have become better understood and treated. Similarly, we think, this second edition will stimulate therapists to investigate further and to treat patients who suffer from primitive states of disruptive agitation associated with much earlier fixations than previously recognized, and therefore incomprehensible in terms of our current concepts. This is a fascinating and exciting clinical area that promises to teach us how psychic structure is acquired in treatment—an excitement that puts us in mind of that we all felt when we first discovered that emotional illness, at least in some instances, is enduringly reversible.

Prefaces to the First Edition

In 1911 and 1914, Freud presented his formulations concerning the psychopathology of the psychoses. He stated that in psychosis there was a break with reality that consisted of a total decathexis of libido from objects of the external world and their mental representations. The libido then became attached to the self. Freud conceptualized that after the psychotic person had regressed to such a narcissistic phase, he gradually recathected mental representations of external objects in a distorted manner, usually through hallucinations and/or delusions. He believed the psychotic was unsuitable for psychoanalytic therapy because of an assumed incapacity to develop transference relations. Since then, clinical observations have indicated that the development of the schizophrenic state is not precipitous in at least a significant minority of cases, and that psychotic individuals develop intense transference relationships.

Freud was aware of a continuum of disorders ranging from psychoneuroses through characterological disorders and borderline conditions to unmistakable psychoses. After 1914 his own use of psychoanalysis as a method of treatment included patients who suffered from severe characterological disorders and, in at least one instance, overt psychosis. The literature of the past thirty-five years reveals that an ever-increasing number of psychoanalysts have used analytic techniques for the treatment of a broadening range of psychopathological conditions, including schizophrenic states, and have reported satisfactory results. Yet the majority of psychoanalysts have continued to abide by Freud's interdiction against the use of psychoanalysis as a method of treatment for people who suffer from borderline and schizophrenic disorders. Their conservatism has been reflected in training programs for psychoanalytic candidates. Some institutes in the United States fail to present varying viewpoints concerning the psychopathology and treatment of the psychoses. In consequence, psychoanalysts and candidates who are interested in exploring various methods of therapy for psychotic patients have had to study alone or in extracurricular groups.

In 1964, the Program Committee for the Biannual Meeting of the West Coast Psychoanalytic Societies, the chairman of which was Dr. Sydney L. Pomer, arranged for a panel discussion entitled "Psychoanalytic Therapy of Schizophrenic Patients" and invited one member from each of the participating societies to take part, with Boyer acting as chairman and Giovacchini an invited panel member. Sufficient interest was evinced in the discussion before the meeting took place so that time allotted for the panel was extended to a full day, although the total congress lasted but a day and a half. The panel members, in addition to the contributors to this volume, were Doctors Bernard S. Brandschaft of the Los Angeles Psychoanalytic Society and Alfredo Namnum of the Asociación Psicoanalítica Mexicana. Dr. Steven Schwartz of the Southern California Psychoanalytic Society was to have contributed but was prevented because of illness. Brandschaft presented a thoughtful and most interesting account of his attempts to understand the psychopathology of the psychoses through application of Fairbairn's viewpoint and of his own experience in treating schizophrenics psychoanalytically. Namnum offered a scholarly review of the role of countertransference in the treatment of individuals who have schizophrenic disorders. Boyer presented a brief historical survey and spoke of his efforts in psychoanalyzing schizophrenics. Giovacchini spoke of the structuralizing effects of interpretation in the treatment of serious characterological disorders and borderline conditions. Hoedemaker gave the paper which is included in this volume [omitted in the new edition]. There ensued a lively discussion that included contributions from many psychoanalysts in the audience in addition to the panel members.

During the ensuing weeks, I (Boyer) received a number of requests from audience members to serve as editor of a book that would present the proceedings of the panel, requests that produced mixed reactions of pleasure and reluctance: pleasure because of the interest elicited in this approach to the understanding and treatment of these disorders and reluctance because I was involved deeply in studying and reporting the data obtained from research in another area and because a larger work than merely an editorial task might be required.

Because of the aforementioned continuum of psychopathological disorders, it seemed advisable to include in a single volume remarks pertaining to the pathology and therapy of the entire range of conditions for which psychoanalysis has been considered to be inapplicable as a treatment method. Because I had limited my research to the application of psychoanalysis to the borderline states and the schizophrenias, I asked Giovacchini to join me in editorship of the proposed volume because he had had a large experience in working with serious characterological disorders, some of whose victims belonged clinically to the borderline states. We soon decided that the panel contributions had dealt deeply with too few areas to delineate adequately the historical, theoretical, and clinical issues. At the same time, if we were to include all the panel presentations, there would be unnecessary duplication of discussion of some issues. We decided to write a book together, and, most reluctantly, to include in it only the contribution of Hoedemaker omitted in the new edition, since his particular approach to the therapy of schizophrenia emphasized elements which were not included in our own work and writings.

We are deeply indebted to Brandschaft and Namnum and

trust we have done justice to their contributions in this volume, although we have not specifically spelled out the areas in which their stimulating ideas have enriched our own thinking.

L. BRYCE BOYER, M.D.
May 1966

The recollection of my own and my colleagues' reactions shortly after beginning psychoanalytic practice brings to mind the confusion we had about the applicability of the psychoanalytic method. True, we had learned from our courses at psychoanalytic institutes, and the pedagogic value of our personal analyses could not be overestimated.

Since the limitations of psychoanalysis had been so clearly spelled out, we eagerly awaited the "analyzable" patient. How often did this type of patient present himself? And, if we were to discuss him at a postgraduate seminar, it was usually decided that his "classical" neurosis was only a superstructure for a basically psychotic core. These nosologic decisions were not rare even when control cases were presented in the classroom.

As the years went by, some of us became convinced that many patients could be treated psychoanalytically; the whole question of what is analyzable and the conceptual basis of the analytic process had to be scrutinized further. I can recall innumerable private conversations with colleagues who "confessed" that they were analyzing patients who traditionally would be considered too sick or not sufficiently motivated. Gradually some of us became bolder and voiced our opinions at workshops and seminars. Although there was often considerable opposition, it usually led to clarification, and it was gratifying that there were many common meeting grounds.

Therefore I was especially pleased to have been invited to present my views to the District Meetings of the Western Psychoanalytic Societies. It was both reassuring and exciting to know that there were analysts in other parts of the country asking similar questions and groping with identical problems.

The purpose of this book is to record systematically what has been discussed in the innumerable private conversations mentioned above. In many instances it is difficult to ascertain where a particular idea came from. So many of our opinions were impressionistic. The panel compelled us to organize our thinking and to recall the clinical data that led to our impressions. This can be a tedious task, but it has its compensations, for not only does this work clarify, but it stimulates further ideas. The stimulating effects of the panel were obvious to everyone, and, in turn, led to many more private conversations, which in time will have to be put in an orderly form.

Our book begins with Dr. Boyer's introduction and review of the literature. The latter was a prodigious task, as is evidenced by the length of his bibliography. However, even here there were gratifications, since one was able to reach some conclusions from the study of Freud's writings in particular, about why there was a reluctance to treat schizophrenia. A more extended view of object relations and a concept of libido that always includes an object, in terms of a developmental spectrum, might have made the absolute distinctions between the transference neuroses and the narcissistic neuroses superfluous.

Dr. Boyer then continues in essentially a clinical fashion and presents the results of his work with schizophrenic patients. He began treating these patients because he believed that the psychoanalytic method would be applicable. As yet there had not been much theoretical understanding of the various facets of the therapeutic process as it related to the treatment of psychotic patients. As mentioned above, the concept of transference as it occurs or does not occur in these patients was, and to a large measure still is, imperfectly understood. Most analysts were aware of countertransference elements, but how they might be utilized was not so much emphasized as their deleterious effects.

In chapter 6, I am concerned with some of the theoretical features of the therapeutic process in order to distinguish what has been referred to as classical analysis from other types of therapy usually designated as supportive. In dealing with cases suffering from severe psychopathology, not necessarily schizophrenia, I attempt to review the applicability of the psychoanalytic method from a theoretical viewpoint. This, of course, is also pragmatic. In so doing, the various concepts that we have crystallized from our focus on ego processes are helpful to our understanding of the therapeutic action of psychoanalysis. We believe that the helpful supportive aspects of therapy are intrinsic to analysis and do not require any (or, as Boyer states, only a minimum of) extra-analytic maneuvers. The mechanism of interpretation and its synthesizing features as part of the intrinsic help analysis offers are also discussed from a conceptual frame of reference.

In the next chapter this exploration is pursued further, and many of the criteria for analyzability are reviewed from an ego-psychological perspective. Many reactions that were once considered contraindications to analysis, such as the negative transference, are now reviewed in terms of their value to the therapeutic interaction.

Finally, and this is an area that has received very little attention, the psychic processes occurring within the analyst as he is analyzing are focused upon. The limitations of analysis have been stressed, but one also discovers that the analytic attitude is often unwarily abandoned. Concentrating on external realities, for example, may shift the therapeutic focus so that the spontaneous elaboration of fantasy is hindered and the unfolding of the transference is so contaminated that further analytic activity becomes impossible. The role of the analyst's primary and secondary processes is also stressed in his understanding of the patient's intrapsychic state and the communication of insight (interpretation).

Naturally, in undertaking a project where the applicability of therapeutic technique is explored from a clinical and theoretical perspective, one cannot expect universal agreement. The reader will note occasional criticism by one author of some of his colleagues' ideas. During the panel discussion the format was purposely set up so there would be discussion and criticism. Here it was felt that each discussion had a theme of its own that should be explicitly stated rather than being merely a point of departure from a critique of the previous paper. However, disagreement is to be expected, and eventually the therapist will choose the conceptual system that offers the best clinical advantages.

It is impossible to thank everyone who was instrumental in writing this book. We have received considerable support and encouragement from our colleagues around the United States. The private conversations the authors found so helpful were held mainly in our home areas, the West and Midwest, but our eastern colleagues' interest at conventions and workshops was also stimulating and reassuring. We wish especially to thank Dr. Gene Borowitz and Dr. Alfred Flarsheim for their painstaking reading of our manuscripts and their innumerable suggestions, both conceptual and editorial, which we did our best to incorporate into the text.

PETER L. GIOVACCHINI, M.D.
May 1966

CHAPTER ONE

Introduction

L. Bryce Boyer

The orientation of modern clinicians generally is that the technical procedures developed by psychoanalysts for the treatment of the transference neuroses are not applicable to the narcissistic neuroses, including the group of schizophrenias. We hope to demonstrate, on the basis of a review of clinical and theoretical data, that the psychoanalytic model, one designed for the transference neuroses, may be the psychotherapeutic method of choice for a large number of individuals whose diagnoses fall within the continuum of states that are included in the group of schizophrenias.

In this first chapter, a number of related subjects will be discussed conjointly: (1) the importance of the schizophrenias from the standpoint of social waste and personal suffering; (2) the historical development of attitudes concerning the genesis of these disorders; (3) the difficulties involved in diagnosis; and (4) an introductory statement about the psychoanalysis of the schizophrenias.

PREVALENCE OF THE SCHIZOPHRENIAS

Throughout history, perhaps the most bewildering and challenging of all the abnormal behavioral syndromes have been those that are now included in the group of schizophrenias. The social significance of such disorders is vast. Today, in the United States, schizophrenia is considered to be the most important of the major psychoses. Individuals who are diagnosed to be schizophrenic constitute 20 percent to 25 percent of first admissions to hospitals for the treatment of mental disorders. Because of the relative youth of patients when first hospitalized and the length of their hospital stay, the group makes up some 55 percent of the residual population in such institutions (Hoch and Zubin 1961).

It is well known that psychosomatic disturbances sometimes mask psychotic conditions, and it is probable that a significant minority of patients who are treated in public institutions for chronic physical and psychosomatic illnesses are afflicted with schizoid conditions.

Numerous observers have held that the incidence of psychotic illnesses increases as cultural conditions become more complex and have concluded that cultural homogeneity and intimate social contacts protect against the development of the schizophrenias (Carothers 1953, Faris and Dunham 1939). Other students note that valid epidemiological surveys have yet to be conducted among nonliterate cultures and that structured social complexity is not necessarily related to subjective complexity (Beaglehole 1940). Maltzberger (1940) believed there had been an actual increase in the incidence of psychosis in the United States, but others stress that evidence is lacking to support the thesis that there has been an increase in the incidence of psychotic disorders attendant on heightened complexity of civilization (Goldhammer and Marshall 1949). Rin, Chu, and Lin (1965) have demonstrated in one Taiwanese area that the severity of psychophysiological changes parallels certain stresses of socioenvironmental milieux and rapid culture alterations. However, schizophrenic disturbances appear to have approximately equal incidence in those areas of the world in which reliable epidemiological surveys have been conducted (Cawte and Kidson 1964). A recent international pilot study to determine the incidence of schizophrenia among diverse cultures indicates that the morbidity rate for schizophrenia in the general population of many countries is about 1 percent (Carpenter et al. 1978, WHO 1973).

Although adequate diagnostic surveys have yet to be made, clinicians estimate privately that perhaps 10 percent of the population of the United States and Western Europe suffer from schizoid states or variously labeled conditions that are characterized at times by transient schizophreniform psychotic episodes, most of which do not require hospitalization. Eisenstein (1951) found some 30 percent of his private patients, whether hospitalized or not, to suffer from borderline psychotic disorders and cited a study that stated that 50 percent of the patients evaluated at the Psychiatric Institute of New York had been diagnosed as latent schizophrenics. Segal (1965) believes that the majority of patients interviewed by psychiatrists in England should be diagnosed as borderline psychotics, but Paz, Pelento, and Olmos de Paz (1975) found far fewer Argentinian patients suffering from similar disorders. Anthropological studies suggest that schizoid personalities and/or transient psychotic episodes are typical for some groups (Bateson and Mead 1942, Fortune 1932).

DIAGNOSTIC DISCREPANCIES

It is common knowledge that a discrepancy exists between American and European psychiatrists in regard to their assessments of the prevalence of the schizophrenias, a discrepancy based upon differences in diagnostic criteria. In general, Americans rely predominantly on Bleuler's "four A's" (1911): autism, ambivalence, looseness of associations, and disturbances of affects. Europeans tend to make their diagnoses on the basis of Schneider's first rank symptoms (1939), which are regarded as secondary phenomena by those trained in the Bleulerian tradition. Freedman (1978b) judges that because of this difference in diagnostic criteria Americans are apt to overdiagnose schizophrenia while Europeans are prone to underdiagnose. In his view, it is possible to derive everything that is unique to the schizophrenias from the cognitive/affective state known as autism and from its immediate developmental successor, narcissism (see also Stierlin 1958).

Kraepelin (1883) and especially Eugen Bleuler (1911) were pessimistic about the prognosis for schizophrenics who presented certain symptoms, particularly deterioration associated with an affective response and heightened autism. It has been argued repeatedly that recovery from schizophrenic symptomatology precludes a diagnosis of schizophrenia (Leonhard 1961).

Numerous clinicians have found the current methods used in establishing diagnoses to be deficient (Hoch and Zubin 1961). They stress especially the difficulties in determining whether individual patients suffer from schizophrenic states. Partly as a result of confusions to be found in present classification standards, there has been a tendency toward diagnostic nihilism. Some psychoanalysts have suggested that use of the word *schizophrenia* be discarded and that regressive reactions be described in terms of which ego and superego functions are pathologically distorted and to what degree (see chapter 7).

The responses of military and civilian populations to the varying stress conditions produced by World Wars I and II demonstrated that many people who previously had functioned adequately underwent regressive responses that included "schizophrenic" symptoms. When the manifestations of such states responded quickly to combinations of altered environment, rest, medicine, and physical treatments such as electroplexy and insulin shock therapy, they were given nonspecific labels. Thus terms like *battle fatigue* found their way into the charts of military personnel, whereas a variety of names were ascribed to the regressive responses of civilians. We now have many diagnostic terms with poorly defined meanings: pseudoschizophrenic neurosis, pseudoneurotic schizophrenia, ambulatory schizophrenia, borderline schizophrenia, borderline states, latent psychosis, schizoid personality disorder, psychotic character. *Frequently the label depends upon the theoretical orientation of the diagnostician, and sometimes a name is applied that reflects social or economic requirements rather than the psychopathological state involved.*

Patients who have been diagnosed to be neurotic undergo transient psychotic episodes during psychoanalysis. When such states respond favorably to further analytic or nonanalytic treatment, they are sometimes called "transference psychosis." If they persist, however, it is usual for the analyst to decide he made a faulty diagnosis and to apply one or another of the labels mentioned above.

The difficulties involved in the diagnosis of mental disorders in general and the schizophrenias in particular can be summarized as follows: (1) the underlying causes of psychopathology have not been defined clearly; (2) no unanimity exists concerning the differentiation between normal and abnormal behavior (Devereux 1956); and (3) there is a continuum of psychopathological states, at one end of which lie the transference neuroses and, at the other, the narcissistic neuroses. Such areas of complexity can be separated arbitrarily for purposes of exposition. We shall deal first with the lack of agreement concerning the basic causes of psychopathology.

IDEAS ABOUT THE CAUSES OF THE SCHIZOPHRENIAS

From time immemorial, mankind has been concerned profoundly with aberrant human behavior and particularly with the manifestations of psychosis. Men have sought to understand its origins and striven to develop rational therapeutic measures. The ancients, as do members of today's nonliterate and nonindustrialized societies, ascribed abnormal conditions to a variety of agents, both natural and supernatural (Zilboorg and Henry 1941). Such causes include noxious environmental influences, hereditary taint, organic disease, demoniacal possession, and loss of mind or soul. The treatments employed to cure illnesses thought to result from natural causes have included medical and surgical procedures, purging, bleeding, cold-water shocks, and removal of supposedly offending organs. Therapy for abnormal behavior ascribed to supernatural causes has included exhortation, incantation and religious ritual, the use of medicines with allegedly magical effects, and various operative procedures, such as craniotomies, which were designed to permit the egress of evil spirits. During various periods and among widely differing cultures, capital punishment has been used, as in the killing of those psychotic people who were called witches (Zilboorg 1935).

The predominant viewpoint of nineteenth-century psychiatrists was that all disorders manifesting psychological aberrations resulted from neuropathological conditions that were the products of inherited, constitutional, and/or degenerative states. The majority of modern psychologists divide psychotic states into two large groups. In the first are those psychoses that are attributable to toxic states or conditions in which neurological abnormalities can be demonstrated. In the second, severe psychopathological disorders are thought to result from the influences of unfavorable environmental milieux that combine with hereditary or otherwise acquired organic abnormalities. The influences of nonsalutary interpersonal relations on the growing human are held to be of paramount importance in the genesis of psychoses of the second group. A minority of psychologists believe that the role of organic states is exclusively determinant. Arduous and continuous investigations have attempted to evince toxic or other organic origins for the schizophrenias. Thus far, no convincing evidence indicates such causes to be present or particularly relevant to our understanding of the psychotic process.

Genetic Factors

The issues are clouded in regard to genetic factors as well. Major problems confronting geneticists are the absence of a satisfactory classification of the group of schizophrenias, the difficulty sometimes entailed in distinguishing so-called nuclear or process schizophrenia from other types, and the uncertainty involved in demonstrating the existence of a definite trait that can be said to be present or absent in probands and their relatives. Another problem that seems as yet to be unsolved is whether the biochemical changes that may be observed in schizophrenics are causative of the affective and thinking disabilities encountered or secondary to them. Among many others, Arieti (1956) and N.Q. Brill (1978) have proposed that schizophrenia be considered as a psychosomatic disorder.

Some earlier geneticists were enthusiastic over their findings: Kallmann (1950) believed schizophrenia to be genetically specific. The data produced by dozens of population studies, such as those of Alanen (1966) and Kety and his associates (Kety et al. 1968), have been interpreted to indicate that schizophrenia and schizoid disorders are differing expressions of the same genotype (Nicol and Heston 1979). Malis (1959) concluded that an endogenous disposition has not been proved to be an essential factor in the genesis of schizophrenia, and the studies of Lidz (1973, Lidz et al. 1965) and Rosenthal (1963) and their coworkers have demonstrated environmental complexities that illustrate that genetic factors need not be predominantly causative. Today's geneticists are virtually uniform in their subscription to a "diathesis-stressor framework" for explaining the appearance of schizophrenia. Diathesis in this case means a genetic predisposition; stressor means something from the outside that makes itself felt eventually at the physiologic and biochemical level.

Theoretical models for the inheritance of schizophrenia are grouped in monogenic, polygenic, and genetic heterogeneity

(Tsuang 1978). Monogenic models generally postulate a single specific schizophrenic gene that may cause the disease to be manifested either in homozygotes only or in both homozygotes and heterozygotes. Most monogenic models posit a dominant gene with a modified effect; the modification may result from other genes at other loci, from reduced penetrance, or from intermediate effects, where schizophrenia appears in 100 percent of homozygotes but only in about 25 percent of heterozygotes. Polygenic theories include both "continuous phenotypic variation" and "quasi-continuous variation" models (Gottesman and Shields 1973). Genetic heterogeneity theories propose that schizophrenia constitutes a variety of diseases that probably have different etiologies and modes of transmission. Some geneticists state that individual cases of schizophrenia may be due to rare genes that are specific for the individual subtypes of schizophrenia but the majority believe that too much remains unknown to permit such definite statements.

Various researchers stress that biochemistry offers the most promise for explaining the possibilities of genetic transmission of schizophrenia, particularly that which studies the various components of neuronal communication (Nicol and Heston 1979). Another avenue of approach deemed to hold promise is the prospective study of individuals who are at a high risk for the development of schizophrenia (Kimling, Cornblatt, and Fleiss 1979).

Biochemical Research

Research into the biochemistry of schizophrenia has crescendoed during the past forty years, with the object of producing specific medicines for its treatment. Many investigators have been encouraged initially in their quest for a metabolite that could be counteracted or a preparation that would replace some metabolic deficiency only to be disappointed later. Representative is the work of Heath and his collaborators, who found schizophrenia to result from a deficiency in the area of amine metabolism and obtained a protein fraction called taraxein from the serum of chronic schizophrenics. They found that the administration of taraxein to nonpsychotic volunteers reproduced in them schizophrenic symptomatology. However, their methodology was criticized adversely and their results were not duplicated by other researchers (Heath et al. 1958). Manfred Bleuler (1978) has said that each year for four decades he has read of a new substance thought to be the cause of schizophrenia.

During the past decade biochemical pharmacology has led to more promising avenues of study and to the development for the first time of specific medications that alleviate to varying degrees and for differing periods in some patients symptoms that reflect both thinking and affective disorders. The study of the actions of enzymes has been particularly interesting, and there appears to be little doubt that monoamine oxidase activity is decreased in chronic schizophrenics (Wyatt, Potkin, and Murphy 1979). Today the actions of neurotransmittors at neuronic synapses receive the special attention of biochemical investigators, and the neurotransmittor dopamine holds center stage. Advances in this field have been so rapid and dramatic that only specialists can hope to keep up with them; they cannot be summarized here (see Nicol and Heston 1979 for a cogent summary and a relevant bibliography).

As was noted earlier, psychoses were ascribed to both organic and psychological causes from the earliest times. Although in recorded history the importance of emotions and interpersonal relations has been acknowledged implicitly and explicitly in the development of syndromes of aberrant human behavior, no comprehensive psychological theories were developed. Modern abnormal psychology can be said to have its origin in the eighteenth century, when Mesmer demonstrated that aberrant behavior can be intentionally induced and removed through the influence of one person on another.

His concept of animal magnetism stirred much interest, but his new technique resulted in general hostility toward himself and his method.

In the middle of the nineteenth century, mesmerism was reintroduced under the term *hypnosis,* and its effects were studied especially by Charcot, Bernheim, and Janet. However, principally because of the limited scope of the theoretical originality of those investigators, their influence on the development of psychology has declined steadily. As will be discussed in chapter 2, Freud's first interest in purely psychological explanations of behavior probably stemmed from his contacts with hypnotists. As is commonly known, no other person has influenced the development of psychology so profoundly as Freud, and psychological theories concerning the genesis of schizophrenia probably stem more from his contributions than from those of any other investigator. Although Freud concluded eventually that the theory of behavior is best understandable in terms of psychology, he never gave up the belief that the link between psychoanalysis and physico-chemico-biological processes would be found ultimately. Nevertheless, Freud's studies were extended beyond his intentions by a group of investigators who eventually disregarded the biological elements of human behavior (see chapter 3). The nineteenth-century viewpoint that the schizophrenias were attributable to genetic, constitutional, and/or degenerative factors was followed in the twentieth century by the antithetical viewpoint that they were the product solely of faulty socialization processes. Today the argument concerning the relative importance of organismal and behavioral development is considered essentially irrelevant by most observers.

It was stated earlier that one of the major areas of difficulty in establishing diagnoses was that no unanimity exists concerning the differentiation between normal and abnormal behavior. Let us now consider this problem.

NORMAL VERSUS ABNORMAL BEHAVIOR

The approaches to defining normal and abnormal behavior and thinking range between polar opposites. Cultural relativists define normality strictly within the context of cultural functionalism, a position that states that conformation with the average expectable behavior of the group is judged as normal (Ackerknecht 1943). The following data illustrate some difficulties inherent in this viewpoint.

Among the Balinese, the tendency of the average person to be withdrawn and to undergo trancelike states is well known (Bateson and Mead 1942, Belo 1960). Presumably due to Balinese social structure and socialization processes, the typical culture member has a personality pattern that could be considered to fit within the group of schizophrenias in other cultures, but the Balinese are fully functioning members of their society.

The Apache of the Mescalero Indian Reservation who would be considered to be most representative of his group by his culture mates has personality traits that, viewed from the standpoint of Western psychiatry, warrant the diagnosis of character disorder with attributes of the hysterical personality and the impulse neuroses (Boyer 1964b). Psychotic manifestations of these Apaches almost always portray schizophrenic characteristics. According to the cultural relativists, the typical Apache would be considered normal.

At the opposite pole is the orientation of those adherents of Freudian thinking who consider mental health and illness from the standpoint of the structural theory. Mental health is defined as mature personality development and depends on the development of ego functions, of an internalized consistent superego, and of differentiation of ego from id.

The following clinical example illustrates exquisitely the difference between the two viewpoints. For some twenty-two years (more than two of which were spent in actual fieldwork, including almost fifteen continuous months), I have cooperated with anthropologists and psychologists in a study of the interactions among social structure, socialization patterns, and personality organization of the Apaches of the Mescalero Indian Reservation in south central New Mexico (Boyer 1964a, 1979). Initially, my principal research method was to conduct investigative interviews in a psychoanalytically oriented psychotherapeutic situation, almost limiting his activities to making interpretations of transferential reactions and of resistance. It was learned that culturally determined fears and phobias are universal among these Indians. An astute Chiricahua man suffered from nightmares and phobias and requested treatment. During some 165 interviews, interpretations related to dependency and unresolved oedipal problems led to his being freed of his presenting symptoms. Thereafter, he was unafraid of ghosts, witches, the dead, and various cultural bogies. Viewed from the standpoint of the cultural relativists, he had become abnormal, although he had become healthier from the viewpoint of those who follow the psychoanalytic orientation.

Whether an individual administrator or clinician subscribes to the orientation of the cultural relativists or that of the followers of Freud may be of great importance to his decision regarding the diagnosis and care of a suffering person. However, when it comes to the practical disposition of a single case, the theoretical stand taken by the administrator or clinician may have little practical relevance. Every major society contains a number of differing although usually overlapping cultural groups, most of which include members of varying ages. In the United States there is a multiplicity of ethnic and religious subcultures, each of which has, in addition to elements that share attributes with the general society, individual patterns with regard to social structure and socialization. The characteristics of behavior and the patternings of mental illness within cultural groups are well known. Additionally, the economic group from which the person derives influences heavily his *Weltanschauung* and the nature of his emotional and/or mental disorders (Hollingshead and Redlich 1958). Furthermore, varying culture groups have instituted differing methods for handling their disturbed members. Montagu (1961, p. 19) wrote, "In some cultures mental illness is institutionalized, by which is not meant that the individual is put into an institution as a sick man, but rather that he and his behavior are incorporated into the society as a normal part of it."

The Apache culture, now a subculture of the major society of the United States, is characteristic. The typical member, as has been noted, is disturbed, but he functions within the framework of his group's expectations. The individual Apache whose behavior is sufficiently deviant from the norm of the group in a manner that disturbs others is treated, at least initially, by a shaman, whose main purpose is to remove transiently the individual symptoms that have distressed the suffering person or other culture members. To the Apache, further treatment of an "insight" nature is thought to be irrational. Eaton and Weill (1953) have demonstrated that the Hutterites have relatively few schizophrenics and many manic-depressives. Depression among them appears to be an intensification of a culturally supported normative trend. The Hutterites internalize their problems and, under stress, are more apt to be antiself than antisocial. The individual submits to community expectations of personal guilt and pacifism. The Hutterites provide within their social framework functional roles for their mentally ill and look askance at treatment from outsiders. Persons from low economic groups generally view insight therapy as nonhelpful. The attitude of the suffering individual and his relatives from such cultural and economic groups is that of the cultural relativists. Whatever the viewpoint of the administrator or clinician, people from such subcultures and economic strata would usually be loathe to undertake prolonged treatment, even were it available.

The age of the suffering person also plays an important part in influencing diagnosis and recommended therapy. Treatment is seldom sought among some groups for children and adolescents whom most psychiatrists would judge to be severely ill but whose behavior does not unduly disturb their parents or others. The same can be said for deviant behavior associated with stress states, such as childbirth and terminal illness.

FURTHER DIAGNOSTIC COMPLEXITIES: PSYCHOANALYTIC IDEAS

As stated previously, the third major difficulty involved in establishing a diagnosis of schizophrenia exists because there is a continuum of psychopathological states lying between the transference and the narcissistic neuroses. Freud conceptualized the psyche as an organ of the body and used the word *neurosis* to indicate a disorder of the psyche, although the use of the word *psychosis* would appear to have been more consistent. He subdivided neuroses into: (1) transference neuroses, by which he meant those in which there is a capacity to transfer feelings or affects to another person; transference neurosis is an alternate phrase for psychoneurosis, and such a state constitutes a psychopathological syndrome, characterized in the main by special combinations of anxiety, compulsions, conversion symptoms, obsessions, and phobias; (2) narcissistic neuroses, in which libido is bound to the self and is not subject to "natural displacement" to another person. The "psychogenic psychoses" are narcissistic neuroses.

Some clinicians, particularly certain neo-Freudian psychoanalysts and their enthusiastic cross-disciplinary followers, have included all of the schizophrenias among the psychogenic psychoses. Others divide the schizophrenias on the basis of their usual clinical courses into two major categories: (1) those that prove refractory to treatment and have a progressive, chronically deteriorating course are named process or nuclear schizophrenia; in general, this group is thought to be of predominantly organic origin; (2) those that lose their overt manifestations with or without treatment, although symptoms may recur episodically, are called psychogenic schizophrenia. Those who so divide the schizophrenias have considerable difficulty in classifying certain chronic, barely progressive or nonprogressive schizoid states and severe, recurrent conditions from which patients apparently recover their prepsychotic personalities. Implicit in the earlier discussion is the modern consensus that there may be no exclusively psychogenic psychoses but instead only psychopathological disorders in which the psychological causes are probably more important than contributory organic tendencies.

Psychoanalysts have long been aware of the difficulty in distinguishing the psychoneuroses from the schizophrenias. Freud's ideas and those of his followers will be outlined in the second and third chapters. Concerning Freud, suffice it to note here that although he considered the use of the classical technique for the treatment of the schizophrenias to be contraindicated, he used it in the treatment of a number of patients who have been rediagnosed as schizophrenic by several later investigators. The literature contains fragments of case histories that reveal that psychoanalysts have unwittingly undertaken the analyses of individuals whom they have diagnosed as neurotic but subsequently have discovered schizophrenic symptomatology; some such analyses were continued with or without technical modifications and reached apparently successful conclusions.

The point of view of psychoanalysts has been that psychoneuroses are products of regressive operations that defend individuals from anxieties stemming from unresolved oedipal conflicts. The hysterias have been considered to exemplify most graphically this hypothesis, and treatment was directed in the past specifically toward the analysis of neurotic symptoms in terms of genital sexual components. Freud (1909b) considered the hysterical attack to be the equivalent of coitus. However, apparently accurate interpretations of the sexual components of hysterical symptoms unmasked intense unresolved oral conflicts (Marmor 1953), and psychotic regression sometimes took place during the analysis of a "classical" hysteric. Some few therapists continued to use the standard technique and learned that, subsequent to the analysis of the psychotic episode, reexamination of the oedipal conflicts led to cure. Today analysts are more reluctant to make a diagnosis of hysteria than was formerly true, having become more acutely aware of the continuum between the hysterias and the schizophrenias.

The 24th International Psycho-Analytical Congress in 1965 was devoted to a reevaluation of the obsessional neurosis. With few exceptions, each presentation that depicted some phase of the analysis of a diagnosed obsessional patient was followed by a discussion of the intermixture of neurotic and schizoid components combined in his psychopathology. Not infrequently a debate ensued concerning whether the patient should be called neurotic or psychotic. The same problem is found in making a clear diagnosis of patients who in past years would have been labeled unhesitatingly psychoneurotic of any of the usual types.

Some analysts have found that the transference relationships of borderline and psychotic patients are different in a specific way from those of neurotics. The borderline and psychotic patients are apt to develop what appear to be intense triadic, oedipal transference neuroses soon after entering into psychoanalysis. However, interpretation of the oedipal conflicts as though they constituted the patient's main problem does not lead to the resolution of the patient's illness as one would expect to take place in the treatment of a psychoneurotic (Boyer 1966, Ornstein and Ornstein 1975, Paz et al. 1975, H.A. Rosenfeld 1966, Volkan 1979). Instead, the patient may develop a frightening, florid erotic transference relationship, which leads either to his stopping treatment or to a serious therapeutic impasse of a less dramatic nature. To the contrary, if the oedipal material is viewed by the therapist as being used in the service of defense against the analysis of internalized, fragmented diadic relationships and its use is so interpreted to the patient, the analysis may proceed fairly smoothly. Following the analysis of such internalized preoedipal relationships and concurrent psychological maturation of the patient, his analysis may proceed like that of the neurotic, in whom preoedipal material is typically used in the service of defense against the analysis of triadic, oedipal relations.

Whereas in the early days of psychoanalysis, the disorders of patients were separated into transference and narcissistic neuroses, this classification was gradually found to be inadequate. In part, this was because it was discovered that, contrary to Freud's early judgment, schizophrenic patients were extremely capable of developing transference relationships, although their manifestations are often quite different from those of neurotic patients. Additionally, it was gradually discovered that underlying the neurotic symptoms was a personality substratum in which pathological traits were built into the character. Frequently the patient was found to be unaware of having a personality distortion; his pathological character traits were larely egosyntonic. Progressively over the years, the term *character neurosis* has come to have a nosological value. Today many analysts use the term *neurotic*, which stresses the egodystonic symptomatology, less and less frequently, and the term *character neurotic*, which emphasizes the personality structure, more and more often. At first, the term *neurotic character* was used to describe a position between the healthy and the clear-cut neurotic personality, although Alexander (1930) stressed the impulsive and compulsive components. Then the character neuroses were differentiated according to their dominant characteristics, and such terms as *hysterical, impulsive, obsessive, paranoid,* and *psychotic character* (or *personality*) *disorder* have become progressively more popular as nosological terms (see chapter 7).

Whereas psychoanalysis in the past was aimed primarily at symptom removal, it has become more generally employed for character modification. Such alteration is thought to result from interpretation and working through of the transference neurosis, which has a different nature in each of the types of character disorder. With the growing emphasis on character analysis, psychoanalyses have gradually become longer, and the personality structures of patients are found to regress in the transference relationship to a point where some of their thinking patterns, object relations, and defensive manifestations are not confined to the analytic situation. In such instances, most analysts are inclined to alter the original diagnosis from neurosis or character disorder to one or another of the psychogenic psychoses, usually one of the schizophrenias. To judge from case fragments in the literature and from informal discussions, some analysts change the diagnosis when the patient manifests some indefinite quantity of primitive thinking. It may be argued that such instances of apparent psychotic regression are not genuine but are artificially induced and therefore spurious. With the present state of nosological confusion, such a position is difficult to maintain. The classification of patients as transference or narcissistic neurotics appears to be untenable in a large number of instances, perhaps in all cases.

BORDERLINE PERSONALITY DISORDER

Prior to the publication of the first edition of this book in 1967, the terms *borderline states* and *borderline conditions* were seldom used as nosological designations. Subsequently they have become popular, and the literature burgeons with articles and books about them, although various observers question their applicability. Some dispute the concept that there is a continuum of psychopathological conditions (Dickes 1974).

Others, including the present authors, believe that the terms are as yet too loosely applied (Maenchen 1968, Meissner 1978). Kernberg (1975a), who has contributed much to the delineation of the syndrome and to the study of its dynamics, formulates that primitive splitting is used typically as a defense in the borderline conditions. Many authors have been adversely critical (Pruyser 1975). The most thorough historical survey of the borderline states is that of Paz, Pelento, and Olmos de Paz (1975, 1976a,b; see also Mack 1975).

The first efforts to define psychopathological conditions which lie between the psychoses and neuroses of Morel (1857), Magnan (1884, 1893) and Kraepelin (1883) consisted only of clinical descriptions. The main attempts to distinguish structural differences have been made by psychoanalysts, probably commencing with Freud. The term *borderland insanity* was introduced by Hughes in 1884 and used later by Rosse (1890) to apply to patients who manifested neurotic symptomatology at some times and psychotic at others. The term *borderline psychosis* appeared from time to time in the literature written in English prior to the middle of this century, but it seems that Eisenstein (1951), Wolberg (1952) and Knight (1953) were the first to write of borderline states and conditions. Knight's delineation and therapeutic recommendations indicate that he effectively equated them with borderline psychoses.

Kahlbaum (1863) formulated what our present paradigm recognizes as disease processes and introduced such terms as *symptom complex*, *cyclothymia* and *catatonia* (1874). One of his students, Hecker (1871), coined the label *hebephrenia*. Kahlbaum (1878) subsequently referred to some adolescent patients who alternately presented neurotic and psychotic symptoms as "heboidophrenic," noting that they had moral but not intellectual deterioration, thus anticipating later writers' pointing to superego defects among borderline patients. The term that has been used most regularly to designate the group of patients whom many now call borderline is Bleuler's *latent schizophrenia*. Many other names have been introduced, but their use has been limited, such as Claude's *schizomanie* (1926), Zilboorg's "ambulatory schizophrenia" (1941), H. Deutsch's "as-if personalities" (1942), Merenciano's *psicosis mitis* (1945), Hoch and Polatin's "pseudoneurotic schizophrenia" (1949), Mahler's "benign psychosis" (Mahler et al. 1949), and Frosch's "psychotic character" (1964).

Guarner (1978, p. 142) stated that the words *borderline case* or its equivalent appeared but once in Freud's complete works, in his introduction to Aichorn's *Wayward Youth* (1925).

The disorders were uniformly considered to be hereditarily or constitutionally generated until Hendricks (1936) and H. Deutsch (1942) stressed developmental defects and particularly difficulties in identificatory processes and suggested that faulty socialization contributed significantly to their causation. Wolf (1957) found borderline patients often came from families in which one or both parents were severely emotionally disturbed, and recent studies indicate that family experiences may contribute substantially to their causation (Shapiro et al. 1975, 1977, Zinner and R. A. Shapiro 1972, Zinner and E. Shapiro 1975). Concerning genetic studies, the research data are as yet too limited and the diagnostic practices followed in existing studies are too varied to allow firm conclusions to be drawn (Siever and Gunderson 1979).

As a result of the contributions of authors already cited and too many others to be individually named, there is a growing tendency to believe that the terms *borderline states* or *borderline conditions* are applicable for a fairly well-defined group of patients (Ekstein and Wallerstein 1954, Rangell 1955, Geleerd 1958, Panel Discussion 1959, S. K. Rosenfeld and Sprince 1963, Kernberg 1967, Boyer 1970, Masterson 1972, 1976, Mack 1975, Hartocollis 1977).

Signs and Symptoms

Kernberg (1975a) described the patient who has a borderline personality organization as follows. He presents himself ordinarily with what appear to be typical neurotic symptoms but at times of stress he reveals a particular combination of neurotic symptoms, none of which is pathognomonic but a combination of two or more of which is strongly suggestive of borderline personality organization. Such patients tend to present chronic, diffuse, free-floating anxiety, especially related to a pervasive sense of loneliness (Gunderson and Kolb 1978, Grinker, Werble and Drye 1968). They may present multiple phobias, obsessive-compulsive symptoms that have acquired secondary ego syntonicity, multiple, elaborate or bizarre conversion symptoms, hypochondriasis, dissociative symptoms, and paranoid and hypochondriacal trends as with any other symptomatic neurosis. Polymorphous sexual trends, perversions, impulse disorders and addictions are common. They suffer from a variety of character disorders: paranoid, schizoid, hypomanic, "cyclothymic" with strong hypomanic tendencies, hysterical, and infantile. Their initial complaints are often of general dissatisfaction and a sense of failure since they feel they have not lived up to their potentialities (Giovacchini 1975a, 1979). These patients have particular difficulties in interpersonal relationships, and there are specific elements in borderline personality psychopathology that engage both family members and therapists in unique ways (Shapiro 1978).

In unstructured social situations and on unstructured projective tests that provide the opportunity for regressive responses, borderline patients reveal evidence of primary process thinking (Gunderson and Singer 1975, M. T. Singer 1977). That they can use an external organizing structure to bolster their thinking has been repeatedly demonstrated. Melvin Singer (1975) suggested the presence of a cognitive disturbance in which these patients lack the capacity to delay, detour, check, and structure their impulses and affects through contemplation, fantasy, reflection, and symbol formation. These findings suggest that borderline pathology is related to problems in the management of impulse and affect, which manifest themselves most characteristically in interpersonal relationships and in relatively amorphous settings. There is diagnostic relevance in the appearance of transference psychoses (Peto 1967, Timsit 1971).

Gunderson and Kolb (1978) found the most useful discriminator between borderline personality organization and schizophrenia is that schizophrenics have diminished affects and this difference is more obvious in the interview situation than in the patients' recent histories. Borderline patients quickly develop intense relationships as a rule and they cannot tolerate the absence of human or animal companionship, whereas the schizophrenic prefers being alone. Both drug abuse and the occurrence of transient psychotic episodes either outside treatment or in the transference situation tend to differentiate between borderline patients and neurotic depressed patients.

The borderline patient has little capacity for realistic appraisal of others and, in the absence of a relationship, experiences others as distant objects to whom he can compliantly adapt. His response in individual therapy is typically marked by gross fluctuations in perception, thinking, and feelings about himself, and both the therapist and patient are usually unaware of contradictions (Robbins 1976).

In the treatment situation he presents narrow, rigid, and unmodulated affects and scant ability to tolerate guilt or internalized depressive affect (Winnicott 1954b, Zetzel 1956a). He has difficulty in distinguishing among physical sensations and emotions and little capacity for delay, impulse control, or frustration and anxiety tolerance. Often, his drives have not been structuralized. Although, unlike most psychotic patients, he is capable of high-level defenses and good reality testing in many circumstances, his unpleasant affects may escalate readily into panic states without the involvement of reliable defensive operations (Pine 1974). In the transference situation or under stress he is apt to regress to transient psychotic states characterized by fantasies of abandonment, destruction, and intense neediness (Adler 1975).

Transference of the Borderline Patient

The transference of the borderline patient may develop with great rapidity, be initially chaotic, and evolve only gradually into a discernible pattern. Modell (1968) described the borderline patient's diagnostic transference response to the therapist as similar to the infant's response to the transitional object. Winnicott (1953) described the child's transitional object-blanket as something that possesses attributes of its own, something "not-me," yet is forbidden to change except at the behest of the child. It is both loved and mutilated by the child, yet both must survive. Modell found the therapeutic relationship to constitute a protective shield between the patient and external dangers and the patient's gradual disengagement to resemble that from the transitional object which represents a phase of the child's gradual separation from the mother (see also Volkan 1979). Further manifestations of the transference-countertransference relationship will be obvious from a discussion of the ego defenses typically used by the borderline patient.

Ego Defenses of the Borderline Personality Organization

H. A. Rosenfeld (1957) has described the use of two specific primitive ego defenses as characteristic for the borderline patient in intimate relationships, splitting and projective identification. Melanie Klein (1946) hypothesized that in the first months of life the infant has an omnipotent fantasy that unwanted parts of his personality and parts of internal objects can be split, projected, and controlled in the external object. Kernberg (1975a) has found that an underlying pattern of sharply polarized relationships is "activated" in the transference of the borderline patient and that the polarization of these fantasies is determined by the defensive maneuver called "splitting." He stated that loving and hating internalized fantasized relationships are split in order that the individual may avoid the anxiety that would result if they were experienced simultaneously. The patient defends himself against anxiety by projecting off unwanted personality aspects onto the therapist in the transference relationship (Volkan 1976).

Some analysts believe that with successful negotiation of the rapprochement phase the child develops the capacity for ambivalence and object constancy (Fraiberg 1969, Mahler et al. 1975, Masterson 1972, 1976, Shapiro, Zinner et al. 1975, Zinner and Shapiro 1975).

While various authors question the value of the idea of splitting as a primary defensive mechanism, there seems to be common agreement that failure to integrate and modify impulses and affects is an important aspect of such patients, which results in their view of the therapist as alternately omnipotent and omniscient and helpless and ignorant.

The second primitive ego defense that has been considered as characteristic of borderline patients is projective identification, a phenomenon that an increasing number of psychoanalysts consider to be most important in understanding the highly complex countertransference relationships typical of therapeutic interactions with such patients and in using countertransference reactions to facilitate the treatment process (Bion 1956, Carpinacci et al. 1963, Carter and Rinsley 1977, Cesio 1963, 1973, Giovacchini 1975b, Giovacchini and Boyer 1975, Grinberg 1962, 1976, 1979, Ogden 1978, Perestrello 1963, D. Rosenfeld and Mordo 1973, H. A. Rosenfeld 1952a, 1954, Searles 1965b). Projective identification involves the dissociation of uncomfortable aspects of the personality, be they of impulse, self-image or superego, and the projection of them onto a person, resulting in identification with him on the basis of the self-elements ascribed to him. Klein (1955) noted that once the split part had been projected onto another person, it was lost to the subject and an alteration of the object-perception process ensued.

Countertransference with the Borderline Patient

In the treatment situation, projective identification creates bewildering situations because this intrapsychic and interpersonal mechanism consists of an attempt to evoke feelings and behavior on the part of the therapist that conform to the projection, as well as the conscious or unconscious willingness of the analyst to accept such attributes as a part or as parts of himself (Grinberg 1979, Malin and Grotstein 1966). Such evocation is particularly characteristic of borderline patients.

The person who uses projective identification as a defense is selectively inattentive to the real aspects of the therapist that may invalidate the projection (Brodey 1965). The therapist, now believed by the patient to be imbued with the disclaimed and projected attribute, is consciously perceived by the patient to be unlike himself, while an unconscious relationship is sustained in which the projected aspect can be experienced vicariously (Zinner and E. Shapiro 1975). Projective identification differs from projection because the individual who uses the former defense maintains a greater degree of contact with that which is projected and seeks unconsciously to develop a relationship with the therapist and to involve him as a collusive partner in conforming to the way the patient has come to perceive him.

Racker (1957, 1968) has written of concordant and complementary countertransference identification and Grinberg (1979) of projective counteridentification, and both authors have discussed their implications for psychotherapeutic impasses and their avoidance. Difficulties arise when the therapist has unknowingly become a collusive partner.

An important but not usually discussed aspect of projective identification in the therapeutic situation is the reintrojection by the patient of that which seemed to have been successfully projected into the therapist. Ordinarily the projection involves the patient's hostility, which he perceives to be exceedingly dangerous. Many patients are particularly interested in how the therapist handles his aggression. They are often unusually sensitive to the presence of hostility in the therapist and how to provoke it. Over time their observations that the therapist's hostility has harmed neither therapist nor patient allow them to view hostility as being less dangerous than they had previously believed. Of course, their acquiring the capacity to make that observation depends on complex interactions of the developing transference and real relationships that take place during interpretive therapy (Loewald 1960). That observation combined with the taming of their own aggression, which is inevitably a result of successful therapy, allows them to reintroject their modified hostility and integrate it into their evolving personalities as it is used in a self-supporting fashion.

However, it is not only hostility that may be viewed as magically dangerous by the borderline patient. Various analysts have described patients who believe their love is destructive and, during treatment, to have had the omnipotent fantasy that they have projected it into the therapist for safekeeping and subsequent reintrojection. Bion (1956), among others, has written on patients' projection of their sanity into the therapist for safekeeping.

Treatment of the Borderline Patient

There tends to be a growing reversal of psychoanalysts' attitudes pertaining to the treatment of borderline patients. In contrast to the position typified by Knight (1953) and Zetzel (1956a), who stressed that psychoanalytic treatment was categorically contraindicated for such patients, many who previously agreed with them now believe that psychoanalysis with as few parameters as possible is the treatment of choice, thus agreeing with the position taken by H. A. Rosenfeld (1952a) and Boyer (1961). Today the point at issue when analysts discuss a prospective treatment program for a patient who is suspected early of suffering from a disorder that might be called borderline is generally the nature and degree of parameters that might be recommended, that is, what deviations if any from orthodox psychoanalysis.

Searches continue for more effective and specific treatments for patients who suffer from all of the group of schizophrenias as well as for those illnesses that lie nearer the neurotic end of the continuum of psychopathological disorders. Within recent years antipsychotic drugs and community involvement have made significant contributions, but it is nevertheless obvious that these relatively new developments in treatment have their limitations. The majority of clinicians emphasize that psychotherapy of some sort holds promise for schizophrenics although they continue to differ radically in their recommended approaches. Thus we find in a recent book such divergent viewpoints as that of H. Y. Meltzer (1975) who believes that milieu combined with drug therapy is optimal and that of Grotstein (1975) who recommends psychoanalysis with as few parameters as possible. Mosher (1975) has discussed at length the difficulties intrinsic in research into the effectiveness of therapeutic modalities and the reasons for research decline.

In the first edition of this book, the introduction included these remarks:

> It would appear, then, that although formal teaching of psychoanalysis continues to recommend psychotherapy of a "supportive" or covering nature for the narcissistic neuroses and classical analysis for the transference neuroses, operationally these technical recommendations are followed irregularly. This is inevitable, since the concept of transference and narcissistic neuroses are so hazy. It seems also that the lack of uniformity of treatment procedures depends upon a growing judgment that the classical technique of psychoanalysis has broader application than is generally recognized publicly. One of the most interesting phenomena to be observed in discussions at psychoanalytic meetings is that the critics who are

> most adamant in their stand that psychoanalysis is not applicable without gross modifications for the treatment of patients suffering from one of the group of schizophrenias are those who either (1) have never attempted knowingly to treat such patients by the classical method, or (2) have altered their therapeutic procedures by introducing extensive parameters or abandoning psychoanalysis altogether when patients originally diagnosed to have neuroses or character disorders have begun to regress seriously in treatment.

It appears that there has been a shift in the teaching philosophies of some analytic institutes during the last decade in the direction of belatedly taking into serious consideration education consonant with the widening scope of indications for psychoanalysis (Stone 1963). As recently as ten years ago, when papers involved data taken from the psychoanalytic treatment of borderline or psychotic patients, the discussant often felt obliged to chastise or ridicule the presenter for his presumed bad judgment in having used such a therapeutic mode. Frequently no other message was forthcoming unless the presenter claimed therapeutic success, in which case he was either nicely or blatantly dubbed a prevaricator or the discussion centered around the issue of whether he understood of what psychoanalysis as a therapeutic procedure consisted. Today scarcely an eyebrow is raised when the presenter or the discussant states that psychoanalysis with as few parameters as may be introduced is the treatment of choice for severe characterological or borderline disorders. Patients' regressions during therapy are apt to be discussed from the standpoint of countertransference problems or regression in the service either of defense or of growth.

SUMMARY AND COMMENT

The schizophrenias probably cause more social waste and personal suffering than any other group of psychopathological conditions. They comprise a wide range of psychical disorders, including acute and chronic psychotic states that are easily diagnosed and a continuum of conditions that are scarcely distinguishable from severe psychoneuroses, characterological disorders, and psychosomatic illness. Although physical and chemical treatments have been devised that are used with some success in restoring the acutely psychotic individual to his previous psychosocial level of adjustment, such therapeutic methods have proved to be ineffectual in reconstituting the personality structure of the schizophrenic and ensuring his psychical maturation.

There is no unanimity among students of the schizophrenias concerning their causation. Some observers believe that hereditary and/or other organic abnormalities are involved. They can be successfully treated only through the use of chemical or physical agents that have yet to be discovered; psychotherapeutic methods at best are palliative. Another group of observers consider the schizophrenias to result from unfavorable interpersonal and social influences and believe whatever pathological organic states may be found to result from as yet undelineated psychosomatic mechanisms. They think that psychotherapeutic methods alone can be used to alter the personality of the schizophrenic in such a manner that he can learn to be pleased with himself and live successfully and productively within the social group. The majority of students, including the present authors, deem an interplay among the myriad potential influences of heredity and socialization to be causative. Some who hold this view, however, believe that such an interplay has led to a psychosomatic state that is irreversible. They agree with the organicists that psychotherapeutic methods can be employed to alleviate some of the symptomatology but not the underlying, ill-defined, so-called schizophrenic process that is part of the psychosomatic disruption. They believe that the patient's environment must be altered so that he will have a minimum of external conflictual, anxiety-provoking stimuli and that psychotherapeutic measures should be limited to vaguely defined supportive and suppressive measures. Others of the third group are more optimistic. They hold that psychotherapeutic steps can be used to reverse the schizophrenic process.

To date, psychotherapeutic methods based on psychoanalytic principles are the only ones that have shown promise in reconstituting personality structure. The psychoanalytic method was devised by Freud and his followers to treat individuals through analysis of transference relations. Interpretation is the ultimate technical procedure that is effective in such analysis. Freud stated that some people are incapable of developing a transference relationship and, therefore, refractory to psychoanalysis. He categorized psychopathologies into two large groups, the transference neuroses, comprising illnesses in which transference can develop, and the narcissistic neuroses, constituting those states in which transference relationships do not develop or are so tenuous that their analysis is impossible. Freud was aware of the continuum of psychopathological states that range between the transference neuroses and the narcissistic neuroses, but he took the conservative position that the psychoanalytic method is applicable solely to patients whose illnesses were clearly definable as transference neuroses.

Freud's classification system was based on clinical observations made during the theoretical period preceding introduction of the revised anxiety theory and the formulation of the structural hypothesis. It has long since been learned that individuals who are incapable of developing transference relationships must be very rare, and recently Freud's original theoretical position concerning the narcissistic neuroses has been questioned by an increasing number of analysts (Arlow and Brenner 1964). The transference relationships of hypothetically simple neuroses are relatively easily understood and are characterized largely by manifestations of thinking and behavior found in individuals who have traversed the oral stage of psychosexual development with only minor psychical injury. The psychoses reflect the effects of severe psychical traumata during narcissistic and oral phases and are characterized by a predominance of primary process mentation, primitive defenses, and immature handling of affects. In the continuum of states lying between the neuroses and the psychoses, there are all gradations and combinations of the capacity to use secondary process thinking, the maturity of defenses, and the stability of affective attachments.

A variety of psychotherapeutic procedures appear to alleviate psychopathological symptoms, and there are a sufficient number of so-called spontaneous recoveries of both obvious psychotic and psychoneurotic symptomatologies that some observers have developed a nihilistic viewpoint concerning the value of psychotherapy.

Psychoanalysts use a different yardstick concerning the value of psychotherapy. In general, they aim at more than mere symptom alleviation and believe that personality modification is necessary for lasting benefit. While some continue to favor the use of the diagnostic term *psychoneurosis* for most of their patients, they know that in the main they are treating personality disorders underlying the neurotic symptoms.

As has been stressed, the personality disorders make up the continuum of states that lie between Freud's transference and narcissistic neuroses. Consequently, psychoanalysts face an enigma that has been discussed frequently, namely the determination of the limits of applicability of the psychoanalytic method. For many years some analysts have continued to use the classical method or have added minor modifications when patients who were diagnosed as neurotic regressed during their treatment; an increasing number of reports in the literature reflect this trend. A few analysts have intentionally used the classical technique with very few alterations for the treatment of psychotic patients or patients with severe characterological problems. Their results have been encouraging.

While it is important that research continue into the causes and treatment of the schizophrenias, the standpoint of this book is that psychoanalysis has more to offer for this group of disorders than has been recognized. We believe that more parameters have been employed in treatment than are necessary and even suspect that sometimes the introduction of parameters itself has resulted in some of the severe regressions seen during psychoanalysis. We have reached our bias through our clinical experience, which has suggested that even patients who are commonly diagnosed to suffer from borderline or frankly psychotic disturbances are susceptible to treatment with psychoanalysis that includes few parameters.

We think that a review of the psychoanalytic literature combined with our own work supports the hypotheses that (1) the so-called schizophrenic process probably is reversible in some instances and its reversibility depends upon the possibility of reconstitution of the character structure; (2) such reconstitution can result from psychoanalytic treatment; and (3) Freud's formulations concerning the psychological aspects of the genesis of the group of schizophrenias need revision. We think that all the characterological disorders are understandable within the framework of the structural theory and that Freud's objections to the psychoanalytic treatment of psychoses are no longer theoretically valid within the framework of the structural hypothesis. This statement does not preclude the possibility that further research will produce better theoretical formulations and therapeutic procedures. It simply presents the viewpoint that for the present there exists no treatment method that offers as much hope as psychoanalysis.

CHAPTER TWO

Historical Development of Psychoanalytic Psychotherapy of the Schizophrenias: Freud's Contributions

L. Bryce Boyer

BACKGROUND INFORMATION

Freud was taught that psychopathological states were the products of neuropathological conditions, which in turn were attributable to hereditary, constitutional and/or degenerative states. His early scientific interests were in the fields of biology, histology, and neurology. He obtained a medical degree with the hope that he might have a better chance to obtain a university appointment, which would enable him to continue his studies in those fields. After Freud received his doctorate of medicine in 1881, he continued his researches in Brücke's physiological laboratory (Jones 1953, pp. 58-77). Despairing of becoming Brücke's successor and pressed for money, Freud reluctantly prepared for the practice of medicine. He devoted himself to neurology, and in 1884 was appointed *Privatdocent* in neuropathology, as the result of his having written six monographs in the fields of histology, pharmacology, and medicine (Kris 1954, p. 16).

Despite his primary interests, Freud evinced curiosity about psychological conditions per se. As a medical student he observed an exhibition given by the magnetist Hansen and, "from noticing that a hypnotized person had been made deathly pale, became convinced that hypnotic phenomena were genuine" (Jones 1953, p. 235). He met Breuer while still a student, and in the early eighties the great physician told his young friend of his therapy of Miss Anna O. (Kris 1954, p. 12), a celebrated case which constituted one of the starting points that led to psychoanalysis (Breuer and Freud 1895).

Between 1880 and 1882, Breuer treated a girl who has been considered generally to have suffered from a classical hysteria, although Reichard (1956) and others have rediagnosed her as schizophrenic. Breuer hypnotized Anna O. when she was in states of altered personality with confusion and found that when she related fantasies and simultaneously released affect, her conversion symptoms disappeared one by one. Breuer called her states hypnoid, and he and Freud attributed them to dammed-up, intracerebral excitation, a concept that both may have learned from Brücke.[1]

Perhaps because of his contacts with Breuer, Freud was led, by his interest in hypnosis and its effects and implications, to use a grant to study under Charcot during four months of 1885-1886. Upon his return to Vienna, he lectured about hysteria in the male (Freud 1886a), but his psychological explanation fell on deaf ears. He continued to do laboratory research, but also undertook the private care of "nervous" patients, primarily neurotics. His first attempts at treatment were with the application of Erb's electrotherapy, a fact that Jones (1953, p. 235) attributed to the influence of Charcot's derogatory attitude toward the cathartic method of Breuer. Freud confined himself to electrotherapy for some months, although he used various adjuvants as well, such as baths and massage. Jones wrote (1953, p. 235), "elsewhere he made the caustic remark that the only reason he could not agree with Moebius in ascribing the results of electrical treatment to suggestion was that he did not find any results to explain."

Despite his discouragement with the results of the therapeutic methods he was using and his contact with Breuer's work, Freud did not use hypnosis in his psychiatric practice until the autumn of 1887 (Freud 1887-1902, p. 53), with Frau Emmy von N. (Breuer and Freud 1895). Hypnosis excited him because he saw in its use the possibility of

1. Freud's later extrapolations from this idea led him to ideas about regulatory mechanisms of the psyche, which belong today to the fundamental assumptions of psychoanalysis (Bernfeld 1944).

"arriving at a purely psychological theory of hysteria, with affective processes in the front rank" (Freud 1914a, p. 18). However, he was unable to alter the mental state of most of his patients. In 1889 he observed Bernheim's demonstration that patients who were in a state of hypnotically induced somnambulism only appeared to have forgotten their somnambulistic experiences. Freud used hypnosis for some eighteen months, but then changed his procedure in order to work with patients in their "normal state." At first he declared they would remember when he put his hand on their foreheads, and although he found the procedure laborious and "unsuited to serve as a permanent technique," he continued to use it until he was certain that forgotten memories are not lost (Freud 1914a, p. 23). Freud looked upon psychical splitting itself as an effect of a process of repelling, which he first called defense and later repression. He gradually developed the relatively noninterfering techniques of psychoanalysis, becoming aware of the roles of regression, infantile sexuality, and, later, transference.

THE DEVELOPMENT OF FREUD'S THINKING CONCERNING THE SCHIZOPHRENIAS

It is not easy to follow the development of Freud's thought in regard to the schizophrenias, partly because his utilization of the words *neurosis* and *psychosis* was not clearly defined. Zilboorg (1954) has suggested that Freud's apparent "nosological laxity and even confusion" resulted from an essential indifference to diagnostic entities. An early example is to be found in Freud's first letter to Wilhelm Fliess, in which, without amplification, he wrote, "In neurasthenia, a hypochondriacal element, an anxiety psychosis, is never absent . . . " (Freud 1887-1902, p. 51). Freud (1911, p. 75-76) also spoke directly to the point with his remark, "it is not on the whole of very great importance what names we give to clinical pictures." In his last work (Freud 1940, p. 195), he wrote, "it is not scientifically feasible to draw a line of demarcation between what is psychologically normal and abnormal."

In an 1893 draft of the paper "On the Grounds for Detaching a Particular Syndrome from Neurasthenia under the Description Anxiety Neurosis," Freud (1895) divided hysterias into hereditary and traumatic and asserted that all cases of "acquired" hysteria had a genital sexual origin. He distinguished between periodic depression, which he regarded as a third form of anxiety neurosis, and melancholia proper, implying that the latter is of an hereditary nature. In Freud's remaining letters to Fliess, his use of the word *melancholia* leaves the reader in doubt as to whether it signified neurotic or psychotic depression. The same looseness of utilization of the term is to be found frequently in the German psychiatric literature of that time.

Freud distinguished between psychopathological states of hereditary and acquired origins, and his early attempts to understand the bases of acquired neuroses and psychoses included organic explanations. By 1893 he had abandoned hypnotherapy and the tedious technique of placing his hand on the patient's head while demanding the production of associations. He was, however, still convinced that acquired psychopathological states were attributable to sexual *noxae*. Nevertheless, in that year he introduced the then revolutionary theory that the symptoms of psychotic patients were understandable in the same way as were the dreams and actions of normal persons and the symptoms of neurotic individuals. In "The Neuro-Psychoses of Defence" Freud (1894a) conceptualized acquired hysteria, phobias, obsessions, and certain hallucinatory psychoses to constitute defensive states that served the purpose of keeping unacceptable sexual ideas from consciousness. One of his obsessional patients suffered from (p. 55) an *Überwältigungpsychose* (a psychosis in which the ego is overwhelmed), another from hallucinatory confusion. In this paper Freud designated his treatment method as "psychical analysis" (p. 47), "clinicopsychological analysis" (p. 53), and "hypnotic analysis" (p. 59), and stated that it could be used to remove conversion, displacement, and splitting of consciousness through counteracting the effects of repression.[2] He was clearly aware of current combinations of neurotic and psychotic symptoms in the same patient. In this first article he presented a hypothetical mechanism of psychosis to which he returned thirty years later in his last papers concerning the same subject. Contrasting two cases with obsessions, in which the defense against an intolerable idea was effected by detachment of the affect, with a case of hallucinatory confusion, in which a "more energetic and successful kind of defence existed," Freud (1894a, p. 58) wrote concerning the latter: "Here, the ego rejects the incompatible idea together with its affect and behaves as if the idea had never occurred to the ego at all. *But from the moment at which this has been successfully done the subject is in a psychosis, which can only be classified as 'hallucinatory confusion.'*" He continued (p. 49), "the ego has fended off the incompatible idea through a flight into psychosis," and added, "The ego breaks away from the incompatible idea; but the latter is inseparably connected with a piece of reality, so that, in so far as the ego achieves this result, it, too, has detached itself wholly or in part from reality."

In 1894 Freud (1887-1902, p. 86-88) included melancholia and mania among the neuroses, although in 1895 he wrote (p. 103), "the typical and extreme case of melancholia appears to be the periodic or cyclical form."

In a draft of a paper written in 1895 entitled "Paranoia," Freud wrote (p. 109), "delusional ideas stand alongside obsessional ideas as purely intellectual disorders, and paranoia stands alongside obsessional insanity as an intellectual psychosis" and "chronic paranoia is a pathological mode of de-

2. Later in the same year he (Freud 1894b, p. 75) used the term *psychological analysis*. *Psycho-analysis* first appeared in the French paper on the etiology of the neuroses (Freud 1896b, p. 151).

fence." At a later time, in his thirty-ninth letter to Fliess, he repeated that theme, as though to reassure himself of its validity (Freud 1887-1902, p. 141), "paranoia is really a defence neurosis." In a draft of a paper written the same year, "The Neuroses of Defence," we find (p. 146): "There are four types of these, and many forms. . . . They are pathological aberrations of normal psychical states of affect: of *conflict* (hysteria), or *self-reproach* in obsessional neurosis, of *mortification* (in paranoia) and of *grief* (in acute hallucinatory dementia)." Freud (1896a) published both drafts as "Further Remarks on the Neuro-Psychoses of Defence," and in that elaboration he presented the case history of a woman who suffered from chronic paranoia or dementia paranoides whom he had treated psychoanalytically. He wrote (p. 175), "This is a psychosis of defence." Freud's laxity in distinguishing neuroses and psychoses remains apparent. Without having in the meantime defined those states with any more clarity, he soon (1898b) stated that psychoanalysis was a method of treatment designed only for psychoneurotics, but later in the same year Freud (1898a) included paranoia among the psychoneuroses.

In 1904 Freud wrote of the limitations of the psychoanalytic method. In his words (1904, p. 257), it "was created through and for the treatment of patients permanently unfitted for life." Patients were to be accepted for treatment only if they possessed a "reasonable degree of education and a fairly reliable character." Analytic psychotherapy was considered unsuitable (p. 258) for the treatment of "neuropathic degeneration" and "psychoses, states of confusion and deeply-rooted (I might say toxic) depression." He suggested that "by suitable changes in the method we may succeed in advancing beyond these hindrances—and so be able to initiate a psychotherapy of the psychoses," and he added (p. 259) that from analytic therapy "no injury to the patient is to be feared when the treatment is conducted with real comprehension." He did not suggest what technical modifications might make the method suitable for the treatment of the psychoses. He supplemented these remarks later, commenting (1904a) that persons with "deep-rooted malformations of character, traits of an actually degenerative constitution," are also unsuitable for psychoanalysis.

It is to be noted that Freud had yet to define what he meant by neurosis or psychosis. Although he had not written directly of acquired versus hereditary psychoneuroses for some years, a picture of his conceptualizations gradually emerged. He believed that psychoanalysis was to be recommended for illnesses that were predominantly, if not totally, caused by traumatic life situations and that psychoanalysis was contraindicated for states stemming from hereditary or constitutional origins. This would seem to indicate that when Freud judged a condition to have been caused by the latter, he included it among the psychoses or severe character malformations. Five years later Freud (1909a) offered a criterion for making such a differentiation, stating, "Psychoanalytical research into the neuroses (the various forms of nervous illness with mental causation) has endeavored to trace their connections with instinctual life and the restrictions imposed on it by the claims of civilization." His implication was that other "forms of nervous illness" have hereditary, constitutional, or degenerative causations, but he did not amplify this point or indicate methods to differentiate between illnesses caused by socialization or by organic factors. There is another implication to be found in his remarks, namely that if a "nervous illness" is predominantly due to the claims of civilization, it should be amenable to psychoanalytic therapy.

Soon thereafter, Freud (1911) turned his attention to an amplification of his libido theory and to the development of a theory of narcissism to which he had alluded at a meeting of the Vienna Psycho-Analytical Society in 1909 (Freud 1914a). He chose as a point of departure a study of the autobiographical account of a paranoic. Freud developed his argument in four steps. He sought (1) to understand the origins of paranoia by an analysis of the phenomenology that characterized

Schreber's illness, (2) to separate paranoia from the schizophrenias, (3) to develop a theory of the psychoses, and (4) to exploit his ideas concerning the psychopathology of the psychoses to clarify his theory of narcissism.

From an interpretive analysis of Schreber's recorded symptomatology and the development of his delusional system, Freud considered the basis of Schreber's illness to have been an outburst of homosexual feeling toward his physician, Flechsig, a father surrogate. After stating that the "father complex" was the dominant element in Schreber's case, Freud noted (p. 59), "But in all of this there is nothing characteristic of the form of the disease known as paranoia, nothing that might not be found (and that has not been found) *in other kinds of neuroses*" (italics added). He maintained his earlier position (Freud 1894a, 1896a) that the symptomatology of the neuroses and psychoses was the result of defensive mechanisms and defined the protective nature of Schreber's paranoid symptoms by adding (1911, p. 59), "The distinctive character of paranoia (or of dementia praecox) must be sought for elsewhere—namely in the particular form assumed by the symptoms; and we shall expect to find that this is determined, not by the nature of the complexes themselves, but by the mechanism by which the symptoms are formed or by which repression is brought about" and "what was characteristically paranoid about the illness was the fact that the patient, as a means of warding off a homosexual wishful phantasy, reacted precisely with delusions of persecution of this kind." He added (p. 62), "paranoics *endeavor to protect themselves against any such sexualization of their social instinctual cathexes.*" He then reviewed the roles of fixation, repression, and irruption of the repressed in the formation of symptoms and wrote (p. 71), "*The delusion formation, which we take to be a pathological product, is in reality an attempt at recovery, a process of reconstruction*" and "the process of repression proper consists in a detachment of the libido from people—and things—that were previously loved."

In his exposition of the significance of such conclusions, Freud then exploited the data to develop a theory of the psychopathology of the psychoses. He noted that the process of repression happens silently and can be inferred only from the later events. He stated (p. 71): "What forces itself so noisily upon our attention is the process of recovery, which undoes the work of repression and brings back the libido again onto the people it had abandoned. In paranoia, this process is carried out by the method of projection. . . . Such libido detachment occurs in other conditions. . . . It is possible that a detachment of libido is the essential and regular mechanism of every repression." He found that (p. 72) "paranoics have brought along with them a *fixation at the stage of narcissism,* and we can assert that the length of *the step back from sublimated homosexuality to narcissism* is a measure of the amount of *regression* characteristic of paranoia." Such libidinal detachment may be partial, or (p. 73) "it may spread to a general one, which will loudly proclaim its presence in the symptoms of megalomania," and (p. 75) "It cannot be asserted that a paranoic, even at the height of the repression, withdraws his interest from the external world completely—as must be considered to occur in certain other kinds of hallucinatory psychosis (such as Meynert's amentia [an acute hallucinatory confusion])."

Here, then, we have the core of Freud's theory of the psychoses. Whereas Kahlbaum (1874) emphasized the motor phenomena in schizophrenia, Kraepelin (1883) the progressive course leading to dementia, and Bleuler (1911) the thought disorder and affective disturbance, Freud considered the patient's changed relationships with people and other objects to be of primary importance. He was particularly impressed by the generally verifiable observation that there is a gross withdrawal of interest from the environment that is reflected in varying behavioral and subjective changes in different forms of psychic disorders. Normal people, when subjected to object loss, do not become ill but find some other objects onto whom or which they can transfer the interest that was attached to the previous love object. Individuals who suffer from hysteria, anxiety hysteria, or the obsessional neurosis—Freud (1911) now refers to this group as transference neuroses—repress the mental representations of the lost libidinal objects, and the cathexis of object-libido to those unconscious mental representations is maintained, revealing itself in the symptoms characteristic of those disorders. In psychotics the situation is quite different. They have the notion that the world about them and the people in it have somehow changed, and sometimes the world appears to them to have been destroyed. Freud later (1924a, 1932) referred to this group of symptoms as the patient's break with reality.

In 1911 and 1914 Freud attempted to explain the psychopathology of the break with reality on the basis of a quantitative or economic factor: the distribution of the patient's libidinal cathexes. He deemed it to be the consequence of the patient's having withdrawn *totally* his libidinal cathexes from the mental representations of his love-objects and having attached the detached object-libido to his self.

Freud then sought to explore what happens to the object-libido, which has been detached from love-objects and invested in the self. He noted the presence in the paranoic and the schizophrenic of megalomanic symptoms and a period of hypochondriasis, a state that ushered in Schreber's paranoia. At the same time, Freud knew of the important part played by regression in psychosis; he had written of the significance of the similarities among sleep, dreams, and psychosis (1900). He had perceived the profound similarities between the psychotic patient and the infant, and he assumed that, in both, cathexes of object representations are either absent or insignificant compared with the quantity of libido invested in the self. He reasoned that the psychotic patient regressed to the stage of narcissism through which every normal child was thought to traverse early in life.

How did Freud attempt to explain megalomania? He wrote

(1914b, pp. 75-75), "What happens to the libido which has been withdrawn from external objects in schizophrenia? The megalomania characteristic of these states points the way. This megalomania has no doubt come into being at the expense of the object-libido. The libido that has been withdrawn from the external world has been directed to the ego and thus gives rise to an attitude that may be called narcissism. But the megalomania itself is no new creation; on the contrary, it is, as we know, a magnification and plainer manifestation of a condition which has already existed previously. This leads us to look upon narcissism which arises through the drawing in of object-cathexes as a secondary one, superimposed upon a primary narcissism that is obscured by a number of different influences."

Let us now follow Freud's argument concerning hypochondriasis. He wrote (1914b, p. 82), "a person who is tormented by organic pain and discomfort gives up his interest in the things of the external world, in so far as they do not concern his suffering. Closer observation teaches us that he also withdraws *libidinal* interest from his love-objects." He "withdraws his libidinal cathexes back onto his own ego, and sends them out again when he recovers." (It should be remembered that in German the word ego has the dual connotation of self and ego.) Freud continued, "Here libido and ego-interest are once more indistinguishable from each other. The familiar egoism of the sick person covers both." He went on (p. 83): "Hypochondriasis . . . has the same effect as organic disease on the distribution of the libido. The hypochondriac withdraws both interest and libido—the latter specially markedly—from the objects of the external world and concentrates both of them upon the organ that is engaging his attention," and (p. 84), "the familiar prototype of an organ that is painfully tender . . . is the genital organ in its states of excitation." Freud, referring to his "Three Essays on the Theory of Sexuality" (1905), suggested that cathected organs become erotogenic organs and wrote (1914b, p. 84), "For every such change in the erotogenicity of the organs there might then be a parallel change of libidinal cathexis in the ego." He noted, "If we follow up this line of thought, we come up against not only the problem of hypochondria, but of the other 'actual' neuroses—neurasthenia and anxiety neurosis," and "we may suspect that the relation of hypochondria to paraphrenia is similar to that of the other 'actual' neuroses to hysteria and obsessional neurosis: we may suspect, that is, that it is dependent on ego-libido just as the others are on object-libido, and that hypochondriacal anxiety is the counterpart, as coming from ego-libido, to neurotic anxiety. Further, since we are already familiar with the idea that the mechanism of falling ill and of the formation of symptoms in the transference neuroses—the path from introversion to regression—is to be linked to a damming-up of object-libido, we may come to closer quarters with the idea of a damming-up of ego-libido as well and may bring this idea into relation with the phenomena of hypochondria and paraphrenia." Noting that damming-up of libido is perceived as unpleasurable, and the degree of unpleasure is dependent upon the quantity of dammed-up libido, Freud continued, "Here we even venture to touch on the question of what makes it necessary at all for our mental life to pass beyond the limits of narcissism and to attach libido to objects."

Let us now return to Freud's theory of psychosis during this period when his orientation was that of the libido theory within the framework of the topographical hypothesis. The repression of the neurotic and the psychotic is silent. Evidence of its existence can be obtained only through an analysis of symptoms that show themselves during the period of improvement. Such symptoms are compromise formations that result from the psyche's attempt to relieve the unpleasure that has resulted from dammed-up ego-libido. With improvement, the psychotic's withdrawn libido becomes gradually reinvested in the outer world and its objects in a pathological manner, that is, delusions and hallucinations. This attempt at reinvestment Freud called the restitutive phase of the psychosis.

The decathexis of object representations, which characterizes the first stage of a psychosis, is the analogue of a neurotic repression, but in the case of the psychotic, repression is a deeper and further-reaching process. It does not simply prevent ideas and memories from reaching consciousness but results in a profound change in the mental representations themselves. The repressed contents of the neurotic's unconscious remain cathected, but the mental representations of the psychotic become truly decathected and no longer exist for him. Freud wrote (1914b, p. 86), "Paraphrenics display two fundamental characteristics: megalomania and diversion of their interest from the external world—from people and things. In consequence of the latter change, they become inaccessible to the influence of psychoanalysis and cannot be cured by our efforts." Freud (1915a) first used the term *narcissistic neurosis* to designate schizophrenia. To paraphrase his view: the schizophrenic cannot reinvest actual external objects; he suffers from a narcissistic neurosis and is incapable of transference. Thus, he cannot be treated by psychoanalysis.

Let me summarize the argument. The break with reality, or complete withdrawal of cathexis from the environment, is the most characteristic single feature of the psychoses. The repression employed by the psychotic is more profound than that of the neurotic and consists of a total decathexis of libido from mental representations. The self-centeredness of the psychotic results from the turning of the decathected libido onto the self, resulting in megalomania when it is attached to the ego and hypochondriasis when it is attached to the body. Following regression to such a narcissistic stage, the psychotic gradually recathects mental representations of external objects in a distorted manner, usually through hallucinations and delusions, in a restitutive phase.

It will be recalled that in the analysis of the Schreber case,

Freud sought also to distinguish paranoia from the schizophrenias, into which group it had been included by Kraepelin and Bleuler. Freud (1911, p. 76), however, believed that "paranoia should be maintained as an independent clinical type, however frequently the picture it offers may be complicated by the presence of schizophrenic features," as it had been in the Schreber case. He gave as his reason, "For, from the standpoint of the libido theory, while it would resemble dementia praecox in so far as the repression proper would in both disorders have the same principal feature—detachment of the libido, together with its regression onto the ego—it would be distinguished from dementia praecox by having its dispositional fixation differently located and by having a different mechanism for the return of the repressed (that is, for the formation of symptoms)," namely, projection. He stated that the attempt at recovery employed in dementia praecox (paraphrenia), in contrast to that used in paranoia, is hallucinatory. Freud stated that the hallucinatory mechanism is hysterical and continued (p. 77), "this is one of the two major respects in which dementia praecox differs from paranoia."[3] A second distinction lies in the natural history of the disorders. It "is shown by the outcome of the disease in those cases where the process has not remained too restricted. The prognosis is on the whole more unfavorable than in paranoia. The victory lies with repression and not, as in the former, with reconstruction. The regression extends not merely to narcissism (manifesting itself in the shape of megalomania) but to a complete abandonment of object-love and a return to infantile autoerotism. The dispositional fixation must therefore be situated further back than in paranoia, and must lie somewhere at the beginning of the course of development from autoerotism to object-love. Moreover, it is not at all likely that homosexual impulsions, which are so frequently—

3. Today we would not consider this argument to be valid, since projection is clearly involved in the process of hallucinating.

perhaps invariably—to be found in paranoia, play an equally important part in the aetiology of that far more comprehensive disorder, dementia praecox."

Freud ended his analysis of the Schreber case by stating (p. 79): "Lastly, I cannot conclude the present work . . . without foreshadowing the two chief theses towards the establishment of which the libido theory of the neuroses and psychoses is advancing: namely, that the neuroses arise in the main from a conflict between the ego and the sexual instinct, and that the forms which the neuroses assume retain the imprint of the course of development followed by the libido—and by the ego." That he considered the same to be true for the psychoses is apparent from what follows.

The onset of Schreber's illness consisted of a state that was labeled hypochondria. Freud considered that during the hypochondriacal phase, Schreber had not "overstepped the limits" of a neurosis. However, he also included paranoia among the neuroses (p. 59). During the unfolding of Freud's argument, which sought to differentiate paranoia from schizophrenia, he indicated his cognizance of another nosological difficulty, writing (p. 77), "Our hypotheses as to the dispositional fixations in paranoia and paraphrenia make it easy to see that a case may begin with paranoic symptoms and may yet develop into a dementia praecox, and that paranoid and schizophrenic phenomena may be combined in any proportion." Freud, then, implied that there is a continuum of states that lie between normality and psychosis, various degrees of neurotic and psychotic mechanisms are employed in the different psychopathological states, and the diagnostic terms applied to different abnormal states depend upon quantitative or economic assessments. In other words, as Freud had indicated before (1896a) and would again later (1924a), the psychic processes in neurosis and psychosis display a fundamental unity. In 1911 and 1914, reasoning from the libido theory, he sought to establish that paranoia lay between neurosis and psychosis, between the transference and the narcissistic neuroses.

Although Freud maintained his position regarding the fundamental unity, he apparently altered another judgment. In the libido theory, derivatives of instinctual drives are inaccessible to consciousness, and the removal of symptoms depends upon making that which has been repressed available to the system *Cs.* In Freud's early letters to Fliess, he held the vastly optimistic viewpoint that all the acquired psychopathologies could be cured through the removal of repression, the only defense he then recognized. He had generally included paranoia among the neuroses and apparently thought some cases to be acquired, that is psychogenic. By 1896 he had become less optimistic regarding the efficacy of psychoanalysis in the treatment of paranoia, and he remarked at the beginning of his analysis of the Schreber case (1911, p. 9) that "paranoics cannot be compelled to overcome their internal resistances."

At this point, let us summarize, up to 1914, the development of Freud's thinking pertaining to the psychoses and the applicability of psychoanalysis to their treatment.

In 1893 Freud (1895) divided psychological illnesses into those of organic and psychological origin, although neither then nor at any subsequent time did he present clearly his criteria for deciding which patients suffered from organically or psychologically caused psychopathological states. In 1894 he (1887-1902, pp. 86-88) included melancholia and mania among the neuroses and in 1895 (1895, p. 141), paranoia. He soon (1896a, p. 175) hinted that identical symptom complexes could result from either predominantly organic or mental causes, placing paranoia among the psychoses. In "Further Remarks on the Neuro-Psychoses of Defence" Freud (1896a) designated as chronic paranoia the illness of a woman whose case material served as the basis for his discussion of paranoia, but in 1924 he added a footnote, naming the condition *dementia paranoides*. Perhaps his early diagnostic label implied that he considered her condition to have been psychogenic and subsequently, on the basis of material omitted from the case presentation, had decided the causes of her psychopathology to have been organic in nature. Two years later Freud (1898b) concluded that psychoanalysis was suitable only for the treatment of neuroses, but he did not state his reasons. Soon (1898a) he included paranoia anew among the neuroses. A few years later Freud (1940b, p. 258) believed psychoanalysis to be contraindicated for "neuropathic degeneration," psychosis, states of confusion, and toxic or "deeply-rooted" depression, implying that it was to be used for the treatment of illnesses not of organic origin. By 1909 Freud (1909a) made this judgment explicit, stating that psychoanalysis was to be used to treat illnesses that had mental causation and implied that such pathological conditions resulted from the claims of civilization. He then (1911) implied that paranoia is not amenable to psychoanalysis when he said that paranoics cannot be compelled to give up their resistances, but he (1911, 1914a) also placed paranoia between the transference neuroses and the psychoses, represented by paraphrenia. In schizophrenia the break with reality constitutes complete withdrawal of libidinal cathexis from the environmental and turning it onto the self. If the decathected libido becomes attached to the ego, megalomania results, and if to the body, hypochondriasis. Such libido withdrawal recreates the early narcissistic state of the infant, and following such regression the psychotic gradually recathects mental representations of external objects in a highly primitive manner, through hallucinations and delusions.

A number of questions are obvious.

How is one to distinguish between psychopathological states of organic and psychogenic origin? If Freud is correct that at least some psychopathologies of mental origin, that is, resultant from socialization, are amenable to psychoanalysis, the answer to this query is crucial. Freud implied that such a differentiation could be made retrospectively by the clinical course of the illness, which in organically caused conditions was gradually deteriorating, but that an early differentiation might have to be devised by scientists of other disciplines. The implication would be that psychoanalytic therapy should be attempted for some unstated period of time, regardless of the patient's state when first interviewed.

During what period is a patient to be considered psychotic? Apparently some degree of decathexis short of total withdrawal of libido is to be found in all other conditions; in them the previous cathexis of persons and things is replaced by cathexis of fantasized objects. But the same phenomenon occurs with the psychotic during the restitutive phase. Megalomania and hypochondriasis are also conditions that can be observed in states other than paraphrenia, as in paranoia.

Why is the psychotic not amenable to psychoanalysis? Freud felt there was insufficient libidinal cathexis available for investment in external objects, and therefore transference would not occur. But what quantity of cathexis has to be available for transference to exist? How can that be determined without an attempt at psychoanalysis? Freud did not say. He implied that psychoanalytic therapy could not be done while the patient was hallucinating and deluded, but this judgment was inconsistent because some of his "hysterical" patients hallucinated and some of his "obsessional" patients were deluded. Before 1911 and again in "On Narcissism: An Introduction" in 1914, paranoia had been included among the conditions that were possibly amenable to psychoanalysis. But then even though the paranoic was not psychotic within the framework of the orientation of the libido theory, he was not subject to psychoanalysis; nevertheless, persons who suffered from acquired melancholia and mania presumably were. Freud also made amply clear his awareness that the symptoms of paraphrenia and paranoia were frequently intermixed, and he remained dissatisfied with his formulations. These and other vexing problems pertaining to a theory of the psychoses, as we shall see below, continued to trouble him throughout his life. We shall now continue to present the unfolding of his thinking concerning the psychoses.

In 1910 Freud (1918) undertook the psychoanalysis of the Wolf Man, who had been hospitalized for various periods with a diagnosis of manic-depressive insanity; the initial period of treatment lasted until 1914, when Freud regarded the case as completed. He considered the Wolf Man's condition to represent a severe case of obsessional neurosis.[4] Freud set an arbitrary date for termination of the analysis because it seemed that this passive patient had become too comfortable in his relationships with Freud, and it appeared unlikely that further movement would take place without his taking an unusually active step. Following the completion of the four-year psychoanalysis, the Wolf Man appeared to be symptom-free during a period of five years; then he returned for another four-month period of analysis, afflicted with a severe case of "hysterical constipation." By that time he had lost his wealth and Freud not only treated him without charge but even arranged to support him and his invalid wife through solicited contributions. Freud continued to present him with money for the next six years.

In 1923 the Wolf Man learned that Freud had undergone an operation on his mouth. Apparently this news caused the Wolf Man to masturbate compulsively. Subsequently he learned that Freud suffered from cancer. In the same year, the Wolf Man's mother developed a wart on her nose and became hypochondriacal. During the next three years he developed a hypochondriacal type of paranoia. He became convinced that his nose had been deformed by a physician whom he equated with Freud. In 1926 he returned to Freud for further treatment and was referred to Brunswick (1928), who analyzed him without fee for four or five months. She found his hypochondriacal ideas to mask persecutory delusions. The Wolf Man had identified both with his mother and a castrated

4. Jones (1955, p. 273) wrote: "The patient suffered from an extremely severe neurosis." Zetzel (1965) stated it to be probable that whenever Freud diagnosed a patient to have been a severe neurotic, that patient was either a borderline psychotic or frankly psychotic.

image of his father. Brunswick wrote (p. 440): "The source of the new illness was an unresolved remnant of the transference, which, after fourteen years, under the stress of peculiar circumstances, became the basis for a new form of an old illness." During his treatment by Brunswick, the Wolf Man overcame his fear of castration and lost his paranoid psychosis. She saw him for a second period of analysis two years later and had occasional interviews with him during the next fourteen years. In 1940 she reported him to be in excellent health, as did Gardiner (1953) some fifteen years later.

The implications of Freud's having accepted the Wolf Man in psychoanalysis are interesting. Despite his use of the label "severe obsessional neurosis," he could scarcely have been unaware of the man's being what we would today call a borderline schizophrenic. The past history was available to Freud, and during the first interview the Wolf Man offered to submit to anal intercourse with Freud and then to defecate on his head. This gives credence to the supposition that Freud probably felt that a trial period of psychoanalysis was indicated for many patients who presented mixed symptomatology, so long as there was evidence that transference could develop. However, we can only infer what constituted such evidence to Freud. He considered psychotic patients to be incapable of transference, at least theoretically. *It would appear that when Freud used the word* transference *in this context, he meant transference reactions that he could trace obviously to oedipal traumata and that did not shift rapidly during the course of the treatment.*[5]

Let us now retrace our steps and consider another facet of Freud's thinking. As we have seen, he did not initially occupy himself with problems of definition of psychopathological states. He was more interested in creating an operational

5. Today we know that psychotic patients are indeed capable of the most intense of transference relationships, except possibly during the brief moment when the silent pathological process of schizophrenia is in operation (Pious 1949).

model of psychical structure, one which would account for the observations he made of his patients' productions. In 1895 in "Project for a Scientific Psychology," Freud (1887-1902, pp. 347-445) sought to represent the psychical apparatus in terms of neurophysiology but became dissatisfied with his formulations and never completed and published the fruits of his efforts. From the early nineties he developed his hydrodynamic libido theory, which, as illustrated above, formed the basis of his theory of the psychoses. However, his thinking went further, and in chapter VII of *The Interpretation of Dreams*, Freud (1900) systematically proposed the topographical theory.[6] His formulations concerning the psychoses have been understood generally by psychoanalysts principally in terms of the libido theory within the framework of the topographical hypothesis and not within that of the structural theory. As we shall see below, Freud attempted, albeit unsuccessfully, to reconcile his theory of the psychoses with the structural hypothesis.

In "The Unconscious," Freud (1915c) began to express dissatisfaction with the topographical theory because he had discovered the existence of unconscious fantasies and found

6. The following synopsis of the topographical theory is taken from chapter VII (Freud 1900) and "The Unconscious" (Freud 1915c). See also Arlow and Brenner (1964). In the topographical theory, the psychical apparatus is divided into the systems *Ucs.*, *Pcs.*, and *Cs.* on the basis of their relationships to consciousness. The elements of the system *Ucs.* are unavailable to consciousness and are governed by the primary process. The elements of the system *Pcs.* are more readily accessible to consciousness. Both the systems *Pcs.* and *Cs.* are governed by the secondary process. The repressing agency that keeps forbidden memories and wishes in the *Ucs.* is the censor of the *Pcs.* The crucial factor in neurotic symptoms formation is of the accessibility to consciousness of mental elements, those elements being unconscious sexual wishes in conflict with the individual's conscious moral standards and practical life goals. Repressed wishes threaten to overcome the repressive forces of the censor; compromise formations result in the production of neurotic symptoms. Only an unconscious wish can be pathogenic. The task of therapy is the removal of repression to make relevant contents of the *Ucs.* accessible to the *Cs.*

they could not be placed rationally in any of the systems provided by his model. Inaccessibility to consciousness was the cardinal criterion for distinguishing between the systems *Ucs.* and *Pcs.* Unconscious fantasies belong by definition to the system *Ucs.*, but such fantasies are composed of definite word and object-representations, and their formal aspects reveal influences of the secondary process; thus they should be assigned to the system *Pcs.* In "On Narcissism: An Introduction," Freud (1914a) had postulated a differentiating grade within the ego, which he called the ego-ideal and later the superego. By the time he contributed "Beyond the Pleasure Principle," Freud (1920) had become certain that both unconscious libidinal and aggressive drive derivatives could result in psychical conflict when they threatened to irrupt into consciousness. The topographical theory had made provisions only for repressed sexual drives. Freud's growing dissatisfactions with the topographical theory led him to revise fundamentally his concept of psychical structure and to create a new hypothetical view of psychical systems that was incompatible with the topographical hypothesis. This led to his publication of *The Ego and The Id* (1923).

In *The Ego and The Id,* Freud postulated a psychical structure with two parts. The id was the repository for the instinctual drives, which included aggressive as well as libidinal drives. The ego, more coherent and organized, mediated between drive-derivatives and the demands of the external world; it contained the antiinstinctual forces of the mind, some of which were unconscious. The ego itself came to have a second division, the superego; this consisted of the moral functions of the ego.

Freud was particularly struck with two sets of clinical observations: (1) in neurotic conflicts, repressive forces are *not* always readily available to consciousness, and (2) a need for punishment may be inaccessible to consciousness. The significance of the first observation was that accessibility to consciousness cannot be used as the basis for dividing the mental apparatus into systems. The second had further meaning. When Freud found an unconscious need for punishment in some patients, he concluded that conflicts existed not only between the demands of id and ego but also between those of ego and superego.

In "Mourning and Melancholia," Freud (1917a) determined that an object that had been lost was reinstated within the ego, that is, that an object cathexis had been replaced by an identification. In *The Ego and The Id,* he (1923, p. 35) concluded, "this kind of substitution has a great share in determining the form taken on by the ego and that it contributed materially towards building up what is called its 'character.'" He added, "In the primitive oral phase of the individual's existence, object-cathexis and identification are hardly to be distinguished from each other." He (p. 36) suggested that such identification might be the sole condition under which the id can give up its objects and that "the ego is a precipitate of abandoned object cathexes and . . . maintains a record of past object choices." In the dissolution of the Oedipus complex, the object cathexis of the mother must be given up and its place could be filled either with an identification with the mother or an intensified identification with the father. The dissolution of the Oedipus complex resulted in the formation of the superego; the identifications were those of the parents' ethical and moral aspects, as they had been perceived by the child.

Thus Freud developed the structural model to account for mental phenomena not explained by the topographical theory. The fundamental changes of hypotheses implied the need of a vast change in the aims of psychoanalytic treatment and, in fact, the effect of the change on psychoanalytic technique has been enormous.

In the topographical theory, the therapeutic task is to make the contents of the system *Ucs.* conscious. Symptom formation results from the failure of repression; the irruption of unconscious instinctual wishes into consciousness threatens. Their derivatives are excluded from consciousness through the substitute expression of wishes in the form of symptoms. Therapy aims at the abrogation of repression to recover forgotten data, especially those pertaining to childhood traumata.

In the structural theory, intrapsychic conflict is viewed as much more than a problem of inaccessibility to consciousness. Since the defenses themselves are frequently unconscious, their analysis is part of the therapeutic task; their automatic actions must be resolved, and the integration of instinctual derivatives and their memories that were previously defended against should be permitted into the normal parts of the ego. In addition to the analysis of id derivatives and ego defenses, it is of great importance to analyze whatever superego manifestations are part of the pathogenic conflict.

Freud was aware of a lack of consonance between his theory of the psychoses and the structural hypothesis. In 1911, when he had not formulated clearly the system ego, he had postulated a complete withdrawal of libido from objects of the external world and a regression to the stage of narcissism in the psychosis. By 1923 he thought that lost objects were reinstated with the ego, or that object cathexes were replaced by identifications. The ego was conceptualized as a precipitate of past object cathexes. In the topographical hypothesis, libido is both withdrawn and detached from objects, whereas in the structural theory libido is conceptualized as being attached *always* to *some* object representation, no matter how primitive and archaic. Insofar as the building blocks of the ego consist of precipitates of internal objects, ego-libido must, of necessity, be attached to such objects. Within the framework of the structural hypothesis libido cannot exist in a vacuum, that is, without an object component. Theoretically, therefore, some degree of transference is possible whenever *any* ego structure persists, insofar as that structure has been developed from object precipitates. Freud's formulations concerning the treatment of the psychoses can be seriously questioned since they rest on the premise that transference is impossible.

Soon after the appearance of *The Ego and The Id,* Waelder (1924) discussed a schizoid mathematician who he believed had made a reasonably successful adjustment by sublimating his narcissistic libido. Waelder reached the practical conclusion that there can be a "union" of narcissistic and object libido and, therefore, transference is possible. Freud read Waelder's manuscript in the spring of 1924 and was stimulated to reconsider his position about the psychoanalytic treatment of the psychoses. A few weeks later he published "Neurosis and Psychosis." In the second paragraph he wrote (Freud 1924b, p. 149): "In connection with a train of thought raised in other quarters which was concerned with the origin and prevention of the psychoses," a reference to Waelder's manuscript (Waelder 1965).

Freud made two brief attempts to apply the structural hypothesis to the theory of the psychopathology of the psychoses, "Neurosis and Psychosis" and "The Loss of Reality in Neurosis and Psychosis" (1924a). They were his last papers that dealt specifically with this subject, although he continued to occupy himself with the dissonance between the formulations he had propounded in 1911 and the structural theory. Nevertheless, he did not totally relinquish his original position concerning the psychoses.

In "Neurosis and Psychosis," Freud considered the role of the superego in the psychoses. In the topographical theory, moral trends were thought to be conscious and governed by the secondary process. He noted that the role of the superego must be taken into account in every form of psychical illness and wrote (1924c, p. 152), "There must also be illnesses which are based on a conflict between the ego and the superego," such as melancholia. He used the term *narcissistic neurosis* for such illnesses and continued, "Transference neuroses correspond to a conflict between the ego and the id; narcissistic neuroses to a conflict between the ego and the super-ego; and psychoses to one between the ego and the outer world." Freud (1915a, p. 124; 1915c, p. 196) had previously used the words *narcissistic neurosis* in connection with his idea of libido withdrawal in the psychoses.

In "The Loss of Reality in Neurosis and Psychosis" Freud stated (1924a, p. 185): "Both neurosis and psychosis are . . . the result of a rebellion on the part of the id against the external world." In both conditions there is a disturbance of the patient's relations with reality due to a failure of repression. In the development of a psychosis, however, a second step is involved. In "The Neuro-Psychoses of Defence" Freud (1894a, p. 58) had written, "The ego rejects the incompatible idea together with the affect and behaves as though the idea had never occurred to the ego at all." Now (1924a, pp. 184-185) he wrote, "The second step of the psychosis is indeed intended to make good the loss of reality, not, however, at the expense of restriction of the id . . . but by the creation of a new reality." Although he used his new concept of the id, he retained the old theory of anxiety, that of the libido theory within the framework of the topographical hypothesis; he continued: "In a psychosis, the transforming of reality is carried out upon the psychical precipitations of former relations to it . . . this relation was never a closed one; it was continually being enriched and altered by fresh perceptions. Thus, the psychosis is also faced with the task of procuring for itself perceptions of a kind which shall correspond to the new reality; and this is radically effected by means of hallucinations." "Probably in a psychosis the rejected piece of reality constantly forces itself upon the mind, just as the repressed instinct does in a neurosis." He determined the role of fantasy to be important in both neurosis and psychosis. In the former condition, disagreeable reality is compensated for by a world of fantasy, but in psychosis, too (p. 187), "phantasy plays the same part . . . it is the storehouse from which materials of the pattern for building the new reality are derived." Thus, "both in neurosis and psychosis there comes into a consideration the question not only of a loss of reality but also of a substitute for reality."

In this attempt to integrate his formulations concerning the psychopathology of the psychoses with the structural theory, Freud appears to have begun to consider the possibility that *the fantasies of the psychotic are tied to those elements of ego structure that have resulted from identifications.* However, he did not amplify this theme or carry it to its logical conclusion regarding transference.

In "Fetishism," Freud (1927) discussed two patients who refused to believe in the deaths of their fathers, but neither had become psychotic. This clinical datum contradicted his thesis that only psychoses are detached from reality. He then wrote (p. 156): "It is true that there is one way out of the difficulty. My formula only needed to hold good where there was a higher degree of differentiation in the psychical apparatus (than in childhood); things might be permissible to a child which would entail severe injury to an adult." However, the patients had not merely "scotomized" their fathers' deaths. They had a split attitude; the attitude of the wish and that of the reality existed side by side. He added, "in a psychosis the one current—that which fitted with reality—would in fact have been absent."

In *An Outline of Psychoanalysis,* Freud's last publication on this subject, he (1940, p. 114) noted that either an intolerably painful reality situation or "extraordinarily intensified" instincts could precipitate the outbreak of a psychosis. Then he reversed his original hypothesis of complete withdrawal of cathexis from mental representations, writing (pp. 114-115): "The problem of psychoses would be simple and intelligible if the withdrawal of the ego from reality could be carried through completely. But that seems rarely if ever to happen. Even so far removed from the reality of the external world as hallucinatory confusional states, one learns . . . that at the time in some corner of their mind, there was a normal person hidden, who watched the hubbub of the illness go past, like a disinterested spectator." He continued (pp. 115-116), "what occurs in all such cases is a split in the mind. Two mental attitudes have been formed instead of a single one—one, the normal one, which takes account of reality, and another which under the influence of the instincts detaches the ego from reality." "If the second is or becomes the stronger, the necessary condition for a psychosis is present. If the relation is reversed, then there is an apparent cure of the delusional disorder. Actually, it has only retreated into the unconscious." Freud, then, suggested once again the existence of a continuum of psychical illnesses, which were to be differentiated from one another largely on the basis of quantitative factors. Additionally, he suggested but did not adumbrate a major revision of the first part of his original formulations concerning the development of the schizophrenias, namely that there is a total decathexis of the objects followed by a restitutional phase. In this final monograph, he suggested the complete withdrawal of cathexis did *not* take place.

Through the courtesy of Dr. Dieter Eicke, we are able to reproduce a translation of a letter written by Freud in 1935.[7] It concerns a patient whom Freud treated psychoanalytically, presumably in the late 1920s and early 1930s. Although the patient was not schizophrenic, according to Freud, he was nevertheless psychotic. From the symptomatology listed, either the diagnosis of schizophrenia or of schizoaffective psychosis seems possible.

Wien 30.6.1935

Sehrgeehrter Herr Doktor,

I was most touched by your news of the death of Mr. X., since he occupied my highest professional interest for many years. I

7. This letter has been published in its original form by L. H. Binswanger (1956). In a personal communication received after this chapter was written, Dr. Binswanger stated that the patient later had an acute "schizophrenic-manic outburst" and subsequently died of "catatonic fever." The patient had had other "attacks" before he was treated by Freud, and after his treatment by Freud he had periods of remission and his "mental state was almost good" but from time to time hospital treatment was required.

was not much concerned about his typical constitution or about classifying him psychiatrically. Like you, I am not satisfied with the diagnosis of schizophrenia in his case. I shall impart to you here what I feel that I understood about the psychic mechanism of his illness.

He complained of a total loss of capacity to work and a decrease of interest in professional and business matters. I was able to bring him back to conducting his business but he was unable to resume his theoretical work. I never made him quite normal. The way he treated symbols in his mind, confused identifications, falsified memories and kept to his delusional superstitions made him always psychotic; his mood was always hypomanic. As for the aetiology, one had certainly to think of constitutional factors, but there was the question of an individual cause of his illness which I was unable to answer. Nevertheless, one day I had the opportunity to observe him more clearly. He was left alone in my room and accused himself of an act of indecent behavior, a fact which he could easily have kept secret. (He had read private notes on my desk.) This confession impressed me deeply. I felt seduced to analyze it. He was then oppressed by something he had done and he was troubled to keep it secret. I recalled then that he habitually spoke vividly of all of the phases and instances of his life, but omitted a great technical invention and its implications. I got the impression there had been something amiss concerning the history of this invention, that he accused himself of something pertaining to it, which he tried to deny. I had no idea what it could be. However, I doubted the advisability of continuing to attempt to lift this denial. With a neurotic this would have been the only correct way and would have promised the end of the illness, but I was probably right in doubting the influence of analysis on a psychotic. In making conscious the conflict I had to fear a new psychotic breakdown which I would then be unable to manage. Therefore I decided to leave the theme and to be satisfied with an imperfect and temporary success.

Soon afterwards the patient left me, pretending that he could no longer stay away from his business. Fortunately for my own future I had refused his invitation to move with him to Berlin. A short time later I heard from a reliable person that the partner of my patient, with whom he had worked on his invention and who was now working in a firm in Czechoslovakia, had accused him of having cheated him out of his right of possession to the patent. He had proposed to my patient an arrangement which he rejected violently. This had happened during the period of his analysis with me, but the patient had never mentioned it and I did not even know of the existence of a partner. My patient instituted and lost a lawsuit. I do not know what happened later. Nevertheless, I felt this material confirmed my suspicion. My patient was a neurotic criminal, that is a swindler with a sensitive conscience. He could not resist the temptation to take more of the rights of the invention than were due to him but he had to pay with useless humiliations for the guilt instigated by his silence. Even his working had the characteristics of self-punishment. All his unconscious attempts to avoid hearing his hatred of himself while he defended himself against his unconscious conscience were fruitless. He then unfortunately got known with such an unscrupulous swindler and exploiter as (name).

With kind regards,
Freud

At least two points relating to Freud's having undertaken the analysis of this patient whom he considered to have "always been psychotic" and to the technique he used are significant. It may be that Mr. X. was the only psychotic patient with whom Freud attempted psychoanalysis, subsequent to his presentation in 1911 and 1914 of his formulations concerning the psychoses. We must wonder why Freud never published this case history, since to have done so would have indicated that his viewpoint was changing concerning the applicability of psychoanalysis to the psychoses and perhaps have encouraged other analysts to engage in such treatment.

Despite Freud's having undertaken this psychoanalysis, he apparently had from the beginning a pessimistic viewpoint, since he wrote, "I was probably right in doubting the influence of analysis on a psychotic." It would seem that the treatment went well until Freud abandoned the classical technique and failed to pursue the unresolved conflict because of his fear of "a new psychotic breakdown." Just what Freud meant by this statement is obscure, when we recall he said the patient was "always psychotic" and that Freud had begun the analysis while, presumably, Mr. X. was in a state of psychotic decompensation. At any event, Freud believed that the lifting of a denial would have been detrimental to the patient, producing a clinical state "which I would have been unable to manage." Why he would have been unable to manage that breakdown is unstated. By implication, he seems to have consigned the patient to permanent psychosis by failing to analyze the defensive nature of the denial and uncovering the unconscious delusions that it no doubt held in check. It seems probable that the patient sensed Freud's pessimism and fear, because soon after the investigation of the denial was abandoned, Mr. X. found reasons to discontinue therapy. It seems reasonable to suspect that this analysis failed *because* Freud abandoned the classical technique.

We have to wonder, in view of Freud's actions with this psychotic patient, whether his analysis of the Wolf Man may also have remained incomplete because of his behavior. To be sure, Brunswick's case presentation and recounting of Freud's technique during the first analysis of the Wolf Man give no such indication. However, it seems unlikely that she would have openly criticized her esteemed mentor. Her explanations for Freud's failure to complete the Wolf Man's analysis seem unconvincing. Concerning the first period of analysis, she attributed it both to Freud's arbitrary setting of a termination date and to a supposed impossibility that the Wolf Man could have been analyzed by a man. Many patients who suffered from deep-seated problems related to latent homosexuality have been analyzed successfully by men. We have scant factual data concerning Freud's ongoing technique during that period of treatment. However, we know that during the second analysis with Freud, the Wolf Man was seen without fee and that Freud even supported him and his wife. Further, we know that during the six-year period when Freud continued to supply him with money the Wolf Man was in possession of family jewels and consciously defrauded Freud. We can surmise that Freud's parameter of paying the patient to come to see him and to continue to have contacts with Freud was not satisfactorily analyzed. When the Wolf Man later said he considered himself to be Freud's favorite son, surely his judgment was not determined entirely by fantasies based on transference. The similarities between the fraudulence of the Wolf Man and the deception of Mr. X. of the 1935 letter are obvious. It seems reasonable to suspect that countertransference involvement combined with Freud's viewpoint concerning the impossibility of cure of psychosis by psychoanalysis may have caused him to abandon classical analytical technique with the Wolf Man as well as with Mr. X. and to raise the question of whether such abandonment was responsible for the incompleteness of both analyses.[8]

SUMMARY

This chapter has outlined the development of Freud's thinking concerning the psychopathology of the psychoses, epito-

8. The development of Freud's thinking about the schizophrenias has been reviewed more recently by London (1973a, 1973b) and Grotstein (1977a, 1977b). Freud's view of schizophrenia as a disorder of conflict, no different from neurosis except in depth, severity, and mode of defense, owes its provenance to the Freud of 1894 through 1911, to Melanie Klein and her co-workers, and to Arlow and Brenner. That orientation has been called the unitary theory by London and the conflict model by Grotstein. Proponents of the unitary theory include Arlow and Brenner (1964, 1969), Boyer (1966), Grinberg (1977), Kubie (1971) and Pao (1973). In his review of Freud's view of schizophrenia as a deficiency disorder, London has traced six different ways in which Freud used the word *decathexis*. Those favoring a specific, defect theory of schizophrenia include Freeman (1970), London (1973a,b) and Wexler (1971). Lidz (1973) thinks of schizophrenia as a deficiency disorder in the sense that the family of the schizophrenic has been remiss in supplying the necessary ingredients to assist the growing child and adolescent to reach psychosocial maturity.

mized by the schizophrenias. That development can be divided into three phases: (1) During the period when Freud was groping with the problem of whether psychopathological states were rationally attributable solely to organic etiologies or their origins could be traced purely to psychogenic causes, he apparently concluded, although he never stated specifically, that some psychical disturbances had their causes in hereditary, constitutional and/or degenerative factors, and the genesis of others could be ascribed to conflicts between instinctual forces and socialization agents. Psychoanalytic therapy was considered to be potentially beneficial to disorders of the second group. (2) Freud then developed the libido theory within the framework of the topographical hypothesis. In the constellation of those postulations, he devised his formulations concerning the psychoses: in psychosis there is a total decathexis of libidinal investment from mental representations of the objects of the external world and an attachment of the detached object-libido onto the self. If the erstwhile object-libido becomes invested in the subject's ego, he becomes megalomanic, and if it be attached to the body, hypochondriasis results. Following regression to such a narcissistic phase, the psychotic gradually recathects mental representations of external objects in a distorted manner, usually through hallucinations and delusions, in a restitutive phase. The implications of this formulation were that psychoanalytic therapy of the psychoses was contraindicated because, as a result of total withdrawal of libidinal cathexis, the development of transference was either impossible or too tenuous to permit lasting relationships with a therapist. (3) After Freud's clinical observations led him to revise his ideas concerning the nature of the mental apparatus and to devise the structural hypothesis with its attendant alterations in instinct and anxiety theories, he sought to bring his theory concerning the psychoses into consonance with his new and profoundly altered position. Although in his last writings he indicated awareness that in the schizophrenias total withdrawal of instinctual cathexis does not take place, he never totally abandoned his theory of the psychoses.

The following chapter will be concerned with the historical development of the thinking of other psychoanalysts concerning the genesis and therapy of the schizophrenias. Arguments will be presented that are intended to indicate that the psychoses are better understood within the framework of the structural theory and that psychoanalytic therapy is logically applicable to the psychoses.

CHAPTER THREE

Historical Development of Psychoanalytic Psychotherapy of the Schizophrenias: The Followers of Freud

L. Bryce Boyer

As outlined in chapter 2, the development of Freud's thinking concerning the psychopathology of the schizophrenias can be divided somewhat arbitrarily into three phases.[1]

Between 1893 and 1910 Freud viewed the psychoses from the aspect of libido development and laid stress on fixation points, defense mechanisms, the aims of the sexual instinct, and object cathexis. During this first period, he groped with the problem of whether psychopathological states could be attributed solely either to organic or psychological causes and apparently concluded that some psychical disturbances had their origins predominantly in hereditary, constitutional, and/or degenerative phenomena but the genesis of others could be ascribed mainly to conflicts between libidinal forces and socialization agents. Psychoanalytic therapy was considered to be useful in the treatment of the second group and to operate by making elements of the system *Ucs.* available to the systems *Pcs.* and *Cs.* through removing repressions.

Between 1911 and 1923 Freud's views concerning the structure of the psychical apparatus changed fundamentally. As he became dissatisfied with the topographical theory, he presented the dual instinct theory (1920) and introduced the structural hypothesis (1923). Concerning the psychoses, he offered a formulation that used the libido theory within the framework of the topographical hypothesis (1911, 1914b). Freud concluded that in psychosis there was a break with

1. See also Rickman (1926, 1927), who divided Freud's contributions into three slightly different phases. Rickman listed 500 references.

reality that consisted of a total decathexis of libido from objects of the external world and an attachment of the detached object-libido onto the self. If the libido, which had been detached from objects, were invested in the subject's ego, he became megalomanic; if it were attached to his body, hypochrondriac. Following regression to such a narcissistic phase, the psychotic person gradually recathected mental representations of external objects in a distorted manner, usually through hallucinations and delusions, in a restitutional phase. Psychoanalytic treatment of psychotics was considered to be contraindicated because, with total withdrawal of libidinal cathexis, the development of transference was either impossible or too attenuated to permit lasting relationships with a therapist.

In 1924, following his revision of the instinct theory and the introduction of the structural hypothesis, Freud (1924a, 1924b) wrote his last papers dealing specifically with the psychoses. In them he began to bring his formulations concerning the psychoses into consonance with his new and basically altered position. He then knew that serious disturbance of ego functions occurs regularly in the neuroses and the psychoses, although he stressed that in the latter conditions they have more serious consequences. When he presented his revised theory of anxiety, Freud (1926) clearly recognized that the disturbances that occur in ego functions are primarily defensive in nature and knew much of their relations to anxiety and the aggressive drive. Nevertheless, he never rejected completely the theory of the psychoses propounded within the framework of the topographical theory, despite the fact that in his last writings Freud (1932, 1940) indicated his awareness that total withdrawal of instinctual cathexis does not take place regularly in the schizophrenias.

In order to maintain his original formulations regarding the genesis of the schizophrenias, Freud had to ignore the fact that the course of development of at least a significant minority of patients does not follow the pattern he had outlined, that is, severe disruption of relations with the environment followed by a restitutive phase.[2] As far as his writings indicate, he did not come to the conclusion that in both neuroses and psychoses various ego functions are disturbed as part of the defensive struggle against instinctual derivatives, self-punitive trends, or both. This is especially interesting, since Freud was well aware of the existence of psychoses that continued from childhood and developed insidiously and gradually; he knew, too, that psychotic persons had various degrees of ego maturity. Tausk, who wrote before the introduction of the structural theory and used the language then in vogue, seemed to understand to a degree that was advanced for his period the contributions of derivatives of libidinal and aggressive drive energies to the development of normal, neurotic, and psychotic components within the same person. He rediagnosed Freud's "hysterical" patient, "Miss Emma A.," as a case of "paranoia somatica." Freud attended Tausk's presentation (1919) of his classical paper before the Vienna Psycho-Analytic Society and raised no objection to Tausk's stand on these matters.

This chapter will be devoted to tracing the historical development of the thinking of Freud's followers concerning the therapy of the schizophrenias. The treatment of schizophrenia involving psychoanalytic principles has developed concurrently in Europe and the Americas. Nevertheless, its course has varied on the three continents. For convenience, this survey will be divided into two parts: (1) The first will deal with the growth of interest and the alterations of technique employed in Europe and Latin America. (2) The second will concern itself with the attitudes of psychoanalysts of the United States. Because psychoanalysts have moved from one continent to another during their productive years, a strict division on the basis of geography is impossible.

2. In one recent population study, it was found that schizophrenia "had an acute onset in approximately 40% of the cases and a periodical course in as many cases" (Hallgren and Sjögren 1959, p. 59).

THE CONTRIBUTIONS OF PSYCHOANALYSTS OF EUROPE AND LATIN AMERICA

The Pre-Kleinian Period

Reading the pre-Freudian psychiatric literature and the writings of investigators of even the first decade of this century provides an exciting adventure—the contrast between the nihilistic attitude toward treatment of patients with psychopathological disorders, which existed during the nineteenth century, and the initially exaggerated optimism reflected in the literature of the early twentieth century is remarkable. The difference between the sterility of theories concerning psychiatric illnesses before Freud introduced the results of his studies and the freshness of various subsequent approaches as reflected in the reports of clinicians who sought to test his ideas reminds one of the contrasting experiences of first viewing a still, arid desert in which but a few bedraggled, gray-green, scrubby bushes dot the landscape, and then a verdant, semicultivated valley in which a shining stream provides sustenance for the growth of a number of species of varicolored plants.

The first group, stimulated by Freud's ideas, that sought to study the psychoses from a fresh viewpoint was headed by Bleuler at Burgholzli. His early thinking was influenced by Wundt. He sought to reconcile the differences between the opposing viewpoints of Wundt and Freud and to determine whether mental disorders could be explained best on an organic or a psychological basis. Bleuler introduced the term *schizophrenia* as a substitute for dementia praecox. He demonstrated the part that autistic thinking plays in the development of paranoia. He studied the language of schizophrenia and explored regressive behavior. He believed the discrepancy between the aspirational level and moderate ability of the individual sets the stage for the development of delusions. E.

Bleuler (1911, p. 1) wrote, "An important aspect of the attempt to advance and enlarge the concepts of psychopathology is nothing less than the application of Freud's ideas to dementia praecox." He also credited Abraham, Jung, and Riklin (1906) as having contributed greatly to the development of his ideas.

Jung found so many similarities between hysteria and dementia praecox that one must wonder whether he clearly differentiated these conditions. Although he considered dementia praecox to be rooted more deeply in organic predisposition, he also considered hysteria to contain (1907, p. 97) "in its innermost essence a complex which could never be totally overcome." His principal therapeutic tool for both seems to have been interpretations aimed at the removal of repressions. He eventually considered schizophrenia to be caused by an unusual strength of unconscious urges, so that an abnormal number of atavistic tendencies resulted in faulty adjustment to modern life.

Jung, although initially influenced heavily by Freud's ideas, deviated sharply later (Freud 1914a, Glover 1950). His viewpoint was essentially biological, and while he paid some attention to the effects of the past life of the individual, he conceptualized the existence of a collective unconscious in which primordial images or archetypes had been deposited as a result of countless recurrences of identical situations in previous generations. Whereas Freud eventually wrote of inherited maturational trends, Jung believed there to be inheritance of thought content.

Abraham (1907) considered the symptoms of hysteria and schizophrenia to be elaborations of sexual fantasies of an infantile character. He (1908) found that dementia praecox destroys the capacity for sexual transference and object-love, a condition that explained indifference to the outer world, but not other symptoms of the disorder. Nevertheless, Abraham mentioned gradations of schizophrenic involvement in different individuals and used interpretations aimed at the removal of repression with at least some patients. He considered the schizophrenic to be "ripe for delusions of persecution" because the patient who has withdrawn libido from objects to himself has set up an antithesis between the outer world and himself; then he loves only himself, and his hostilities are projected onto persons who were previously loved. Abraham explained delusions of grandeur and overvaluation of the self on the basis of the attachment to the self of libido after its decathexis from love-objects. Thus the sexual overestimation that had returned to the ego was the source of the delusion of grandeur. He differentiated between hysteria and schizophrenia as follows: in the autoerotism of dementia praecox there is a return of the libido to the self, but in hysteria, object cathexis is exaggerated; in the former there is a loss of the capacity to sublimate, and in the latter there is increased sublimation. Although both conditions have an innate psychosexual constitution, that of schizophrenia depends on an inhibition of development. Abraham thus anticipated parts of Freud's formulation (1911, 1914b) concerning the psychoses.

In his 1908 presentation, Abraham did not consider the psychotic to be incapable of hostile transference. Within a few years he discussed a schizophrenic male. The patient had identified his father with the sun (as had Schreber). He wrote (1913, p. 175): "The patient had also transferred to the sun his ambivalent attitude toward his father in a remarkable way. He disliked the light of the sun but loved its warmth." Thus, by 1913, Abraham no longer considered schizophrenics to have totally decathected libido from love-objects and thought them to be capable of transference of libido as well as hostility.

Maeder found delusions of persecution to reflect projection and unresolved homosexuality; he thought delusions of grandeur to result from an introversion of libido that coincided with regression to a state in which all wishes could be satisfied in a world of fantasy, following removal of the inhibitions imposed by reality. He (1910) wrote (Payne 1913-1914, p. 202):

In psychosis "the content is strongly determined by individual thought elements [and] the motives for actions are relatively few and . . . most of them belong to the instinctive life of the infantile period."

Bertschinger (1911, p. 176) found that the schizophrenic patient can "regain control of his subconscious sphere by correction, resymbolization and evasion," and considered the outbreak of psychosis to constitute "the eruption of the subconscious into the conscious." He did not report actual treatment of schizophrenics.

Ferenczi (1911) supported Freud's position regarding homosexuality, as had Maeder, but he also wrote (Payne 1913-1914, p. 89): "It turns out that the paranoic mechanism is not set up as a defence against all possible investment of the libido but according to present observations is directed only against the homosexual object choice." He thought paranoia in general to be "nothing else than distorted homosexuality."

Bjerre (1911) reported the intensive treatment during forty interviews of a patient who suffered from chronic paranoia. He detailed his method of therapy and was enthusiastic about its results. He wrote (Payne 1915, p. 94): "[I worked] through the details of the patient's whole life from earliest childhood to the present, pointing out the proper value of everything false therein, sowing thousands of seeds of doubt concerning the delusions and then gradually bringing the unconscious complexes to light and setting them free." Initially Bjerre was careful to avoid becoming the target of the patient's hostility. He was "sympathetic" and showed "not the slightest doubt" that the patient was persecuted. After the paranoic considered Bjerre to be his ally, he began to interpose explanations during the patient's recitals. Transference interpretations were made indirectly if at all. Bjerre felt the patient's feeling of security with him was a great factor in the eventual improvement. He considered interpretation to have been the principal effective tool of therapy but added (Payne 1915, p. 100) that in the treatment of psychotics "One must also, and this in particular, take account of the immediate influences which the physician, often unconsciously, exercises by his person." Despite the tone of optimism so obvious in his presentation, Bjerre's forty-three subsequent articles and books do not include contributions that deal specifically with the treatment of psychotics.

Prior to Tausk's contribution (1919), the writings of other analysts offered but minor amplifications of Freud's views. They supported his position that the symptoms of the psychoses can be understood in the same way as those of the neuroses and that paranoia is either the product of, or closely related to, unresolved homosexuality. Fantasies and behavior were interpretated in terms of unconscious sexual meanings. Occasional analysts concerned themselves with the characteristics of schizophrenic language. Few articles demonstrated actual technical procedures employed in treatment. Most analysts who spoke directly of having treated schizophrenics wrote a single article; it usually presented an optimistic viewpoint concerning the usefulness of the procedure in producing improvement.[3] However, since they contributed but one article, it would seem that their optimism waned.

From 1919 onward, there seems to have been a renewed interest by psychoanalysts in the study of various aspects of the schizophrenias.

Boven (1921) appears to have been the first psychoanalyst to study in a systematic manner the home environment of patients who became psychotic. Storch (1922, Storch and Kulenkampf 1950) wrote extensively of the archaic forms of inner experience and thought in the schizophrenias. Hoop (1924) attributed the archaic elements of projections to the effects of the collective unconscious. Ophuijsen (1920) and

3. The following contributions are representative: L. Binswanger 1910, Birnbaum 1909, Chijs 1919, Delgado 1937, Grebelskaya 1912, Hitschmann 1912, Jones 1909, Markus 1911, Morichau-Beauchant 1912, Nelken 1912, Oppenheim 1912, Simmel 1909, Stärcke 1904, Ter-Ogannessien 1912, Wanke 1919.

Stärcke (1919) wrote of the origin of the feeling of persecution. They found the presumed attack by a homosexual love-object to be a later development of an earlier fear of attack by the skybalum. The persecutor became the personification of the fecal mass and the sensations it produced. Few psychoanalysts wrote in detail of their treatment methods.[4] Nunberg (1921) was an exception.

Nunberg wrote at length of the treatment of a schizophrenic patient. He considered the active fostering of a "positive transference" to be mandatory, a position supported by Alexander (1931) and Federn (1933). Nunberg's therapeutic procedures had much in common with Federn's, to be outlined below.

As discussed in chapter 2, Waelder (1924) suggested that certain schizophrenic patients might be benefited by psychoanalysis without gross modifications, and Brunswick (1928) tacitly supported his stand. Landauer, whose publications spanned seventeen years, wrote (1924) of his procedure in treating schizophrenics, stressing the beneficial results of relatively "passive techniques." He recommended gradual education of the patient concerning his uses of projective mechanisms and active interpretation of hostile transference reactions. Positive transference manifestations were to be ignored. In dealing with auditory hallucinations, Landauer discovered that asking questions about them as if they had originated from a third person resulted in improved reality testing, the patient identifying with the therapist's attitude and feeling pleasure by "overcoming" the analyst.

Laforgue (1926) outlined a complex defensive system that he considered to be of great importance in the development of schizophrenia. His argument was the following: During the stage of psychological weaning, if the child in times of stress is refused refuge by the mother, he responds by attempting to create a narcissistic substitute for her. He introjects two

4. Bumke 1924, Caravedo 1924, Delgado 1937, Hartmann and Stumpfl 1930, Minkowski 1927, Stärcke 1921, Wilmanns 1922.

images of his mother and scotomizes the real mother, from whom he withdraws and whose care he denies he needs. One introjected image is that of the caretaker, and the other is of the idealized mother who demands perfection of behavior and achievement, the mother-ideal. The development of the narcissistic substitute enables the child to avoid the sufferings of the process of psychological weaning and to neutralize the feelings of inferiority inevitable during that process. However, the child is unable to tolerate future frustrations and remains fixated at the anal-sadistic phase. He develops a personality split that Laforgue called schizonoia. He remains an individual who is easily traumatized by frustrations and yet attempts to live up to the self-demands imposed by the introjected mother-ideal; he cannot do so and feels guilt and worthlessness. The child also identifies one aspect of the introjected mother with excrement. In order to kill the frustrating parents, he withdraws from life; in order to castrate them, he thus castrates himself. He depersonalizes people, make them into feces and then chooses feces as his libidinal objects. He becomes receptive to all that has to do with destruction and scotomizes that which is constructive. He chooses his own ego as a love object, but he dissects every thought until nothing remains. While he indulges in this sort of mental digestion, he projects the persecutor.

Laforgue, then, was among the first to stress the role of the sadistic and archaic superego in schizophrenia, although he did not mention that part of the psychical structure by name. At a later time (1935) he presented a case history which outlined his treatment method.

Odile was a schizophrenic girl who made repeated attempts at suicide and was eventually hospitalized after she shot herself in the head, producing a superficial wound. Her illness had begun with an obsession about germs. She urinated in public, drank her urine, and ate slugs; she raged with incoherent words and suffered obstinate constipation. She was awkward and slow physically. She was brought to Laforgue's office by force and was mute. She was seen four times weekly.

Odile lived with a sister who cared for her. During the first weeks of treatment, she was panicky in Laforgue's presence and frequently ran into the waiting room to be with her sister. Since she was mute, he judged her emotional state by her pulse rate, posture, and actions. During the first months Laforgue made his interpretations in the presence of the sister. At first he said only that she feared being alone with him. Later he said she feared love and equated it with excrement; that her constipation was connected with her disgust about sexual things. He said her guilt was great and that she hated herself for having bodily needs. He also told her that she could not collect within herself forever her physical and mental excrement.

After some months, Odile remained in the office with him, but she maintained almost complete silence. She continued to make suicidal attempts, but in such a way as to be prevented by her sister. She began to talk and to lose her constipation. She developed severe insomnia; Laforgue said she remained awake lest a man enter her room. Eventually, references to sexual things did not make her pulse race. The analyst strove to lessen her guilt about sexual thoughts and about her hostile, controlling behavior toward her family. After a year she slept well, was sociable with her family, and went regularly and spontaneously to the toilet. Suicidal behavior continued.

During a vacation period, she tried to throw herself under a train; there were no further attempts to take her life. She then began to lie on the couch and to report her dreams. Progress in locomotion was noticeable; she began to skate and to sew deftly. Nevertheless, she seemed not to exist as a feeling person; sensibility was interdicted. Her verbal productions were memories; there was no thought synthesis. Irrational fears were replaced by "rational" ones, such as being near high windows and skating on thin ice.

As she improved, her sister became glum, so Laforgue treated her as well. After he interpreted to the sister her resentment of loss of authority over the patient and said she had used her relationship with Odile to avoid men, the relationship between the sisters changed. Odile went into a rage at her sister; it was determined that the rage was at all women who couldn't have children and were thus inferior. Soon thereafter Odile became interested in the analyst and asked for personal information. Laforgue did not state whether he answered her questions, but he did give her mouth wash upon her request. The subject matter then went to her germ phobia, thence to her compulsory adolescent masturbation. Guilt concerning masturbation had led first to the phobia and then to the schizophrenic regression. Except for the giving of the mouth wash and perhaps some personal information, the treatment technique apparently changed to orthodox analysis after the understanding of the rage at the sister.

Bychowski (1928) suggested that psychoanalytic principles be employed in the treatment of the schizophrenias, although he considered the introduction of varying modifications of the "passive technique" (Landauer 1924) to be essential. Bychowski's contributions to the literature pertaining to the schizophrenias spanned more than forty years (Bychowski 1923, 1966). Although his earlier writings appear to have been oriented within the framework of the topographical theory, he progressively shifted his viewpoint to the structural hypothesis. He has contributed valuable information concerning the roles of the introjects in the ego of the preschizophrenic and the schizophrenic. Nevertheless, he believes that the introduction of technical modifications is necessary in the treatment of both borderline and psychotic patients.

Garma (1931) thought psychoanalysis could be used successfully without gross modification of technique. He has been using psychoanalysis in the treatment of psychotics for the past forty-five years, employing the couch and using interpretations as his principal therapeutic tool. As with psychoneurotics, he seeks to analyze systematically the transference relationships and the defenses. He was one of the first to introduce the idea that in schizophrenia the superego is extremely punitive and archaic; he postulated that the severity of the superego was in large part responsible for the repression of libidinal and aggressive drive derivatives. He became influenced strongly by Kleinian thinking and joined Rascovsky et al. (1960) in his extension of her system into a study of fetal psychology. Garma (1978) continues to advocate psychoanalysis with few parameters for the treatment of the schizophrenias.

Federn[5] was also a psychoanalyst who consistently treated schizophrenics over a long period. He (1933) presented specific recommendations for the therapeusis of the schizophrenias, and many of the technical procedures he recommended have been accepted by numerous therapists.

According to Federn, if the patient is to be helped, the family or some substitute individual must give active cooperation to the therapy. If the schizophrenic is hospitalized, the nurses and attendants should have been schooled in psychoanalytic principles. Treatment must be directed toward the patient's reason insofar as he maintains it. The transference situation of the schizophrenic is even more important than that of the neurotic, and every possible step must be taken to have the patient's attitudes toward the therapist remain positive. If the doctor-patient relationship becomes hostile, the therapist cannot be effective. Without defining just what he meant by transference or countertransference, Federn wrote (p. 210): "Psychotic patients are accessible to psychoanalysis at all, first, because and in so far as they are still capable of transference; secondly, because and in so far as one part of their ego has insight into their abnormal state, and thirdly, because and in so far as a part of their personality is directed towards reality." The second part of this statement depends on whether the patient has temporary remissions. The chief precaution is to avoid regression wherever possible. Free

5. Federn (1952) developed a theory of ego psychology that is at variance with Freud's. It will not be outlined here because it seems to have had little influence on the theoretical position of very many analysts.

associations and the use of the couch are contraindicated, and the "countertransference" must not be withheld. After the patient has learned what is wrong with his causal behavior and can dissimulate normal behavior, the analyst may cautiously investigate deeper material.

The dependency of the litigious psychotic can be exploited in the therapy. The analyst should help him in the actual affairs of his life. He should seek the connections between the patient's psychotic utterances and his symptoms and between the actual occurrences of his life and his symptoms. After these phenomena and the "actual occurrences of transference situations in his life" are determined, the analyst can explain to the patient the real motives that actuate his behavior and thinking.

While the patient who is not in analysis is benefited by the opportunity for a normal sexual life, Federn considered sterilization by ligature of the oviducts or vas deferens to be indicated in the treatment of some patients. Consistent attempts must be made to avoid flight into introversion. At the same time, "we must suffer" the affect-charged conflicts of rage; after explosions have occurred, they can be analyzed. Only then "we can aim at substituting abreaction according to the analytic method." The psychotic must never be depreciated or treated as a child. We must fully respect the patient's right to his own personality. At the same time, the analyst should gratify the patient's oral cravings and show him hospitality. (Federn sometimes had patients live with him.) He recommended the use of a female helper and lasting postpsychotic contact and help.

The aim of Federn's treatment was to encapsulate "permanent psychotic reactions," to accomplish what occurs in "spontaneous" recovery. That he considered the psychosis itself to be incurable is implicit. Although he called his treatment "The Analysis of Psychotics," he employed very wide deviations from psychoanalysis as it is practiced with neurotics. He conducted psychotherapy in a psychoanalytical framework. Some of his technical modifications were obviously not analyzable, as is consistent with his orientation and treatment goal.

Some remarks concerning the influence of Ferenczi's technical deviations from classical psychoanalysis are in order. No systematic presentation of his ideas pertaining directly to the treatment of the psychoses has come to my attention. Nevertheless, his modifications are evident in the work of analysts both in Europe and the United States, especially Melanie Klein and Harry Stack Sullivan and their followers.

Ferenczi (1929, 1931), Rank (1929), and W. Reich (1933) were dissatisfied with the efficacy of the psychoanalytical treatment of the neuroses. They considered Freud to have understressed the significance of the emotional relationship of the patient and the analyst in the therapeutic situation. Ferenczi emphasized above all that the psychoanalytic situation involved the interaction of two personalities and that its outcome depends upon resolution of both transference and countertransference phenomena. He felt the dynamic train of analytic experience to be dependent upon three precepts (de Forest 1942, Thompson 1943): (1) An emotional relationship between patient and therapist must be fostered and maintained, in part by overt "befriending" of the patient by the use of open reassurances given by the therapist, and by the use of a dramatic dialogue, including "forced fantasies" rather than the usual explanations and interpretations of the analyst-teacher. (2) The analyst must make himself the center of each association and action of the patient. At the same time, he is at liberty to validate the patient's notions about him and to disclose his own feelings. (3) To bring the critical dramatic moments of the analysis to the surface, care must be taken to avoid alleviating emotional tension. Technical terms are to be avoided, and interpretive explanations are to be used most sparingly.

Thompson (1943, 1955) felt that Ferenczi's entering into the transference mood of the patient and his dramatizing interpersonal relationships may have precipitated psychotic episodes when used with borderline patients, and she doubted the value of open reassurance. It is obvious that his departures from ordinary analytic technique were gross and that some of the interventions he employed were not analyzable. Klein was heavily influenced by the thinking of Ferenczi, and many of her followers seem to frame every intervention or interpretation given to the psychotic patient within the context of the transference relationship.

The Kleinian System

The development of child analysis as a specialized branch of psychoanalysis began in the 1920s. With its growth, investigators divided into two major groups, whose divergent theoretical and technical orientations have significantly influenced psychoanalytic thinking regarding the genesis and treatment of the schizophrenias. The work of Anna Freud and her colleagues has contributed substantially to the unfolding of ego psychology and amplification of the structural hypothesis; they have been accepted by one group of European analysts and the vast majority of clinicians in the United States. The studies of Melanie Klein and her supporters have taken a different direction; they have shaped the philosophies of a second major group of European analysts and most of those of Latin America. Kleinian ideas have stimulated more clinicians to work psychoanalytically with psychotics without the use of extraanalytic procedures than have those of Anna Freud.

According to Glover (1945), the findings of the early child analysts were more corroborative of Freud's analysis (1909a) of Little Hans than original in scope. Glover wrote:

> Child analysis was in the first instance a branch of applied psychoanalysis, a behavioristic study. . . . As far as infancy is concerned it must remain an observational study, for until the

> child's mind has reached the stage of development at which it can understand the meanings of interpretations, the psychic system between the child and the analyst remains one of spontaneous or, at the most, of developed rapport only. [p. 76]

Before the 1920s, Freud had delineated positive and negative aspects of the Oedipus situation and outlined the structure of the mind during that phase. His analysis of the obsessional neurosis (1909c, 1913, 1917b) had enabled him to understand the stage immediately preceding the Oedipus phase. However, between the anal phase and the earliest stages of infantile psychosexual activity, a gap remained in the understanding of psychical structure; it was but tenuously outlined by the adumbration of various steps in the development of the libido, conceptions related to the development of object relations and etiological formulations pertaining to paranoia and melancholia (Freud 1905, 1911, 1914b, 1917a). Those steps were expressed principally in terms of libidinal development, although such terms as *oral-sadism, anal-sadism,* and *ambivalence* indicated some understanding of the role played by aggression. To repeat, there were in essence no clearly depicted cross-sections of the mind of children of less than three years of age comparable with those that had been constructed for the child of three to five years. Concepts of id, ego, and superego were first described in terms of the classical oedipal phase. Hypotheses concerning preoedipal regulatory systems were undelineated. Ferenczi (1925, p. 267) had combined the idea of the anal-sadistic stage of the libido with that of the superego by describing "sphincter morality," but this concept was not well correlated with ego structure.

Melanie Klein, whose life and work have been discussed recently by Lindon (1972), was a highly intuitive child-analyst pioneer with great clinical acumen. She set herself the important task of filling the gap left unexplored by Freud (between birth and the second or third year of life), to elucidate the preoedipal phases of physical development.[6]

Klein (1948) became aware earlier than most analysts of the importance of aggression and depression in psychical development. Whereas Freud (1905) had attributed the sources of sexual excitement in the young child to physiological sources, Klein sought to explain them on purely psychological grounds. In his discussion of the metapsychology of psychotic depression, Abraham (1924) had indicated clearly the important role of objects that had been introjected in an ambivalent or hostile manner in the genesis of depressive states. Klein found evidence of animistic fantasies that involved the uses of introjection and projection in her treatment of both children and borderline and psychotic adults (1930). She wrote of her conceptualization of the development of the psychology of the preoedipal child in *The Psycho-Analysis of Children* (1932).

Applying the concepts of projection and introjection and becoming ever more convinced of the importance of the role of aggression in the development of anxiety that occurred with oral frustration, Klein concluded that the infant's life is dominated by alternating processes of introjection and projection. These mechanisms overcome the baby's anxiety with regard to his aggressive fantasies, chiefly through the development of libido and its fusion with aggression. Simultaneously she hypothesized that these fantasies had specific contents, that they contained elements of an oedipal conflict at a period that far antedated the classical oedipal period. Then she suggested that the depression that she attributed to the early months of

6. In this inadequate review of her thinking, only a few aspects are considered. The comments regarding her theories presented here lean especially on the evaluations made by Bibring (1947), Glover (1945), Kernberg (1972), Waelder (1937), and Zetzel (1953, 1956a, 1956b, 1964a, 1964b, 1967). See also Alexander (1933), Bergman (1962), Blum (1953), Brierley (1942), Ekstein (1949), Geleerd (1963), Guntrip (1961), Pasche and Renard (1956), and Wisdom (1962).

life could be compared in all essential aspects with the structure of depression in the postoedipal period as described by Abraham (1924).

Klein's point of departure was the effect of early anxiety situations on the development of the child. The infant's reactions to painful experiences were thought to be highly significant. Repeated and extreme oral frustrations intensified reactive feelings of sadness, anger, and rage. In the functioning of the primitive ego, intensified oral-libidinal needs merge with oral sadism, leading to internal as well as external frustration; the infant reacts with anxiety to both and considers its own destructive impulses to threaten its existence (1932, p. 184). The resultant tension prematurely mobilizes defense mechanisms, especially projection. Consequently the external frustrating object becomes a destructive agent, and fears are focused on it. However, ejection and projection of aggression are inadequate defenses, and the panic-stricken ego seeks to protect itself from the dangerous objects through destroying them. In the oral stage this attempt is expressed by the sadistic need to devour the breast and its contents. In this conceptualization, oral-libidinal, oral-aggressive, and self-preservative tendencies are blended into a functional whole. Since the infant is thought to hallucinate gratifications of its needs and the hallucinations are assumed to have the value of reality, the infant believes it has truly destroyed the object. However, the fact remains that the motor discharge of the infant's tensions is limited and that hallucinated gratification is even more limited; the destructive defense is illusory. At this point, another defense mechanism sets in: the accumulated aggressive-libidinal trends spread to all bodily functions, which become vehicles of sadism. This spreading of tension, as Bibring (1947, p. 73) notes, constitutes a theoretical conception of the first order in Klein's reconstruction of development. Its taking place can be conceptualized as a mechanical spreading from a point of high tension to that of a lower one, or it is actively distributed by the ego. Klein gives preference to the latter method.

The spreading of oral-sadistic tensions takes place in two directions: in cross-section onto a variety of existing functions and in longitudinal section along developmental lines. Abraham (1924) explained the relationship between the oral-libidinal and oral-sadistic phases by assuming that frustration at the sucking stage increased the need for gratification in the biting stage that followed; the biting stage supplanted the frustrated energies of the sucking stage and was intensified by them. The cannibalistic phase made up for the frustrations of the sucking stage. According to Klein, sensations or impulses that appeared at the beginning of dentition are not only immediately intensified by and fused with the oral tension complex but also forced to unfold.

The hypothesis of spreading, however, includes spreading to genital sensations and ideas at this very early age. Klein wrote (1932, p. 188): "In the early analyses we find . . . that oral frustration arouses in the child an unconscious knowledge of sexual pleasure." The orally frustrated infant girl withdraws from the disappointing part object, the nipple, and hallucinates a completely satisfying huge nipple, capable of filling the whole mouth. This fantasy forms a transitional link between the nipple and the phallus. The infant is fully capable of the "unconscious understanding" of symbols. Klein wrote (p. 271): "This equation of penis and breast, accompanied as it is by a displacement from above downwards, activates the oral, receptive qualities of the female at a very early age." The nipple-penis is desired simultaneously in the mouth and vagina, the existence of which has been conceptualized from the extension of oral tension to the vaginal area. The concept of developmental spreading opposes the Freudian idea of development in steps or stages. In his view, the various psychosexual stages develop constitutionally in more or less typical succession. In the Kleinian hypothesis, there are no stages but a continuous development from one "position" to another. There is a genetic continuity that is a kind of chain reaction along an uninterrupted line of transitional links.

The activation process differs in girls and boys. The girl is forced to know of the vagina by her symbolic equation of nipple and phallus and her desires to have her mouth and vagina filled. In the boy, the biting impulses arouse penetration impulses of the penis. Secondary process logic is ascribed to the infant boy who, since he has the impulse to penetrate with his penis, conceptualizes the vagina as a receptor organ. Thus internal data such as obscure reference sensations and impulses lead to knowledge of such external facts as complementary sex organs. Bibring (1947, p. 79) called such "knowledge" "sensation or impulse knowledge."

Klein assumed this sensation knowledge to play an important role in further development of boys and girls. According to her, oral frustration arouses in the child an "unconscious knowledge" that its parents enjoy sexual pleasures, originally conceived to be of an oral sort. She wrote (1932, p. 188): "It appears that an unconscious knowledge . . . about sexual intercourse between the parents, together with fantasies concerning it, already emerge at this very early stage of development." With this newfound "knowledge" the infant enters the painful period of the early oedipal conflicts. The girl's fellatic idea is associated with the knowledge that sucking gets milk (or semen) and, from the child's alimentary experience, reaches the concepts also of excrement and baby. The nipple-penis or milk-semen are taken in and a feces-baby are made of it. Jones (1933, pp. 22-23) later wrote "the girl's wish to have a child . . . is a direct continuance of her autoerotic desire for the penis. She wants to enjoy taking the penis into the body and to make a child from it." "The insertion of the nipple into the mouth is followed by the anal-erotic pleasure at the passage of feces." He did not suggest that such mentation exists during the first year of life. The child, with the assistance of sensations and symbolic equations, comes to know of procreation, parenthood, and children, of the roles of the parents in procreation, of elimination and birth processes, etc. All of this information becomes available to the child of six to twelve months of life.

In this formulation, infantile development is precipitous. The ego develops in advance of the libido. The impetus of development is the tension resultant from oral frustration; when once set in motion, it is an intrapsychic process and not the result of further interplay of growth and environment. The development of drives and some ego functions can be accelerated far beyond the total development of the child as a nearly completely independent unit. An implicit assumption in this system of thinking is that maturation, the principle of growth, does not apply to the unconscious.

Bibring (1947) has taken issue with these concepts. He noted that factors such as frustration, accumulation and intensification of tension and anxiety that strongly influence the development of the ego and the drives are familiar to psychoanalysis. Succeeding instinctual interests can be modified by preceding stages, and such factors can have a formative influence on even infants of a few months of age. However (pp. 84-85), "it is difficult to accept the proposition that such emergency factors represent all or the most important 'motors' of development. Development is more than a defense mechanism, and the 'motors' of development something more than tensions and anxieties." Bibring also found the exclusive role ascribed by Klein to the importance of endopsychic development, which is largely independent of any external stimulation, to be deficient, pointing to experimental observations of the development of instincts in animals, which show that phylogenetically determined instincts are predominantly directed toward external stimuli. Such stimuli are, as a rule, typical and specific, producing phylogenetically determined responses; their absence during a particular stage of development may result in the nonappearance or loss of certain instinctual functions.[7]

Zetzel (1956a) believed that Klein or her followers should indicate how true reality testing and secondary process thinking can be understood in terms of the basic Kleinian premises and how maturation plays a role in the different stages of development. Without such elaboration, Klein's work cannot be correlated within the main body of analytic theory. Zetzel noted that confusion results when concept and content are not clearly distinguished.

In the opinion of the majority of psychoanalysts whose theoretical orientation has followed the mainstream of analytic thought, those who have followed Klein have extrapolated backward from observations made during the treatment of children who can verbalize and of borderline and psychotic patients and have developed a psychology that is incompatible with the structural theory. They believe that, while hypothetical reconstructions of the mind in early infancy can increase the plausibility of clinical interpretations, thus giving the therapist a feeling of confidence that may be exceed-

7. According to Hess (1964), two types of learning have been differentiated: imprinting and associational learning. The evidence summarized by Hess has established that such different learning processes and characteristics exist in birds. Washburn (1965) states that studies of anthropoids indicate the existence also of imprinting and associational learning, although the time periods involved are longer for mammals than avians. The brain of birds is almost mature at birth and includes scant cortical structuration. Learning of the imprinting type appears to take place during the period that precedes the expansion and myelinization of the cortex. Associational learning takes place in the presence of a more highly developed cortex.

It may be that Bowlby's concepts (1958) of primary object seeking and primary object clinging, as parts of the id, may be understood within a conceptualization of human imprinting.

Klein (1932) clearly ascribed associational thinking to the infant. However, Piaget's observations (1924) indicate that associational learning depends upon a physical development of the nervous system beyond that of the infant of the first few months of life.

ingly important in his establishment of contact with his psychotic patient, such interpretations are not subject to validation from observational studies or from the memories of the patients. They may lead to confusion, which frequently follows from the blending of fantasy and fact. Hartmann and Kris (1945) pointed out that the retrospective method was in the past in a position to direct attention to new areas in the child's life and that there is no reason to believe that this function of pointing to the essential is exhausted. However, the retrospective method can do no more than to establish interconnections between experiences that are bound to escape observers who have less intimate insight. Some followers of Klein have extrapolated her hypotheses even further backward and held that determinate fantasies and perhaps even psychic structuralization exist *in utero* and perhaps in the ovum (Rascovsky et al. 1960).

However, few analysts who do not follow the so-called English School believe that the existence of such fantasies in infants can be validated. Glover (1945) was especially harshly critical of this retrospective extrapolation. In his judgment the Kleinian group has reduced to confusion Freudian concepts of the mental apparatus and has undermined basic distinctions between unconscious and conscious systems and the primary and secondary processes of mentation. With Bibring (1947), Glover considered them to have departed from the Freudian theory of nosogenesis. He suggested that the Kleinian theory of a central depressive position that develops between the third and fifth months of life is a "closed system," which if it were generally accepted, would arrest all possibility of correlating normal and abnormal manifestations of adult life with stages of development in infancy; he also thought that such a stand subverts all standardly accepted concepts of development from the unorganized to the organized. Many analysts agree (Zetzel 1953) that while the superego of the classical Oedipus phase has forerunners and that Klein performed a valuable service with her focusing attention on that neglected area, her formulations depend on dogmatic assumptions.

In 1932 Klein had stated that the phase of maximum sadism occurs toward the end of the first year of life, and she spoke of the importance of introjection and projection of good or bad part objects and of the denial of reality. Soon thereafter, Klein (1935) stated that a depressive position develops at the stage of passing from "part object" to "whole object" relations, between the third and fifth months, at which time there is an increase in projective processes, which have the purpose of preserving the love-object inside the self. Rivière (1936) then stated that all neuroses are different varieties of defense against the fundamental anxiety of the depressive position. This position appears to have been accepted generally by the Kleinians. Segal (1954) considered infantile neuroses to constitute means of working through earlier psychotic anxieties of both paranoid-schizoid and manic-depressive natures. Such a position would seem to confirm Glover's comment (1945) that the Kleinian group had committed themselves to a monistic theory of psychopathogenesis. Anna Freud (1943) found "these new theories" to be bewildering. She noted that although the Kleinians maintained that their system of thought constituted local extensions of the thinking of Abraham, Ferenczi, Freud, and Jones, while some existing analytic concepts were stated to be retained, they were concurrently denied.

It is interesting to speculate why this system of thinking, which was found to be so controversial and stimulated such bitter antagonism, came to have so powerful an influence over a large group of psychoanalysts. Glover suggested that support of Kleinian viewpoints was due to a lack of objective evaluation of the conceptual implications of her extrapolations from fantasy contents that had been ascribed to infants. He thought that psychoanalysts who had been eager to have problems of early development solved for them had uncritically accepted the Kleinians' statements that their ideas were logical extensions of the thinking of the aforementioned analysts. Others have considered the personality of Klein to have played an important role in the acceptance of her ideas by a devoted coterie. Whatever the truth may be, we might recall that she introduced her theories during a period that followed Freud's presentation of the structural theory, and ego psychology was in its infancy. The lack of understanding of the structural theory and its implications was widespread during the period in which Klein introduced her ideas. Additionally, at that time the work of scientists in other disciplines, notably ethology and neurophysiology, was not so relevant to psychology as is true today, and there was less evidence with which one could compare Klein's theories.

Regardless of the degree of logic one ascribes to the Kleinian system of thought, it cannot be denied that the thinking and the technical procedures used by Kleinians in the treatment of children have had great influence on the development of the psychoanalytic treatment of the schizophrenias.

During the 1930s and 1940s, Klein and her followers continued to apply her concepts to studies of children, and some articles appeared that delineated studies of psychotic children (Isaacs 1939, Klein 1946). Fairbairn (1936) treated bor-

8. Fairbairn has extended Klein's conception of internalized objects, "which traces its scientific origin to Freud's theory of the superego" (1944, p. 70) and developed the hypothesis that libido is not primarily pleasure seeking, but object seeking. To him, the anal and phallic phases are artifacts. The schizoid and manic-depressive states are not to be regarded as defenses but as states to be defended against. The outstanding feature of infantile dependence is its unconditional character, which is focused on a single object. The intrauterine state is the most extreme form of dependence; "on its psychological side it is characterized by an absolute degree of identification," and "Normal development is characterized by a process whereby progressive differentiation of the object is accompanied by a progressive decrease in identification" (Fairbairn 1941, p. 269). He thought the fetus to be aware of its dependence on the mother, a viewpoint that seems once again highly questionable and to be subject to the charge that he

derline or psychotic individuals and used Kleinian concepts. His technical approach remained initially closely aligned with that of orthodox psychoanalysts.[8] From the mid-forties onward, an increasing number of the so-called English School have involved themselves in the treatment of schizophrenia; they have reported their therapeutic methods and been optimistic regarding the results of their procedures.[9] The work of Rosenfeld is most widely known; he has been treating psychotic patients of various types, using psychoanalysis that has included the minimum number of parameters and extraanalytic steps he deemed necessary. He, like Garma, has aimed at the systematic analysis of the transference relationships and of the patient's resistances.

In general, Kleinian analysts have not insisted that borderline and psychotic patients lie on the couch, although it seems that patients frequently assume the reclining position soon after a working relationship has been developed. As is consistent with Klein's stress on the analysis of introjective-projective mechanisms, their use is emphasized in treatment in the form of analysis of projective identification, and all interventions and interpretations appear to be made strictly within the context of the transference situation. The majority

---

has attributed to the fetus psychical capacities known to apply to children who are old enough to talk. His ideas on the awareness of dependence of the fetus and newborn baby are hard to bring into consonance with Spitz's studies (1946) concerning eight-months' anxiety, for example. Fairbairn's ideas have been used in an attempt to understand some behavioral and ideational productions of schizophrenic patients and they have been discussed critically (Abenheimer 1955, Balint 1957, pp. 281-291; Guntrip 1961, C. T. Sullivan 1963, p. 56 *et seq.*).

9. Representative contributions are those by Abadi 1954, Aslan and Horne 1966, Bion 1954, 1956, 1957, Garbarino 1966, Garcia Vega 1956, Gioia and Liberman 1953, Kusnetzoff and Maldovsky 1977, Liberman 1952, 1957, Nöllman 1953, Pichon Rivière 1947, Rolla 1957, 1959, H. A. Rosenfeld 1965, Segal 1950, Szpilka 1967, Uchôa 1967).

of analysts stress the need for vigilance on the part of the analyst for evidence that he, too, is using projective identification in dealing with his patient; there seems to be no consistency among these analysts in regard to whether they communicate their own feelings verbally to the patient. From the standpoint of the non-Kleinian, one of the most interesting technical procedures commonly employed is early interpretation from the side of the id and the analyst's verbalizing his understanding of what he considers to be the patient's unconscious fantasies even during the initial interview. An illustration of the emphasis on projective identification combined with early interpretation of what the analyst considered to be the patient's unconscious fantasies follows (Avenburg 1962, pp. 351-352).

All the analyst knew of his patient was that his parents were living, that he had a sweetheart, and that he had a brother who was two years younger than he. The patient was twenty-five years old, and the day before the first analytic session he had terminated a course of insulin shock therapy. He was interviewed four times weekly, face to face. At the beginning of the fourth interview, the patient waited for a short time before the analyst opened the door of the consultation room, perhaps waiting for the handshake with which the analyst opened and ended each interview.

He waited in silence, observing his surroundings and making his movements very hesitantly. After a short time I interpreted to him:

> A: You are observing what happens inside me.
>
> P: What happens inside me.
>
> A: What happens to your parts which are located in me.
>
> P: I wish to see why I am mute; today I was dumb with everybody. (He remained in silence, hanging on my movements.) Do you believe that it is possible to converse without speaking?

> A: That would be what you are doing with me.
> P: I think so, but if I would not be very worried.

Avenburg interpolated: "What has occurred to this moment? He has located determinate parts of his own inside me, although we do not know what characteristics they have, but we are able to see his conduct because of them: he wishes to maintain himself isolated (mute) but not too removed; he must at the same time control those parts with conversation which does not include talking. At this time I interpreted to him:

> A: You are in touch with the spirit but you are afraid of physical closeness because you fear my penetration. [Author's translation; later in the article, Avenburg said he had meant "reintrojection" when he used the word *penetration*]

Another step employed by some Kleinian analysts is illustrated by the following example. A woman patient had been taken from the breast when three months old. During an interview in which it became clear that she was envious of her analyst, he first made her conscious of her feelings, and then said to her, "You feel now just as you did when you were at your mother's breast and there was not enough milk for you."

Both of these interpretations are consistent with the Kleinian framework of thinking as outlined above. No doubt they have some degree of accuracy. However, it seems to me that the analysts arbitrarily interpreted their patients' associations to fit their theory. Regressed patients are most apt to ascribe omniscience to their analysts, especially when the therapists make statements with an attitude of certainty. One must wonder whether the use of such technical procedures constitutes the most important element leading to their improvement, or whether introjection of projections or of distorted aspects of the analyst's personality is more responsible for the reconstruction of the ego of the patient, or at least for his symptomatic improvement.

As was made clear in the foregoing pages, the majority of ego psychologists have been prone to find fault with Kleinian contributions. To the contrary, Kernberg (1972, pp. 78-80) has stressed the areas of possible convergence between the ego-psychological and the Kleinian orientations. No doubt he has been led to do so because of his work in both Chile and the United States and because of his having studied and treated borderline patients. Kernberg finds those aspects of theory that have been accepted and integrated into the mainstream of psychoanalysis to be:

1. Ego-psychological analysts now acknowledge the importance of early object relations both in normal and pathological development, and the importance of the development of a potential for depressive reaction during the first year of life and its significance for future development. They stress the concept of the simultaneous development of narcissism and object relations in contrast to the older model of an objectless state of development (van der Waals 1965).

2. Psychoanalysts who have worked analytically with borderline and psychotic patients recognize the importance of the defensive operations described by Kleinians as paranoid-schizoid, depressive and manic. At the same time, they are critical of what they consider to be Kleinian neglect of later defensive operations such as repression, reaction formation, and other operations of the fully developed ego. Selective use of the new understandings of early defensive operations provided by the Kleinians, such as splitting and projective identification, has improved our diagnostic and therapeutic armamentarium (see Introduction and Kernberg 1966, 1967, 1975a).

3. The importance of aggression in early development is now generally recognized although with less emphasis than was accorded it by Klein.

4. There is a general tendency to accept early superego formation, probably beginning during the second year of life,

and to recognize the importance of early superego structures on early and later psychic development (Jacobson 1964).

5. The relationships between early genital development and pregenital conflicts and the influence of pregenital factors on the sexual development of both sexes and on the pathological sexual developments in severe character pathology have been integrated by many non-Kleinian contributors. The presence of oedipal conflicts from the second or third year on has been acknowledged by ego-psychological child analysts (A. Freud 1951).

Kernberg finds the following aspects of Kleinian technique to have been accepted by ego psychologists:

1. The application of classical psychoanalytic technique to children is a generally acknowledged and major contribution of Melanie Klein. There is a growing consensus that children are able to develop full-blown transference neuroses (Harley 1966).

2. There is a growing technical utilization of the new understandings of early defensive operations provided by Klein and her followers, including the interpretation of splitting of ego states as a defense, the explanation of negative therapeutic reaction as a possible consequence of unconscious envy, the focus on projective identification and its relationship to countertransference, and the explanation of omnipotence and devaluation as narcissistic defenses (Searles 1963, Winnicott 1962).

3. The understanding of the above-mentioned mechanisms and other early defensive operations as the predominant problem in the transference development of borderline and psychotic patients has led to increased diagnostic refinement and therapeutic hopefulness.

4. The focus on regressive features and the activation of early defensive operations in the opening phase of psychoanalysis have been acknowledged as important contributions from the Kleinian orientation (Zetzel 1967).

Contributions of Non-Kleinian Analysts in the 1940s

At the same time that followers of Klein became active in the psychoanalytic treatment of schizophrenia, other analysts continued their studies. It is interesting to note that few of them have tried to use psychoanalysis which does not include gross deviations from the classical technique.

Schwing (1940) provided therapeutic optimism to psychiatrists who seemed to have resigned themselves to treating severely disturbed patients with what amounted to custodial care after ordinary physical and supportive treatments had failed. Her procedure consisted essentially in providing what she called a "loving environment." She was permissive and attended to the patient's bodily needs, an act that may in itself have been therapeutic, since the patients with whom she worked sometimes were incapable of recognizing their own bodily needs. Interpretation played a scant role in treatment. She encouraged the development of dependency and then sought to gratify the patients' demands by direct, nonsymbolic actions. Eissler (1943) believed her therapy was effective because it provided a marked contrast to the care the patient had received from his parents. He suggested that her treatment relieved guilt feelings. While this mechanism may have applied to some of the patients, one wonders why patients who were concurrently depressed were not relieved of guilt by the accusatory and rejecting attitudes to which they had been subjected. It seems possible that some of the improvement can be attributed to relief of anxiety through environmental support of paranoid ideation of mistreatment. Stone (1955) considered treatment to have proceeded only to the level of establishing contact. Schwing's case reports suggest that the nature of that contact did not progress much beyond that of supportive dependency.

Sechehaye (1947) treated a seriously regressed schizophrenic girl. During the first three and one-half months, treatment was of a tentative nature. When Sechehaye made her intention to continue clear, Renée, her patient, said she now had a mother. During the first two years, treatment consisted essentially of explaining, reassuring, and bodily contact. Sechehaye wrote (p. 42): "I resolutely take the side of the ego against unconscious self-punishment." Verbal interpretations were given rarely and seemed to have no effect. Eventually it became necessary to rehospitalize Renée. Then Sechehaye began to give her in symbolic form things she considered to have been factually withheld from the patient during her early life, such as an apple for a breast. "Taking an apple, and cutting it in two, I offer Renée a piece, saying, 'It is time to drink the good milk from Mummy's apples'" (p. 51). "The first symbol which represented Renée was a little plush monkey which I had given her." "It personified the ego still dominated by the impulses of the 'enlightening'" (p. 55). Sechehaye reasoned (pp. 142-143):

> The "loving mother" had to find something other than the verbal method of psychoanalysis, because the initial conflict had occurred before the development of spoken language and because the patient had regressed to the stage of magical presymbol participation. The only [mode] that could be used was that which is suitable to the baby: expression by the symbolic signs of gestures and movements.

Sechehaye's writings (1960, 1965) on this subject now reach over a period of some thirty years.

Various therapists have utilized a combination of the treatments recommended by Schwing and Sechehaye. For example, in Canada, Azima and Wittkower (1956) thought that an aspect of pathogenesis can be understood as the real or imagined frustration of basic needs at the oral and anal levels. Accordingly they designed a method of treatment that was supposed to gratify needs in an "appropriate setting and with appropriate objects." They provided milk, baby bottles, brown clay, and mud to provide a miniature infantile situation in which "appropriate" feelings can be expressed. They stated that subsequent to the establishment of this type of relationship with the therapist, progressive ego interpretation is made possible or at least potentiated. Von Staabs (1954) stated that she dealt with the behavior and verbalizations of the patient less by interpretation than by her own reactions.

During the past twenty-five years, European analysts have become less pessimistic regarding the treatment of schizophrenia. Many of them have used therapeutic procedures that have included interpretation as an essential element,[10] and the role of transference has been studied more frequently than before.[11] As was the case previously, many articles have continued to present general remarks and to reflect concern about establishing diagnoses and the relative roles of heredity and environment in the pathogenesis of the schizophrenias.[12] Isolated articles have studied the state of the ego of schizophrenics (Freeman, McGhie, and Cameron 1957). Hallucinations have been viewed from various aspects (Benedetti 1955, Häfner 1954), and the roles of disordered perception, thought, and consciousness have been considered (Benedetti 1955, Davie and Freeman 1961a). Some authors have sought to combine aspects of existentialism and psychoanalysis.[13] Winnicott, who believes Klein's depressive position to be logically defensible as a theoretical and clinical

10. Representative articles are: Amendola and Garzillo 1955, Bash 1957, Benedetti 1955, 1965, H. Binswanger 1954-1955, Boroffka 1958-1959, Ernst 1957, Fornari 1963, Khan 1960, Margat 1956, Matussek 1956, 1960, Müller and Benedetti 1965, Müller and Masson 1963, Rycroft 1960, Schindler 1955, 1960, Stengel 1957, Tolentino 1956, Tolentino and Callieri 1957, Vangaard 1955, M. Winkler 1960, W. T. Winkler 1966.

11. Benedetti 1963, Davie and Freeman 1961b, Schindler 1955, W. T. Winkler and Häfner 1954.

12. L. Binswanger 1945, 1957, Cargnello 1947, Faergemann 1946, Kielholz 1951, Schultz-Hencke 1952, Stengel 1957a, Vowinckel 1930, Winkler and Wieser 1959, Zapparoli 1957.

13. L. Binswanger 1958, Boss 1958, Ey 1958, Storch 1930.

construct (1958b, pp. 21-23), has indicated in various articles that he has used psychoanalysis in the treatment of frank psychoses (1958a). He believes that character disorders range between conditions in which the presenting syndrome masks neurotic illness and those in which the hidden illness is psychotic in nature (1963, pp. 206-207). The existence of character disorders, according to Winnicott, indicates the capacity of ego stucture to bind energies "that belong to the stunting of maturational processes and also the abnormalities in the interaction of the individual child and the family" and warns of the likelihood that a character disorder might break down "into paranoia, manic depression, psychosis or schizophrenia" (1963, p. 210) during psychoanalytic therapy. Nevertheless, he considers psychoanalysis to be the treatment of choice for such conditions. Winnicott has striven to bridge the theoretical gap between Melanie Klein and Anna Freud concerning the psychosexual and psychosocial development of the preoedipal child. His concepts of transitional objects and phenomena (1953) have proved valuable in the understanding and treatment of the schizophrenic disorders.

I will now present abstracts from the writings of some of the authors who have used interpretations as their principal therapeutic tool.

Perrier (1955) noted that in schizophrenia, verbal representations prevail over object relations in the sense that when object relations are abandoned, the investment in the verbal representations of the objects is maintained. The schizophrenic who does not recognize himself in a mirror has rejected and lost his capacity for self-representation; he cannot differentiate himself from the outer world. When the therapist imposes himself on the patient in such a stage of undifferentiated narcissism, his verbal products are made partly communicative by the actions of the therapist. Perrier stated that he made himself into a mirror and reflected to the patient what was meaningful in his productions, an action that made the patient gradually look at himself as he was. He found the patient's aggression to express itself first in retention and then in explosions. He found the last fundamental resistance was the symbiosis that the patient demanded; that if the symbiosis were accepted, the patient becomes "eager to cure himself through us." However, in contrast to Schwing and Sechehaye, Perrier thought the patient must be given the initiative and feel that his reconstituted image was accepted. During the period when the symbiotic behavior was "rejected," that is, dealt with through interpretations, the patient's aggressions were found to become more intense. Perrier noted that during this phase of treatment the therapist's countertransference causes the most serious problems.

Glover (1955, pp. 244-251) found schizophrenics with depressive features to be suitable for psychoanalysis but paranoid cases to be refractory. As a procedure for treatment he recommended first an estimation of the factors that prevent development of a stable transference and then an attempt to deal with such traumatic reactions "as appear to have obstructed those particular channels of libido." He believed that manifestations of love, as Ferenczi advocated in his rapport therapy, were unnecessary. Faced by psychotic crises, the analyst should limit alterations of the analytic situation to those which do not prejudice resumption of the ordinary psychoanalytic technique: Eissler's parameters (1953a). As a general procedure, he suggested: (1) reduction of traumatic reactions to past and present situations of excessive stimulation, which he felt could be best done by giving preference to the depressive aspects of the case, (2) then turning attention to projective manifestations, which will have been rendered more accessible by the preliminary work on pathogenic introjections. He thought that if the pathogenic introjective and projective systems are reduced, the regressive products will diminish without direct analysis.

Glover's final statement is tantalizing and seems tautological since he did not specify just what he did to accomplish such reduction, and the essence of successful therapy could be defined to be the reduction of pathogenic systems.

Nacht and Lebovici (1955) recommended classical analysis for some cases, excluding paranoia and hypochondriasis. Analysis was said to be indicated in various cases, regardless of the diagnostic label, when the anxiety is related to the fear of the superego and in which the ego is strong, but not when anxiety is of instinctual origin and the ego is weak. Lebovici reported cures of three cases of manic-depressive psychosis using a classical technique.

Nacht and Lebovici seem to agree in general with Glover. However, their article is somewhat confusing since they do not make clear either what constitutes anxiety of instinctual origin or a strong or weak ego.

THE CONTRIBUTIONS OF PSYCHOANALYSTS OF THE UNITED STATES

The Period Before Sullivan and Fromm-Reichmann

The development of psychoanalytic thought concerning the genesis, nature, and treatment of the schizophrenias in the United States paralleled in several respects that which took place in Europe. There was a period during which Freud's ideas were spread and therapists who attempted to use them seemed to be guardedly optimistic. Subsequently a system of psychology was developed that was based to some extent on psychoanalytic principles, and its appearance encouraged many therapists to turn their serious attention to the psychological treatment of these disorders. Then psychoanalysts who followed the mainstream of Freudian thinking became more interested in determining whether the scope of psychoanalytic therapy should be broadened to include the treatment of the borderline states and the schizophrenias. At the same time, various groups arose which stressed one or another aspect of Freudian thinking to explain or justify their handling of borderline or schizophrenic patients.

If any single psychoanalyst can be singled out as the most influential disseminator of psychoanalytic thought regarding this group of disorders, that man must be Brill. His relevant writings extended over a period of thirty-three years (A. Brill 1908, 1925, 1941). He strove to demonstrate the presence of psychological factors in the schizophrenias through the presentation of case histories. Brill indicated similarities and differences between the neuroses and psychoses and attempted to demonstrate the limitations of psychoanalytic therapy when it is applied to schizophrenic disorders. Brill's orientation seems to have remained consonant with the topographical theory.

Campbell (1909, 1935), Jelliffe (1907, 1927), Meyer (1911, 1921-22), and White (1910, 1926), influenced by Freudian thinking, were among the first to stress the psychological aspects of the genesis and treatment of the schizophrenias. Arieti (1955, p. 7) has considered Meyer, along with Bleuler, Freud, Kraepelin, Jung, and Sullivan, to have been responsible for the evolution of our current concepts of schizophrenia. Sullivan at one time credited White with having been his most influential teacher.

Coriat shared the optimism of the European psychoanalysts who first used psychoanalytic methods in the treatment of schizophrenia. He wrote (1917, p. 327): "The only hope of combatting the disease must rest on the conception of interpreting it purely as a psychogenetic disease." He thought psychoanalytic treatment could cure mild cases and relieve the symptoms of severe and chronic instances. He recommended that psychoanalysis be tried for all cases and stated that the chance for cure depended upon a "thorough psychoanalysis of the entire content of psychosis." Clark (1919) was less optimistic and recommended great caution in the use of psychoanalysis for the treatment of schizophrenias. He continued to emphasize the need for the use of technical modifications (Clark 1926, 1933).

Others dealt with various aspects of the application of psychoanalytic thinking to the schizophrenias. Gordon (1917, 1951) and Silk (1920) studied the meanings and defensive uses of delusions and hallucinations; Osnato (1918) concerned himself with pathogenesis; Gordon (1912) and Greenacre (1918) investigated schizoid phenomena in affective disorders; Hassall (1915), Menninger (1920, 1922), Shockley (1914), and Wholey (1916) wrote of the roles of sexual complexes in schizophrenia and paranoid ideation; and Karpas (1915-1916) and Lehrman (1919) studied the meanings and uses of various schizophrenic mechanisms.

In the 1920s Barkas (1925) wrote of the treatment of psychotic patients in institutions in the light of psychoanalysis and agreed with Nunberg (1921) that the staff should be oriented psychoanalytically. Lewis (1923) believed he had demonstrated pathology in the vascular and endocrine systems of schizophrenics, and O'Malley (1923) contributed a very superficial study of the transference relations of psychotics. So far as the psychoanalytic treatment of these disorders was concerned, writers continued to recommend its use with gross modifications and were guarded in their estimates of its efficacy.[14]

The Approaches of Sullivan and Fromm-Reichmann

Harry Stack Sullivan (1925, 1931, 1947) entered the psychiatric world in 1920. From the beginning he worked primarily with psychotics and predominantly with schizophrenics. Some of his early innovations paralleled those of Ferenczi, but the two investigators probably had little influence on one another (Thompson 1952). Sullivan credited Freud, Meyer, and White as most significantly guiding his psychiatric thinking, but in his later years he wrote (1940, p. 88): "Aside from

14. Cassity 1925, Hinsie 1930, Lewis 1936, 1949, Lundholm 1932, Malamud 1929.

Freud's discussion of the Screiber [sic] case and Groddeck's *Das Buch vom Es* . . . my subsequent reading of more purely psychoanalytic contributions has fallen under the law of diminishing return."

He became aware earlier than most psychoanalysts of the characteristics of schizophrenics that must be taken into account in their treatment (Brody 1952, pp. 39-88). He knew that Freud's position that schizophrenics are unreachable because they do not develop transference was clinically refutable. He understood that the physician's communications may carry more aggression than the patient's special vulnerability makes him capable of withstanding without panic or unsalutary regression; he also knew that this is a complex issue because the schizophrenic also projects hostility onto the therapist. Sullivan stressed the tenuous nature of emotional relationships of schizophrenics and stated that stimulation of the libidinal needs of the patient evokes his destructive impulses. He thought it possible that the basic fear of the schizophrenic is that he or his physician may be in danger of magical destruction, usually by oral means, reminiscent of the ideas of Klein and her followers and Lewin's hypotheses (1950) related to eating and being eaten.

Sullivan also stressed that the first step in dealing with the schizophrenic is the establishment of meaningful contact and sought to approach the patient by any possible means (M. J. White 1952). He agreed with and antedated Stone (1963), who stated that any number and degree of parameters can be introduced where they are necessary to meet special conditions and so long as they are directed to producing the ultimate purposes and processes of the analytic end. Anna Freud (1954) has agreed, although she warned that many variations of technique are occasioned by the analyst's outlook and theoretical position, a fact demonstrated previously in this chapter by the examples of Kleinian techniques. Sullivan did not believe that the positive transference must be maintained. He found the psychotic to attempt to make contact through reenacting in a highly distorted manner the events of his childhood with the therapist and the split representatives of the psychiatrist, the other members of the hospital staff. He thought the difference between the neurotic and psychotic transference to be largely quantitative. He viewed almost all the behavior of the chronic psychotic to constitute transference, an opinion that has found much support (Searles 1963). Sullivan noted that the therapist is conceived by the schizophrenic as an important person of his past. From this he concluded that the actual person and personality of the therapist are highly important, as had Ferenczi and Rank, although their avenues of reaching that judgment differed from his. Other therapists have stressed that kindness, strength, and fairness (Betz 1950), dissimilarity of the physician to actual life figures from the patient's past (Kolb 1956), frankness (Federn 1933), sincerity, insight, and self-control (Kempf 1919), and altruism (Schwing 1940) are desirable qualities. Sullivan would have agreed with all of them, although his emphasis might have varied. He stressed the need for a high degree of tolerance, one that will enable the psychoanalyst to permit the patient to seek individual ways of satisfying his needs, so long as they do not transgress the rights of others. With Menninger (1940) and Schwartz and Stanton (1950), Sullivan thought the psychiatrist's overdependency on cultural standards causes him to disparage rather than to investigate the genetics and dynamics of the patient's productions.

Sullivan never presented a systematic account of his theoretical ideas, and the efforts of his critics and apologists have not succeeded in making them clear and consistent.[15] It would appear that the most significant differences between his constructions and those of Freud lie in the relative importance placed by each on the vicissitudes and nature of drives

15. Bromberg 1954, pp. 225-233, M. Cohen 1953, M. R. Green 1962, Mullahy 1940, Salzman 1964, Thompson 1952.

and their importance in the psychic structure. Sullivan was apparently unable to penetrate to basic psychoanalytic concepts and discoveries (Jacobson 1955). He failed to take into account such phenomena as infantile sexuality. To him there was no Oedipus complex, no infantile masturbation problem, and no castration conflict. He conception of sexuality is reminiscent of the pre-Freudian period and surely no more advanced than that of Jung (1907). Jacobson noted (1955, p. 151): "Sullivan's complete unawareness of the part that instinctual life plays in child development is the prerequisite for his theory of anxiety and fear."

It has been implied (Mullahy 1940) and overtly stated (M. J. White 1952) that Sullivan's idiosyncratic terminology obscured the fact that he was developing a dynamic theory of ego psychology, but Jacobson (1955, p. 150) has noted that to Sullivan structural concepts are unacceptable. He was heavily influenced by anthropologists, notably Margaret Mead and Edward Sapir. According to Sullivan, the child conforms to the standards of his culture essentially from fear of estrangement from individuals in his environment. The role of the superego is obviously depreciated.

Although Sullivan's theory of personality deviated sharply from Freud's in regard to therapy, his views have been widely influential in shaping the procedures of therapists who have been more sympathetic to Freudian views (Mullahy 1948, Perry and Gawel 1953, Sullivan 1940). Thompson wrote:

> If by psychoanalysis one means recognition of unconscious motivation, the influence of repression and resistance on the personality and the existence of transference, then Sullivan's thinking fulfills all requirements for being considered psychoanalysis. [1952, p. 107]

However, recognition of transference, repression, and resistances constitutes a most incomplete statement of what psychoanalysis as a therapeutic method is: recognition is not systematic analysis and repression is not the only defense.

Resistance and unconscious motivation obviously had meanings to Sullivan vastly different from what they have to Freudian psychoanalysts.

Thompson (1952, p. 107) stated that Sullivan's unique contribution to the treatment of psychotics was his stressing the need to convey the therapist's respect to the patient. He considered demonstrating the fallibility of the psychiatrist to be important, and when he requested amplification, he also inquired whether he had missed something. Neither of these attitudes was new with Sullivan, being implicit or explicit in many articles in the German psychoanalytic literature. Sullivan did not know German well and apparently was unaware of many contributions that appeared in that language.

He considered "why" questions to be incomprehensible and inadvisable, because the patient interprets such interrogations as accusatory. In this regard his viewpoint was similar to Arlow's (1952). He interpreted expressions of guilt and directed the patient's attention to an understanding of events that transpired, especially during the interview situation. Such an approach and the nature of his interpretations were consistent with his conceptualization of personality. He thought that "To gain satisfactions and security is to have power in interpersonal relations [and that] the self comes into being because it is necessary that one's interests be focused into certain fields that 'work'" (Mullahy 1940, p. 121). He stated "free" association to be unsuitable for schizophrenic patients, at least insofar as dealing with the patient during the period of establishing meaningful contact is concerned, a position that agrees with recommendations forwarded by most analytic therapists.

At the same time, Sullivan emphasized the importance of "marginal thoughts," and he used directed associations in attempts to catch distortions.

Sullivan was not active in every interview, and at times long periods transpired during which there was little intervention. In general, he controlled interview situations by his movements, vocalizations, questions, and minimal interpretations.

In unfolding the patterns of living that had led to the patient's difficulties in getting along with others, Sullivan worked first with the "peripheral field," the relationships with relatively innocuous people. He confronted patients with their distortions of what he and they had said previously, and sometimes he made deliberately false statements, designed to be corrected by the patient. At the same time, he recommended complete honesty with the patient and felt it advisable to communicate overtly his feelings, a viewpoint that has been popular with many therapists of schizophrenics. Such a procedure may abet the patient's retention of the unconscious bases for delusions and hamper reconstruction of his personality; indeed, the same procedure was recommended by Federn (1933) as a means of encapsulating the psychosis. It will be recalled that Federn considered the schizophrenic patient to be, in the strict sense, incurable.

Sullivan considered it mandatory to give positive recognition of the patient's forward moves. With catatonics he was reserved, gentle, and kindly; with paranoids he was distant and cold (Mullahy 1940, M. J. White 1952). Bartemeier (1965) remembered him to have been "very agressive towards his schizophrenic patients, and that he combined this attitude with an equal amount of tenderness, affection, and understanding." Despite his advocacy of frankness concerning the therapist's personal feelings, he also stated that he did not reassure except with his attitude of kindly reserve, since he considered the psychotic to interpret overt reassurance as evidence that the therapist considers the patient to be hopeless. It will be noted that this idea is at sharp variance with the usual recommendation that the psychotic requires "ego support," using the term within its popular connotation. After he listened to "primitive pregenital material" for some months during which the working alliance was established, Sullivan began to disparage such communications and to insist that the patient "leave the neologistic hoop-la and discover when he began to feel frightened" (M. J. White 1952, p. 147). However, it will be remembered that Sullivan did not acknowledge the existence of infantile pregenital or genital sexual activity, as the terms are used within ordinary psychoanalytic parlance. According to him, sexual pleasure is genital "lust" and gains importance only at puberty (Jacobson 1955, p. 151). Additionally, just what he meant by the working alliance is not quite clear from his writings.

Nevertheless, Sullivan's work with psychotics was highly intuitive and apparently effective; it stimulated much interest and kindled optimism in psychotherapists, and the present author believes that *this* was his cardinal contribution.

Fromm-Reichmann, too, began to work with psychotics in the 1920s. The principles she worked from were based upon a general dynamic and psychoanalytic orientation, derived from her training in and experience with the application of Freud's concepts of psychoanalytic therapy with neurotics. However, she found Sullivan's operational interpersonal conceptions to be of great value in the treatment of psychotics. She, with Alexander (1954) and many others, postulated a continuum, with no discernible or practical line of demarcation, between psychoanalysis and dynamic psychotherapy (Fromm-Reichmann 1954).

Fromm-Reichmann agreed with Sullivan's stand regarding the need to convey respect to the patient. However, she found additionally that the "exaggeratedly sensitive, cautious overpermissive approach to the patient," which had been advocated by Alexander, Federn, Nunberg, and Schwing, as examples, was lacking as a technique to establish an effective treatment background. Such an approach addresses itself to the rejected child in the schizophrenic and encourages perpetuation of regression. She recommended that the therapist address himself to the patient's adult aspects, as had Sullivan with his disparagement of neologistic productions. Fromm-Reichmann (1948) recommended respect and understanding relevant to the patient's chronological age. She also found that when the therapist discourages the expression of hostile feelings toward himself, the patient understands such behavior to indicate that the therapist fears the patient's and his own hostility. Such an ascription supports the schizophrenic's attribution of magical qualities to hostility.

Fromm-Reichmann (1950, 1952) found the interpretation of content to be of secondary importance in the treatment of the schizophrenic and said that interpretation should be directed toward an understanding of the genetics and dynamics that determine content. Her conceptualization and dynamics were much more in consonance with Freudian hypotheses concerning personality development than were Sullivan's. She was very much concerned with the importance of the security and personality of the therapist himself and focused strongly on the importance of countertransference. The therapist must not be bound for his security on the "denizens of the society and the culture of the area," and feel impelled to have the patient conform to them. The recovery of the schizophrenic often depends on the psychoanalyst's freedom from convention and prejudice (1949).

Like the work of Melanie Klein, that of Harry Stack Sullivan and Frieda Fromm-Reichmann has permeated the psychotherapeutic techniques employed by the vast majority of dynamic therapists and psychoanalysts. This does not mean to imply that psychoanalysts who use such techniques agree with the theoretical orientations upon which they were originally based.

More Recent Contributions

As was noted previously, Kleinian ideologies have found little acceptance in the United States, and child analysts have remained sharply cognizant of the "fact that a lifelong, albeit diminishing, emotional dependence on the mother is a universal truth of human existence" (Mahler 1963, p. 307). They have aligned themselves with those who place cardinal importance on the actual life experiences of the growing person. Their observations have been made in longitudinal studies of the child with normal and pathological psychological development,[16] as well as typical analytic situations that provide reconstructive material and hypotheses. Such studies have led to the increasing corroboration of the validity of the structural theory of psychical organization; they have led to the stand taken by Mahler:

> The biological preparedness of the human infant to maintain its life separately conditions that species-specific prolonged phase which has been designated the "mother-infant symbiosis." I believe it is from the symbiotic phase of the mother-infant dual unity that those experiential precursors of individual beginnings are derived which, together with inborn constitutional factors, determine every human individual's unique somatic and psychological make-up.[17] [1963, p. 307]

Understanding of symbiotic phenomena required following the child into a later stage of the mother-infant relationship, the "separation-individuation" phase

Normal separation-individuation is conceived to be the first crucial prerequisite for the development and maintenance of the sense of identity (Mahler, Pine, and Bergman 1975).

Such longitudinal studies, combined with reconstructive efforts, have indicated that the libidinal availability of the mother, because of the emotional dependence of the child, facilitates the optimal unfolding of innate potentialities and

16. Significant references are to be found in the bibliographies of Korner (1964) and Mahler, Pine, and Bergman (1975).

17. The unique contributions of individual organic endowments in the infant on the nature of the development of the object relationships between the child and his environment have been stressed in such contributions as that of Bergman and Escalona (1949) who stressed the role of unusual sensitivities in young children (see also Boyer 1956b, Korner 1964).

contributes to or subtracts from harmonious synthesis of the autonomous functions in the service of the ego, the neutralization of drives, and sublimation, by activating or hindering the flux of developmental energy (Kris 1955).

But the child does not grow up solely under the influence of his mother. With increasing impact he comes meaningfully in contact with other members of his immediate and extended family and then other individuals and institutions in his environment. The impact on the personality and the demands and supports that emanate from this widening circle of environmental influences has led to a crescendoing series of longitudinal studies performed by scientists of various social disciplines.

The psychoanalytic treatment of psychotics was formerly conducted largely in the hospital situation. In such an environment, it was learned early that the patients behave as though various hospital personnel and other patients were their actual family members. This finding was probably serendipitous at first. Historically psychoanalytic therapies of patients had been conducted within the framework of a one-to-one relationship between patient and analyst. The varieties of techniques employed in that predominantly dyadic situation were aimed at enabling the individual to be reconstructed through rectification of earlier pathological relationships, predominantly those of the mother-child dyad, through various means of educative contact, actual and symbolic, and through interpretation.

As has been emphasized frequently, psychoanalytic treatment techniques influence and are influenced by the theoretical positions taken by analysts. With the renewed focusing of attention on the individual's relationships with members of his environment, therapists, extrapolating from dynamic theories of child development, heeding their own intrahospital observations, and borrowing from the findings of researchers in other disciplines, have been increasingly interested in devising techniques of treating psychotics within the framework of a family situation. At first, such efforts were directed to including patients only in group situations and later actual family members were brought into the treatment situation and research milieu.[18]

All these contributions have been combined with the observations of psychoanalysts in order to understand various aspects of schizophrenia such as the relative contributions of heredity and environment to the genesis of these disorders, the role of object relations in influencing psychic structuralization, and the genesis, defensive uses, and adaptational functions of such phenomena as language and hallucinations. The nature of the psychotic process, its manifestations, and the use of transference and countertransference phenomena have also been studied.[19] A detailed discussion of these contributions is not possible within the framework of this chapter.

Let us return to the therapy of schizophrenia. As has been true in the past, the practical problem of whether to hospitalize the patient has proved to be troublesome. As A. Brill (1929) had before him, Boyer (1961, 1966) has advocated avoidance of hospitalization whenever possible. Nevertheless, the need of some families to keep patients ill is a well-known phe-

18. Ackerman 1960, 1964, Alanen 1958, 1966, Alikakos, Starer, and Winnich 1956, Bateson et al. 1956, Bion 1961, Böszörmënyi-Nagy 1962, Böszörmënyi-Nagy and Framo 1963, Delay, Deniker, and Green 1957, Jackson 1961, Lidz 1973, Lidz, Fleck, and Cornelison 1965, Schaffler et al. 1962, Shapiro, Shapiro et al. 1977, Shapiro, Zinner et al. 1975, Singer and Wynne 1965, Stierlin 1969, 1974, Uchõa 1968, Wynne 1967, Wynne and Singer 1963a,b, Zinner and E. R. Shapiro 1975, Zinner and R. A. Shapiro 1972.

19. Bak 1939, 1954, Bellak 1948, Bellak and Benedict 1968, Bellak and Loeb 1969, Boyer 1978, Hartmann 1953, Hollender and Böszörmënyi-Nagy 1958, Jacobson 1964, 1969, Kasanin 1944, Kasanin and Hanfmann 1942, Katan 1939, 1950, 1954, 1969, Marcondes 1966, Modell 1956, 1958, Nadelson 1977, Pious 1949, 1961, Prado Galvão 1966, Savage 1961, Searles 1965a, Spence 1967, Szalita-Pemow 1955, Volkan 1976, Wexler 1951a,b, 1971, Will 1959, 1962, 1964.

nomenon.[20] The special problems connected with hospital management have been the object of numerous and penetrating studies.[21]

One of the most spectacular deviations from ordinary psychoanalytical technique to have been introduced in the United States is the "direct analysis" of Rosen (1962), who has claimed that his procedures are a logical extension of Freudian hypotheses. His techniques have proved sufficiently stimulating to a group of supporters and followers that a special foundation and school continue his research and teachings; an international congress of direct psychoanalysis was held (Scarizza 1965).

Rosen's major description (1947) of his technique was presented in 1947. He felt "called upon" to converse with the patient in the language of the unconscious and to untwist, "clear down to the earliest ontogenetic and even philogenetic roots," each symptom, remark, and symbol. He reasoned that when the symbol was clearly unmasked to the patient, it would become purposeless and the patient would be able to relinquish it for more mature ways of handling his drives. Rosen felt the task to be incomplete until the "transference is as completely worked out as we aim to do in ordinary analytic procedures." During the initial period of treatment he spent several hours each day with his patients and literally fed, bathed, and otherwise cared for their presumed needs. He claimed cures following treatment of three days to eleven months; the average period of treatment lasted two to three months. Needless to say, Rosen's conceptions of what constitutes working through a transference relationship must be considered to be very different from those of most analysts, and his ideas concerning the development and uses of symptoms, too, are radically different.

Horwitz et al. (1958) reviewed and followed nineteen of

20. Bychowski 1963, Jackson 1959, 1961, Ryckoff, Day, and Wynne 1959.

21. Brody 1952, pp. 57-74, Fromm-Reichmann 1947, Morse and Noble 1942, Stanton and Schwartz 1954.

Rosen's original thirty-seven cases and noted (p. 783): "Whatever the merits of direct analytic therapy for schizophrenia, the claim that it results in a high degree of recovery remains unproven" (see also Sagredo 1955, Scheflen 1961).

It has been remarked frequently that there appear to be as many approaches to the psychological treatment of the schizophrenias as there are individual therapists.[22] Yet today it appears that all therapists in the United States have been influenced by various aspects of the techniques of Federn, Fromm-Reichmann, Klein, Nunberg, and/or Sullivan, regardless of their individual theoretical position. Psychoanalysts who deal with schizophrenics now seem to be divided into three general groups: (1) Those who agree with variants of Freud's original formulations. These therapists in general offer supportive therapy and environmental manipulation, although some interpretations may be employed. The majority tend to use extraanalytic or parametric procedures to handle anxiety-laden or anxiety-producing situations; many also use medicines. They seem to aim at encapsulation of the psychosis. Some of these therapists, as Knight (1953), suggest that whenever the physician suspects that the patient's symptomatology masks a borderline condition, he should have psychological tests done; if unusual regressive tendencies are discovered, the patient should have supportive therapy rather than psychoanalysis, although certain patients may, after a suitable period, be given a trial analysis. Eissler (1953a,b) has written at length on the effect of the structure of the ego and the emotionality of the patient and their relation to technique. As mentioned before, Bychowski believes that the introduction of parametric and extraanalytic procedures is mandatory, but his treatment method more nearly approaches that of the classical analytic than is true of the majority of the therapists of this group. Kolb (1956) has listed the "necessary" modifications of analytic technique for the

22. For varying approaches see Brody 1952, R. Cohen 1947, Ekstein 1955, Feigenbaum 1930, Karpman 1944, Myerson 1939, Wexler 1951b.

treatment of the schizophrenias. (2) Those who have greater reluctance to shift analytic technique because of their patients' exhibition of regressive tendencies. The writings of many analysts reveal that they are now knowledgeably treating borderline and psychotic patients with techniques that use interpretation as their principal therapeutic tool and systematically analyze resistances and transference relationships.[23] (3) Those who have turned to family therapy techniques.

SUMMARY

In this chapter I present a survey of the thinking of psychoanalysts other than Freud pertaining to the therapy of borderline and schizophrenic conditions. The chapter is divided into two main sections, dealing with the development of thought of European and Latin American analysts, and those of the United States. However, parallels exist that make it possible to present a unified summary.

Before Freud introduced his formulations concerning schizophrenia and stated that psychoanalysis was inapplicable as a method of treatment, many European clinicians used psychoanalytic techniques and were enthusiastic about their results. After Freud's pronouncement, however, there was a period of almost a decade when few articles appeared in which the treatment of schizophrenia was discussed in any detail. After Tausk questioned Freud's diagnosis of one of his "hysterical" patients, there was again an upsurge of therapeu-

23. Aronson 1968, 1977, Atkins 1967, 1968, Bettelheim 1965, 1975, Caruth and Ekstein 1964, Ekstein 1966, 1968, Ekstein and Caruth 1967, 1972, Ekstein and Friedman 1968, Ekstein and Wallerstein 1954, Flarsheim 1967, 1972, 1975, Grotstein 1975, James 1964, 1972, Kernberg 1975a, 1976b, 1978, Langs 1973, 1974, 1975a, 1976, Malin and Grotstein 1966, Modell 1963, 1968, Roth and Blatt 1975, Searles 1965a, 1975, Sperling 1955, 1974, 1978, Volkan 1976, 1979, Wilson 1968.

tic attempts. In the United States, before 1920 psychoanalytic principles were used in an attempt to understand various facets of paranoia and the schizophrenias, but very few writers indicated they had attempted to use psychoanalysis as a treatment method; their conclusions varied from those of Coriat, who was enthusiastic, to Brill and Clark, who were much less optimistic.

During the 1920s, analysts of both continents became more adventurous, and a few turned their attentions strongly toward the use of psychoanalysis in the treatment of these disorders. In Europe, Nunberg treated psychotics using gross parameters and extraanalytic procedures; Waelder, Landauer, Laforgue, and Brunswick overtly or implicitly suggested that techniques close to those of classical analysis could be used, and Bychowski thought that analytic techniques could be used for the treatment of some borderline and schizophrenic disorders, but that various modifications were mandatory. In the early 1930s Garma and Laforgue recognized earlier than most analysts the nature of the schizophrenic superego and the need of the therapist to reduce its archaic and sadistic qualities; they recommended the use of orthodox analysis once adequate contact had been made between patient and therapist and a working alliance had been established. However, the work of Federn was much more influential; it was similar to that of Nunberg, who, with Alexander, believed that a "positive transference" must be maintained if the analyst is to do effective work. In the United States, Sullivan began his intensive work with psychotics and extrapolated therapeutic methods from psychoanalytic theory as he understood it, demonstrably imperfectly, combined with his own brilliant clinical observations. The vast majority of psychoanalytic therapists who worked at all with schizophrenics used techniques such as those recommended by Nunberg and Federn.

Also in the 1920s, child analysis made its appearance as a specialty. Although the work of the Anna Freud school did not stimulate an upsurge of the use of psychoanalysis for the treatment of the schizophrenias, the work of Melanie Klein clearly did, both in Europe and later, after Garma's migration, in Latin America. Her system of thought, which seems difficult to synthesize with the point of view of the structural hypothesis, gave a number of analysts a feeling of assurance that they understood infantile fantasy, enabling them to interpret the behavior and mentation of borderline and psychotic patients. A sizable number of analysts, particularly in Great Britain and South America, have undertaken the psychoanalytic treatment of patients who suffer from such disorders, apparently without the use of gross parameters or extraanalytic procedures such as those advocated by the vast majority of analysts whose thinking has followed more closely that of the mainstream of psychoanalysis. Perhaps the best known of the Kleinian analysts who treat psychotics are Bion, Rosenfeld, and Segal.

In the United States, too, a group of analysts developed a deviant school of thought, that of the neo-Freudians, which has, in the viewpoint of the followers of the structural theory, overemphasized the role of socialization processes and understressed the biological equipment of the infant. Sullivan has been the most influential of this group. The Sullivanian school, as the Kleinian, stimulated far more interest in the treatment of the schizophrenias than did the analysts of more orthodox orientation; both schools have heavily swayed the treatment techniques of other analysts who treat psychotics. Following Sullivan, the work of the much better trained psychoanalysts Frieda Fromm-Reichmann and Harold F. Searles appears to have been most influential in the development of treatment methods of United States analysts.

During the past quarter century, interest in the psychoanalytic psychotherapy of the schizophrenias has increased. In Latin America, Klein's thinking has predominated in determining technical procedures and some of her theoretical and technical orientation has begun to influence the mainstream of psychoanalysis. In Europe and the United States a number of different approaches have been used or developed. Schools of divergent thought have arisen over the years: In Europe, in addition to the analysis of Klein and others of the so-called British School of Psychoanalysis, there have been psychosynthesis and existential analysis; in the United States, in addition to that of Sullivan, there has been the direct analysis of Rosen. More orthodox analysts have divided themselves into three main groups in both geographical areas: (1) Those whose philosophy has elements of Freud's early formulations or who for other reasons believe that the schizophrenias are essentially incurable. This group uses psychoanalytic principles in their work to some extent, but they believe that uncovering techniques are generally contradicted and hold that dealing with the transference relationship per se is ill advised. They offer support of existing defenses, environmental manipulation, reassurance, and various symbolic or real gratifications, as did Schwing, Sechehaye, and Azima and Wittkower. (2) Those who are more optimistic regarding the curability of individuals who suffer from borderline and schizophrenic conditions. Some of these work in hospitals with chronically regressed patients, and some see patients in their consultation rooms. Both groups attempt to use as few extraanalytic procedures and parameters as they can in establishing contact and developing a working alliance and seek to analyze systematically the transference neurosis and psychosis and the defenses. (3) Those who have turned their attention to group and family therapies for the borderline and schizophrenic states.

CHAPTER FOUR

Office Treatment of Schizophrenic Patients: The Use of Psychoanalytic Therapy with Few Parameters

L. Bryce Boyer

This chapter is the first of two largely clinical presentations that illustrates the development of my theoretical and therapeutic orientations during the past thirty-odd years. It consists of a slightly modified paper written in 1965,[1] after I had conducted for some seventeen years a study directed toward evaluating the efficacy of psychoanalytic therapy with few parameters in the office treatment of severely disturbed individuals. All prospective patients under the age of fifty who suffered from borderline or overt schizophrenia or schizoaffective psychoses were included. The seventeen patients who supply the data for this report exclude chronically regressed, "back-ward" individuals, and all had average or superior intelligence. Some were seen at reduced rates. No waiting list was kept; patients were accepted when they were referred and therapeutic hours were open.

Bychowski (1957, p. 129) subsumed under the term *psychotic core* three points of special interest for the understanding of future psychotic development:

> 1. Persistence and prevalence of archaic forms of functioning such as magic thinking and thinking on the original concrete level;

1. This chapter is a modification of papers that have been presented before the Department of Psychiatry, University of Illinois at the Medical Center, Chicago, May 1963; the Extension Division of the San Francisco Psychoanalytic Society, October 1963 and November 1964; the Los Angeles Psychoanalytic Society, February 1964; the West Coast Psychoanalytic Societies, San Diego, October 1964; the Utah State Department of Mental Health, February 1965.

2. Persistence and prevalence of such primitive mechanisms as introjection, primary identification, and projection, though of universal significance for every mental functioning, in individuals under consideration they assume the leading role and culminate in paranoid formations; and

3. Splitting of the ego, occurring according to the original, highly ambivalent attitudes of the child toward essential figures of his environment.

The psychotic core, then, consists of primitive internalized object- and relationship-representations and is reflected in the transference situation by the projection of dyadic, preoedipal phenomena. Because all but three of the fifteen patients whose external circumstances permitted continuation of their treatment developed transference neuroses that were predominantly triadic and oedipal in nature after they had been in analysis for two or at the most three years, I assume that their psychotic cores had been fundamentally altered in that span of time.

It is postulated that psychoanalysis can be used for the successful treatment of borderline and schizophrenic patients of the types included in this study. On the basis of the empirical data, I believe that countertransference problems may constitute the major obstacle to the psychoanalytic treatment of such patients. On the basis of this investigation, it remains questionable whether successful outcome depends upon special qualifications of the therapist. The data suggest that the professional and theoretical orientation of the analyst is a major determining factor.

THEORETICAL ORIENTATION

As outlined in chapter 2, Freud stated that complete decathexis of mental representations followed by a restitutive phase was the most characteristic single feature of the schizophrenic psychoses. He never changed explicitly his formulations to make them consistent with the structural theory. As has been noted by Arlow and Brenner (1964), interpretations based upon Freud's formulations do not abet thorough understanding of the defensive nature of psychotic regression and withdrawal. Federn (see chapter 3) believed the psychotic process to be irreversible and used various so-called supportive techniques in the treatment of patients who suffered from this group of disorders. He strove to encapsulate the psychosis.

The roots of all functional psychoses have been traced to the qualities of the symbiotic and separation-individuation phases described by Mahler and her co-workers. The structure of the ego and superego results from the interaction of inborn and socialization factors, which determines the nature of their introjects. Deprivation in infancy alone, whether due predominantly to hereditary and/or constitutional defects within the babies or psychological defects within their mothering figures, does not produce all the schizophrenias. The schizophrenic has traversed to some degree all phases of psychosexual and psychosocial development, has manifold areas of development failure and fixations, and uneven levels of ego and superego development, and the various ego functions are affected differently from patient to patient. As observed by Arlow and Brenner (1964) and Glover (1955), defensive regression typically transpires in response to adolescent or postadolescent stresses that reawaken unresolved oedipal conflicts.

No human action can be conceptualized to be free of hereditary factors. The hypothesis that schizophrenia is due especially to environmental influences has led to many investigations of schizophrenic patients and their families (see chapter 3). Research has shown that schizophrenic behavior serves various functions in particular kinds of family organizations and cultural groups and that serious impairment of ego functioning may be related to the failure of parents to transmit properly the usual communicational tools of the society. The families of schizophrenic patients have discouraged the learning methods of communication that are based predominantly on secondary process logic and include generally understood, rather than idiosyncratic, symbolic connotations. Individuals who have been reared in such unfavorable milieux do not learn to exchange information well in extrafamilial or cross-cultural situations. It seems likely that they regress defensively when confrontation with their message-sending and message-receiving difficulties is superimposed upon already existent intrapsychic conflicts.

Consistent with this bias regarding the origins of schizophrenia is the notion that the primary therapeutic task is to restore and/or develop a reasonable ego and superego. Theoretically this can be accomplished by modifying or replacing cold, unloving, and archaic ego and superego introjects. The introjects of those psychic structures must be warm, loving, and reasonable in order for the individual to be capable of loving himself and others. Simultaneously, therapy must be directed toward the growth of intrapsychic and interpersonal communication techniques. With these orienting notes in mind, let us turn to the methodology that has been employed in the present controlled observation.

METHODOLOGY

I shall first describe my procedure with prospective patients who appeared at the office. All individuals of the groups mentioned above were accepted for treatment except those for whom there was inadequate time or who could not pay minimal fees. Once the diagnosis was made, the patient was told that the object of therapy was to make him comfortable with himself, that treatment was to be of an experimental nature, and that an indefinite period might be spent in our collaborative work. During the vis-à-vis hour or hours, I explained the analytic procedure as one does with neurotics. In addition, clear criteria were set regarding vacation periods, interview attendance, and payment arrangements (Boyer 1961, pp. 390-392).

Couch treatment was begun after the patient had been seen no more than four times, usually after one or two face-to-face interviews. Free association techniques were used from the beginning. Once couch therapy was instituted, few parameters were employed, and they were, with one exception, of ordinary varieties used in the analyses of neurotics, as the arbitrary setting of the termination date in one instance, the demand bills be paid on time in two cases, and the instruction to face a phobic object in several analyses (Boyer 1961, pp. 392-393). None of the seventeen patients who are included in this series was given medicine at any time while being seen in the office. Telephone contacts were discouraged and occurred rarely, except in two of the three cases with whom failures resulted. Direct communication with relatives was rare and almost nonexistent after office treatment was undertaken. Patients were not called by their first names. They were seen four times weekly, except for one of the two women whose treatment failed; she was seen five or six times weekly during some months of treatment. As Searles (1963) has noted, the techniques employed in the care of the patients included in this study have more nearly approached orthodox psychoanalytic treatment than has been reported previously in any detail in the literature.

Five of the six patients who were first interviewed in hospital were under the care of other psychiatrists at the time. A fragment of the case history of the sixth is included below. With that exception, I did not involve myself in the physical or drug therapy of any of those patients. I restricted my activities to observation and interpretations; all of these cases then came to the office for therapy and, although they were still actively psychotic, were begun in analysis, after having been given the conditions of therapy while still in the hospital. Only two of the patients included in this study were hospitalized during treatment with me. Aside from the one mentioned below, one woman was immured and treated by a psychiatrist while I was absent from my office for a period of two weeks. Her hospitalization was at her request.

Although the treatment of these patients constituted a continuum, for purposes of amplification it can be divided conceptually into two phases. In the first, reasonably stable, loving introjects appear to be established within the patient. Coincidentally, psychotic thinking patterns and behavior are removed or their cathexes are markedly diminished. At the end of this artificially divided first period, a transference neurosis has developed.

The words *transference, transference neurosis, transference psychosis,* and *countertransference* are used with variant meanings in the psychoanalytic literature. The following paragraphs will clarify their use in this contribution.

French (1946, p. 71) noted that the word *transference* has been used to include everything from the transference neurosis proper to the "emotional relationship existing between patient and analyst" to the "treatment situation as a whole." When Freud used the word *transference,* he meant reactions to the analyst as though he were not himself but some person from the patient's past. Such a definition implies that a patient's transference to the analyst is but that part of his reaction that repeats his responses to an individual who has previously played an important role in his emotional life. When a patient is neurotic, his continuing, predominant partial misidentification of the analyst is properly said to constitute a transference neurosis. During the course of analysis with most neurotics, the therapist is reacted to for varying periods, usually for months or years, as though he were one or another person from the patient's past. In addition, the patient responds realistically toward the analyst and also with phenomena that are properly called transferences. Derivatives of the repressed may be attached to various individuals and situations in the environment so that in everyday life, too, there are transference situations. When the word *transference* is used in this sense, it means an irrational repetition of a stereotyped reaction that has been adjusted to the present situation.

Countertransference is likewise a term used with variant meanings (Orr 1954). In its most nonspecific application, countertransference means all of the analyst's reactions to his patient. Freud's first reference to it (1910a, p. 289) said: "We have begun to consider the 'countertransference' . . . arising as a result of the patient's influence on (the physician's) unconscious feelings." In this conceptualization, countertransference corresponds to the word *transference* as used above, although it may mean more. Sometimes analysts unconsciously identify patients with important persons from their own pasts. In this communication the word *countertransference* will be used to designate those reactions of the analyst that correspond to the transferences of the patient and the phrase *countertransference neurosis* will be used to indicate the state in which the analyst has unconsciously identified the patient with an important person from the life of the therapist, and that identification has remained unconscious for a period of weeks or months. This formulation appears to agree with Greenson's latest formulations (1965). The counter-identifications described by Fliess (1953) would appear to form one group of the countertransference neuroses.

Psychotics, too, develop transference reactions to the therapist. They have been called *transference psychosis* (H. A. Rosenfeld 1954) and *delusional transference* (Little 1958). Searles (1963, p. 251) has written:

> The difficulty of discerning the transference aspects of one's relationship with the (chronically schizophrenic) patient can be traced to his having regressed to a state of ego-functioning which is marked by severe impairment in his capacity either to differentiate among, or to integrate his experiences. He is so incompletely differentiated in his ego-functioning that he tends to feel not that the therapist reminds him of or is like his mother

> or father . . . but rather his functioning toward the therapist is couched in the unscrutinized assumption that the therapist *is* the mother or father.

The matter is further complicated by the fragmented nature of the patient's introjects that are projected onto the therapist, so that the analyst may, during the course of even a few minutes, be reacted to as though he were an actualization of a mental representation of a part of first this person and then that. Additionally, under the influence of the primary process, cathexes are sometimes loose and easily displaceable, so that an intense reaction present at one moment may be misjudged by the therapist to indicate a more serious involvement with the introjected and usually distorted aspect of the person represented than later analysis will indicate to be the case.

One further datum should be indicated. The psychotic patients who are included in this study had, at all times, areas in which their regressions were similar to the regressive level of neurotics. Thus, intermixed with the use of transferences and the presence of the transference psychosis that developed during the treatment of each, elements of transference neurosis were present simultaneously. A very complicated transference relationship was the rule. Some patients who had been hospitalized immediately before entering analysis quickly projected fragmented introjects onto me. At the same time, their relationships with other individuals had varying degrees of objectivity. Others, who appeared to be less psychotic, first developed a relationship in which a transference neurosis was evident and only later were transference psychosis elements obvious. Since those individuals simultaneously functioned better in their everyday lives by that time, it was considered to be a sign of progress when they began to focus their reexperienced infantile emotions onto me, rather than maintain them in their previously generalized state.

Psychotherapists have sought usually to avoid states of

further regression in the treatment of psychotic patients. I believe the data provided by this study indicate that the patient's ability to regress in a controlled manner in the therapeutic situation is a sign of development of trust and psychic structuralization. It would seem that if no psychotic transference develops to be analyzed, there is little likelihood of cure: the most one can hope for is isolation or encapsulation of the psychotic process.

The course of the treatment, then, constituted a continuum that can be viewed from the side of changing transference relationships. After there had been more or less controlled regression to a stage where psychotic transference elements were obvious and these had been effectively analyzed, a neurotic transference relationship ensued. Sometimes this neurotic transference seemed to have the same content as that which had developed before the regression to the psychotic transference state, but the bases of the initial neurotic transference had been cleared of parts of their meanings, and they could be analyzed from the standpoint of a more advanced period of psychosexual development.

To state the case slightly differently, the second phase of the arbitrarily divided continuum constituted the analysis of the neurotic character disorder and its attendant symptomatology. Most therapists of psychotics have not sought to continue treatment to the resolution of these elements. However, the patients included here gave no indication of a desire to discontinue therapy after they had lost their psychotic symptomatology and thinking patterns. I wished to continue the investigative procedure because of the possibility that neurotic elements might be masking further psychotic mechanisms or process, inasmuch as a goal of this controlled observation was to test the hypothesis that psychoses can be cured by the use of psychoanalysis. My remarks in this chapter are directed to the first of the artificially divided phases, since there appeared to be little to distinguish the second phase from the usual analyses of neurotics. Nevertheless, during the second phase, in times of stress, the patients sometimes defensively recathected psychotic thinking and behavioral patterns for short periods, but the intensity of such recathexis was less than that observed during the first phase and, when the reasons for such regressions were determined, quickly abated.

As the result of more than two decades of work with schizophrenics, I believe that few, if any, patients are truly inaccessible. In the present series, no chronically and severely regressed schizophrenics are included because none applied for treatment when time was open. At the present time, such a patient is being analyzed, and the course of events supports the stand just mentioned, but it is too early to report details of his treatment. Nevertheless, the seven patients who had been hospitalized just before they began the study believed in the reality of their hallucinations and/or delusions; thus they belonged to Eissler's "acute" group (1951). Four had received courses of electroplexy and one had undergone insulin shock therapy. Seven cases were borderline schizophrenics whose psychotic thinking became obvious only after they lay on the couch. Examples of the emergence of psychotic thinking in such patients have been published previously. I quote from the case fragment of a woman whom I thought to be a classical hysteric before the following material emerged:

> During the second week of a trial period of psychoanalysis, as she lay on the couch, she heard noises outside the window. A gardener was filing his shovel. What she thought she heard was a man's hand rubbing a "hard object." A dog barked outside. Her interpretation of this sound was that I was rubbing my hand on some "hard object," probably a thick, long stick of wood. Her dream that night depicted a man masturbating. She insisted that she could recall seeing her father masturbate when she was about 4 years old, while her mother was pregnant. She was convinced that I was masturbating openly behind her; nevertheless, she had no inclination to leave my care.

> As she lay speaking of such things, she thoughtfully rubbed her pubic area. [1956a, p. 459]

Psychological tests were done and interpreted to be diagnostic of schizophrenia, the accuracy of which judgment was ascertained during her subsequent successful but lengthy treatment.[2]

Therapy during the first phase is directed toward the replacement or modification of undesirable introjects, that is, to restoration and/or development of a reasonable ego and superego. Clearly, the first step in preparing the patient to accomplish such goals is to establish meaningful and lasting contact with him. Aside from the common denominators inherent in systems of referral and the patient's first interviews, each psychiatrist has techniques that are more or less individual. I strive to make contact in an atmosphere of abstinence and through the use of interpretation. I believe that such a technique is most apt to offer true ego support, through the integrative and structuralizing effects of interpretation (see chapter 6), and through the immediate establishment for the patient of an atmosphere in which symptoms are treated calmly and as subjects for investigation. I shall present a vignette of the effects of interpretation with a floridly psychotic patient. I do not mean to imply that her

2. This case is the only one whose analysis was not conducted solely by me. The psychotic core seemed to have been resolved after about two and a half years of analysis; a transference neurosis developed in which I was reacted to as though I were her mother and she were a pregenital child. A year and a half later her care was transferred to another analyst, Dr. Charles B. David, because I was leaving the area for a year and a half to be involved in a research project of a different sort. During her analysis with me, the mother-transference had been analyzed almost completely, and she was beginning to view me as a father figure. Dr. David was reacted to from the first as a father substitute. Her analysis with him reached successful conclusion after another four years; there has been no regression of any kind during the ensuing seventeen years.

dramatic response is typical, but only that it can occur under some circumstances.

A thirty-six-year-old woman had suffered intermittently from a psychosis manifested by hebephrenic, depressed, and manic behavior for fourteen years, requiring almost constant care by psychiatrists and repeated hospitalizations. She had undergone insulin shock therapy. I saw her first while she was slightly confused from electroplexy. I asked her to tell me the history of her illness. When she could not remember dates, she became flirtatious and joked. I said she tried to hide her embarrassment because of memory deficiency by seeking to divert my attention through humor. She gratefully responded that she had always sought to make people laugh when she thought they might be angry with her. She was able to eschew such behavior for the rest of the interview. During the next week, she regressed seriously. She spent most of her time in seclusion, hallucinating, soiling herself, and terrified.

Her husband was a physician who had undergone a period of psychoanalysis for assistance with a psychosomatic complaint. He subsequently "forgot" his reason for undertaking therapy, read a great deal, and convinced himself he had studied analysis for intellectual reasons and became a "nonpracticing analyst." Accordingly, he knew that psychoanalysis is not recommended commonly for the treatment of psychotic conditions. However, it was generally known that he interfered grossly with psychiatrists' care of his wife and he was unable to obtain the services of anyone else for her care.

The patient was aware of her husband's actions and the nature of his relations with me before I saw her again.

The second interview took place in a seclusion room. We sat on the floor. She faced away from me and talked through clenched teeth about the dangers of gamma rays. I asked whether she feared she might harm me, were she to face me and open her mouth. She turned toward me, agreed, and asked if I were going to "buckle" her. I ignored the sexual connotation of her question, choosing to hear instead, "Are you going to put me in a straitjacket?" I said if she were afraid she would harm people on the ward, she could ask directly to be put into seclusion and that it was unnecessary for her to be noisy, silly, and provocative as a means of getting there. After she smiled, I said if she controlled her behavior for a while, we would start interviews in my office, although she could return to the hospital if she chose.

Following that interview, she refused further sedatives and voluntarily requested seclusion when she became fearful. I saw her for five further interviews but made no additional interpretations. Then she came to my office, accompanied by a nurse. She lay on the couch after the third hour and left the hospital soon thereafter.

During this initial period of interchange between the patient and me, I made two interpretations: (1) I suggested a reason for her flirting and joking and (2) I implied that I understood her attribution of magical qualities to her hostility and was unafraid. However, it is obvious that the interpretations were made in a framework that had other significant elements. I believe that her startling improvement and the establishment of contact which, as it proved, quickly developed into a working relationship, cannot be ascribed solely to the effects of the interpretations. My objective, observing, optimistic, and relatively calm attitude was important and promptly introjected in part; she also responded to my appeal to her own ego strength, her self-control. I believe these elements to be the most relevant in the framework within which the interpretations were made and that it is not possible to distinguish their relative positions of importance. The example serves to illustrate that from the beginning of my contacts with psychotic patients, I strive to make contact especially through the use of interpretations. Nevertheless, we cannot forget that all interpretations made by psychoanalysts while acting in their positions as therapists are made in special contexts (see chapter 6 and Boyer 1961, p. 394).[3]

Throughout this project I have considered that the primary initial goal of therapy is to enable the patient to develop altered introjects. At the same time, I have attempted to use interpretations as the ultimate therapeutic tool. I have attempted from the beginning to present consistent examples of

3. This woman's psychotic core was greatly alleviated after about two years. The psychotic transference was less florid than might have been expected, and after a few months she reacted to me largely as though I were her pregenital mother. During this period, much of her self-punishing behavior and thinking had disappeared and her previous sense of worthlessness and emptiness had been greatly modified. She then made of me a father figure and worked through some of her heterosexual incestuous conflicts. As a result, she began to be consciously aware of sexual urges toward her husband, who had denied her physical contact throughout her analysis. His need to keep her ill had been patent from the beginning, and his overt support of her self-evaluation as being dirty and without value had been disruptive. When she indicated she might be a better sexual partner than erstwhile, he informed her he had had mistresses for many years and was planning to divorce her to marry one with whom he had been intimate for the duration of her analysis. She responded by recathecting psychotic thinking for a brief period and her ideas of worthlessness for a longer time. While she again considered herself to be valueless, he proceeded with the divorce action. She refused to get a lawyer of her own and accepted as joint attorney a close personal friend of her husband's, a man whom she knew to be a misogynist. In consequence, her husband was awarded their children on the basis of her past mental illness, and she accepted a meager alimony settlement that provided for but six months of a further medical or psychiatric care. During the last six months of a three-year-long analysis, she made substantial strides in regaining self-esteem. Two years after she left analysis she remarried and was happy in her new relationship, which proved to be successful for the ensuing ten years. During that period she never sought an appointment. We have had chance meetings in which her embarrassment indicated to me that the erotized oedipal transference relationship that was being analyzed when she stopped treatment was incompletely resolved. However, it was clear that there had been no psychotic regression. No subsequent information about her has reached me.

the scientific attitude, a quality the patient gradually acquires. In doing so, he develops an attitudinal shift from a predominant primary process orientation to one in which he achieves the capacity of self-observation. The patient learns to view his conflicts as subjects for study and develops a working alliance (see chapters 6 and 7).

Thus, treatment begins with steady but gentle confrontations with distortions, contradictions, and other abandonments of reality, coincident with interpretations that are, as a rule, of the defensive functions of the products of his psychotic thinking. However, a review of the research data indicates that I have gradually shifted my technique over the years in the following ways. Initially, I responded rather indiscriminately to the patient's productions, interpreting defensive products of the derivatives of both sexual and aggressive drives. Now, I tend to ignore indications of positive transference or of the development of an oedipal transference relationship, unless a highly erotized transference threatens to develop or has suddenly made itself manifest. I have come to assume that such material is being used in the service of defense against the analysis of preoedipal, dyadic relationships. In the presence of such an erotized transference, I interpret its defensive functions. I find I have come, by and large, to restrict my interpretations during the early period of analysis to the aggressive aspects of whatever material is being presented. Of course, at the same time, such interpretations are made through the technique of stressing the object relationship aspects of the utilization of such aggressive drive derivatives.

Another shift in my technique over the years has been in the direction of choosing to deal with depressive material when possible in preference to persistently pursuing the products of paranoid ideation, an approach which has been recommended by Glover (1955) and others (see chapter 3). Both changes in technique reflect my growing conviction that ego introjects cannot be altered efficiently unless simultaneous changes take place in the superego introjects, in the direction of reducing the archaic, sadistic nature of that psychical structure. However, in contrast to Wexler (1951a) and others, I do not give direct superego support. The delineation of specific rules of conduct during treatment constitutes an indirect support. As another example, I stress the patient's anxiety when he factually has transgressed morality and label asocial and antisocial actions by their common names. When his "sins" have been moral infringements in thought only, I ask him to consider whether his thoughts have harmed anyone. Within the framework of the therapeutic situation, such support is not limited to the prohibitive functions of the superego.

I have called the initial period of treatment the "noisy phase." It is unusual that such patients can tolerate my silence for long periods. When they seem to be developing too great anxiety, I make noncommittal noises or request amplification. Almost any sound seems to reassure the patient that he has not been deserted or magically committed murder. I believe, with Arlow (1952) and Fromm-Reichmann (1950, 1952), that interpretations of content that emphasize forbidden or frightening wishes are not of primary importance during the period while the patient is still psychotic, although to make them is technically expeditious at times. In general, an interpretation regarding such content arouses feelings of guilt, whereas one concerning defense gives the patient the sense that the therapist, whom he perceives to a large degree as a superego figure, appreciates how much he struggles against his impulses. However, content interpretation can at times serve as a means for regaining contact with the patient when it becomes necessary to demonstrate to him that the therapist does understand some small part of what he tries to communicate. In addition to the use of content interpretation as a gambit, there are times when one has no choice. Occasionally neurotic symptoms will demand attention. The following case fragment serves as an example.

A woman underwent a paranoid and depressed psychotic

regression during the last months of pregnancy and became excited and confused following childbirth. A psychiatrist hospitalized her twice and administered electroconvulsive therapy. Soon after her second hospital discharge, she fled from his care and was included in this study.

During one of her early interviews, she recalled having seen her mother and a maternal uncle having sexual relations when she was a small child and confessed that she had wanted to take the place of each of them in the act. Her feelings had caused her to wet her pants. She was startled that I was not disturbed by her accurate screen memory and did not reprimand her because she wanted to urinate on the couch as she recalled the scene. She was also incredulous that her recitation did not excite me and thus make me want to urinate. She then related that, while hospitalized, she thought her psychiatrist was really her father and that he had sexual relations with her in the presence of a nurse while she was unconscious from the shocks. Although she ascribed the actions to his lechery, at the same time she was aware that she had awaited each electrical treatment in a state of sexual excitement and was a willing victim. She withdrew from his care in part because she was afraid they would have sexual relations in his office while she was awake and responsible for her acts. Then God would kill her as punishment for the overt incestuous crime.

Soon thereafter, she decided that she had distorted the event in which her mother and uncle had cohabited, and she began to picture her mother as asexual, forgiving, kind, calm, and supremely intellectual and to have had an attitude of "scientific detachment." Although her mother may have had such qualities to some degree at times, she was factually a chronic manic-depressive psychotic whose dominant characteristics were quite otherwise. The patient had ascribed her evaluation of me to her mother. She then began to describe herself to me in the same terms, a distortion as great as had been her picture of her mother. This series of events illustrates an early modification of archaic, sadistic superego introjects, no doubt preoedipal and maternal in origin, combined with or followed by projective identification (see Introduction).

She then had a dream in which she obviously combined the figures of her mother and me, and when she entered the office the following day she was startled to see that I was factually a man. She promptly developed a street phobia, a symptom that was new for her. One of its purposes was clearly to prevent her coming unaccompanied to the office; she wanted to be brought by a woman. My interpretation of that defensive aim of the neurotic symptom relieved no anxiety. I then suggested that her perception of me as a woman had been motivated in part by her fear that she would be unable to distinguish me from her father, whom she visualized as sadistic, lewd, stupid, and totally dedicated to satisfying his own lusts. I said she was now afraid that what she had feared would happen with the psychiatrist whom she had fled would now transpire with me in my office. She was vastly relieved, and the street phobia disappeared, never to return. During the next interviews she recalled having seen while a teenager her father making love to a neighbor woman. The patient had tried soon thereafter to get her father to make sexual advances to her and was bitterly disappointed that he rejected her thinly veiled offer. The preoccupation with her parents' sexual lives then disappeared from the content of the interviews for some time, and her attention turned to a closer examination of her relations with her husband. The therapy moved along smoothly for some weeks.

As has been stressed, the intended purpose of the first phase of the treatment of these patients is conceived to be the replacement or modification of introjects. Both case fragments illustrate descriptively some results of this process, with larval evidence of concomitant taming of drives. It may be that in the first of the examples, there was simultaneously a redirection of the aggressive drive toward self-control or mastery.

Numerous writers have called attention to the fact that in the presence of inadequate differentiation of id and ego, tensions are frequently fixed to physical phenomena. In the treatment of psychotics, the analysis of the meanings of phenomena that result from automatic actions of bodily systems that are innervated by the voluntary and involuntary nervous systems is sometimes mandatory before further differentiation of id and ego can transpire. Reference is made to skeletal muscular tensions, postures, and gestures (Deutsch and Murphy 1955, W. Reich 1933), emotional attitudes (Greenson 1949, 1951), and the so-called psychosomatic disorders (Alexander and French 1948, Sperling 1955, 1974, 1978). My practice has not included patients who have suffered from severe and chronic psychosomatic disturbances. In the analysis of muscular tensions, postures, and gestures, I have found the extraanalytic and parametric procedures recommended by Braatøy (1954) to be unnecessary. Such analysis is usually indicated during the period while the patient is psychotic; like Searles (1963) I have found it to be an essential step during the resolution of the transference psychosis. Subsequently, as in the case of recathexis of psychotic thinking and behavior during the second phase (see above), defensive regression to the utilization of such phenomena must be repeatedly analyzed.

It is a noteworthy and mysterious fact that no patient to whom participation in this controlled observation was offered has refused. This datum gives evidence that in these cases a potentially favorable transference relationship existed from the beginning. Whether this can be attributed to the nature of the individual cases or of the referrals, or to the patients' initial contacts with me, I cannot say. It was quickly evident that many patients projected megalomanic expectations onto me; they ascribed omniscience and omnipotence to the analyst and expected some form of magical performance. The data I have that are relevant suggest that such ascription resulted in part from my apparently successful attempt to treat the patients' productions with calm and neutrality. Those subjects who have spoken to this point have stated that they interpreted my not having been upset by their recitations of material that seemed extremely dangerous to them to signify that I was too strong and wise to be made anxious. I have had some experience in dealing therapeutically with people whose healers are shamans (Boyer 1964b) and have been struck by the similarity of expectations of those Indians and my schizophrenic patients.

Various authors have discussed the importance of accurate interpretations in dealing with the schizophrenic. Fromm-Reichmann (1950, 1952) in particular has emphasized the dangers of incorrect interpretations. However, what constitutes an accurate or a wrong interpretation presents a most complex problem. At times I have made statements that were subsequently determined to have been dynamically, economically, and reconstructively wrong. Patients have responded to them in widely varying manners, ranging from no evident reaction to acute, although brief, psychotic regression. Not infrequently I have found faulty interpretations to have been accidentally beneficial. Sullivan (1940) consciously used misstatements for the purpose of having the patient correct them, and I, too, have used this technical procedure for the purpose of having the patient reconsider data and remove distortions, thereby strengthening his powers of discrimination. However, here I write of unintentionally faulty statements. One patient, commenting to this point, said:

> When your understanding of what I've said is just wrong, I'm not bothered at all. If it has been partly right, I am angry and frightened because I expect you to be completely right when you're right. What disturbs me most, though, is when you have overestimated how much *I* can understand and have been *too* right when I wasn't quite ready.

In general, in my experience, accurate interpretations are more detrimental to the course of treatment than are totally inaccurate or partially wrong statements and explanations, when the correct statements are faulty as to *timing*, that is, when they pertain to phenomena not near enough to the conscious, economic, or dynamic agenda, to paraphrase Loewenstein (1956).

Fromm-Reichmann has also written of the dangers of pretense of understanding. When I think I have failed to understand, I let the patient know of my lack of comprehension and invite him to amplify and clarify. Additionally, I never consciously play a role.

It is obvious that I disagree with Alexander (1927, 1931), Federn (1933), and Nunberg (1921), who advocated nonanalytical and parametric methods of fostering a "positive transference" as a means of establishing contact. The schizophrenic is terrified of the potential destructiveness of his impulses, and when the emergence of hatred of former love objects is discouraged, he interprets the therapist to fear the patient's or his own hostility. I refer here to hostility that is expressed in words or symbolically and not that which shows itself in assault. No patient has ever attacked me in the office, and when I have been attacked or threatened obviously with attack by a hospitalized patient, and have been unable to mollify the patient's panic or rage by interpretive means, I have commanded cessation or directed attendants to calm the patient physically. When hostility is expressed in words or symbols, they are interpreted from the standpoint of their defensive or testing functions. The appearance of hostility is not discouraged, but the rate and intensity of its emergence are slaked by the timing of interpretations.

Patients who no longer ascribed magical destructiveness to their aggressive impulses commented that during the courses of their treatments they considered their repetitive and timid attempts to express hostility to have been beneficial and necessary. It is known that children's repetitive activities are highly cathected and that interruption of practice or prevention of completion of acts sometimes upsets a tenuous balance of psychic energy. Hartmann, Kris, and Loewenstein (1946) suggest that experiments on act completion in normal adults and obsessional patients indicate that the same may be true of man's life.

The child's tendency to respond aggressively when he experiences restraint can be modified, usually without great difficulty, by the behavior of the restraining adult, or, in the therapy of the psychotic, by that of the parent-substitute. When the child is distracted by nonhostile, loving attention, cathexis that was directed previously toward action is transformed into loving cathexis. When the psychiatrist recognizes that the patient's release of aggression, here viewed as a practice phenomenon, is accompanied by too-great anxiety, he can shift the patient's attention considerably to possible meanings of his behavior. This, then, would constitute a learning situation, lead to psychic structuralization, encourage the development of object cathexis, and make possible further mastery of reality by reducing the patient's fear of his own hostility.

Above all, I wish to emphasize the importance of consistency in attitude and technique; my attitude and technique can best be described by the terms *calmness, indirectly communicated optimism,* and *scientific detachment.* All these phenomena are superimposed, obviously, on a capacity to understand productions that are influenced heavily by primary process thinking and some knowledge of why they are used at the times they are employed. I periodically remind patients that interpretations are made tentatively and solicit answers to enigmas. This procedure enhances the development of at least the observing and synthesizing functions and reduces the severity of the patient's primitive superego introjects by permitting him to view his new parent-model as fallible.

Let us now turn to the results of this study to the present.

RESULTS

The treatment of this series of seventeen patients was terminated at least two years ago, except for one patient who took hiw own life. Fourteen appear thus far to have outcomes that can be classified as satisfactory, or, in some cases, most encouraging. Because of numerous reports of spontaneously remitting schizophrenias, perhaps some of them might have encapsulated their psychoses (to use Federn's term) without such therapy. In addition, the number of cases involved and the shortness of time that has elapsed since their termination of treatment makes this an interim report.

It has been noted regularly that psychotic states that include overt anxiety and mood changes, particularly depressive manifestations, have a better likelihood of therapeutic success. All the patients in this series, manifested overt anxiety, and the majority could well have been labeled as suffering from schizoaffective psychoses, with depressive aspects prevailing over manic, although several patients experienced periodic hypomanic episodes.

Glover (1955) found schizophrenics who manifested depressive elements to be the most suitable for psychoanalytic therapy. Nacht and Lebovici (1955) recommended classical analysis for cases of schizophrenia, excluding paranoia and severe hypochondriasis. They, as had Glover, felt that anxiety due especially to fear of the superego was a favorable sign. In all the cases in the present series, evidence of an extremely punitive superego was present. However, in my experience, this state has been observed uniformly. Authors have discouraged regularly (since about 1908) the use of analytic therapy for paranoid schizophrenics. In this series, two patients, both male, had systematized persecutory delusions. In one, there had been hallucinations during a period of late adolescence and early adulthood, symptoms of which reappeared during one phase of his selective analytic regression, but the other man never experienced hallucinations and in previous years might well have been labeled as paranoiac. Both recovered from their paranoid states although they both remained hampered by obsessive-compulsive character disorders. Each man had been psychotic for many years before analysis; neither has regressed since termination of analysis. The treatment of one man lasted six years and ended ten years ago; that of the other lasted five years and was terminated eight years ago. Each reentered analysis at a later time for relief of depressive symptomatology and received further assistance in overcoming obsessive-compulsive rigidity.

Three cases of this series ended in outright failure. The lack of success with two of them appeared to have been related more to my problems than theirs; I believe the third failed because of faulty judgment on my part.

I shall present two clinical abstracts that illustrate apparent success. I have chosen these cases above others because they show that analysis can take place with the same therapist after a change in treatment method, whereas in the other instances of apparent success only analytic therapy was used. Each of these patients had been treated by me before I decided to conduct this controlled observation.

A twenty-nine-year-old woman sought treatment because she thought she was going insane; she had numerous obsessive fears. She was afraid she would bite her tongue off if she were openly angry and that she would jump from windows; she barricaded those of her apartment. She also suffered from claustrophobia and had an intense fear of pregnancy. She was sexually anesthetic.

Her parents had immigrated from a southern European country and were ardent Catholics of peasant stock. They had never been happy together and lived apart during most of her life. The mother resided in a city with the children and the father attended a vineyard in the country. He came home on weekends when she was small and at much rarer intervals as she grew older. From puberty, she sided with her mother and avoided her father.

She was the youngest of many children, being seven years younger than the next sibling. She was treated always as though she were an incompetent baby; her decisions were made for her, and she was protected from all extrafamilial dangers. She was a devout Catholic and sincerely believed in the healing effects of confession. Her principal libidinal outlets were in the home and the church. There were no sanctioned aggressive outlets except contempt for the father and outsiders. At the same time her extended family, succumbing at last to the ideals of their new cultural environment, pressured her into becoming its only college graduate, a role perceived to be masculine. She did well in school, was popular and apparently happy.

Following her graduation from college, she was rewarded with a trip to an eastern city. She had dated when in the university but experienced no sexual encounters beyond nonpassionate kisses and had never drunk liquor more intoxicating than watered wine. The female relative with whom she lived led a relatively Bohemian life. In that environment, the patient drank too much one evening and had the first genital experience she remembered during all of her psychotherapy and subsequent analysis. She believed she was in a trancelike state while she was being kissed and fondled. She knew the man's penis touched her legs, but did not know that she had intercourse. However, she was impregnated.

She remained in the East, had her baby without letting the man or her family know of her pregnancy. She confided her state to a schizoid man whom she had known while she was in school, with whom her relations had been platonic. He asked her to marry him, the marriage being contingent upon her getting rid of the baby. She had her baby adopted out. The man joined her in the East and she returned to her home environment as a housewife.

Following her homecoming, she became withdrawn, obsessive, phobic, and depressed, and retired from church and family activities. The marital partners had little personal contact and almost no sexual life. He worked during the night by choice, and she during the day. He had affairs and otherwise his social life was spent with his widowed mother, who dominated him through her hypochondria. The patient was terrified of pregnancy but both partners insisted on the rhythm system of contraception. Although her husband never threatened overtly to betray her to her parents, she always felt she must obey him implicitly and did so, achieving some semblance of expression of hostility and independence only through passive aggression and the use of her fears.

In her work she was grossly inefficient, but the general pattern in her office was lax. She had no friends. She felt her miserable life was just retribution for her sin. Her social life consisted largely of rare visits to her mother and an older sister, who were solicitous and nondemanding.

After eight years of marriage, her husband became more than usually interested in some woman and the patient feared he would leave her. She then began to fear she would go mad and sought psychotherapy.

During two years (150 hours) of vis-à-vis psychotherapy, she was an exceedingly tense, largely silent patient. Treatment was directed toward making her aware of her suppressed and repressed hostility and her manipulative uses of passive aggression and fears.

When treatment began, she stopped taking sedatives. She made me into an omniscient and omnipotent figure and used my words, perceived at times as concrete phenomena, as protective amulets. Her behavior outside the interviews did not seem to change, but her anxiety abated. Eventually she began to have vague sexual fantasies concerning me and began to demand sedatives. It was clear that the demand for pills reflected an equation of genital and oral gratifications. Various data indicated she had blamed herself for her parents' separation and believed her father left home to avoid succumbing to her sexual desires. Oedipal interpretations were ineffective, and she discontinued treatment.

In conjunction with a separate research project, all my patients were required to undergo psychological tests, which were administered by a colleague at six-month intervals. The test protocols of this patient were interpreted to mean that she suffered from undifferentiated schizophrenia throughout this period of treatment. There were also strong indications of hysteria and depression.

She was seen at six months, one year, two years, and five years following treatment, at my request. She seemed much improved. Although all the old complaints persisted with the exception of the fear she would go insane, there was little anxiety. She apparently lived with me, quite totally, in fantasy. We held long conversations, no matter what else she was doing, and I cared for her and guided her as though she were a small child. Psychological tests done at the same intervals indicated no change.

Seven years after she left treatment, she became intoxicated with her husband one night and got pregnant, again without knowing for certain whether she'd had intercourse. When she ascertained that she was pregnant, she tried to reach me, but I was out of town. She presented herself at a hospital where she had learned I sometimes treat patients and was admitted as my patient. She was terrified that she was going insane and would rip her tongue out. She had the delusion that I was God and had impregnated her. During the two days before I saw her, she regressed into a catatonic state and there were vaguely systematized persecutory ideas. When she first saw me, her terror left, and she was discharged from the hospital the next day.

She was then included in the project. Her delusion promptly disappeared. Thereafter, attention was directed primarily toward alleviating superego pressures. She soon resumed church activities, including confession. No clear-cut oedipal memories ever emerged. Under the influence of reconstructive remarks, she seemed to attain some intellectual understanding, although I was never sure that she was not simply responding to what she interpreted to be suggestions or commands. Concurrently, her obsessions and fears were alleviated to a large extent.

Her pregnancy proceeded without difficulty and she delivered a son. Her period in analysis lasted for one year (140 hours). She had become grossly involved in the care of her son and seemed otherwise symptom-free. Analysis was terminated, however, because of absence of funds and because her husband's hostility toward her involvement in her treatment, superimposed upon that toward the baby and the church, led him to threaten to leave her and to tell her family about her first pregnancy if she didn't stop.

Soon after termination, she became pregnant through choice and was unafraid. She became reconciled with her father.

She was seen again at the follow-up intervals described above. Psychological tests done on termination and at those intervals revealed no evidence of psychosis. It is twenty-five years since termination. During the first five years she was a doting mother and seemed very happy. She was able to enjoy some of her sexual experiences. Aside from a letter she wrote seven years after termination, there have been no further contacts with me. In that missive, she said she had resumed working, was no longer so preoccupied with her children, and getting along better with her husband, who had become a devoted father.

A second married woman was thirty-two years old when first interviewed. Material concerning her history and care has been published previously (Boyer 1955, 1961). She was customarily timorous, intensely dependent, grossly inhibited in both the sexual and aggressive spheres, and received pleasure primarily from serving her demanding, arrogant, and bullying husband and their young sons. Although she had graduated from college with honors, following her marriage she had become more and more like her withdrawn, complaining, bored and boring mother and had no interests outside the home. The apparently stable marriage had assumed a sadomasochistic quality in which the symptoms of each spouse supported the psychopathology of the other. Following a business reversal, her husband's dependency on his female relatives was heightened, and she became fearful that he would desert her.

She underwent an acute excited catatonic episode, which I eventually treated by electroplexy. She improved rapidly and explained her improvement on the basis of her having equated the shocks with punishment for her hostile wishes toward her husband (Boyer 1952). She was seen in supportive therapy for three months but suffered another acute catatonic excitement when she became aware of murderous wishes toward her husband when she feared he was incestuously involved, or might become so, with his sister. I treated her a second time with electroconvulsive therapy after a few weeks of hospitalization, during which there was no improvement. It was at that time in my career that I decided to undertake the experiment to determine whether psychoanalysis with few parameters might prove to be beneficial to schizophrenic patients. After a few more months of supportive therapy, which was frustrating to both her and to me, I asked whether she wished to be included in the study and she eagerly agreed.

She was in analysis for four years, being seen 750 hours. Her treatment went smoothly. Although Rorschach tests continued to reveal evidence of schizophrenic thinking, there was no clinical evidence of psychosis after a year or so. During much of that year, her parents, brother, husband, and I were all perceived by her as idealized, good-mother projections, while her husband's mother and sisters were viewed uniformly and indiscriminately as bad-mother projections. As she became able to tolerate ambivalence, she became freer in self-assertion and other modes of expressing aggression and lost some of her sexual inhibitions. She resumed educational pursuits and allowed herself to pursue aesthetic interests that she had previously denied to herself. She had done so both because of her fear of maternal disapproval as well as that of her husband and his family. She also felt guilt at seeking selfish pleasures rather than devoting her life solely to the service of her husband and sons. A third reason that she had denied herself such pursuits was that she was afraid she would lose her sense of personal identity if she were to relinquish the self-martyring maternal introject. During the last year and a half or so of her analysis, a full-blown transference neurosis unfolded, in which I represented principally her oedipal father. These changes frightened her husband, who began to behave destructively toward their sons. She terminated her analysis prematurely because she felt there was no other way to help him behave more like a loving father.

She remained at the same level of integration for the next four years, although her annual Rorschach tests continued to reveal diminishing signs of schizophrenic thinking. During that period I saw her once annually at my request; we had no other contacts although I knew of her welfare from another source and that she was happy and stable. Then during a period when I was away, she responded to one of her husband's temper tantrums by undergoing a schizomanic regression. She was hospitalized for two weeks and treated with nonspecific sedatives during those days when the palliative effects of the phenothiazines and lithium were as yet unknown. Upon my return, she reentered treatment with me.

Soon after the resumption of analysis, while she was still hypomanic, her husband had a sudden, life-threatening illness. She responded with great guilt and severe depression. Interpretations pertaining to her ascription of magical powers to her hostility and sexual fantasies enabled her to continue office treatment. New material related to her early life emerged, and her childhood ideas that her sexual wishes toward her father had resulted in various catastrophes, including his imprisonment and her mother's becoming a lifelong, severly withdrawn hypochondriac, were analyzed. The second period of treatment lasted thirteen months (225 hours). At its end her sexual inhibitions were greatly relieved, and her fears of her aggression had lost their magical qualities. When the analysis was discontinued, Rorschach tests revealed no evidence of psychotic thinking.

She then enrolled in graduate school to prepare for a career, since her husband's life prognosis was tenuous. Soon after she enrolled, he had another acute attack, but she remained well. She obtained her degree and has been a talented and successful worker in the mental health field for more than twenty years. Her husband died soon after she received her degree, but she handled his demise well. She reappeared for a few months of vis-à-vis therapy for mild depression about four years after the second termination of analysis but has had no further need of treatment.

DISCUSSION

Psychoanalysis was designed for the treatment of neurotics, and in its classical milieu their projections are analyzed. The neurotic who assumes the couch position is invited to regress selectively. When a psychotic takes the couch, certain facets of his ego and superego are already in a deeper state of regression than we usually expect the neurotic to reach in his therapy. He reenacts the early mother-child relationship, although the areas of ego and superego regression that permit such a reliving differ from patient to patient. We recall that the unfolding of conflict-free ego spheres is dependent upon the mother-infant relationship. In the treatment situation, identification with the actual frustrator is enhanced, and there exists a danger of the patient's becoming too like the therapist and being unable to develop subsequently in a manner optimal to his personal potential. The therapist appears for a time to become a variant of Winnicott's transitional object (1953). Hopefully, the second phase of treatment eradicates much of this danger. Empirically none of the individuals in this study has become professionally like me, but one. The ego and superego structures of a number appear now to approximate my own. The psychotic, I believe, makes the treatment situation, as he probably does of many others, one in which he acts in terms of innate strivings toward ego maturation. He also reaches for new objects to replace the old ones to which he ambivalently clings.

When a person lies down on the couch, his contacts with the therapist are diminished abruptly, and he maintains contact primarily through hearing. Thus, the attitudes of the analyst, as reflected in his words, voice tones, and other sounds, assume great importance and cannot be disguised. As with the pregenital child and particularly the child who has not yet learned to communicate in words, the introjections of the analysand are dependent upon the actual attitudes and qualities of the analyst. The psychotic patient wishes consciously to validate his auditory perceptions through other perceptual experience, notably visual and tactile, and sometimes presses to be allowed to sit. When he is met with questions concerning his desire to sit, he develops anxiety, which stimulates the emergence of data, serving the analytic purpose. Patients have verbalized subsequently their gratitude that they had not been encouraged to face or touch me. As an example, during the third year of the analysis of a borderline schizophrenic who had used every technique I have ever witnessed in her attempts to seduce me to abandon following rigorously the analytic technique, she suddenly blocked in her associations and had an intense desire to sit and look at me. I asked her to tell me what her wish to see me brought to her mind. She became furious and hurled the following words at me. The transition in her vocal expression mirrored the change in the content of the sentence. First she shouted a few words, then her voice tone became scathingly sarcastic, then softer and ultimately loving. She said:

> You God-damned rat fink, you buddy, you pal, you dear sweet kind man. Do you know that if you had not been incorruptible

> throughout my analysis, I'd have been dead long ago? I used to be afraid, too, that you'd grate off like a potato. I'm so glad you're ungratable and haven't been destroyed.

Patients have commonly said that their remaining on the couch had made them aware of the magical nature of their fears of being destroyed by me or of destruction of me which at times they sought to achieve through fusion through tactile or visual contact.

A therapist cannot remain completely objective about a patient. My patients' introjection of my attitude that they were worth helping served the valuable purpose of increasing their feelings of self-worth. I did not tell them overtly that I liked them. During the early period of treatment, the most important step, in my judgment, has been their introjection of my relatively calm, hopeful, expectant attitude with its consistent implication that gratifications can be postponed, or even renounced, with benefit.

The question has been raised frequently, "How can introjection take place in a milieu designed for the analysis of projections?" This query implies that introjection takes place principally through visual perceptions of the psychiatrist's overt communication of factual data concerning himself. Discussants have offered such a viewpoint as a reason to have the patient face the therapist. The results of this study surely affirm that successful introjection can take place as a result of auditory perceptions. Such information has long been available to us, since congenitally blind people, too, develop ego structures (Blank 1957, Fraiberg 1968, Fraiberg and Freedman 1964, Freedman 1978a).

It is my impression that the notion that visual and/or tactile contact is of primary importance in the treatment of psychotics has been overstressed. In infants such contact promotes the differentiation of id and ego. In certain acute episodes of psychotic regression, such contact is also mandatory for the reestablishment of some degree of autonomy, as is evident by the terror expressed by patients at some times when they are deprived of the sight or touch of the therapist. However, it is my opinion that the helplessness of the psychotic is exaggerated in the minds of many therapists and that their attitudes encourage patients to remain deeply regressed at times by rewarding them for such infantile behavior, that is, by their supplying the secondary gains sought by the patients. When we work with psychotics, in order to develop a working alliance, it behooves us to appeal to the more mature aspects of the patient's ego whenever possible. Clearly, in the presence of too great anxiety, no analysis can take place. I am suggesting that in the analysis of psychotics, especially during periods of acute regression, too little importance has been placed on the value of words and therapists have underestimated the resiliency of their patients. They appear to have forgotten sometimes that the psychotic patient is not all psychotic and that he has both normal and neurotic aspects that can be called into service by directing attention to them.

Freud's original formulation was that the aim of psychoanalytic therapy was to lift amnesias. Since psychoanalysis has come to consider the result of defenses other than repression, the need has arisen to understand the role of the synthetic and organizing function in the therapeutic process. Now we aim not merely at bringing into consciousness but at gaining analytic insight. We seek to produce changes in the ego that make warded-off functions available to the conflictless sphere of the ego, a process that entails both the bringing into consciousness and the reestablishment of connections (Bibring 1937, Fenichel 1937, Kris 1950, Loewenstein 1951, Nunberg 1937). The role of language is of cardinal importance in the accomplishment of this goal.

The psychoanalytic dialogue differs from all others and is made unique by the fundamental rule and the role of the analyst. The patient is asked to relinquish the aim-directed nature of conscious thinking. A controlled regression of the ego (Kris 1950) results, and elements of the Preconscious are made available to the Conscious. The analyst protects the patient and draws certain affects of the patient onto himself, but his main role is of lending his own ego functions to the weakened, although to some degree autonomous, ego of the patient. All of these functions are, of course, even more graphically portrayed when the patient is psychotic. The analyst forms what might be characterized as a variant of the maternal protective barrier (Boyer 1956b). He supplies the knowledge of mental phenomena, the understanding, and the objectivity that help the patient to understand them (see chapter 8).

Loewenstein (1956) has differentiated among three functions of speech: the cognitive function, the expressive function, and the function of appeal. In the neurotic the first two functions predominate at first and that of appeal emerges soon thereafter. In the psychotic the latter two functions predominate initially. The analyst refrains insofar as he can from responding to the appeal function. He attempts, through using interpretations, to transform the appeal function to the expressive function. He demonstrates to the patient that he expresses something about himself when he speaks of other persons or things. The analyst attempts to exclude both the functions of expression and appeal from his own speech.

Nunberg (1932) wrote of the magical function of speech and also of speech as a substitute for action. With the psychotic the analyst seeks to reduce belief in the magical effects of speech. While his nonverbal behavior assists the patient to accomplish this goal, I believe the analyst's interpretive words to be of more lasting benefit.

Superego, id, and ego contribute unequally to the actions of speech. So far as the superego is concerned, the confession of acts or intentions may lead to an actual change in the person when such admissions do not create anxiety and retributive acts on the part of the confessor. Communication through speech is often in the service of the id. Speech may be a poor substitute for sexual gratification but so far as the expression of aggression is concerned, words may indeed constitute actions. As discussed earlier, the patient's being encouraged to express his hostility verbally serves various purposes; here attention is called to its discharge function in an atmosphere of safety. The role of speech from the standpoint of the ego is perhaps of more interest at this point.

Our patients teach us that a barrier exists between the *Ucs.* and the *Pcs.*, but also between the *Pcs.* and the *Cs.*, since they frequently delay relating known information. No doubt this barrier results from fears of loss of love and esteem or other punishments. The analyst is both a superego and witness to the patient; these roles are of inestimable importance in the treatment of the psychotic. As witness, he serves as an accessory, reminding memory, an autonomous ego. When the patient has verbalized data, those data become more real and more easily remembered, which may result, in part, from auditory perception. The analyst stores previously imparted data and recalls them to the patient at appropriate times. Communicated private data become objective and social data, especially if they are not allowed to become repressed.

It has long been known that catharsis in analysis is not enough. The experiencing of emotions must be followed by their verbal expression, and for ultimate structuralization they must be connected with specific contents. Then the affects can be reintegrated as parts of defenses as well as of drives. In the formation of analytic insight, verbalization is an essential step, and the interpretive role of the analyst is his most important function.

Language plays a decisive role in the formation and development of thought processes. In analysis the thought processes of especial interest are those dealing with self-knowledge. When words bring to conscious awareness a previously unconscious thought and an affect, language performs the function of a scaffolding that permits thought to be built inside. Interpretations given by the analyst also provide such a scaffolding, although interpretations may also be misused in the service of resistance. Possibly when such is the result, the interpretations have been made when some aspect of them is untimely. The receptivity of hitherto pathogenic memories into consciousness makes them become harmless because insight and verbalization subject them to reality testing and unravel the effects of pathogenic entwinement between past and present (Loewenstein 1956).

Particularly with psychotic patients and those with characterological disorders it is necessary consistently to analyze idiosyncratic efforts at making himself understood in order that the patient may learn to communicate in a generally acceptable manner. The analyst's understanding of the meaning of the patient's communications enables him to break through resistance and to learn about interpersonal and intrapsychic realities. In addition, the patient's becoming consciously aware of his use of attitudinal and bodily language helps him remove body-ego deficiencies and to separate self from nonself.

Many analysts have stressed the role of the superego in schizophrenia (Hoedemaker 1955, Pious 1949, Wexler 1951a). I have spoken of my means of giving superego support. In general, I communicate indirectly my philosophy that guilt is appropriate when one's behavior, without rational cause, jeopardizes the rights and comforts of others.

A major thesis that the empirical data supplied from the present controlled observation have strongly suggested is the following: revision of faulty ego and superego structures in certain psychotic patients can be accomplished by the analytic process. The success of that process is dependent upon two main phenomena: (1) In a controlled situation, qualities of the new parent-model, the therapist, can be introjected, and such introjection can alter unhealthy nuclei (Glover 1930) of the patient's ego and superego. (2) Interpretation has a structuralizing effect (see chapter 6). Clinical observations have revealed that schizophrenic patients partly fear omnipotent results of their rage; that they worry that their aggressive tendencies will destroy the object or, projected onto the object, result in their own destruction. Hartmann, Kris, and Loewenstein (1959) believed that the internalization of neutralized aggression into the ego and superego made their structuralization possible and that "tamed" aggression made their functioning possible. It is probable that interpretation is the principal tool that leads to neutralization of the aggressive drive and to its being made available for such internalization. These data suggest that, in contrast to the prevailing attitude of psychoanalysts regarding the therapeutic procedure of choice for such patients, the analytic method, modified as little as possible, may be not only preferable but mandatory if the psychotic processes of the patients are not to be merely masked or isolated.

Clearly the internal security of the therapist is of signal importance. If he is too anxious, it is unlikely that a lasting therapeutic alliance can be attained. Since his attitudes and relative lack of anxiety will affect his understanding and judgment, he must understand himself well, be proud of his skills and accomplishments, and be optimistic. Surely if he understands primary process thinking and has the capacity to regress selectively in the service of the therapeutic process, he will be better able to understand his patient's productions and to elicit additional usable data from that patient. I would assume that most properly trained psychoanalysts could become relatively free of anxiety while dealing with psychotic patients and proficient at treating them.

A number of therapists have stressed that the role of countertransference is of great importance for the successful outcome of treatment of schizophrenics (Fromm-Reichmann 1950, Rosenfeld 1952b). My analysis of one patient was supervised. When treatment had reached a frustrating plateau, it became obvious that the problem lay within myself. I returned to analysis, where I learned more than intellectually that I had entered the practice of psychiatry and later psychoanalysis for the unconscious purpose of healing an important person of my past who had periodically regressed into psychotic states. I learned that when dealing with patients whose conflicts struck literally too close to home, I developed a countertransference neurosis. My return to analysis made possible the resurrection of the treatment of my patient. The therapy of two individuals who are included in this study had failed previously. Review of their case histories and the course of their treatment made amply clear that I had acted out with them, too.

The third failure may be attributable to bad judgment on my part. The young male patient had had a particularly tense oedipal period. His father had been absent from the home much of the time, and the patient had believed his father had abandoned him to the sexual desires of his mother. In treatment he was in the midst of a transference psychosis in which he believed I was his father. At the same time, he was having great difficulty in restraining himself from sexual activities with a relative whom he periodically believed to be his mother, a woman who he thought had strong sexual desires for him. This was the state of affairs when I announced to him that I was to be away from the office for a few days, some weeks thence. The patient seemed to take the news well, and I misinterpreted his turning to other subject matter. Nevertheless, I arranged for him to be able to call a psychiatrist whom he knew and trusted and for him to enter a hospital if he were frightened during my absence; he was aware of these provisions. One day after I left, he went to stay with family friends. He became fearful he would harm himself and was taken to a hospital where a psychiatric resident decided he did not require hospitalization. The next morning he killed himself.

SUMMARY

For seventeen years I have treated borderline and overtly schizophrenic patients by the analytic method that has ordinarily been reserved for the treatment of neurotics. In seminar groups, colleagues have remarked at times that I was more strictly and consistently analytical while treating psychotics than they were with neurotics. In this chapter I discuss the theoretical orientation upon which this study has been based, the methodology, and the results.

The patients included were all of average to superior intelligence; the symptom picture of almost all of them included strong depressive tendencies. No chronically regressed, withdrawn patients were studied.

Although the cases number only seventeen and the time elapsed since termination is not long, fourteen of the cases have achieved satisfactory or striking improvements, and there has been no psychotic or serious neurotic regression among them during periods which range from sixteen to twenty-four years. The data suggest that with patients such as those included, therapists have used more parametric and extraanalytic procedures than have been either necessary or, perhaps, advisable.

It is suggested that the psychotic process is reversible in some patients and that we, as analysts, might aim not at encapsulation of at least some psychoses but at their cure. Stone (1963) voiced the opinion that the analyst shirks his responsibility at times if he does not give decisive help beyond interpretation. To me, as it does to Giovacchini, such a statement implies that we have something better to offer than psychoanalysis. Hartmann and Kris (1945, p. 12) wrote: "Those who do not appreciate the importance of genetic interpretations change their technique." It is emphasized here that the role of genetic interpretations is at least as important in the treatment of psychotics as it is with neurotics and that the likelihood of successful therapy will be enhanced by the therapist's taking only such actions as do not jeopardize subsequent use of interpretations.

CHAPTER FIVE

Working With A Borderline Patient

L. Bryce Boyer

It is now thirty years that I have been engaged in the outpatient care of individuals who suffer from disorders that were long considered untreatable by psychoanalytic therapy.[1] As was illustrated in chapter 4, my therapeutic procedures have involved minimal use of parameters (Eissler 1953a) and have excluded the use of supportive and nonanalytic procedures such as those advocated by Federn (1952) and Nunberg (1932). It has been my good fortune to have worked with some thirty patients whose diagnoses have ranged from clearly schizophrenic to what are now labeled borderline personality and severe narcissistic personality disorders. For the same length of time I have supervised residents, the majority of whose

1. This is an amplified version of a presentation made before the American Psychotherapy Seminar Center, New York, December 1975, the Los Angeles Psychoanalytic Society and Institute, May 1976, and other groups.

2. In Kernberg's words (1976b, p.xiv), this intermediate position would describe object relations theory "as a specialized approach within psychoanalytic methodology, one that stresses the building up of dyadic intrapsychic representations—self- and object images—reflecting the original infant-mother relation and its later development into dyadic, triadic, and multiple internal and external interpersonal relations in general. This focus stresses the simultaneous building up of the self and of internal objects (or object representations), with particular emphasis on the essentially dyadic—or bipolar—nature of all internalizations, which are established in the context of a particular affective disposition or interaction."

This intermediate definition "reflects the views of such theoreticians as Erikson, Jacobson and Mahler within the ego-psychological approach; Fairbairn, Winnicott, Bowlby and Melanie Klein within the so-called British schools of psychoanalysis; and, to some extent, Harry Stack Sullivan and the more relevant work of Talcott Parsons."

patients had similar personalities. My work has involved the application of the intermediate position regarding object relations defined by Kernberg.[2]

Whereas in previous communications I have focused principally on the articulation between theory and technique (Boyer 1956b, 1961, 1971, 1976, 1978), in the present article I shall emphasize technique and my own experience while treating a difficult case. It is possible to do this with some degree of accuracy because, like Greenacre (1975), I take notes during each session. I record the general theme of the patient's productions and often note some elements in detail, particularly dreams, fantasies, and nonverbal communications; I note my own emotional reactions and fantasies, whether they remain private or are in some manner communicated to the patient. The fragment of the case history that follows involved culling through some two thousand pages of handwritten notes.

I have found my recording rarely interferes with the patients' communications, and such interferences are generally easily nullified by relevant interpretations. My method is beneficial to patients in two ways: it helps them to believe their communications are valuable and enables them to develop a sense of objectivity about their messages.

A large majority of my patients have benefited from our work. This is confirmed by follow-up information in some instances of more than twenty years. Nevertheless, I have found it difficult to assess what in the therapeutic situation has led to successful results.

I grew up suspicious of the words of others and with a deep need to determine realities by personal observation and research. When I reviewed the development of Freud's thinking and that of his followers pertaining to what were called the narcissistic neuroses (see chapters 2 and 3), I became certain that the treatment of such disorders within the framework of the structural hypothesis was feasible, and I undertook their treatment on an experimental basis while still a candidate.

Initially I was disheartened by my mentors in my then ultraconservative training institution. They deemed my efforts to be wild analysis and motivated principally by rebelliousness and counterphobic tendencies. Yet what I was doing seemed to me to be logically consistent and to benefit my patients; so I persisted. Given my need for external approval, I was encouraged by the responses of North Americans who were similarly engaged in such searchings, notably Bychowski, Giovacchini, Hoedemaker, Lewin, and Searles, by Europeans and Latin Americans, especially Eicke, Garma, Rosenfeld, and Rolla, and by the appearance of literature that supported my thinking, such as the contributions of Arlow and Brenner (1964, 1969).

On the basis of my research, I have reached some general conclusions. In agreement with Giovacchini (1975a, 1979), Grinberg (1962, 1979), Kernberg (1975a, pp. 146-149), Langs (1975b), Racker (1968), Searles (1958), and others, I am convinced (1) that failures in the treatment of such disorders are often iatrogenic, resulting from problems in the countertransference or the therapist's failure to use his emotional responses adequately in his interpretations; (2) that the success of treatment depends on accurate, empathic, and timely confrontations, interventions, and reconstructions that lead to relevant genetic interpretations; and (3) that success also depends on the rectifying emotional and cognitive experience of the patient's development of new object relations with the therapist (Dewald 1976, Garma 1978, A. Green 1975, Loewald 1960). With adequate treatment it is possible for the patient to replace archaic and sadistic ego and superego introjects and identifications with more mature ones, to develop higher-level defense mechanisms and adaptations, and to progress from regressed positions and developmental arrests.

I have found with the Ornsteins (1975), Rosenfeld (1966) and many others that premature oedipal interpretations preclude the re-creation of the preoedipal transferential states. The latter must be worked through before character modifications can proceed. These are the states that Freud deemed unanalyzable.

I find that my handling of transference interpretations is in accord with the principles set forward by Kernberg (1975b): (1) the predominantly negative transference is systematically elaborated only in the present without initial efforts directed toward full genetic interpretations; (2) the patient's typical defensive constellations are interpreted as they enter the transference; (3) limits are set in order to block acting out of the transference insofar as this is necessary to protect the neutrality of the therapist; (4) the less primitively determined, modulated aspects of the positive transference are not interpreted early since their presence enhances the development of the therapeutic and working alliances (Dickes 1975, Kanzer 1975), although the primitive idealizations that reflect the splitting of "all good" from "all bad" object relations are systematically interpreted as part of the effort to work through these primitive defenses; (5) interpretations are formulated so that the patient's distortions of the therapist's interventions and of present reality, especially of the patient's perceptions during the hour, can be systematically clarified; and (6) the highly distorted transference, at times psychotic in nature and reflecting fantastic internal object relations pertaining to early ego disturbances, is worked through first in order to reach the transferences related to actual childhood experiences.

I consider the understanding and pertinent interpretation of the unfolding transference to be of the utmost importance. I have come to contemplate each interview as though it might have been a dream and material from recent interviews as part of the day residue.

CASE REPORT

This report deals with the treatment of a patient whose presenting life pattern and personality included almost all those elements commonly considered to carry a poor prognosis and to contraindicate psychoanalytic treatment, except that there was no evidence of ego-syntonic antisocial behavior. Much of the following history was obtained during the first two vis-à-vis interviews.

History

Fifty-three years old when first seen, Mrs. X was a twice-divorced Caucasian, friendless, living alone, and almost totally impulse dominated. She looked and dressed like a teenage boy. She had been a chronic alcoholic for some twenty years and had been hospitalized repeatedly with a diagnosis of schizophrenia. She had been jailed many times and while in the "drunk tank" had masturbated openly, smeared feces, and screamed endlessly. She had lived dangerously, having on various occasions provoked sexual assault by gangs of black men in ghettos. In the last twenty years she had had many forms of psychiatric care (excluding shock therapies), but without effect. She had lived for about a year in a colony designed for faith healing, led by a guru. There appeared to be but two redeeming features when she was first seen: (1) She had concluded that her problems were based on unconscious conflicts and wanted an orthodox analysis. (Various respected analysts had refused her.) (2) Having been told by the most recent therapist of her psychotic son that her interactions with him kept him sick, she wanted very much to stop contributing to his illness.

Her forebears were wealthy aristocrats and included Protestant religious figures. The males all graduated from prestigious universities, and the females, products of noted finishing schools, were patrons of the arts. Her parents treated those who were not their social peers as subhumans. Her bond salesman father's chronic alcoholism resulted in the loss of his and his wife's fortunes during the patient's late childhood. From then on her nuclear family lived on the largesse of relatives.

Her mother was highly self-centered and throughout the patient's childhood and adolescence remained in bed during the daytime for weeks on end, depressed, hypochondriacal, and unapproachable. She vacillated between two ego states. In one, she lay with her aching head covered by cold cloths, moaning and complaining about mistreatment by all, but particularly her husband. In the other, she lay in reveries, reading romantic novels. Much later in treatment the patient remembered that when her mother was in such a dreamy state, she permitted the child to lie with her and perhaps fondle her mother's genitals, manually and with her face. The mother's withdrawals seemingly could be interrupted only by the temper tantrums of two of the sisters, when parties were being planned for social lions, or when she was planning to take the "grand tour" alone. She often left unannounced for her annual European jaunts, but sometimes she would confide in the docile Mrs. X that she was leaving and swear her to secrecy, assigning her the task of tending the other children, who voiced their objections dramatically when they knew of their mother's impending departure.

The patient was the second of four sisters, born three years apart. All were reared by a senile woman who had been the mother's nursemaid. The oldest remains a frequently hospitalized alcoholic spinster. The younger two are vain, childless divorcées who live on generous alimony and who continue to have a succession of young lovers. All five females were contemptuous of the father, whom the mother divorced after the patient was married. Thereafter the mother gave up her depression, hypochondriasis, and withdrawal and became a spirited woman. She had platonic affairs with young male authors whom she sponsored. The father married a warm woman, became abstinent, and returned to work. After many years he regressed to serious depression and committed suicide by throwing himself in front of a train. This was one year before the patient first saw me. She had had no contact with him since his remarriage and thought of him only with contempt. When she heard of his death and burial, she felt totally detached. At the beginning of therapy, she indiscriminately idealized her mother and devalued her father.

When she was less than three years old, an incident occurred on board an ocean liner. Something happened in a stateroom that frightened the child, so she fled crying to her mother, who was breakfasting with the ship's captain. Her mother ignored her anguish, but a black waiter comforted her, holding her and giving her a cube of sugar. The patient explained to me that she felt the outcome of her treatment hinged on the recall of that memory and on my capacity to accept what she had to tell me without disgust, anger, or anxiety.

Before attending school she was an avid reader of fairy tales, and in her first year she did well. But during the second, she became incapable of learning. She read unwillingly and with great difficulty and was unable to learn the simplest mathematics. She never passed a single test during her grammar or finishing school years. This was unimportant to her parents; they taught her that her obligation to the family was to be charming, to exploit her beauty and wit, and to get a rich doctor as a husband who would support the family.

During the second year of schooling she became sexually involved with a swarthy chauffeur who wore black gloves, but she did not reveal their frightening activities, believing that risking death was somehow in the service of her sisters' getting parental love.

During her latency period she was exceedingly docile and well behaved. She had a severe obsessive-compulsive neurosis and believed that her family's lives depended on her thoughts and actions. She was a religious martyr who projected onto her parents the wish that she die so that her sisters would be the recipients of all her parents' love. In this way the sisters would become less disturbed.

When she was eleven she was sent away from home for the first time to attend finishing school. She soon lost her previous nighttime terrors of attack by something vague and unvisualized and gave up her endless nocturnal rituals. While there, she became enamored of a popular girl who seemed perfect, although she knew of her hypocrisies and manipulations. She was content to be one of an adoring coterie of this popular girl so long as the girl's attentions were equally divided among her worshippers. When the patient was sixteen, however, her idol became enamored of another girl, and the patient went into a catatoniclike state. She was sent home from school, and for the next five years remained passive, felt mechanical, and went through the motions of living.

She never had any boyfriends and was awkward at parties. She wistfully reveled in her mother's attractiveness as hostess and vaguely wished that she would someday be her mother's social equal.

While she was in her teens, her father, an outcast at home, spent much time boating. The patient, in her role of family protector, willingly went with him, taking the helm while he got drunk in the cabin. She believed her parents wanted her dead and that she should be killed. She went with her father not only to look after him but to make it easy for him to murder her for the good of her sisters.

When her older sister was able to get a rich medical student to propose marriage, the patient was galvanized into activity and got him to choose her instead. Once married, she was sexually passive and anesthetic. On their honeymoon her husband became so infuriated by her sexual passivity that he sought to murder her, being thwarted only by chance. She felt no resentment and never told anyone, thinking his act had been further evidence of the validity of her being destined to be the savior-martyr.

She lived with his parents in one city while he continued medical school in another. He sent her occasional letters in which he depicted his affairs with sensual women. She was vaguely disappointed. His senile father, a retired minister, considered her passivity to be the result of her having been possessed and sought to exorcise her by giving her enemas while she was nude in the bathtub. This was condoned by her mother and her husband. She felt neither anger nor excitement. She wondered at times if he were getting some sexual or sadistic pleasure from his actions and fantasized seducing him or committing suicide in order to humiliate him by exposing him—all for the good of others.

Following his graduation, her husband joined the military, and they moved to another part of the country, whence he was shipped abroad. She was utterly without friends or acquaintances. His letters were rare and included accounts of his affairs with uninhibited women. She bore him a defective daughter and could not believe she was a mother. She feared touching the baby, leaving her care to maids. She felt the baby's defect to be her fault, which was somehow associated with her actions with the chauffeur. She began to drink in secret. On leave, her husband impregnated her and she bore another daughter who again she could not believe was hers and whom she could not touch. She began to frequent bars and to pick up men to whose sexual demands of any nature she would submit, always with total subsequent amnesia. She learned of her actions by having them told to her by the children's nurses. Then she bore a defective son who became an autistic psychotic. She was totally helpless in the face of his unbridled hyperactivity and feces smearing. He was hospitalized at about three years of age and remained so until his early adolescence, rarely acknowledging her existence in any way. Her husband divorced her, her daughters were sent away to institutions, and she lived alone.

For twelve years and periodically later her life was occupied with bar activities and sexual encounters for which she continued to have amnesia. She would pick up black men and submit to their manifold sexual abuses. She passively assented and at times encouraged them to take her money and jewelry. One of her many therapists suggested that she would feel less worthless if she were to prepare herself for some occupation and stop living on what amounted to charity. She managed to complete a practical nursing course and then worked in various psychiatric hospitals where she felt she was of some use because she could understandingly care for psychotic and senile patients. She was fired from a number of positions for being absent and for appearing on the job while intoxicated or hung over.

In one of the hospitals where she worked, she met a male patient who was her physical counterpart, even to the color of her hair and eyes. They were so alike she wore his clothes. He was addicted to various drugs, including alcohol, and totally dependent on his family and welfare. She soon began to live with him. She adored him as she had her mother and the girlfriend of teenage years. She knew of his many faults but totally idealized him. She felt complete and rapturous with him and at times believed they were psychological and even physical continua. They were married, and the idyllic fusion persisted. Periodically they bought whiskey and went to bed where they remained for days, engaging in polymorphous sexuality to the point of exhaustion, occasionally lying in their excreta. While she never had an orgasm, she felt complete. Such episodes were especially pleasant to her when she was menstruating and she and her partner were smeared with blood, which she sometimes enjoyed eating. After some nine years of marriage, he divorced her for reasons she never understood, particularly since she supported him financially. Then she became a mechanical person once again and resumed her pursuit of men in bars.

A year before treatment began, she obtained an undemanding job as a file clerk, where her superiors tolerated her lateness and incompetency. She lived on her meager salary and placed no value on material possessions. She believed that she had never had a hostile wish and that throughout her life she had invariably sought to help others.

Course of Treatment

Over the years, I have gradually come to accept for treatment almost solely patients whose activities are apt to influence the lives of others, such as educators, physicians, and professionals who work in the mental health field. Yet it did not occur to me to refuse her request to try psychoanalytic treatment. I found appealing her determination to undergo for predominantly altruistic purposes a procedure that she well knew would be painful. And I felt comfortable with her.

She was seen at what she knew to be reduced rates three times weekly on the couch for about five years, payments being made from a small endowment from a deceased family friend. After a trial six-month interruption she resumed treatment on the couch twice a week for two more years, making a total of over 800 interviews in seven and a half years.

Before analysis is undertaken with such patients, I tell them that our work is to be cooperative and of an experimental nature and that we cannot expect to set a time limit; that they are to make a sincere effort to relate aloud whatever comes to their minds during the interviews and to report their emotional states and physical sensations; that I do not send statements and expect to be paid what is owed on the last interview of the month; that they will be charged for cancellations unless their scheduled interviews are filled by another patient; and that I am away frequently for short periods and one long period during the course of each year and will inform them of the expected dates of absence as soon as I know of them. When an occasional patient inquires what is to be expected of me, I state that I shall keep the scheduled interviews and be on time; that I do not give advice unless I deem it necessary; that I see my role as seeking to understand as much as I can about the patients and will tell them what I have learned when I consider them ready. I explain that I expect to be wrong at times and that the final validation will depend on the patient's responses and memories. For these patients I have found such specific conditions offer needed ego and superego support.

As is common with patients with borderline personality disorders (see Gunderson and Singer 1975), during the first two structured vis-à-vis interviews, Mrs. X's productions were but slightly tinged with primary process thinking. However, there was a periodic affective disparity that confused me; I was undecided whether it constituted *la belle indifférence* or schizophrenic dissociation.

During her third interview she eagerly lay on the couch, her speech promptly became heavily influenced by primary process thinking and she was at times incoherent. Her verbal productions were highly symbolic, and her language was often unusually vulgar. She made tangential references to fairy tales, fusing elements of *Beauty and the Beast, Cinderella, Hansel and Gretel,* and *Snow White,* and told a story that involved a good witch who transported children through a magical opening into a paradisiacal world in which the protagonists fused and became perpetually indistinguishable and parasitic, needing no others for their constant bliss. She also alluded to a white elephant and a spider.

She did not seem frightened by her productions or her style of presentation. There was some embarrassment about her foul language, but her principal reaction was one of mild curiosity as to why she talked so strangely. My own reaction to her behavior was one of mild surprise at the degree of such prompt regression, of empathy with her embarrassment, and of detached intellectual curiosity.

I felt at ease with this patient. I have devoted many years to the study of folklore (Boyer 1964a, 1975, 1977, 1979, Boyer and Boyer 1977) and know most of the psychoanalytic literature dealing with the fairy tales to which she referred, as well as that dealing with the spider.

I understood from her behavior and verbal productions that her conflicts referred to attempts at mastering early primal scene traumata and fusions with aspects of various people, to oral and anal sadism, and to intense sibling rivalry. I thought that the actual, affect-laden recovery of primal scene memories would be crucial in her treatment and assumed that her vulgarity indicated that they had occurred in connection with the period of cleanliness training or had become attached to experiences that occurred then. I attributed some of her easy regression to a toxic alcoholic brain syndrome and was dubious about the oft-repeated diagnosis of schizophrenia.

I had the uncanny feeling that she had talked to me in a distorted childish language as though I were an actual loved figure from her early life. Retrospectively I regret not having validated my hunch. Had I done so, I might have been aware that she had globally identified me with the only person of her childhood whom she could trust (her maternal grandfather); and my added comprehension would both have made her progress in treatment less mystifying to me and perhaps precluded a near-disaster.

In the fourth interview she came to the office drunk, although I had the impression that she was less intoxicated than she seemed. Her lips were painted black and there were white streaks on her face. She was dressed in garish, revealing clothes which exposed filthy underpants. She screamed and cursed and threatened to attack me with outstretched claws. I felt as though I were observing a puppet show. There was an obscure reference to my being a vampire. She threw harmless objects, aimed narrowly to miss me so that I felt unthreatened. She then picked up a heavy stone ashtray and menaced me with it. I felt no anxiety, but sat still and remained silent and observant. When she found me unafraid, she cried and threw herself on the couch, spread her legs apart and partially bared her tiny breasts. When I remained passive and silent, she sat at my feet, hugged my legs and eventually touched my penis. She seemed surprised that it was not erect. I then removed her hand and said it was unnecessary for her to express her conflicts physically and advised her to tell me her problems with words. She reacted with rage and tried to claw my face. It was easy to fend her off; I effortlessly held her at arms' length. If she had chosen to do so, she could have easily kicked my genitals as she threatened to do. Her strange behavior and dress seemed to be designed to test the level of my tolerance of what she felt would be anxiety provoking or disgusting. I viewed her allusion to me as a vampire as indicative of splitting and projective identification.

I have come to understand the operational functions of projective identification in rather simple terms. I agree with those who believe that what is projected remains to a degree unrepressed and that the patient maintains some level of continuing to be preconsciously aware of what he imagines the analyst to experience. The therapist is used as a repository for projected internalized objects and attitudes that make patients feel uncomfortable, and they believe they have succeeded in locating them within the analyst. Patients fear that their hostile wishes or thoughts may result in the destruction of the therapist or retributive damage to themselves (Grinberg 1976). Once they believe that such hostility is a part of the analyst, they watch the analyst's behavior. Over time, effective interpretations, combined with patients' observations that their projections within the therapist have not proved deleterious, enable them to reintroject what they have projected in a detoxified form and to integrate them into their evolving personalities. Some patients fear that their love is destructive and project it onto the therapist for safekeeping; similarly, with treatment these patients come to view love as not dangerous (Giovacchini 1975b).

Discussants have often wondered about my relative lack of fear of attack by psychotic patients. I have never been actually attacked, although I have been frightened at times. In my own past, one of my important love objects suffered from a borderline personality disorder and periodically regressed into acute paranoid psychotic episodes. That person was impulsive and violent; as a young child, I learned to judge the degree of physical danger and to stay away from potential murderous attacks.

In the fifth interview Mrs. X remembered none of what had happened. When I told her what she had done, she was aghast. She vowed spontaneously not to come drunk to the office again. Most of the interviews ol the first year, however, took place with her either mildly intoxicated or hung over.

For several months many interviews included periods of incoherency that were at times grossly vulgar and talk that was obviously symbolic of early primal scene observations. Periodically I inquired whether her interview behavior was designed to test my level of tolerance, to determine whether she could disgust or anger me or make me uncomfortable. Such queries usually resulted in a temporary cessation of her blatant vulgarities and "crazy" talk.

At times she ascribed her speech content or immodest behavior to my will, and from the outset I used such material to help her learn about her splitting mechanisms and projective tendencies and their defensive uses. An example follows.

The physical set-up of my consultation room is such that a shared waiting room has a sliding door that separates it from a tiny hallway that has three other doors, one opening into my office, one into my private lavatory and one to an exit. Mrs. X had the first interview of the day, and it occurred at an hour when I had to unlock the office building. I generally arrived early enough for other activities before seeing her. She customarily arrived for her interview just on time, making enough noise so that she could be heard entering the waiting room, although the sliding door was shut. One morning when I emerged from the lavatory some ten minutes before she was expected, I noted that the sliding door was ajar, but I assumed I must have left it so. At the time her appointment was to begin, she buzzed to announce her presence. Since I had not heard her before the buzz, I suspected some acting out had transpired. During the first few minutes of her hour, her talk dealt manifestly with hostility-laden events in her office on the previous day and included the interjection "Oh, shit" and the phrase "He pissed me off." I then assumed that she had been repeating spying activities of her childhood pertaining to adults' uses of the toilet, but I did not choose to direct my inquiries to the past. Instead I asked how long she had been in the waiting room before she buzzed, and I obtained some previously withheld information. It had been her wont to arrive some minutes before I opened the building and to park where she could watch me unseen. On that particular morning she had noiselessly followed me into the building, entered the waiting room, opened the sliding door, and eventually heard the toilet flush.

Discussion of her behavior and its motivations on that day occupied several interviews and the analysis of some dreams. It developed that she had contradictory views of me. In one I was a sadistic voyeur who had become a psychoanalyst in order to spy on the "dirty" activities and thoughts of my patients, to titillate myself and to learn how to frustrate patients by determining precisely what they wanted of me, so that I could torture them by refusing to accede to their desires. I "got my jollies" by means of subtly exhibitionistic behavior that excited in my patients those wants that I frustrated. At the same time, I had had a traumatic childhood and had undergone much suffering because of exhibitionistic and frustrating parents and wanted, as a psychoanalyst, to relieve my patients of their misery. It was as if I were two people. I was at times totally hateful, bad, and hurtful and at other times solely loving, good, and helpful, and my alternating personalities determined my totally unpredictable behavior. It was my will that she observe my every act so that she could become exactly like me and arrive at social and professional success, but it was also my will that she should not embarrass me by letting me know that she had read my mind and was following instructions.

When I indicated to her how she had ascribed to me precisely the qualities that she had previously described as her own, she was impressed, and for a time she could more clearly contemplate her self-view as all good and all bad and her projective tendencies. It was then possible to review the events in the office on the day that preceded her acting out and to delineate ways in which her behavior with me and her ascriptions to me had been in the service of defense against anxiety and guilt over behavior and wishes related to people in her work setting. She had acted toward me as she felt her co-workers had acted toward her. I suggested that she had sought to master a feeling of helplessness through identification with the aggressor, and I postulated that this behavior constituted a lifelong pattern. I did not have sufficient cathected data to make a more specific statement.[3]

At times she was flirtatious in her dress and actions and sought to entertain and amuse me, imitating, as it developed, her mother's party behavior and obeying her parental injunctions about how to "hook" a rich doctor. At the same time she had fused sensations of urinary or fecal urgency and, despite a hysterectomy some years before treatment began, felt blood on her legs and expressed the wish to smear me with it. Sometimes there was vaginal itching. Occasionally, she spread her legs and began to undress, meantime rubbing her pubis. When I asked her about her thoughts and feelings, it became apparent she was unaware of her actions. On a few occasions, she wondered whether I felt lonely and wanted my face in her crotch. When I commented that she seemed to believe she had put part of herself into me, she recalled what she believed to have been early childhood and latency experiences of lying with her mother and palpating her mother's genitals with her hands and face; she remembered the feeling

3. It will be noted that my inclusion of a genetic interpretation was tentative. While I believe the inclusion of genetic aspects of interpretations is essential from the outset, I hold that genetic interpretations are meaningful to patients only after they have become well acquainted with their uses of various primitive defensive mechanisms and with the current reasons for their appearance. This is in marked contrast to the technical approach of many Kleinians who, from the outset, seek to interpret unconscious motivations in terms of the id rather than of the ego. (See chapter 3.)

of pubic hair on her nose and cheeks. In her sober interviews, she was often largely withdrawn and "headachy" or had other somatic complaints, which we came to understand as her imitating one part of her mother's periodic daytime bed behavior. I also focused on her primitive wish to fuse with me as a representative mother.

For many months she picked up men at bars and submitted to their sexual demands. When I tried to show her that these men were father figures, she regularly corrected me, making me aware that they represented the phallic and nurturant mother with whom she sought to fuse. However, she gradually became cognizant that her conscious contempt for her father covered rage at him, and with amazement she slowly recovered memories of boating with him. During one session she misinterpreted a noise to mean I was masturbating behind her. I remarked that perhaps there had been a time when she had seen her father masturbate. Over a period of weeks, she recovered the memory of her actions with the chauffeur, which included placing her hands on his erection, while he wore black gloves. Then she gradually recalled with much embarrassment that during adolescence on the boating excursions with her father, she had watched him masturbate in the cabin; she slowly became aware of her anger that he had preferred masturbation to using her sexually.

In the interviews that followed, material continued that involved nighttime dreams and overt or covert themes of mutilations, murder, and desertion. There was obvious blurring of ego boundaries. My interpretations, as always, were transferential and as genetic as I deemed advisable and aimed at reinforcing previous interpretations of the defensive use of splitting. She gradually became aware that she had much anger that she had denied and uncritically projected onto policemen and other establishment figures. Now she began to be more critical of her automatic devaluation of them as parental representatives. Later she would be able to comprehend a pattern of projection of aggression and reintrojection of aggressively determined self- and object images and the subsequent use of splitting operations.

In this early period I delayed focusing on the fusion of anal, vaginal and urethral sensations, judging that data pertaining to this evidence of lack of structuralization of drives would be remembered at a later time when interpretations would be more meaningful. I believed that the content of her primary process thinking during the third interview had already heralded the fact that primal scene traumata were partial organizers of her particular ego structure. Periodic interpretations of her wish to fuse with me were gradually understood and elaborated by her. For example, she often responded that she wished to be taken into one or another of my orifices, even including my pores, and to circulate in my blood, to lodge in my brain and govern all my activities, while secretly spying on my actions to learn from them how I handled those elements that she had projected onto me. Only much later, after she had reintrojected detoxified versions of those projections, did she see this fantasy as self-destructive. She then strove to clarify actual differences between us.

About five months after Mrs. X was first seen, she learned that I had an interest in anthropology and asked to borrow a magazine from the waiting room that included an article on stone-age humans. She had lost her capacity to read easily and with comprehension after the first grade, and I suggested that she wanted permission to learn to read understandingly again and to develop herself as a person rather than to follow the assigned role of dumb-blond doctor-seducer. She promptly enrolled in high school, then college, and slowly developed the capacity to read and write with comprehension. During the following years she received only *A*s in her extension division college courses.

After she had been in treatment for about six months, I left for a period of six weeks. She had known of my planned absence from the beginning of her sessions, and I had thought her anxiety about the separation had been well understood before I left since we had dealt extensively with her reactions to her mother's European jaunts. However, immediately after my departure, she attempted suicide by taking an overdose of pills, which I had not known she possessed. She was rescued, so far as could be determined, by chance. It was noted in her hospital chart that she had mentioned her mother's father. During my absence she had no remembered thought about me until the day before her scheduled appointment; when she appeared for her interview, she seemed surprised that I was alive. She had not died, therefore I must have. When she entered the room, she looked everywhere for something but when I inquired what she was trying to find, she declined to tell me. Much later, I found out that she had sought a white elephant.

She had hoped that her death would result in my professional destruction. She now viewed her father's drunkenness and affairs as ways of risking death in the hope that he would thereby get even with her mother for her contemptuousness. She also recalled the Oriental custom of committing suicide on the doorstep of the wronging person.

Soon after my return, poignant memories of her early relationship with her mother's father emerged. Apparently, her relationship with that loving man was the only consistently dependable one of her childhood. It formed the basis of the element of basic trust that enabled her to develop psychologically as far as she did. He had held her on his lap, listened to her seriously, and was always considerate of her needs. One time, when she was envious of one of her sisters' having received a soft, stuffed animal as a present, she told her grandfather that she wanted a similar toy, which she could care for as though it were a baby. He responded by telling her the story of an orphan baby elephant in India that was adopted by a boy whom it loved and always obeyed, no doubt a variant of Kipling's "Toomai of the Elephants." He promised to get her a white elephant for Christmas. In fact, he gave her another white stuffed toy, but she retained the belief that he would eventually give her the living pachyderm. When she was almost seven years old, he died; but she had the set idea that when she got a white elephant someday, she would also find her grandfather and once again have a dependable, loving relationship with a kindly person who did not misuse her.

She apparently entered a satisfactory early latency period adjustment, but the death of her grandfather caused her to lose her capacity to learn and to use fantasy constructions in an adaptive manner (Sarnoff 1976). She had not been taken to his funeral where she might have viewed the corpse and thus been confronted with the reality of his demise. Her loss of the capacity to learn had been based on her wish to deny having learned of his death; she would never again learn anything if she had to accept this learning.

I shall now turn to an example of how my coming to understand my emotional response enabled me to change an impasse into a beneficial step. When her son as a young child had come home from the hospital for brief periods, she had taken men home with her and in a drunken state performed fellatio and submitted to sodomy before him. She had no memory of her actions but would be informed by the nurses. Sometimes when she was unwittingly angry with me, she would return to her shameful feelings on being told by the nurses what she had done. I gradually noted that I began to respond to such recitations by irritation and sleepiness; I found myself being subtly punitive toward her. For some weeks there was a therapeutic stalemate, during which her acting out increased and our rapport all but disappeared. I regretted having accepted her for treatment and wondered why I had done so. I fell into a brief trancelike state during an interview with her, and when I became fully alert again, had repressed the content of my reverie. That night I had a dream that reminded me of my own past. I had learned in prior periods of personal analysis that I had become an analyst with an unconscious motivation of curing the important but psychologically disordered and dangerous love object to whom I have alluded previously. Analysis of my dream made me aware of another reason: I had sought to protect a younger sibling from the love object. I then knew that I had accepted Mrs. X in treatment to effect changes not only in her but in her psychotic son. Then I became aware that I had identified myself with her abused child and was expressing my anger by withdrawal and by refusing to recognize her, as she had previously reported her son to have done. Such knowledge permitted me to regain my objectivity. Finally I could interpret her wish to provoke me to abuse her. She responded by remembering dreams and hypnopompic fantasies in which she was forced to watch women being raped anally or having huge phalluses shoved into their mouths. Three years later I was able to interpret her behavior as an attempt to master her terror and her feelings of dissolution when she had watched the sexual activities of her parents.

Soon she began to experience choking sensations during the interviews. Analysis of dreams showed her use of the body-phallus equation and her wish that I would force her to reintroject both good and bad aspects of herself, which she had projected onto me. Affect-laden memories of her experiences with the chauffeur appeared. Following her grandfather's death, she had turned to that black-gloved man (whom she partly confused with the Negro who had comforted her during the shipboard experience) in an effort to regain a loving relationship with a man who would take her on his lap, as her father refused to do. He had forced his phallus into her mouth, causing her to choke. She had concealed their activities, rationalizing that she was supposed to die through choking in her effort to provide her sisters with their parents' finite love. She also now remembered nightly efforts to determine whether her parents were alive by checking to make sure they were breathing while they were asleep. The choking conversion symptom disappeared.

She now recalled with emotion nightly rituals during her latency period. Her family's house was very old. While electrical contrivances had been installed in her third-story bedroom, there remained a gas jet. At night it was permissible to have illumination from the jet, but the lights were not to be used. She was terrified that a vague, never visualized something would attack her from the dark. She feared even more that leaking gas would poison her. She engaged in endless prayers for her own salvation and for the other members of the family. She engaged in counting rituals that were supposed to influence God to save them. She used the rituals to stay awake, believing that she was safe from attack so long as she remained alert. She had a collection of dolls and stuffed animals that covered most of her bed, and she tenderly put them to sleep with caresses and cooings. She endlessly repeated, "Now I lay me down to sleep, I pray the Lord my soul to keep," applying the theme to her dolls and consciously equating being asleep with being dead. While doing so, she sometimes believed she was Christ, grandfather-God's protector of children, and felt her pubis repeatedly to determine whether she had grown a penis. She had to check many times to be sure the window was tightly locked, because if she were to fall asleep with it open, she might throw her babies (dolls) and herself into the snow on the ground below. Her own death would have been acceptable because of its altruistic motives; but to have murdered her babies would have made her a sinner and unsuitable to rejoin her grandfather and have God keep her soul.

Her treatment had begun just before a Christmas separation, and her reactions to my first absence had not been decipherable (Boyer 1955). As our second Christmas separation approached, she returned to thinking of her mother's departures for the grand tour of Europe. Now those memories became cathected with feelings of rage and then with loneliness. She sought to remove the loneliness by joining a singles group and resuming the drunken activities with men she picked up. For the first time, she could remember what she did with her partners. She was exceedingly aggressive, insisting on assuming the superior position. She demanded that the man be passive while she pumped up and down on his erection, at times believing his penis was hers and was penetrating him. I interpreted this behavior as representing a continuation of her efforts to save me from her anger for deserting her like a parent.

The following summer when I left her for another extended period, she went on a prolonged drunk and behaved so crazily that she was jailed. She requested hospitalization and rejoined her second husband, whom she knew to be in the hospital. There she entered a fusion state with him. She had no conscious thought of my existence until the week before our scheduled appointment. Then she arranged her release and met me on time.

She explained that in her rage at my leaving her she had wanted to humiliate me by killing herself or getting murdered; but she protected herself by getting hospitalized and joining her husband. Thus she deemed her behavior to have been adaptive and was pleased with herself. She now valued her contacts with me above all else.

Throughout her treatment until this time, there had been rare contacts with her mother, sisters, daughters and their young children, whom she had never been able to touch, fearing she would kill them. When the third Christmas came, she was able to spend more time with her mother and sisters and feel less uneasiness than before. She also had one of her daughters bring her family to visit for the holidays. She found herself infuriated with the excited pleasure and selfishness of the young children. Now she recalled with intensity childhood Christmases that had been immensely frustrating for her, not only because she felt her sisters got more than she, but particularly because she did not turn into a boy or get a penis so she could be Christ, the martyred favorite son of all mankind. She began to realize that her fears of harming her own babies disguised a wish to kill them, as they represented her siblings. Then she became closer to her daughters and enjoyed holding their children. Also her relations with her mother and sisters improved. She invited her son to visit her periodically on leave from a distant psychiatric hospital. Over the next few years during subsequent visits they developed a calmer and mutually affectionate relationship.

She now eschewed alcohol for long periods and only occasionally had sexual relations with men. Her interests were limited to job, school, and analysis. She was gradually promoted at work. There was a growing interest in the lives of her female bosses, and fantasies pertaining to them I interpreted as displaced fantasies about my life. The previous flirtatiousness with me resumed as did the pattern of coming to the office in altered ego states; the fusion of vaginal, urethral, and anal sensations reappeared. I suggested that her childhood pattern of checking on her parents' breathing was the result of her having been disturbed by noises in their bedroom that she assumed to have occurred during their sexual activities. She then recalled that during preoedipal years, her bedroom was separated from theirs by a bathroom in which her mother's douche tip and bag, which she believed to have been used to give her enemas, hung on the wall and that sometimes mother's bloody menstrual rags were in a bucket of water. Then I guessed that she had repeatedly observed their activities and had experienced excitement, which she discharged with urinary and fecal activities, during the night. My ideas were accepted with equanimity. She gradually recalled with much feeling repeated childhood observations of their sexual actions, which included sodomy, cunnilingus and fellatio, always accompanied by her mother's groaning protests. She had interpreted their actions in anal-sadistic and oral-fusional terms and had thought that each had a penis like a sword which would kill the other. She had reacted with fused oral, anal, and vaginal excitement and had sought to interrupt her parents by noisy bathroom activities.

In the fifth year of treatment she gradually repressed the primal scene memories and the observations of father's masturbating on the boat. She did well at work and school, had occasional dates and developed the capacity to have mild orgasms during nonfrantic intercourse. During my summer absence she briefly reentered a relationship with her second husband, now devoid of its fusional aspects. He was ill, and she cared for him considerately. She began to have vague and emotionally uninvested fantasies about me. Therapy appeared to have reached a plateau in which she was functioning well but retaining a primitive idealization of me, interpretations of which had no effect. She was quite cognizant that I made mistakes and assumed that I had secret faults that she could not verify, but I remained an idol like her mother. I decided to use the parameter of a trial separation in an effort to dislodge the primitive idealization. Accordingly I recommended that, beginning with my summer absence six months thence, we remain apart for six months and resume treatment just after the following Christmas. She was gratified but apprehensive because she had not recovered the shipboard memories.

She decided to have an earlier trial separation by making a hiking trip with an organized group in the Himalayas and returning to treatment a month before I was to leave for the summer period. During her preparation for the trip, she began to have occasional dates with a black gardener who, she thought, had previously been a chauffeur, her first contact with blacks since she began treatment. She recalled that she had turned to the swarthy chauffeur at the age of seven after her grandfather's death in an effort to replace him with another sustaining object. Before her trip to India she had passing thoughts about seeking a white elephant and wondered whether she might be seeking a magical reunion with her grandfather. En route to the Himalayas, she went for the first time to the site of her father's suicide and could cry and miss him. She also visited with her mother, sisters, children and grandchildren and had warm interchanges with them. After her return she said she had seen her family to say farewell, since she expected to have some accident and die while in India, hoping thereby to be reunited with her grandfather.

On the journey, she was very happy. However, she took fragments from shrines and worried that she had desecrated the dead. She bartered with Tibetan women for their jewelry and felt she corrupted them by buying their religious objects, one of which included a white elephant. When she came back to treatment, we discussed her wish to return to the loving relationship with her grandfather, but she experienced little affectual release.

In the last interview before our trial separation, she had a fantasy of using the stone fragments as a memorial stele for my grave. Thus she would have me near her and available for her alone; she would commune with me in time of need.

She did not contact me after six months as we had planned. In January I wrote a note inquiring about her progress. She was intensely gratified and requested further therapy. She had not made the memorial shrine and had again forgotten my existence, being sure that I had died.

Her relationship with the black man had intensified. Over Christmas she had the delusional conviction that her visiting mother and a sister had sought to take him from her. She was furious and tried to hurt them in various ways. When she got my note, she partially decathected her delusion and viewed it as a subject for investigation.

During the next eighteen months, the vicissitudes of her jealousy were worked through fairly well. The death of her grandfather and her subsequent seeking to join him in the Himalayas were cathected, but true mourning did not take place; unconsciously she still did not accept the fact of his death (Wolfenstein 1966, 1969).

She had earlier been unaware of fantasies during masturbation or sexual relationships and had focused solely on the physical seeking for orgasm. Following a reported episode of masturbation, I asked her to visualize what she might have fantasied were she able to shift her attention from the physical experience and her fear that either she would not have orgasm or that if she did, she would convulse and explode into fragments. She closed her eyes and saw oblong geometric forms. During subsequent interviews the forms became rounded and unified as a hand and an arm, tearing at her vagina. She revealed that for years she had awakened at night, clawing her perineum. She was sure she continued to have invisible pinworms from childhood. When stool examinations were negative, she understood the fantasized oblongs in terms of projected sadistic part objects. She now revealed that she kept her apartment like a pigsty and ate her meals standing up when she was alone. She also found it interesting that she had never learned to wipe herself and always had feces on her perianal hair and underpants. When she deemed this behavior to reflect a continuing wish to be totally taken care of, she felt humiliated and began to straighten up her apartment and keep herself clean.

During an interview in which she recalled the fantasy of the fragmented geometric, dehumanized hand-arm symbols, she returned to the terrifying experience on board ship. She had gone to the head and seen her father having intercourse *a tergo* with a nursemaid. She had been shocked, and she felt that her face had become wrinkled and flat and had then slid off her head, to lie on the floor like an emptied breast (Isakower 1938, Lewin 1946, Spitz 1966). She recalled also that her father had seen her watching him and looked aghast. His face seemed similarly to disintegrate. She had thought both of them were dissolving. Now she remembered early childhood episodes of watching her father's masturbation and having experienced a halo effect (Boyer 1971, Greenacre 1947).

She dreamed that she was being decapitated as she was in danger of being swallowed by huge waves. These she equated with her mother's vaginal labia. Her remembered seekings to get into her mother's vagina face first were recathected. Dressed like a teenage boy, she lay rigid on the couch. She feared she would vomit, ejaculate with her whole body, and that I would cut off her head in retribution for her ambivalent wish to render me impotent by making her treatment a failure. Soon she saw these ideas in terms of an early wish to de-masculinize her father as her mother's behavior had effectively done. She became intensely aware of having identified herself with her father's phallus and was both stunned and relieved. She had the fantasy that if she could supplant her father's sexual role with her mother, then her mother would need no one but her and they could live together in an idyllic symbiotic union. On the other hand, such a situation would be dangerous because a fusion with her mother would mean a destructive loss of personal identity.

When she did not regress during my summer absence, she decided to terminate before the annual Christmas separation. During the final six months, she continued to function well, except that she eschewed relationships with men other than the black lover from whom she was detaching herself. She recathected her jealousy of women at work, mother and sister surrogates, but her behavior remained appropriate and her murderous wishes were confined to fantasies. She became relaxed in her relationship with me, which essentially became that of an old friend. While my behavior remained strictly analytic with her, I shared her feelings and her fantasies that when we were apart, we would miss each other and wish each other well.

Just before termination she brought me a tiny bonsai tree, representing herself, and in the pot was one of the Himalayan shrine stone fragments. She wanted to remain with me, to have me continue to help her mature. She planned to return in another six months, to sit and talk with me as old friends, and perhaps then we would tenderly hold one another. She understood that this wish included an element of finally telling her father she loved and missed him.

During the last interview she sat on the couch, looking at me through much of the interview, saying she now securely felt herself to be a separate and real person and could view me as a real person. At its end she hugged me and kissed my cheek. Then she told me she had to touch me during the drunken interview to be sure I was not the product of her mind but had some separateness from her.

By the end of treatment she was a vastly changed woman, capable of warm, responsible, calm relationships with the members of her family. She drank socially, had progressed in her work to a position of authority, and was on the verge of obtaining a baccalaureate. She was very proud of herself and happy. However, she had not developed the capacity to have lasting mature relationships with men and had neither completely worked through her idealization of me nor truly mourned the death of her grandfather.

A year after termination Mrs. X requested follow-up interviews because she was uneasy about the Christmas season. She had renounced her relationshp with the black lover, had begun to have dates with men who were more eligible for marriage, had lost much of her idealization of me, and appeared to have satisfactorily mourned her grandfather. She no longer felt compelled to get her baccalaureate, which she now deemed to have been a goal set with the idea that by achieving it she would be more pleasing to me. Rather, she now took courses solely for her own pleasure. She announced her intention to return for interviews early in the holiday season each year until she felt more secure with her emotional responses to Christmastime.

DISCUSSION

The discussion will be limited to three issues: the diagnosis, the effects of the therapist's absences, and the question of the influence of the therapist's personality on the outcome of treatment.

Diagnosis

I view the classical psychoanalytic technique to be the model for the psychological treatment of psychiatric disorders; the purpose of evaluative interviews is to work out which variations of that technique are necessary for the individual patient. But the early establishment of a diagnosis may tend to predetermine the nature of treatment and to reduce the therapist's plasticity. In my opinion the therapist should assume that underlying the presenting symptomatology are untapped ego strengths and a capacity for maturation that might allow a working alliance and the development of a technical approach close to the analytic model.

There have been continuing efforts to refine diagnostic categories, which might lead to more suitable therapeutic procedures. Kernberg's dynamic definition of the borderline personality is a particularly useful contribution. When the term is used as he advocates, it ordinarily makes the nature of the characterological dysfunctioning more easily comprehensible. His recommendations concerning the modifications of psychoanalytic technique are sound, although, in my opinion, fewer deviations are necessary than he advocates.

The establishment of a diagnostic label for Mrs. X continues to plague me. It may be that her having been diagnosed as schizophrenic predetermined to some extent the nature of her treatment before I saw her and resulted in her having been denied the opportunity to undergo the therapy that would have led to her improvement. To be sure, there were good reasons to apply that label to her. Her reaction to our first prolonged separation was to try to kill herself so that I would continue to exist. Her surprise that I remained alive although she had not died was dramatic evidence that the self-representation of being a martyr was delusional. She underwent a catatonoid regression during her teens when she felt deserted by her primitively idealized girl friend and lived in a withdrawn, almost machinelike state for six years. After her first marriage she passivly accepted her husband's attempt to murder her. And later she accepted enemas from her father-in-law. The seriousness of her subsequent regressive behavior, however, was complicated by a toxic brain state from chronic alcoholism.

In Mrs. X we have a very complicated concatenation of ego structures. She apparently retained from very early childhood split maternal introjects that she then sought to project onto various people in her environment, as evinced by her primitive idealization and devaluation (Volkan 1976). There remained an ego-syntonic drive to fuse with loved ones whom she could equate with the good-mother projection, and her self-worth was enhanced by her self-view as martyr. We can suppose that the persistence of the goal to fuse represents a wish to regain the mother of the symbiotic phase (Mahler, Pine, and Bergman 1975). Her self-identification as martyr may be considered as an attempt to be at one with a primitive ego ideal, a phenomenon that Kernberg (1975a, pp. 227-262) views as evidence of pathological narcissism. However, she retained an internal bad-mother introject that she sought to externalize.

Her actual life models served to reinforce her primitive split internalized object relations. Her parents served predominantly as bad models with whom to identify in contrast to her grandfather who, before me, provided her sole consistent good model. The imposition of traumatizing primal scene experiences and her comprehension of those events at the level of her psychosexual maturation (oral-aggressive, fusional and anal-phallic-sadistic) served as an ego organizer, determining the manifest nature of her need to adjust to the retained split introjects. One root of her faulty sexual identity and ego-syntonic striving to become Christ lies in her striving to achieve a sense of intrapsychic unity and wholeness.

But, although it was easy for her to identify with her autistic son, Mrs. X did not become an autistic psychotic. She had the capacity to develop a hierarchy of defenses, including rationalization and repression, and object relationships that varied in their levels of maturity.

A case could be made for schizoaffective psychosis, with masked depression stemming from the incomplete mourning of her lost grandfather, combined with cognitive regression. Her fundamental characterological pathology may have had its roots in her relationships with mothering objects in the latter half of her first year of life.

To conclude, the course of her life and transference responses seem to me to indicate the diagnosis of borderline personality organization. Before the introduction of that label I would have said she suffered from a severe hysterical personality disorder with schizoid, depressive, and impulsive trends.

The Absences of the Therapist

Separations imposed by the therapist are generally thought to be detrimental to therapy with regressed patients. The topic has been touched on by various writers, who usually focus on its adverse effects (Federn 1952), but also on the possibility of useful interpretations resulting from countertransference experiences (Langer 1957) and on the setting of a termination date as an impetus to analysis (Orens 1955).

During all the years of my research in treating regressed patients, I have imposed separations frequently, being absent as a rule at least ten times yearly for periods of a few days to ten weeks at one time. This procedure resulted initially from my involvement in other research, but then I learned that such imposed absences were generally helpful. However, many colleagues feel that emergency contacts between interviews by telephone or actual meetings are necessary. They hold the view that the therapist's role includes "real" good parental caretaking to substitute for the presumed poor past-life experience of their patients (Azima and Wittkower 1956, Federn 1952, Nunberg 1932, Schwing 1940). But I have not been readily available for emergency contacts; it is my view that the best substitute parenting one can afford the patient is to hew as closely as possible to the classical analytic model.

Before the analytic contract has been reached, I inform the potential patient of my planned absences, a move that motivates analysis of reactions to impending separations and their involvement in the transference. From the outset the issue of being deserted is an implicit or explicit focus of investigation. Although most patients respond with anxiety, the forms of which and defenses against which can be studied and used integratively, I have found almost regularly that the patient has heard another message to which he responds with conscious or unconscious encouragement: that the therapist does not consider him to be as helpless as he deems himself.

Not infrequently, soon after a patient has been informed of my planned absences, his anxiety takes the form of overt or veiled requests for permission for emergency contacts. In general, it suffices for me to make an interpretation that he wants to be reassured that the therapist still exists. Patients have not usually telephoned me after this interpretation has been made. When such calls have occurred, I have listened long enough to determine whether an actual emergency has arisen; only rarely have I considered the patient in danger of engaging in some harmful acting out that might warrant overt limit setting or undergoing such a regression that intramural care might be indicated.

In the instances in which I have deemed no true emergency to exist, I have simply asked whether the patient did not feel it would be better to wait until the next interview to discuss the matter in question. This maneuver has regularly occasioned relief and gratitude.

There have been, however, as in the case of Mrs. X, suicide attempts associated with separations. In no such instance had the patient sought telephone contact. The suicide attempt of Mrs. X came as a total surprise to me and caused me concern and self-searching. I still wonder whether, if I had checked my hunch after the third interview that she had been speaking to me as though I were an actual loved person of her past, material pertaining to the death of her grandfather might have emerged and been subject to analysis. This might possibly have averted her attempt by self-destruction to unite with him and keep me alive.

The Personality of the Therapist

The quantitative study of the outcome of the Psychotherapy Research Project of the Menninger Foundation (Kernberg et al. 1972) stressed the importance of both the therapeutic technique and the skill and personality of the therapist in the treatment of patients with serious ego weaknesses and the need of a "fit" between therapist and patient for a successful outcome.

It has never been established whether a combination of a satisfactory personal analysis, adequate training, and experience are sufficient to enable a therapist to work with seriously regressed patients in a manner that approaches the psychoanalytic model, or whether preconditioning, idiosyncratic life experiences provide an indispensible extra element. For us to know would require publication of confidential information. This is unlikely to happen since it would have to come from training analysts who disclosed confidential data or from a large number of personal autobiographical accounts. I can only speculate.

Early in my psychiatric and later psychoanalytic experience I became aware that I had an unusual capacity to understand primary process products and simultaneously to retain a degree of objectivity that made me feel comfortable with seriously regressed patients and able to behave in such a manner that they benefited from our contacts. At that time, knowing of my special past, I seriously entertained the idea that reasonably successful survival of a potentially pathogenic childhood might be a prerequisite for such an aptitude.

My subsequent intimate contacts with others who have done successful psychoanalytic work with such patients, combined with extensive teaching experiences, have changed my view. It is my more mature opinion that such an individual past may make the early efforts of trainees less discomfiting and more effective, but a good personal analysis, subsequent training, and experience are entirely adequate as prerequisites for the successful work with borderline and psychotic patients.

CHAPTER SIX

Psychoanalytic Treatment of Character Disorders: Introduction

Peter L. Giovacchini

The psychoanalyst seldom sees cases similar to those reported in the early literature. Reichard (1956) questioned whether Breuer and Freud's cases (1895) were hysterics. Instead of classical hysteria the analyst is faced with a variety of conditions that are sometimes called character disorders. These patients usually complain of an inability to adjust to their milieu. They feel as if they are misfits, that there is no purpose to their existence, and that in general they "do not belong." When they are studied in analysis, the psychoanalyst does not see the usual neurotic preoccupation with manifestations of intrapsychic conflict and defense. Such patients may not complain of discrete symptoms, but one notes confusion about their identity and special problems in dealing with reality.

A seminar, under the auspices of the Chicago Institute for Psychoanalysis, has been studying these clinical entities for the past five years. Although we have learned much about their ego structure and the problems encountered in the analytic setting, very little progress has been made in distinguishing these cases from psychoses. Most of us agree that there must be nosologic distinctions, but when we attempt to enumerate differences in terms of narcissistic fixations, object relations, and a variety of ego functions, we find we are unable to construct sharp and definite boundaries.

However, here it is not particularly relevant to be too concerned about exact diagnostic categories since the focus in this chapter will be to consider the applicability of the psychoanalytic method to patients suffering from severe characterological problems regardless of whether they might be phenomenologically psychotic.

In 1896 Freud (1896a) believed psychoses could be treated psychoanalytically, and he stressed the defensive techniques of a case of paranoia. He had not as yet distinguished between the narcissistic and the transference neuroses or made precise nosologic distinctions. Today, as noted above, one is faced with a similar diagnostic vagueness. However, when Freud was evaluating patients from a psychodynamic viewpoint exclusively, he felt that the psychoanalytic method was applicable to most cases. He (1898a) stated that psychoanalysis was a method of treatment designed only for psychoneurotics, but later in the year (1898b) he included paranoia as well as the hysterias and the obsessionals among the psychoneuroses.

CONTRAINDICATIONS TO ANALYSIS AND WITHDRAWN LIBIDO

Later, in "Freud's Psychoanalytic Procedure" (1904a), contraindications to analysis are discussed, and although psychoses are not specifically mentioned, it is apparent that cases suffering from severe psychopathology are not considered suitable. The following year (1905) he states that psychoanalysis is indicated for cases with a "normal mental disposition" and contraindicated for psychoses as well as other groups of patients. While constructing a model for paranoia (1911), he concludes that the paranoid patient is difficult to analyze. This is due, Freud explains in a discussion of narcissism (1914b), to the psychotic patient's withdrawal of libido from the external world and his inability to form a transference. This formulation emphasized that libido becomes detached from an external object and defensively turns toward the self, a megalomanic-hypochondriacal phase. But Freud elaborated his theoretical model into the structural hypothesis, one that considered the ego as a precipitate of past object relations. At least once in *The Ego and The Id* Freud writes of withdrawn libido and the introjected object as occurring together.

One finds considerable discussion of withdrawn libido in "On Narcissism" (1914b), "Instincts and Their Vicissitudes" (1915a), and "Mourning and Melancholia" (1917a), but it is with his final formulation of the structural hypothesis that Freud (1923) stresses the role of the object, internal and external. Although Freud does not explore the subject of transference in this context, it is theoretically compatible that even in cases of withdrawn libido (the beginning phase of Freud's model for psychosis) transference can develop. Since libido that is returned to the ego is still connected with object-representations, or insofar as it is projected back onto the outer world in the restitutional phase, it can once again attach itself to objects even though this may occur only in the context of a delusion. Arlow and Brenner (1964) have pointed out that the structural hypothesis enables one to construct a model different from the hydrodynamic model that will account for the formation of transference, although Freud also stressed that not all the libido is withdrawn from objects in the paranoid psychosis as it might be in dementia praecox.

Nonetheless, even though transference has been reported to occur in patients with severe psychopathology, the question of whether the classical psychoanalytic technique is feasible is an unsettled one, since there are factors other than transference necessary to conduct an analysis. One also has to distinguish between a transference neurosis and a transference psychosis.

Consequently one must reevaluate the applicability of the psychoanalytic method. Insofar as these patients have been so deprived and traumatized during their development, some therapists feel that they have to modify their technique to give the patient an experience that makes up for or corrects the effects of early disruptive object relations. Other analysts,

Boyer (1961) in particular, believe that the so-called classical technique is effective in the treatment of schizophrenia, whereas Eissler (1953b) believes that one can concentrate on an interpretive approach after having introduced some modifications that lead to psychic integration, modifications that are required before the patient can benefit from introspection. Jacobson (1969), Little (1958), Searles (1963), and Modell (1963), among others, believe that they can work with the psychotic transference, but they specify how their therapeutic activity differs from the treatment of the neurotic patient. Hoedemaker (1960) illustrates how such patients attempt to intrude into the therapist's "ego activity" and demonstrates how he handles such a complication, mainly by not allowing the patient to do anything disruptive to analysis, emphasizing by his behavior that he values the psychoanalytic method and will not permit the patient to devaluate it.

Aside from such pragmatic considerations, the reevaluation of psychoanalytic technique is a natural extension of the theoretical elaborations of ego psychology. As any science progresses and its ramifications become widespread, both pragmatically and heuristically, there comes a time to reexamine basic fundamentals and premises. Psychoanalysis started a general reevaluation of its theoretical scaffold with the development of ego psychology and the examination of the ego operations of the therapeutic process.

Freud (1911-1915) was the first scientist to design a method of psychotherapy founded on a consistent theoretical rationale. It is therefore logical to attempt to integrate the theoretical extensions of ego psychology with the conceptual framework that underlies psychoanalytic treatment. Concentrating on the ego and using it as a framework causes us to sharpen our metapsychological focus of the therapeutic process. Many questions regarding the applicability of the psychoanalytic method to the treatment of characterological defects and psychosis can be restated as we understand the underlying treatment problems in terms of ego psychological theory.

THE DICHOTOMY BETWEEN HELPING AND ANALYZING

Frequently one hears about two types of therapy, one concentrated upon supporting the ego and the other focused on uncovering, which is the essence of classical psychoanalytic technique. The definition of classical technique, however, is an ever-evolving one. Freud outlined certain practical tenets but naturally could not, in the early days of psychoanalysis, discuss treatment in a comprehensive theoretical fashion that would include modern ego concepts. Freud was aware of the integrative features of interpretation, but some recent writers point out there is a dichotomy between helping the patient and analyzing him.

For example, Stone (1963), in his monograph "The Psychoanalytic Situation," believes the analyst is shirking his responsibility if he doesn't give "decisive help beyond interpretation." He is talking about patients in general and not restricting himself to characterological and psychotic disorders. Although interpretation is not dismissed as valueless, one gets a definite impression that it is insufficient. If interpretation is the essence of psychoanalytic technique, he implies that analysts have something better to offer than analysis. Nacht (1962) believes the analyst has to feel some kind of love for the patient. Because the patient has been traumatized by life experiences, the analyst is in some way supposed to make up for resulting developmental deficiencies.

In the treatment of patients with characterological defects, it has often been stated that the patient cannot turn to external objects in order to receive gratification. In early developmental stages his parents or guardian have failed him in one way or another, and the patient has later manipulated himself into similar positions. Still, very often such patients have made appeals to persons who have not helped. That may be one of the reasons he comes to analysis. Do we have any special qualifications to gratify the patient when everyone else has failed?

Deviations from analysis in patients suffering from severe psychopathology are often referred to as a more human approach than classical psychoanalytic technique, implying that analysis for these patients is inhuman and that the analyst has to step outside his role of "mirrorlike" anonymity and relate as a "real" object. These are unfortunate distinctions, for every analyst is familiar with the patient's needs, based on transference projections, to distort his perception of the analyst. The distortion itself becomes the central theme of the analysis, and the "real" presence of the analyst may confuse the picture. On the other hand, there are cases where, even though the analyst has maintained strict anonymity, the patient will not be able to involve himself in a workable transference. It may be natural to want to help the patient, but we can utilize our professional approach in order to give such help. Commitment to analysis by being receptive to the patient's projections is more important than gratifying his curiosity or being primarily interested in "helping" him. The maintenance of a professional attitude is potentially helpful, even though at the beginning of treatment it may seem that what the analyst offers is different from what one would ordinarily consider helpful.

Such questions cause us to examine our concepts of what constitutes analytic help. I feel, as do Gitelson (1962) and other writers, that help is intrinsic to the analytic process and need not involve any extraanalytic factors. Winnicott stresses the same point when speaking of reassurance, a feeling of security the patient experiences because he is in "a reliable setting with a mature person in charge, capable of making penetrating and accurate interpretation, and to find one's personal process respected . . . " (1955).

Being helped, as with any psychic transaction, can be considered in terms of a spectrum arranged in a hierarchical continuum. The continuum can be correlated with different stages of psychosexual development. For example, during the early neonatal period the mother's care is global, the infant's survival depending (anaclitically) almost exclusively upon her. One can view this type of help in terms consonant with this early developmental period, that is, a megalomanic kind of help where boundaries between self and outer world are not yet established and the mother's role is cosmic. With psychic differentiation this initial state of cosmic fusion is changed into a more circumscribed one, and the child becomes able to make some discrimination about the source of help that up to now has been synonymous with the nurturing substance. The child begins to differentiate the sources of homeostasis, the milk, the warmth, or the soothing kinesthetic or equilibratory sensations. Later the person (the parent) who supplies is specifically identified, and the presence or absence of this person becomes the mediator of satisfaction or of disruption and frustration. Summing up momentarily, with psychic development there is greater structure and differentiation of perceptual ego systems associated with more highly structured needs and increasingly more sophisticated means for their gratification.

Both the needs and the techniques of satisfaction acquire greater coherence, flexibility, and mastery, attributes characteristic of the secondary process. Delay and postponement of gratification, qualities that are the essence of reality testing, promote autonomy and make the psyche less dependent upon external objects.

Piaget (1952) draws a hierarchical continuum when discussing the development of thought processes, the beginning point consisting of a sensory-motor modality and characterized by egocentricity and the most advanced stage being what he refers to as formal thought, a form of thinking characterized by self-observation. In other words, such thinking is reflective and involved with an awareness of what is occurring within the self, a process that occurs with introspection. To understand what is going on within the psyche becomes, according to Piaget, the most advanced form of thinking.

To draw an analogy, understanding the nature of one's needs represents the advanced continuum of our need-satisfaction series. Thus, I am postulating a gamut from biological satisfaction to self-knowledge and awareness of our psychic requirements. The latter is self-understanding and is associated with a well-integrated, autonomous ego.

It is precisely this kind of understanding that the analyst offers. Analytic help is associated with the highest order of development where self-observation is dominant. To know about one's needs is of greater adaptive significance than the narrower gratification of the need. The former puts matters, in the context of structure, on an objective level and enables ego systems to be aware of all the implications of internal requirements and outside gratifying facilities.

The study of cases with characterological defects and of psychoses highlights the lack of awareness of inner needs, of understanding what they need and want as well as the lack of experience of ever having felt understood. In order to develop basic ego capacities, a person must have some satisfying and gratifying relationships in early life. The psychotic patient has never felt understood. His early relationships were characterized by a lack of empathy for his needs. His mother or his guardian never really understood his needs; instead she reacted only to her own needs, and he experienced either rejection or assault. As a consequence, his ego development is both narrow and defective, and the hierarchical development of needs is also a constricted one. Many so-called borderline cases complain of never knowing what they want and experience a hopeless dejection, not simply because they feel the outer world to be frustrating, but because they do not feel anything. This lack of feeling applies to such elemental sensations as hunger, heat or cold, excretory functions, etc. A patient who had been diagnosed as a character disorder was aware in a gross way of such feelings, but he was not aware of any finer sensory discriminations. Not being able to feel was often experienced as nonexistence and a complete alienation from objects, a state of panicky dissolution. The patient felt dead (but still panicky) and believed that no one could see anything within him, that is, understand him, because there was nothing there to see or understand.

To be understood, therefore, has many implications and offers the patient the type of help he has never had before. Kind and helpful friends may try to give him wise counsel, but their needs are somehow also involved. The analyst tries to make the patient aware of his needs and conflicts, but he does not take sides in his ambivalence. The patient begins to learn that the analyst's understanding indicates that there is something within him worth understanding. As the analyst recognizes the patient's inner processes and reveals them to him by integrative interpretations, he is pulling together (synthesizing) disparate fragmented elements and thereby helping the patient to structuralize what was previously felt as vague, diffuse, and perhaps painful. *The analyst has not only helped the patient become aware of something within himself but also, by synthesizing fragmented elements, helped create a need.* The previous sense of emptiness is, to some extent, alleviated as the patient begins to develop an ability for self-observation. Patients with ego defects do not use repression as much or as effectively as the psychoneurotic, one reason among others being that the ego is insufficiently structuralized to support the function of repression. For both types of patients, however, interpretation has an integrative effect that expands the self-observing function and, in cases with character disorders, also leads to a structuralization of needs.

Granted many such patients have only a limited ability to form a therapeutic alliance and, instead, demand some form of nurturing. However, their frustration is eventually intensified if the analyst tries to minister to their needfulness. These patients will inevitably experience a disruptive agitation since they demand an omnipotent, megalomanic type of help. They will find it impossible to maintain the delusion that the analyst is supplying magic. A conflictual and primitive need is then experienced in the transference. To be aware of its existence, rather than attempting to gratify it, shifts the patients' cathexis from the product that they think would bring gratification to the phenomena of the existence of such a need and its constricting effects. This can be compared to a creative achievement because psychic equilibrium is achieved by adding a segment (insight) to the ego, resulting in an ego expansion. This is the essence of the unique quality of analytic help.

TECHNICAL FACTORS

Boyer (1961), Will (1964), and Eissler (1953b) conceptualize the treatment of schizophrenia as consisting of two phases: (1) a more or less supportive phase in which the therapist attempts to get the patient sufficiently oriented so it is possible to work with him analytically, and (2) a phase that can be considered analytic in which the emphasis is on interpretation and insight formation. This same type of division into two phases is considered applicable to nonpsychotics who suffer from ego defects. This separation strikes me as being an artificial one, although perhaps of value in organizing one's thinking; but clinically the two phases are so merged that they are indistinguishable. Still, many therapists would disagree and remind one of the patient who is so excited or withdrawn that it is impossible to make analytic contact.

Although such cases rarely come to the analyst's consulting room, they still exist, usually in institutional settings, and consequently cannot be dismissed in any discussion of clinical interaction and therapeutic process. There are cases so completely inaccessible that it would be utter folly and even ludicrous to attempt a standard analytic approach. Still one wonders whether many cases thought of as being far out of reach would be amenable to analysis if it were tried. For example, cases have been recorded where the initial phases of therapy have been extremely stormy. The patient has been distrustful and suspicious, and his behavior has been antagonistic and rejecting. The therapeutic approach has been viewed as an assault and an intrusion. Under these circumstances the therapist has often tried to make himself felt as a person, indicating his interest and concern for the patient's welfare. Until a "real" relationship is established, it is felt that interpretive work is impossible; the patient's libido is so narcissistically fixated and withdrawn that transference projections will not occur. However, as has often been the case, when the patient regards the therapist as an intruder and sees him in a negative light, this is already of tremendous value and an important and significant step in the establishment of a transference relationship. The severe paranoid distinguishes between good and evil. By projection he constructs a bad and persecutory external reality, one he hopes to escape from. Although this defense is primitive, it also means that the patient is able to make some evaluation of internal distress and has methods at his disposal that might achieve some equilibrium.

What is being described appears, on the surface, to be withdrawal. But this does not indicate that the patient's libido is completely introverted. On the contrary, very often such patients have turned away from us in anger, and this means that the therapist has been connected with his destructiveness. By so doing, the patient reveals an investment in the therapist, one that he hopes will give him relief from internal tension. This also implies that a concept of the future exists and that the patient is able or has the capacity to be able to imagine or fantasy a situation less painful or more pleasurable than the current one.

A hostile rejection of the analyst has an element of structure to it and can eventuate into a workable transference situation if the therapist can keep these feelings focused on himself and prevent them from becoming generalized. *The analyst, by making himself available for the projection of negative feelings, which are often embodied in destructive introjects, is removing an obstacle to psychic development.* The analytic process is, therefore, set into motion from the very first contact with the patient.

A clinical vignette to illustrate the above point describes a young man in his middle twenties who, although he came to therapy voluntarily, was extremely suspicious of what the analyst would do to him and felt vulnerable, fearing that he might be taken advantage of and exploited. During the middle of the first hour he became very angry about doctors in general. He believed they made much more money than he did, and he decided not to go on with the interview because he did not want to contribute to what he considered to be my already sizable financial estate. He had revealed considerable paranoid ideation about several people, especially his immediate superior on his current job. I showed an interest in his rejecting and hostile attitude and conjectured as to whether there might not be some advantage in feeling exploited by me, that this might represent some security rather than having to feel at the mercy of and vulnerable to his boss. After all, he could leave me, but he would have more difficulty leaving the job upon which his livelihood depended. He visibly relaxed at this point and nothing more was said about discontinuing therapy for a long time.

I will not go into the details of this patient's interesting analysis but will mention one particular crisis that emphasized the analytic gains that can occur when the patient is hostile and rejecting and seemingly analytically inaccessible. This patient had an acute delusional episode following an important business success, where he thought he had destroyed his immediate superior and, in a sense, he had, insofar as he demonstrated that his employer's judgment was faulty. He became angry and disappointed with me because I was unable to protect him from being overwhelmed by destructive feelings, and at this point he had an acute paranoid episode. He heard tormenting voices accusing him of being a homosexual and sneering and laughing at him. He heard babies crying through the ventilator system in his apartment building, and he suffered from uncontrollable waves of panic. He became so agitated that his relatives finally called the police and had him dragged bodily to a hospital. He quickly calmed down, but continued to be plagued by his own thoughts and the voices. All of this happened over a weekend, and, surprisingly, despite all the turmoil, he asked for permission to keep his appointment with me. The attending psychiatrist granted it, and the patient came alone to my office. At first he would not lie down on the couch and insisted on maintaining a distance of at least fifteen feet between us. I pointed out that he need not fear for my safety, that he wouldn't destroy me, whereupon he shouted he wasn't concerned about my safety but was worried about his own and what I might do to him. Nevertheless he lay down and revealed that he felt I was his persecutor, exploiting him, picking his mind and becoming rich, since I was being paid 100 thousand dollars a year by a business rival to drain all his mental abilities from him. This other person and I would learn a good deal from him, but he would be intellectually destroyed. I had, up to this point, asked some questions as to the details of his paranoid delusion, but when I was satisfied that I understood its content, I asked him why he had to bring another person into the picture, why did I have to be paid such a large sum of money to persecute him? He was astonished at my question and interpreted it as meaning that I wanted exclusive rights to persecute him, but he also saw the humor in this interaction and was able to recognize the transference projection. After he left the hour, he signed himself out of the hospital and continued his analysis as previously.

His delusions disappeared with partial transference resolution. A patient who reacts in this fashion may not be considered as a typical example of a seriously disturbed schizophrenic; still, if all the details of this patient's delusional system were given, not only during this particular episode but including those present at the onset of therapy, he would be indistinguishable from any bizarre, paranoid schizophrenic, at least on a phenomenological level. This raises an interesting question, because patients who have been to some extent analytically influenced are considered nosologically different from another group where it is postulated, in fact it is a criterion of diagnosis, that analysis is contraindicated.

There is a very important difference between this patient and many other patients who reject their therapists. I feel it is highly significant that he sought therapy on his own and was able to come to my office. This particular capacity may be of crucial significance, and it cannot be denied that no matter how correct our interpretations may be, there are some patients who will not respond to our efforts to conduct analysis. These patients are so withdrawn, as in some catatonic stupors, that external objects are either not recognized or completely denied. One can raise the question, however, as to whether any form of psychotherapy will be effective. To repeat, is there anything better than analysis that can be offered within the frame of reference of psychotherapy if analysis is ineffective? Other therapeutic approaches may be relevant, but we are limiting ourselves in this discussion to the consideration of outpatient relationship type of therapy, and at this point we are not considering the environment outside of the analysis.

In the beginning of treatment, interpretations may not involve much in the way of specific content. However, from the very first interview, the patient is making projections, some quite obvious, and others subtle. By constantly interpreting the projection, one causes an internalization of conflict. The analyst's purpose is to focus on the intrapsychic, and when the patient succeeds in doing likewise, he has gained considerable security. The following vignette is an example of the reassurance a patient can receive by converting external chaos to a topic for intrapsychic consideration.

This middle-aged housewife had been rejected as analytically unsuitable by two different analysts in another city. Although neither one of them believed she was psychotic, they felt that the degree of narcissistic fixation was so sufficiently intense that she could be considered a borderline character. The patient had been in a state of utter confusion and despair for many years and had reached a point where she was incapable of carrying out routine activities. She was unable to care for the house, the children, do the shopping, etc. She lay in bed crying all day and complained of numerous physical symptoms including migraine headaches.

She arrived fifteen minutes late for her first appointment and presented herself in a state of utter dissolution and chaos. She was dirty, dishevelled, and her face had a pained, agonized expression. She gripped her stomach, moaned, and, in a helpless feeble voice, asked where the nearest toilet was because she didn't know if she could get through the session without having to rush out. She then pleaded for something to alleviate her distress and intense pain. Throughout all of this I kept looking at her and, despite this display of helplessness, I could not feel any sense of urgency. I was puzzled and felt immensely curious as to why she was behaving in this fashion and what it could mean. I motioned her into the consulting room and made what I felt to be an interpretation. I told her that she wanted something from me but she didn't know precisely what it was because she was unable to put it into words. She had a need to create confusion and make others feel anxious. On the basis of all this we would have to try to find out why she had to go to so much trouble making herself sick for my benefit. She looked me straight in the eye, accepting this challenge of putting matters on an intrapsychic level, composed herself and indignantly said she felt fine. This immediate change was striking, one that I considered a resistance. However, she lay down on the couch and, without any instruction, started free-associating. It became apparent that the patient was attempting to manipulate and destroy the analyst with her helplessness as she had done with everyone else. By relating her behavior to a transference situation, I was able to make certain observations that were designed to internalize a conflict. What the patient presented was seen as a phenomenon that both the patient and therapist could study together. In this instance the interpretive activity consisted of indicating that her seeming chaos had: (1) an intrapsychic origin and (2) adaptive significance. This activity was integrative and one can say it was also supportive, *but it was supportive because it was analytic.*

Pointing out to the first patient that he was afraid of killing me was an interpretation of a defense. He was basically afraid of being killed, but both the fluidity of his ego boundaries, which made the distinction between the two of us a blurred one, and his projective defenses caused him to feel panicky, fearing he would destroy me. Still, his basic fear was that he would destroy part of himself, the hated part that he had projected onto me. His agitated response to my comment highlighted the more basic fear of being destroyed. The fact that one could talk about all of this and relate it to the transference enhanced his self-observing tendencies.

THE STRUCTURALIZING ASPECT OF INTERPRETATION AND THE PSYCHOANALYTIC SETTING

In self-knowledge and awareness of inner processes a structuralizing experience in its own right? Perhaps it can be, but this can occur only in an ego that has considerable resources and is capable of functioning at high levels of autonomy. In schizophrenia and characterological defects, structuralization does not occur *sui generis*, and autonomous boundaries cannot be established without a positive object relationship.

However, this does not mean that one has to give support in addition to interpretation. Interpretation is more than just a verbal exchange between analyst and patient, and as the clinical examples demonstrate, the giving of an interpretation conveys an attitude, an integrative one based on understanding. Furthermore, effective interpretation, that is, therapeutically useful interpretation, can occur only in the setting of the transference. Therefore, intrinsic in interpretation is an object relationship composed of various elements. Interpretive content cannot be pulled out of context and viewed as a disembodied stream of words. Rather, it is a communicative aspect of an object relationship, and its integrative value is to some extent due to its object relationship qualities.

The object relationship qualities of the transference consist of many different levels. The patient's perception of the analyst is determined by a projection of infantile archaic imagos as well as reactions to current impressions. Projected archaic imagos, however, are not exact reproductions of early introjects, since any introject undergoes numerous revisions throughout the course of psychic development. The essence of the transference neurosis at any particular moment depends upon what aspect and level of a particular introject is projected onto the analyst. During the course of analysis there is a broad spectrum of transference projections, ranging from primary process infantile elements to relatively nondistorted secondary process percepts.

The ego gains structure by the formation of functional introjects. Through the incorporation of satisfactory and gratifying object relationships, the ego's adaptive capacities are increased. The introject at the highest level represents an operational technique that leads to mastery rather than simply being a nurturing object. The transference neurosis is an introjective-projective process, and the patient's perception of the analyst, one that contains many levels, is finally incorporated into his ego. Once result of the introjective aspect of the transference is the formation of what I have referred to as the *analytic introject,* and I believe that Zetzel's concept (1960) of the therapeutic alliance includes the formation of such an introject. The analytic attitude, one that scrutinizes intrapsychic processes and archaic fixations, leads to integrations. The patient, by incorporating this observational quality identified with the analyst's interpretive activity, can look at his problems to some extent objectively and place them in their proper perspective.

Integration takes place, and what had previously been fragmented, disparate, and inchoate, is now brought together into a synthesis that can be definitively experienced and structured as a coherent goal-directed drive. Loewald (1960) believes this type of synthesis is a cardinal feature of the analytic relationship.

Is a patient with severe characterological defects and intense narcissistic fixations capable of forming and sustaining an analytic introject? The above clinical examples indicate that even a severely disturbed patient may rather quickly identify with the analyst's viewpoint, which also includes the ability to respond to interpretation. Still one has to consider what general factors are important in determining the limits of analyzability. Three variables, the patient, the environment, and the analytic setting, are conditions that have to be explored relative to each other before one can conclude whether analysis is possible. This chapter emphasizes the integrative effects of analytic activity, but the patient and the environment cannot be dismissed, although they are not focused upon here. Insofar as the environment intrudes into the analysis or the patient's ego is totally involved, defensively or otherwise, with an infantile relationship with the external world, the patient is decreasingly analyzable. *Specific psychopathology is not the chief determinant as to whether analysis is possible, but the reciprocal interplay of the patient's psychic organization, the supportive or disruptive factors in his environment, and the constant nonanxious reliability of the analytic setting all have to be included in our final assessment.*

However, in terms of the analytic setting the analyst is not overwhelmed with anxiety because what the patient consciously or unconsciously perceives as dangerous is considered as an intrapsychic phenomenon that has become the focus of intense interest. The analyst, by wanting to understand the intrapsychic, is not responding to it as a reality that the patient fears but as a subject deserving of his analytic skill. Even when the ego is precariously balanced, the patient gains considerable reassurance and esteem by being treated as a person worthy of study rather than a pitiful human tragedy. This occurs in a steady, reliable setting (Winnicott 1955), which in itself promotes integration. The analytic atmosphere is characterized by calmness, which fosters introspection. The analyst does not share and consequently does not contribute to the patient's inner sense of urgency. He is particularly effective in achieving the latter, which is also reassuring to the patient since he related in an entirely different frame of reference than one determined by the content of the patient's intrapsychic conflicts.

Freud (1910b) emphasizes the futility of giving a patient direct advice aimed at gratifying instinctual impulses. Winnicott (1954b, 1960) repeatedly points out that the unstructured ego reacts to many external stimuli as if they were traumatic impingements. Very often the helpful analyst unwittingly interferes with the patient's autonomous potential. The patient may not be aware that he feels "assaulted" by good advice and direction, although the character disorders, in particular, with their poorly formed identity sense, tend to react sensitively to external manipulation.

The analyst listens to free associations derived from all levels of the psychic apparatus, representing varying proportions of primary and secondary process. A particular association will be predominantly characteristic of a specific developmental phase, but it will also include to a lesser degree other phases and systems of the psychic apparatus. Patients with severe psychopathology produce associations that often lean heaviest on the side of the primary process, but the analyst is perceiving and responding from all levels of his psychic organization. Intuition may be due to the primary process element of the analyst's response to similar elements in the patient. On the other hand, the analyst is simultaneously reacting with his secondary process too. As in creative activity, he is refining and synthesizing primary process-oriented stimuli into terms that have the integrative and coherent features characteristic of secondary process activity. Elevating the analyst's perception to a verbal level and communicating it to the patient involve the progressive abstraction of psychic elements that are responses to primitive aspects of the patient's intrapsychic organization. The interpretation, therefore, is an upward extension of an aspect of the patient's psyche and in the character disorders a psyche whose range of development is narrow. The interpretation by superimposing the analyst's secondary process upon the patient's primary process adds a significant element to the patient's adaptive capacities. The patient's ego gains organization and structure as the analyst supplies an auxiliary secondary process through his interpretations. The integration, which replaces the previous inner chaos, leads to a solidification of the analytic introject. There has to be some degree of ego synthesis before introjection can occur, be maintained, and be functionally significant. The introject, in turn, because of its emphasis on introspection and understanding, creates order from the previous primary process disorder and thereby leads to further structuralization. This process constitutes a positive feedback for, insofar as the ego gains structure from an interpretation, its capacity to form an analytic introject is increased; the introject leads to further integration, which enables the ego to introject more effectively and expansively and respond to further interpretations.

With reference again to patients with a poor identity sense, one often notes eagerness to identify with the analyst in order to obtain some coherence for their self-representations. What one frequently sees at the beginning is not a true identification, since the analyst is not smoothly incorporated and integrated into the patient's ego. Rather, one sees a somewhat clumsy imitation of the analyst, but as the analysis continues to focus on observing and understanding the patient's inner chaos, what was an unsynthesized and unintegrated incorporation becomes gradually integrated and contributes to a more secure identity sense. This does not mean that the analyst is imposing his standards or values on the patient. *The analyst's main interest is to foster the patient's autonomy, and it is this aspect of the analyst that the patient ideally incorporates.* The analyst represents autonomy or the patient's hope for autonomy, a feature that is the essence of a secure, well-delineated self-representation.

Interpretation, therefore, leads to structuralization. It has an intrinsic supportive value. From another viewpoint, it is also educational in the sense that the patient learns new adaptive techniques, but he does so by correcting inner distortions. This adds to the patient's capacity for reality testing. From this viewpoint one can take the position that the analytic method is indicated for patients who have defects in reality testing, that is, schizophrenics and character disorders, who particularly need the integration intrinsic to analysis. The superimposition of the analyst's secondary process upon the patient's primary process is especially valuable for a patient who has only a minimum of his own secondary process. Much that is considered as being extraanalytic can be achieved by adherence to analytic principles, principles that become sharper as we clarify our theoretical framework rather than by altering our role.

SUMMARY

Early dictums concerning the applicability of classical psychoanalytic technique to the treatment of cases with severe psychopathology assert that these patients are not suitable for such an approach. With the theoretical expansions that have occurred with increasing focus on ego psychology, one must reexamine the metapsychology of the therapeutic process relative to the psychopathology of ego defects.

As the treatment process is examined from such a viewpoint, the integrative and supportive aspects of interpretation become apparent. For a fuller understanding of the effects of interpretation, one has to define more precisely, in operational terms, what constitutes analytic help. Help can be considered along a broad spectrum, ranging from the gratification of needs associated with primitive levels of psychosexual development to analytic help conveyed through interpretation. Analytic help leads to introspection, resulting in a broadened perception of inner needs and their integration with the perceptions of the outer world rather than in the narrower constricting gratification of the need.

Interpretation is then understood as a special aspect of an object relationship with the analyst. As the analytic imago is introjected and as interpretive activity becomes internalized, the patient's range of secondary process functioning is expanded. The analyst superimposes his secondary process upon the patient's primary process, leading to greater ego structure. In a positive feedback sequence this enables the patient to introject more helpful aspects of the analytic relationship, which in turn leads to further structuralization and then to greater ability for internalization, etc. This increase in secondary process activity gradually extends to the patient's everyday life and no longer requires analytic reinforcement.

Patients with faulty ego structure are in particular need of auxiliary secondary process activity. The analytic method is an integrative one and need not be altered to supply greater structure. These patients have had only a minimum of understanding during their childhood; the analyst's willingness to focus exclusively upon his intrapsychic processes constitutes an acceptance that he had never had before. To scrutinize content of conflictful needs leads to resistance, but wanting to understand how the patient's mind works fosters the therapeutic alliance. Giving the patient an awareness of what goes on within himself, to help him see himself as a psychic phenomenon rather than as a human tragedy, not to participate or take sides in archaic self-destructive conflicts and defenses, in other words, to analyze him and to make him understand there is a core within him worth analyzing, is treating him with the greatest dignity and highest respect possible, and represents, in my mind, the ultimate in human responses.

CHAPTER SEVEN

Some Elements of the Therapeutic Action in the Treatment of Character Disorders

Peter L. Giovacchini

The extension of the classical psychoanalytic method for the treatment of cases with characterlogical disorders is intellectually exciting, and its successful application is of tremendous clinical significance. However, as with any innovation, one does not expect universal acceptance. There will be and should be a certain amount of disagreement on both major and minor issues.

It must also be recognized that, in presenting a particular viewpoint, we are working within a frame of reference not necessarily the most comfortable one for another investigator. The symposium in California responsible for this book was addressed exclusively to psychoanalysts, but psychoanalysis does not impose homogeneity upon its practitioners, especially in regard to technical issues. As Boyer has demonstrated in his review, there are many "schools" stemming from the mainstream, each encompassing a discrete theoretical orientation and each claiming some therapeutic validity. Others may prefer to work within a theoretical subsystem founded on principles that differ from classical analysis but are still related in some way to the psychoanalytic realm. Undoubtedly there is much to be learned from such differences and similarities, but at the moment it seems premature to attempt a rapprochement. Our task is not one of evaluating but of focusing on our approach and exploring its rationale.

In dealing with patients with character disorders we have found it unnecessary to alter the basic psychoanalytic model Freud provided. However, there are areas of metapsychology referring to the therapeutic process that are vague and require both extension and clarification. In our pursuit of theoretical and therapeutic clarification, we must expect differences of opinion even between the two authors of this volume. Although basically we are very much in agreement, it is precisely at the junctures where our ideas differ that we hope to open up vistas that will not only lead to new insights but also cause us to look at our therapeutic interactions in a new perspective. This can lead us to make explicit many attitudes and strategies of which we may have been previously unaware or have not considered as being particularly important in the treatment setting.

GRATIFICATION OF INSTINCTUAL NEEDS

Boyer (see chapter 4) believes that at times it is necessary to behave in a manner aimed at direct gratification of the patient's instinctual needs. He does not, however, consider this activity therapeutic in and of itself. He believes that in some cases it is necessary to gratify the patient, such gratification leading to a situation in which analysis becomes possible. Boyer considers this a parameter, but a minimal one. As with all parameters, the sooner it can be eliminated, the less hampered will be the course of analysis.

The gratification of instinctual needs in an emotionally deprived patient has frequently been considered desirable for its own sake, since it is postulated it may bring about an equilibrium favorable for psychic development. As mentioned above, this does not impugn the value of an interpretive, introspective approach, but merely emphasizes that there may be necessary conditions before interpretation can be effective, and these conditions, in addition to the transference neurosis, may be an important aspect of the treatment of patients suffering from characterological defects. Winnicott (1955) believes that the analyst offers the patient a reliable setting that leads to an organized regression. The latter is valuable and becomes the subject of transference interpretations, but it would not have occurred without a secure setting.

Various nonanalytic psychotherapeutic approaches attempt to gratify basic needs as well as to reinforce defenses without the utilization of insight or the aim of altering character structure. The purpose of such therapy is to provide symptomatic improvement and to facilitate adjustment to reality. Such treatment is occasionally considered a preparation for analysis. This is not what Boyer describes.

Nevertheless, since this issue is encountered so frequently in clinical discussions and in the psychoanalytic literature, it behooves us to examine it as a phenomenon rather than casually to accept such "supportive" interaction as a therapeutic necessity.

Instinctual frustration contributes to ego defects and fixations. Can psychoanalysis undo these deleterious effects? To put the question more cogently, is it possible for the analyst to give a patient gratification that would have been appropriate during his infancy or childhood and would have led to psychic growth? Does such gratification lead to emotional development when one attempts to give it in the analytic setting? Many therapists have made the casual assumption that they have the capacity to undo childhood trauma by a direct response to the patient's needs. If we are to assess the effectiveness of the attempt to gratify such needs, they must be considered in terms of the psychosexual stage to which they are appropriate. Through the transference projection the patient relives infantile conflicts. He relates to the analyst as if he were a significant person from the past, one who can withhold and frustrate or minister to his needs and provide what is required for emotional sustenance. The types of needs the transference regression evokes are related to earlier stages of psychosexual development and are characterized by a preponderance of primary process elements. In order to gratify these needs, the analyst would have to be able to respond to primitive elements within the patient's personality while at the same time being able to maintain his own professional orientation.

The transference regression is not an exact replica of a childhood state that is revived and projected into the analytic setting. The patient is biologically an adult and has been exposed to a variety of experiences throughout the course of his life that have had their effect upon his psychic structure. He has acquired many skills and adjustive techniques that were not present during his infancy. During the therapeutic regression there is a selective loss of these later accretions, but not a total one. Although the patient may feel a need to make up for his infantile deprivations, he is considerably more complex despite his regression, and his current requirements have many elements that could not have been incorporated and integrated by his infantile ego.

He needs more than he once did. Mother's milk is no longer an adequate nutriment even though the patient may not know it while in the regressed state. His dietary requirements include a variety of substances that would not have been digestible when he was an infant. Similarly, at the psychic level, an attempt to give the patient something that would have been appropriate for an earlier developmental period is not adequate or even relevant to his current needs. Trying to gratify the patient does not fill a gap in his psyche, nor does it correct the traumatic and disruptive effects of early frustration, for even if the analyst were able to gratify infantile needs, what would enable the patient to benefit from it? Undoubtedly the patient has had many subsequent experiences that had adjustive and developmental potential, but because of intrapsychic conflicts, disruptive, constricting introjects, and ego defects, he was not able to profit from them and to use them for the expansion of various ego systems. Without the resolution of these archaic conflicts, activities designed to satisfy relatively primitive drives neither gratify them nor promote psychic structure, as noted by Freud (1910b) in his paper "'Wild' Psychoanalysis."

The patient frequently demands gratification of what he considers to be urgent needs. This may be expressed as a cry for help or by clinging to the analyst for succor. He often is asking whether the analyst will be able to rescue him from his destructive self. He feels helpless and vulnerable as well as hateful and unlovable. The analyst is cast in the role of an omnipotent savior sufficiently powerful to counteract the patient's "badness." The patient's needs are megalomanic in quality and dominated by primary process elements. To be consonant with such needs a response would have to be preponderantly primary process in quality. One is then faced with the situation where a primary process-oriented need is responded to with a primary process-oriented reaction. Can such a transaction lead in the direction of secondary process structure? It is difficult to conceptualize how experiences founded on primitive infantile expectations can lead to the acquisition of adaptive techniques, techniques that are the consequence of ego structure and that enable the patient to master the complex and subtle problems involved in relating to external reality.

Any attempt to give the patient something that may have been required during childhood is a way of relating to him as if he *really* were a child. This interaction emphasizes his helplessness and vulnerability and enhances his potential for the projection of omnipotence. Similar to disruptive and constricting introjects, this kind of activity may result in corresponding fixations. To attempt to relate directly to such needs is perceived by the patient to be an acceptance of their reality. Not infrequently patients complain subsequently of having felt depreciated and threatened because they believed the analyst shared their fear of their disruptive impulses. Even though they may ascribe omnipotent powers to the analyst, they often resent it if he assumes such powers, and one finds that the analysis of the transference becomes inordinately complex.

The patient regresses during analysis. But as Winnicott (1955) emphasizes, there are different types of regression, some analytically useful and other types disruptive to analysis. In a previous communication (1965) I discuss how the regressed state can create a setting in which the ego is not hampered by destructive, constricting introjects and can incorporate experiences that enhance self-observation. In contrast, relating to the patient on the basis of infantile needs leads to a hypercathexis of archaic introjects. The corresponding regressed ego state is then unable to incorporate and synthesize ego-expanding experiences because of the fixation on these primitive introjects.

A frequent objection regarding the utilization of the analytic method in the treatment of patients suffering from severe psychopathology is that the patient will not be able to tolerate it. It is felt that the use of the analytic method may lead to serious repercussions, such as further decompensation or a complete psychotic breakdown. The author has found that even incorrect and poorly timed interpretations, by and of themselves, do not lead to psychotic disintegration. It is not easy to penetrate prematurely the patient's resistance so that primitive underlying impulses will flood the ego and cause a state of psychic dissolution. However, stepping outside the analytic role and making promises that cannot be kept or further hampering the patient's autonomy by trying to run his life in the interest of helping him, according to the experience of many analysts, is more likely to lead to disruptive panic states and psychotic decompensation. The patient's ego becomes inflexible and nonadaptive when he places himself in an infantile setting and lets the analyst take over basic caretaking functions. Insofar as his dependency on the analyst is such a total one, his vulnerability is intensified if the analyst disappoints him. He sacrifices his autonomy for the promise of omnipotent nurture. His adjustment, therefore, hangs on the thread of the analyst's power to supply, and, at best, is in a state of precarious balance.

THE EFFECT OF THE ANALYST'S PERSONALITY UPON THE PSYCHOANALYTIC PROCESS

Some clinicians believe that the psychotherapist who is able to remain within the psychoanalytic frame of reference while treating psychotic patients may need special personality qualities. It is important to consider whether this is a question of degree or whether there are differences in kind. Should the analyst have a specific characterological or psychodynamic constellation that contributes either to his skill or capacity to deal with what are generally considered to be difficult patients? This question is, of course, of interest regarding psychoanalysis in general, but is there something additionally specific to what is required of one who treats patients who have been so traumatized during childhood?

While I agree that the analyst had to be very much in tune with the patient's needs and to some extent even have some fondness for him, I do not believe this is above and beyond what one must feel for every patient. There are patients who ostensibly seek help but are insincere or have ulterior motives (usually some manipulative needs) and who are so unlikable that the analyst finds himself unable or unwilling to work with them. I doubt whether such patients are more common among those nosologically categorized as suffering from character disorders. In fact, the needy person is less apt to have sufficient structure to resort to subtle manipulative maneuvers. His hatred and self-hatred, however, may reach disturbing proportions and evoke rejecting responses in those about him.

One has to consider the question of what enables us to tolerate patients at all. Is it solely some specific internal need of our own? The desire to help the patient sometimes represents a desire to help ourselves at an emotional level that may be at approximately the same level of fixation as the patient's. One would hope, however, that our needs are not too deep or intense, and that our desire to treat patients is based largely on mature motives; otherwise, we would run the risk of indulging in a neurotic interaction that does not lead to analysis and psychic development.

If the analysis of patients with severe psychopathology demands specific personality features of the analyst, then the "standard" analytic method is inadequate. It is implied that analysts without such qualities and yet able to use the psychoanalytic method will not, in spite of their technical skills, be able to deal with these patients. What is required is both special emotional features and technical psychoanalytic skills. The analyst's personality will, of necessity, affect his psychoanalytic style. If it is assumed that he has to have specific emotional features, then his psychoanalytic style will reflect them. This would constitute a modification, for although the personality of the analyst is to some extent always reflected in his technique, here we are considering the effects of special personal qualifications. When one speaks of qualifications, one is not necessarily speaking of skills that are the outcome of optimal development and training. Oftentimes we are referring to a residual or core of severe psychopathology that has been to a large measure resolved and that can now be used to empathize with the patient.

Searles (1965b), Staveren (1947), and Szalita-Pemow (1955), among others, emphasize the importance of the analyst's reactions and the extent of personal involvement with the patient based on the analyst's intrapsychic requirements. However, what is being described is often idiosyncratic. It is a moot question whether one's "deeper" motivations hinder or help one's analytic capacity, although to separate motivations completely on the basis of the level of the personality from which they stem is an artificial dichotomy. In creative activity optimal conditions consist of a balance between primary and secondary process operations. Our motivation springs from all levels of our psyche, but the clinical situation determines which attitudes are appropriate in terms of psychic level and the proportionate amount of primary and secondary process.

If our assumption that the psychoanalytic method need not be altered, or only minimally altered for the treatment of borderline and some psychotic patients, is correct, then the analyst's personal orientation should not be a distinguishing factor. There may be some homogeneous factors found in all analysts, but one is also impressed by the diverse qualities compatible with sincere motivation and analytic competence. Consequently if we are to be consistent in our assertion that these patients can be treated analytically, it must be postulated that no particular type of intrapsychic orientation or psychopathology is a necessary condition for conducting analysis with either psychoneurotics or patients suffering from characterological defects. Conversely, if special emotional constellations are required of the therapist, then the treatment of the latter group cannot be effective without some radical revisions of our psychotherapeutic approach.

The above does not mean, however, that there are not psychic constellations and forms of psychopathology that hinder one's capacity to analyze. There may also be regressions and acting out by the patient that may evoke feelings within the analyst incompatible with analysis. Such feelings have to be examined by the analyst and brought sufficiently into focus so that he will not allow the analytic situation to be disrupted.

IS THE PATIENT SUFFICIENTLY MOTIVATED?

Hoedemaker (1960) makes some interesting points about the disruptive aspects of his patient's behavior. He emphasized that certain types of acting out may preclude analysis, and the patient has to be able to curb his behavior if he is to continue. This idea brings several issues to the fore, a particularly important one being that of motivation.

Analysts often gauge analyzability by an assessment of the patient's motivations for treatment. Such an assessment is often impressionistic and intuitive. If there isn't a "proper" amount of motivation at the onset, it is sometimes believed that analysis is not feasible, and this supposedly occurs more often with "sicker" patients. Commitment to analysis is a progressive step, one that is realistically oriented insofar as it involves a judgment and appraisal of one's emotional state and the recognition that something can be done about its painful and self-defeating aspects. Patients with characterological defects are not very skillful at making such appraisals, and this deficiency, which is in part due to faulty reality testing, will be reflected in their seeming motivation for analysis. The character defect itself handicaps the patient's desire to be analyzed.

Lack of motivation is similar to any attitude or behavior that is a consequence of intrapsychic conflict or an ego defect. The patient brings many varied attitudes to the consulting room that are determined by specific emotional constellations and conflicts. Usually these are symptomatic, and the analyst uses attitudes, behavior, and symptoms to assess what is going on within the patient. This is material, and it would be unrealistic to expect the patient not to have symptomatic manifestations or to expect him to give up some of his symptoms if he is to be analytically acceptable.

The patient's motivation for treatment, to repeat, is a manifestation of attitudes that are the outcome of his psychic organization. From one viewpoint, it is a symptomatic manifestation, and as with all symptoms one can question the wisdom of expecting modification as a condition of acceptance for treatment. Granted there may be certain qualities to the patient's behavior that may preclude analysis (to be discussed later), but can one make relevant a priori judgments about motivation per se before the formation of an operable transference neurosis and analysis?

It is valuable to consider motivation in terms of its object relationship qualities as well as its intrapsychic determinants. The patient must be willing to involve himself in a relationship with the analyst; whatever anxieties and defenses were directed to significant objects from the infantile past will be repeated in the transference neurosis. The patient has some awareness of what is going to happen and is understandably reluctant. Even in the first interview (sometimes even before the patient has met the analyst), there is already some projection of archaic imagos, that is, an object relationship is partially established that to some extent is imbued with the same conflicts present during a vulnerable childhood. Motivation, therefore, has to be considered in the context of a setting that is object directed. The patient undergoes some regression, even at the beginning, and his judgments are already impaired. His sense of discrimination and reality testing will function at the level of his ego state of the moment, one that has infantile elements. These important ego functions will be influenced more by primary process operations than usual and cannot be taken at face value. As with earlier object relationships, the patient's motivations will be unstable insofar as he is either manifestly wary and distrustful or extremely positive because of projection of omnipotence and idealization of the analyst. In either case, these attitudes represent psychopathologically distorted perceptions and are only of limited value in judging the patient's suitablility for analysis.

The analyst's response to the patient is of crucial significance. Considering motivation as an aspect of an object relationship brings the analyst's reactions into focus. Motivation is no longer considered as something that happens exclusively to the patient. The analyst is involved too, and his reactions, conscious and unconscious, are communicated to the patient at some psychic level. Hesitancy or reluctance to analyze are reacted to by the patient, who may then withdraw. The analyst's indecision and scepticism stimulate a similar indecision and scepticism in the patient, which are manifested as insufficient motivation. What has to be emphasized is that this lack of motivation is not a singular phenomenon, but one that exists in both the analyst and the patient. Rather than viewing this situation in an absolute sense, one may consider it as a subject worthy of investigation. As with all analytic material, countertransference attitudes also must be assessed.

The manifest expression of motivation and the actual circumstances that bring the patient to analysis are often deceptive. It has often been stated that one of the worst possible circumstances for beginning treatment is when the patient is forced to do so. The patient ostensibly does not seek treatment; due to circumstances, someone has imposed it upon him. In some instances, in spite of an apparently impossible obstacle, treatment may proceed in a relatively unobstructed fashion.

For example, a young man in his early twenties was apprehended by a policeman who let himself be homosexually approached in a public washroom. The patient was well educated and held a position of responsibility. The judge was sympathetic and wanted to spare him a jail sentence and the jeopardy of public disgrace. Still he was firm in his insistence that the patient get psychiatric treatment and made treatment a condition for a suspended sentence. The patient was to report to a probation officer every three months so that the latter could ascertain that he was still in treatment. If not, he would be put in jail immediately. A court edict not only demanded that the patient start treatment but also imposed the further condition that he couldn't discontinue treatment if he so desired. Many therapists believe that the patient has to have the freedom to leave therapy in order to foster his autonomy.

In spite of these severe circumstances, this patient's treatment did not present any unusual problems. The problems encountered were related to intrapsychic conflicts and defenses, and the external situation did not seem to enter into the therapeutic interaction. This, in itself, was pertinent, and only later in the analysis did it become apparent why he showed such little resentment at having analysis imposed upon him. He remembered having been rebuffed during childhood and, at times, physically attacked if he dared to ask for anything. This developed into a component of his masochistic submission and homosexuality, in which he was usually the passive partner. On occasion, he would use reaction formation, as in the washroom, and at least momentarily adopt the aggressive role. It is tangential to the thesis to go into any further details of this patient's analysis except to mention briefly that the patient really wanted treatment but had to manipulate himself into a situation where he was "ordered" to do what he was afraid to ask for directly.

One might conclude that this case is an exception, but when it was presented at a seminar, other members of the group reported similar experiences. Such cases should cause us to pause and wonder when we are presented with material that seems to indicate a lack of motivation and to try to understand the patient's reactions in terms of the intrapsychic rather than being discouraged. The fact that the patient comes to the analyst's office often indicates sufficient "motivation." A court order "forcing him" to seek help or a painful symptom may each be sufficient reason for analysis. The analyst is interested in the patient's reasons for wanting treatment, and a court order and a symptom may be equivalent.

SHOULD RESISTANCE BE ELIMINATED?

There are many other kinds of reactions that have been considered by analysts as incompatible with analysis. Hoedemaker (1960) presented examples of actions he considered to be attempts by the patient to sabotage the analytic relationship. What his patient did might be considered a resistance, one that threatened to be totally disruptive. He described the case of a middle-aged woman who ignored his interpretations. Whenever he attempted to point out what she was doing, she paused to let him speak and then went on without overtly acknowledging that he had spoken. Finally Hoedemaker became irritated and expressed his anger. He banged his hand on his chair and insisted that the patient listen to what he had to say, not just for the sake of making himself heard, but to convey what he felt was going on within her.

Hoedemaker knew why the patient ignored him and was able to understand that she was reenacting in the transference neurosis an infantile relationship with her mother. The patient always felt ignored by her and couldn't get through to her; in the analysis she reversed roles, identifying with her mother and rejecting the analyst as she perceived she had been rejected. The analyst broke through this pattern by "insisting" he be "heard."

I will direct myself to the wider implications of behavior similar to that of Hoedemaker's patient, behavior that has been viewed as resistance and which is frequently considered to be detrimental to analysis.

Freud presented several viewpoints about the nature of resistance. In "Remembering, Repeating and Working-Through" (1914c), he states that overcoming of resistance is a major therapeutic task. The resolution of "resistance due to repression" leads to a filling in of memory gaps. Acting out, which is accentuated by resistance, is a further obstacle to remembering and impedes analytic progress. He concludes that the aim of removing resistance distinguishes psychoanalytic therapy from other forms of treatment.

The transference neurosis became the center of Freud's interest in his two papers "The Dynamics of Transference" (1912) and "Observations on Transference Love" (1915b). In the former, he remarked that as one approaches the unconscious sources of the patient's associations, resistance occurs. However, transference enters the picture at this point. We need not pursue the process of transference development here, except to point out that Freud believed the transference itself to be a potent form of resistance. Specifically, in the case of the erotic transference, the patient tends to suppress or to repress it. In the latter paper, Freud notes that a frequent manifestation of the transference is that the patient falls in love with the analyst. He asks the pertinent question as to whether the analyst should prohibit or exhort the patient to overcome these feelings, since they present a resistance to analysis in that the patient wishes to destroy the analyst as analyst and convert him into a lover. He answers his questions by concluding that such an attitude merely would be asking the patient to repress, while the aim of analysis is to undo repression. Such an exhortation would be contrary to analytic principles.

Consequently one is impelled to reexamine the concept of resistance in terms of whether one should seek to eliminate it. We have a situation in which, on the one hand, it is acknowledged that resistance is a hindrance to analytic progress, and, on the other hand, to attempt to get "rid" of resistance introduces parameters that may in themselves obscure material necessary for the understanding of the patient's intrapsychic processes. Freud resolved this dilemma by not resorting to parameters. He expressed this by advising against any deliberate role taking and suggesting that resistances must be viewed as material to be analyzed.

If one follows Freud's line of reasoning, one may view resistance as something of analytic value. The patient has to reveal himself, and there is nothing more revealing than his characteristic defensive modes. Resistance, according to Freud, is the way the patient manifests his defenses in the therapeutic setting. He defends himself against his unconscious, and the defense manifests itself in behavior that is reflected in object relationships. The analytic relationship is also an object relationship that fosters a variety of infantile elements depending upon the dominant transference theme. Resistance becomes part of the transference, insofar as projected archaic imagos contain the reactions and defenses the infantile ego constructed against the more disruptive aspects of the threatening persons of the past. These reactions and defenses constitute resistances when projected onto the analyst and reveal characteristic adjustive ego modalities. In cases with characterological defects, the distortions and defects of the ego's adjustive modalities reveal the personality style and highlight the psychopathological core. Consequently in this group of patients the development and quality of resistance is especially important to the significant transference trends. Resistance is an important aspect of an ego state that reveals as much about the patient as does any other type of material.

THE ANALYST'S REACTIONS AND COUNTERTRANSFERENCE

The specific questions stimulated by Hoedemaker's clinical material are intriguing. In his clinical example, he emphasizes the value of the hostile transference and discusses personal reactions that include some countertransference elements. He also discusses behavior that he feels was in his own best interest but, as a consequence, was in the patient's best interest, too.

The type of transference described, that is, the patient identifying with her mother and treating the analyst in the same way her mother treated her, involved projection of the memory of an infantile self-representation and is typical of character disorders. It is also found, however, in the psychoneurotic patient. Frequently neurotic patients bring in dream material where the roles of analyst and patient are reversed. Usually this represents a reaction formation against passive dependent or passive homosexual impulses. Anna Freud (1936) described a similar role reversal when she described the important defense of identification with the aggressor.

Hoedemaker recognized that he felt irritated by his patient, and then he responded accordingly; he did not suppress his anger, but instead coveyed it to the patient in the context of not letting her devalue the analytic situation. He felt that the analytic interaction was important and that he must not allow her to ignore him. Being ignored meant being depreciated and represented the destruction of his analytic role. He felt his interpretations were integrative and did not allow the patient to reject them, the essence of his response being, "I have an idea you haven't looked at."

Other analysts have written of their reactions to patients, and discussion of the countertransference in recent years has proved to be fruitful. The analyst's response should be examined, especially when the patient is able to provoke anger. Of course, any affective reaction, positive or negative, is meaningful, and sexual responses in particular have to be considered.

Analysts are, after all, human, and patients are usually, for defensive purposes, quite skillful in discovering their sensitive spots. They learn rather quickly how to evoke a response from the therapist. Once the analyst is able to place the patient's behavior in an analytic frame of reference, the particular affective reaction often disappears immediately. If he can understand that the patient at some level wants to evoke such a response and if he is able to see this as an aspect of a transference projection, the analyst is adopting a viewpoint that goes beyond any constrictive personal reactions. For example, as Freud described, an hysterical patient may wish to manipulate and destroy the analyst by evoking erotic feelings within him. The analyst may actually feel sexually stimulated by a patient who is able to be seductively attractive. But once he understands that being chosen a sexual partner or the victim of her seduction is representative of a fantasied relationship with some figure of her infantile past, and that the patient has to behave in this fashion because it has adaptive and defensive significance to her, then his outlook becomes clinical and no longer a personal sexual one. This shift in attitude eliminates responses that could be disturbing and interfere with the course of analysis, but does not create an affectless state. The analyst is then looking at the patient from an entirely different viewpoint. She is still the subject of intense interest but now it is an analytic interest, one aimed at understanding the patient's behavior and needs rather than reacting to them.

There is no consensus as to whether it is always necessary to respond first with affect, and then to use such a response as a stimulus to place the patient in a clinical perspective. Winnicott believes that with the psychotic patient the analyst has to feel "objective" hate, and this response can eventuate in a constructive experience for both the analyst and the patient. He views the analyst's feelings as an intrinsic aspect of the therapeutic interaction. Once the psychotic patient can feel hated, then it is possible that, at some future time, he can feel loved. Winnicott (1947) reminds us that in order to experience affect there has to be considerable ego structure, so an interaction founded on a degree of structure greater than the initial fixed state represents an advance. The experience of being hated is potentially constructive, according to Winnicott, if it is conscious and if the reasons for it can be recognized by both the analyst and patient.

That the analyst's response can act as a "signal" to place the patient in a clinical perspective has been discussed; but is it absolutely necessary to have such a signal (a potentially disruptive affect such as hate) to set the analytic process in motion? With greater experience and familiarity with patients' defensive and adaptive modalities, the therapist can adopt a clinical viewpoint from the very beginning. The analyst may perceive the patient's material in a total perspective in addition to the primary process qualities he detects. He may be familiar with a total pattern, a gestalt, that enables him to make an immediate evaluation. His secondary process is brought into play, and his ego continues to function with high degrees of integration and synthesis. His psychic balance is maintained without any disruptive affects.

In considering Winnicott's proposition about the psychotic patient needing to feel hated before he can experience love, the analysis of the transference projection might achieve the same result without the analyst necessarily having to hate the patient. When hatred occurs, it has to be analyzed and its countertransference components have to be recognized and resolved. This viewpoint, contrary to Winnicott's, stresses that hatred, by and of itself, is an impediment to analysis. The analyst had to overcome this feeling, which hampers his ability to analyze. Once he recognizes what factors within the patient stimulated certain personal inner conflicts, he has gained considerable understanding that can be analytically useful. The same kind of understanding, even with the psychotic patient, could conceivably be achieved without the analyst having to feel threatened. If he is able to continue viewing the patient's material in the context of transference projections, then he can maintain objectivity and his analytic role. He still has considerable feeling for the patient, but it is feeling founded on his desire to analyze rather than on the basis of other personal intrapsychic needs.

Hoedemaker emphasizes that he sometimes has to react forcefully in order to preserve the therapeutic relationship. In his clinical example, he felt it necessary to intervene and stop his patient from ignoring his interpretations. This case presents us with a fascinating paradox. If the patient defends herself by not hearing the analyst's interpretations, then she will be unable to learn from them and to achieve analytic integration. Besides feeling frustrated, Hoedemaker felt it necessary to intervene in order not to allow the patient such a total withdrawal and insulation. On the other hand, the patient was reliving (with a reversal of roles) an early relationship with her mother. In other words, this was a transference projection that included a defensive reaction to a maternal imago. The analytic relationship is set in motion by just such a transference projection. Is it advisable then to interrupt a pattern that is part of the spontaneous unfolding of the transference?

Phrasing the question in such a manner carries an implicit answer. Since the unfolding of the transference neurosis is our most valuable therapeutic tool, one should use it and analyze it rather than attempt to eliminate it. In Hoedemaker's case, the nature and content of the transference neurosis would seem to preclude analysis. One wonders, however, if he had persisted in interpreting the transference implications of her ignoring him whether it might have been possible for the patient to integrate it. She might not immediately have changed her behavior, but making explicit the adaptive value of what she was doing might have made her behavior less constricting and eventually capable of integrating the analyst's interpretations.

THE ANALYST'S LIMITATIONS AND CONDITIONS FOR ANALYSIS

One may still ask whether there are certain types of behavior and acting out that, in spite of being important elements of the transference neurosis, are so designed that it is not possible to subject them to analytic scrutiny? Hoedemaker's patients may have furnished us with an example of such behavior. Other patients may act out with such violence that the analytic decorum is disrupted and analysis cannot proceed. In other instances, the analyst may not be able to tolerate the analysand's behavior and thereby loses his analytic objectivity.

The latter, of course, involves countertransference. In spite of countertransference elements, there are conditions that every analyst imposes upon the patient, conditions he feels are necessary in order to conduct analysis. One expects the patient to be able to get to the office most of the time and to pay his bills. He should be reasonably presentable and not do anything that would unduly disturb the analyst. These are general conditions most analysts require. In addition, there are other conditions, more subtle and idiosyncratic and determined by the analyst's specific personality patterns. In the optimal analytic relationship these conditions are kept at a minimum. But it still is important to recognize that we make some demands that impose limits on what we permit the patient to present to us, and on what we choose to analyze. No therapeutic relationship is completely spontaneous and uninhibited, and the unfolding of the transference neurosis is, to some extent, guided by some extraneous factors.

If then, the patient's behavior reaches unmanageable proportions, that is, unmanageable for a particular analyst, what avenues are open to the therapist? He may forbid the patient to continue with such behavior. As Hoedemaker states, such curtailment is in the analyst's best interest, but as a consequence it may then be in the patient's best interest, too. If, for example, a patient makes a gesture threatening the analyst's life, no matter how free from conflict the analyst might be or how immersed he might be in viewing the patient's behavior as an intrapsychic phenomenon, he will still feel anxious. An adolescent boy picked up the letter opener from my desk and using it as a dagger made threatening gestures with it. At first I could view what he was doing with relative analytic calm, but when he came dangerously close to my chest my previous objectivity left me and I became frightened. Because of my anxiety, I could no longer function as an analyst, and in spite of the rich transference significance of what the patient was doing, it was no longer available to either of us. This patient by frightening me succeeded in disrupting the analytic relationship. In order to preserve it (and perhaps my life), I had to stop this behavior. As one might suspect he wanted limitations imposed upon him, so I forbade him to continue what he was doing. However, I made it quite plain that I could not tolerate such behavior because by exposing personal vulnerabilities he would destroy my role as analyst, and this I could not permit. He could either stop voluntarily, or I would call the police and have him taken away. I admitted this was unanalytic behavior on my part, but I had to deviate from the usual interpretive procedure in order to be able to return to it later, if he decided this was what he wanted. To persist in such behavior would stimulate such levels of anxiety within me that I might never again be able to look at him with analytic detachment. H stopped acting so flamboyantly, and we were then able to look at some of the provocative and self-defeating elements that were inherent in his behavior. This was possible because I was again able to look at his behavior as a transference phenomenon as he became relatively less threatening and as my anxiety gradually diminished. As we were able to shift back to the analytic frame of reference, he stopped altogether and went back to the couch, where he continued free-associating. This is an extreme case, but even though extreme it was possible to make a prohibition, one made in the context of preserving analysis. Many other less traumatic but thoroughly disruptive situations occur, especially in the analysis of cases suffering from severe psychopathology. In these cases, setting limits might be helpful, but this is necessary only if the patient's behavior cannot be handled in an analytic context and if the analyst feels that he cannot otherwise continue functioning in a professional capacity.

In some instances the patient cannot stop himself, and the analyst is unable to influence him. Under these circumstances, it may be necessary to temporarily discontinue therapy. The patient may unconsciously want to sabotage treatment and seeks rejection. Nevertheless it is often possible to demonstrate to him that discontinuing treatment is not the same as termination and that this course of action is taken specifically because the analyst does not want the treatment to degenerate into a confused, unworkable relationship. The patient makes the decision when to return, the analyst keeps himself available, and the interruption may be only for a very short period of time, and sometimes only the interval until the next scheduled session. An instance of this kind occurred when another adolescent patient drove to my home office on a hot summer day. He was wearing a beach robe, and after having entered my consulting room, he took it off. He was completely naked and mockingly taunted me; insofar as he was supposed to reveal himself, he was now displaying himself and hiding nothing. I was taken completely by surprise and shocked. I was also "analytically" speechless and not able to think in terms of exhibitionism, homosexuality, and the other implications of his behavior. All I could do was react to his provocativeness, and I refused to go on with the interview. I told him that he was making a travesty of his treatment and that I could not work with him under these circumstances. I, therefore, asked him to leave and not to return until he felt that he wanted to meet my conditions for analysis (in this case I simply meant wearing clothes). He left but returned for his next appointment appropriately dressed. He was then able to discuss the meaning of his previous bizarre behavior.

Would it have been possible to have dealt with his nakedness during the previous hour and not have had to send him away? Perhaps some analysts could have worked under these circumstances and have been able to view the patient's behavior in an analytic context, that is, use it as material at the time it occurred.

Are there specific kinds of behavior that are unusually disruptive of the analytic situation? Different analysts can tolerate different types of responses. Behavior cannot be classified as disruptive on an absolute basis but only in terms of the interaction between the patient and the analyst, which includes the analyst's unique responses. Some therapists have a particular tolerance for certain types of behavior. This does not necessarily mean that they are more tolerant of all types of acting out. On the contrary, they may find it difficult to relate to patients whom most other analysts would not find troublesome. The analyst's reaction is, to a large measure, idiosyncratic. At this point the analyst has to evaluate the extent of his personal contribution to the unmanageable therapeutic situation. If it is significant, it may be best that the patient be sent to another analyst who has greater tolerance, or, at least, different kinds of idiosyncracies.

The ultimate resolution of any kind of acting out is achieved when the patient is able to view it as a phenomenon that has an intrapsychic origin, as will be detailed in the next section. This optimal situation requires the ego to be using its self-observing faculties, an ego function that the analyst augments. In acting out and in extreme regression the patient's self-observing capacities are presumably minimal and not available for insight formation.

THE SELF-OBSERVING FUNCTION

The ego's self-observing function, like any psychic formation, may be considered in terms of a hierarchical continuum (see chapter 6, pp. 000-000 for discussion of the hierarchical continuum of analytic help) and its qualities described in terms of phases of psychosexual development. As the ego achieves greater structure throughout the course of spontaneous maturation or analytic integration, all the ego functions become more efficient, including the ability for self-observation. In the primitive ego state characterized by gross disturbances in reality testing or profound withdrawal, which is often found in psychotic patients, one wonders whether there is sufficient capacity for self-observation to make the patient analytically accessible.

Regression and fixation do not reproduce ego states identical to the phase of psychosexual development to which they correspond. The regressed ego state contains pathological distortions and defensive superstructures. The phase of specific capacity for self-observation will undergo considerable distortion while being incorporated into the ego's defensive and distorted operations during regression. On the other hand, there are many acquired adaptive techniques that are not completely lost in the regressed state. These skills are, in some way, involved in relating to both the outer world and inner needs. A gross example is the ability of most psychotic patients to talk and make observations considerably beyond the level of sophistication of the neonate. These skills, although they may be subjected to considerable distortion, will still enable the patient to make observations compatible with analysis. Although the general level of ego structure may be extremely primitive and the chief adjustive modalities may operate with a preponderance of primary process, there still may be self-observing elements that have survived the regression and include later acquired secondary process factors.

What the patient observes about himself is determined, in part, by his psychopathology. However, insofar as the regressive path is an uneven one and the ego consists of various parts operating at different developmental levels, some aspects of the patient's self-awareness are enhanced. If all ego systems are operating at approximately the same developmental level, then the perceptual system is relatively unaware of the internal psychic state in the same way that one is not ordinarily aware of a bodily appendage. Where there is a somatic dysfunction that leads to pain, then one is very much aware of the soma. Similarly, insofar as the perceptual systems does not undergo the same degree of regression of some other ego systems, the patient's self-awareness, although very much distorted, may be accentuated. Such distortions are not necessarily contraindications to analysis since they are dealt with in the context of the transference.

The analytic setting, by stimulating regression, also enhances self-awareness. Even before treatment most patients show considerable self-preoccupation. Whether this self-preoccupation, which may be a pathologically distorted self-awareness, can be made analytically useful is a crucial question, but can this be determined at the onset by making a diagnostic evaluation? Some regressed states may be characterized by a defensive turning away from any kind of introspection. Analytic flexibility, however, is preferable to a priori judgments, and the analytic regression and the introjective-projective aspects of this regression often lead to the development of a useful self-observing function that would not have been predictable during the first few interviews.

If the patient refuses to relate to the analyst, then analytic regression can not take place and the capacity for self-observation will not be enhanced. The inaccessible patient has been briefly discussed (see chapter 6), but now I am emphasizing the factors that might determine whether a patient becomes engaged in analysis to the point where he regresses as described above, or whether he remains rigidly fixated and withdrawn from the analytic setting. In order to involve himself in the analytic process, the patient has to feel, to some extent, that he has made an autonomous choice. To feel that treatment is imposed equates the analytic situation with the threatening external world in general, and the patient's ability to make discriminations about what's occurring within and outside of the psyche is impaired. However, insofar as he had made a choice, therapy becomes a situation that he believes will gratify desires. Because of the constant reliability of the analytic setting, one that is different from the projected external world, the patient becomes able to look inside himself. Therefore, according to this thesis, the patient has to have some autonomy in order to develop the capacity for analytic self-observation.

There are different degrees of autonomy, and patients suffering from characterological defects have only a minimum amount. One of the purposes of analysis, however, is to foster autonomy. One cannot expect or demand that a patient have a considerable degree of a function, the absence of which is a manifestation of psychopathology. If the patient can walk voluntarily from the waiting room into my consulting room, I consider him to have sufficient autonomy to consider analysis. A colleague told me of various experiences in which a resistive patient was able to choose to walk through the door into the consulting room and thereby isolate the analytic situation from the imposing external world that forcibly brought him to the waiting room. Such patients are able to discriminate between two frames of reference, the painful environment and the analytic setting. Such a discrimination makes the development of further self-observation possible.

In primitive ego states the boundaries between the self and the outer world are blurred. It is generally believed that in the phase of infantile omnipotence the neonate does not recognize the existence of an external reality, one apart from himself. His universe is presumably a homogeneous one; but in disrupted ego states, characterized by tension resulting from psychic trauma, it is one that is homogeneously bad, consisting of a hostile, attacking, persecuting outer world and a hateful, unlovable self. The distinction between the self and the outer world is still blurred, but the perceptual system is, nevertheless, functioning, and everything is felt as hateful and associated with disruptive rage. This is not an unusual outcome of the fixation and regression seen in so many character disorders and psychoses.

Since the patient perceives everything as bad, he indiscriminately attacks external objects and himself. This occurs because of faulty ego structure and introjective-projective mechanisms. In view of such blurring of ego boundaries, one may question whether there is sufficient therapeutically useful self-observing ego function available to conduct analysis.

The manifestations of such an ego state as it occurs in an adult patient are presented to the analyst, sometimes quite vociferously. This ability to communicate, however, is evidence of sensory awareness and some secondary process. What the patient expresses (hatred, rage, self-disgust, etc.) are qualities he perceived about himself, even though he may have projected many of them onto others. This type of awareness has rudimentary features that can develop into an analytically operational self-observing function.

Describing something hateful about the self indicates the acceptance of the existence of a self and the capacity to make an evaluation. In a sense he is scrutinizing and describing destructive and disruptive introjects. This constitutes a self-observation of internal pathological factors. Similarly his ability to blame the external world indicates he has the capacity to blame the analyst, perhaps a necessary step for the formation of a workable transference state. To be able to recognize that he is projecting is necessary for the resolution of the transference, and patients suffering from characterological defects often find it difficult to make such a distinction. Insofar as his universe is a homogeneous one, the analyst is often not distinguished from the self either, and an inoperable transference psychosis may occur. Nevertheless the patient's ability to feel hatred and rage signifies that he can feel and has the capacity to experience other feelings. Whether he hates himself or the projected outer world, there are some object-directed qualities to such an affect. Consequently he has the further capacity of making more than one kind of observation about himself.

The ego progresses from operating primarily on the basis of the pleasure-pain principle to a state where ego boundaries are established, and through gradations of identifications with various external objects, object and self-discrimination develops. The ego identifications contain relative amounts of pain and pleasure, and such identifications are responsible for the formation of the superego, a psychic agency that has self-observing qualities. If the superego introjects are cathected with intense hostile feelings, they may be projected during an ego regression so that the self-observing function is externalized, which results in the belief of being watched by a hating persecutor. This belief may be precariously masked by its opposite; the patient insists that he feels only sentimental love for the exclusively benign persons by whom he feels surrounded. These are familiar manifestations of the transference regression of many patients who have a psychotic core, and insofar as the analyst is kept externalized, there is only a minimum of identification and a moderate degree of ego splitting. However, although with hostility, the patient is at one level relating to an external object, the analyst. This cathexis of an external object signifies that the patient has the potential to distinguish between the self and the outer world, that is, he is able to make assessments about himself in regard to an external object (even though delusional).

The capacity to experience diverse feelings about the self and projected and disowned parts of the self is associated with the ability to discriminate between the self and the outer world. Such patients can also value what they hate. Hostile, destructive introjects that have been impediments to psychic development are projected onto the analyst. The analyst is then valued specifically because he has lessened the tension the patient experiences in hating himself. This leads to a dual perception of the analyst. The patient, by being able to relate to the analyst from two different perspectives, a hating one and one that is valued because he has adaptive significance, is beginning to involve himself in an operable transference. The value of projecting is that it can eventuate into analytic self-observation, and in the therapeutic setting it can be thought of as the *anlage* of the self-observing function. By being capable of experiencing another type of feeling, the patient is developing an ability to compare different percepts of the analyst. Eventually he may be able to distinguish the analyst from what he has had to project onto him—to experience the positive side of the ambivalence. When this occurs, the patient has progressed, and his ego has gained structure.

The ability to be aware of the self begins early in the course of ego development and can be considered the *anlage* of the self-observing function that is indispensable for analysis. Obviously, to observe the self one has to be able to make some discrimination between self- and object-representations. Just as there is a continuum between early recognition of part objects and viewing objects as synthesized whole objects, the awareness of the self undergoes progressive secondary-process refinement to an optimal development for analytic work. The self-representation, in fact, develops from the fusion of self-object representations, and the awareness of objects is paralleled by the awareness of the self. In the analysis of psychotic patients, the transference is often characterized by a symbiotic fusion with the analyst, and one notes sequences of progression and regression, the analyst at times not being distinguished from the self and at times, with ambivalent object differentiation, being viewed as a hating persecutor or an omnipotent savior. If the patient is able to experience object relations as ambivalent part objects, then he has sufficient ego organization to be potentially capable of developing a self-observing function that can lead to transference resolution.

The perception of different levels of tension is a perception of an internal state, and one from which self-observation can develop. With further ego structure one acquires the concept of time and the ability to distinguish between past, present, and future. The patient may feel miserable in the present, but even misery has to have some frame for a differential comparison. It cannot be experienced in a vacuum. This implies a concept of a better state that may be projected into the future. Feelings have to be compared with other feelings, and it is the possibility of a better ego state that makes a patient feel so terrible in the present, especially if he believes that future happiness is unattainable. However, as long as one's unhappiness can be related to the awareness that somewhere a state of happiness exists, then the patient has the capacity to develop hope. It is this capacity that the patient uses for analytic integration and that leads to self-observation. Since the patient can feel one ego state and compare it with another, which for the moment may be unobtainable, his universe is no longer homogeneous. This disruption of homogeneity can, on the one hand, be the outcome of psychic trauma or, on the other, of structuralization and may lead to further development.

As one can see, the scrutiny of the various elements involved in therapeutic interaction leads to a discussion and elaboration not only of technical factors but also of many basic fundamental theoretical issues. Both require further exploration, a pursuit that should eventually clarify our conceptual basis of the therapeutic process.

CHAPTER EIGHT

Further Theoretical and Clinical Aspects

Peter L. Giovacchini

At this point it becomes pertinent to examine our concepts about the psychopathology of the group of patients we have discussed. Some analysts have raised the question as to whether we are describing a homogeneous group, and Monke (1964) asked how useful a diagnosis, or rather the word *schizophrenia,* is, especially when we attempt to orient our thinking in a therapeutic frame of reference.

DIAGNOSTIC DISTINCTIONS

When we examine the patient in a therapeutic context, nosologic distinctions recede into the background. A striking example of how the diagnostic classification of the patient was minimized occurred in a postgraduate clinical seminar where Dr. S. Lipton was presenting a case. He had described in detail a patient's behavioral aberrations, which were definitely paranoid in quality, and then went on to describe the transference interaction. At no time had he said anything about diagnosis. Finally one of the members of the seminar group asked, "But haven't you considered schizophrenia?" Dr. Lipton, after a short pause, replied, "Of course I have, but it didn't help," and he then went on to give further details about the unfolding of the transference neurosis. Schizophrenia was not mentioned again, and the group felt much more comfortable when it was made explicit that we were not going to burden ourselves with a constricting adherence to diagnostic issues.

Should we, therefore, discard diagnosis entirely and in its place emphasize the patient's particular intrapsychic conflicts, especially as they shape the course of the transference neurosis? The latter certainly requires emphasis, but this does not mean that we should discard all diagnostic concepts. A "therapeutic" diagnosis replaces the traditional diagnostic label. It may have elements similar to the usual nosologic categories, but it is not static; the patient's response to the therapeutic setting, an ever-evolving one, is the main diagnostic criterion.

Recently it has become increasingly clear that the diagnostic category *schizophrenia* no longer refers to a group of cases that is as homogeneous as we once believed. Bleuler (1911), many years ago, questioned homogeneity when he wrote about the group of schizophrenias, and today we are impressed by the diverse types that are labeled schizophrenia. Practically everything concerning this so-called entity has been questioned: etiology, course, developmental and environmental aspects, and constitutional and hereditary factors. Immense quantities of data have been collected from many research approaches, including those conducted in biochemical and physiological laboratories. However, these studies have not added particularly to our understanding of how to relate to such patients in a therapeutic setting.

The problem is compounded when we broaden our vista to include cases that have been referred to by a variety of labels, such as character disorders, borderline cases, or ambulatory psychoses and pseudoneurotic schizophrenia. Again one has to inquire as to whether we are dealing with specific and distinct categories that have some value in predicting the therapeutic course or in determining the prognostic outcome. These labels are comparatively recent, although the cases to which they refer have been with us for a long time. Most likely we have become more aware of such cases because the usual formulations applying to the "classical" neurosis are not particularly helpful in understanding this group. The label "character disorder" is especially confusing because in the past it has been considered synonomous with Alexander's concept (1930) of the neurotic character, which refers to a patient whose intolerance of tension leads to externalization and acting out. The types of patients described here may resort to primitive functioning and acting-out behavior, but this has not been considered a distinguishing feature. Instead we have referred to a characterological defect as a common denominator.

In seminar discussions the question of definition of the cases being studied always comes up, especially when we compare schizophrenia with character disorders. How do these cases, which are identified by the existence of a characterological defect, differ from those cases that are phenomenologically identified as schizophrenia? Schizophrenics also suffer from faulty ego structure, which results in a variety of characterological defects. Both groups show narcissistic fixation and difficulties in relating to the external world. On the other hand, many investigators believe that there is an advantage in distinguishing patients with characterological defects from overt psychoses and, within the former group, believe there is a further advantage in separating the character disorders from the so-called borderline cases.

The character disorders are distinguished chiefly by an ego defect that leads to distortions in the perception of various areas of the external world. The defect to some extent involves all ego systems, and consequently the patient's interactions with the external world are also affected. One sees adjustment problems accompanied by dissatisfaction with the self and a poorly integrated identity sense. However, one does not see well-systematized delusional systems or hallucinations as are sometime found in the psychoses. In a sense the latter seem to have more structure than we encounter in the character disorders, even though the psychotic is further removed from reality. Furthermore, the character disorders, according to some analysts, do not readily become psychotic.

Gitelson (1958) believed that certain ego systems become "hypertrophied" as part of their defect and enable the patient to deal with the traumatic features of his reality. Even though this leads to a pathological adjustment, it is still adaptive and not easily disrupted. In other words, the ego defect may have defensive elements or a defensive superstructure, which prevents the ego from undergoing a psychotic dissolution. These defensive elements, unlike the defenses erected against unacceptable id impulses, are ego mechanisms that are involved in relating to the vicissitudes and the demands of both internal needs and the restrictions of the outer world and external objects. Insofar as they are ego mechanisms that deal with a traumatic reality,[1] they have become part of the character structure and are characterological defenses and adaptations.

When studying the borderline patient, one also finds a defective ego, but not as well defended as that of the character disorders. His defenses rarely involve the development of a "hypertrophied" ego segment that can be used adaptively. He is more apt to use primitive mechanisms of defense, such as denial and projection, although to a lesser degree than the clinically psychotic patient. His projections tend to be more diffuse than those seen in the classical paranoid, who frequently demonstrates systematized focalized delusions in addition to generalized projection. The borderline patient tends to project with less intensity and organization. Nevertheless, his reality testing is tenuous; trauma can cause him to "strengthen" his defenses to the point where he becomes clinically psychotic. In some instances a psychosis occurs after a decompensation, one that is fixed by the formation of a systematized delusional system instead of a return to the previous shaky defenses.

The behavior of the borderline patient reflects the influence of the primary process more obviously than that of the person

1. The traumatic reality of early childhood has become incorporated into the ego as destructive, constricting introjects that later are projected onto the outer world and then defended against.

who suffers from a character disorder. He is often referred to as schizoid, a term that indicates withdrawal of cathexis from external objects. The borderline patient does not appear to attempt to involve himself with some facet of the external world in order to "pull himself up by the boot straps." His orientation is more autistic. He finds it difficult to even fantasize the possibility of receiving gratification from an external object. He deals with objects in terms of megalomanic manipulation or withdrawal. Those who have character disorders also manipulate and have megalomanic expectations, but there are still more qualities to their object relationships, which indicate there is recognition of the object as separate from the self.[2]

Hard and fast distinctions are impossible to make. These conditions constitute a continuum, and there may be little value in distinguishing two diagnostic categories. In this book we have been prone to consider our cases as belonging to a single general category. Our belief is that our theoretical and therapeutic formulations apply to a large group of cases, including character disorders, borderline cases, and some psychotics. The common denominator is that there has been a profound disturbance of emotional development reflected in manifestations of defective structuralization of the adult's ego. This discussion attempts to scrutinize small differences in ego operations and defensive readjustments of this group of patients. These may assume some importance in the therapeutic interaction, and our alertness to subtle variations may broaden our comprehension of the specific vicissitudes that enter into the formation of the transference relationship. Understanding the various ego systems in terms of defensive "hypertrophies" or lacks of adjustive techniques helps the therapist to focus on what is most relevant in determining our therapeutic response.

2. The psychic mechanisms differentiating various forms of character disorders and psychoses are discussed in extensive detail in my recent book, *Treatment of Primitive Mental States* (1979).

PRECOCIOUS DEVELOPMENT OF EGO SYSTEMS AND CHARACTEROLOGICAL DEFENSES

Very often such patients give the impression of particular efficiency and talent in some area, which is then exploited to the fullest as an adjustive modality. This is frequently seen in the intellectual area, and one finds a history of intellectual precocity. It also becomes apparent that the only way they can relate to the world is "through their mind," and this method compensates for an inability to feel and to become affectively involved in meaningful object relationships. These patients are too frightened of the latter and are, therefore, unable to give or receive love. Intellect becomes a defense against the fear of becoming emotionally involved. At first the display of intellect may resemble strength, but one becomes aware of its desperate and constricting qualities.

Closer examination also reveals that even in the intellectual area there is considerable fragmentation and, at times, not much accomplishment. There is often a hollow, empty quality to their pursuits, and little is achieved. Projects are started, but the patient lacks the organization or the drive to bring them to successful completion. In other instances there is an obsessional rigidity that never enables the patient to go beyond the preliminary stage, or if he can be productive, he lacks the mobility and flexibility characteristic of creative accomplishment. Since the patient has so few resources available to him, he cannot enjoy his intellectual pursuits for their own sake; instead he clings to them for psychic survival, so he is unable to relax and has to maintain rigid control over them. This results in vast expenditures of energy and psychic constrictions similar in their manifestations to those caused by countercathexis.

Patients with character disorders suffer from intense feelings of worthlessness, a self-appraisal that is commonly found in psychopathological states where the ego is poorly structured and primitively fixated. Characterological defenses such as "hypertrophied" intellectualism often do not work, for several reasons. As has been mentioned, because of a general lack of integration the ego is impaired in its executive capacity. This leads to a tremendous discrepancy between what the patient feels he needs and what he can accomplish, for in many instances the patient hopes to "save" himself through his intellectual efforts. The patient has to be rescued from his inner "badness." In order to achieve this he needs an omnipotent "goodness," a savior of omnipotent and godlike proportions to elevate him from a state of helpless vulnerability to one where he can feel worthy. To feel worthy, however, requires cosmic acceptance, so the patient has to produce something of universal significance. A patient in a professional field feels he has to make a great discovery that will win him international acclaim. Since he is always in pursuit of omnipotence, he is always disappointed. His preconscious or unconscious preoccupation is focused exclusively upon the acclaim he hopes to gain rather than on the work itself, so projects are seldom completed.

These patients often find that life consists of a repetitive and continual pursuit of tasks that always lead to the same blind alley. What is most impressive is the dull monotonous quality they find to be pervasive in all their activities. Basically they are constantly frustrated in trying to prove that they are worthwhile, that is, in attempting to establish a structured identity. Their behavior varies. It may range from a direct acknowledgment of worthlessness and impotence in the management of their daily lives to attempts at restitution and overcompensation, which may be manifested by intellectualism, paranoidlike projection, or a defensive arrogance.

COUNTERTRANSFERENCE REACTIONS CAN BE THERAPEUTICALLY USEFUL

The specific defenses that characterize patients with ego defects are, of course, prominent in the therapeutic interaction as well as in daily life. The analyst's responses to unusual and sometimes bizarre elements in the patient's behavior have to be understood and can be viewed from the frame of reference of ego psychology.

The analyst's reactions have been scrutinized as "countertransference phenomena," and this has been valuable. As previously discussed (see chapter 7), the limits of analyzability cannot be separated from certain conditions required by the analyst so that he can relax sufficiently in order to conduct analysis. In some instances these are conditions based upon countertransference attitudes.

Countertransference has received much attention in the recent literature but has not been consistently defined. Here I would like to distinguish it from other responses that occur within the analyst. Countertransference for our purpose is simply the analyst's reactions as they are primarily determined by unconscious factors. These tend, to a large measure, to be irrational and idiosyncratic reactions based upon conflictful intrapsychic elements within the analyst. If he becomes aware of such reactions or if they are limited in scope, they need not seriously interfere with analysis. In fact it is conceivable that they may even augment analytic progress if the analyst is able to recognize the irrational response and then use his newly found insight to empathize with the patient because he is now aware of a similar or complementary problem. The interplay of the analyst's unconscious with the patient's free associations is a fascinating topic that also has received little attention in the literature.

In order to elaborate upon the psychological processes occurring within the analyst, it is useful to distinguish between other reactions occurring during therapy from countertransference. The analyst responds to the patient from many different levels, and some of his responses are not founded exclusively on the basis of irrational or conflictful elements characteristic of deeper layers. Of course every mental construct has its unconscious substrata, but there are some reactions that are primarily determined by secondary process factors and are the outcome of experience and training. The unconscious (see chapter 7) contributes to the process that eventually leads to understanding of what is occurring within the patient, but the ego is still operating with synthetic and integrative systems simultaneously. Still the distinction between a countertransference response and other responses is relative, and every presumably autonomous response has some countertransference element in it. It is the degree of countertransference involvement that is important.

The ego psychology of therapeutic activity cannot be explored without considering the stimuli the patient provides. Unlike the discussion in chapter 7, we are not now concerned with the analyst's idiosyncratic (countertransference) responses to unique features within the patient's personality that are perhaps characteristic of severe psychopathology. The emphasis now is on how different kinds of material stimulate specific types of mental operations within the analyst, operations that involve a variety of structures such as memory traces, integrative and synthetic systems, as well as activities such as fantasy formation and reality testing.

Our therapeutic response is dependent upon many factors and influenced by the combination of various levels of stimuli. Insofar as patients with characterological defects have considerable trauma during infancy, it becomes relevant to inquire what effects specific knowledge and documentation of the past have upon the analyst.

REALITY AND REALITY TESTING

It has been emphasized that understanding of both the current and past realities is important. An ego defect causes perceptual and cognitive distortion of current reality. In such cases a major part of the therapeutic activity consists of pulling together fragmented percepts in order that they may become synthesized into a gestalt that is an accurate appraisal of the external world. One can raise the question as to whether the analyst's synthetic functions are able to construct fragmented reality elements into a whole. Implicit in his question is a division of analytic activity into two types, one dealing with phenomena that are chiefly conscious and preconscious and the other with phenomena mainly unconscious. Does such a division occur in the analyst's psyche, causing him to make such a dichotomy?

Again one has to acknowledge that everything the patient presents has its unconscious determinants. However, to speak of helping the patient by strengthening reality testing is to emphasize the relationship between his ego and the outer world and to minimize the relevance of unconscious drives and mental operations. The analyst views the patient's percepts of reality and compares them with his own as they are determined primarily by secondary process factors. When the patient and analyst are able to look at the same segments of reality, it is easy to make comparisons, and one can assume that the analyst's perceptions are more objective and correspond better to the actual situation. Then the analyst is able to recognize how the patient has distorted and fragmented percepts. Presumably the analyst's more realistic perceptions are communicated to the patient and cause him to function with better reality testing than previously. This transaction supposedly meets one of the most basic requirements of cases with ego defects since their reality distortions are fundamental to their pathology and are the consequence of early developmental disturbances and faulty object relationships.

Can reality testing be achieved by virtue of the analyst's superior ability to be objective?

First one has to consider whether the analyst's ability to be objective is really superior and, if it is, whether it is relevant to the therapeutic process. Relevance would be determined by the analyst's ability to communicate his synthesizing elements to the patient and the patient's capacity for integrating this synthesis within his psychic framework. Even in the frame of reference of the transference neurosis, the question still remains whether the patient can gain an ego function, so to speak, when one's attention is exclusively directed toward the development of such a function. This is an educative role in spite of the fact that it occurs within the context of the transference neurosis. One would also have to make the dubious assumption that the contamination of the transference neurosis is minimal and that it can be handled analytically.

From the viewpoint of the analyst's psychic operations, one has to inquire from what primary process foundations his secondary process stems. He perceives the external world objectively, but there is no such phenomenon as total objectivity. Secondary process cannot exist without an underlying primary process. As discussed in chapter 6, the work of interpretation consists of superimposing primary process responses within the analyst upon the patient's primary process, but with the additional factor that the analyst's secondary processes are added onto this congruence. The secondary process accretion is organized, coherent, and verbal, and constitutes the interpretation. Still what has happened is essentially a response to the patient's primary process, at least initially. This is an entirely different situation from what has been described as strengthening of reality testing by educational measures.

The analyst's secondary process evaluation of the external world is now determined on the basis of his primary process and not the patient's, when he assumes an educative role. So, the reality conveyed to the patient is one founded upon the analyst's personal orientation. He is, in effect, attempting to correct the patient's secondary process distortions and to synthesize fragmented elements by responding only to the patient's secondary-process lacunae and not to their primary-process basis, adaptive value, or meaning of these distortions. If he attempted to do the latter, he would be relating to the patient in an analytic and interpretive fashion, and this would not be considered primarily a reconstructive, educative experience aimed specifically at improving the patient's reality testing.

It becomes understandable that the patient may find it difficult to accept the analyst's personal percepts as his own. He has to incorporate the analyst's reality into his own ego, but it becomes difficult to amalgamate within his psyche because, in a sense, it is a foreign body. It is not an upward, hierarchically structured extension of the primary process and, as with any foreign body, it is not functional. Unless one can deal with the patient's primary process too, that is, deal with primitive introjects that have impeded and distorted the upward extension of the secondary process, it becomes difficult to understand how these distortions can be corrected. It becomes especially difficult to see how a "frontal asault," a direct confrontation of the analyst's secondary process with the patient's secondary process, can be effective, even temporarily.

Many analysts agree that this type of confrontation does not lead to a significant character change, but, nevertheless, it has a supportive value, one that is essential for such cases so that analysis can follow. This activity is considered preparatory to analysis since the patient is so out of touch with reality that he cannot even perceive the reality of his treatment. The patient is in need of auxiliary secondary process in order to be able to function in the therapeutic setting.

How effective such a maneuver might be and its possible drawbacks has been discussed (see chapter 6), but it can be pursued further. It must be granted, however, that there are some patients who need someone to manage some facets of their chaotic situation to effect sufficient stabilization so that therapy can proceed. Whether this can be done by the analyst while preserving the necessary conditions for therapy already discussed (see chapter 6), is still an unsettled question.

THE ANALYST AS AN ADJUNCTIVE EGO

Our interest now is to emphasize the analyst's psychic operations. What are his reactions if he assumes the role of an alter ego? Is he achieving his purpose of creating a setting that is stable for analysis, or is he perhaps unconsciously defeating this aim? This may be only a temporary defeat, and, as with any parameter, a deviation from analysis is relinquished as quickly as possible. But still this question must be pursued not only in terms of the effects strengthening of reality has upon the patient but also in terms of what changes this type of relationship has upon the analyst's psyche. Does it help, as he hopes, or does it hinder his ability to relate to the patient from an analytic perspective?

I feel there are at least two factors that must be examined. The analyst is oriented toward fostering the patient's autonomy. By analyzing within the context of the transference neurosis, he hopes to create a setting favorable for the awakening of the patient's autonomous potential. He addresses himself to removing obstacles to the patient's spontaneous development. He also demonstrates his faith in the patient's capacity for emotional development by his continued interest in understanding the intrapsychic and by not assuming that he is helpless and has to have someone tell him what direction his emotional development should take. He does not deprive him of the opportunities for autonomous choice, so the patient can develop an identity that is truly his own, even though he may have identified with some aspects of the analytic interaction.

When the analyst becomes an adjunctive ego, he is projecting his ego operations onto the patient. If he is able to augment the patient's reality testing, then the patient has been able to introject them, but by the same token the analyst has had to have been able to project. I doubt that any relationship can be completely one-sided, that is, where one person relates to another with a particular psychic mechanism and the other person is relating exclusively on an entirely different plane without reciprocity or complementarity. This one-sided interaction is even less likely to occur when the analyst's purpose is to have the patient incorporate aspects of himself. In other words, such activity by the analyst may cause him to function at a primitive level that corresponds to the patient's psychopathology. Anyone who puts himself in the role of supplying adjustive techniques and assumes the position of a teacher is always giving something of himself to the other person. This, of course, occurs to some extent in any analysis, but the analyst is conveying an attitude, one of exploration and interpretation, rather than showing the patient how to adjust or doing it for him. If the analyst "gives" the patient such techniques, how does it affect his capacity for conveying a self-observing, introspective attitude to the patient? To return to the analogy of the teacher, if he directs and sometimes actually does the work for the student, he is not allowing him the opportunity to discover for himself. The good teacher guides with the aim of helping the student to work independently. True, he supplies him with techniques, but these are all means by which he can then master problems without his help. This is often done by correcting bad habits as well as supplying new information, but never before he feels the student is able to integrate it and make it his own.

The analyst is confusing his role of fostering the patient's autonomy with that of projecting an aspect of himself onto the patient. This projection does not foster the patient's autonomy; it also hampers the analyst's autonomy. Projection, as with any other object-directed ego mechanism, does not occur in a vacuum. In other words, with every projection there is a corresponding introjection, even though it may be of a considerably lesser degree. When the analyst is confronted with a patient who has a fragmented reality sense, he has to identify with this aspect of the patient, at least partially so, in order to recognize the problem. This partial identification has to occur to some extent in every relationship whose purpose is to help another person, whether by psychoanalysis, psychotherapy, or even a student-teacher relationship. But it is the quality of the identification that differs in these various relationships.

By directing himself to that aspect of the patient's personality that has led to faulty reality conceptions, the therapist is also fragmenting his observations. Instead of relating to the patient with free-floating attention, one that might be considered a holistic type of observation, he is limiting himself to only one particular area of the patient's psyche. From time to time the analyst may *choose* to focus upon a particular aspect of the patient's psyche, but when he has felt it necessary to limit himself to one area, this leads to a constriction of his autonomy. He feels impelled to "remain" with reality, and until some improvement is noted, he cannot deal with any other level of the patient's personality. Some analysts feel that it would be even dangerous to make such an attempt. Consequently even though the restriction is self-imposed, his analytic mobility and autonomy are hampered.

THE ANALYST'S AUTONOMY

The above assumes that analytic mobility can be equated with autonomy and the corollary that whatever is done to hamper this mobility also has a significant effect on the analyst's autonomy. It makes the further, but perhaps more obvious, assumption that restrictions on the therapist's autonomy would also affect his attitudes toward the patient, specifically those attitudes aimed at fostering the patient's autonomy.

The first assumption would involve us in a general discussion of autonomy, one that would carry us into interesting but not relevant areas. Here I wish to confine myself to the concept of professional autonomy. Having to change one's analytic approach to a preparatory, supportive one, constitutes, in my opinion, an impingement, to use Winnicott's expression (1955), upon analytic autonomy. Although this opinion does not ignore the fact that the analyst has assessed the clinical situation and then reached a decision, I do not feel that it is an autonomous decision, that is, one without some coercion. The patient has been able to convince the analyst that in some vital respects he is helpless. Whereas in analysis the analyst and patient are cooperating with each other and looking at intrapsychic phenomena, in trying to supply the patient with an ego function, there is a differential between the analyst and patient. Looking at something together, even though the analyst is better able to integrate and understand than the patient, is still relating to each other in the same frame of reference, one that constitutes a therapeutic alliance. To accept the patient as needing something and then believing it can be supplied puts the analyst on a "higher" level, helping someone who has fewer or less-structured ego mechanisms. When one is confronted with such a situation, he is, in a sense, forced to respond. To some extent the need to respond to someone's helplessness is always experienced as an imposition. There is not the same degree of reciprocity in such an object realtionship as there is when the participants are operating on an approximately similar level. There may be immense satisfaction in giving a person help that is appropriate to early developmental phases, but there is always some resentment. There are maneuvers by which the resentment is minimized, ranging from the fee to the "end of the hour," as Winnicott describes (1947), but to feel resentment implies that to some extent one's autonomy feels threatened and one has to compensate for this loss. These compensations can, in themselves, be satisfying, but they are of a different order from those experienced in a reciprocal relationship where one does not feel imposed upon.

Why does one have to feel imposed upon in offering a patient a concrete form of help? Benedek (1959) pertinently points out that the mother's successful motherliness in helping her child develop is a developmental experience for her too, although Winnicott, who does not disagree with this thesis, points out that the mother also feels imposed upon. Benedek emphasizes that the mother's ego reaches higher levels of development that are associated with higher levels of autonomy. To nurture her child and to create conditions for ego structuralization by her nurturing is a task that is intrinsic to a structured, well-integrated developmental level. Such nurturing is one of the functions (operational aspects) of this advanced developmental phase. To give help, that is, the type of help associated with early developmental stages, need not be an imposition and hamper autonomy, but can instead lead to the attainment of higher levels of autonomy.

The analyst, however, does not operate in the same frame of reference as the mother-child dyad. Harris (1960) has pointed out similarities, but there are significant differences. Reference has already been made to ways in which the adult patient's fixations are not replicas of the corresponding stages of childhood. Another significant difference is that the analyst does not wish to be a mother; he is not aspiring to reach a developmental level that has the same quality as motherliness.

His analytic work furthers his development, but this occurs because as he is discovering new intrapsychic relationships, he is adding segments to his own ego. This is an ego expansion and constitutes psychic development, an expansion that occurs because all levels of his personality are involved. To restrict himself only to a secondary process appraisal and response is not a creative accomplishment. It is not an operational aspect of a higher level of psychic integration. Therefore, the gratifications the analyst receives from helping the patient in this exclusively secondary process fashion are not felt as deeply, nor are they as rewarding as analytic activity. It is this distinction, this differential of satisfaction, that determines whether one feels imposed upon or whether the therapeutic relationship is characterized by mutuality and reciprocity, that is, where both participants can continue their emotional development despite the fact that they begin from different starting points. Without such mutuality the analyst is not an autonomous agent if, for no other reason, than that he does not feel free to pursue "higher" levels of autonomy, but must remain fixated to the one particular function of secondary process elaboration.

The analyst responds to the primary process elements of a patient's associations and subjects them to secondary process synthesis and refinement as discussed in chapter 6. One cannot analyze and give form to material that is at the same level of psychic operations. Secondary process cannot add new integration to other secondary process material; it can correct distortions, but it does so within the same frame of reference. There is no further structuralization. The difference is similar to maintenance and repair as contrasted with creating something new. A patient expressed this situation in an apt fashion. Crab grass ruins lawns, and one can spend much time and energy, even ingenuity, in getting rid of it. This is, however, not the same as beginning with black dirt, grass seed, and shrubbery and creating an original landscape arrangement. The analogy breaks down when discussing a patient, since inherent in the raw material of the primary process is an arrangement, but the analyst makes it possible for the patient to give it form. But the point remains that one cannot analyze when there is not a differential in the material. If one is dealing with the end product, so to speak, then there is nothing to analyze. Filling in lacunae, repair, correcting distortions, and the like, do not constitute an activity where something is "added" to the patient's or the analyst's psyche.

The same comments can be made about an ego defect as were made about resistance and motivation (see chapter 7). The behavioral manifestations of the defect are brought into the treatment and influence the course and development of the transference neurosis. Consequently it behooves the analyst to use this material for analytic purposes rather than doing away with it by correcting distortions. Such material can be disruptive to analysis, but this involves the analyst's reaction and, at times, his idiosyncrasies, as discussed (see chapter 7).

THE "OBJECTIVE" PAST

There are situations, as Serota (1964) reminds us, where the patient attempts to give objective information about his background in order to help us correct his distortions. They sometimes bring the analyst photographs from the family album, home movies, or, in one case, a tape recording of the patient's father trying to teach him mathematics when he was a young child. There are many points of view from which one can discuss this interesting topic. Our focus here is again to inquire how such material can be used analytically and how it influences the analyst's psychic operations and his ability to analyze. Patients with characterological defects have had an especially traumatic past, so one wonders how an objective appraisal of it is relevant to analysis.

Material such as photographs and movies is considered to be objective evidence of the patient's past, but just how objective is it? Relatively speaking, since it refers to a past that can be seen or heard, it is less prone to be distorted than free associations, which have more unconscious determinants. Still, is the photograph unbiased? One has to consider the photograph from two viewpoints, the subject and the photographer. When an artist is painting a picture, he is putting a good part of himself into the painting. Photography, although much more objective, still has artistic elements, and even the rankest of amateurs projects some features of his personality into the picture. Our viewpoint is much too psychically deterministic to believe that the clicking of a shutter is a purely mechanical phenomenon. From the subject's or patient's viewpoint, the particular period of his past or the setting he chooses to present to the analyst may be so designed as to becloud a variety of reality features. This, too, is revealing, but then it is material that resides in the same frame of reference as the patient's associational material and not particularly representative of an unbiased reality.

The analyst has signaled, directly or otherwise, that he is

interested in such material, or the patient is being manipulative and acting out some facet of the transference relationship. The motivation behind bringing the analyst some memento, as with everything else, is multidetermined. One determinant may be a response to the analyst's interest, or it may constitute a resistance against further exploration of the transference relationship. Frequently patients tend to defend themselves against disruptive and frightening currently experienced transference feelings by returning to their genetic antecedents. It is a commonly encountered situation with some female patients to talk about their sexual feeling toward their father, rather than having to face disturbing erotic feelings toward the analyst. Similarly, the exposing of the past, or even better, a synthetic externalization of the past, can be used in the service of resistance against exposing himself in the present to the analyst.

As previously emphasized, resistance can be valuable and need not be avoided. What one has to caution against is that the analyst does not contribute to the resistance. An analyst can often directly respond to the patient without augmenting his resistance or allowing himself or the patient to lose sight of the fact that one is dealing with some defensive or manipulative activity. In this instance the analyst might respond with curiosity or have the response that the patient wanted to provoke and still discuss the situation analytically. It is not always necessary to frustrate the patient in order to preserve the analytic interaction. One could, for example, answer a personal question or look at a photograph and still maintain an analytic decorum. He can still weave the interaction into an interpretive framework.

Whether analysis can be preserved if one still responds to some aspect of the patient's resistance depends upon how the analyst responds. He can respond to content and, at the same time, maintain himself in another frame of reference. In other words, he can relate to the patient at one level and still be an observer appraising how he and the patient are relating to each other. If he can maintain this dual frame of reference, then he can preserve his analytic demeanor. However, it must be recognized that there are certain types of interaction where it is no longer possible to be both participant and observer. The analyst, because he becomes involved in some way with the patient or because his percepts of the patient have been channeled into specific areas, may find it difficult to maintain his role of observer. Are there certain types of stimuli that either enhance the therapist's ability to analyze or, on the negative side, impede him? Are there optimal conditions that enhance the analyst's ability to analyze? Such a favorable condition is a well-developed transference neurosis. How does learning about a "concrete" reality affect analytic activity?

The ever-hovering attention that characterizes analytic receptivity involves an interplay of secondary process synthesis and fantasy activity. The latter brings into focus a number of mnemic images, reconstructions the analyst makes about present and past events that encompass the significant figures in the patient's life, imagos that have been projected into the transference setting. To better understand dreams, for example, one often attempts to visualize the dream as the patient reports it and then fix an image of both the action and the various dream elements in our mind. This activity is possible because of the analyst's ability to construct visual images that are, in part, determined by free-floating fantasy activity.

Analytic activity requires mobility, and one must be able to tolerate, as has been frequently stressed for creative activity, considerable ambiguity and lack of closure. The analyst must be able to combine the visual image he has constructed in response to the patient's free associations with a variety of his own memory traces. Some are derived from his past, and some are reflections of material he has collected since he started treatment with the present or other similar patients. This combination and juxtaposition of memory traces and recent constructs need not be entirely conscious (preconscious), and its operations can be predominantly primary process. Simultaneously, integrative and synthetic ego systems are operating with considerable quantities of psychic energy. Once this free-floating fantasy activity has undergone sufficient secondary process elaboration, it eventuates into an insight that, when communicated to the patient, constitutes an interpretation.

The analyst's responses may also include the auditory modality. Individual personality styles or other factors inherent in the therapist's psychic structure determine whether auditory or visual factors are predominant in his response to the patient's material. However, I would conjecture that the visual modality is most frequent, and reports from creative scientists indicate their creative activity is primarily visual. Visual activity, as Freud (1900) frequently stated, is closer to the primary process and, therefore, more mobile.

Since what is subjected to secondary process activity involves many visual elements that are reflections of fantasy material and since the transference is characterized by projections of imagos that have no corresponding objects in either the past or the present, one wonders how knowledge about a concrete reality affects analytic activity. Freud's early papers on technique (1910b, 1914c) stressed a mirrorlike anonymity, a concept that has in recent years frequently been misunderstood and criticized. Freud felt that if the patient knew too much about the analyst's personal life he would be hampered in his ability to make transference projections and later to recognize them as transference manifestations. The same recommendation applies to the analyst also. Although on the surface it may seem paradoxical, there may be a disadvantage in the analyst's knowing too much about the patient.

Consequently one has to determine which types of information are pertinent. The acquisition of exact knowledge of the patient's past does not impress me as being particularly useful. The concrete reality of past situations and object relationships is not directly relevant to the analysis, in contrast to the reality of the object relationship with the analyst, which determines the form and content of the transference neurosis. The patient never relives an exact replica of his past in the transference. The early imagos associated with the infantile ego differ from the external object. The patient reenacts relationships that are the result of a combination of early introjects with subsequent experiences. These later experiences, as well as developmental and maturational factors, cause revisions of infantile imagos. The objective past has undergone considerable elaboration and distortion by the time it is projected in the transference. The patient's distorted perceptions of past reality have led to constrictions and fixations, and it is precisely these percepts that have to be distinguished from the present reality. The analyst's judgment as to how they distorted the past is not meaningful or useful in the context of analysis, although in other studies this may be crucial.

The attempt to gather objective data about the patient's past, as in extensive history taking or the use of ancillary methods such as casework studies with relatives, can become impediments to analysis since it may hamper the analyst's capacity for free-floating fantasy. A confrontation with objective reality introduces a secondary process element. As such, it cannot be subjected to the mobility of the primary process; if it is, then it is no longer objective or real, and it is representative of the analyst's intrapsychic structure rather than the patient's. In some instances, such a percept may interfere with the juxtaposition of the patient's archaic imagos with corresponding primary process organized memory traces of the analyst. For example, I saw a patient walking down the street with his mother, who was small, thin, and frail. She impressed me as being weak, and her demeanor seemed kind and gentle. It was hard to reconcile this image with that of a hostile, devouring ogre, the patient's childhood and current impression of her. Undoubtedly, she had changed considerably, and the mother the patient spoke of no longer existed. Perhaps she had never existed as the witch he had described, his version being the result of considerable elaboration. Nevertheless she stood for something very important in his psychic economy. The witch role he had assigned to her had to be dealt with, and the fact his mother is not a witch and never really was didn't make much difference from a therapeutic viewpoint.

Having a picture of a crucial person in the patient's life, one different from the one he presents, could introduce a complication. Whenever he spoke of his mother, it became difficult to go along with his associations and to maintain the primary-process mobility mentioned above. The image of the sweet old lady intruded itself when he began describing processes that indicated he was able to encapsulate considerable amounts of rage in the mother imago. This "objective" percept tended to minimize my recognition of the constricting and damaging effect of what the patient experienced as a disruptive introject.

However, the introduction of external reality, whether past or present, need not hamper analytic activity and freedom. The analyst may be able to dissociate himself from such percepts just as the patient is able to view the analyst, to some extent, from two different viewpoints. The analyst can never and should never aim to be a total mirror; the patient always knows something about him in addition to his role as analyst, and this knowledge will not be harmful as long as the analysis does not contribute to a potential confusion of roles. Similarly, the analyst can keep the two realities separate; as long as he is involved in and dedicated to analytic activity, other items of information will not matter. What is important is to recognize in terms of analysis that this kind of information is not helpful, is addressed to a layer of the personality associated with secondary process activities, and corresponds to later developmental aspects of the psychic hierarchy.

THE MIND AS A HIERARCHICAL CONTINUUM

All these clinical considerations are consistent with the model of the psychic apparatus that stresses a hierarchical organization. It is not essentially different from the one Freud constructed, although he frequently introduced modifications. However, this model tends to emphasize the ego and its operations. Freud was cognizant of the importance of the ego, and the works of modern ego psychologists are extensions of Freud's metapsychology. These extensions emphasize autonomous ego operations, adaptation, and a variety of energic factors.

All the above topics are sufficiently important to deserve detailed consideration, but insofar as this chapter deals primarily with clinical phenomena and technical and theoretical aspects of treatment, only one aspect of the psychic model will be scrutinized, that is, its organization from the viewpoint of a continuum.

Viewing the psyche as a multiplicity of levels highlights the importance of ego functions that are closer to the uppermost layers. These functions are of special significance for the study of cases with characterological defects since they are characterized by disturbances of such functions.

Ego functions imply structure and are included in Freud's first model, a stimulus-response one. Ego systems are designed to be aware of and to respond to stimuli that have their origin both in the external world and within the organism. Both the technique and methods of response, and what has been responded to, have to be placed in their proper perspective. Psychopathology as well as normal development involves these aspects of the psychic apparatus.

Every aspect of the psychic apparatus, structure, and function can be included in a hierarchical continuum. When studying functions, one is dealing with the products of the ego's executive systems, which, when directed to the external world, determine the patient's behavior.

Whatever a person does, or, in the case of verbal behavior, says (as when free-associating), can be placed in a definite spot on the hierarchical continuum. In other words, both the form and the content of the patient's productions can be considered first in general terms, whether it is primitive, corresponding to early developmental states, or adaptive, coherent, and reality oriented, qualities associated with later highly integrated well-structured developmental stages. Then, more specifically, one can roughly assess the relative amounts of primary and secondary process and which of these two modes of operation is predominant. When one makes such evaluative judgments about behavior, one is simultaneously assessing the structure of the ego systems that have initiated the behavior. Consequently one can associate a response with a particular ego state. The latter can be described in the same terms of relative amounts of primary and secondary process and the stage of psychosexual development to which it predominantly corresponds. It has become increasingly apparent, especially since the formulation of the structural hypothesis, that structure and function cannot be separated. Freud (1923) formulated the concepts of id, ego, and superego in operational terms.

Needs can be placed in a similar continuum (see chapter 6). One can adopt a frame of reference of progressive structuralization without having to deal with a specific instinct theory or to bring in concepts of epigenesis as Spitz (1959) has done, nor is it necessary to distinguish whether the stimulus is internal or external since every need passes through all layers of the psychophysiological apparatus, beginning with the most primitive. An internal need may be stimulated by an external situation or may primarily arise because of physiological requirements that have a periodic rhythmicity, although even needs arising primarily "within" the organism frequently have an external component, too, as in sexual stimulation. In any case, as the need, which in the stimulus-reponse model can be equated with the stimulus, impinges on sensory systems and traverses the various layers of the psyche, it undergoes a hierarchical elaboration. What began as a result of a disruption of a homeostatic equilibrium due, for example, to metabolic cyclical physiological requirements, normally becomes progressively elaborated. At first the response to such a disruption is at a biochemical, physiological level. But before it can be experienced as a definitive need, it has to be felt, that is, reach sensory awareness. This can be achieved only when this initial homeostatic imbalance attains mental representation. The latter is a structured, sophisticated elaboration of what can be conceptualized as having been an elemental somatically bound stimulus and, in terms of total organization, represents the advanced end of a hierarchical spectrum.

The process of becoming aware of what initially is a physiological requirement involves a hierarchical elaboration of this inner need, which, when having reached the highest levels of ego organization, is experienced in socially adaptive terms and cathects appropriate executive systems that respond with reality-attuned behavior designed to gratify the need. If there are defects in the ego organization, then the need is experienced in a distorted fashion and correspondingly the executive systems, insofar as they, too, are defective, and because they are responding to a pathological, distorted stimulus, respond in an inept fashion that is essentially frustrating to the organism. The executive apparatus may achieve sufficiently for survival, but this does not usually involve pleasurable satisfaction.

If the range of development of the psychic apparatus is a narrow and constricted one, then the hierarchical elaboration of the need (similar to the hierarchical elaboration of help; see chapter 6) is also narrow and constricted and closer to what has been defined as the primitive end of our spectrum, the physiological, biochemical level. This constriction of the hierarchical development of needs has many manifestations that are clinically important and are indicators of the faulty development of various ego systems.

The above indicates there is a parallel between the ultimate elaboration of a traumatically induced need and emotional development. This emphasizes that all the patient's productions, what he feels as well as what he does, recapitulate the course of his development, and in the therapeutic interaction the analyst is in a particularly favorable position to determine the relative participation of different developmental levels. What the patient brings to analysis is, in a sense, a miniature replica of the balance between the primitive and the more highly structured that is characteristic of the psychic organization of the moment. The nature of this balance determines the functional adequacy of the ego.

A psychic model based primarily on the concept of a structural and functional hierarchy is especially useful in evaluating the clinical phenomena that one encounters most often in cases of severe psychopathology. Clinical interaction and theoretical elaboration are dependent upon one another; neither is meaningful without the other. Theoretical understanding causes us to study our rationale and to bring into focus problems that would have been unnoticed if one did not conceptualize beyond the simple level of observation. Regarding the therapeutic process in the context of a logically consistent theoretical system, one founded on the principle of structural hierarchies, causes us to reexamine our ideas about the necessity of modifying the therapeutic approach to patients suffering from characterological defects. Such theoretical considerations sharpen our concepts about the processes underlying the psychoanalytic method, and, as this chapter stresses, the more we learn about the psychoanalytic method, the wider is its range of application, one that includes a variety of clinical conditions at one time considered analytically inaccessible.

CHAPTER NINE

Primitive Agitation and Primal Confusion

Peter L. Giovacchini

As clinicians become more relaxed in treating patients fixated at primitive mental states, they also become aware of new or previously unnoticed types of therapeutic limitations. In my own case, just as soon as I had begun feeling comfortable in relating analytically to patients suffering from character disorders (and even to some psychotic patients), I found that my usual formulations of structural defects and the projection of parts of the self were not particularly useful when applied to these patients. For some time I passed this off as a countertransference impasse or an unusual rigidity on the patient's part that obscured the therapeutic interaction. It often happened that the passage of time and the holding elements of the analytic setting would lead to insights (within both participants) that loosened the countertransference constriction or caused the patient to be sufficiently introspective to be understood within a familiar conceptual framework.

In some instances this did not occur. At such times I felt confused, but was nonetheless convinced that I was confronted with something exciting. I was intrigued. As usual, patients became teachers and eventually explained what was going on within their psyches.

As happens so often in the history of a science, progress in psychoanalysis is made when problematic phenomena are viewed from a new perspective. This book is the result of just such a shift in point of view. Conceptually, we moved from id psychology to ego psychology. We do not, however, consider this in any way a radical departure. Some analysts have recently contended that Freudian metapsychology must be abandoned and other systems adopted that are more akin to what they consider to be modern science; this usually means communication and information theory. As a clinician, I find these transformations esoteric and not at all helpful as I begin to see my next patient.

What I am proposing is not so much a revision as a conceptual extension aimed at understanding this perplexing group of patients. We are simply extending our researches further back along the developmental continuum.

Clinicians have become aware of the wide range of ego states that can be observed in a nonintrusive, insight-oriented therapy. If the therapist or analyst does not interfere with the spontaneous unfolding of the transference, the levels of regression may extend as far back as the preverbal, and presymbiotic. That is to say, we may encounter orientations that are essentially psysiological. These are prementational states in which there is very little psychological elaboration.

Frequently the patient reaches a presymbiotic developmental phase during the regressed state. The disruption that is characterisitic of agitation and trauma at such early levels may be a transient phenomenon seemingly created by the therapeutic relationship. These patients are often fairly well integrated and adapt adequately to the outer world, in some instances even in a superior fashion. Other patients are examples of very severe character disorders, including psychoses, whose behavior in the consultation room is not particularly different from the way they react in the outer world. The degree of regression of this group is not as great as in better integrated personalities; since they are primitively fixated and their usual organization is based upon early ego states, they have less distance to travel in this regard.

Some of my colleagues have considered all such patients psychotic. Indeed, patients suffering from character disorders may reveal so many bizarre qualities that this diagnosis often seems justified. Still, they do not replace reality with their own private delusional reality; they recognize the outer world as it is, but simply have no place in it. This is a frequent complaint of adolescents whether they are patients or not. The intensity of their reactions is in part the outcome of the instability and fragmentation often associated with the psychopathology of adolescence. The interplay of the ordinary disruptive forces of the adolescent process and the primordial vulnerability of early ego states creates a striking syndrome that taxes the patient's psychic stability to the utmost.

Therapists are familiar with the alienated patient (Giovacchini 1979). The clinical pictures to be discussed here include alienation, but they also contain many elements that puzzle and disconcert us. Interestingly enough, our reactions may be viewed as reflections of the patient's psychopathology. But until we can put them in their proper context, we may unproductively absorb much of the patient's inner disruption. These patients may be especially bewildering to young therapists who have recently begun treating patients. This perhaps is generally to be expected, but there are unique reasons why it should be so.

I recall experiences during my residency and my early days in practice when I would occasionally encounter a patient who defied my attempts at making a psychodynamic formulation. I attributed this to my lack of experience and naivete, and hoped that with time I would acquire the skills that would enable me to deal with these difficult clinical situations. I will give examples later, but will for the moment simply mention the reaction of my teachers when I turned to them for supervision; they either admitted similar puzzlement or provided formulations that seemed forced and unconvincing.

In the group of patients I choose to discuss, psychopathology is the outcome of preverbal disturbances; its manifestations are also preverbal. The differentiation between the thing cathexis and the word cathexis that Freud (1915) postulates does not pertain when these primitive levels emerge during the therapeutic interaction. Because of such preverbal elements, we might not expect these patients to seek psychotherapy. We could conclude that they would be unable to fantasize or free associate, and this is frequently the case. However, even prementational states can become part of the transference interaction as they become associated with later mechanisms and structures that enable the patient to communicate verbally. They attach themselves as riders to a more sophisticated organization.

The tension these patients experience is contagious. It has a jarring quality. In regressed states the patient behaves as though he has lost control of feelings. He is not always overwhelmed with anxiety, though this happens often enough. The therapist feels in turn—and I mean "feels" literally, since he experiences a disruption which parallels the patient's—that he is witnessing a psyche that is no longer in a state of homeostatic equilibrium. The regulatory mechanisms that organize perceptions and responses to perceptions seem lost; the patient's agitation is pervasive. In addition, his behavior is often quite primitive and bizarre. In the light of what are usually considered the indications for psychoanalysis, this type of patient appears out of reach. And yet—many such patients desperately seek psychoanalytic treatment, raising issues that can best be discussed in a clinical context.

DISRUPTIVE PSYCHIC STATES AND COUNTERTRANSFERENCE REACTIONS

I wish to present several clinical vignettes. Some of these patients came to me when I first started practice and others much later. I will also contrast my difficulties then with those I have now. I believe I can best illustrate this difference by introducing an adolescent patient whom I saw for four years and who then, feeling satisfied with his progress, terminated treatment only to return fifteen years later. I begin with this patient because, though some of his symptomatic behavior is commonly encountered, the degree of regression he achieved during his second period of treatment would cause us to view him as an unusual case. He did not appear so during the original period of treatment, but I am now convinced that my anxiety and insecurity prevented me from providing him an analytic setting in which he could regress.

He was a seventeen-year-old college student when I first saw him. At that time he appeared typical of the patients seen in a university student health service. He was anxious about examinations, was uncertain of a career choice, and believed he was too shy with girls. He had complaints in many areas and in general felt alienated from the campus milieu, but he was his most uncomfortable around girls. He had dated infrequently, had participated in only a bit of light petting, but had never had sexual intercourse. This was not unusual for college students of his era, but he had strong sexual urges and felt frustrated because he was too inhibited to seek a sexual relationship. I thought in terms of conflict and repression and began what I believed would be a fairly standard analysis. I had consulted with a senior supervisor who agreed that I was dealing with an oedipal neurosis that was suitable for analysis.

To my surprise, I soon found the patient's material tedious. He brought in many dreams which I could not understand. They were replete with sexual symbols, penises, vaginas, breasts, and all kinds of situations that had erotic overtones, but any interpretation that occurred to me seemed bland, or I was made to feel that all I could think of were crass clichés. For example, he once brought in a dream in which several women in a saloon were smoking cigars. He quickly associated to fellatio and expressed how much he would like to have a girl suck his penis. I had the conviction that this was valuable material but was unable to do anything with it.

What gradually became apparent was that although the patient was making numerous id interpretations about his behavior, dreams, and associations, I could not connect any of them to me. I was unable to discover a transference focus. As he continued, my confusion intensified as all my attempts at explanation—explanations I was giving myself, not the patient—failed. At first I had speculated that he was intellectualizing, but this proved ludicrous, as his pronouncements were accompanied by considerable and sometimes immense amounts of affect. It was impossible to pass them off simply as histrionic emoting.

His material can be briefly summarized. He saw penises and vaginas in everything. Every protuberant object was a penis and every concavity represented a vagina. He fantasized such objects as coming out of the wall as he lay in bed. He would react with anxiety bordering on panic. Often he experienced these genital symbols as engulfing him, which created great anxiety. During this period of treatment, which lasted several months, he spoke of no responses whatsoever to any persons, in either the present or the past.

My supervisor tried to convince me that I was dealing with primal scene material that had erupted prematurely. He believed that I should not have used the couch, so he encouraged me to have the patient sit up and to give him supportive psychotherapy as preparatory to analysis. Today I would be less clear as to what was meant by supportive psychotherapy, but generally speaking he was suggesting that I direct the patient's attention to current reality and that I guide and help him in his everyday relationships. The purpose was to stimulate a dependent relationship which in turn would stimulate oral-dependent defenses against a fundamental oedipal problem complicated by primal scene trauma. Even though I did not like abandoning the couch, because even then I was more comfortable when the patient was lying down, these formulations helped organize my thinking so that I felt less confused. I must confess, however, that the primal scene elements did not seem as obvious to me as they did to my supervisor, an experienced and renowned psychoanalyst. Furthermore, my mentor insisted that the patient was behaving defiantly and was guilt-ridden, but I had no impression that he was either.

Still, I bowed to superior authority and was thankful for the help. I had the patient sit up, became much more active, and directed the patient's attention to his present life. The patient was somewhat puzzled and a little irritated with our change of method, but he assumed I knew what I was doing and went along. As had been predicted, he rather quickly formed a dependent attachment to the treatment. He indicated this by asking me many questions and by bringing up material which indicated his fondness for me, as well as some idealization. This was the first clear indication of transference, and his previous periods of agitation and excitement had for the moment completely disappeared. After six months of this regime, my supervisor decided we could have the patient lie down once again and resume the analysis on a more formal basis.

The patient complained about the couch because he felt it disturbed our former state of being "locked in" with each other. I did not know what "locked in" meant but assumed that it had something to do with a dependent tie such as that between mother and infant. Consequently, I interpreted his dependence. Once again, he became disturbed.

In supervision, we concluded that this disturbance was to be expected. The interpretation upset his surface dependent defenses and now the underlying sexual feelings with their attendant conflicts were energized. This neat formulation, however, helped neither me nor the patient very much.

His agitation mounted and he continued with material similar to that he had concentrated on prior to my having him sit up. In other words, it was no longer object directed and it made very little sense. During one session, for example, he talked about a penis coming into his ego and winding its way into the superego. He emphasized that he was describing a mode of communication.

I tried to understand this material in terms of phallic invasiveness and the formation of the oedipal superego. I can almost still see him in that session, patiently shaking his head at my obtuseness. He lamented that I was trying to make sense out of something that intrinsically made no sense. I also recall how dismayed I felt at the end of that session.

From that point on I was increasingly aware of an inner disruptive excitement in myself, that is, of an overstimulated state, during the sessions. In part this was due to my attempts "to make sense out of something that makes no sense," and in part to my feeling completely ignored by the patient. He listened to me politely when I attempted to interpret and clarify something he brought up, but then he went on as if I had said nothing. He made absolutely no reference to my presence. At first I believed this was a typical adolescent defense, the outcome of a fear of intimacy, and decided to interpret this to him. My rationale was that he was involving me in the oedipal triangle and had to protect himself by defensively withdrawing. This time he did not ignore me. He regretted that he never thought about me outside of sessions and he was hardly aware of my presence during sessions. He stated further that this had nothing to do with withdrawal. On the contrary, he would like very much to get close to me, but he simply could not. He could not hang onto my mental image, and, unless he looked at me directly, he did not remember what I looked like. He then lamented that this was not a unique situation: he felt this way toward everybody. I continued feeling anxious.

This material puzzled me, but I persisted in thinking about withdrawal and regression as I remained in a psychodynamic frame of reference and was encouraged by my supervisor to do so. The patient protested, but I dealt with his protests as resistance. Gradually he seemed to accept my viewpoint, indicating to me rather expressly that he was working through his dependent defenses. This was accompanied by verbal and behavioral signs that in fact this was taking place. The sexual material continued, and I tried to view it in phallic and oedipal terms. The patient reported that he felt more at ease with girls and had chosen a vocation as graduation was approaching. He was feeling indifferent about analysis and decided that he had achieved what he wanted. Consequently, we discontinued treatment on amiable terms.

For many years I had mixed feelings about this patient. He behaved as if he had had a successful analysis, and for the most part his symptoms had disappeared. In fact, toward the end of the analysis he had started dating and having sexual relationships. Nevertheless, I had a nagging doubt that I had really understood what was happening between the two of us. Perhaps I had put him in a Procrustean bed.

These doubts were further strengthened by other patients who presented material I could not understand. Not that I believe a therapist always has to understand; indeed, I have emphasized that an analyst has to have the ability to sustain ignorance (Giovacchini 1975, 1979). Still, at some point the therapeutic interaction has to be understood in terms of the transference focus and the emergence of the traumatic infantile environment, that is, the repetition compulsion. With some patients, I never felt confident that I was able to grasp our interaction in such terms, and as the years went by I became familiar with many other clinical situations in which the kind of formulations I had discussed with my supervisor proved inadequate.

In spite of what I know now to be inappropriate explanations, the patient improved clinically. Many of his symptoms disappeared. Perhaps this was itself a resistance, a flight into health both to please me and to get rid of me as an analyst. Nevertheless, I still recall with some amazement a fair number of presentations in a clinical seminar when I was a beginning student at a psychoanalytic institute. We were all clumsily groping around to achieve security in the analytic setting and to feel comfortable in our interactions with patients. We were trying to refine our technique and to make accurate and relevant interpretations. Most of us, however, were more astute at picking up the errors of our colleagues than our own. Candidate after candidate presented material that indicated they had missed the point entirely; their interpretations were either meaningless or wrong. It was painful to listen to this, but the progress of the treatment, that is, the development of the transference, often seemed to follow the expected course, as it represented the unfolding of psychopathology, despite rather than because of our crass interpretations. We are all impressed with the power of the analytic process and how resistive it is to intrusive interventions.

My patient's reactions could not all have been based upon a flight into health. To some extent, the strength of the analytic process must have had its effects upon him, because fifteen years later he called me for an appointment. I learned on the telephone that he was married, had four children, and was engaged in a job that required considerable training and skill. Difficulties at work precipitated his present difficulties. I was eager to see him since I had on many occasions wondered about him.

He was also glad to see me. He told me his story in a rapid, almost staccato fashion, which was a sign of how intensely anxious he was feeling. As had occurred many years ago, I soon became aware of the fact that I was unable to link his anxiety to any precipitating events or to conceive of his affective upheaval as the consequence of the return of the repressed. He felt anxious, bordering on panic, and the only response he could give to my questions of what he was afraid of was that everything, that is, the whole world, frightened him. He was emotionally paralyzed and dreaded going to work. He feared that he would have to give up his job, and then he and his family would starve to death. The only bit of information that could possibly be viewed as a precipitating factor was that previously in his job he had had a private office in which he was able to carry on his duties without any human contact; now, however, he had been transferred to a cubicle where he could not maintain his isolation. He stressed how he could not stand any social relationships, preferring to remain in what seemed to be the protective confines of his family. Again, I felt confused.

As in his earlier period of treatment, he brought in all kinds of material with sexual content. More striking this time was the amount of anxiety he exuded. He was terrified during every session and never felt better, only worse. He had "never felt worse" than during the current session. Inasmuch as I could not make sense of his material, I began to absorb some of his anxiety and felt frustrated and irritated.

There was no question as to the overwhelming quality of his feelings. He would scream and convulsively sob on my couch. Once he rolled off it onto the floor and started chewing on a loose throw rug. I had to stop him since he was creating a pervasively disruptive atmosphere and we were both feeling agitated.

In addition to these affective explosions, he introduced a modality of communication that he had not used during the earlier period of analysis. He often reported visual images, pictures he conjured during a session, which he would describe in considerable detail. At some point during his description he would be overcome by a wave, a "tidal wave," of affect and would start screaming and sobbing. Once more I was unable to connect what he was describing with the emotional explosion.

I was reminded of early Freud (Breuer and Freud 1895) and abreaction. Perhaps the patient obtained some relief, but not much. The following episode proved crucial. The patient pictured a room that was part of a house he had lived in during his first six years. It was filled with penises and breasts. Some were floating loose and others were part of a three-dimensional wallpaper. Surprisingly, this was related in a calm, softly modulated voice. Without warning, his throat seemed to convulse, as if a sob were building up deep down in his trachea and slowly ascending. It became louder and louder and then intensified to a terrifying scream. Now his whole body shook in rhythm with his crying.

The copious visual material made me think of what my supervisor, years ago, had interpreted as the outcome of the primal scene. The patient also confessed that during adolescence he was a voyeur, but that this had stopped during his first analysis.

One week later, he confused me further with a similar outburst following the production of similar pictures. However, in addition to floating breasts and penises, he had a series of images of toy sailboats in a pond, which did not seem to corroborate an hypothesis involving the primal scene. Instead, it seemed to point to another type of childhood experience.

I then recalled that he had discussed a potentially tragic incident that occurred when he was very young. He was vague as to when it had happened or whether he actually remembered it. Perhaps someone in the family had told him about it. At first he stated that he was eighteen months old, a toddler, when he had had the experience. This would make it highly improbable that he could recall it, but then he said that possibly he was three years old. He described the following incident. There was a small fountain in the yard of his home, a replica of the one in Brussels of a young boy urinating. A neighbor, most likely a four or five year old boy, climbed the enclosing fence, since he was not allowed there, and had put a piece of wood with a small sail into the pool. The patient's parents called their son to come into the house. The neighbor child was frightened on hearing their voices and, since he was trespassing, hid in the bushes. The patient was so absorbed with this floating piece of wood that he either did not hear or ignored his parents' calling him. Instead of responding, he leaned forward to touch the boat. He lost his balance and fell face first into the pool. Apparently he panicked and thrashed around, but was not able to pull himself out. He started drowning. The parents, angry at his not responding, went outside to find him and found him struggling in the pool swallowing more and more water. They stood there watching him, completely immobilized, unable to do anything to save him. The neighbor boy, hiding in the bushes and anxiously watching this scene, could no longer stand it. In spite of his fear of exposing his trespassing, he finally rushed to the pool and pulled the patient out. Then he ran out of the yard as fast as he could. The parents continued being paralyzed and did not move toward the patient. He lay on the ground, coughing and spluttering and trying to regain his breath. His parents did not touch him or thank the neighbor, nor did they remove the dangerous fountain.

The apparently disconnected outbursts now made sense. He was gripped in the throes of the terror of annihilation and both sets of images related to some aspect of the inner catastrophe that was overwhelming him. They also had transference connections.

Breasts and penises, among other things, fundamentally represented mother and father. They also signified the external world, a world which surrounded him totally and threatened to engulf him. He had emphasized how these breasts and penises were moving toward him. He had on other occasions concentrated on breast sucking and fellatio fantasies, but these were unpleasant and frightening associations. He reported sucking his lips and was obsessed with the thought that they were grotesquely large. Actually, I had never seen him suck his lips and his lips did not appear to be in any way unusual. However, after he reported these images, I recalled the many occasions when he spent most of the session talking about fellatio fantasies and his preoccupation with his mouth and lips.

He was breast-fed for the first two months of his life, but he did not believe this meant that his mother was devoted to nurturing him. Apparently very soon after she started nursing him, she developed a breast abscess. She weaned him abruptly. Later, when he was seven months old, she left him for four months. To this day he does not know why; even though he asked, he was never given a definite answer.

The focus of his anxiety as he spoke of the pool incident was on how completely surrounded he felt. During the session, he relived the terror of suffocation. He had a very specific emphasis that is not particularly unique for a drowning person, but in view of his material I believe it noteworthy. He experienced the external world as coming closer and closer and finally filling him up completely through his mouth. During moments of anxiety he often gagged. He compared his feelings to those of geese being force-fed so they would develop fatty necrosis of the liver to produce *paté de foie gras*. He equated drowning in the pool with having penises and breasts stuffed in his mouth and choking to death. He carefully made the distinction that he would be choked from within, as his body was invaded, rather than having his throat constricted and crushed from the outside. This seemed to be related to the intensely traumatic impact of the memory of the childhood incident.

The parents' inability to help also intensified the effects of the near drowning. Their impotence and noninvolvement must have augmented his helpless vulnerability immensely. He was terrified. His parents simply watched him, being either unwilling or unable to do anything to help him.

In my office, he relived this terror and was able to bring it into the transference, making his feelings fit in the analytic setting. I did not know at the time what was happening, but this, far from hindering the transference, actually aided its development. Like his parents, I was just watching him at the height of his vulnerability and terror, and like them I was unable or unwilling to do anything about it.

My initial reason for not responding was simply that I did not understand what was happening. I did not know that he was creating an important transference focus. He was constructing a setting within analysis similar to his infantile environment. I am not postulating the sort of traumatic theory of neuroses that Freud held in the early days of his researches. The patient did refer to a traumatic event that supposedly occurred, and presumably his other images and outbursts could be related to similar incidents, but I do not believe it is the incident itself that is important. Rather, I find it easier to view the trauma he reported as a paradigm that reflects in concrete, encapsulated form the general ambience that surrounded him. For this purpose a fantasied traumatic event would serve as well. The images and the abreactive qualities of his associations do not require traumatic moments; they can be explained in terms of specific ego defects related to the inability to integrate and maintain mental representations. The patient's ego lacked the psychic mechanisms that would protect him from invasive external stimuli. The latter were experienced as intrusive because the parental modality was unable to provide the protection of an external stimulus barrier (Boyer 1956). The resulting excitation was felt internally as painful and disruptive, and was not connected to specific intrapsychic conflicts. He could not organize external percepts and achieve equilibrium. *He could not be soothed.*

I was placed in the position of a person who could not help him, but unlike his parents I was trying. I had also absorbed some of his agitation, but once I understood it in these terms I regained some calm. The patient was able to accept the connection between my feeling helpless toward him with his infantile orientation.

He still felt anxious but was able to find relief in the therapeutic relationship. He eventually could hold a mental representation of me outside the sessions and found that it had a calming effect. He spoke of this as constructing an internal soothing mechanism.

I will not pursue the course of this analysis further since it did not present any other features relevant to agitation and structural problems. He progressed beyond the prementational stage and achieved the ability to project the helpless and vulnerable parts of the self-representation into me, but these processes were understandable and did not cause me to feel disrupted or agitated.

HOMEOSTATIC REGULATION AND THE HOLDING ENVIRONMENT

Winnicott's concept of the holding environment (1955) is useful when we attempt to understand these primitive agitated states. I wish to stress the protective aspects of this maternal function. As Freud (1920) indicated, the neonate is bombarded with stimuli from which he requires shielding. Freud postulated that the mother provides a stimulus barrier, a *Reizschutz,* against external stimuli. The mother modulates and filters incoming sensations. According to Winnicott (1956), the mother, who is tied to her infant almost biologically, just as she was during gestation, intuitively resonates with her child and can sense when tension is mounting. She responds by soothing the infant and at the same time soothes herself.

Soothing is accomplished in many ways. She may hold, cuddle, rock her child when the infant needs it, that is, when the homeostatic equilibrium begins to be upset. She knows when to initiate action as she absorbs her child's beginning agitation.

The child experiences an altered internal state when stimuli impinge from either the inside or the outside. Concerning the former, the mother knows when her child needs nurture. The child, for example, might signify a need for relief from the discomfort of an external sensation, such as a cold, wet, and soiled diaper. Undoubtedly there are also peaks of excitement produced by diurnal and circadian rhythms that require soothing.

What I am discussing, I repeat, are tension states not linked to specific psychological content. They are created both by internal stimuli (mainly physiological, without any notable degree of mentational elaboration) and by potentially disruptive external stimuli. Regarding external stimuli, the ego is still too immature to process these impingements. In other words, it is not yet able to organize these external stimuli as percepts. Without the mother's soothing, the child cannot integrate certain external sensations and feels agitated. He does not have sufficient ability psychologically to work over stimuli so that they do not upset homeostasis. The infant does not have sufficient internal regulatory mechanisms in this prementational phase.

Internal needs also cannot be integrated without the mother's intuitive responses. The child does not have established memory traces of satisfying (in this instance, nurturing) experiences that will maintain him as he seeks gratification of what Freud (1915) referred to as instinctual tension. However, the facet of the patient's character I am exploring here has more to do with the mother's filtering of external stimuli, an element of the holding environment, rather than with her nurturing function. Of course, the two are intimately related, as I have discussed elsewhere (Giovacchini 1979).

As mentioned at the beginning of this chapter, the regression induced by treatment often reaches back to these early prementational states. Regression of this sort occurs in patients with well-integrated levels of adaptation as well as in some with primitively fixated egos. Many ego states that have been considered affective disturbances to be explained on the basis of intrapsychic conflict are, I believe, better understood as the outcome of prementational agitation. Such agitation is often expressed in a dramatic and puzzling fashion, and not infrequently through somatization. For example, a nineteen-year-old college student complained of a constant and painful state of tension. He thwarted me immediately when, thinking in terms of Erikson's identity diffusion syndrome (1959), I tried to make connections to his leaving home. He protested that he had been depressed and anxious all his life. He stressed the depression much more than the anxiety, which I found interesting: though visibly distressed, he did not seem at all depressed. His voice had an urgent frightened quality, and he spoke of many physical symptoms, such as headaches and periodic disturbances of the gastrointestinal system. It sounded as if he might be suffering from some type of colitis. He viewed himself as a sickly, vulnerable child.

He emphasized that he would have to interrupt treatment once a year during the later summer months because he suffered from unbearable hay fever and would have to go to Arizona. For as long as he could remember, he had had on both wrists a visible rash that he was constantly scratching. His overt agitation and frenetic scratching made the atmosphere in my consultation room rather turbulent.

The patient reported further that he compulsively masturbated, anywhere from three to eight times a day. In the psychic sphere, he feared that he would not be able to graduate, since he had tremendous difficulties in remembering anything for more than an hour.

As with the previous patient, I was not able to connect his distress to any conflicts or, for that matter, to any particular feelings. When he mentioned feeling anxiety or depression, I would ask him to describe exactly what he felt. His descriptions had no resemblance to organized affects, even disturbed affects. Instead he emphasized states of excitation and sensations of inner "jarring." He felt that his internal organs were whirling around inside him, banging and knocking against each other. His descriptions were vivid, but he was well aware that he was using metaphors for the sake of communicating. These were not somatic delusions, although it was easy to suspect that they were because of the intensity of his reactions.

I present this patient in order to emphasize how his agitated state confused and obscured my therapeutic vision. I viewed him in terms that were appropriate to a level of organization he had not achieved. He did not cause me, as did the previous patient, to attach specific psychological content to the behavior he displayed in my office. Nevertheless, I was ascribing certain qualities to a feeling which, if they were there, would make it possible to formulate the patient's psychopathology as the outcome of intrapsychic conflicts or even higher-level ego defects. I had initially considered his reactions as expressing affects, but further examination proved that this was not so.

His masturbatory activity also seemed devoid of psychological significance. He had no accompanying fantasies and received no sexual pleasure from ejaculation. He experienced only a transitory calming effect.

I will make only a few brief remarks about this patient's treatment, since I wish to report in greater detail a patient whose problems were similar but who presented me with particular countertransference difficulties of a sort I believe many clinicians commonly experience (see next section). Here I wish merely to note how closely connected the present patient's agitated state was to his somatic symptomatology.

The patient began treatment with me in the autumn. By late spring he had been able to achieve a modicum of comfort in the consultation room. There were sessions during which he felt tranquil. He relaxed and stretched on the couch and enjoyed the temporary respite from tension. Sometimes he could sustain this freedom from agitation for as long as a week and a half. I noted that during such periods the rash completely disappeared and he no longer scratched. When the agitation returned, both the rash and the scratching would reappear. Simply by looking at his wrists before a session, I was able to predict his psychic state. Psychic equilibrium obviously had a neutralizing effect on whatever organic processes affected his skin. His bowel symptoms also disappeared during these periods of calm and he took some pride in the competence of his body. At the same time he became able to retain impressions in his mind, and he was reassured that he could learn in school. When his agitation returned, his somatic symptoms and inability to hold a mental representation were exacerbated.

After eighteen months of treatment, it occurred to me that the patient had not gone to Arizona for the hay fever season, as he had informed me in his first session he would. When I asked him about his allergy, he replied that for the first time since he had developed hay fever symptoms he had been entirely free of discomfort. This complete remission has persisted throughout the years.

The young man's agitation was all-pervasive. To contain it, to quiet his painful excitement, he masturbated frequently and took drugs. And yet he also sought situations that would create excitement. This had adaptive features but not in the usual sense. Usually when we speak of adaptation, we are referring to ego executive techniques designed to achieve equilibrium. In this instance, however, we seem to have a paradox. The excitement fills a void, an inner emptiness, and provides the patient a sense of existence, but it also represents a loss of equilibrium. I will return to this seeming paradox in the next section, when it becomes involved in the therapeutic process and produces disturbing countertransference reactions.

SPECIFIC TECHNICAL COMPLICATIONS

If we are really dealing with presymbiotic preverbal states, how can therapists expect to treat such patients in insight-oriented therapy? Much of the material presented by patients in treatment consists of thoughts, feelings, fantasies, and dreams, all couched in words and indicative of psychological processes. Since in the patients I am describing the verbal linkage has not yet occurred, we are confronted here with unique problems in the therapeutic interaction.

But though these technical problems are complex, they are not impossible. Despite these patients' early fixations, they still have many structured ways of relating available to them. In many, a considerable overlay of psychic structure is present, although others are fixated at primitive levels. Nevertheless, higher levels of psychic structure can become the vehicles by which earlier levels become involved in the treatment process. I will give an example of how a trauma occurring during a preverbal phase expressed itself in the transference interaction with an adult patient.

A middle-aged lady suddenly reported feeling warm. She felt as though she were sinking into the couch. It was slowly engulfing her, she said, and she began experiencing painful excitement. The initial feeling of warmth intensified so that it too was painful, and as she approached a state of frenzy her excitement culminated in an orgasm. Naturally, I was curious. I knew that she had a phobia of fires that could be explained in fairly conventional psychodynamic terms that are irrelevant for our purposes. I asked her if this experience had any specific antecedents.

The patient then told me about an accident that occurred when she was one month old. Her mother had misjudged the temperature of the bathwater and put her in a hot tub. The patient was scalded and required medical attention. Fortunately there were no residuals. She had been told about this event, but had not thought about it for years. It had never come up in her analysis.

I am not maintaining that this early trauma is of direct etiological significance in the production of the patient's orgasmic experience. To me and the patient it was simply an intriguing and useful connection. After I helped her bring the early event into focus with what had occurred on the couch, she was completely convinced that she had experienced in an erotically organized fashion a primeval terror that was depicted in an actual event. It was her conviction that I found most impressive. In any case, patients have methods available, techniques stemming from later developmental acquisitions, to communicate the impact and effects of early preverbal traumas.

In a similar fashion, other primitive parts of the psyche emerge during treatment, but they may cause confusion and in some instances lead to therapeutic impasses. There may perhaps be a natural reluctance for some therapists to become involved with early ego states, as they may have to reach into the deeper layers of their personality in order to achieve empathic understanding. Many authors have devoted themselves to this topic, Searles (1965a), Khan (1969), and Winnicott (1947) in particular. Often the therapist attempts to change frames of reference. The patient is reacting and feeling on one level and the therapist forces his interpretations and understanding to a higher level. This is tantamount to denying the archaic early elements of the personality, and the patient may react with despair. For his part, the therapist may sincerely believe that by focusing upon the patient's achievements and capabilities, he is offering hope and reassurance. Here patient and therapist are, in more than one sense, out of phase.

This is an easy dilemma to fall into, and in the treatment of some patients it may be inevitable. I am referring specifically to the therapist's being out of phase with the patient. This leads to special technical problems, as illustrated in the treatment of the following patient.

The patient, a young woman in her twenties, had succeeded in alienating four psychoanalysts. She was bitter about her experiences and felt exploited and victimized. She felt taken advantage of all of her life.

She is the daughter of wealthy suburbanites. Although her parents live under the same roof, they behave as though they are strangers to one another. The house is large enough so each has a separate apartment, and they have lived secluded from each other since she was six years old. At that time, her father attached himself to another woman and moved in with her to another house in the same suburb.

The patient was bitter about his deserting the family. She felt angry at the task that was suddenly imposed upon her, that of taking care of her mother. Her mother seems hypochondriacal, as evidenced by her many incapacitating illnesses for which no physical basis has ever been found. After her father's departure, the patient felt as though she had to wait upon the mother and manage the house even though she was only six years old. That is how she felt, although there were a maid and a houseman who must actually have looked after the house and her two brothers, one two years younger, the other two years older. The patient remembers that she felt responsibile for their care, especially that of the older brother, who had a "nervous breakdown" when the father left.

The patient visited her father and his paramour for several years, and believes that she finally persuaded him to return to the home, if not to his wife. Even after he returned, she felt she was in charge of the situation. She summarized her childhood as a period of life in which she had to look after everyone else's needs while no one acknowledged that she had any of her own. She could maintain a relationship with her father only by constantly chasing after him. Otherwise he would drift away and disappear. Her mother was "hopeless." The patient believed that she had to take over the maternal role toward both her mother and her siblings. The mother was depicted as being afraid of life: hypersensitive, withdrawn, and "afraid of everything." That is, the simplest, most pedestrian situations were transformed into crises. The patient felt she was constantly "bailing her out." In many ways, she became her mother's "pacifier," an ironic situation because she described herself as always being distraught. She could not concentrate and found school overwhelmingly difficult because she "had no memory." Unable to remain calm, she was also unable to learn.

Her agitation was all-pervasive. She was always on edge but not able to see any relationship between her inner feelings and the external situation. The same vagueness applied to her memory of the onset of these disturbed states. First she stated that they dated back to the age of six when her father left home, but this was amended during treatment to as far back as she could remember.

Shortly after menarche, at the age of twelve, she developed a rash on her chest as well as a low-grade fever ranging from

99.8 degrees to 101. The rash was correlated with her menses. It would appear seven to ten days before each period, but her temperature was always elevated. She had a complete medical work-up, a procedure that was repeated many times over as different medical specialists were consulted. Her diagnosis included such esoteric entities as periarteritis nodosa and toxoplasmosis. At one time the doctors considered the possibility of lupus erythematosis, but this entity was ruled out. In truth, there was no convincing explanation of her fever.

She was anxious to have therapy, but in view of her past experiences, she was wary. She wondered whether she was capable of being treated. Through her previous therapists, she had learned that her behavior did not make her a good candidate for psychoanalytic psychotherapy. For the last several years, the patient had been a heavy user of such drugs as marijuana, Quaaludes, barbiturates, and on rare occasions LSD. She seldom drank and was afraid of hard drugs such as heroin. Her sexual behavior, wildly promiscuous, had occasioned two pregnancies and two abortions.

During all her sessions of the first year of treatment, she was unrelenting in her criticism of me. Nothing about me or my office was right. If I coughed or moved in my chair, she would conjecture that I was bored with her or was concerned with some personal problem that caused me to feel anxious. I felt immobilized as she continued reviling me. Her anger filled the room. She was always scowling, and her tone of voice was harsh and shrill as she protested that I was useless and incapable of understanding her.

At first, I felt relatively comfortable since this form of relating by patients was not unfamiliar (Giovacchini 1975). I viewed her behavior as the outcome of projection of the hateful and vulnerable aspects of the self-representation. I had learned from experience with other patients that it was best to let her continue developing this projection before interpreting it. Interpretation would interfere with the process, and patients need the relief that the unburdening of these painful elements of the self affords them.

Later I learned that this patient did not experience relief. She viewed my silence as distance and, as she stated, she felt I was defensively drifting away from her. Her anger persisted and intensified, and I realized that I was becoming uncomfortable. I was aware of being agitated.

I finally interpreted to her that she had a need to put what she viewed as the bad parts of herself into me. Even as I was making this interpretation, I had the feeling I was wrong, not necessarily about the content of what I was saying but rather about my timing. My observation was directed more toward obtaining some relief from my discomfort than toward unambivalently understanding what was happening in the transference interaction. In any case, the patient let me know that I was wrong on all counts.

She insisted that I was "interpreting upward" and ignoring her basic needs, which she considered fundamental and primitive. She lamented that I did not really understand the depth of her misery and how intensely needful she felt. She increased her barrage of criticism and reviled me all the more, but instead of feeling hurt I began feeling more comfortable. In some mysterious way I regained my equanimity.

What now struck me as peculiar was that even though she accused me of being a bad analyst, withdrawn and unempathic, she in the same breath called me nonintrusive, warm, and objective. I was given the interesting impression that I did not understand and was not in touch with her feelings, and yet that at the same time I was being a good therapist. I then realized that I had been drawn into a repetition compulsion.

She was reliving with me early object relationships in which she had no security that anyone was relating to her on the basis of her needs or recognized that something inside of her was clamoring for emotional sustenance. Neither of her parents (she emphasized her father) had any intuitive feelings that she was needy. I in turn, by focusing upon the more structured aspects of her psyche—by "interpreting upwards," as she put it—was not in contact with the basic elements of her personality. Whatever these might be, the important factor was that I was not in intuitive resonance with her. I now realize, however, that this was a situation she created.

To be forced into the position of being nonintuitive creates countertransference difficulties. It is contrary to our professional ego ideal, which is predicated upon empathic understanding. Here I was faced with a situation where I should not interfere with the re-creation of infantile constellations, that is, where I should allow the transference to develop. In so doing, however, I was transformed into a withdrawn, insensitive, and nonintuitive person, clearly the opposite of how I like to view myself, especially when treating patients. This caused me to feel discomfort, and the patient's agitation was unabated. She was seriously thinking of discontinuing treatment.

Finally I saw the dilemma. I realized the importance of the role I had assumed for the patient. My being nonintuitive at one level was being intuitive at another. I was responding to the patient's expectations that I fail her, but she did not realize that it was intrinsic to the therapeutic process that she experience this expectation as fulfilled. I was able to point out this intuitive-nonintuitive paradox to her. I stressed the infantile parts of herself that were reaching out for sustenance and soothing, as well as how thwarted she felt in this desire. It was, I told her, a frustration and bitter disappointment that she had to live out with me. This time she listened and added that I had survived her anger, an anger that was in itself binding, that gave some organization to her agitated state and thereby had a calming effect.

She gave up drugs and her sexual behavior was almost chaste in comparison to what it had been, She responded to our sessions by feeling tranquil. She saw the consultation room as a place in which she could get relief from her agitation. At this point in treatment, all of her physical symptoms disappeared, including her premenstrual rashes. To me the most interesting finding was that for the first time in many years her temperature became normal.

As might be anticipated, her feeling of tranquility during sessions varied with the state of the transference. When she felt agitated, all her physical symptoms, including the fever, returned, whereas when she could obtain relief from inner disruptive feelings through the therapeutic reaction her temperature was normal and she felt generally well.

During a tranquil period she had the following dream. I was hypnotizing her. She went into a trance, but the trance had very special characteristics. In it, all her sensory modalities—visual, auditory, and tactile were mentioned—would stop functioning. This was experienced as peaceful. She felt absolutely nothing, a state of complete void characterized by a total absence of agitation. She was deaf and blind, but this was not frightening. I told her that the trance would last only a few hours and then sensations would return, but in a gradual fashion. Light would first be perceived in a filtered fashion, that is, she would begin by seeing dimly as if a low-wattage bulb were illuminating the scene. Then it would slowly increase in intensity until she could see in a normal fashion. The same sequence would occur with other sensory modalities. For example, the first sounds heard would be low in volume and then gradually become louder until they reached a comfortable level. She felt reassured and then awakened from the dream. It is an interesting aside that after this dream the patient's taste in music abruptly changed. No longer did she listen to loud rock and roll. She now preferred melodious classics and semiclassics.

Even now the patient would sometimes feel agitated; then, as stated, her physical symptoms, including the fever, would return. Most of the time, however, she could use the treatment relationship to soothe herself, to create a relative calm that was not always simply a quiet state. Often she felt considerable excitement, but now it was a comfortable and organized excitement.

The patient frequently commented on her ability to feel equilibrated and excited at the same time. Now she believed that her inner feelings had meaning and that I was capable of understanding them. *From a developmental viewpoint, the organization of feelings from a state of disruptive agitation to controlled excitement achieved psychological content for these feelings, a progression from a prementational to a mentational phase.*

This created a background which permitted therapy of a more conventional nature to continue. By more conventional I mean that she could now discuss her problems in terms of developmental vicissitudes and disturbed object relationships as these were recapitulated in the transference interaction.

Had I insisted upon viewing her agitation in terms of psychological content, had I not accepted the importance of being put in the position of a nonintuitive therapist, the transference-countertransference tension would probably have increased to the point of premature termination.

Because of the all-pervasive nature of her anger, the beginning phases of treatment were especially trying. I believe that her previous therapists stopped seeing her because they could not tolerate the discomfort she created. I know I often wished to dismiss her, but apparently I must have sensed how important it was for her to have a setting in which she could display such feelings. The fact that four other treatment situations had foundered encouraged me to adjust to her explosions, a tactic that proved to bind and organize her agitation.

Other feelings may also destroy the therapeutic relationship. For example, another patient, again a young woman in her twenties, had been involved with three therapists, each treatment ending badly. With each of them, she would sit in the office, smoking cigarettes and looking disdainful. All three therapists were male, and they admitted feeling agitated and uncomfortable because of sexual feelings toward her. The patient is pretty and somewhat provocative, but this alone does not explain the degree of discomfort these therapists felt. I had treated the patient's mother and therefore knew something of her background.

I will outline the bare essentials of the mother-daughter relationship. The mother sought therapy because she felt uncontrollable tension that could be relieved only with copious amounts of alcohol. Regarding her daughter, she once described to me how she would pick her up as an infant to feed her. Apparently she put her hands around the child's waist without any support for her head and back. Then she would swing her in a wide arc and literally shove the bottle in her daughter's face. She illustrated this in pantomime and at the same time hummed, as presumably she did to soothe her daughter. This humming sounded very much like wailing; I found it jarring rather than calming.

The daughter gained solace at noisy, smoked-filled discotheques. She could not be alone and always sought crowds, but she had practically no social relationships. Like her mother she was an alcoholic and drank continually throughout the day. She seemed anesthetized most of the time. She reported the following fantasy. She is sitting in a locked car illegally parked on ice in a lot adjacent to her high school. She is calmly smoking cigarettes while several policemen are hovering around her car, enraged because they are locked out and can not get to the patient.

This fantasy is clearly reminiscent of her therapeutic experiences. Unlike the policemen, her therapists were not enraged, but they were irritated because they felt blocked out and uncomfortably agitated because of their sexual arousal. This patient has others absorb her excitement and lived in paradoxes. She obtained comfort from the coldness of ice rather than from warmth, as depicted in the fantasy. Discordant noise soothed her. These reactions make sense when we recall how her mother related to her as an infant.

The mother fed her child, but the atmosphere in which nurturing occurred was turbulent. Instead of creating a calm, comfortable setting that would make the feeding experience pleasant, or at least equilibrated and modulated, one where mother and infant are in resonance with each other, she caused her child to feel painfully agitated. Being fed and being held should ideally be smoothly synchronized. With this patient, they were highly discordant. What should have been calming led to disruptive excitement, a situation I have referred to as *primal confusion.*

Her therapists felt confused. The patient's calmness as she sat coolly smoking cigarettes made them extremely uncomfortable. At first they felt irritated because they viewed her as being aloof and condescending. Their anger soon became erotized and they felt sexually attracted to her. Her most recent therapist was plagued with rape fantasies which he found so disturbing that he sought consultation and then terminated her treatment. The patient then moved to another city and married. Occasionally she comes to Chicago for a consultation with an older therapist, an experience she finds pleasant and sustaining.

The two young women I have just described highlight specific countertransference difficulties. Both employed affects to bind disruptive feelings of inner agitation. The first patient pervaded the consultation room with her anger. I finally absorbed her agitation, and she in turn achieved some equilibrium, some inner harmony. The second created an atmosphere that was a mixture of anger, manifested as condescending haughtiness, and erotic provocativeness. Her therapists absorbed her agitation, but in this case it was experienced in terms of sexual excitement. *The therapist's task is to survive the ambience the patient produces without being submerged by it.*

DISCUSSION

Prementational developmental phases become manifest in treatment if therapists do not interfere with their emergence.

These stages represent the most primitive levels of the psyche and can easily be overlooked in the treatment relationship. More accurately, they are not exactly overlooked; frequently they are misinterpreted in terms of higher psychic structures.

Work with these prementational stages requires that the therapist make contact with primitive parts of himself. Inasmuch as this might involve absorbing the patient's disruption, therapists may be reluctant to put up with such potentially painful ego states. Consequently, we can deny that anything occurs in treatment that can not be explained on the basis of intrapsychic factors, or decide that an insight-oriented therapy is not useful for these patients.

These patients, however, are frequently encountered. Early prementational phases become manifest during the transference regression of patients who have achieved high levels of development and fairly sophisticated adaptive techniques, but are characteristic also, as some of my clinical examples make clear, of primitively fixated psyches. It is possible to deal psychotherapeutically even with the more fixated group, provided we are aware of our countertransference responses.

Before enumerating the difficulties that typically arise, I wish to raise once again the question as to whether disruptive countertransference reactions are necessary to resolve the psychopathology inherent in primitive mental states. In the light of my clinical experience, the question is superfluous. I could not help feeling as I did. Still, since having worked with such phases in several patients, other patients prove less threatening. With experience, our being in resonance with the patient need not be unpleasant.

Nevertheless, there are special difficulties in the therapeutic relationship intrinsic to countertransference responses to prementational ego states. Frequently therapists view such patients as untreatable by any modality that depends upon the acquisition of insight into the transference interaction. This is sometimes done on the basis of diagnosis. The patient is given a label, such as borderline, schizoid, or even psychotic, that ipso facto precludes analysis. True, often enough such patients are in fact not amenable to analytic approaches; but many have been rejected who have eagerly sought such a relationship and who, although difficult patients, have proven treatable. The therapist's reluctance should therefore be examined and taken into account as well as diagnostic and prognostic considerations regarding the patient.

Other patients, those diagnosed as psychoneurotics, may also create problems, usually unanticipated. Again the therapist feels confused and agitated. For example, some obsessional and hysterical patients produce what seem insurmountable difficulties in treatment. Usually this has been explained as the outcome of incorrect diagnosis. Underneath a neurotic superstructure, it is argued, lies a psychotic core. This means that the therapist was mistaken in his choice of treatment and must abandon the analytic approach.

Many such patients have been able to reach back to prementational levels during the transference regression only to have their therapists react with specific countertransference difficulties that could have been resolved if understood. Undoubtedly there are many patients whose psychotic core is so rigidly fixed that the transference focus is too obscure to be used toward therapeutic resolution. On the other hand, some clinicians have had frequent experience with patients who have been rejected by other therapists for these very reasons, and who have nonetheless revealed prementational ego states that could be dealt with in the treatment interaction.

Still, no matter how much experience we as clinicians accumulate, there seem to be certain natural urges we have toward patients, primitively fixated patients in particular. We find the suffering of others painful and want to do something to alleviate it. Intellectually, we may realize that these tense states have to be lived through in treatment, but they are not at all easy to tolerate. Hopelessness in a physically healthy and often bright person is especially poignant.

Ostensibly to relieve the patient, but really to relieve ourselves, we attempt to reassure the patient that the situation is not hopeless. We refer to the adaptive elements in the patient's behavior and otherwise focus on higher psychic levels. This is interpreting upward, as my patient stressed, a procedure that introduces subtle complications in the therapeutic course. Such interpretations are effective only when directed to transference interactions in which early adaptive constellations are being reenacted. Their purpose is not to dispel states of painful agitation, nor are they effective when designed to reassure either patient or therapist.

Perhaps the most difficult factor in preventing ourselves from defensively retreating to higher levels is that we inadvertently, almost reflexively, slip into this pattern. We deceive ourselves into believing that we are relating to the patient in a nonanxious, calm, and objective manner. We view our emphasis on the hopeful aspects of the patient's personality as a synthesizing attitude that is an important constituent of the therapeutic ambience or holding environment (Winnicott 1955).

But often we are rationalizing when we couch our defensiveness in these professional formulations. This is particularly true when we are dealing with reactions to the anger and sexual provocativeness so commonly experienced in therapeutic relationships. I am again emphasizing the pervasive qualities of the affective climate these patients produce. It is difficult to keep in mind that often what is felt as destructive by the therapist is for the patient a binding, synthesizing, and often soothing experience. The patient may seem agitated, but the therapist's agitation is often greater. An affect has at least some structure and organization, certainly more so than the patient's otherwise unintegrated, disruptive perceptions. This situation causes even greater problems for the therapist, because, in contrast to the situation in which he interprets upward, here he misses the organizing qualities of what appears to be chaotic. In these instances, the therapist fails to recognize structure because the therapeutic relationship seems to point to primitive disintegration. He may then assess these patients as being so primitively fixated that they can not be treated in the transference context. We might consider this as an example of *interpreting downward.*

Occasionally the patient creates a paradox in the sense that Kumin (1979) describes. Kumin conjectures that the toleration of opposites, that is, of an unresolved paradox, is found in the mature ego. He is stressing a psychic area that does not strive toward synthesis. The agitated patient sometimes attempts to resolve the therapist's agitation while at the same time maintaining his own. The therapist who feels overwhelmed by synthesizing anger or sexual provocativeness may cause the patient to take countermeasures. The patient may wish to preserve the treatment and is impelled to do something to calm the therapist. Frequently this represents the repetition of an infantile relationship.

I recall a patient who first began treatment as an adolescent. She reported that one of her earliest memories, a traumatic memory, was of her mother waking up from nightmares. In her fright she turned to her young daughter for solace. The patient believes she was three years old at the time, perhaps younger, but her memory could not go any further back. The patient now resented this reversal of roles, a resentment manifested by tantrums and self-destructive behavior.

However, the reenactment in treatment of the patient's precocious soothing responsibilities led to an interesting and at first puzzling situation of a sort that I believe frequently occurs but often goes unrecognized. The patient would bring in material that was directed more to my interests than to hers, although she made them her interests. For instance, she would give me news, even gossip, about colleagues which was amusing. As she captured my interest, I could feel myself relaxing. I knew that I would not deal with the content of her material directly. I suppose I should have wondered more about her motivations for bringing it to me. Eventually she would become exasperated with herself because she was entertaining me. She was making me "feel good" whereas I should have been helping her. She reacted by feeling sad and agitated. We finally understood these elements of our relationship as a repetition of the reversal of roles that characterized her infancy.

She took this understanding into the external world, so to speak. She attached herself to an older woman and started looking after her. She learned that they could both of them survive dependency and enjoy it. She was able to achieve calm.

The paradoxical behavior of some patients may have a similar basis. We are often confronted with people frenetically involved in activities related to helping others. Whatever else such activity may signify, it often represents an attempt to establish equilibrium and harmony. One patient felt he had volcanoes erupting inside him, but he did not need an explosion, as we might expect if he were referring only to anger. Instead, the volcano had to be made extinct. It is striking how helpful and sympathetic these patients can be to others and yet themselves be so obviously needy.

My patient's relationship with a maternal woman was in the service of therapeutic resolution. It was an attempt at working through. Similar patients report experiences which indicate that they are attempting to re-create childhood experiences in which they had to soothe their parents instead of being soothed themselves. Too often this group develops manifest psychopathology even in the presence of these attempts at re-creation. The patients I have seen indicate that these experiences are not sufficient. They have not been able to work through the traumatic effects of their early experiences by repeating them. They had first to be experienced in the transference.

Apparently, agitated patients have to realign the tempos of their relationships—that is, they have to modulate their sensory input. Perceptions have to be toned down sufficiently to be integrated. Being able to soothe the therapist and to survive the experience produces a benign ambience characterized by calm rather than turbulence. Patients indicate the need for these transference interactions in their dreams and fantasies.

I have already mentioned the dream in which a patient dreamt I was hypnotizing her. Another patient had a fantasy of being submerged in water. This was a situation of complete sensory deprivation, in exactly the same fashion as in actual experiments. He first felt threatened by the feeling of complete isolation, but then, unlike what actually happens in the laboratory, he found this state of insensibility quite pleasant. This was due to the further elaboration of the fantasy, in which he had himself slowly brought back into the sensory world. As with other patients, the emphasis was on the gradual reintroduction of stimuli.

These clinical situations are examples of a structural inability to organize and integrate stimuli. This primitive, defective functioning is the outcome of primal confusion. These patients who were nurtured in an environment that could not soothe them found no relief from their inner excitation.

If we keep in mind the division of the neonatal environment into two components, holding and nurturing, then it becomes obvious how important it is for the developing infant that they are in synchrony. The feeding experience should be soothing. Not only does the nurturing substance, the milk, alleviate the internal hunger pangs, but the mother's calming influence, her holding, protects the infant from any impingements from the external world. This combination leads to true satisfaction.

The psychopathology I have been examining is precisely the outcome of a lack of synchrony between these components. The child is nurtured and hunger is satiated, but because the mother, instead of providing a stimulus barrier, has herself been an irritating stimulus, there has been no reestablishment of psychic equilibrium. What should have been calming is perceived as internally disruptive, and here we have the anlage of confusion.

This primal confusion has dramatic effects later in life. A calming environment, since it has never coexisted with nurture, is experienced as disruptive or discordant. If these patients feel internal agitation, responding with external soothing only increases the disruption. What allows them some degree of equilibrium is a jarring, discordant environment similar to what they knew in infancy in the nurturing situation. While to the observer this hardly seems to be equilibrium at all, still these patients do sometimes manage to acquire a degree of calm in chaotic circumstances, an achievement that to us seems incomprehensible. They experience in the present discord a resonance with the earlier one, a paradoxical "harmony" based on a primal confusion.

SUMMARY AND CONCLUSIONS

As we follow the transference regressions of these seemingly incomprehensible patients, we reach ego states that are mainly prementational in character, that is, they have minimal psychological content. The patient brings considerable tension and agitation into the consultation room while at the same time preventing the therapist from making contact with him. This often becomes an extraordinary situation in which the patient wants to get in touch with the primitive elements of his psyche.

The analyst wants to form a meaningful bond with the patient, but more often than not both patient and analyst feel they have failed miserably. The patient is unable to get through to the therapist, who in turn feels frustrated because he can not see what the patient is so desperately trying to show him.

Inasmuch as we are trained to view clinical phenomena in

terms of psychic determinism, we are impelled to interpret these agitated states as the outcome of intrapsychic forces, forces that can be put in a psychological context. The patient insists that we "are trying to make sense out of something that does not make sense." The therapist, by "interpreting upwards," misses essential primitive elements, and consequently the patient feels misunderstood.

Patient and therapist do not communicate with each other; their mode of relating is discordant. The patient experiences the therapist as nonempathic. What is frequently overlooked is that this treatment impasse is a necessary part of the therapeutic process. The treatment is recapitulating early failures in which the nurturing relationship was discordant, in which maternal responses were not in intuitive resonance with the infant's needs for both nurture and soothing. These failures led to a state of primal confusion.

Countertransference factors gain further prominence as the patient uses affects to control painful agitation. An affect has some degree of psychic organization and is usually directed toward an external object or situation. I have given examples in which anger, as an affect, is used to bind, to achieve some cohesion of otherwise unorganized tension. The patient's anger pervades the consultation room, and this may lead to countertransference problems. The therapist unknowingly absorbs the patient's agitation and finds himself succumbing to the engulfing anger. He finds it difficult to survive.

This devastating situation threatens the therapist's professional ego ideal. Everything he does seems to be wrong, and he is made to feel as if he understands nothing. This is significantly different from situations in which patients project the devalued and hated parts of the self "into" the analyst. This can be understood as a valuable adaptation and promotes the further unfolding of the transference. With the agitated patient, by contrast, neither patient nor analyst obtains any relief. The therapist continues being uncomfortable, as he feels himself out of resonance with the patient.

Sexuality, as a binding force, can be used similarly. Again this leads to disruptions, as the therapist's sexual excitation interferes with therapeutic calm and objectivity. Here too the therapist's ego ideal is threatened, as he believes he is more concerned with his own needs than with the patient's. In both instances, that is, whether the therapist feels inundated by anger or sexually stimulated, the treatment relationship recapitulates the infantile environment of early maternal failure.

Recognition of the treatment as a re-creation, through the repetition compulsion, of the generally traumatic infancy can become a turning point. This insight calms the therapist as he regains a therapeutic perspective and realizes how important it is to survive anger and accept the role of being nonintuitive. The therapist continues to absorb the patient's agitation, but now he can calm himself. *By so doing, he also soothes the patient.*

Initial prementational agitation now acquires psychological content. The soothing experience becomes organizing, and disruptive stimuli can be integrated within the psyche. Mahler (Mahler, Pine, and Bergman 1975) discusses similar processes as they occur in the subphases of separation-individuation. I am describing much earlier ego states and am emphasizing that later experiences associated with psychological content become associated with the newly acquired organization that is the consequence of the soothing experience.

More is involved in the acquisition of psychic structure than the patient's agitation being absorbed. This is important, but equally important is the re-creation during treatment of the early nonempathic environment. The quality of traumatic infancy emerges, as was demonstrated by my patient who reported nearly drowning in the pond. Even if this incident had not actually happened, he demonstrated his vulnerability in my office as he thrashed on the floor, and I responded with the same helplessness and ineptness his parents must always have felt.

Therapists are becoming increasingly aware of the influence of early developmental phases on later stages and their importance in determining the course of the therapeutic interaction. Many patients appeal to us to get in touch with the primitive elements of their psyche. They know, unconsciously or otherwise, that if these prementational agitated states are not dealt with in treatment, they will not be able to achieve a synthesis that will allow them autonomy, and that will shape their basic and fundamental humanity.

Epilogue

Peter L. Giovacchini

The examination of clinical phenomena leads to many interesting ramifications that, when viewed from an historical perspecitve, enable the investigator to form a dim awareness of future developments. Here we hope to indicate a direction that will extend our concepts of what is considered psychoanalytically treatable. The usual clichés of fragile ego, shaky defenses, psychotic core, among others, need to be seen in another perspective, primarily an ego-psychological one. What have been considered contraindications could be the most important factors that, in some instances, make analysis mandatory.

THE EXTENSION OF PSYCHOANALYTIC PRINCIPLES

What is being proposed may at first seem to upset and contradict well-established principles. This is certainly not our purpose; the fundamental tenets of psychoanalysis, I believe, are strengthened rather than modified or undermined by our study of characterological problems. In fact, the thesis of this book emphasizes the use of the classical approach instead of introducing changes that are purportedly necessary because this group of patients may "decompensate" if analysis is attempted. Here the theoretical basis of the psychoanalytic process has to be understood in the context of an ego-psychological focus.

In the classroom the student may complain that principles,

as those discussed here, are the antithesis of everything they have been taught. Even though this is an overstatement, the fact that they are confused is obvious. They feel the same way I once did when at a psychoanalytic meeting the principal speaker presented his thesis in a logically sound, convincing fashion. The formal discussant then proceeded to present an opposite hypothesis in an equally coherent rational fashion, so at the end of the evening I had the feeling they were both correct.

Returning to our hypotheses, we can understand that a person who has been taught the distinctions between the transference and narcissistic neuroses and the therapeutic limitations of the latter might feel that we are being iconoclastic, at least from a theoretical perspective. Our residents show their discomfort when faced with a dilemma that overstrains their tolerance for ambiguity.

Such ambiguities, however, are not uncommon as scientific investigation progresses. Sometimes antithetic concepts are the outcome of the particular observational frame. Classical Newtonian concepts have been "contradicted" by both relativity physics and quantum mechanics. Physicists, especially in the earlier part of this century, found these theoretical disagreements exciting as well as perplexing. The scientific atmosphere was highly charged and characterized by enthusiasm. Ambiguity had its advantages and became an incentive for scientific progress.

The new concepts and the older physics are not mutually exclusive. It depends upon what part of the field is being examined, where in the spectrum between the infinitesimal and the infinite our attention is directed. Certain experiments indicate that light is corpuscular (matter) and others that it is a wave. Absolute time and space are concepts that are relevant to ordinary movement, whereas they do not apply to speeds that approach that of light. In spite of such incompatibilities, theoretical integrations follow that are able to include these seemingly disparate constructs and phenomena.

Here we are proposing an extension of the psychoanalytic method to patients who, according to psychoanalytic theory, cannot be so treated. Rather than being iconoclastic, as discussed above, such a proposal may cause one to feel that we are being more Catholic than the Pope, or it has been thought of as representing a reactionary position opposed to innovation and experimentation with new treatment approaches. But to use the psychoanalytic method where it has been previously believed to be inapplicable in itself represents an advance. Since this procedure would be in conflict with the existing theory, theoretical modifications and integrations are required. Ego psychology furnishes us with an observational approach that is particularly pertinent to the study of patients with characterological problems, whereas concentration upon the id and psychodynamic factors has greater explanatory significance for the psychoneuroses. Each approach complements the other, and the inclusion of character structure and ego mechanisms as well as conflictful forces between the ego and the id adds dimensions to our concepts of psychopathology that cause us to extend our concepts about the applicability, as well as the theoretical basis, of the psychoanalytic process.

Psychoanalysis is ready for an examination of its theoretical edifice. There is no danger that basic foundations will have to be rebuilt. Freud was too deterministically minded and too skillful a scientist to rest his system on flimsy assumptions based upon ad hoc reasoning. Revisions of later accretions, however, have been formulated gradually during the last fifty years, the main revisionist being Freud himself.

If students can be faced with contradictory statements that seem to have considerable merit, then we should recognize that we are living in exciting times. There is no harm in being confused as long as we are not dismayed. The interest that has been shown in the ideas in this book indicates that there are many analysts who share our enthusiasm, not necessarily accepting our ideas in toto but agreeing that there are questions to be asked and problems to be delved into. The subject of the treatment of characterological and schizophrenic disorders is far from closed.

THE LIMITATIONS OF THE PHENOMENOLOGICAL APPROACH

As Boyer and I have emphasized, a phenomenological approach to clinical problems limits one's appraisal of therapeutic possibilities. When Freud concentrated on intrapsychic processes rather than upon nosological classifications, he was more optimistic about the efficacy of the psychoanalytic procedure. General psychiatry had erected diagnostic categories, systems of classification, that were based almost exclusively on observable behavior and the patient's mental status. Freud's unique contribution was to understand the purpose of the patient's behavior in terms of unconscious motivation rather than simply categorizing. As a consequence he was able logically to extend his formulations to a theoretically plausible treatment method. Although diagnosis was only of minor importance, Freud later believed that his method was especially suited for the psychoneuroses, the transference neuroses, which he distinguished from the narcissistic neuroses, a group that included the psychoses and patients that today have been referred to as character disorders.

If the difference between the transference neuroses and the narcissistic neuroses is that the latter do not form transferences either when psychoanalytic treatment is attempted or in their mode of relating to objects in general, then such a distinction is not valid. Many analysts have reported and documented intense transferences in psychotic and borderline states, patients that would be definitely considered to be examples of narcissistic neuroses. If the existence of transference is to be the criterion that separates these two groups, then there is no advantage in designating one group the narcissistic neuroses. These patients may have unique types of transferences, but this does not vitiate against the possibility that their transference neuroses or psychoses can eventually be resolved. The concept of transference also has to be clarified (see below).

The contributors to this book have found that most of their patients have had characterological problems and did not fit the psychodynamic mold of the psychoneuroses as described in the early literature. True, their problems could be viewed from a psychodynamic perspective but, as reviewed in previous chapters, their difficulties could best be understood in terms of ego defects involving the identity sense and perceptual and executive ego systems. Insofar as we seldom saw a patient who could be formulated in terms similar to those outlined by Freud, the question as to whether the "classical" psychoneurotic patient existed or just how frequently one encountered such a patient had to be asked. Frequently the course of therapy reveals that what seems to be a psychoneurosis primarily based upon an oedipal conflict masks underlying primitive pregenital problems and ego defects. One cannot come to any definite conclusions, but this book raises the question as to whether psychopathology has been modified, perhaps because of cultural changes, or whether our further understanding of transference phenomena, because of insights gained from the structural theory and ego psychology, has enabled us to see aspects of psychopathology that were not previously apparent.

Our initial chapters (Boyer) are clinical, but the interplay of a structural theoretical approach, an ego-psychological perspective, and the patient's behavior is constantly stressed. The model that is worked out later is one that emphasizes a hierarchically ordered psychic apparatus

THE CYLINDER MODEL OF THE MIND: A STRUCTURAL HIERARCHY

In order to stress structural differentiation, I have constructed a model, purely for classroom exposition, called the "cylinder" model. The geometric figure of the cylinder is apt because it is three dimensional, and one can view a psychic state in terms of both breadth and depth.

As many others have stressed, the organism can be conceptualized as consisting of numerous levels beginning roughly with the molecular and after traversing through various physiological systems of increasing complexity (biochemical, cellular, hormonal, organ, organ system, etc.) finally merging with psychological systems. The latter are our primary interest and can also be arranged in an order of increasing complexity, one end of the spectrum consisting of a relatively undifferentiated id and the other end containing various ego systems that are involved in reality-attuned, secondary-process appraisal and behavior, which may include consciousness. The bottom part of the cylinder represents the undifferentiated (psychologically) end of our spectrum, whereas the uppermost part refers to integrative and synthetic ego functions, both perceptual and motor. The only reason for viewing what is essentially a serial hierarchy as a cylinder is that one can vary its height and width, emphasizing that any psychic element has varying degrees of primary- and secondary-process elements. For example, a psychic state may be characterized by a preponderance of primary process, the upper part of the cylinder being relatively small. This would, of course, represent psychopathology, whereas a cylinder where there is a minimum of primary-process elements may represent a well-functioning ego but possibly a constricted one. Defenses also have relative amounts of primary- and secondary-process operations.

In Figure 2 one might be describing a person who has a rigid hold on reality but no flexibility. He has strong restrictions

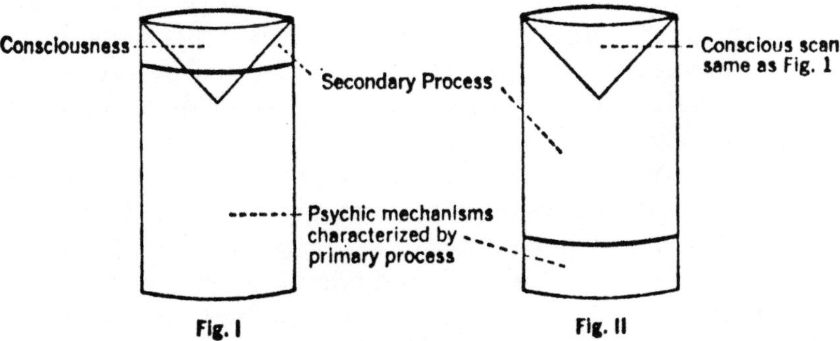
Consciousness
Secondary Process
Psychic mechanisms
characterized by
primary process
Conscious scan
same as Fig. 1

Fig. I

Fig. II

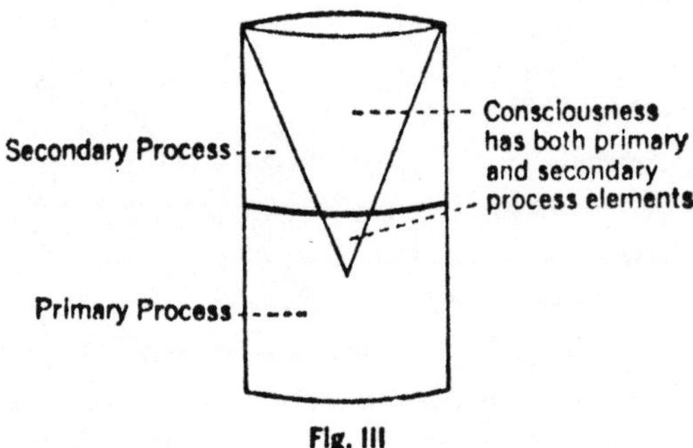
Secondary Process
Primary Process
Consciousness
has both primary
and secondary
process elements

Fig. III

that are the outcome of intense repression and a lack of primary-process mobility. Figure 1 might depict a schizophrenic patient or a person who has regressed and decompensated. A well-functioning, expansive, flexible psyche is characterized by a balance of primary-process and secondary-process forces. In terms of the cylinder, it would be longer and wider and the span of consciousness would plunge deeper (Figure 3).

Any psychic element can be considered in terms of such a structural and functional hierarchy. Ego states, drives, as well as the patient's behavior and associations, can be examined from the viewpoint of this model.

By stressing a structural hierarchy, the hydrodynamic energy theory and the concept of discharge are not needed when describing the satisfaction of an instinctual need. Needs traverse the psyche from the bottom of the cylinder to the uppermost layers. In so doing they acquire greater structure as they gain further psychological components and mental representation. Needs, therefore, can also be thought of in terms of a structural hierarchy and as containing varying degrees of development. Chapter 6 discussed the development spectrum of dependent needs and how a particular ego state requires a characteristic mode of gratification.

The organism, because of an anabolic-metabolic rhythmicity, as well as external stimuli, becomes aware of a homeostatic disturbance that affects various physiological systems. The cylinder model, which adapts itself to a stimulus-response sequence, can depict such a homeostatic disturbance as affecting psychic as well as physiological systems. When describing an impulse traversing through layers of increasing complexity, one is speaking metaphorically. A homeostatic imbalance does not create an impulse that then travels through various layers of the psychic apparatus and finally is discharged in conscious action. A physiological imbalance sets off a variety of responses that also impinge on sensory systems, causing conscious awareness and responses by the ego's integrative, synthetic, and executive systems. In other words, such a need makes itself felt at all levels, from the physiological to the psychological. Any psychic construct can be looked upon from different frames of reference, from the molecular, so to speak, to psychological approaches. The latter can be further subdivided, and a person's behavior, free associations, symptoms, general adaptation, and the like, can be considered in terms of its id component or its ego factor. Within the ego sphere, defensive, integrative, and adaptive mechanisms might be stressed. None of these approaches are mutually exclusive; the clinician may choose to focus upon one particular level because he believes it will lead to therapeutic benefit. On another occasion he may find it necessary to focus upon a different level as there are shifts in the transference neurosis and the ego state.

With severe psychopathology, as the cylinder model depicts, a psychic element may have led primarily to the activation of the primitive aspects of the mental apparatus and not have involved the so-called higher ego systems. In characterological disorders and schizophrenic states these systems are only minimally developed, and the range of development of any psychic element, including instinctual needs, is narrow and constricted. There are limitations of structural and functional differentiation in these clinical entities.

Terms such as *primitive and advanced* or *higher and lower* are imprecise and used loosely. There are, nevertheless, some advantages in considering the psychic apparatus as containing primitive elements that are contrasted to reality-attuned secondary-process mechanisms. The former refer to structures and functions that are characteristic of early developmental phases, although in the neuroses and psychoses they have become pathologically distorted. Similarly in the somatic sphere some systems, based on embryological development and function, are considered as being less differentiated than certain highly specialized groups of cells, for example, such as those found in the central nervous system.

Returning to clinical problems, the patient's maladaptations reflect characterological problems when the psychic apparatus is seen in terms of the above model, insofar as it stresses a structural and functional hierarchy. Boyer (chapter 3) quotes various authors who have reviewed Freud's cases and other patients who have been considered from a psychodynamic viewpoint and who, as discussed above, have been found to be narcissistically fixated and, at times, phenomenologically psychotic. In fact, some British analysts believe that most if not all psychopathology has to be explained in terms of a basic psychotic core, neurotic defenses being only a surface superstructure.

The above may be an overstatement, but overstatements tempered with moderation can sometimes have merit. Rather than making sweeping generalizations about clinical entities, we might be prudent to study our patients without preconceived judgments about psychopathology. This also means that we must not take for granted that the patient's problem is a regression from a primarily oedipal conflict. The psychodynamic approach continues to be valuable, but the ego apparatus has to be also included in our appraisal (a characterological approach).

TREATABILITY AND TRANSFERENCE

Regardless of our ultimate conclusions about psychopathology, the pragmatic question about treatability inevitably arises. Can we reconcile our theoretical formulations about characterological defects with metapsychological aspects of the treatment process? Several chapters in this book express the opinion that we can, and this question is discussed from various perspectives.

Any discussion of treatability must review the concept of transference. Freud's recognition of transference phenomena was undoubtedly one of the most significant and valuable discoveries about the psychotherapeutic interaction. Transference occurs in many object relationships, but in psychoanalysis it is our point of greatest resistance and yet our most powerful therapeutic tool. Therefore the transference reaction has to be examined further in patients suffering from characterological and schizophrenic disorders over and above the question as to whether it does or does not occur.

If the transference neurosis is defined as the projection of impulses characteristic of the oedipal phase onto the analyst, then the cases discussed here obviously do not form transference neuroses. Similarly if the concept of transference requires that intrapsychic elements are exclusively projected onto the analyst, our patients do not fulfill this condition either.

Freud and his early followers considered transference as the projection of an infantile imago. Granted that it may be advisable to distinguish between transference, transference neurosis, and transference reaction, our concern now is whether some relationship toward the analyst exists and whether it can become therapeutically useful.

The patient's early object relationships are important determinants regarding the establishment and the course of the relationship with the analyst. The study of object relations are an aspect of ego psychology that has led to valuable insights about psychopathology as well as emotional development.

Since the formulation of the structural theory there has been a tendency to put the external nurturing source in its proper place, developmentally and defensively. The external object and its internal representation is not in early stages of emotional development perceived in its totality, that is, as a whole object. Most psychoanalysts accept the thesis that there is a gradual progression from viewing objects as part objects to whole objects.

If transference is defined as the projection of an archaic imago, then one is referring to the projection of a part object.

Freud also drew a continuum of object relations from autoerotic preobject states to narcissistic object choices, and finally to relationships with external objects.

The schizophrenic patient is narcissistically fixated. Consequently one would expect him, in treatment or with persons in general, to relate to objects on the basis of a narcissistic object choice. Can a narcissistic object choice lead to a therapeutically useful transference relationship?

Some analysts believe that a patient who relates to the outer world primarily on a narcissistic basis does not form transference relationships. But the concept of the archaic imago does not restrict how archaic the imago might be. If the patient relates to the analyst as if the latter were an extension of himself, this still represents the projection of a primitive self-representation, which consists of introjects of early objects, usually destructive, assaultive part objects. In addition to the projection of these early self-object fusions there have been innumerable revisions of these introjects due to later experiences and relationships that are also projected.

The narcissistic transference relationship involves a fusion of the patient with the analyst, which can strengthen delusions of omnipotence, or if the patient is able to differentiate himself from what he has projected onto the analyst, he may be able to synthesize fragmented parts of the self, parts that had not achieved cohesiveness and unity because of nonfunctional, destructive introjects. The latter are impediments to psychic development that when projected onto the analyst may permit the release of a previously submerged developmental potential. Of course there are many factors that contribute to therapeutic integration. For the moment the point is being stressed that the projection of archaic part objects may lead to a therapeutically useful transference relationship.

Some analysts believe that transference reactions have to be directed exclusively toward the analyst. If the patient projects elsewhere, then one does not have an analytic relationship. The neurotic conflicts with the outer world are replaced by a transference neurosis where the analyst becomes the recipient of infantile impulses. Other persons become less important, and the patient's problems are fairly well contained in the consulting room. If he expresses his conflicts in his everyday life, he is acting out and being resistant to analysis.

The exclusive projection of infantile impulses onto the analyst represents an ideal therapeutic situation, one that never occurs initially in patients suffering from characterological defects. I doubt that it occurs spontaneously with any patient. Insofar as transference for patients suffering from severe psychopathology consists of the reliving of part-object relationships, it is plausible that they fragment their object relationships. Different feelings are not directed toward one object since the regression that is further stimulated by analysis leads to an ego state that has not fully attained the capacity to experience diverse feelings toward the same object. The patient's psychopathology is manifested in object relationships that are in some instances not sufficiently structured to achieve the synthesis that is the outcome of ambivalence. When the patient is able to project both sides of the conflict onto the same person, he has made considerable progress. However, one cannot expect the patient to behave in a fashion that is beyond his emotional capacity. Such behavior is a goal of treatment and not a precondition.

The inability to relate to persons as whole objects and the fragmentation of the transference has been considered a contraindication to analysis. Therapy is designed to support defenses and is supposed to have an educative influence. Frequently, however, the therapist moralizes against symptoms, exhorting the patient to give them up. The fact that they have adaptive significance and are of value to the patient seems to be ignored. Similarly, transference is not allowed to unfold spontaneously. The therapist encourages the patient to repress the negative transference. The projection of destructive introjects onto the therapist is implicitly discouraged.

We have stressed the complications that often occur when the therapist's desire to support defenses is misconstrued as omnipotence by the patient. Unimpeded transference often assigns omnipotence to the analyst; to attempt to support the patient may reinforce this spontaneous tendency and lead to ego disruption. The negative transference, on the other hand, can also cause considerable discomfort and provoke unpleasant countertransference attitudes.

Manipulation by the therapist distorts the transference insofar as deliberate role playing cathects infantile imagos that would probably not have been projected without the analyst's intervention. Mirror-like anonymity, for the patients as sensitive as those described here, can be misconstrued as rejection and coldness and create a tense and inhibited atmosphere. Where does one draw the line? Can the analyst be comfortable and natural and still not intrude his personality so that the transference can spontaneously develop?

THE ANALYTIC INTROJECT AND ANALYTIC INTENT

There is no clear-cut answer to this question. The individual style and personality of the analyst is important, and years of experience with patients as well as other factors "teach" the analyst to be comfortable with his patients. The analyst, of course, has to be comfortable in his role as analyst. He is dedicated to analysis and all his conduct is guided by an analytic intent conveyed to the patient from the first interview. Eventually a situation of nonanxious calm occurs, one that fosters introspection and understanding.

Again one can not outline precisely how this self-observational attitude is fostered. The patient's regressed ego often reverts to primitive modes of adaptation. Introjection as well as projection are characteristic techniques of early developmental phases, phases that are relived in the transference relationship. Insofar as destructive introjects can be projected onto the therapist, the ego becomes relatively unimpeded in the introjection of new imagos. During the course of analysis (usually very early) the patient perceives the analyst's nonanxious observational attitude. Even though regressed, he is able to some extent to incorporate this attitude and establish what I have referred to as the *analytic introject.* This is similar to such recent concepts as the therapeutic or working alliance, but I prefer emphasizing the structural and object relationship qualities of the analytic interaction. An alliance refers also to object relationships, but besides interpersonal factors, the concept of an introject has advantages. The formation of such an introject is a continuing process, and its "absorption" (internalization) into perceptual, integrative, and even executive systems is the outcome of successful analysis. There is an analytic progression from superficial imitation of the analytic attitude, to the discrete formation of an analytic introject, and finally to the amalgamation of an introspective, self-observing, understanding attitude into all ego systems. The latter extends the patient's perceptual sensitivities and his object relationships may become warmer and empathic.

Analytic intent is conveyed to the patient, and a person suffering from characterological problems gains considerable reassurance to have someone whose exclusive interest is focused upon him. As long as the analyst maintains his analytic intent, the fact that he is a human being in other respects, too, will not interfere with the course of analysis. The question of mirrorlike anonymity is not relevant. The analyst can reveal many aspects of his personality because not to do so would create an artificially strained atmosphere. From the analyst's viewpoint mirrorlike anonymity would be role playing and would constrict his analytic mobility. As long as his "analytic personality" is dominant, other aspects of his emotional makeup will not interfere with his availability for transference projection.

Freud provides us with an excellent example of where he related to his patient (Rat Man) in a nonanalytic fashion, and yet this did not seriously interfere with the course of analysis. Dr. Jerome Beigler, at a seminar, called our attention to Freud's therapy notes on the Rat Man. On one occasion his patient began his session by telling Freud that he was hungry, whereupon Freud gave him something to eat. The ensuing discussion was lively and opinions were divided. Some believed that Freud introduced a parameter, stepping out of the analytic role by attempting to gratify his patient's wishes. The next few treatment hours were characterized by omnipotence; some of the group maintained this was an artifact stimulated by Freud's response, which caused the patient to believe in the omnipotence of his wishes. Even though the patient had such an omnipotent attitude about himself anyway, Freud's response supposedly brought it to the surface prematurely, before it could be subjected to analytic integration.

Other members of the group had different ideas. For Freud not to feed a hungry man would have been out of character. Those more familiar with the middle-European attitude about eating pointed out that it is quite natural to offer food, a small courtesy that is not particularly meaningful. Their final conclusion was that as long as Freud had no therapeutic purpose in feeding his patient, then it would not interfere with the course of analysis. He was not role playing, and therefore he could keep separate one aspect of his personality from his analytic intent.

I do not know which of the points made at this seminar is more correct. However, the latter principle is apt and applicable especially to the treatment of patients suffering from severe psychopathology. Insofar as their egos are not well structured and their sense of discrimination poorly developed, they have difficulty in that they confuse the multiple facets of the analyst's personality with each other. A well-developed ego, because of its better ability to differentiate, would be less apt to confuse the analyst as analyst with other levels of his personality. This leads us to formulate one of the antithetical conclusions mentioned at the beginning of the Epilogue. Patients suffering from characterological and schizophrenic disorders, if in any way therapeutically accessible, cannot tolerate a nonanalytic approach. To deviate from analysis may cause complications that vitiate against the possiblity of progressive character change. This does not mean that there are not many nonanalytic therapeutic interactions where the patient has benefited considerably. In these instances there may be symptomatic improvement, and the patient to a large measure may become socially rehabilitated. However, there is seldom much character change, and the patient-therapist relationship sometimes is maintained on the basis of a delusional belief in the therapist's omnipotence. Such a relationship may be stabilizing, but it is also precarious. Stepping outside the analytic role in this group of patients is a frequent source of decompensation. Many suicides have occurred because the analyst in his eagerness (and anxiety) to save and rescue the patient has unwittingly promised the patient omnipotence, a promise that eventually led to bitter disappointment, a repetition of innumerable childhood traumas.

THE INFANTILE PAST, PROJECTION AND EXTERNALIZATION

The traumatic aspects of the past are reflected in the transference, and as they become the dominant transference theme, the therapist may lose sight of the fact that he is dealing with transference phenomena. Some patients need to construct a personal universe that is similar to the frustrating, traumatic one of childhood. This need is defensive and may contain masochistic elements, but it is also vital for the total equilibrium. All defenses, to some extent, require some aspect of the environment to support them. There has to be some ego-outer world syntonicity to maintain the defense. What is being described is different in that the need for general psychic equilibrium goes beyond being congruent with a relatively structured defense such as masochism. The patient externalizes adaptive mechanisms and requires an outer world that he has learned to cope with. He does not have adjustive techniques that can deal with a relatively benign nonfrustrating world. All he has known is a depriving assaultive environment, and he has learned to survive at a primitive level that is in resonance with such surroundings.

This constellation has to be recognized especially because of its implications for the transference. The patient attempts to convert the analyst into the same frustrating environment he knew in childhood. Can this be considered transference? Anna Freud distinguishes between this process, which is called externalization, and transference.

I believe two points have to be briefly clarified: (1) the relationship between externalization and the defensive mechanism of projection, and (2) the above question regarding the distinction between this process and transference. Concerning projection, one usually limits this mechanism to attributing impulses, affects, and some aspects of psychic structure such as self- and object-representations to some external objects. Externalization is distinguished in that it is considered to be the projection of psychic mechanisms such as the controlling aspects of the superego, the patient constructing a critical prohibitive environment. Similarly, if an important adjustive mode is repression, the patient may attempt to relate to repressive segments of his environment. These distinctions become important as we examine the concept of transference. If the environment has to be constructed in a particular fashion so the ego can maintain itself, it is not surprising that the patient would attempt to convert the analytic situation into a familiar one with which he can cope. Making the analyst into a replica of the early environment and the projection of archaic imagos are related activities. An object, whether part or whole, internal or external, is never an isolated entity; it is always in an environmental context. When the child introjects, he not only internalizes a person but also incorporates the setting that is characteristic of the object. Conversely, when later in life the object is projected onto the analyst, the setting is an important aspect of this projection. There is no advantage in designating the projection of the object artificially separated from its setting as transference. The internal object in its adaptive or disruptive setting is a fundamental mechanism that determines the ego's adjustment. The object plus the setting constitute a gestalt that is projected onto the therapist. In the character disorders the fact that the assaultive setting is emphasized rather than a discrete object does not require that we modify our views about transference. Somewhere in the setting one will eventually find an archaic imago, which in schizophrenic patients is often represented as an environmental element, such as water, sun, the wind, storms, and the like. In any case, as long as we view all the patient's reactions as transference, the therapist continues the analytic interaction.

The above implies that, among other factors, transference *is a point of view.* All the patient's productions contain transference elements or defenses against these elements. Any relationship as previously discussed can be understood in terms of a structural hierarchy. The perceptual system, as well as other ego systems, functions on the basis of a broad spectrum with admixtures of primary- and secondary-process types of operations. Its range of perception includes viewing external objects in a reality-oriented, coherent fashion with an accurate appraisal of their role in a contemporary setting, to distorted impressions based upon a confusion with objects of the infantile past. These distortions are the essence of transference. Insofar as introjects affect the functioning of all ego systems, including perception, some aspect of our impressions about contemporary persons will be determined by these early introjects. The archaic imago will cause distortions of what we perceive and then will also contribute to our reactions to the external world. The contribution, both perceptual and motor, may be minimal. It may also apply to other persons besides the analyst. Nevertheless, in all behavior there is a transference element.

THE CREATION OF TRANSFERENCE

The analyst orients himself around these transference elements no matter how minimal or diffuse they may be. By constantly relating to how the patient's mind works, by being dedicated to understanding what is going on inside the patient, the analyst is fostering the development of transference. The analytic situation, because of its constant reliability, is conducive to regression. The regressed ego is less structured, and infantile introjects become highly cathected. Consequently, in a sense the analyst has helped create the transference. Minimal transference elements receive impetus from regression and the analyst's fostering of introspection. The patient's relationship to the therapist may at first contain only a small "percentage" of transference but the analyst's integrative interpretations lead to the further cathexis of archaic imagos. Insofar as the analyst becomes partially identified with the primitive, the patient tends to displace feelings directed toward these imagos onto him. If the analyst, for the purpose of the treatment, chooses to see some transference in all the patient's productions, he becomes representative of an approach that attempts to understand transference implications of behavior. The analysand eventually identifies with this attitude and examines his distorted feelings toward the analyst. What was previously a minimal transference element, by shifting one's focus and identifying with the analyst's attitude, now becomes the predominant theme.

Of course the analyst has not "caused" transference, but he has created a setting where it can develop. The spontaneous unfolding of the transference is not necessarily spontaneous; the analyst has to foster its development by not doing anything to interfere. This sounds like a tautology, but there are many subtle interactions between patient and therapist where the analyst unwittingly has shifted his interest from understanding how the patient's mind works to telling him how to run his life, that is, shifting from exploring the expectations of and conflicts about the analyst-introject fusion to the assumption of a role that is identical to the introject's. *Not to interfere by trying to manage the patient's life is hard work and demands analytic skill.*

DEVELOPMENTAL PROGRESSION

In the final chapters of this book there is considerable discussion about the therapeutic benefits derived from the recognition of the intrapsychic origin of behavior and its adaptive qualities. How does the analytic interaction lead to ego development? How does the projection of archaic imagos onto the therapist benefit the patient?

To some extent these questions were considered when the therapeutic process underlying interpretation was discussed (chapter 6). The superimposition of the analyst's secondary process onto the patient's primary process leads to structure and ego expansion. There are, however, many subtle aspects to the analytic interaction that makes this topic inexhaustible.

The aim of analytic treatment is achieved by interpreting the transference. Once the patient recognizes how intrapsychic forces have led him to distort his perception of the analyst, he is in a better position to evaluate and respond to the tasks that are imposed upon him by the external world and inner needs.

The patient, in the process of transference resolution, develops the capacity to recognize that he has projected archaic imagos. Since these imagos and the conflicts attached to them are now, in a sense, outside himself, he is better able to examine them. The transference projection creates distance, and as the patient recognizes that he has constructed his picture of the analyst on the basis of feelings within himself, his capacity for objectivity increases. It is much more difficult to perceive and appraise feelings and situations when one is close to them. Putting psychic elements into the analyst furnishes the patient with a repository for his feelings and in a sense he has "stepped outside himself." This is not the same situation as a frightening dissociation but instead represents an integrative experience.

Objectivity is enhanced by the analyst's participation. An ego that has projected destructive introjects is partially relieved of some pressures. Early traumatic object relationships cause ego fixation. The traumatized ego introjects disruptive and depriving experiences and is unable to incorporate subsequent experiences that have an adaptive potential. With the projection of nonadaptive, constricting introjects, the ego gains some ability to incorporate aspects of the analyst's secondary process. The archaic imagos within himself interfere with acquiring what is essentially a learning experience; attributing the disruptive qualities of these early experiences to the analyst lessens their effect upon the patient since their projection causes a partial decathexis of their representation within the patient. Consequently the recognition that he has projected and the fact that he is able to examine the content of his projection allow the patient to integrate the analyst's secondary process and to use it, in a positive feedback sequence, for further evaluation of the projected introjects. The progressive decathexis of the archaic imagos that follows releases the previously constricted developmental drive and further synthesis and integration are achieved.

There are other reasons why it is adaptive to project inner

disturbing forces onto the analyst. Since these early relationships were experienced as assaultive and destructive, their internal representations are considered dangerous, and the ego has to expend enormous quantities of energy to defend itself against them. The ego's balance is precarious because it is the victim of self-destructive forces. To project these feelings onto the analyst gives the patient some protection and some of the energy used for countercathexis becomes available for integration and the incorporation of positive experiences.

Patients with characterological and schizophrenic disorders frequently look around to see if the analyst is still alive. They are often very sensitive to what seems to be a rejection and abandonment by the analyst, but analysis reveals they are also concerned about having killed the analyst. They are frightened that the analyst will not be able to survive their projection.

Insofar as the analyst is able to survive the projection, he is "stronger" than the dangerous introjects. What had previously been self-destructive impulses, because of the transference projection, are now destructive impulses toward the analyst. They are manifested as negative transference. The patient gains considerable security in that he no longer feels as threatened, and since the analyst is not destroyed, the patient no longer believes that his hostility is overwhelming and uncontrollable. The analysis of the negative transference for patients suffering from severe psychopathology is invaluable and gives the patient considerable support.

The thesis stressed throughout this book is that support is an intrinsic aspect of the psychoanalytic process, and one need not introduce extraanalytic procedures in order to give the patient sufficient stability so that therapy can proceed. The unfolding of the transference and the analyst's observing orientation can become very important stabilizing experiences.

The process of projecting and externalizing and then discussing the adaptive value of projecting as well as identifying the conflicts attached to the archaic imagos shift the patient's orientation from one of experiencing and suffering to observation. The analyst makes himself available for the patient's projections and finds them fascinating instead of dangerous and repulsive. For example, a young schizophrenic patient constantly talked about killing himself. From a superficial viewpoint such a preoccupation was ununderstandable. Realistically he had everything to live for; he is personable, bright, and wealthy, so there was no rational reason why he should want to commit suicide. The fact that he wanted to and the further puzzling feeling that he was somehow going to please me by killing himself presented me with an extremely interesting enigma. Rather than responding directly to the content of the material, I found myself absorbed by it. I saw it as a phenomenon that demanded understanding that could be supplied only by learning about the unconscious intrapsychic factors underlying this impulse. Its adaptational value was also kept in mind. The patient soon realized that I was not dismayed but interested in examining valuable material, and he gradually developed the same attitude about his feelings that I had. He also became very curious as to why he felt the way he did, and together we were able to examine his impulses. He had succeeded in shifting from the position of being a helpless victim of his feelings to an observational frame of reference. He now shared my enthusiasm for examination, and the transference projection became the central focus of our attention. That I should be pleased by his death became the riddle that required explanation, and soon the projected introjects underlying this feeling became apparent.

The development of the self-observing attitude parallels the decathexis of internal disruptive forces. These processes are the essence of working through that results in an ego that has gained greater structure and has considerable free energy in store to master the problems of everyday living. The decathected internal representations of the projected imagos become fragmented and cease to exist as discrete entities that provoke defensive reactions and energy expenditure. Instead they become relatively harmless and less painful memories that are no longer pathologically operational (at least much less so). It is as if the introjects were "dissolved" into the ego, being able to maintain their destructiveness only when they have discrete boundaries. A depressed patient graphically illustrated this process in a dream. Throughout the years he would be plagued by many dreams where his dead father appeared, always in a threatening, frightening context. After several years of analysis he dreamed of the resolution of this conflict. As usual, his father appeared in the dream looking very much as he did during the patient's childhood. He did not, in contrast to earlier dreams, appear threatening. Instead he had a shadowy, filmy quality that when viewed from a certain angle reminded him of my "shadelike" presence. Then his father literally broke up into innumerable small fragments and as an entity disappeared. The patient, even during the dream, felt that an enormous weight pressing on him had been lifted, and from the time of the dream he no longer felt depressed. He reported feeling energetic in contrast to his previous lassitude.

The energy required to maintain the introject was now available for other purposes. A nonfunctioning introject becomes an adaptive technique that is amalgamated into the ego and is incorporated by various ego systems.

In therapy, changes do not occur abruptly. Prior to reporting the above dream, the patient had been working on his problem as it was relived in the transference. The dream was a manifestation of years of analytic work.

THE ANALYST'S EMOTIONAL ORIENTATION

A final theme of this book focuses upon the analyst's emotional orientation. Analysis is a two-person relationship, and the analyst's participation from the viewpoint of his psyche also has to be investigated. Countertransference elements have been frequently discussed in recent years, but other elements of the analyst's psyche, while he is analyzing, have not received much attention. An ego psychology of the analyst's psychic operations as the transference neurosis unfolds is an essential aspect of the conceptual model underlying the therapeutic process. As the analyst "dips" into his primary process, the effects of both current and past reality have to be weighed. The mobility required for free-floating fantasy is often hampered by a concentration on secondary-process factors, as when assuming an educational role.

Patients are more or less educable. The analyst may point out and correct distortions. In some instances he may provide the patient with information he did not previously possess. Possibly what the analyst has "taught" the patient may be useful.

Some analysts are not content with the role of educator per se. This may be a question of different styles, which reflects the therapist's personal orientation. Nevertheless, many analysts feel more comfortable if the analytic role is confined to correcting distortions by interpreting their inner source. This can be educative insofar as the patient is then able to synthesize previously unavailable psychic elements and has expanded his armaentarium of adjustive techniques. To learn directly from the therapist may cause the patient to correct bad habits in a parrotlike fashion, but his ego has not gained new structure.

There are parallel reactions in the analyst's psyche. Analytic activity is fulfilling when it is a creative experience. The patient gains accretions to his ego, but the analyst's ego also gains. Every creative endeavor leads to an ego expansion, although the psychic levels that are further structuralized in the patient are different from the levels of the analyst's psychic apparatus that undergo expansion. The former involve the acquisition of basic adjustive techniques, whereas hopefully the analyst effects an aesthetic synthesis as he attains the standards of his ego ideal.

The analytic experience is beneficial to both the patient and the analyst. The patient, if analysis is successful, achieves autonomy. Relatively speaking, he is better able to choose how he will relate to both inner and outer pressures, whereas previously he had no choice because of constrictive introjects. The analyst gains an increasing respect for the fascinating and subtle operations of the unconscious. He learns with each case that the patient is a human being worthy of study, a scientific but not cold and detached attitude. He does not feel hopeless even though the patient may at first. Underneath the chaos and turmoil the analyst discovers a developmental core that must not be impinged upon. Every patient increases the analyst's confidence in the psychoanalytic process, which is reflected in his therapeutic attitude of calm optimism. By not reacting to the patient with sorrow and pity, he is not degrading him; rather his interest and desire to analyze enhance the patient's dignity. The analyst, by not interfering with the development of the patient's autonomy, is also enhancing his own. The analysis of cases suffering from characterological and schizophrenic disorders is a profound and moving experience for both participants.

DISRUPTIVE AND AGITATED STATES

Chapter 9 represents a beginning exploration of primitive mental states that represent fixations at very early levels of psychic development. Up until now no one has considered psychoanalysis as a method of treatment for psychopathology which is the consequence of predominantly presymbiotic elements. The argument usually advanced is that these preverbal mental states cannot be analyzed since analysis deals with psychological content, that is, mental phenomena that can be represented visually or verbally. Traumatic circumstances that have occurred so early in life do not form mental representations that can become involved in transference projections.

Frequently these patients suffer from states of painful agitation that cannot be understood in conventional terms such as reactions to uncontrollable feelings or the emergence of states of helpless vulnerability associated with specific traumatic constellations. As therapists we try to understand them in some such fashion but are often rebuked by the patient for "trying to make sense out of something that does not make sense." The latter threatens our deterministic orientation.

The treatment of patients suffering from primitive mental states has demonstrated that this "senseless" agitation can become attached to mental content that does make sense and can be analyzed. This occurs during treatment and as a consequence of treatment. These primitive preverbal states acquire psychological significance as they become associated with later developmental phases. Chapter 9 illustrates how this happens through clinical examples that emphasize that the psychoanalytic process, in addition to resolving intrapsychic conflict, can also lead to the *acquisition of psychic structure.*

To add psychological content to what can basically be thought of as an organic disruptive agitation is the same as elevating an essentially concrete orientation to a symbolic level. The assaultive infantile environment is experienced in a global fashion in the newborn. At these early stages, there are no mental representations, not even of internal states. Neither homeostatic equilibrium nor a loss of equilibrium can be registered in a memory system or be expressed by symbols.

Concreteness and global feelings characterize these patients. I recall a patient who constantly sought situations that could "account" for her anxiety. She was always getting involved in crises to justify her feeling anxious. She described a feeling of internal disruption for which she had to find a cause. She was looking for an object on which to focus her anxiety. At first, it was difficult for me to view her painful tension and behavior the way she wanted me to. I kept thinking in terms of masochism and in the conventional psychodynamic frame of reference, but the patient kept insisting that I was trying to see more than was there. She protested that she lacked such sophistication.

How can treatment achieve the creation of mental representations? If it can, is it still psychoanalytic? These questions have often been asked in regard to character disorders and in fact stimulated us to write the earlier version of this book. These questions, when asked about the patients Freud subsumed under the rubric of narcissistic neuroses, took the form of inquiries as to whether psychic structuralization would occur in the context of a narcissistic or psychotic transference. Are other factors involved besides interpretation within the transference context? Furthermore, o the narcissistic neuroses and now these presymbiotically fixated patients require maneuvers that are considered extraanalytic?

Psychoanalytic treatment has two components—the setting and the process. Much has been written about the process, but except to emphasize holding qualities—that is, Winnicott's holding environment (1955)—very little has been written about the analytic setting. To my mind, this is an area that psychoanalysts will give increasing attention to in the future. It has many implications, not only for the treatment of patients with primitive mental states, but also for constructing a rational treatment milieu for hospitalized patients.

We are becoming less concerned with the question of what is extraanalytic. Rather, we wish to concentrate upon what is therapeutic and at the same time maintain respect for the patient's autonomy and avoid repeating the intrusions of the traumatic infantile environment. This is the essence of the analytic process and does not require maneuvers beyond transference interpretation. Perhaps the only difference in the treatment of patients fixated at such primitive levels is the degree of countertransference involvement.

Our excitement and our despair often parallel similar feelings within the patient. Many analysts are reluctant to become involved in such treatment situations because they sense that they will feel the same disruption the patient does. This can be painful. However, pain can be converted into pleasurable excitement as our patients begin to acquire psychic structure and achieve the ability to form and hold mental representations. The alleviation of our pain is the outcome of a process that is in resonance with the patient's overcoming the crushing impact of the early environment.

The emergence of early developmental levels during the transference regression is a fascinating phenomenon if we are aware it is happening. Often we are misled and feel personally threatened, but once we can explain the treatment interaction as the outcome of the repetition compulsion, that is, the patient's attempt to repeat early infantile orientations and to re-create the early environment in the consultation room, then we can restore our analytic equanimity.

These patients can be very helpful. They are tolerant of our blind spots and do their best to get us on the right track. Patients are good teachers. Those suffering from early developmental fixations are especially good teachers, as they patiently tell us how to preserve our analytic orientation in the face of material that seems incapable of being analyzed. They demand that we experience the same agitation that constantly disrupts them, but they do not want us to despair as they do. Our analytic orientation contains our despair and furnishes us with the hope these patients so desperately need.

Bibliography

Abadi, Mauricio (1954). Consideraciones psicoanalíticas acerca de algunos aspectos de una psicosis con amaurosis congénita. *Revista de Psicoanálisis* 13:21-40.

Abenheimer, Karl M. (1955). Critical observations on Fairbairn's theory of object relations. *British Medical Journal* 28:29-41.

Abraham, Karl (1907). On the significance of sexual trauma in childhood for the symptomatology of dementia praecox. In *Clinical Papers and Essays on Psychoanalysis*, pp. 13-20. New York: Basic Books, 1955.

——— (1908). The psychosexual differences between hysteria and dementia praecox. In *Selected Papers on Psycho-Analysis*, pp. 64-79. London: Hogarth Press, 1948.

——— (1913). Restrictions and transformations of scoptophilia in psycho-neurotics, with remarks on analogous phenomena in folk-psychology. In *Selected Papers on Psycho-Analysis*, pp. 169-234. London: Hogarth Press, 1948.

——— (1924). A short history of the development of the libido. In *Selected Papers on Psycho-Analysis*, pp. 418-501. London: Hogarth Press, 1948.

Ackerknecht, Erwin H. (1943). Psychopathology, primitive medicine and primitive psychiatry. *Bulletin of the History of Medicine* 14:30-67.

Ackerman, Nathan W. (1960). Family-focused therapy of schizophrenia. In *The Outpatient Treatment of Schizophrenia*, ed. Sam C. Scher and Howard R. Davis, pp. 156-173. New York and London: Grune and Stratton.

——— (1964). Family therapy in schizophrenia: theory and practice. *International Psychiatric Clinics* 1:929-943.

Adler, Gerald (1975). The usefulness of the "borderline" concept in psychotherapy. In *Borderline States in Psychiatry*, ed. John E. Mack, pp. 29-40. New York: Grune and Stratton.

Aichhorn, August (1925). *Wayward Youth. Psychoanalysis in Corrective Education.* New York: Viking, 1935.

Alanen, Yrjö O. (1958). *The Mothers of Schizophrenic Patients: a Study of the Personality and the Mother-Child Relationship of 100 Mothers and the Significance of These Factors in the Pathogenesis of Schizophrenia.* Copenhagen: Munksgaard.

——— (1966). The family in the pathogenesis of schizophrenic and neurotic disorders. *Acta Psychiatrica Scandinavica* 42 (Supplement 189).

Alexander, Franz (1927). *Psychoanalysis of the Total Personality.* New York and Washington: Nervous and Mental Disease Publishing Co., 1930.

——— (1930). The neurotic character. In *The Scope of Psychoanalysis: Selected Papers of Franz Alexander*, pp. 56-73. New York: Basic Books, 1961.

——— (1931). Schizophrenic psychosis: critical considerations of psychoanalytic treatment. *Archives of Neurology and Psychiatry* 26:815-826.

——— (1933). Book review of *Die Psychoanalyse Des Kindes* by Melanie Klein. *Psychoanalytic Quarterly* 2:141-152.

——— (1954). Psychoanalysis and psychotherapy. *Journal of the American Psychoanalytic Association* 2:722-733.

Alexander, Franz, and French, Thomas M., eds. (1948). *Studies in Psychosomatic Medicine.* New York: Ronald Press.

Alikakos, Louis C., Starer, Emanuel and Winnich, William (1956). Observations on the meaning of behavior of a group of chronic schizophrenics. *International Journal of Group Psychotherapy* 6:180-192.

Amendola, E. and Garzillo, C. (1955). Psicoanalisi delle schizofrenie. *Rassegna di Neuropsichiatria* 9:479-496.

Arieti, Silvano (1955). *Interpretation of Schizophrenia.* New York: Brunner.

——— (1956). The possibility of psychosomatic involvement of the central nervous system in schizophrenia. *Journal of Nervous and Mental Disease* 123:324-333.

Arlow, Jacob A. (1952). Discussion of Dr. Fromm-Reichmann's paper. In *Psychotherapy with Schizophrenics: a Symposium*, ed. Eugene B. Brody, and Fritz C. Redlich, pp.112-120. New York: International Universities Press.

Arlow, Jacob A. and Brenner, Charles (1964). *Psychoanalytic Concepts and the Structural Theory*. New York: International Universities Press.

——— (1969). The psychopathology of the psychoses: a proposed revision. *International Journal of Psycho-Analysis* 50:5-14.

Aronson, Gerald (1968). Discussion. *Treatment of Schizophrenia*, ed. Philip R. A. May, pp. 294-297. New York: Science House.

——— (1977). Defence and deficit models: their influence on therapy of schizophrenia. *International Journal of Psycho-Analysis* 58:11-16.

Aslan, Carlos, and Horne, B. (1966). La destrucción del objeto bueno en triunfo maníaco. In *Psicoanálisis de la Manía y la Psicopatia*, ed. Arnaldo Rascovsky and David Liberman, pp. 171-175. Buenos Aires: Editorial Paidos.

Atkins, Norman B. (1967). Comments on severe psychotic regressions in analysis. *Journal of the American Psychoanalytic Association* 15:584-605.

——— (1968). Acting out and psychosomatic illness as related regressive trends. *International Journal of Psycho-Analysis* 49:221-223.

Avenburg, Ricardo (1962). Modificaciones estructurales en un paciente esquizofrénico a traves del primer mes de análisis. *Revista de Psicoanálisis* 19:351-365.

Azima, Hassan, and Wittkower, Eric D. (1956). Gratifications of basic needs in schizophrenia. *Psychiatry* 19:121-129.

Bak, Robert C. (1939). Regression of ego-orientation and libido in schizophrenia. *International Journal of Psycho-Analysis* 20:64-71.

——— (1954). The schizophrenic defence against aggression. *International Journal of Psycho-Analysis* 35:129-134.

Balint, Michael (1957). *Problems of Human Pleasure and Behavior*. London: Hogarth Press.

Barkas, Mary (1925). The treatment of psychotic patients in institutions in the light of psychoanalysis. *Journal of Neurology and Psychopathology* 5:333-340.

Bartemeier, Leo (1965). Personal communication.

Bash, Kenower W. (1957). Descensus ad infernos. Aus der Analyse eines Falles von Schizophrenie mit katamnestischen angaben. *Psyche* 11:505-525.

Bateson, Gregory, Jackson, Don D., Haley, Jay, and Weakland, John. (1956). Towards a theory of schizophrenia. *Behavioral Science* 1:251-264.

Bateson, Gregory, and Mead, Margaret (1942). *Balinese Character: a Photographic Analysis.* New York: Special Publications of the New York Academy of Science.

Beaglehole, Ernest (1940). Cultural complexity and psychological problems. *Psychiatry* 3:330-332.

Bellak, Leopold (1948). *Dementia Praecox. The Past Decade's Work and Present Status. A Review and Evaluation.* New York: Grune and Stratton.

Bellak, Leopold, and Benedict, Paul K., eds. (1968). *Schizophrenia: a Review of the Syndrome.* New York: Grune and Stratton.

Bellak, Leopold, and Loeb, Laurence, eds. (1969). *The Schizophrenic Syndrome.* New York: Grune and Stratton.

Belo, Jane (1960). *Trance in Bali.* New York: Columbia University Press.

Benedek, Therese (1959). Parenthood as a developmental phase. *Journal of the American Psychoanalytic Association* 7:389-417.

Benedetti, Gaetano (1955). Il problema della conscienza nelle allucinazione degli schizofrenici. *Archivio di Psicologia, Neurologia e Psichiatria* 16:287-312.

——— (1963). Übertragung and Schizophrenietherapie. *Schweizer Archiv für Neurologie und Psychiatrie* 91:112-128.

——— (1965). Le probleme de la regression psychotique dans la psychotherapie individuelle. In *Psychotherapy of Schizophrenia,* 3rd International Symposium, 1964, eds. Christian Müller and Gaetano Benedetti, pp. 168-176. New York and Basel: Karger.

Bergman, Paul (1962). The "dissident schools." *Psychiatry* 25:83-95.

Bergman, Paul, and Escalona, Sibyl K. (1949). Unusual sensitivities in very young children. *The Psychoanalytic Study of the Child* 3-4:333-352.

Bernfeld, Siegfried (1944). Freud's earliest theories and the school of Helmholtz. *Psychoanalytic Quarterly* 13:341-362.

Bertschinger, H. (1911). Process of recovery in schizophrenia. *Psychoanalytic Review* 3:176-188.

Bettelheim, Bruno (1965). *Love Is Not Enough.* New York: MacMillan.

——— (1975). The love that is enough. In *Tactics and Techniques in*

Psychoanalytic Therapy, II. Countertransference, eds. Peter L. Giovacchini, Alfred Flarsheim, and L. Bryce Boyer, pp. 251-278. New York: Science House.

Betz, Barbara J. (1950). Strategic conditions in the psychotherapy of a person with schizophrenia. *American Journal of Psychiatry* 107:203-215.

Bibring, Edward (1937). Symposium on the theory of the therapeutic results of psychoanalysis. *International Journal of Psycho-Analysis* 18:170-189.

——— (1947). The so-called English school of psychoanalysis. *Psychoanalytic Quarterly* 16:69-93.

Binswanger, Herbert (1954-1955). Zur Theorie und Praxis der Psychotherapie Schizophrener. *Zeitschrift für Psychosomatische Medizin* 1:253-260.

——— (1956). Freud's Psychosentherapie. *Psyche* 10:357-366.

Binswanger, Ludwig (1910). Über Neuropsychosen. *Deutsche Medizinische Wochenschrift*, no. 50, and *Zentralblatt für Psychoanalyse* 1:250.

——— (1945). Zur Frage des Häufigkeit der Schizophrenie im Kindesalter. *Zeitschrift fur Kinderpsychiatrie* 12:33-50.

——— (1957). *Schizophrenie.* Pfulligen, Germany: Neske.

——— (1958). Daseinsanalyse, Psychiatrie, Schizophrenie. *Schweizer Archiv für Neurologie und Psychiatrie* 81:1-8.

Bion, Wilfred R. (1954). Note on the theory of schizophrenia. *International Journal of Psycho-Analysis* 35:113-118.

——— (1956). Development of schizophrenic thought. *International Journal of Psycho-Analysis* 37:344-346.

——— (1957). Differentiation of the psychotic from the nonpsychotic personalities. *International Journal of Psycho-Analysis* 38:266-275.

——— (1961). *Experiences in Groups and Other Papers.* London: Tavistock; New York: Basic Books.

Birnbaum, Karl (1909). Dementia praecox und wahnpsychosen der degenerativen. *Zentralblatt für Nervenheilkunde und Psychologie* 20:429-433.

Bjerre, Poul C. (1911). Zur Radikalbehandlung der chronischen Paranoia. *Jahrbuch für Psychoanalytische und Psychopathologische Forschung* 3:795-847.

Blank, H. Robert (1957). Psychoanalysis and blindness. *Psychoanalytic Quarterly* 26:1-24.

Bleuler, Eugen (1911). *Dementia Praecox, or the Group of Schizophrenias.* New York: International Universities Press 1958.

Bleuler, Manfred (1978) *The Schizophrenic Disorders: Long-Term Patient and Family Studies.* New Haven: Yale University Press.

Blum, G.S. (1953). *Psychoanalytic Theories of Personality.* New York: McGraw-Hill.

Boroffka, Frieda L. (1958-1959). Bericht über die Behandlung einer schizophrenen Patientin mit psychoanalytisch orientierter Psychotherapie. *Zeitschrift für Psychosomatische Medizin* 5:182-188.

Boss, Medard (1958). The role of psychotherapy in schizophrenia. *Indian Journal of Psychiatry,* second series, S. 1-12.

Böszörmënyi-Nagy, Ivan (1962). The concept of schizophrenia from the perspective of family treatment. *Family Process* 1:103-113.

Böszörmënyi-Nagy, Ivan, and Framo, James L., eds. (1963). *Family Treatment of Schizophrenia.* New York: Harper and Row.

Boven, William. (1921). Études sur les conditions du developpement au sein des familles, de la schizophrenie et de la folie maniaques. *Archives Suisses de Neurologie et Psychologie* 8:89-116.

Bowlby, John (1958). The nature of the child's tie to its mother. *International Journal of Psycho-Analysis* 39:350-373.

Boyer, L. Bryce (1952). Fantasies concerning convulsive therapy. *Psychoanalytic Review* 39:252-270.

——— (1955). Christmas "neurosis." *Journal of the American Psychoanalytic Association* 3:467-488.

——— (1956a). Ambulatory schizophrenia. Some remarks concerning the diagnosis. *Kaiser Foundation Medical Bulletin* 4:457-459.

——— (1956b). On maternal overstimulation and ego defects. *The Psychoanalytic Study of the Child* 11:236-256.

——— (1960). A hypothesis concerning the time of appearance of the dream screen. *International Journal of Psycho-Analysis* 41:114-122.

——— (1961). Provisional evaluation of psycho-analysis with few parameters employed in the treatment of schizophrenia. *International Journal of Psycho-Analysis* 42:389-403.

——— (1964a). An example of legend distortion from the Apaches of the Mescalero Indian Reservation. *Journal of American Folklore* 77:118-142.

——— (1964b). Psychological problems of a group of Apaches. Alcoholic hallucination and latent homosexuality among typical men. *Psychoanalytic Study of Society* 3:203-277.

——— (1966). Office treatment of schizophrenic patients by psychoanalysis. *Psychoanalytic Forum* 1:337-356.

——— (1970). Estados fronterizos: una revisión del concepto y sus applicaciones. (Relatos de mesas redondas). *Revista de Psicoanálisis* 27:865-886.

——— (1971). Psychoanalytic technique in the treatment of certain characterological and schizophrenic disorders. *International Journal of Psycho-Analysis* 52:67-85.

——— (1975). The man who turned into a water monster. A psychoanalytic contribution to folklore. *Psychoanalytic Study of Society* 6:100-133.

——— (1976). Meanings of a bizarre suicidal attempt by an adolescent twin. Adolescent Psychiatry 4:371-381.

——— (1977). Mythology, folklore and psychoanalysis. In *International Encyclopedia of Psychiatry, Psychology, Psychoanalysis and Neurology*, ed. Benjamin B. Wolman, vol. 7, pp. 423-429. New York: Aesculapius Publishers and Van Nostrand Co.

——— (1978). Countertransference experiences with severely regressed patients. *Contemporary Psychoanalysis* 14:48-72.

——— (1979). *Childhood and Folklore. A Psychoanalytic Study of Apache Personality*. New York: The Library of Psychological Anthropology.

Boyer, L. Bryce, and Boyer, Ruth M. (1977). Understanding the patient through folklore. *Contemporary Psychoanalysis* 13:30-51.

Braatøy, Trygve (1954). *Fundamentals of Psychoanalytic Technique*. New York: John Wiley and Sons.

Breuer, Joseph, and Freud, Sigmund (1895). Studies on hysteria. *Standard Edition* 2:1-252.

Brierley, Marjorie (1942). "Internal objects" and theory. *International Journal of Psycho-Analysis* 23:107-112.

Brill, Abraham A. (1908). Psychological factors in dementia praecox, an analysis. *Journal of Abnormal Psychiatry* 3:219-239.

——— (1925). Schizoid and syntonic factors in neuroses and psychoses. *American Journal of Psychiatry* 4:589-598.

——— (1929). Schizophrenia and psychotherapy. *American Journal of Psychiatry* 9:519-542.

——— (1941). The etiological relationship of trauma to schizophrenia. *Medical Record* 153:159-162.

Brill, Norman Q. (1978). Schizophrenia: a psychosomatic disorder? *Psychosomatics* 19:665-670.

Brodey, Warren M. (1965). On the dynamics of narcissism. I. Externalization and early ego development. *Psychoanalytic Study of the Child* 20:165-193.

Brody, Eugene G. (1952). The treatment of schizophrenia: a review. In *Psychotherapy with Schizophrenics*, ed. Eugene B. Brody, and Frederick C. Redlich, pp. 39-88. New York: International Universities Press.

Bromberg, Walter (1954). *Man Above Humanity*. New York: Lippincott.

Brunswick, Ruth Mack (1928). A supplement to Freud's *A History of an Infantile Neurosis*. *International Journal of Psycho-Analysis* 9:439-476.

Bumke, Oswald (1924). Die Auflösung der Dementia Praecox. *Klinische Wochenschrift* 3:437-440.

Bychowski, Gustav (1923). *Metaphysik und Schizophrenie. Eine Vergleichend-Psychologische Studie*. Berlin: Karger.

——— (1928). Über Psychotherapie der Schizophrenie. *Nervenarzt* 1:478-487.

——— (1957). From latent to manifest schizophrenia. *Congress Report, 2nd International Congress for Psychiatry* (Zurich) 3:128-134.

——— (1963). Schizophrenic partners. In *Neurotic Interactions in Marriage*, ed. Victor Eisenstein, pp. 135-147. New York: Basic Books.

——— (1966). Obsessive-compulsive facade in schizophrenia. *International Journal of Psycho-Analysis* 47:189-197.

Campbell, C. Macfie (1909). A modern conception of dementia praecox, with five illustrative cases. *Review of Neurology and Psychiatry* 7:623-641.

——— (1935). *Destiny and Disease in Mental Disorders with Special Reference to the Schizophrenic Psychoses*. New York: Norton.

Caravedo, Baltazar (1924). Actitudes regresivas en los esquizofrénicos. *Revista de Psicología* (Lima) 5(2).

Cargnello, Danilo (1947). La schizofrenia con turba della personalità. *Archivio di Psicologia, Neurologia e Psichiatria* 8:333-393.

Carothers, J. C. (1953). *The African Mind in Health and Disease*. Geneva: World Health Organization.

Carpenter, William T., Bartko, John J., Strauss, John S., and Hawk, Alan B. (1978). Signs and symptoms as predictors of outcome: a report from the international pilot study of schizophrenia. *The American Journal of Psychiatry* 135:940-945.

Carpinacci, Jorge A., Liberman, David, and Schlossberg, Norberto (1963). Perturbaciones en la comunicación y neurosis de contratransferencia. *Revista de Psicoanálisis* 20:63-69.

Carter, Linnea, and Rinsley, Donald B. (1977). Vicissitudes of "empathy" in a borderline patient. *International Review of Psycho-Analysis* 4:317-326.

Caruth, Elaine, and Ekstein, Rudolph (1964). Certain phenomenological aspects of the countertransference in the treatment of schizophrenic children. *Reiss-Davis Clinic Bulletin* 1:80-88.

Cassity, John H. (1925). Comments on schizophrenia. *Journal of Nervous and Mental Disease* 62:477-484.

Cawte, J. E., and Kidson, M. A. (1964). Australian ethnopsychiatry: the Walbiri doctor. *Medical Journal of Australia* 2:274-284.

Cesio, Fidia R. (1963). La comunicación extraverbal en psicoanálisis. Transferencia, contratransferencia e interpretación. *Revista de Psicoanálisis* 20:124-127.

——— (1973). Los fundamentos de la contratransferencia. El yo ideal y las identificaciones directas. *Revista de Psicoanálisis* 30:5-16.

Chijs, A. van der (1919). Über halluzinationen und psychoanalyse. *Internationale Zeitschrift für Psychoanalyse* 5:274-284.

Clark, L. Pierce (1919). Some practical remarks upon the use of modified psychoanalysis in the treatment of borderline neurosis and psychoses. *Psychoanalytic Review* 6:306-308.

——— (1926). The phantasy method of analyzing narcissistic neuroses. *Medical Journal Record* 123:154-158.

——— (1933). Treatment of narcissistic neuroses and psychoses. *Psychoanalytic Review* 20:304-326.

Claude, Henri (1926) Schizomanie à forme imaginative. *Éncephale* 25:715-727.

Cohen, Mabel B. (1953). Introduction. In *The Interpersonal Theory of Psychiatry of Harry Stack Sullivan*, ed. Helen S. Perry and Mary L. Gawel. New York: Norton.

Cohen, Robert A. (1947). Management of anxiety in a case of schizophrenia. *Psychiatry* 10:143-157.

Coriat, Isadore H. (1917). The treatment of schizophrenia by psychoanalysis. *Journal of Abnormal Psychology* 12:326-330.

Davie, James M., and Freeman, Thomas (1961a). Disturbances of perception and consciousness in schizophrenic states. *British Journal of Medical Psychology* 34:33-41.

——— (1961b). The non-psychotic residue in schizophrenia. *British Journal of Medical Psychology* 34:117-127.

Delay, Jean P. L., Deniker, P., and Green, R. (1957). Essai de description et de definition psychopathologique des parents des schizophrènes. *Congress Report: 2nd International Congress of Psychiatry* 4:189-232.

Delgado, Honorio F. (1937). *Psicopatología y Delimitación Cliníca de la Esquizofrenia*. Lima.

Deutsch, Felix, and Murphy, William F. (1955). *The Clinical Interview*. New York: International Universities Press.

Deutsch, Helene (1942). Some forms of emotional disturbance and their relationship to schizophrenia. *Psychoanalytic Quarterly* 11:301-321.

Devereux, George (1956). Normal and abnormal: the key problem of psychiatric anthropology. In *Some Uses of Anthropology: Theoretical and Applied*, pp. 23-48. Washington: Anthropological Society of Washington.

Dewald, Paul A. (1976). Transference regression and real experience in the psychoanalytic process. *Psychoanalytic Quarterly* 45:213-230.

Dickes, Robert (1974). The concepts of borderline states: an alternate proposal. *International Journal of Psycho-Analytic Psychotherapy* 3:1-27.

——— (1975). Technical considerations of the therapeutic and working alliance. *International Journal of Psycho-Analytic Psychotherapy* 4:1-24.

Eaton, J. M., and Weill, R. J. (1953). Some epidemiological findings in the Hutterite Mental Health Study. In *Interrelations between the Social Environment and Psychiatric Disorders*, pp. 222-234. New York: Milbank Memorial Fund.

Eisenstein, Victor M. (1951). Differential psychotherapy of borderline states. *Psychiatric Quarterly* 25:379-401.

Eissler, Kurt R (1943). Limitations to the psychotherapy of schizophrenia. *Psychiatry* 6:381-391.

——— (1951). Remarks on the psychoanalysis of schizophrenia. *International Journal of Psycho-Analysis* 32:139-156.

——— (1953a). The effect of the structure of the ego on psychoanalytic technique. *Journal of the American Psychoanalytic Association* 1:104-143.

——— (1953b). Notes on the emotionality of a schizophrenic patient, and its relation to problems of technique. *Psychoanalytic Study of the Child* 8:199-251.

Ekstein, Rudolph (1949). Ideological warfare in the psychological sciences. *Psychoanalytic Review* 36:144-151.

——— (1955). Vicissitudes of the "internal image" in the recovery of a borderline schizophrenic adolescent. *Bulletin of the Menninger Clinic* 19:86-92.

——— (1966). *Children of Time and Space, of Action and Impulse: Clinical Studies on the Psychoanalytic Treatment of Severely Disturbed Children.* New York: Appleton-Century-Crofts.

——— (1968). Impulse—acting out—purpose: psychotic adolescents and their quest for goals. *International Journal of Psycho-Analysis* 49:347-352.

Ekstein, Rudolph, and Caruth, Elaine (1967). Distancing and distance devices in childhood schizophrenia and borderline states: revised concepts and new directions in research. *Psychological Reports* 20:109-110.

——— (1972). Keeping secrets. In *Tactics and Techniques in Psychoanalytic Therapy,* ed. Peter L. Giovacchini, pp. 200-218. New York: Science House.

Ekstein, Rudolph, and Friedman, Seymour W. (1968). Prolegomenon to a psychoanalytic technique in the treatment of childhood schizophrenia. *Reiss-Davis Clinic Bulletin* 5:107-115.

Ekstein, Rudolph, and Wallerstein, Judith (1954). Observations on the psychology of borderline and psychotic children. *Psychoanalytic Study of the Child* 9:344-369.

Erikson, Erik H. (1959). *Identity and the Life Cycle.* New York: International Universities Press.

Ernst, K. (1957). Praktische Probleme der individuellen Psychotherapie in der Anstalt am Beispiel einer Schizophreniebehandlung. *Acta Psychotherapeutica, Psychosomatica et Orthopaedagogica* 5:297-305.

Ey, Henri (1958). Les problemès cliniques des schizophrènes. *Évolution Psychiatrique* 2:149-212.

Faergemann, Paul M. (1946). Early differential diagnosis between psychogenic psychoses and schizophrenias. In *The Memorial Volume to Professor H. Helweg*. Copenhagen: Ejnar Munksgaard.

Fairbairn, W. Ronald D. (1936). The effect of the king's death upon patients under analysis. *International Journal of Psycho-Analysis* 17:278-284.

——— (1941). A revised psychopathology of the psychoses and psychoneuroses. *International Journal of Psycho-Analysis* 22:250-279.

——— (1944). Endopsychic structure considered in terms of object relationship. *International Journal of Psycho-Analysis* 25:70-93.

Faris, Robert E. L., and Dunham, H. Warren (1939). *Mental Disorders in Urban Areas. An Ecological Study of Schizophrenia and Other Psychoses*. Chicago: University of Chicago Press.

Federn, Paul (1933). The analysis of psychotics. *International Journal of Psycho-Analysis* 15:209-215.

——— (1952) *Ego Psychology and the Psychoses*. New York: Basic Books.

Feigenbaum, Dorian (1930). Analysis of a case of paranoia persecutoria. Structure and cure. *Psychoanalytic Review* 17:159-182.

Fenichel, Otto (1937). On the theory of the therapeutic results of psychoanalysis. *International Journal of Psycho-Analysis* 18:133-138.

——— (1945). *The Psychoanalytic Theory of Neurosis*. New York: Norton.

Ferenczi, Sandor (1911). Stimulation of the anal erotic zone as a precipitating factor in paranoia. Contribution to the subject of homosexuality and paranoia. In *Final Contributions to the Problems and Methods of Psychoanalysis*, pp. 295-298. New York: Basic Books, 1955.

——— (1913). Entwicklungsstufen des Wirklichkeitssinnes. *Internationale Zeitschrift für Ärtzliche Psychoanalyse* 1:124-138.

——— (1925). Psychoanalysis of sexual habits. In *Further Contributions to the Theory and Technique of Psycho-Analysis*, pp. 259-297. London: Hogarth Press, 1950.

——— (1929). The principle of relaxation and neocatharsis. In *Final Contributions to the Problems and Methods of Psychoanalysis*, pp. 108-125. New York: Basic Books, 1955.

——— (1931). Child analysis and the analysis of adults. In *Final Contributions to the Problems and Methods of Psychoanalysis*, pp. 126-142. New York: Basic Books, 1955.

Flarsheim, Alfred (1967). Resolution of the mother-child symbiosis in a psychotic adolescent. *Bulletin of the Chicago Society for Adolescent Psychiatry* 2:6-16.

——— (1972). Treatability. In *Tactics and Techniques in Psychoanalytic Therapy*, ed. Peter L. Giovacchini, pp. 113-134. New York: Science House.

——— (1975). The influence of psychoanalytic treatment upon a woman's attitudes toward sex and motherhood. In *Tactics and Techniques in Psychoanalytic Therapy, vol. II: Countertransference*, ed. Peter L. Giovacchini, Alfred Flarsheim, and L. Bryce Boyer, pp. 326-338. New York: Science House.

Fliess, Robert (1953). Countertransference and counteridentification. *Journal of the American Psychoanalytic Association*, 1:268-284.

deForest, Izette (1942). The therapeutic technique of Sandor Ferenczi. *International Journal of Psycho-Analysis* 23:120-139.

Fornari, Franco (1963). L'io nelle psicosi schizofreniche. In *Nuovi Orientamente delle Psicoanalisis*. Milan: Feltrinelli, 1966.

Fortune, Reo (1932). *Sorcerers of Dobu: The Social Anthropology of the Dobu Islanders of the Western Pacific*. New York: Dutton.

Fraiberg, Selma (1968). Parallel and divergent patterns in blind and sighted infants. *Psychoanalytic Study of the Child* 23:264-300.

——— (1969). Libidinal object constancy and object representation. *Psychoanalytic Study of the Child* 24:9-47.

Fraiberg, Selma, and Freedman, David A. (1964). Studies in the ego development of the congenitally blind child. *Psychoanalytic Study of the Child* 19:113-169.

Freedman, David A. (1978a). The blind. In *Social and Emotional Development: the Preschooler*, ed. Norbert B. Enzer and Kennith W. Goin, pp. 157-167. New York: Walker Press.

——— (1978b). Current psychoanalytic issues in schizophrenia: one analyst's perspective. In *Phenomenology and Treatment of Schizophrenia*, ed. William E. Fann, Ismet Karacan, Alex D. Pokorny, and Robert L. Williams, pp. 325-340. New York: Spectrum Publications.

Freeman, Thomas A. (1970). The psychopathology of the psychoses: a reply to Arlow and Brenner. *International Journal of Psycho-Analysis* 51:407-415.

Freeman, Thomas, McGhie, Andrew, and Cameron, John (1957). The state of the ego in chronic schizophrenia. *British Journal of Medical Psychology* 30:9-18.

French, Thomas M. (1946). The transference phenomenon. In *Psychoanalytic Therapy*, ed. Franz Alexander and Thomas M. French, pp. 71-95. New York: Norton.

Freud, Anna (1936). *The Ego and the Mechanisms of Defense*. New York: International Universities Press, 1946.

——— (1943). Discussion before the British Psycho-Analytic Society, January.

——— (1951). Observations on child development. *Psychoanalytic Study of the Child* 6:18-30.

——— (1954). The widening scope of indications for psychoanalysis. *Journal of the American Psychoanalytic Association* 2:607-620.

Freud, Sigmund (1886). Beobachtung einer hochgradigen hemianasthesie bei einem hysterischen Manne (Beiträge zur Kasuistic der Hysterie. I.). *Wiener Klinische Wochenschrift*, 36, no. 49, 1633.

——— (1887-1902). *The Origins of Psychoanalysis. Letters, Drafts, and Notes to Wilhelm Fliess*. New York: Basic Books, 1954.

——— (1894a). The neuro-psychoses of defence: an attempt at a psychological theory of acquired hysteria and obsessions and of certain hallucinatory psychoses. *Standard Edition* 3:45-61.

——— (1894b). Obsessions and phobias: their psychical mechanism and their aetiology. *Standard Edition* 3:69-82.

——— (1895). On the grounds for detaching a particular syndrome from neurasthenia under the description anxiety neurosis. *Standard Edition* 3:87-117.

——— (1896a). Further remarks on the neuro-psychoses of defence. *Standard Edition* 3:159-188.

——— (1896b). Heredity and the aetiology of the neuroses. *Standard Edition* 3:141-156.

——— (1898a). The psychical mechanism of forgetfulness. *Standard Edition* 3:287-297.

——— (1898b). Sexuality in the aetiology of the neuroses. *Standard Edition* 3:259-285.

——— (1900). The interpretation of dreams. *Standard Edition* 4/5:1-361.

——— (1904a). Freud's psychoanalytic procedure. *Standard Edition* 7:247-254.

——— (1904b). On psychotherapy. *Standard Edition* 7:255-268.

——— (1905). Three essays on the theory of sexuality. *Standard Edition* 7:122-243.

——— (1909a). Analysis of a phobia in a five-year-old boy. *Standard Edition* 10:3-149.

——— (1909b). General remarks on hysterical attacks. *Collected Papers* (Fifth Impression), 2:100-104.

——— (1909c). Notes upon a case of obsessional neurosis. *Standard Edition* 10:151-249.

——— (1910a). The future prospects of psycho-analytic therapy. *Standard Edition* 11:139-152.

——— (1910b). "Wild" analysis. *Standard Edition* 11:219-230.

——— (1911). Psychoanalytic notes on an autobiographical account of a case of paranoia (dementia paranoides). *Standard Edition* 12:1-82.

——— (1911-1915). Papers on technique. *Standard Edition* 12:89-170.

——— (1912). The dynamics of transference. *Standard Edition* 12:97-108.

——— (1913). The disposition of obsessional neurosis. *Standard Edition* 12:311-336.

——— (1914a). On the history of the psychoanalytic movement. *Standard Edition* 14:3-66.

——— (1914b). On narcissism: an introduction. *Standard Edition* 14:67-102.

——— (1914c). Remembering, repeating and working-through (further recommendations on the technique of psycho-analysis). *Standard Edition* 12:145-156.

——— (1915a). Instincts and their vicissitudes. *Standard Edition* 14:103-140.

——— (1915b). Observations on transference love. *Standard Edition* 12:157-171.

——— (1915c). The unconscious. *Standard Edition* 14:159-215.

——— (1917a). Mourning and melancholia. *Standard Edition* 14:237-258.

——— (1917b). On transformations of instinct as exemplified in anal erotism. *Standard Edition* 17:125-133.

——— (1918). From the history of an infantile neurosis. *Standard Edition* 17:1-222.

——— (1920). Beyond the pleasure principle. *Standard Edition* 18:3-66.

——— (1923). The ego and the id. *Standard Edition* 19:12-68.
——— (1924a). The loss of reality in neurosis and psychosis. *Standard Edition* 19:183-190.
——— (1924b). Neurosis and psychosis. *Standard Edition* 19:147-153.
——— (1924c). A short account of psycho-analysis. *Standard Edition* 19:191-212.
——— (1926). Inhibitions, symptoms and anxiety. *Standard Edition* 20:75-124.
——— (1927). Fetishism. *Standard Edition* 21:147-157.
——— (1932). New introductory lectures on psycho-analysis. *Standard Edition* 22:5-184.
——— (1940). *An Outline of Psychoanalysis*. New York: Norton, 1949.
Fromm-Reichmann, Frieda (1947). Problems of therapeutic management in a psychoanalytic hospital. *Psychoanalytic Quarterly* 16:325-356.
——— (1948). Notes on the development of schizophrenia. *Psychiatry* 11:263-273.
——— (1949). Notes on the personal and professional requirements of a psychotherapist. *Psychiatry* 12:361-378.
——— (1950). *Principles of Intensive Psychotherapy*. Chicago: University of Chicago Press.
——— (1952). Some aspects of psychoanalytic psychotherapy with schizophrenics. In *Psychotherapy with Schizophrenics, a Symposium*, ed. Eugene B. Brody and Frederick C. Redlich, pp. 89-111. New York: International Universities Press.
——— (1954). Psychoanalytic and general dynamic conceptions of theory and therapy: differences and similarities. *Journal of the American Psychoanalytic Association* 2:711-721.
Frosch, John (1964). The psychotic character: clinical psychiatric considerations. *Psychiatric Quarterly* 38:91-96.
Garbarino, Héctor (1966). Algunas consideraciones acerca del acting out en la enfermedad maníaco-depresivo. *Revista Uruguaya de Psicoanálisis* 8:363-374.
Garcia Vega, Horacio (1956) Algunos aspectos del análisis de una psicosis paranóide. *Revista de Psicoanálisis* 11:77-92.
Gardiner, Muriel (1953). Meetings with the Wolf Man. *Bulletin of the Menninger Clinic* 17:41-48.

Garma, Angel (1931). La realidad exterior y los instinctos en la esquizofrenia. *Revista de Psicoanálisis* 2:56-82.

——— (1978). La esquizofrenia. In *El Psicoanálisis. Teoría, Clínica y Práctica*, 3rd ed., pp. 191-216. Buenos Aires: Editorial Paidós.

Geleerd, Elisabeth R. (1958). Borderline states in childhood and adolescence. *Psychoanalytic Study of the Child* 13:279-295.

——— (1963). Review of Melanie Klein's last book: *Narrative of a Child Analysis*. *Bulletin of the Philadelphia Association of Psychoanalysis* 13:39-41.

Gioia, Gina, and Liberman, David (1953). Una sesión psicoanalítica de un paciente esquizofrénica. *Revista de Psicoanálisis* 10:372-378.

Giovacchini, Peter L. (1963). Integrative aspects of object relationships. *Psychoanalytic Quarterly* 32:393-407.

——— (1965). Some aspects of the development of the ego ideal of a creative scientist. *Psychoanalytic Quarterly* 34:79-101.

——— (1975a). *Psychoanalysis of Character Disorders*. New York: Jason Aronson.

——— (1975b). Self-projections in the narcissistic transference. *International Journal of Psychoanalytic Psychotherapy* 4:142-166.

——— (1979). *Treatment of Primitive Mental States*. New York: Jason Aronson.

Giovacchini, Peter L., and Boyer, L. Bryce (1975). The psychoanalytic impasse. *International Journal of Psychoanalytic Psychotherapy* 4:25-47.

Gitelson, Maxwell (1958). On ego distortion. *International Journal of Psycho-Analysis* 39:245-258.

——— (1962). The curative factors in psycho-analysis. *International Journal of Psycho-Analysis* 43:194-206.

Glover, Edward (1930). Grades of ego-differentiation. *International Journal of Psycho-Analysis* 11:1-11.

——— (1945). Examination of the Klein system of child psychology. *Psychoanalytic Study of the Child* 1:75-118.

——— (1950). *Freud or Jung?* New York: Norton.

——— (1955). *The Technique of Psychoanalysis*. New York: International Universities Press.

Goldhammer, Herbert, and Marshall, Andrew H. (1949). *The Frequency of Mental Disease. Long-Term Trends and Present Status*. Santa Monica, CA: The Rand Corporation.

Gordon, Alfred (1912). Differential diagnosis between manic-depressive psychosis and dementia praecox. *Journal of Nervous and Mental Disease* 39:24-41.

——— (1917). Obsessive hallucinations and psychoanalysis. *Journal of Abnormal Psychology* 12:423-430.

——— (1951). Transition of obsessions into delusions. Evaluation of obsessional phenomena from the prognostic standpoint. *American Journal of Psychiatry* 107:455-458.

Gottesman, Irving I., and Shields, James (1973). Genetic theorizing and schizophrenia. *British Journal of Psychiatry* 122:15-30.

Grebelskaya, Sch. (1912). Psychologische Analyse eines Paranoiden. *Jahresbericht Über Psychologische und Psychopathologische Forschung* 4:116-140.

Green, André (1975). The analyst, symbolization and absence in the analytic setting (on changes in analytic practice and analytic experience). *International Journal of Psycho-Analysis* 50:1-22.

Green, M. R. (1962). The roots of Sullivan's concept of self. *Psychiatric Quarterly* 36:271-282.

Greenacre, Phyllis (1918). Content of the schizophrenic characteristics occurring in affective disorders. *American Journal of Insanity* 75:197-202.

——— (1947). Vision, the headache and the halo. In *Trauma, Growth and Personality*, pp. 132-148. New York: Norton, 1952.

——— (1975). On reconstruction. *Journal of the American Psychoanalytic Association* 23:693-712.

Greenson, Ralph R. (1949). The psychology of apathy. *Psychoanalytic Quarterly* 18:290-302.

——— (1951). Apathetic and agitated boredom. *Psychoanalytic Quarterly* 20:346-347.

——— (1965). The working alliance and the transference neurosis. *Psychoanalytic Quarterly* 34:155-181.

Grinberg, León (1962). On a specific aspect of countertransference due to the patient's projective identification. *International Journal of Psycho-Analysis* 43:436-440.

——— (1976). *Teoría de la Identificación*. Buenos Aires: Editorial Paidós.

——— (1979). Countertransference and projective counteridentifications. *Contemporary Psychoanalysis* 15:226-247.

———, ed. (1977). *Prácticas Psicoanalíticas Comparadas en las Psicosis*. Buenos Aires: Editorial Paidós.

Grinker, Roy R., Sr., Werble, Beatrice, and Drye, Robert C. (1968). *The Borderline Syndrome: a Behavioral Study of Ego-Functions.* New York: Basic Books.

Grotstein, James S. (1975). A theoretical rationale for psychoanalytic treatment of schizophrenia. In *Psychotherapy of Schizophrenia,* ed. John G. Gunderson and Loren R. Mosher, pp. 175-204. New York: Jason Aronson.

——— (1977a). The psychoanalytic concept of schizophrenia. I. The Dilemma. *International Journal of Psycho-Analysis* 58:403-426.

——— (1977b). The psychoanalytic concept of schizophrenia. II. Reconciliation. *International Journal of Psycho-Analysis* 58:427-452.

Guarner, Enrique (1978). *Psicopatología Clínica y Tratamiento Analitico.* Mexico: Libreria de Porrua Hnos. y Cia.

Gunderson, John G., and Kolb, Jonathan E. (1978). Discriminating features of borderline patients. *American Journal of Psychiatry* 135:792-796.

Gunderson, John G., and Singer, Margaret T. (1975). Defining borderline states. *American Journal of Psychiatry* 132:1-10.

Guntrip, Henry J. S. (1961). *Personality Structure and Human Interaction: the Development Synthesis of Psychodynamic Theory,* pp. 192-245. New York: International Universities Press.

Häfner, Heinz (1954). Zur Psychopathologie der Halluzinationischen Schizophrenie. *Zeutschrift fur Gesamte Neurologie und Psychiatrie,* 192 (154):241-258.

Hallgren, Bertil, and Sjögren, Torsten (1959). A clinical and genetico-statistical study of schizophrenia and low-grade mental deficiency in a large Swedish rural population. *Acta Psychiatrica et Neurologica Scandinavica,* vol. 35, supplement 140.

Harley, Marjorie (1966). Transference developments in a five-year-old child. In *The Child Analyst at Work,* ed. Elisabeth R. Geleerd, pp. 115-141. New York: International Universities Press.

Hartmann, Heinz (1953). Contributions to the metapsychology of schizophrenia. *Psychoanalytic Study of the Child* 8:177-198.

Hartmann, Heinz, and Kris, Ernst (1945). The genetic approach in psychoanalysis. *Psychoanalytic Study of the Child* 1:11-30.

Hartmann, Heinz, Kris, Ernst, and Loewenstein, Rudolph M. (1946). Comments on the formation of psychic structure. *Psychoanalytic Study of the Child* 2:11-38.

——— (1949). Notes on the theory of aggression. *Psychoanalytic Study of the Child* 3-4:9-36.

Hartmann, Heinz, and Stumpfl, F. (1930). Psychosen bei einigen Zwillingen. *Zeitschrift für die Gesamte Neurologie und Psychiatrie* 123:251-298.

Hartocollis, Peter, ed. (1977). *Borderline Personality Disorders: the Concept, the Syndrome, the Patient.* New York: International Universities Press.

Hassall, James C. (1915). The role of the sexual complex in dementia praecox. *Psychoanalytic Review* 2:260-276.

Heath, Robert G., Leach, Byron E., Byers, Lawrence W., Martens, Sten, and Feigley, Charles A. (1958). Pharmacological and biological psychotherapy. *American Journal of Psychiatry* 114:683-689.

Hecker, Ewald (1871). Die hebephrenie. *Archive fur Pathologie, Anatomie und Physiologie*, vol. 52. Cited by Gregory Zilboorg and George W. Henry in *A History of Medical Psychology*, p. 448. New York: Norton, 1941.

Hendricks, Ives (1936). Ego development and certain character problems. *Psychoanalytic Quarterly* 5:320-346.

Hess, Eckhard H. (1964). Imprinting in birds. *Science* 146:1128-1139.

Hinsie, Leland E. (1930). *The Treatment of Schizophrenia.* Baltimore: Williams and Wilkins.

Hitschmann, Edward (1912). Swedenborg's paranoia. *American Imago* 6:45-50.

——— (1913). Paranoia, Homosexualität und Analerotik. *Zentralblatt für Psychoanalyse und Psychotherapie* 1:251-254.

Hoch, Paul H., and Polatin, Philip (1949). Pseudoneurotic forms of schizophrenia. *Psychiatric Quarterly* 23:248-276.

Hoch, Paul H., and Zubin, Joseph, eds. (1961). *Comparative Epidemiology of the Mental Disorders.* New York and London: Grune and Stratton.

Hoedemaker, Edward (1955). The therapeutic process in the treatment of schizophrenia. *Journal of the American Psychoanalytic Association* 3:89-109.

——— (1960). Psycho-analytic technique and ego modifications. *International Journal of Psycho-Analysis* 41:34-46.

Hollender, Marc H., and Böszörmënyi-Nagy, Ivan (1958). Hallucination as an ego experience. *Archives of General Psychiatry* 80:93-97.

Hollingshead, August B. and Redlich, Frederick C., eds. (1958). *Social Class and Mental Illness.* New York: John Wiley and Sons.

Hoop, Johannes H. van der (1924). Über die Projection und Ihre Inhalte. *Internationale Zeitschrift für Psychoanalyse* 10:276-288.

Horwitz, William A., Polatin, Philip, Kolb, Lawrence C., and Hoch, Paul C. (1958). A study of cases treated by "direct analysis." *American Journal of Psychiatry* 114:870-873.

Hughes, Charles H. (1884). Borderland psychiatric records—prodromal symptoms of psychical impairment. *Alienist and Neurologist* 5:85-91.

Isaacs, Susan (1939). A special mechanism in a schizoid boy. *International Journal of Psycho-Analysis* 20:333-339.

Isakower, Otto (1938). A contribution to the pathopsychology of phenomena associated with falling asleep. *International Journal of Psycho-Analysis* 19:331-345.

Isham, Mary K. (1920). The paraphrenic's inaccessibility. *Psychoanalytic Review* 7:246-256.

Jackson, Don D. (1959). Family interaction, family homeostasis and some implications for conjoint family psychotherapy. In *Science and Psychoanalysis,* ed. Jules Masserman, pp. 112-141. New York: Grune and Stratton.

——— (1961). Family therapy in the family of the schizophrenic. In *Contemporary Psychotherapies,* ed. Morris I. Stein, pp. 272-287. Glencoe, Ill.: The Free Press.

Jacobson, Edith (1955). Sullivan's interpersonal theory of psychiatry. *Journal of the American Psychoanalytic Association* 3:102-108.

——— (1964). *The Self and the Object World.* New York: International Universities Press.

——— (1969). *Psychotic Conflict and Reality.* New York: International Universities Press.

James, Martin (1964). Interpretation and management in the treatment of preadolescence: the handling of pre-oedipal and oedipal material in child development and psycho-analysis. *International Journal of Psycho-Analysis* 45:499-511.

——— (1972). Preverbal communications. In *Tactics and Techniques in Psychoanalytic Therapy,* ed. Peter L. Giovacchini, pp. 436-454. New York: Science House.

Jelliffe, Smith Ely (1907). The signs of dementia praecox: their significance and pedagogic prophylaxis. *American Journal of Medical Science* 134:157-182.

——— (1927). Mental pictures in schizophrenia and in epidemic encephalitis: their alliances, differences and a point of view. *American Journal of Psychiatry* 6:413-645.

Jones, Ernest (1909). Psycho-analytic notes on a case of hypomania. *American Journal of Insanity* 66:203-218.

——— (1933). The phallic phase. *International Journal of Psycho-Analysis* 14:1-33.

——— (1953). *The Life and Works of Sigmund Freud, 1856-1900. The Formative Years and Great Discoveries.* New York: Basic Books.

——— (1955). *The Life and Works of Sigmund Freud, 1901-1919. Years of Maturity.* New York: Basic Books.

Jung, Carl G. (1907). *The Psychology of Dementia Praecox.* New York: Nervous and Mental Disease Monographs.

Kahlbaum, Karl Ludwig (1863). *Die Gruppierung der Psychischen Krankheiten und die Einteilung der Seelenstörungen.* Danzig: A. W. Kaufman.

——— (1874). *Catatonia.* Baltimore: Johns Hopkins University Press, 1973.

——— (1878). *Die Klinisch-Diagnostischen Gesichtspunkte der Psychopathologie.* Leipzig: Breitkopf and Härtel.

——— (1890). Uber Heboidophrenie. *Allgemeine Zeitschrift für Psychiatrie* 46:461.

Kallmann, Franz J. (1950). The genetics of psychoses. *American Journal of Human Genetics* 2:385-390.

Kanzer, Mark. (1975). The therapeutic and working alliances. *International Journal of Psychoanalytic Psychotherapy* 4:48-73.

Karpas, Morris J. (1915-1916). Paraphrenia erotica. A contribution to the study of synthetic psychiatry. *American Journal of Insanity* 72:291-296.

Karpman, Benjamin (1944). Hebephrenic phantasies, relations to two basic crime trends: analysis of techniques used in one case. *Journal of Nervous and Mental Disease* 100:480-506.

Kasanin, Jacob S., ed. (1944). *Language and Thought in Schizophrenia.* Berkeley and Los Angeles: University of California Press.

Kasanin, Jacob S., and Hanfmann, Eugenia (1942). *Conceptual Thinking in Schizophrenia.* New York: Nervous and Mental Diseases Monograph Series.

Katan, Mauritz (1939). A contribution to the understanding of schizophrenic speech. *International Journal of Psycho-Analysis* 20:353-362.

——— (1950) Structural aspects of a case of schizophrenia. *Psychoanalytic Study of the Child* 5:175-211.

——— (1954). The importance of the nonpsychotic part of the personality in schizophrenia. *International Journal of Psycho-Analysis* 35:119-128.

——— (1969). A psychoanalytic approach to the diagnosis of paranoia. *Psychoanalytic Study of the Child* 24:328-257.

Kempf, Edward J. (1919). The psychoanalytic treatment of a case of schizophrenia: report of a case. *Psychoanalytic Review* 6:15-58.

Kernberg, Otto F. (1966). Structural derivatives of object relationships. *International Journal of Psycho-Analysis* 47:236-253.

——— (1967). Borderline personality organization. *Journal of the American Psychoanalytic Association* 15:641-685.

——— (1972). Critique of the Kleinian school. In *Tactics and Techniques of Psychoanalytic Therapy*, ed. Peter L. Giovacchini, pp. 62-93. New York: Science House.

——— (1975a). *Borderline Conditions and Pathological Narcissism.* New York: Jason Aronson.

——— (1975b). Transference and countertransference in the treatment of borderline patients. *Strecker Monograph Series*, no. XII. Philadelphia: Institute of Pennsylvania Hospital.

——— (1976a). Foreward. In *Primitive Internalized Object Relations*, Vamik D. Volkan. New York: International Universities Press.

——— (1976b). *Object Relations Theory and Clinical Psychoanalysis.* New York: Jason Aronson.

——— (1978). Contrasting approaches to the psychotherapy of borderline conditions. In *New Perspectives on the Psychotherapy of the Borderline Adult*, ed. James F. Masterson, pp. 75-104. New York: Brunner/Mazel.

Kernberg, Otto F., Burstein, Esther D., Coyne, Lolafaye, Appelbaum, Ann, Horwitz, Leonard, and Voth, Harold. (1972). Psychotherapy and psychoanalysis. Final report of the Menninger Foundation's Psychotherapy Research Project. *Bulletin of the Menninger Clinic*, vol. 36, nos. 1-2.

Kety, Seymour S., Rosenthal, David, Wender, Paul H., and

Schulsinger, Fini (1968). The types and prevalence of mental illness in the biological and adoptive families of adopted schizophrenics. In *The Transmission of Schizophrenia*, ed. David Rosenthal and Seymour S. Kety, pp. 345-362. London: Pergamon Press.

Khan, M. Masud R. (1960). Clinical aspects of the schizoid personality: affects and technique. *International Journal of Psycho-Analysis* 41:430-437.

——— (1969). On symbiotic omnipotence. *Psychoanalytic Forum* 3:137-147, 157-158. Reprinted in M. M. R. Khan, *The Privacy of the Self: Papers on Psychoanalytic Theory and Technique*, pp. 82-93. New York: International Universities Press, 1973.

Kielholz, Arthur (1951). Von Zweisinn. *Schweizerische Zeitschrift für Psychologie und ihre Anwendungen* 10:97-116.

Kimling, L. Erhenmeyer, Cornblatt, Barbara, and Fleiss, Joseph (1979). High-risk research in schizophrenia. *Psychiatric Annals* 9:79-102.

Klein, Melanie (1930). The psychotherapy of the psychoses. *British Journal of Medical Psychology* 10:242-244.

——— (1932). *The Psycho-Analysis of Children*. London: Hogarth Press.

——— (1935). A contribution to the psychogenesis of manic-depressive states. *International Journal of Psycho-Analysis* 16:145-174.

——— (1946). Notes on some schizoid mechanisms. *International Journal of Psycho-Analysis* 27:99-110.

——— (1948). *Contributions to Psycho-Analysis*, 1921-1945. London: The Hogarth Press and the Institute of Psycho-Analysis.

——— (1955). On identification. In *New Directions in Psycho-Analysis*, ed. Melanie Klein, Paula Heimann, and R. E. Money-Kyrle, pp. 309-345. London: Tavistock.

Knight, Robert P. (1953). Borderline states. In *Selected Papers of Robert P. Knight*, ed. Stuart C. Miller, pp. 208-222. New York: Basic Books, 1972.

Kohut, Heinz (1971). *The Analysis of the Self*. New York; International Universities Press.

Kolb, Lawrence C. (1956). Psychotherapeutic evolution and its implications. *Psychiatric Quarterly* 30:579-597.

Korner, Annaliese F. (1964). Some hypotheses regarding the

significance of individual differences at birth for later development. *Psychoanalytic Study of the Child* 19:58-72.

Kraepelin, Emil (1883). *Dementia Praecox and Paraphrenia.* Edinburgh: Livingston, 1925.

Kris, Ernst (1950). On preconscious mental processes. *Psychoanalytic Quarterly* 19:540-560.

——— (1954). Introduction. In *The Origins of Psychoanalysis: Letters, Drafts, and Notes to Wilhelm Fliess,* Sigmund Freud. New York: Basic Books.

——— (1955). Neutralization and sublimation. Observations on young children. *Psychoanalytic Study of the Child* 10:30-46.

Kubie, Lawrence S. (1971). The relation of psychotic disorganization to the neurotic process. *Journal of the American Psychoanalytic Association* 15:626-640.

Kumin, I. (1979). Developmental aspects of opposites and paradoxes. *International Review of Psycho-Analysis* 5:477-485.

Kusnetzoff, Juan C., and Maldavsky, David (1977). Aportes del estudio de una paciente borderline de base esquizóide. Análisis componencial y consideración de los "lugares psíquicos." *Revista de Psicoanalisis* 34:803-842.

Laforgue, René (1926). Scotomization in schizophrenia. *International Journal of Psycho-Analysis* 8:473-478.

——— (1935). Contribution à l'étude de la schizophrénie. *Évolution Psychiatrique* 3:81-96.

Landauer, Karl (1924). "Passive" technik. Zur analyse narzissistischer erkrankungen. *Internationale Zeitschrift für Ärztliche Psychoanalyse* 10:415-422.

Langer, Marie (1957). La interpretación basada en la vivencia contratransferencial de conexión o desconexión con el analisado. *Revista de Psicoanálisis* 14:31-38.

Langs, Robert J. (1973). *The Technique of Psychoanalytic Psychotherapy.* Vol. I. New York: Jason Aronson.

——— (1974). *The Technique of Psychoanalytic Psychotherapy.* Vol. II. New York: Jason Aronson.

——— (1975a). The patient's unconscious perception of the therapist's errors. In *Tactics and Techniques in Psychoanalytic Therapy, II. Countertransference,* ed. Peter L. Giovacchini, Alfred Flarsheim, and L. Bryce Boyer, pp. 239-250. New York: Jason Aronson.

——— (1975b). Therapeutic misalliance. *International Journal of Psychoanalytic Psychotherapy* 4:77-105.

——— (1976). *The Bipersonal Field*. New York: Jason Aronson.

Lehrman, Philip R. (1919). Mental mechanisms in the psychoses and neuroses. *New York State Journal of Medicine* 110:150-152.

Leonhard, Karl (1961). The cycloid psychoses. *Journal of Mental Science* 107:633-648.

Lewin, Bertram D. (1946). Sleep, the mouth and the dream screen. *Psychoanalytic Quarterly* 3:61-73.

——— (1950). *The Psychoanalysis of Elation*. New York: Norton.

Lewis, Noland D. C. (1923). *The Constitutional Factors in Schizophrenia*. New York and Washington: Nervous and Mental Disease Monograph Series #35.

——— (1936). *Research in Schizophrenia (Past Attainments, Present Trends, and Future Possibilities)*. New York: Committee on Mental Hygiene.

——— (1949). Criteria for early differential diagnosis of psychoneurosis and schizophrenia. *American Journal of Psychotherapy* 3:4-18.

Liberman, David (1952). Fragmento del análisis de una psicosis paranóide. *Revista de Psicoanálisis* 9:413-454.

——— (1957). Interpretación correlativa entre relato y repetición: su aplicación en una paciente con personalidad esquizóide. *Revista de Psicoanálisis* 14:55-62.

Lidz, Theodore (1973). *The Origin and Treatment of Schizophrenia*. New York: Basic Books.

Lidz, Theodore, Fleck, Stephen, and Cornelison, Alice R. (1965). *Schizophrenia and the Family*. New York: International Universities Press.

Lindon, John A. (1972). Melanie Klein's theory and technique: her life and work. In *Tactics and Techniques in Psychoanalytic Therapy*, ed. Peter L. Giovacchini, pp. 33-61. New York: Science House Press.

Little, Margaret (1958). On delusional transference (transference psychosis). *International Journal of Psycho-Analysis* 39:134-138.

Loewald, Hans W. (1960). On the therapeutic action of psychoanalysis. *International Journal of Psycho-Analysis* 41:16-34.

Loewenstein, Rudolph M. (1951). The problem of interpretation. *Psychoanalytic Quarterly* 20:1-14.

——— (1956). Some remarks on the role of speech in psychoanalytic technique. *International Journal of Psycho-Analysis* 37:460-468.

London, Nathaniel J. (1973a). An essay on psychoanalytic theory: two theories of schizophrenia. Part I: review and critical assessment of the two theories. *International Journal of Psycho-Analysis* 54:169-178.

——— (1973b). An essay on psychoanalytic theory: two theories of schizophrenia. Part II: discussion and restatement of the specific theory of schizophrenia. *International Journal of Psycho-Analysis* 54:179-193.

Lundholm, Helge (1932). *Schizophrenia.* Durham, North Carolina: Duke University Press.

Mack, John E., ed. (1975). *Borderline States in Psychiatry.* New York: Grune and Stratton.

Maeder, Alphonse E. (1910). Psychologische Untersuchungen an Dementia Praecox. Kranken. *Jahrbuch für Psychoanalytische und Psychopathologische Forschung* 2:185-245.

Maenchen, Anna (1968). Object cathexis in a borderline twin. *Psychoanalytic Study of the Child* 23:438-456.

Magnan, Valentin J. J. (1884). *Le Délire Chronique.* Cited by A. Dureau, *La Grande Encyclopédie: Inventaire Raisonné des Sciences, Des Lettres et des Artes* 19:950. Paris: H. Lamirault, 1886-1902.

——— (1893). *Lecons Classiques sur les Maladies Mentale.* 2nd ed. Cited by A. Dureau, *La Grande Encyclopédie: Inventaire Raisonne des Sciences des Lettres et des Artes* 19:950. Paris: H. Lamirault, 1886-1902.

Mahler, Margaret S. (1963). Thoughts about development and individuation. *Psychoanalytic Study of the Child* 18:307-324.

Mahler, Margaret S., Ross, John R., Jr., and DeFries, Zira (1949). Clinical studies in benign and malignant cases of childhood psychosis (schizophrenia-like). *American Journal of Orthopsychiatry* 19:295-305.

Mahler, Margaret S., Pine, Fred, and Bergman, Anni (1975). *The Psychological Birth of the Infant: Symbiosis and Individuation.* New York: Basic Books.

Malamud, William (1929). The application of psychoanalytic principles in interpreting the psychoses. *Psychoanalytic Review* 16:62-68.

Malin, Arthur, and Grotstein, James S. (1966). Projective identification in the therapeutic process. *International Journal of Psycho-Analysis* 47:26-31.

Malis, G. Yu (1959). *Research in the Etiology of Schizophrenia.* New York: Consultants Bureau.

Maltzberger, Benjamin (1940). *Social and Biological Aspects of Mental Disease.* Utica: State Hospital Press.

Marcondes, Durval (1966). A regressão na contratransferencia. *Revista Brasileira de Psicanálise* 2:11-21.

Margat, P. (1956). Détail d'une psychotherapie de schizophrène. *Évolution Psychiatrique* 3:717-749.

Markus, Otto, (1911). Über Assoziationen bei Dementia Praecox. *Archiv für Psychiatrie und Nervenkrankheiten* 48:344-393.

Marmor, Judd (1953). Orality in the hysterical personality. *Journal of the American Psychoanalytic Association* 1:656-671.

Masterson, James F. (1972). *Treatment of the Borderline Adolescent: a Developmental Approach.* New York: John Wiley and Sons.

——— (1976). *Treatment of the Borderline Adult: a Developmental Approach.* New York: Brunner/Mazel.

Matussek, Paul (1956). Psychotherapie bei Schizophrenen. In *Handbuch der Neurosenlehre und Psychotherapie,* ed. V. E. Frankel, V. E. von Gebsattel, and J. H. Schultz, pp. 385-417. Berlin: Urban and Schwarzenberg.

——— (1960). Der schizophrenie Autismus in der Sicht eines Kranker. *Psyche* 13:641-666.

Meissner, William W. (1978). Notes on some conceptual aspects of borderline personality organization. *International Review of Psycho-Analysis* 5:297-311.

Meltzer, Herbert Y. (1975). Regression is unnecessary. In *Psychotherapy of Schizophrenia,* ed. John G. Gunderson and Loren R. Mosher, pp. 123-138. New York: Jason Aronson.

Menninger, Karl A. (1920). Paranoid psychoses. *Journal of Nervous and Mental Disease* 51:35-40.

——— (1922). Reversible schizophrenia. *American Journal of Psychiatry* 1:575-587.

——— (1940). Psychoanalytic psychiatry: theory and practice. *Bulletin of the Menninger Clinic* 4:105-123.

Merenciano, W. (1945). *Psicosis Mitis.* Madrid: Diana Artes Gráfica.

Meyer, Adolf F. (1911). The nature and concept of dementia praecox. *Journal of Abnormal Psychology* 5:274-285.

——— (1921-1922). Constructive formulation of schizophrenia. *American Journal of Psychiatry* 1:355-364.

Minkowski, Eugene (1927). Sur le rattachement des lésions et des processus psychiques de la schizophrénie a des notions plus générales. *Revue Francaise de Psychanalyse* 1:21-23.

Modell, Arnold H. (1956). Some recent psychoanalytic theories of schizophrenia. *Psychoanalytic Review* 43:181-194.

——— (1958). The theoretical implications of hallucinatory experiences in schizophrenia. *Psychoanalytic Review* 43:181-194.

——— (1963). Primitive object relationships and the predisposition of schizophrenia. *International Journal of Psycho-Analysis* 44:282-293.

——— (1968). *Object Love and Reality*. New York: International Universities Press.

Monke, J. Victor. (1964). Personal communication.

Montagu, Ashley (1961). Culture and mental illness. *American Journal of Psychiatry* 118:15-23.

Morel, Benedict Augustin (1857). *Traité des Dégénérescences Physiques, Intellectuelles et Morales de L'Espèce Humaine*. Cited by Gregory Zilboorg and George W. Henry, *A History of Medical Psychology*, 1961, p. 402. New York: Norton.

Morichau-Beauchant, R. (1912). Homosexualität und Paranoia. *Zentralblatt für Psychoanalyse und Psychotherapie* 2:174-176.

Morse, Robert, and Noble, Douglas (1942). Joint endeavors of the administrative physician and psychotherapist. *Psychiatric Quarterly* 16:578-585.

Mosher, Loren R. (1975). Psychotherapy research. In *Psychotherapy with Schizophrenics*, ed. John G. Gunderson and Loren R. Mosher, pp. 243-252. New York: Jason Aronson.

Mullahy, Patrick (1940). A theory of interpersonal relationships and the evolution of psychiatry. In *Conceptions of Modern Psychiatry*, Harry Stack Sullivan, pp. 119-147. Washington: The William Alanson White Psychiatric Foundation, 1947.

——— (1948). *Oedipus, Myth and Complex*. New York: Hermitage Press.

Müller, Christian, and Benedetti, Gaetano (1965). *Psychotherapie der Schizophrenie*. Basel: Karger.

Müller, Christian, and Masson, D. (1963). La psychotherapie clinique des schizophrènes. *Évolution Psychiatrique* 28:609-615.

Myerson, Abraham (1939). Theory and principles of "total push" method in chronic schizophrenia. *American Journal of Psychiatry* 95:1197-1204.

Nacht, Sacha (1962). The curative factors in psycho-analysis. *International Journal of Psycho-Analysis* 43:206-212.

Nacht, Sacha, and Lebovici, Serge (1955). Indications et contre-indications de la psychanalyse. *Revue Francaise de Psychanalyse* 19:135-204.

Nadelson, Theodore (1977). Borderline rage and the therapist's response. *Archives of General Psychiatry* 134:748-751.

Nelken, Jan (1912). Analytische Beobachtungen über Phantasien eines Schizophrenen. *Jahrbuch für Psychoanalytische und Psychopatologische Forschung* 4:504-562.

Nicol, Susan E., and Heston, Leonard L. (1979). The future of genetic research in schizophrenia. *Psychiatric Annals* 9:32-53.

Nöllman, Jorge (1953). Consideraciones psicoanaliticas acerca de un enfermo esquizofrénico con mecanismos hipocrondriaco-paranoídes. *Revista de Psicoanálisis* 10:37-74.

Nunberg, Herman (1921). The course of the libidinal conflict in a case of schizophrenia. In *Practice and Theory of Psychoanalysis*, pp. 37-74. New York: Nervous and Mental Disease Publishing Co., 1948.

——— (1932). *Principles of Psychoanalysis: their Application to the Neuroses*. New York: International Universities Press.

——— (1937). On the theory of the results of psycho-analysis. *International Journal of Psycho-Analysis* 18:161-169.

Ogden, Thomas H. (1978). A developmental view of identifications resulting from maternal impingements. *International Journal of Psychoanalytic Psychotherapy* 7:486-506.

O'Malley, Mary (1923). Transference and some of its problems in psychoses. *Psychoanalytic Review* 10:1-25.

Ophuijsen, J. H. W. van (1920). On the origin of the feeling of persecution. *International Journal of Psycho-Analysis* 1:235-239.

Oppenheim, Hans (1912). Zur Frage der Genese des eifersuchtswahnes. *Zentralblatt für Psychoanalyse und Psychotherapie* 2:67-77.

Orens, Martin H. (1955). Setting a termination date—an impetus to psychoanalysis. *Journal of the American Psychoanalytic Association* 3:651-665.

Ornstein, Anna, and Ornstein, Paul H. (1975). On the interpretive process in schizophrenia. *International Journal of Psychoanalytic Psychotherapy* 4:219-271.

Orr, Douglas W. (1954). Transference and countertransference. *Journal of the American Psychoanalytic Association* 2:621-670.

Osnato, Michael (1918). A critical review of the pathogenesis of dementia praecox, with a discussion of the relation of psychoanalytic principles. *American Journal of Insanity* 75:411-432.

Pacheco, Mario A. (1979). Neurotic and psychotic transference and projective identification. Paper presented at the 31st International Psycho-Analytical Congress, New York, August.

Panel Discussion: Neurotic Ego Distortion (1959). Presented at the 20th Congress of the International Psycho-Analytical Association, Paris, 1957. *International Journal of Psycho-Analysis* 39:243-275.

Pao, Ping-Nie (1973). Notes on Freud's theory of schizophrenia. *International Journal of Psycho-Analysis* 54:469-476.

Pasche, F., and Renard, M. (1956). The reality of the object and economic point of view. *International Journal of Psycho-Analysis* 37:282-285.

Payne, Charles R. (1913-1914). Some Freudian contributions to the paranoia problem. *Critical Digest* 1:76-93, 187-202, 308-421, 445-451.

——— (1915). Some Freudian contributions to the paranoia problem. *Critical Digest* 2:93-101, 200-202.

Paz, Carlos A., Pelento, María L., and Olmos de Paz, Theresa (1975). *Estructuras y Estados Fronterizos en Ninos, Adolescentes y Adultos. I. Historia y Conceptualización.* Buenos Aires: Ediciones Nueva Visión.

——— (1976a). *Estructuras Y/O Estados Fronterizos en Niños y Adultos. II. Casuistica y Consideraciones Teoricas.* Buenos Aires: Editorial Nueva Vision.

——— (1976b). *Estructuras Y/O Estados Fronterizos en Ninos y Adultos. III. Investigacion y Terapeutica.* Buenos Aires: Editorial Nueva Vision.

Perestrello, Marialzira (1963). Um caso de intensa identificacão projetiva. *Jornal Brasileira Psiquiatrica* 12:425-441.

Perrier, Francois (1955). Sens du transfert dans les psychotherapies de schizophrene. *Acta Psychotherapeutica, Psychosomatica et Orthopaedagogica* 3 (Supplement): 266-272.

Perry, Helen S., and Gawel, Mary L., eds. (1953). *The Interpersonal Theory of Psychiatry*. New York: Norton.

Peto, Andrew (1967). Dedifferentiations and fragmentations during analysis. *Journal of the American Psychoanalytic Association* 15:534-550.

Piaget, Jean (1924). *The Language and Thought of the Child*. New York: Harcourt, Brace, 1930.

——— (1952). *The Language and Thought of the Child*. London: Routledge and Kegan Paul.

Pichon-Rivière, Enrique (1947). Psicoanálisis de la esquizofrenia. *Revista de Psicoanálisis* 5:293-304.

Pine, Fred (1974). On the concept "borderline" in children: a clinical essay. *Psychoanalytic Study of the Child* 29:341-368.

Pious, William (1949). The pathogenic process in schizophrenia. (1) ego pathology. (2) Relation of super-ego to aggression and ego organization. (3) Instinct theory. *Bulletin of the Menninger Clinic* 13:152-159.

——— (1961). A hypothesis about the nature of schizophrenic behavior. In *Psychotherapy of the Psychoses*, ed. Arthur Burton, pp. 43-68. New York: Basic Books.

Prado Galvão, Luiz de A. (1966). Contratransferencia frente a regressão. *Revista Brasileira de Psicanálise* 2:22-34.

Pruyser, Paul W. (1975). What splits in splitting? *Bulletin of the Menninger Clinic* 39:1-46.

Racker, Enrique (1957). The meanings and uses of countertransference. *Psychoanalytic Quarterly* 26:303-357.

——— (1968). *Transference and Countertransference*. New York: International Universities Press.

Rangell, Leo (1955). (Reporter) The borderline case. Panel discussion of the American Psychoanalytic Association, 1954. *Journal of the American Psychoanalytic Association* 3:285-298.

Rank, Otto (1929). *Will Therapy in Truth and Reality*. New York: Knopf, 1945.

Rascovsky, Arnaldo, deFerrer, Susana L., Garma, Angel, de Mendes, Susana A., Mujica, Carlos P., Borrero, Hernando P., de Rascovsky, Matilda I. W., Tomas, Jaime, and Wencelblat, Simon (1960). *El Psiquismo Fetal*. Buenos Aires: Editorial Paidós.

Reich, Wilhelm (1933). *Character Analysis*. New York: Orgone Institute Press, 1945.

Reichard, Suzanne (1956). A re-examination of "Studies in Hysteria." *Psychoanalytic Quarterly* 25:155-177.

Rickman, John (1926). A survey: the development of the psychoanalytical theory of the psychoses, 1894-1926. *British Journal of Medical Psychology* 6:270-294.

——— (1927). A survey: the development of the psycho-analytical theory of the psychoses, 1894-1926. *British Journal of Medical Psychology* 7:94-124, 321-374.

Riklin, Franz (1906). Beitrag zur Psychologie des Kataleptischen Zustände bei Katatonie. *Psychiatrische-Neurologische Wochenschrift* 8:32-33.

Rin, Hsion, Chu, Hung-ming, and Lin, Tsung-yi (1965). Psychophysiological reactions of a rural and suburban population in Taiwan. *Acta Psychiatrica Scandinavica* 42:410-473.

Rivière, Joan (1936). On the genesis of psychic conflict in earliest infancy. *International Journal of Psycho-Analysis* 17:395-422.

Robbins, Michael D. (1976). Borderline personality organization: the need for a new theory. *Journal of the American Psychoanalytic Association* 24:831-853.

Rolla, Edgardo (1957). Análisis de una esquizofrenia. *Revista de Psicoanalisis* 14:72-75.

——— (1959). Actualización, psicoanálisis de psicóticos. *Revista de Psicoanálisis* 16:72-83.

Rosen, John N. (1947). The treatment of schizophrenia psychosis by direct analytic therapy. *Psychiatric Quarterly* 21:3-37.

——— (1962). *Direct Analytic Therapy*. New York: Grune and Stratton.

Rosenfeld, David, and Mordo, E. (1973). Fusión, confusión, simbiosis e identificación. *Revista de Psicoanalisis* 30:413-423.

Rosenfeld, Herbert A. (1952a). Notes on the psycho-analysis of the super-ego conflict of an acute schizophrenic patient. *International Journal of Psycho-Analysis* 33:111-131.

——— (1952b). Transference-phenomena and transference-analysis in an acute catatonic schizophrenic patient. *International Journal of Psycho-Analysis* 33:457-464.

——— (1954). Consideration regarding the psycho-analytic approach to acute and chronic schizophrenia. *International Journal of Psycho-Analysis* 35:135-140.

——— (1957). Supervisión colectiva de un caso fronterizo. Buenos Aires: mimeographed.

——— (1965). *Psychotic States: a Psycho-Analytical Approach.* London: Hogarth.

——— (1966). Discussion of office treatment of schizophrenia by L. Bryce Boyer. *Psychoanalytic Forum* 1:351-353.

Rosenfeld, Sara Kut, and Sprince, Marjorie P. (1963). An attempt to formulate the meaning of the concept "borderline." *Psychoanalytic Study of the Child* 18:603-635.

Rosenthal, David, ed. (1963). *The Genain Quadruplets: a Case Study and Theoretical Analysis of Heredity and Environment in Schizophrenia.* New York: Basic Books.

Rosse, Irving C. (1890). Clinical evidences of borderland insanity. *Journal of Nervous and Mental Disease* 17:669-683.

Roth, David, and Blatt, Sidney J. (1975). Ego structure, psychopathology and spatial representations. In *Tactics and Techniques in Psychoanalytic Therapy, Vol. II. Countertransference,* ed. Peter L. Giovacchini, Alfred Flarsheim, and L. Bryce Boyer, pp. 281-292. New York: Science House.

Ryckoff, Irving M., Day, Juliana, and Wynne, Lyman C. (1959). Maintenance of stereotyped roles in the families of schizophrenics. *Archives of General Psychiatry* 1:93-98.

Rycroft, Charles (1960). The analysis of a paranoid personality. *International Journal of Psycho-Analysis* 41:59-69.

Sagredo, Oscar (1955). Psicoterapia de esquizofrenia (método de Rosen). *Archivos Médicos de Cuba* 6:173-193.

Salzman, Leon (1964). Socio-psychological theories in psychoanalysis: Karen Horney and Harry Stack Sullivan. *American Journal of Psychoanalysis* 24:131-144.

Sarnoff, Charles (1976). *Latency.* New York: Jason Aronson.

Savage, Charles (1961). Countertransference in the treatment of schizophrenics. *Psychiatry* 24:53-60.

Scarizza, Spartaco, ed. (1965). *Proceedings of the First International Congress of Direct Psychoanalysis (1964).* Doylestown, Pa.: The Doylestown Foundation.

Schaffler, Leslie, Wynne, Lyman C., Day, Juliana, Ryckoff, Irving M., and Halperin, Alexander (1962). On the nature and sources of the psychiatrist's experiences with the family of the schizophrenic. *Psychiatry* 25:32-45.

Scheflen, Albert E. (1961). *A Psychotherapy of Schizophrenia. A Study of Direct Analysis.* Springfield, Ill.: Charles C Thomas.

Schindler, Raoul (1955). Übertragungsbildung und Übertragungsführung in der Psychotherapie mit Schizophrenen. *Acta Psychotherapeutica, Psychosomatica et Orthopaedagogica* 3 (Supplement): 337-344.

——— (1960). Klinische Psychotherapie von Psychosen. In *Therapeutische Fortschritte in der Neurologie und Psychiatrie*, ed. Hans Hoof, pp. 379-396. Vienna: Urban and Schwarzenberg.

Schneider, Kurt (1939). *Psychischer Befund und Psychiatrische Diagnose*. Leipzig: G. Thieme.

Schultz-Hencke, Harald (1952). *Das Problem der Schizophrenia: Analytische Psychotherapie und Psychose*. Stuttgart: Thieme.

Schwartz, Morris S., and Stanton, Alfred H. (1950). A social psychological study of incontinence. *Psychiatry* 13:399-416.

Schwing, Gertrud (1940). *A Way to the Soul of the Mentally Ill*. New York: International Universities Press, 1954.

Searles, Harold F. (1958). The schizophrenic's vulnerability to the therapist's unconscious processes. In *Collected Papers on Schizophrenia and Related Subjects*, pp. 192-215. New York: International Universities Press, 1965.

——— (1963). Transference psychoses in the psychotherapy of chronic schizophrenia. In *Collected Papers on Schizophrenia and Related Subjects*, pp. 654-716. New York: International Universities Press, 1965.

——— (1965a). *Collected Papers on Schizophrenia and Related Subjects*. New York: International Universities Press.

——— (1965b). Feelings of guilt in the psychoanalyst. *Psychiatry* 29:319-323.

——— (1975). The patient as therapist to his analyst. In *Tactics and Techniques in Psychoanalytic Therapy. Vol. II. Countertransference*, ed. Peter L. Giovacchini, Alfred Flarsheim, and L. Bryce Boyer, pp. 95-151. New York: Science House.

Sechehaye, Marguerite A. (1947). *Symbolic Realization*. New York: International Universities Press, 1951.

——— (1960). Technique de gratification en psychotherapie analytique des schizophrènes: indications et contreindications. In *Psychotherapy of Schizophrenia* (2nd International Symposium), ed. Gaetano Benedetti and Christian Müller, pp. 221-254. New York: Karger.

——— (1965). Les divers aspects du moi schizophrénique. *Évolution Psychiatrique* 30:299-316.

Segal, Hanna (1950). Some aspects of the analysis of a schizophrenic. *International Journal of Psycho-Analysis* 31:268-278.

——— (1954). A note on some schizoid mechanisms underlying phobic formation. *International Journal of Psycho-Analysis* 35:238-241.

——— (1965). *Introducción a la Obra de Melanie Klein*. Buenos Aires: Paidós.

Serota, Herman M. (1964). Home movies of early childhood: correlative developmental data in the psychoanalysis of adults. *Science* 143:1195.

Shapiro, Edward R. (1978). The psychodynamics and developmental psychology of the borderline patient: a review of the literature. *American Journal of Psychiatry* 135:1305-1315.

Shapiro, Edward R., Shapiro, Roger L., and Zinner, John (1977). The borderline ego and the working alliance: indications for family and individual treatment in adolescence. *International Journal of Psycho-Analysis* 58:77-87.

Shapiro, Edward R., Zinner, John, Shapiro, Roger L., and Berkowitz, David A. (1975). The influence of family experience on borderline personality development. *International Review of Psycho-Analysis* 2:399-411.

Shockley, Francis M. (1914). The role of homosexuality in the genesis of paranoid conditions. *Psychoanalytic Review* 1:431-438.

Siever, Larry J., and Gunderson, John G. (1979). Genetic determinants of borderline conditions. *Schizophrenia Bulletin* 5:59-86.

Silk, S. A. (1920). Compensatory mechanisms of delusions and hallucinations. *American Journal of Insanity* 77:523-542.

Simmel, Ernst (1909). *Kritischer Beitrag zur Aetiologie der Dementia Praecox* (dissertation). Rostock: Rats- und Universitäts-Buchdruckerei von Adlers Erban G. M. B. H.

Singer, Margaret T. (1977). The borderline diagnosis and psychological tests: review and research. In *Borderline Personality Disorders*, ed. Peter Hartocollis, pp. 193-212. New York: International Universities Press.

Singer, Margaret T., and Wynne, Lyman C. (1965). Thought disorder and family relations of schizophrenics. IV: results and implications. *Archives of General Psychiatry* 12:201-212.

Singer, Melvin (1975). The borderline delinquent: the interlocking of intrapsychic and interactional determinants. *International Review of Psycho-Analysis* 2:429-440.

Spence, Donald P., ed. (1967). *The Broad Scope of Psychoanalysis: Selected Papers of Leopold Bellak.* New York: Grune and Stratton.

Sperling, Melitta (1955). Psychosis and psychosomatic illness. *International Journal of Psycho-Analysis* 36:320-327.

——— (1974). *The Major Neuroses and Behavior Disorders in Children.* New York: Jason Aronson.

——— (1978). *Psychosomatic Disorders in Childhood.* New York: Jason Aronson.

Spitz, René A. (1946). The smiling response. *Genetic Psychology Monographs* 34:57-125.

——— (1959). *A Genetic Field Theory of Ego Formation.* New York: International Universities Press.

Stabbs, Gerdhild von (1954). Die Behandlung einer Schizophrenie unter besonderer Berücksichtigung der Handhabung der Übertragung. *Acta Psychotherapeutica, Psychosomatica et Orthopaedagogica* 2:314-333.

Stanton, Alfred H., and Schwartz, Morris S. (1954). *The Mental Hospital. A Study of Institutional Participation in Psychiatric Illness and Treatment.* New York: Basic Books.

Stärcke, August (1904). *Psychoschisis.* Amsterdam: Staatsdrukkerij.

——— (1919). The reversal of the libido-sign in delusions of persecution. *International Journal of Psycho-Analysis* 1:231-234.

——— (1921). *Psychoanalyse und Psychiatrie.* Leipzig and Vienna: Internationale psychoanalytische Verlag.

Staveren, Herbert (1947). Suggested specificity of certain dynamics in a case of schizophrenia. *Psychiatry* 10:127-135.

Stengel, Erwin (1957). Die Rolle der Psychoanalyse in der Behandlung der Psychosen, insbesondere der Schizophrenie. In *Das Psychoanalytische Volksbuch,* ed. Paul Federn and H. Meng, pp. 305-311. Bern: Hans Huber.

Stierlin, Helm (1958). Contrasting attitudes toward the psychoses in Europe and in the United States. *Psychiatry* 21:141-147.

——— (1969). *Conflict and Reconciliation. A Study in Human Relations and Schizophrenia.* New York: Doubleday.

——— (1974). *Separating Parents and Adolescents. A Perspective on Running Away, Schizophrenia and Waywardness.* New York: Quadrangle.

Stone, Leo (1955). Two avenues of approach to the schizophrenic patient. *Journal of the American Psychoanalytic Association* 3:126-148.

——— (1963). *The Psychoanalytic Situation.* New York: International Universities Press.

Storch, Alfred (1922). *The Primitive Archaic Forms of Inner Experiences and Thought in Schizophrenia.* New York: Nervous and Mental Disease Publishing Co., 1924.

——— (1930). Die welt der beginnenden schizophrenia und die archäische welt. Ein existential-analytischer versucht. *Zeitschrift für die Gesamte Neurologie und Psychiatrie* 127:799-810.

Storch, August, and Kulenkampf, Caspar (1950). Zum Verständnis des "Weltuntergangs" bei den Schizophrenen. *Nervenarzt* 21:102-108.

Sullivan, Charles T. (1963). Freud and Fairbairn: two theories of ego psychology. A Doylestown Foundation Paper. Doylestown, Pa.: The Doylestown Foundation.

Sullivan, Harry Stack (1925). Affective experience in early schizophrenia. *American Journal of Psychiatry* 6:467-484.

——— (1931). Environmental factors in etiology and course under treatment of schizophrenia. *Medical Journal Record* 133:19-22.

——— (1940). *Conceptions of Modern Psychiatry.* Washington: William A. White Psychiatric Foundation.

——— (1947). Therapeutic investigations in schizophrenia. *Psychiatry* 10:121-125.

Szalita-Pemow, Alberta B. (1955). The "intuitive process" and its relations to work with schizophrenics. *Journal of the American Psychoanalytic Association* 3:7-18.

Szplika, Jaime I. (1967). Consideraciones sobre el marco y el proceso psicoanalítico en la psicosis. *Revista de Psicoanálisis* 24:899-923.

Tausk, Victor (1919). On the origin of the "influencing machine" in schizophrenia. *Psychoanalytic Quarterly* 2:519-556.

Ter-Ogannessien, Elizabeth (1912). Psychoanalyse einer Katatonie. *Psychiatrisch-Neurolgische Wochenschrift* 14:299-302, 309-312.

Thompson, Clara (1943). The therapeutic technique of Sandor Ferenczi: a comment. *International Journal of Psychoanalysis* 24:64-66.

——— (1952). Sullivan and psychoanalysis. In *Contributions of Harry Stack Sullivan,* ed. Patrick Mullahy, pp. 101-115. New York: Hermitage House.

——— (1955). Introduction. *Final Contributions to the Problems and Methods of Psychoanalysis,* Sandor Ferenczi. New York: Basic Books.

Timsit, Meyer (1971). Les états limites. Évolution des concepts. *Évolution Psychiatrique* 36:679-724.

Tolentino, Isidor I. (1956). Aspetti psicogenetici della schizofrenia. Studio clinico. *Rivista Sperimentale di Freniatria e Medicina Legale Della Alienazioni Mentali* 80:1-10.

Tolentino, Isidor L., and Callieri, Bruno (1957). Contributo clinico all 'impostazione psicodinamica della depersonalizazione. *Rivista Sperimentale di Frenetria e Medicina Legale Della Alienazioni Mentali* 81:615-639.

Tsuang, Ming T. (1978). Genetic counseling for psychiatric patients and their families. *American Journal of Psychiatry* 135:1465-1475.

Uchõa, Darcy de M. (1967). A adaptacão regressiva do ego en esquizofrenia. *Revista Brasileira de Psicanálise* 1:116-126.

——— (1968). *Psiquiatria e Psicanalise.* Sao Paulo: Sarvier.

van der Waals, Hermanus G. (1960). *Chronic Schizophrenia. Exploration in Theory and Treatment.* Glencoe, Ill.: The Free Press.

——— (1965). Problems of narcissism. *Bulletin of the Menninger Clinic* 29:293-311.

Vanggaard, Thorkil (1955). A discussion of the basic principles of psychoanalytically oriented psychotherapy of schizophrenia. *Acta Psychiatrica Scandinavica* 30:507-527.

Volkan, Vamik D. (1976). *Primitive Internalized Object Relations. A Clinical Study of Schizophrenic, Borderline and Narcissistic Patients.* New York: International Universities Press.

——— (1979). The "glass bubble" of the narcissistic patient. In *Advances in Psychotherapy of the Borderline Patient,* ed. Joseph LeBoit and Attilio Capponi, chap. 10. New York: Jason Aronson.

Vowinckel, Edith (1930). Der heutige Stand der psychiatrischen Schizophrenieforschung. *Internationale Zeitschrift für Psychoanalyse* 16:471-491.

Waelder, Robert (1924). The psychoses: their mechanisms and accessibility to treatment. *International Journal of Psycho-Analysis* 6:254-281.

——— (1937). The problem of the genesis of a psychical conflict in earliest infancy. *International Journal of Psychoanalysis* 18:406-473.

——— (1965). Personal communication.

Wanke, Georg (1919). *Über Die im Gewöhnlichen Leben Wichtigste Geisteskrankheit: Jugenirresein, Dementia Praecox (Kraepelin), Schizophrenie (Bleuler), Paraphrenia (Magnan, Freud), Zweisinn (Bresler) für Arzte, Juristen und Erzieher.* Halle: C. Marhold.

Washburn, Sherwood L. (1965). Personal communication.

Wexler, Milton (1951a). The structural problem in schizophrenia: the role of the internal object. *Bulletin of the Menninger Clinic* 15:221-234.

——— (1951b). The structural problem in schizophrenia: therapeutic implications. *International Journal of Psycho-Analysis* 37:157-166.

——— (1971). Schizophrenia, conflict and deficiency. *Psychoanalytic Quarterly* 40:83-100.

White, Mary J. (1952). Sullivan and treatment. In *The Contributions of Harry Stack Sullivan*, ed. Patrick Mullahy, pp. 117-150. New York: Hermitage House.

White, William A. (1910). The etiology of dementia praecox. *Journal of the American Medical Association* 46:1519-1521.

——— (1926). The language of schizophrenia. *Archives of Neurology and Psychiatry* 16:395-413.

Wholey, Cornelius C. (1916). A psychosis presenting schizophrenic and Freudian mechanisms with scientific clearness. *American Journal of Insanity* 73:583-595.

Will, Otto A., Jr. (1959). Human relatedness and the schizophrenic reaction. *Psychiatry* 22:205-223.

——— (1962). Hallucinations: comments reflecting clinical observations of the schizophrenic reaction. In *Hallucinations*, ed. Louis J. West, pp. 174-182. New York: Grune and Stratton.

——— (1964). Schizophrenia and the psychotherapeutic field. *Contemporary Psychoanalysis* 1:1-29.

Wilmanns, Karl (1922). Die Schizophrenie. *Zeitschrift für die Gesamte Neurologie Und Psychiatrie* 78:4-5.

Wilson, C. Philip (1968). Psychosomatic asthma and acting out. A case of bronchial asthma that developed *de novo* in the terminal phase of analysis. *International Journal of Psycho-Analysis* 49:330-335.

Winkler, Monica (1960). Erfolgreiche analytische Kurztherapie bei einem Schizophrenen. In *Psychotherapy of Schizophrenia* (2nd

International Symposium), ed. Gaetano Benedetti and Christian Müller, pp. 30-46. Basel and New York: Karger.

Winkler, W. T. (1966). Indikation und Prognose zur Psychotherapie der Psychosen. *Zeitschrift für Psychotherapie und Medizinische Psychologie* 16:42-51.

Winkler, W. T., and Häfner, Heinz (1954). Kontakt und Übertragung bei der Psychotherapie Schizophrener. *Zeitschrift für Psychotherapie und Medizinische Psychologie* 4:179-184.

Winkler, W. T., and Wieser, S. (1959). Die Ich-Mythisierung als Abwehrmassnahme des Ich, dargestellt am Beispiel des Wahneinfalles von der Jungfraülichen Empfängnis und Geburt bei paraphrenen Episoden. *Nervenarzt* 30:75-81.

Winnicott, Donald W. (1947). Hate in the countertransference. In *Collected Papers. Through Paediatrics to Psychoanalysis*, pp. 194-203. New York: Basic Books, 1958.

——— (1953). Transitional objects and transitional phenomena. In *Collected Papers. Through Paediatrics to Psycho-Analysis*, pp. 229-242. New York: Basic Books, 1958.

——— (1954a). Metapsychological and clinical aspects of regression in the psycho-analytical set-up. In *Collected Papers. Through Paediatrics to Psycho-Analysis*, pp. 278-294. New York: Basic Books, 1958.

——— (1954b). Mind and its relation to the psyche soma. *British Journal of Medical Psychology* 27:201-209.

——— (1955). Clinical varieties of transference. In *Collected Papers. Through Paediatrics to Psycho-Analysis*, pp. 295-299. New York: Basic Books, 1958.

——— (1956). Primary maternal preoccupation. In *Collected Papers. Through Paediatrics to Psycho-Analysis*, pp. 300-305. New York: Basic Books, 1958.

——— (1958a). *Collected Papers: Through Paediatrics to Psycho-Analysis*. New York: Basic Books.

——— (1958b). Psychoanalysis and the sense of guilt. In *The Maturational Processes and the Facilitating Environment*, pp. 15-28. New York: International Universities Press, 1963.

——— (1960). The theory of the parent-infant relationship. *International Journal of Psycho-Analysis* 41:585-596.

——— (1962). A personal view of the Kleinian contribution. In *The Maturational Processes and the Facilitating Environment*, pp. 171-178. New York: International Universities Press, 1963.

——— (1963). *The Maturational Processes and the Facilitating Environment.* New York: International Universities Press.

Wisdom, John O. (1962). Comparison and development of the psychoanalytical theories of melancholia. *International Journal of Psycho-Analysis* 43:113-132.

Wolberg, Arlene R. (1952). The borderline patient. *American Journal of Psychotherapy* 6:694-710.

——— (1973). *The Borderline Patient.* New York: Intercontinental Medical Book Corporation.

Wolf, Alexander (1957). Discussion of Dr. Bychowski's paper, "Psychic Structure and Therapy of Latent Schizophrenia." In *Schizophrenia in Psychoanalytic Office Practice,* ed. Alfred H. Rifkin, pp. 135-139. New York: Grune and Stratton.

Wolfenstein, Martha (1966). How is mourning possible? *Psychoanalytic Study of the Child* 21:93-123.

——— (1969). Loss, rage and repetition. *Psychoanalytic Study of the Child* 24:432-460.

World Health Organization (1973). *International Pilot Study of Schizophrenia. Vol. I.* Geneva: World Health Organization.

Wyatt, Richard J., Potkin, Steven G., and Murphy, Dennis L. (1979). Platelet monoamine oxidase activity in schizophrenia: a review of the data. *American Journal of Psychiatry* 136:377-385.

Wynne, Lyman C. (1967). Family transactions and schizophrenia. II. Conceptual considerations for a research strategy. In *The Origins of Schizophrenia,* ed. John Romano, pp. 165-178. Amsterdam and New York: Excerpta Medica.

Wynne, Lyman C., and Singer, Margaret T. (1963a). Thought disorder and family relationships of schizophrenics. I. Research strategy. *American Archives of General Psychiatry* 9:191-198.

——— (1963b). Thought disorder and family relations of schizophrenics. II. A classification of forms of thinking. *American Archives of General Psychiatry* 9:199-206.

Zapparoli, Giovanni C. (1957). Note sui meccanismi metapsicologici della Schizofrenia. *Rivista di Psicoanalisi* 3:107-150.

Zetzel, Elizabeth R. (1953). The depressive position. In *Affective Disorders,* ed. Phyllis Greenacre, pp. 84-116. New York: International Universities Press.

——— (1956a). An approach to the relation between concept and content in psychoanalytic theory (with special reference to the work of Melanie Klein and her followers). *Psychoanalytic Study of the Child* 11:99-121.

——— (1956b). Current concepts of transference. *International Journal of Psycho-Analysis* 37:369-376.

——— (1960). Discussion at the American Psychoanalytic Association Panel on Criteria for Analyzability, New York, December.

———(1964a). The analytic situation. In *Psychoanalysis in the Americas: Original Contributions from the First Pan-American Congress for Psychoanalysis*, ed. Robert E. Litman, pp. 86-106. New York: International Universities Press.

——— (1964b). Discussion of Herbert A. Rosenfeld's paper, "Object Relations of the Acute Schizophrenic Patient in the Transference Situation." *Psychiatric Research Reports* 19:75-79.

——— (1965). Personal communication.

——— (1967). Psychosis and the very young infant. Review of *Psychotic States: a Psychoanalytical Approach*, Herbert A. Rosenfeld, 1965. *Contemporary Psychoanalysis* 12:126-128.

Zilboorg, Gregory (1935). *The Medical Man and the Witch During the Renaissance*. Baltimore: Johns Hopkins Press.

——— (1941). Ambulatory schizophrenia. *Journal of Nervous and Mental Disease* 94:201-204.

——— (1954). Personal communication.

Zilboorg, Gregory, and Henry, George W. (1941). *A History of Medical Psychology*. New York: Norton.

Zinner, John, and Shapiro, Edward (1975). Splitting in families of borderline adolescents. In *Borderline States in Psychiatry*, ed. John E. Mack, pp. 103-122. New York: Grune and Stratton.

Zinner, John, and Shapiro, Roger A. (1972). Projective identification as a mode of perception and behavior in families of adolescents. *International Journal of Psycho-Analysis* 53:523-530.

Index

Peabody Institute Danvers, MA
3 1397 10149 2422

D0699068

LOOKING FOR MR. GILBERT

Also by John Hanson Mitchell

Ceremonial Time

Living at the End of Time

A Field Guide to Your Own Backyard

Walking Towards Walden

Trespassing

The Wildest Place on Earth

Following the Sun

Looking *for* Mr. Gilbert

THE REIMAGINED LIFE OF AN AFRICAN AMERICAN

John Hanson Mitchell

Shoemaker & Hoard *Washington, D.C.*

Library of Congress Cataloging-in-Publication Data
Mitchell, John Hanson.
Looking for Mr. Gilbert : the reimagined life of an African American / John Hanson Mitchell.
p. cm.
ISBN 1-59376-026-4
1. Gilbert, Robert Alexander, 1870–1942.
2. Brewster, William, 1851–1919—Friends and associates.
3. African Americans—Massachusetts—Boston—Biography. 4. African American photographers—Massachusetts—Boston—Biography.
5. Photographers—Massachusetts—Boston—Biography.
6. Boston (Mass.)—Biography. I. Title.
F73.9.N4M58 2005 974.4′61′00496073-dc22
2004017305

Text design by David Bullen
Printed in the United States of America

Shoemaker SH Hoard
A Division of Avalon Publishing Group, Inc.
Distributed by Publishers Group West

10 9 8 7 6 5 4 3 2 1

For my father

James Archibald Mitchell

1892–1967

Contents

Looking *for* Mr. Gilbert

CHAPTER ONE

The African Charioteer

A PHOTOGRAPH IS ONLY A FRAGMENT, AND WITH THE PASSAGE OF TIME ITS MOORINGS BECOME UNSTUCK. IT DRIFTS AWAY INTO A SOFT ABSTRACT PASTNESS, OPEN TO ANY KIND OF READING. . . .

Susan Sontag

Concord River, 1911

April 6, 1911, Concord, Massachusetts:

As far as the eye could see that day, nothing moved. In the foreground, a dog, a black spaniel, stands immobilized, nose pointed forever toward the horizon. Beyond the dog, a river, stilled to a rippled skein of marble, winds through the landscape. The halyard on the mast of a skiff pulled up on the riverbank hangs in a lifeless curve; streamside trees and shrubs are caught in mid sway, and on the other side of the river, the land rolls westward in a rising wave, fields, farmhouses, and distant woodlands eternally fixed in early spring and unchanged even after a hundred seasons of growth. It's a sleeping kingdom waiting for some future prince to break through the thorn hedges and set the world in motion.

The shutter snaps. The river resumes its flow. The halyard begins to flutter. The inanimate dog breaks into a bounding run, and the photographer, a trim black man in a dark suit and a bowler hat, removes the plate holder and slips it into an oblong carrying case at his feet. He straightens himself and, with one hand resting on the oaken tripod, stares out at the landscape he has just trapped, his alchemy accomplished.

There are two other men in the field that day, both white. One has a neat, graying beard and is dressed in rumpled tweeds and high-topped calfskin boots, much worn from years of outings. The other wears a blue cotton overshirt and a heavyweight Winslow German vicuña cloth sport coat and woolen trousers. These two stand apart from the black man, squinting toward the scene that will reappear at some future point fixed on the glass plate the black man has just extracted from the camera. The white men have field glasses with them, and as they look out across the landscape they raise the glasses periodically to sight the ducks that wheel and settle over the river in small hammering flocks.

This is early spring in New England. It is a sunny, warming day, about eleven o'clock in the morning judging from the shadows cast by the standing dog. Somewhere up the hill, behind the little group of men, you can hear the sound of a piano emanating from the half-opened window of a farmhouse. Inside the house, in the parlor, a copper-haired woman dressed in a nobby shirtwaist of silk Duchess satin is leaning over the keyboard, tentatively sounding out the opening bars of Edward MacDowell's "To a Wild Rose." Somewhere, off beyond the low hill to the south, a horse whinnies; somewhere the sad three-note whistle of a song sparrow sounds off.

Across the river a flight of red-winged blackbirds rises up from the marshes and resettles, a small flock of ducks comes whistling down the flood, and the white men shift in place, raise their field glasses, and then agree to move on. Their intention today is to sail upstream to the wide waters of Fairhaven Bay to look for birds. The black man waits, then unscrews the camera, packs it into a square-shaped leather case, folds the tripod and hoists it over his shoulder, and the three of them walk toward the river. The dog is first, criss-crossing the path, snuffling everything, then the white men, then the dark man in the rear, carrying most of the equipment. You see them drop below the hill, legs first, then midriffs, then their shoulders, their hats. And then they are gone.

The woman at the keyboard sounds a full D-minor chord. A strand of auburn hair comes loose and falls over her smooth forehead. She has China blue eyes and hums softly to herself as she plays.

✠

Alternatively, you might reverse the flow of time and begin on the morning before the photograph was made.

The 8:42 train from Boston, via Cambridge, Belmont, and Lincoln, heaves into view around a curve, slows, and with much squealing and steaming halts at Concord Station. A natty little man with a round, balding head and darting eyes jumps briskly onto the platform and looks around expectantly. This is Mr. Samuel Henshaw, executive director of Harvard University's renowned Museum of Comparative Zoology and a man known for his orderliness and punctuality.

In spite of the fact that Concord is a mere fifteen miles beyond

Cambridge, this amounts to a trip to the wilderness for Mr. Samuel Henshaw, and, always prepared, he carries with him on this occasion a heavy twisted hickory walking stick and wears his newly purchased two-buckle rolled lumberman boots in case of possible encounters with savage dogs or snakes, possibly both.

Henshaw is greeted at the station by a tall, imposing figure with a high forehead, a rudder-straight nose, serious dark eyes, and a well-trimmed beard. This would be William Brewster, the ornithologist, founder of the Nuttall Club, the American Ornithologists' Union, president of the recently organized Massachusetts Audubon Society, and a well-known figure at the Harvard Museum.

The two men shake hands, Henshaw formally, the heels of his new boots snapped together, and the two of them walk to the front of the station, where Mr. Brewster's new Model T Ford touring machine is awaiting them.

Lounging against the high doors of the vehicle, his legs crossed and arms folded, is a dapper black man, who straightens slowly when the two white men appear. This is Brewster's manservant, known to the white community by his surname, "Gilbert"—better known among his peers in the Cambridge black community where he lives as Mr. Gilbert. Mr. Robert A. Gilbert, that is, the pianist.

This man, in his current guise as "Gilbert," opens the driver's-side door for the white men, who, after some deliberation as to who should enter first, settle themselves in the backseat. Gilbert leans into the automobile and sets the spark and throttle levers, then walks slowly around to the front of the car and slips his left forefinger through the choke loop. He waits for a second, then yanks the ring and at the same time throws the crank mightily with his right hand. The engine barks, sputters to life.

It should be noted that in the year 1911 this process is an art fraught with many pitfalls—failed or false starts, occasional broken arms from the kickback of the crank. But for Mr. Gilbert the act is carried out with an air of balletic grace, a slow dance in the palm courts of the Ritz.

7

THE AFRICAN CHARIOTEER

Now in the driver's seat, Mr. Gilbert releases the emergency hand brake, presses down the low-speed pedal with his left foot, and, as the machine begins to growl and roar, eases up the pedal and shifts into high gear. They move off from the station, riding high above the throng, passing through the rural streets of Concord town like European dignitaries, the only machine that will pass that morning. They are headed northward to Monument Street and Brewster's country home, "October Farm."

Henshaw would spend the day and the night there with Brewster and Gilbert, ranging the fields and water meadows of the Concord River in search of birds. He would pass the night at Brewster's "camp" by the riverside (and shiver the night through—partly from cold, partly chilled by the ghostly hooting of the surrounding owls) and then return on the morning train the next day. We know all this because a few days after his return Henshaw wrote up an account of the visit, inscribed in vaguely mock heroic phrases, as if he were ascending some undiscovered tributary of the Amazon. Henshaw described Brewster's automobile as a chariot, the village as an outpost, and the Concord open lands as wilderness tracts. He also described the driver of the automobile—Brewster's "African Charioteer"—who conducted the two of them through the wild interior of the province of Concord and ultimately to the country hacienda of William Brewster.

Suffice to say that this Henshaw was not a well-traveled individual.

The so-called African charioteer was a small, well-formed man, aged 42 at the time. He wore a dark wool four-button jacket, a white starched shirt with a detachable collar, and a black tie. For this occasion, and perhaps for his own entertainment (Brewster would not have cared what he wore), he had donned a conductor's cap with a freshly polished black leather visor and a hatband with two brass buttons. Inasmuch as they were traveling eastward, toward the sun, he wore the cap at a slight, almost unnoticeable angle, the shiny visor pulled down to shade his large dark eyes. Gilbert, it appears, was good at roleplaying. Like most men and women of his race living in the United States of America in 1911, he had to be.

Gilbert drove with a relaxed, although formal poise, both hands on the wheel, head fixed forward, his eyes glancing left and right, reviewing the familiar landscape of Concord as the vehicle rolled on. There was some banter between the white men in the backseat, and at one point Brewster leaned forward and jokingly admonished Gilbert to drive with care. Top speed of a 1910 Model T was all of twenty miles an hour. But these carriages were noisy and still new to the streets of Concord; the local horses were suspicious and tended to bolt.

The air was clean and fresh that sunny day, and as they swept eastward through the town, they passed small white houses set back from the street behind picket fences, freshly whitewashed for the coming season. They passed the old brick-front market, with the wooden bins of local vegetables set out on the sidewalk for the shoppers. They puttered by the livery, and the mill dam, and Wright's Tavern, where, one hundred and thirty-six years earlier, local farmers and tradesmen had assembled to plot resistance to what they viewed as the repressive government on the other side of the Atlantic.

The two white men in the backseat chatted formally as they rode along, perhaps even uncomfortably. Henshaw was a bit of a problem at the museum, carefully attending to more details than were necessary, even down to the number of paper clips doled out to the hardworking secretaries. There had been talk among the staff members at the museum, even at the upper levels, and Brewster knew it. But Mr. William Brewster, as far as I can determine, was a man who kept his opinions to himself. His field notes describe what he saw, not what he thought, and his personal diary, which he maintained along with his field journals for over twenty-five years, are a circumspect accounting of birds seen, of dogs, of works in progress at his farm, or the arrivals and departures of his houseguests.

Did Gilbert eavesdrop as these two chatted in the backseat? Did he size up this Henshaw for his known flaws? Gilbert and Brewster were intimates in a manner that we now, in the early twenty-first century, would be hard-pressed to understand, an interdependency that fed the daily lives of each. They had spent nearly every day together for fifteen years, either in town at Brewster's locally famous bird museum on Brattle Street in Cambridge, or in the field and camps on the river at Concord, or sometimes on expeditions into the wilds of Maine and northern New Hampshire. If anyone knew of the little tempests at the museum it would be Mr. Gilbert, even if Brewster had not shared a word with him. Gilbert was a good listener and reader of character, and he had a sharp eye for white behavior. But he too was circumspect, kept his own counsel, was ever polite, knew when to make his appearance and when to stay in the shadows, when to speak and when to remain ignorant. Or feign ignorance.

Even at home, among his own people, he was formal, an inscrutable presence. His inner emotions, it was said, were expressed at the keyboard, and even there he favored airs and arias, the theme from Ponchielli's *La Gioconda,* Chopin mazurkas, the new piano works of Amy Beach and Edward MacDowell, and sentimental popular songs such as "The Roses of Picardy." On Sundays he consented to Baptist and Episcopal hymns. And once or twice a year, at night, when he was in a certain mood and alone in the house with his wife, Anna, Mr. Gilbert descended to the lower depths and deigned to play a few of the currently popular low-class rags, his left hand arcing across the keys in the bouncing, offbeat stride style, and he, almost, but not quite, smiling.

Gilbert was not fond of jazz, even though he was an accomplished pianist, was not given to histrionics, or boasts, or, what seemed to him, the loud braying laughter one sometimes heard on the streets from his people. His employer, William Brewster, also despised the new form of music known as jazz, eschewed theater, rarely went to church, except at Christmas and even then only at the behest of his wife, Caroline. He avoided clubs, rarely drank, and ironically, given the fact that he now owned one, hated the new machines known as automobiles.

Gilbert quite agreed.

The souls of these two men, master and servant, one white and born with the proverbial silver spoon in his mouth, one black and from humble beginnings, had, by some fluke of fate or history, been forged in the same smithy. Nevertheless, the vast divide of the American social and racial chasm yawned between them. As the African American scholar Cornel West wrote, race matters. And as F. Scott Fitzgerald pointed out, the rich are different.

✢

Gilbert proceeded up Monument Street, passing en route the farms and vegetable plots of Concord. Three miles along, he turned right up a long unfinished drive and halted at the main house. Here, with Gilbert's assistance, arrangements were made for the outing. Gilbert carried out the rucksacks, field gear, thermoses, and field glasses. He packed an older model 8 × 10 mahogany Perfection Viewing Camera and a plate holder in a leather carrying case, and thus burdened the three of them set out down the old cow path beyond the house, past a field of birches, over the hill to a meadow above the Concord River.

Below this spot, by the side of the river, Brewster maintained several outbuildings landscaped with native trees, flowers, and shrubs. Here, he would commonly pass his days and visit with his guests—of whom there were many in those years. The little group of friends would often eat at the site, and sometimes even sleep there rather than return to the confines of the big house on the hill.

The cabin by the river was the third of Brewster's various abodes, the fourth if you count a houseboat he maintained on Lake Umbagog in northern Maine. The first was his mansion "The Elms" on Tory Row on Brattle Street, in Cambridge. The second was the large, well-appointed farmhouse on Monument Street, set back from the river.

Brewster was a man who, in some circles at least, might be described as a traitor to his class. Although he was moneyed and never had to work, he had no interest in Society matters, was uninterested in politics. And although he was the founder and first president of a number of bird organizations and had many friends and allies, he avoided social events and the frivolous men's clubs of Boston. Furthermore, although he was of good stock, that is to say a descendant of the Brewsters of Plymouth, because of poor eyesight in his youth, he was educated at home by his mother and did not attend Groton or Harvard—something that was de rigueur for most Boston Brahmin males. He was most comfortable out in the field observing birds. Very comfortable, in fact. Obsessed.

As the three of them worked their way toward the river they stopped often to observe the birds of the season. Gilbert acted as spotter on these occasions as would some local guide in the wilds of the North Woods. He spoke quietly, even casually, to Brewster.

—I believe I hear a bobolink, Mr. Brewster—

And a second later, there would be said bobolink, rising up from the field, fluttering and sailing only to drop down again into the long grasses.

Gilbert had a sharp eye and a good ear for calls. At one point in an open area, near a copse of trees, the little troop stopped. A medium-sized bird with a brown back and a red breast rose up, chirping, and landed on a branch at the edge of the woods, flicking its wings and tail and continuing to cluck.

—What would that be?—Henshaw asked.

Did Gilbert look over at Brewster briefly before answering? Was there an exchange of glances?

—That was a robin—Gilbert said haltingly, adding, *sotto voce*—Sir.

There must have been a certain undertone to all this. Samuel

Henshaw's brother, Henry, was a popular and well-known bird man and a good friend of William Brewster and his company of ornithologists. Samuel, by contrast, was an innocent afield.

"We were guided through the dense forests of Concord," he wrote in his account of the day, "by Brewster's faithful colored friend and helper, the redoubtable Gilbert, a skilled field observer and factotum for the great man."

Slung over his shoulder on a thick leather strap Gilbert carried the oakwood tripod and, in his right hand, the leather, boxlike case with the camera and plate holders. In the meadow above the river, the three of them stopped while Gilbert set up the tripod and screwed the camera onto the brass plate. He swung the lens toward the river and stopped, eyeing the scene on the ground glass:

Roll of meadow in the foreground.

The river beyond, banked by black willows and buttonbush.

He framed the scene, fixed the high sweep of pasturelands, walls and woods beyond.

Tree swallows flitted above the river, chattering flocks of blackbirds started up and settled on the opposite shore. Above them, the great sky rose in cerulean blue. Behind them, at the house, the woman with the copper-colored hair struck an opening chord.

Gilbert sank beneath the black camera hood, twisted the knobs of the rack and pinion focusing devices, and then, as he focused, the dog bounded into the scene. Gilbert raised his head, whistled, brought him to a halt, and squeezed the shutter bulb.

The river freezes. Swallows halt in midair. The willows cease to sway. The spaniel turns to black marble.

Mr. Robert Alexander Gilbert, pianist and photographer, servant, valet, factotum, and gentleman's gentleman for the estimable William Brewster, has stopped forever a small, isolated piece of the world as it stood at eleven o'clock in the morning of April 6th, 1911, in the village of Concord, Massachusetts.

For all we know he left something of himself upon the scene in the process.

13

THE AFRICAN CHARIOTEER

✠

Inasmuch as we know anything about the undiscovered country of the past, we know about the events of that day as a result of the invention in the 1830s of an ingenious device that had the capacity to concentrate light waves and permanently fix images on a chemically coated glass or tin plate. The camera is in fact an alchemist's mortar and pestle or a shaman's drum. It can alter realities. It can reorder the accepted flow of hours and days and arrest any given moment in the flight of time. The photographer, in the role of alchemist or shaman, has the ability to stop the world and hold everything in place, unmoving—the land, streets, people, skies, clouds, running rivers and streams, wind in the trees, flowing grasses, all stilled in midcourse, lovers caught forever in that ecstatic music, forever young. Whatever happened before the image was exposed and what happens afterward is open to interpretation. This means, among other things, that we, the invaders from a time yet to come, observing one of these captured segments, can make of it what we will. The photograph is not really an image incised by light on celluloid film or a glass plate. It is an imaginary history.

And so we can say with as much authority as any other extant record of that day that the three men spent the rest of the afternoon on the river, spotting birds, and that, toward dusk, they rowed and sailed back down the river to the bend at Ball's Hill, where the cabin was located, and that here, roughing it (in the view of Henshaw), they had a dinner of eggs and canned SS *Pierce* meats, with mustard and white bread, prepared by Mr. Gilbert, who, it should be noted, this being the relatively broad-minded environment of Concord, sat at the table with the white men.

The following morning Gilbert drove Henshaw back to the 9:22 train at Concord station and then returned to the farm.

A few days later Henshaw received a short note in the mail.

My Dear Mr. Henshaw,

I found five dollars under a pitcher in your room this morning. Fearing you may have left it by mistake I am writing to ask what disposition you wish made with it.

Respectfully yours,

R. A. Gilbert

The handwriting is small, scrolling left to right. Also neat. The passive voice regarding money, the distancing, the formality, are intentional.

CHAPTER TWO

Attic Archaeology

TIME PRESERVES EVERYTHING, BUT AS IT DOES SO, IT FADES THINGS TO THE COLORLESSNESS OF ANCIENT PHOTOGRAPHS FIXED ON METAL PLATES. LIGHT AND TIME ERASE THE CONTOURS AND DISTINCTIVE SHADING OF THE FACES. ONE HAS TO ANGLE THE IMAGE THIS WAY AND THAT UNTIL IT CATCHES THE LIGHT IN A PARTICULAR WAY AND ONE CAN MAKE OUT THE PERSON WHOSE FEATURES HAVE BEEN ABSORBED INTO THE BLANK SURFACE OF THE PLATE.

Sandor Marais

Near Bethel, Maine. Robert A. Gilbert, far right

The main object of this quest first appeared to me in the form of a silvery-white image on a nineteenth-century glass plate negative. At the time I was in the process of assembling early photographs of the New England landscape for a book project and had heard that there were some old wooden boxes containing glass plate negatives stored in the attic of an estate in Lincoln, owned by the Massachusetts Audubon Society. Leads of this sort sometimes unearth rich reserves, so I made arrangements to have a look.

The property in Lincoln was originally owned by a family named Gordon who had come into money in the late nineteenth century, and, along with other Boston families of means, began moving out from the city in the early 1900s, primarily, I believe, to escape the influx of Italians and Irish who were then moving uncomfortably close to some of the enclaves of Bostonians of the proper sort. The house was a vast Georgian-style building with a wide central foyer floor laid in ancient Cambrian sedimentary stone, still embedded with the curled fossils of trilobites and crinoids. The attic stretched the full length of the building and was ill lit by two mullioned eyebrow windows on the gable ends and a single naked bulb that looked as if it had not been changed since the 1940s.

One of the characteristics of the Boston Brahmin class, who were the founders of the Massachusetts Audubon Society, was a reluctance to throw anything away. Here, lining the eaves and positioned so as to form a veritable labyrinth of corridors and passageways, lay the evidence of this custom—row upon row of shelves and filmed-over glass cabinets containing phalanxes of stuffed birds with moth-eaten, patchy feathers and glazed, dusty eyes. Piled on the floor were chairs constructed from sticks and twigs, with frayed rattan seats, stacks of old books, cartons of bulletins of extinct natural history organizations, framed bird and mammal prints, old manual typewriters, a brass microscope, and oaken filing cabinets containing the minutes from society meetings held back in the 1950s.

As I worked through the clutter, just to the north of the west-facing eyebrow window, I spotted a row of long narrow boxes lurking in the shadows, like the caskets in some ancient sepulcher. Inside the boxes, stacked vertically, some still wrapped in the glassine envelopes in which they had been packed, were twenty glass plate photographic negatives.

I drew out one of the plates and held it up to the window. There, gleaming in the dull light, was the ghostly image of a house and garden, complete with what appeared to be full blossoming hydrangeas and a little dog, all in silvery reverse. I selected another plate, and then another, and then moved on to inspect another box. My pulse quickened as I worked. An acquaintance of mine had just discovered over three hundred glass plate negatives of Civil War regiments under similar circumstances and I thought I was onto something.

In the end, I uncovered more than two thousand photographic plates, most of them taken between 1888 and 1917 and credited, as I later learned, to William Brewster, who was, among other things, the first president of the Massachusetts Audubon Society, which had been founded in 1896 by two socially prominent women who had become outraged by the slaughter of innocent birds for the frivolous purpose of adorning women's hats.

After some negotiation, I gained permission to borrow a few of the plates, and one rainy autumn afternoon printed them to see what they were all about. I laid the first negative on a sheet of photographic paper, flashed the plate briefly with the enlarger, and then placed the paper in the development bath.

For those who do their own darkroom work there is a certain, almost mystical tension in the moment when a new positive image first swims into view. This sense of anticipation is all the more powerful when you are working with historic glass plates from an age long past and created by some anonymous individual long since dead and buried. You feel like an archeologist breaking into the sealed tomb of a lost culture in a distant country, except that there is something more animated about a photograph. As you watch, an actual slice of past life slowly sharpens into reality from the pale nothingness of the light-sensitive photographic paper—landscapes, hills, skies, buildings, dogs, people, the decisive moment, forever stalled in the flux of time.

As I watched, alone in the dull red light of the darkroom, a moment from the late nineteenth century slowly ghosted up into the twentieth century. The image showed a group of men and women dressed in tweeds and tam-o'-shanters, posing beside canoes pulled up on a reedy riverbank on a late summer day in 1898. I printed a few more. There were views of landscapes, pictures of the nests of birds, gardens, full-skirted women in flowering hats standing in the forest with bouquets of wildflowers, wooded roads, the wilder shores of rivers, and quiet, tree-lined Cambridge streets. There was no order to the photos in the boxes, only a few indications of dates and places on some of the plates, but otherwise no identifications—only images, arrested time, a kinetic moment from an unidentified past, temporarily stopped and stored as potential energy, waiting to be liberated.

In those photographs that showed groups of people, I was interested to see from time to time a handsome, white-bearded man with a quizzical, aristocratic look who I later learned was Mr. William Brewster himself. But I was especially interested in one particular plate. The negative image suggested a portrait of a group of people standing and sitting in front of a lean-to structure somewhere deep in the woods. Most of the faces of the figures in the negative were dark black, except for their shining eyes. But there was an image of a smaller man there, who, in contrast to the others, stood out in a bright silvery white. I didn't quite understand why he shone forth with such an angelic glow until I printed the negative and studied it.

The positive print showed a group of well-attired white people. But standing slightly off to the side of the group, in front of one of the cedar posts, was a small, handsome black man. He was younger than the others, but he stood with them, as if he were a member of the party. He was not wearing the apron or work clothes of a servant but, like the others, was dressed properly in a dark suit, white shirt, and a black tie. Furthermore he appeared comfortable with his surroundings; he stares out at the photographer with large, serious eyes and a no-nonsense, almost cynical look, a certain assuredness in spite of his youth and the fact that he is the only black among a company of whites somewhere in the wilds of Maine or the Adirondacks.

My discovery of these plates occurred in the autumn of a uniquely rainy year that somehow seemed to match the sepia tones and grays of the plates and prints I was working with. Photo researchers that year seemed to be having good luck. One had found a collection of plates taken in the late nineteenth century around Cummington, Massachusetts, by two local photographers who had documented the region and the people around their community. A huge collection of some 7,000 turn-of-the-century plates by the Concord photographer Herbert Gleason had recently been assembled. A tireless photo hunter in rural Maine had discovered a new batch of glass plates by the marine photographer Nathaniel Stebbins, and, along with the Brewster plates, I myself had discovered a variety of negatives and prints taken in the Swift River Valley towns in central Massachusetts in the early 1900s. These latter were particularly poignant. The subjects were long dead, of course, but more to the point, by 1939 the whole valley, virtually all the meadows, woodlands, farmhouses, graveyards, and in fact the sites of five whole towns, lay beneath the waters of the Quabbin Reservoir that now supplies drinking water for Boston.

Partly because of my work and partly because of the constant rain, I went around that year with a somber nineteenth-century sort of mood. In a sense I took up residence in the world of sepia photographs. Wherever I went in New England I found myself hunting out those lost landscapes I knew from old photographs —isolated arched stone bridges, hayfields, old woodlands with massive hemlocks, mountain roads in the Berkshires, and mirror-still lakes with graceful Rob Roy canoes and pulling boats eternally stilled in midstream. I became haunted by the fact that this whole world, once filled with peace and solitude, color and light, and the energy of human interactions, was gone forever. And throughout all this I kept wondering about the black man. Who was he? And why was a young black person socializing with a group of well-appointed whites out in the middle of the wilderness of the Northeast? I slowly became obsessed with this man. Where did he come from. Where did he end?

✠

The land use project was completed in the mid-1970s, and to celebrate the publication of the book there was a little gathering at a Boston hotel. All the bright lights of the late twentieth-century city were glittering in the well-appointed function rooms, and generations of people swept through the space in their swirling tropic muumuus and garish floral-patterned neckties. Here and there you could see a few of the remnants of the old Brahmin class of Boston to which Mr. Brewster belonged. They sailed ever upright through the crowd, with their clipped gray hair and their subdued gray tweeds, like the lofty ships that once carried the slaves and the rum and molasses that had earned them their family money. Much chatter, much clinking of cocktail glasses, the high sparkle of lights, and the smell of old wool and whiskey, and then, from within the crowd, I saw an unlikely figure.

A tall man dressed entirely in denim and a cowboy hat, with

flowing chestnut hair falling around his shoulders, was determinedly working his way toward me through the happy throng. Once he had me cornered he fixed my eye with a know-it-all smile and asked if I was the one who had written the credit lines for the photographs taken by William Brewster, which had been published along with some of the other nineteenth-century photographs.

I said I had.

"Well you got them wrong," he said bluntly. "Those pictures were taken by his manservant, a black guy named Gilbert."

There was a lot of noise at this event, much braying laughter, and the loud bird twitter of happy voices. I thought I had missed something and leaned closer.

"Taken by who?" I asked.

"I said the photographs were taken by a black man, not by Brewster. He was the valet for Brewster. You got the captions wrong. They were taken by Gilbert. Robert A. Gilbert."

He was practically shouting.

An ear-piercing whinny of laughter sounded out next to us.

"How do you know?" I shouted back.

"I know . . ."

"Let's go to the bar . . . ," I said.

In spite of his swagger and his all-outdoors deportment, this apparent pioneer was a research assistant who worked in the dark inner forests of the stacks at the Museum of Comparative Zoology at Harvard. Over the past few months he had been assembling and filing the correspondence of William Brewster for the library and said he had found evidence that Brewster was simply the point man in the field, and that this Gilbert, his valet, his gentleman's gentleman and jack-of-all-trades, would do all the work, and then some. The photos, all two thousand of them, he claimed, were the work of this talented young man.

"Gilbert and Brewster were inseparable," he said, "they went together everywhere, and before he died, Brewster arranged to have

Gilbert taken on as assistant to the curator at the museum. He came along with Brewster's entire collection of bird skins. Gilbert stayed on there until he died. He was known to everyone. The Brahmins made a pet of him. There are obituaries."

Having informed me of this fact, he announced that he must be on his way, rose from his chair, and ambled out.

That at least answered part of the mystery. The small black man was the servant. But was he also the photographer? If he was, this new information helped explain how it came to pass that Brewster appears in some of his own photographs. Furthermore, none of the plates and none of the few surviving prints were signed. I only heard they were Brewster's by word of mouth, that is to say, I heard that Brewster owned them. No one ever said he took them.

The thought that I might have discovered a trove of photographs by a heretofore unknown African American photographer was intriguing, all the more so since, as far as I knew, although there were many black photographers at the turn of the last century, not one was making photographs of landscapes—let alone birds' nests.

✠

During this period I had a Cambridge-based friend named Tremont Williams, an avid historical researcher who seemed to know half the people in Boston and Cambridge and was a skilled, if somewhat thinly spread, scholar who, it was said, could find anything you needed to know about anything. Tre, as his friends called him, was a unique species. To all outward appearances he was a white man. He had Caucasian features, light green eyes, and slightly wiry black hair. He looked more like one of the Black Irish you see around Boston, the purported descendants of Spanish sailors, shipwrecked on the Irish coast during the Armada. But Tre claimed he was actually African American, his white appearance resulting from some genetic throwback from some distant white relative who mixed his or her genes in with his basic African roots. To prove his lineage, he showed me once a photo of his parents, two handsome, dark-skinned people of obvious African heritage. He was descended, he said, from one of the original African families who lived on the northeastern side of Beacon Hill in Boston, in a district known as New Guinea in the seventeenth century. His father had attended Harvard, he said, but Tre himself had fled to Washington and had spent several years there socializing with an equally upper-class coterie of blacks. He now supported himself by research contracts and consultancies, and when he wasn't otherwise employed he spent his time investigating overlooked black historical figures. It was Tre's opinion that nearly every successful American had at least a drop of African blood in his or her veins. In this regard he was the opposite of certain whites who argue that all successful black people have at least a trace of white blood. Tre's theories on the number of famous white people with African roots ranged from certain members of the fifteenth-century Medici family, to John James Audubon, Alexander Dumas, and even America's blue-eyed boy, William Jefferson Clinton.

I had met Tre through a mutual friend and calculated that he would be able to help me with this newly garnered information about Mr. Brewster's manservant. So I made a few more prints and arranged to meet him, showed him the pictures, and explained the background.

He looked them over indifferently.

"This kind of thing was common," he said, pushing back the prints. "Sad, but common, especially in nineteenth-century America."

Nineteenth-century naturalists and explorers, he explained, often had talented, and generally unrecognized, assistants ("usually black," he said, although I'm not sure that was true) who are rarely mentioned in the official histories and biographies. Darwin had a black manservant who worked as his taxidermist. More to the point (and more contemporaneous with Gilbert and Brewster) was the emerging story of Matthew Henson, the African American assistant of Admiral Robert Peary. Tre claimed there was good evidence that Henson was actually the first man to the pole.

"So where do I begin?" I asked.

"You begin at the beginning, with his parents' birth records, if you can find them, and then work back through the Middle Passage, if you can find any records, and then forward until you come to the end, with his death records. Then you fill in the rest by hunting through the extant documents, which in this case will undoubtedly be those recorded by the white man and therefore sketchy. Just a bunch of puzzle pieces," he said.

And then, as I knew he would, he began to spew out leads and theories and countertheories, and then he looked at the photos again, most of which were of local environments around Cambridge, Belmont, and Concord.

He studied one photo in particular, leaned closer, turned it slightly.

"Do you have data on the glass plates?" he asked.

"On some of them, yes," I said.

The one he was holding showed a road passing a stone wall, with a large elm on the left.

"That one happens to be Concord, 1905," I said. "But that's all I know."

"Why don't you attempt a rephotographic survey of the environment that these two worked in," he said. "It's all the vogue now. I think there are a couple of guys rephotographing all the western landscapes taken in the nineteenth century by Timothy O'Sullivan, and what's his name—William Henry Jackson. Maybe you'll learn something."

It sounded like a good idea, and certainly far more attractive from my point of view than spending my summer days in the dark interiors of library stacks. So following Tre's suggestion, I began a sporadic, disorganized attempt to retrieve those landscapes for which I had some documentation. I would seek out places between Cambridge and Lancaster, Massachusetts, where certain documented images, exposed between 1893 and 1915, had been, as the curious phrasing has it, "captured." Later, as I learned more about the travels of Brewster and Gilbert, I expanded the range of my resurvey to the forests of Maine and New Hampshire, south to Virginia, where Gilbert was born, and even to France, where Gilbert apparently spent some years. The survey began to take on a life of its own and slowly I was drawn deeper and deeper into the search.

Several years after I discovered the plates, the Massachusetts Audubon Society acquired yet another estate with rural property (it already had four or five such holdings). This one was a substantial house in Canton, Massachusetts, that was once owned by a sometime painter and natural history filmmaker named Mildred Morse Allen. Over the years, along with the various properties, the society had also been acquiring artwork from its generous donors, including a large number of the original hand-colored first and second edition Audubon prints. To house these treasures, the organization decided to build a climate-controlled archive and exhibit hall in the Allen house and turn the property into a center for the visual arts. The Brewster glass plates were subsequently moved there from the questionable environment of the attic in Lincoln. Following this, as a result of yet another generous donation, the society obtained a state-of-the-art computer and began the long process of digitalizing all the glass plate negatives.

Compared to the slow, step-by-step process of creating a positive print in a darkroom, once a negative is digitalized, this ingenious computer allows a viewer to put an image on the screen in a matter of seconds. Furthermore, the device allows you to move into the image, and then, like an explorer in a lost country, move slowly through the landscape, enlarging various sections, inspecting details, lightening darkened areas to reveal things that perhaps even the photographer had not seen. One plate I found, for example, showed a pleasant view of a vine-covered house with a darkened surround of a porch. Wandering through this summery environment with the aid of the computer, I decided to lighten the dark porch to look for architectural details. To my surprise, from the deep obscurity a human face emerged. There was an old woman sitting in a rocking chair on the porch, glaring out at the cameraman angrily, her gray hair pulled severely back on her head. I'm not even sure the photographer—whoever he was—knew she was there.

Having gained permission to use this computer, I began moving ever inward into the world of the nineteenth century, wandering down country roads, following the tracks of a one-horse shay, or the wide, double lines of a Model T Ford. I looked at the incised scrollwork on the brooch of a woman sitting with a group of men in a tent somewhere in the North Woods. I inspected the loose shutters on a house in Lancaster, Massachusetts, and the hammers of a double-barreled shotgun held in the hands of a guide in the wilds around Lake Umbagog, in Maine. But mostly I looked at the lost landscapes of faces, the lines about the eyes, the unsmiling, steady set of lips, the cast of light on a woman's cheek. And ultimately, it was through these images that I found the man.

✠

Brewster's retreat, "October Farm," was located on Monument Street in Concord. The property ran down to the banks of the Concord River and included a long stretch of riverbank where Brewster had Swedish and Irish workers construct a series of small lean-tos and cabins. There is a trail that now runs along the west bank of the river and one day in summer, scouting along this path, I came across an odd structure set at the foot of the prominence known as Ball's Hill. It was an arched stone doorway that led back into the bank of the hill and resembled one of those long barrows where the Neolithic Beaker People of the British Isles buried their dead. The interior of the arch was a dark tunnel with a soggy rotten leaf floor and thick with old cobwebs, but I pushed in. Inside, on the south wall, scratched in cement, I saw a graffito: "W.B. Sept 9 1916."

At least I knew I had the right spot.

Just above the barrow I saw what looked like the remnants of a buried stone wall peeking out of the forest duff and began to clear away some of the soil. Slowly, the shape of a foundation emerged. Nearby was a similar ruin that I also cleared. From the riverside, I angled the camera up the hill to the foundation, where the floor would have been, and where, in one of the Brewster photos, you see a group of men and women seated in a line. Now it's all trees and shrubs—old hemlocks, American filbert, some buckthorn (an alien plant that would not have been present in Brewster's time), and also highbush blueberry, with silver maples, red maples, and buttonbush along the riverbank.

A little beyond the ruins of the cabins and the boathouse, I came upon an old wagon road leading away from the river and followed it. The road dipped down into a muddy hollow laced with horse tracks, and then rose up to higher ground. Soon I was passing through a landscape of dry pines and began coming upon strange twentieth-century archeological artifacts, fenders and discarded wheels of old cars, various machine parts, an engine, and here and there a few car bodies, mostly antique, and many of them foreign —Renaults, a Morris Minor, an old Volvo. I pushed on, rounded a bend, and saw ahead of me an ancient barn. Inside, in the half-light, I could see the gleam of a large, well-cared-for Stanley Steamer.

Beyond the barn was one of the most ramshackled dwellings this side of Appalachia. It was a seventeenth-century house with a hogbacked roof and broken windows. The door stoops and the sills were bowed and leaning back to earth, and there was a shredded curtain blowing out of an upstairs window like a ghost. The house appeared to be uninhabited, but as I approached I saw a frail old man standing in the bare front yard, looking at me quizzically. He was dressed in torn coveralls and a tattered work shirt, and was wearing a pair of eyeglasses that had been repaired with Scotch tape that covered half of the lens of his left eye.

I approached tentatively, introduced myself, made my excuses and soon fell into conversation with him and learned that his name was Sanfred Bensen. One of the first things he told me was that he was "eighty-five years of age" and that he had been born in that very house in the late nineteenth century.

"I have rarely left here," he said. "By choice, you understand. Once, in the year nineteen and fifty three, my sister and I undertook a journey to Lawrence, Massachusetts, but I shan't do that again, I can tell you. There were too many signs, and the automobiles were moving at a very high rate of speed."

Lawrence, it should be noted, is no more than twenty-five or so miles from Concord. In fact, it turned out Bensen rarely went even to the town of Concord, a distance of no more than two miles.

I spent over two hours with the old man talking about the old days on the Concord River and his adventures—such as they were. He seemed to have an indefatigable ability to stand in one spot, telling stories. At no point in our conversation, however, did he invite me to sit down in one of the kitchen chairs that were strewn about the yard, and he did not invite me into the house for tea, which, given the condition of the exterior of the house, was perhaps a good thing. He rambled on interminably about times past, the late afternoon sun glistening off the single, scratched lens of his untaped eyeglass as he spoke. How he was able to see anything was a mystery; in fact, he rarely fixed my eye, which made me wonder if he was perhaps legally blind.

While we were talking I did a little private calculation and figured that he was probably old enough to have known William Brewster, who would have been his nearest neighbor when he was a boy. At the appropriate moment, I asked.

"Oh, yes, indeed," he said in his reedy old voice, "I knew Dr.

Brewster well, and I am here to tell you that he was as fine a man as ever walked the earth."

This generated a litany of the qualities of old "Dr." Brewster. More than I thought I could endure at this point. I had been on my feet for a few hours already, I was dying of thirst, my legs were crumbling beneath me, and yet I knew I had struck a rich find—someone who actually knew the supposed photographer of the lost plates.

"I am here to tell you that Dr. Brewster had the kindest eyes of any man who walked the earth," Bensen said.

This appeared to be a favorite phrase of his: "Dr. Brewster was the gentlest soul of any man who walked the earth," he said. "Dr. Brewster was among the most generous people who ever walked the earth."

Bensen's father had been employed by Brewster and as a boy Sanfred would help out around October Farm. Finally, at great risk to my legs, I ventured to ask him if, by any chance, he had ever heard of a man named Gilbert?

"Why, Gilbert was my best friend when I was a boy," he said enthusiastically.

I had been digging around in attics and libraries of Cambridge and Boston for over a year when I first met Sanfred Bensen, and here in my own backyard, it seemed, I had found the equivalent of a talking library devoted entirely to Gilbert and Brewster.

Although Gilbert was older, Bensen told me, the two of them spent a lot of time together whenever Gilbert was out at October Farm. He said the man I was searching for was a success in everything he did. Inasmuch as he was the personal servant of Brewster and therefore exposed to city lights, influential people, and distant venues, he was far more cosmopolitan than his young friend Bensen, and the two of them would often sit by the riverbank while Gilbert spun out stories of his various adventures at home and abroad. Bensen said that Gilbert was a favorite of the wealthy Bostonians and would commonly associate with them during expeditions to the North Country.

"He was invited to parties with the finest of them. He ate at table with linen cloths and silverware, and he knew how to drink claret wine, and how to hold a glass. He was a perfect gentleman among gentleman, always wore dark suits of the finest wool and starched collars, even here in the countryside. And he knew his birds better than Dr. Brewster, I can tell you. He could name any song he heard, and if you saw a mere flash of a birdwing, why, he would know what bird that was."

"Did he ever take photographs?" I lifted my camera suggestively.

"Oh, yes, indeed. I would see him sometimes on the river with Dr. Brewster. They had a large camera there, set on legs, don't you know. Dr. Brewster carried field glasses, like a general. He would point to scenes. And Gilbert would set up the camera. He could do anything—Gilbert knew everything."

According to Bensen, Gilbert was a Harvard graduate who later took a position with Brewster as assistant researcher and bird spotter and manager of a small bird museum Brewster had constructed behind his main house at 145 Brattle Street in Cambridge. He learned the art of photography and served as the field assistant to the great naturalist. Bensen claimed that many of Brewster's successes in life were in fact due to this man.

"Gilbert, you see, was his right-hand man. He was here all the time, often when Brewster was not present. He acted as the supervisor at these times, ordering the Irish around. There was an older man here, Patrick was his name. Patrick was fond of strong drink, I believe, and would consume a great deal of whisky and would sometimes sleep on the job, so Mr. Gilbert would wake him up. Or try to. He spoke softly, Mr. Gilbert. He was ever so polite. Everyone liked him. Especially old Patrick."

Having informed me of these facts, Bensen leaned forward intimately.

"Did you know, by the way," he asked in his clipped broad A'd New England accent, "that Gilbert was one of these *colored* fellows?"

He said this as if there were perhaps three or four thousand black people in all the world.

Later in life, Bensen said, the resourceful Gilbert invented a specialized shoe polish formula that he took to Stockholm in the years just before the Great War. Once in Europe, freed from racial discrimination and through his natural intelligence, he acquired a fortune, Bensen said.

"But the war came along. He lost the supply of fat he required for his shoe cream. Sales fell off, and Gilbert had to give up the business. He lost his fortune. After the war, he went to Paris and fell in with a low group, I'm afraid. Musicianers and that sort. I only saw him once after that. Some months after Dr. Brewster departed this earth, Gilbert returned. He came back to these fields with Mr. Daniel French, who was a childhood friend of Dr. Brewster's. Gilbert told me that Mr. French was a well-known sculpturer and that they had come to find a suitable granite boulder to place over the burial site of Dr. Brewster."

He paused here and looked eastward toward the river.

"Someday I should like to visit that grave."

I had been to Brewster's grave in Mount Auburn Cemetery. Rather than shape the stone, a fine block of pink granite, French had decided to leave it in its natural condition.

"I have seen that very stone; it's beautiful," I said. "I could even take you there someday."

"Well, I shall have to prepare myself," Bensen said.

"Have you ever been to the city?" I asked.

"Yes, once, Colburn drove me that way in his Stanley Steamer. We got all the way to Bedford."

(Bedford is the town on the opposite side of the river and is twelve miles west of Cambridge.)

Colburn, he explained, was his nephew. He sometimes spent

the night at the house with his uncle, and was a collector of Stanley Steamers and Indian motorcycles, as well as any other machine not constructed after the year 1931, it seemed. The more I looked around the yard and the building, the more evidence I could see of this Colburn—many old cars, ruined chairs, engine bodies, an old clinker-built, flat-iron rowboat, various and sundry bits of farm machinery, hay rakes, plows, hay tedders, and the like, plus a huge, somewhat ominous, empty dog chain.

"What's the heavy chain for?" I asked. "Do you have a large dog?"

"Yes, I do," he said. "She's there in the house."

I saw two eyes flash briefly in the darkened interior of the open door. Bensen whistled sharply and a tiny streak of brown and white fur dashed out from the gloom and launched itself in a long leap into the arms of Sanfred Bensen and began licking his grizzled cheeks.

"This is Muffin," the old man said. "And she is my constant companion."

I saw the opportunity.

"Might I take her picture?" I asked.

"Oh by all means," he said. "Look at the camera, Muffin," he said, turning her head with his hand.

I raised the camera, focused, and began to make kissing noises. The dog perked up her ears. I snapped the shutter.

But it wasn't Muffin I was hunting, needless to say. It was the character of weathered old Bensen with his single glinting eyeglass and his tattered shirt.

✠

I left him, promising to make arrangements to drive him to Mount Auburn Cemetery and wondering how much of this accounting was true and how much was the imagination of an old man who lived alone by the side of a river.

Entr'acte

Robert A. Gilbert, born 1869, Rockbridge County, Virginia

In 1870 the first African American senator and representatives were elected to the 41st and 42nd Congresses. Seven years later, Frederick Douglass was appointed Marshall of the District of Columbia by President Rutherford Hayes, no particular friend of black Americans. He ended Reconstruction and worked to gain the southern vote. Certain southern states were granted the right to control their own affairs. Great rise during this period of the terrorist organization known as the Ku Klux Klan. The Black Codes in full force.

In 1871, Richard Leach Maddox invented a process known as the gelatin dry plate silver bromide, which meant that photographic plates no longer had to be developed immediately after exposure. By 1880 the Eastman Dry Plate Company was founded, by 1884 flexible paper-backed film was invented, and four years later Eastman introduced a roll-film camera.

Congress by this time had passed legislation establishing—in 1872—the first National Park at Yellowstone. Two years later the Sierra Club was founded, with John Muir as president. This was the height of the back to nature movement, especially among the friends and allies of the likes of Mr. William Brewster—much lauding, during this period, of the beneficial effects of open air, and many expeditions into the "wilds"—such as they were—of the Adirondacks.

The Wild West variety show was all the rage when Gilbert was born, as were minstrel shows. New York's first elevated railway was opened in 1870, the Pullman Company introduced a "hotel car" and hired black porters, who would later organize into the first black labor unions. The telephone had been invented by this time and an outdoor demonstration of its function was carried out in

Salem, Massachusetts, in 1877. No one believed it was real and reporters had to be posted at each end of the line to prove that there was no deception. Mr. Thomas A. Edison gave a demonstration of his new phonograph at the White House the following year and did not leave until three in the morning. A year later Edison demonstrated the first practical electric lamp.

In 1881, P. T. Barnum opened the Greatest Show on Earth; there was a Great Fire in Chicago, and the White Star line launched the first of the modern luxury liners. No blacks hired.

CHAPTER THREE

Down in the Valley

PHOTOGRAPHS, WHICH CANNOT THEMSELVES EXPLAIN ANYTHING, ARE INEXHAUSTIBLE INVITATIONS TO DEDUCTION, SPECULATION, AND FANTASY.

Susan Sontag

New England landscape, c. 1903

The place, as far as I can determine, was Lynchburg, Virginia, the time undocumented, but probably around 1868, a few years after the liberation of the descendants of those citizens of Africa who had been captured and held in bondage by the Americans. The photograph shows six men standing in the courtyard of a brick building in front of a two-wheeled horse cart loaded with long planks. Five of the men are staring directly at the camera, but the sixth, one of two black men in the image, stands apart, near the head of the horse, and is looking at something beyond the frame of the photograph, as if contemplating some distant, imagined world. He has a well-trimmed set of sideburns and a mustache and is wearing a dark jacket and a muffler, and he stands with his hands at his side, relaxed, his deep-set eyes staring off beneath the brim of a cap with a shiny visor.

Another photograph, which I found one autumn afternoon in the archives of the Rockbridge County Historical Society in Lexington, Virginia, is an image of this same man. He has the same confident air, but in this photo he is staring directly at the camera, his right hand curled over the arm of a chair, left hand relaxed, the thumb extended, fingers curled gently at the knuckles. He is wearing a fine pressed wool suit, a dark silk tie, and a flared, high-collared shirt and waistcoat. Judging from his demeanor, he could be the ambassador from some recently liberated African nation, save that there were, in the late 1860s, no recently liberated African nations. In this case, the subject of the portrait is identified. His name is William Gilbert and he is the father of Robert Alexander Gilbert, who was born in 1869 in the valley of Broad Creek in Natural Bridge, Virginia.

William Gilbert, as far as I can tell, was freeborn, and even if he wasn't it would be difficult to imagine this man bonded to anyone but himself. He has a kingly, proud air. For all I know he is descended from the line of Yoruba nobility who trace their ancestry back to a leopard who mated with the great princess of Dahomey, Adja-Tado.

The kings and queens who followed from this union always cut claw marks into their temples in remembrance of their patrimony and commanded fierce companies of female warriors who donned lizard-skin capes and conducted slave raids on the weaker tribes of the interior. At some point between the mid-1600s and 1800, the years of the slave trade, one of their number happened to be at the wrong place at the wrong time and was captured in a counterraid, chained, marched to the beach at Ouidah, sold as property, and shipped to Charleston, South Carolina. Slave or free, though, I would not wish to joke with the proposed descendant of this powerful family were I transported to his august presence. He is the type whom you would address formally, as an old deposed king.

Along with the photographs, I also found in the archives an 1853 map of Rockbridge County, showing the roads and dwellings of Natural Bridge, which lies just to the south of Lexington. One of the houses on the map was marked with the name Gilbert, the only Gilbert listed in Natural Bridge and presumably the birthplace of Robert. The house was located somewhere in the bottomlands in the valley, on the inside of a curve created by Broad Creek and just east of a straight path on the west, known as the Plank Road. The valley itself lies west of the Lee Highway not far from a farm now owned by a Korean family who specialize in Asian pears. Tourists traveling by car down from Lexington to the famous stone arch at Natural Bridge will pass the orchard, and then, less than a mile beyond, a narrow road that leads down into the valley of Broad Creek, dipping and weaving through a sharp-hilled landscape.

Early photographs of this valley, taken around the time of Gilbert's birth, show the classic Virginia idyll—rolling hills, peaked haystacks, small, southern vernacular houses with shading front porches, dogs in the front yard, and, in one image I found, a log schoolhouse plastered and much whitewashed, with a scraped, bare-earth yard. This particular structure served as the local school for blacks and the remnants of the Monacan Indian children, the original people of the valley. It is the nearest school to Broad Creek and is probably the place where the education of Robbie Gilbert began.

In our time, the valley is still characterized by the typical hardwood mesic forest of the Blue Ridge, great-boled white oaks and straight-trunked tulip trees soaring skyward, butternuts and sweetgum, a few persimmons, with sycamores in the bottomlands, and all of it interspersed with cutaway meadows, dense green hollows with clear streams gurgling through, and pastured cows lingering in the shade. Curious at first, they edge toward you and then spook easily when you approach, sensing somehow a foreigner.

This is a glacial-free section of North America, no ice-scraped granite outcroppings here as you would find in the Concord region of Mr. Brewster. It's a warm country, sweet smelling in the spring, wafted with zephyrs from the south, deep soils, and a generally mild climate, matching the slow, soft lilts of the local accents. It used to be said that the rural blacks who left the region during the Great Migration at the end of the nineteenth century—Mr. Gilbert among them—longed for that remembered childhood of southern country mornings, the rich scents, the tapestry of color, birdsong, and the evening lowing of the cattle at the gate. Up north, they may have gained ambition, self-respect, freedom from the yoke, maybe, but never could retrieve that soft spring mothering Southland. Some died with the image behind their eyes and the smell of the woods permeating their bedrooms in their last hours.

There is an old Presbyterian church dating from the eighteenth century at the northeastern end of the valley; not far from the church is a local graveyard, and just to the east, there is a little clearing with an outing club called the Hootyville Blue Grass Club. On certain days here, I'm told, you can hear the banjos ringing even from a mile away, and trucks from all over the hollows pull in and debouch lank-jawed hill people in jeans and work boots who are not averse to a taste of red-eye from an old fruit jar.

On my third visit to this valley in search of Mr. Gilbert, I parked my rented car at the side of the road near the site marked "Gilbert" on the 1853 map, and carried my camera back into the October woodlands to look for a house, or at least a foundation, or perhaps an old burial site. This was typical southern bottomland, moist-soiled, and dense with fox grapes and the cries and whispers of gnatcatchers sounding out against that immense rural silence of the Blue Ridge. I sat down on a fallen branch for a while and waited —half hoping that something would happen to roll back the curtain of time and allow me to glimpse for a second or two a vibrant family of four or five black people with the surname Gilbert. It was nearing dusk by this time, an autumnal stillness was suspended over the valley, with a blue-green sky still apparent above the trees, fading to pearl gray in the east and darkening the woods in the hollows. The whole countryside was putting itself to sleep, lending an air of mystery and possibility to the little hollow.

A jay called, and then a large dark bird swept by, landed somewhere out of sight, and began hammering on a dead tree trunk—a pileated woodpecker, a bird the local blacks used to call the Lord-to-God bird. High above, lit from beneath by the lowering sun, a vulture tilted past a clearing in the butternuts.

More gnatcatchers. The call of titmice, and then a silence.

"Mr. Gilbert?" I said aloud to the nothingness of the woodland. "You there?"

Only the gnatcatchers and a flight of chickadees and titmice, working in the greenwood tangle.

It was getting dark, so I rose to thread my way back to the car. When I got there, I saw a dented yellow van with a hand-painted sign on the body: "Pokey's Electric." Nearby was a square-jawed man with a tangle of yellow curls, standing in the road staring at the mud-splattered Dodge I had rented.

"You all right?" he asked.

"Fine," I said. "I was just back in the woods looking for a house foundation."

I showed him the 1853 map and then to fill the space, asked if he had ever heard of a family named Gilbert. I didn't say black or white, just Gilbert, and he thought for a while, and looked up the road, rubbing his elbow and not saying anything, and then he turned and looked down the road. Thinking.

"Gilbert?" he asked.

"Gilbert. Maybe William."

I explained my mission more fully.

"You go on up the road there and ask Mr. Hugh Morgan, he knows everyone in this valley better'n me. He's older too."

"Which is his house?"

"You know the one," he said. "Just up there a mile or two at the bend. You'll see it. Everabody knows where it is."

Armed with these detailed directions I began casting about on the rutted roads of Broad Creek valley with no one to ask for more coordinates other than the cows. The electrician had said that the house lay just beyond the stream and a bend in the road, and although there were many streams and many bends in the road, I took a chance on a likely turning and followed an increasingly rough dirt road to a well-lit house with a big open garage and a lighted door inside, leading to something. Dogs boiling up from everywhere even before I got out of the car—a big one with the look of an Australian cattle hound, little yappy ones, old blueticks lying in the dust, too lazy to even raise their heads, and a snappy mid-sized thing who I judged to be the only biter in the group.

Traditionally, when a stranger pulls up to a remote house in the hollows of the Blue Ridge, a barefoot distiller, coveralls cut off at the shins, comes out on the splintery porch with a shotgun crooked in his elbow and says "Git," just in case you're a revenuer. In this case a cherry-lipped woman in her sixties, alerted by the cacophony of barking, came to the door and told me to come on in even before I had time to say why I was there.

More dogs inside, scrambling around my ankles, snuffling. Also many babies, one tiny one being nursed on a couch by a pretty young woman who looked to be about twenty. Another sleeping on the lap of someone who must have been the mother's older sister. And standing backlit in a doorway in contraposto, a sexy woman with a come-hither look, red lips, heavily made-up blue eyes, and a mane of black hair.

"Aren't there any men 'round here?" I wanted to ask but of course didn't.

From the darkened room in back there came then a full cavalry charge of more dogs and young children, some in droopy diapers even though they were clearly too old for diapers. Cats were poised on every available empty space, wet newspapers on the floor, a sad canary, and the old lady asking everybody where on earth has Hugh got hisself to.

In time, down a narrow hallway came a rangy man in his stocking feet, adjusting his crotch and wearing a billed tractor cap and a blue flannel plaid shirt. I think he had been asleep. This, I gathered, although no one introduced him, was Mr. Hugh Morgan, and after elaborate explanations on my part, he said he did know a family named Gilbert, but as far as he knew they had all died. Died or gone away.

"Why you looking for them again?" he asked, indifferently.

I explained once more, adding this time that the Gilbert family that I was after was African American.

He smiled apologetically. "Gilberts I knew was white," he said.

He didn't say this as if to indicate that this was a good thing or a bad thing, just a fact of history. I might have even caught a tinge of regret, but maybe that was just his normal delivery, a lament for times gone by. He tipped his head to the side and clucked his tongue.

"Up on Diamond Hill is where most the old freeborn families live now," the woman I presumed to be Mrs. Morgan said. "Even since before the War, you got your black families living in the big houses up behind the graveyard."

I had heard this in town. One family of free blacks in particular had made money in the local restaurant business in the nineteenth century and even before Emancipation had purchased a large white house with a clerestory, from a white family down on their luck. I had learned this at the visitor's center in town. The local guide there, a retired gentleman with neatly trimmed gray hair, who should have known better, referred to the Diamond Hill area as "colored town."

"Weren't Johnnie's mother named Gilbert before she married?" one of the younger women asked.

Johnnie, I learned, was a sometime black handyman who used to work on farms in the valley and had a taste for drink. He would disappear for weeks on end and then show up again. But he was a popular character, a good worker, they said, when he chose to work. Sometimes he didn't even bother to collect his pay before disappearing, and was almost guaranteed to disappear once he was paid. Or so they said.

It was a good lead. I asked who would know such a thing.

"Go on up the church on Sunday and talk to the preacher," Hugh Morgan said. "Might be some church records maybe. Church's been there since the old days."

The children began squalling at this point, and then the dogs rose up again, barking, and went scrambling out through a torn screen door, sounding off, and a second or two later I heard a truck pull up, a door slammed, and in came a wiry little rooster with tattoos on his forearm who smiled at me, showing a row of broken teeth, and walked on by to a back room. The high staccato of a wild mountain banjo spilled down the hallway, and then another man ambled in, a fat one, dressed in faded dungaree overalls. He waddled through, nodded politely, touched the bill of his cap, and disappeared down the hall.

Lewis was his name.

Except for the odd mission that I was engaged in, no one seemed to care that I was in their kitchen on a Saturday evening, a stranger from a distant country where, in order to enter a house in this manner, one must, to be polite at least, arrange appointments by telephone in advance and check calendars and arrive at the proper time, or slightly late. Introductions would proceed accordingly, there would be small talk, some of it perhaps pertaining to lineage, before getting down to the business of finding out more about Mr. Gilbert and his company. Tea would likely be served, and any reference to the color of the main player in this little drama would be met with liberal-minded approval.

No tea here. No beer. Not even a snort of white lightning. But Mr. Morgan and his wife finally expressed some passing interest in my mission and turned the tables on me, in a friendly manner, and asked again why, exactly, I was sniffing out some black family what lived back in the valley just after the War, the war being, of course, the only war in these parts, the so-called War of the Northern Aggression, or in some quarters, "the recent unpleasantness."

"Was he some kind a relative of yourn?" Mr. Morgan asked.

✠

Lexington, Virginia, lies in the heart of the Shenandoah Valley near the northern end of the Blue Ridge Mountains. Local legend, no doubt the invention of some local white settlers and not the Monacan Indians, has it that the beauty of the Shenandoah Valley so awed the heavens that each star cast the brightest jewel from its own crown into the valley's limpid waters. Thus arose the valley's name: Shenandoah—Clear-Eyed Daughter of the Stars. In 1716, Virginia's Governor Spotswood and a company of explorers first noticed the valley from the peaks of the Blue Ridge, and by mid-century Scotch-Irish and German immigrants from Pennsylvania began to settle along a well-worn Indian path known as the Great Wagon Road that ran down the center of the valley.

In spite of the fact that Lexington is the spiritual home of Stonewall Jackson, the location of the Virginia Military Institute, which supplied any number of the officers to the war, and also the home of Washington and Lee University, the valleys and towns of western Virginia were not great supporters of the Cause. This was not plantation country, there were not very many large slaveholders in the region, and the industries were based mainly on iron-making and the existence of the North River Barge Canal, which brought iron down the James River to Richmond. Families had slaves, but usually not more than four or five, and they would often live in the house with their white owners and would even be hired out to odd jobs, from which, in certain circumstances, they could earn their own money. In some cases, they would work in the iron forges side by side with their owners. Partly because of this, there were many freeborn blacks in the region. There were even free black families in the valley who were wealthy enough to have had slaves of their own.

Robbie Gilbert spent the first eleven or twelve years of his life in the hill and dale countryside around Broad Creek. He was born in a short period of grace for African Americans, when federal laws and the presence of liberal white reform-minded teachers in the schools of the rural South made things slightly easier for the newly liberated slaves. Things would get worse within a decade, though. Robbie's mother must have died when he was young—there are scant records of her after the 1870s—and Robbie, his father, his older brother, William, an older girl named Mary, and someone named Jackson Gilbert all lived together at the curve of the creek. Contemporary photographs of the makeshift villages of freeborn blacks, which turned up in the 1990s in a historical society near Boston, show the environment in which Gilbert lived. Unpainted clapboard shacks, loose boards held down with stones as roofing, surrounding ditches to keep the floodwaters at bay during wet periods, as well as barrels, strewn lumber, chickens, and bands of little children in cutoff coveralls and bare feet. They spent their days in summer ranging the nearby woods, fishing in the creek, and on summer afternoons sitting by the doorstoop, where the old men related again and again over a period of ten hot summers the old Yoruba stories—“How the Monkey Saved Lion,” “Why Lion Is Not the Real King,” and “The Elephant and the Bush Dog”—stories later transformed from the collected slave tales by the white storyteller Joel Chandler Harris.

The voices that told these stories to Robbie and his company must have had the same cracked timbre as those recordings of former slaves collected by Roosevelt’s Works Project Administration researchers in the 1930s, the hill and valley lilt of intonation, the West African grammatical constructions, interspersed with words bastardized from Woloof and Ibo, and all bound together in a flow of phrasing that would later work its way into the call and response sermons that Gilbert grew up with, and the jagged, broken rhythms that later would resurface in ragtime and jazz and blues. Accent became a badge, an identification almost as powerful as skin color, but, as Gilbert later learned, it would have to be obscured and obliterated to get by in the world into which he was headed.

Lexington is perhaps best known for the presence of the Virginia Military Institute with its long and illustrious history, and also Washington and Lee University, with its own long and illustrious history. The other famous local source of legend is the presence of one of Lexington’s finest, the Civil War general known as Stonewall Jackson. He’s really only an adopted child, having moved to the area as an adult, but he so loved the place that he indicated in his will that he wished to be buried there, no matter where he died. After he was accidentally shot in the arm at the battle of Chancellorsville, he was brought home and died in bed of pneumonia. The arm, which had to be amputated, is buried in one site; his body is buried in the south end of town in the eponymous Stonewall Jackson Cemetery. Here the proud general still stands, embodied in bronze, gazing off to the hills to the west and south, field glasses in one hand, sword in the other, a flare of autumnal trees surrounding him.

Stonewall was an upright sort—religious, devoted to his family, and as far as I can determine from what I learned of the gentleman, a profoundly boring man. He memorized his lectures on ordnance for his classes at the VMI and spoke in cadenced, uninflected tones, and so believed in the higher laws of his Protestant faith that he was willing to break the current laws of the state of Virginia and teach slaves how to read. Nothing to do with liberation on this earth, mind you; the idea was that they would then be able to read the word of God. He had his eyes on the next life.

Young Robbie Gilbert, who was educated in Lexington between 1876 and 1883, would indirectly benefit from Jackson's magnanimity. There were colored schools in the town in the late nineteenth century and by the time he left middle school, Robbie Gilbert could read, which put him ahead of most people of his race in the South in those years.

The war did not entirely liberate people of African descent from slavery, it simply altered the exterior. In fact for some, on certain plantations, and for those in certain family situations in western Virginia, African Americans may have been better off before the war. The dreaded Black Codes, forerunners of the only slightly looser Jim Crow laws governing segregation, were stricter in some states than local governances controlling slaves. If you were black you could not move through certain counties without a pass, for example, could not rent or keep a house, could not preach, "exhort, or otherwise declaim to congregations of colored people, without special permission in writing," and you could not sell or even barter merchandise without written permission. The word "owner" as in "slaveowner," in these codes, was simply replaced with the word "employer."

In Lexington, the codes were looser, but nonetheless there was no school for black children beyond the sixth grade, and so, at an age of eleven or twelve, Robert Gilbert's education would have been completed at this point, except that someone in his family, perhaps even the ambitious Robert himself, must have had grander ideas. He was taken down to Lynchburg by his father, where there were schools of higher education for blacks.

Sometime in the autumn of 1880, Robert and the Old King made a journey by mule back, wagon, and then barge boat, from Lexington down to Lynchburg, where, for the first time, he met his grandmother, Fanny, a woman who must have loomed in his imagination as a female equivalent of the Old King himself. She was a former slave, but a "house nigger" (as even the blacks would phrase it), the ruler of a great airy kitchen on a plantation somewhere in the Tidewater, and an Amazonian commander of the bands of children, white and black alike, who moved to and fro, from house to yard, to field and forest, and ruler even, it was rumored in the legends told to Robbie by his father, of the white misses, whom she had nursed and nurtured from their babyhoods. The one outstanding story among the many was that she had, on one occasion by way of revenge for some offense, served the family a stew prepared from the meat of one of the old hounds that hung around the slave quarters, a dish that was pronounced as savory by the mistress. Ol' Massa himself withheld judgment, which left Fanny wondering for years whether he in fact knew the contents. This same Massa was said to be a kindly, sad-eyed man who would remain sleepless on the night before he required himself to whip a recalcitrant slave and was once seen weeping bitterly, his head buried in his hands, after he had beaten a nameless field hand.

Fanny, who is officially listed in the 1884 census records as Fanny Hardrich, dressed in motley, a huge outflowing combination of multicolored cloth that began high on her neck and swept floorward in a vast rounded series of mountains and valleys. She had, the stories say, strong white teeth and curiously elongated canines, which gave her the appearance of a lioness whenever she smiled or yawned. She could read and write, was churchly, and enfolded young Robbie Gilbert entirely in her great riverlike brown arms when he was first introduced to her and held him there an inordinate length of time, rocking him and kissing him on his round cheeks and forehead when she laid him down to bed in the big central room where she, the Old King, and three other children of indeterminate relation to young Robbie slept. There was a big iron cooking stove in the room with a box behind it where Fanny was nursing a sick hen, and there was a mother cat who slept with her litter of kittens near the chicken. Wood floors, unpainted, unvarnished, and splintering, newspapers lining the walls, a portrait of Jesus torn from a church calendar on a wall shelf near the stove.

Robbie slept in the bed with a strange cousin, a boy half his age, and probably slept fitfully that first night. His father left two days later, and when the dark came on and he was put to bed, Robbie grew silent and troubled and Fanny sat with him till he fell asleep, her hand on his shoulder. She sang to him in a low honeysweet contralto:

And when my time has come to die,
Jus' take me back and let me lie,
Close to where the James goes rolling by . . .

The room haunted his dreams for years thereafter.

I went up to the Broad Street Presbyterian Church one Sunday, just as the morning service was letting out and all the parishioners were standing around talking to the preacher, who was a thoroughly modern minister, dressed in a casual blue silk shirt, no jacket, his white dog collar shining in the bright autumnal light. There was a tall man there with a lantern jaw, short gray hair that he combed forward in bangs like a Viking warrior, or a character out of a Bergman film, also a younger man of about thirty-five with a wispy blond mustache, wearing wraparound dark glasses, and two women, one short and round-faced, with massed gray curls and rosy apple cheeks. They all glanced over as I climbed the hill toward the church, but attempted to carry on with their conversation, feigning indifference in order to be polite. They were the types with long memories, the sort who settle in a place and then, having found fertile ground and a benign climate, come war and flood and famine and the foibles of the almanac, stay put. Many families in the valley had been there since the eighteenth century.

Before I could even say hello the minister extended his hand and introduced himself enthusiastically. I explained my presence and this brought on an ad hoc assembly of the parishioners. The tall man with the Viking bangs seemed to be their leader; he was the oldest and appeared to know the most about the valley.

"They was a Gilbert family in this valley, but Leroy, he's dead," he says. "And Mary Gilbert, her body lives up in the nursing home but her mind dwells elsewhere."

I asked about the black families that used to attend this church and sit up in a balcony in the back of the church.

"Sure enough," one of the older women said. "There were blacks all up and down the Plank Road. Black families, living back I don't know where. Miss Brown—she lives over there—she says there was a Negra burial ground up the hill behind her farm and she remembers the last funeral. They carried a heavy old pine box up that hill to the woods somewhere, but had to rest on the way up."

"Who was in the box?" I asked.

"Don't know who that was. Was it ol' Johnnie maybe?" She threw this question out to the assembly.

"Johnnie's dead?" I asked, as if I had known the man.

"Old Johnnie died ages ago," they said.

I asked if anyone knew Johnnie's last name. And this induced much discussion, and many tributaries of gossip, and many stories of tenant farmers and sometime workers, and then dogs, and who owned the mule—or was it a horse?—who kicked Johnnie on that Sunday afternoon and he didn't come back into the valley for the next year and when he did, first thing he wants to know is whether that old mule is still around. But then, no, they in't anybody left here who knows Johnnie's last name. Just Johnnie. Later Old Johnnie. Earlier, until it became politically incorrect, Uncle Johnnie.

"Wasn't Gilbert?" I ask.

"Wasn't Gilbert. No. They was all white."

"And gone to boot," the rosy-cheeked woman said.

✠

The way to the purported burial ground lay beside a stream close by a small neat house, seemingly deserted. By now it was midday and hot, with the cows in the bottomlands sheltering under the sycamores and the sweetgums, the cicadas calling, and somewhere far off a chainsaw at work. Holding my camera close to my chest, I ducked under a rusty barbed wire fence and scrambled down the bank to the stream, crossing on slippery moss-grown rocks, then climbed the steep hill, stepping over blowdowns and stray boulders all the way up.

This did not seem a likely spot for a burial ground, but then I had heard that the Monacan Indians, who lived in this valley, customarily buried their dead on hilltops, and inasmuch as the local Africans, if they got free, tended to mix with the Indians, it was possible that the custom spilled over into the black community. There were no blacks buried up in the Broad Creek Cemetery, I was told at the church, which explained why I couldn't find Gilberts on any of the headstones. The one exception they told me was a little black boy who died sometime in the 1870s, around the time that Gilbert himself was born. They said that the custom of the grave commission was to bury anyone whose family requested burial there, so they put him there even though he was the wrong color. They buried him outside an iron fence, though, and never marked the site so no one knows where he is now. He could have been Robbie's brother for all anyone knew.

At the top of the hill I went around kicking over limbs and looking at any stone larger than a football in hopes of finding some sort of an inscription—or even a pattern of stones. I was guided in this search by a seventeenth-century Christian Indian burial ground I knew of on Martha's Vineyard where the bodies are marked by simple, unchiseled, unmarked stones—no way to know who lies where.

I gave up finally and sat down to think.

Only the shush of the cicadas for company, the drift of vultures in the hot blue sky, lilting over the crossed branches of the hickories. My subsequent photos of the place reveal nothing—the upward sweep of the tree trunks. Smooth sky above. Fallen limbs littering the ground, and the roll of the dark stream below the hill.

You could read a metaphor in the images, I suppose: The solid earth. The heaven seeking plants, soaring upward, and below, the dark, ever-flowing stream of time.

Later in life, at Saint Bartholomew's Church in Cambridge, after he had successfully established himself, Mr. Gilbert used to sing an old Episcopal hymn: "Time like an ever-flowing stream, bears all our cares away . . ."

✠

From the Broad Creek valley I drove back through the hills to Lexington. It was Old Alumni Day at Washington and Lee and tweedy parents in good shoes were in the streets and cafés and restaurants. There had been a VMI victory on battlefields of a football game and a pent electricity was in the air, later expressed in the bars and fraternity clubs all across the city. The African thrumming of the slit drums and rap filled the warm night, police cars drifted by, lights flickering, huge rains of beer cans fell, the clash of broken whiskey bottles, night and transfiguration for young America. The war years were over in the Valley of the Shenandoah, the bonded Africans were liberated to make their way in the world, and down on the south side of town old Stonewall, who died resisting the emancipation, stood through it all, staring westward across the hills, his sightless bronze eyes fixed on the Holy Land.

CHAPTER FOUR

Self-Reliance

. . . THE PHOTOGRAPH MERELY REPEATS WHAT IS BEING SAID IN WORDS.

John Berger

Road passing October Farm, Concord, Massachusetts

Put the case that on a frosty autumn morning in 1886, when he was seventeen years old, Robbie Gilbert went down to Lynchburg's Percival's Island station accompanied by his father and his grandmother to board the northbound Skyland Special for Washington, New York, Boston. Imagine further that the three of them waited on the platform making small nervous talk, until the blot of the train hove into view, crossed the trestle bridge over the James, and slowed to a halt at the station platform. Much hissing of steam, much loading and unloading, and then, we can presume, there was a handshake with the Old King, his father, who maintained a strong, reassuring grip on the boy's shoulder and placed a kiss on his forehead. And then, following this formality, that Robbie was all but buried by the great encircling arms of old Fanny, who wept bitterly to see her grandchild go off so young, a little boy really. This was the second parting for Fanny and the Old King. The first took place a year earlier when Gilbert's older brother, William, broke ground and rode this same train north to Boston to a better life. They had an auntie in Boston, their mother's sister, Elizabeth, and she had enticed the two boys with her letters.

Then comes the fateful call from the white conductor, instructing all to board, and, his gut churning, holding back tears for all I know, and frightened by the image of the cruel steel of the grated step, Robbie Gilbert, having now transformed himself to Robert, boarded and then turned toward the rear of the train into the shoddy colored cars at the back, a space so familiar to so many northbound black children. He was washed by the steamy interior, the sea of tight-jawed faces, sprinkled here and there with a few cocky bullies, just as frightened maybe, but better defended, as we would say now. Some black passengers on these northbound trains never slept, some jumped and jigged all the way to their destinations, it was said—free at last and Boston bound.

He sits by a window, on the west side of the train, overlooking the platform and the sloping cliffs on the west side of the James.

They were still at the station, waiting to see him off, the tall king, upright, with his regal sweep of whiskers, and Robert's fully-rounded grandmother, swathed in motley, the tears streaming freely now, and seeing this he can't hold it in anymore and that great lump in his throat breaks out into one loud, bark of a sob as the train bumps, shudders once, and clacks off northbound into the unknown.

Once the rhythmic clack starts pacing off the miles, he settles in, empty.

Such partings were not unique. All across the South in those years the familial sacrifice was the same, the cutting of family bonds for financial or psychological reasons, a milder recapitulation of the old auction block, the knot of waiting to see who would be sold and who would not, although this parting was kinder, self-inflicted, and was always softened by the hope of return, of money, and of a modicum of respect in the benign racial climate of this so-called Negro Paradise up in Boston, where you could ride with the whites on the trolleys, even side by side in the same seat, it was rumored, and where the white people, the richer ones at least, would fight for the legal rights of Negroes. It was the obverse of Virginia, where laws were designed to limit the freedom of people of color.

But none of this could blot out the break. Black families were giving up to the industrial north the gift of their talented children. No matter what success they would taste in that cold snowy climate, they would remain exiles.

✠

Digging through photo archives for another project I was chasing, I once came upon a picture of a city square in Boston's South End, taken in 1858. The image shows two women in hooped skirts crossing in front of a double-banked fountain with rain-clear sparkling water cascading in the sun, a tall, spired church just beyond, and peeking out here and there between the young trees, glimpses of the square-topped Italianate towers of town houses with iron fences. There is a sense of balance, of the architecturally desirable elements of space, air, and light, which would become the driving doctrine of the landscape architects who would later design the winding riverways and chain of green parks known as the Emerald Necklace in Boston.

The South End neighborhood had been laid out in the 1850s and was based on the English town plan models of London and Bath. It consisted of a series of grassy squares and plazas, with many fountains and statues, interspersed with tree-lined streets and brick, bow-fronted row houses, all neat and painted and freshly mortared and waiting for new residents.

The new district, which was an early effort at the urban restoration projects that were beginning in this period (Central Park was constructed in New York about the same time), was originally built to give the Brahmin families of Beacon Hill a little breathing room from the hordes of Irish who were settling perhaps too close for comfort in the central city. But even though the South End was a pleasing section of the city, it never attracted very many of the Brahmins. The problem was perhaps that it was, in the socially conscious climate of the era, something of a mixed neighborhood. Although a few of the Beacon Hill Brahmins took a chance and settled there, midlevel merchants of a lesser sort also moved in. These were, in the eyes of the old shipping families, a decidedly different species of animal. The situation is accurately summed up by one of the great fictional characters—or caricatures—of the Brahmin world, J. P. Marquand's George Apley, whose family settled in the South End early in George's life. One day George's father stepped out on the stoop and saw, across the street, an abomination: "Tarnation," he ejected. "There's a man over there in his shirtsleeves." Apley's father sold the house the next day.

The Brahmins moved out of the South End, and after that a

flight of the upwardly mobile merchants began, then the working classes moved in to fill the space, and following this, the South End sank further. By 1886, it was in decay—if ever there was an example of glory in decline it was here. The old mansions were refurbished as rooming houses, cheap restaurants opened, and the area became a notorious, even dangerous, slum. There were some 30,000 lodgers, mostly males of the underclass, stacked into squalid little airless rooms jammed with wooden-framed woven wire cots with stinking mattresses covered with dirty sheets.

It was in this district that Gilbert settled when he first arrived in Boston. He moved in with his brother William at number five Sussex Street, right in the heart of the action. Price for the room was roughly twenty-five cents a night and this was one of the better places, a residence designated for sober men only, "No Drunken Men Admitted," as one advertisement for a similar rooming house announced. Number five Sussex Street still stands and, although set in a shadowed alley, seems slightly more substantial than some of the other dwellings; it's a brick-fronted, two-storey place with tall narrow windows and a very narrow front door, facing east. Nowadays it is surrounded by bland urban renewal projects, most of them still new and not yet fallen into decay.

Although the South End is experiencing renovation and upscale development in our time, the crime rate in certain sections here is still high. One December afternoon I was poking around the district looking for Mr. Gilbert and turned a corner onto a narrow half-lit alley not far from Sussex Street. This was late afternoon, dusk settling in, and as I started down the alley I could see ahead of me a car idling in the center of the street, surrounded by what the police reports often refer to as "black males." Loud thumping chants, driven by a deep basso profundo and rhythmic spoken verses, echoed off the dripping, rain-squalled walls and reverberated through the street. As I drew closer I could see all the regalia of pop violence—baggy black trousers, silver chains, black doorags tied tightly around shaved heads, heavy buckled boots, and the music blasting louder and louder.

Two of the young men looked up and glared at me as I came on.

What to do on this narrow alleyway, turn on my heels and run? That, in my culture, is an abject statement of racism. So I walked on slowly, pretending not to notice the heavy chains, the bulging, suspicious pockets, the noise. I even quickened my step, walked more assuredly. The music churned, I was close enough now to catch a few words: "Kill," "Fuck," "Whiteman," "Police." Twenty yards ahead of me, a huge, dull-looking fellow in a puffy winter coat stepped out of a doorway and joined the crew, looking at me directly as he crossed my path. The group was leaning into the car talking to someone, more or less blocking my passage and leaving only a narrow space between their backs and the wall. But as I drew nearer two of them straightened and glanced back at me casually.

"God bless you bro'," one of them said indifferently as I squeezed by.

✠

Gilbert's attempt at finding a sober, quiet place in the South End may not have made much difference given the nature of the district in 1886. It was a noisy sector by night, catfights in the alleyways, rats in the walls, knifings out on the streets on Saturday nights, and the periodic clang of the police vehicle known as the Black Maria. It says something about the conditions of certain neighborhoods in the city of Boston that this infamous vehicle, which was to become the bane of revelers in the speakeasies in the 1920s, was named for "a brawny negress" called Maria who kept a rooming house and was much feared by the local police. They would often call upon her for assistance to help subdue rowdy criminals in her district.

The late 1880s was no doubt a rough period in the rural area around Natural Bridge, with the infamous and violent independence of the white family clans who lived in the hollows around Broad Creek, and the increasingly common lynchings that were taking place in the region. But Boston must have made Gilbert's stomach churn. Here he was, still in his teens, up from the clean airs of rural Virginia; he must have wondered what he had gotten himself into at first. But he could find work, and even though the purported "Negro Paradise" was not all he had imagined, he could at least eat in restaurants with white people and sit wherever he liked on the trolleys.

Gilbert first worked as a waiter, and then the following year as a shipper for an establishment at 259 Washington Street, and then, in 1887, got a job as a bellboy at the U.S. Hotel. Finally, in the same year, he began work as an usher at the Grand Opera House.

Here was something he never had experienced in the small town environment of Lexington. The Opera House was located on Washington Street between West and Boylston Streets and was surrounded by other famous theaters of the period, the Lion, the Gaiety Theater, a museum of curiosities, any number of minstrel halls, and later the new Boston Opera House and the Savoy. Perhaps for the first time in his life Gilbert would have been exposed to the lively popular and light classical music of the era. The actor Edwin Booth, brother of the infamous John Wilkes, played the stage in the Washington Street theaters; Caruso sang in the Opera House; Gustav Mahler conducted there, so did the pianist Ignace Paderewski, and Sara Bernhardt appeared on the stage in the district.

Also located here, not far from the Grand Opera House, was the photographic studio of Southworth & Hawes, which in the late nineteenth century was the best known and most fashionable studio in the United States. On his way to work each afternoon, Gilbert would have walked by the establishment, and I wonder if he did not see, passing from these doors, those few members of the

Boston elite who would stoop to have their images preserved by the esteemed studio. Perhaps he even studied the formal portraits that were on display.

Somewhere in this district at night, or perhaps in the squalid Sussex Street rooming house where he slept, Gilbert heard for the first time the colorful chatter of foreign languages spoken by the European immigrants from Italy and Eastern Europe, and he must have attended the minstrel shows that ran every night on Washington Street. And even though he was probably familiar with the humor, he winced perhaps at the blatantly racist jokes—although tolerance for racial humor even among blacks was more common in those unfortunate years. For all we know he may still have been enough of a country boy to enjoy the performance, with all its color and high-stepping music and slapstick action.

Gilbert was already trained in music by this time and one wonders whether he was not tempted to join one of the chorus groups, or find a minstrel hall that needed a fill-in piano player. He would have been familiar with the form of entertainment.

Minstrelsy, which was the most common and cheapest form of amusement in the Washington Street district, sprang directly from music and dance that emanated from the slave quarters after dark and on Sundays—events that were sometimes witnessed by proud, affirming plantation owners who would entertain guests by demonstrating the talents of their slaves. Whites picked up the antics of these events, blackened their faces with burnt cork, tuned up the banjos, struck the bones, and pretended to be Africans. They danced the same jigs and the high-stamping jumps that by the 1920s evolved into popular dance steps such as the Charleston. The white performers spoke in the same broken Pidgin English dialogues and acted out the parts of slow-witted field hands, shuffling porters, and dandified dudes strutting their stuff on city streets in plaid suits. They also played the roles of slatternly women, and in fact the whole show was often underlain by a subtext of sexual energy.

There were also groups of all-black performers who, according to the rules created by some bizarre psychology of racism, were required to blacken their faces in order to be allowed to appear on the stage in front of white audiences. One of the best known of these black troops was known as the Original Black Diamonds, which was based in Boston in the theater district where Gilbert worked. One of the composers for these musicals was a middle-class African American named James Bland, who wrote, among other popular melodies, "Carry Me Back to Old Virginny," which Gilbert no doubt heard on the stages of the halls and which, given his economic situation at the time, must have had some resonance.

Gilbert moved into this colorful world as observer, not as player. He may have recognized the characters and the music and the accents from the environment of his youth, although he was trying to leave all that behind when he stepped off the train at South Station. Nevertheless, on certain winter evenings, when the gas lights hissed and the air was thick with the perfumed presence of both black and white ladies—the Boston audiences were integrated—and the lights on stage were warm, and the painted, shuffling dancers dressed in colorful motley coursed across the stage, he must, at least once, have allowed that slow, repressed smile to emerge.

Back on the street, though, he straightened up, adjusted his black cravat, and proceeded down Washington Street to his Sussex hovel. People who saw him, the newly arrived southern blacks at least, might have straightened up themselves when he passed. There went a man with a destiny—Ain't no shufflin' porter—the recent arrivals muttered when they saw him walk by—there go a *Boston* man—.

The Washington Street theater district offered more than music. In this era, before the moving pictures eclipsed the live performances, the American stage was rich with variety. There were cheap comic and tragic plays every night, and people would attend the theater as much as once or twice a week in these years, in the same ways that movie buffs would attend the movie houses in the years before videos kept them home. Crowds would fill a music hall to hear live recitals of classical poetry. There were recitations of monologues, stand-up comics, drolleries, and magic shows. In its early years, the Massachusetts Audubon Society could pack a hall with performances by a certain "Mr. Avis," with his whistled imitations of birdsongs. Along with the cheap entertainments there were also performances of light musicals, which ranked somewhere above the minstrel shows, and there were also performances of European operas—which could also pack a house.

Gilbert, I suspect, had his eyes on this higher culture even before he came to Boston. In the tolerant racial atmosphere of the city he would have been permitted to attend performances of the Boston Symphony Orchestra, which was formed in 1881 by Henry Lee Higgonson, one of the prime movers behind the abolitionist movement and a supporter of the arts. When Gilbert first moved to the city the symphony orchestra played at the Boston Music Hall on Tremont Street, in what is now the Orpheum Theater. Higgonson had personally set aside blocks of seats for those with little money so that they could go to the symphony for a token fee and, given Higgonson's politics, black people would not be turned away at the door.

For a year or so Gilbert lived in the brightly lit glare of this nightlife, and although he must have learned a great deal about theater and music while he was there, he also must have retired to his little warren with his head spinning each night. He was still, withal, a country boy, and must have yearned from time to time for the open air, a wide view, reminiscent of the distant hills of the Blue Ridge.

In 1892 he acted on this whim and, in what may have been a step up financially, found a job as a porter on a steamship line, one of the opportunities available for blacks in the period. Passenger steamships were the rail, bus, and local airlines of the late nineteenth century. They ran up and down the coasts on regular schedules, and Boston was the center for shipping in the Northeast; by the 1880s some 1,700 domestic steamer arrivals were reported at the city piers. Naturally these steamers required crews, not only to handle the vessel but also to serve the passengers, and by the time Gilbert arrived in Boston, African Americans were beginning to replace the whites who worked on these vessels as cooks, stewards, and seamen.

Whenever he was in port on Sundays during this time Gilbert would attend the 12th Baptist Church on Beacon Hill, a popular African American church. One Sunday morning in May, in the pew in front of him, seated to the right, he noticed a woman in a stylish but subdued blue velvetta hat with a dipped front and a crown of lighter blue taffetine rosettes. He noticed first, the hat. Then saw in profile the face beneath the brim. She had a high forehead, large doe eyes, and full lips, and her skin was silky smooth, the color of milk chocolate.

Gilbert looked over again when the congregation stood to sing a rollicking version of "Stand Up for Jesus." He watched as she smoothed her skirt to be seated for the litany. And when the parishioners bent to pray, moved though he may have been by the spirit, he opened his eyes and squinted over again

—Oh Lord—said the preacher at the end of the prayer—Oh Lord, in Thy Wisdom, we beseech Thee. And then came the sermon.

Leaving the pulpit, the preacher high-stepped out to the altar and then back to the pulpit, where he began a riff on the theme of standing up.

—Stand up—said the preacher—stand up for Jesus.

—Stand up—said a few of the older men in the congregation.

—You know to stand up when He walks in—said the preacher—You got to stand.

—Yessuh—they cried in response.

—Got to stand—said the preacher.

—Stand up for that Man—they shouted back.

—Stand up when He walks into your life—said the preacher.

Gilbert watched the woman in the blue velvetta hat. She said nothing, only nodded slightly in response to the preacher, as if to say "yessuh," but she did not shout like the others around her. He liked that. He himself was not given to histrionics in church.

—You got to walk with Him—said the preacher—You stand up now brothers, stand up sisters, stand up when He comes in and walk with him—

—Walk on—they said in return—Walk with that man—

—Just take a closer walk—said the preacher.

—Yeaah—they all shouted.

Somebody whistled.

Somebody said Amen. Clapped.

Gilbert said nothing.

Minister began to sing aloud then. Organ poured out a chord.

"Just a closer walk with Thee . . ." He was singing now in a deep baritone. *"Grant it, Jesus, is my plea."*

Gilbert stood up with the others. He watched the woman in the hat, and then he too began to sing.

"In this world of toil and snares. . . ."

They swayed, clapping in slow unison. Hard on the downbeat, a few starting in on the offbeat, setting up a counterrhythm. And she began to sway with them. She had a fine straight back, narrow waist, and flaring hips, he noticed. And they were all singing now, full voice, the little church rafters absorbing the hammerdown clapping of their hands, and the counterharmonies of the women, the choir sidestepping left—dip—and then right, white and black robes swirling with each dip.

"Grant it, Jesus, is my plea . . . ," they sang.

She was with an older woman dressed in serge, and wearing a wide-brimmed somewhat overdecorated Sunday crown, festooned with feathers and sweeping ribbons. The older woman began to step forward and backward, then side to side, and she was clapping with the beat and throwing her head to the left with each offbeat.

Her mother? he wondered.

The noise increased.

"Guide me gently, safely o'r to Thy kingdom's shore . . . ," they sang.

On certain Sundays for no apparent reason Gilbert would be swept into the great ocean currents of this music. Some powerful, dreamlike memory of his youth and the collected voices of the people of the Plank Road would surface. Like others of his class, he was putting all that behind him now, but the multilayered complexities of pure rhythm would sometimes carry him off—carry anyone off for that matter, African or Anglo—into some other world, and he would join in the tumult of clapping and shouting and stamping in spite of himself. But now, watching her, he was cooled. Here was a creature who walked outside of the dark jungles of their common pasts. Hers was a cooler religion, a more subdued, northern, intellectual faith. More Bostonian.

He liked that too.

Gilbert spoke to her afterward in front of the church, positioning himself in such a way that they would encounter each other, seemingly by accident.

—It was a fine sermon, was it not, and—yes, it was—and doesn't that Reverend Mister Wilson have a class singing voice, and—yes, that he does—and, so do you live around here?

And she does, and not that far from Sussex Street, and her name, she says, is Anna Scott, and this is her mother, Mrs. Scott.

—Well then—he said—did she know so-and-so who was a friend of William Gilbert. She says she does, and did she know that William was his older brother, and she says

—William is your brother?—And he says—yes, he is—.

And finally, after all the small talk, he asks if he might call on Miss Scott next Sunday afternoon inasmuch as he will be back in the port of Boston, his regular schedule being such that he is offshore most of the week, sailing to Portland on Monday morning from Lincoln Wharf, and if she happened to be in that area she might see them put off; it was always a special day, the white folks waving their hats, he said, and it is a sight to see if she hadn't seen such a thing. Sometimes, he said, the white people cry. *The Star of the East* has a regular run, he said, and the seas are smoother now that the winter is over.

And when she says, why, yes, you may call at home next Sunday if you like, his stomach tightens.

So he comes back the next weekend and knocks on the front door and talks again with Miss Scott's mother, a strong dark woman named Rose who was dressed that day in a wool Venetian Eton jacket. She eyes him like a predatory bird with a fearsome glint that makes him polite. They had tea and they talked about church. Which church is better, the 12th Baptist or the old African Meeting House—and where are they all from originally and he learns they are from Lynchburg, Virginia, and did Mrs. Scott ever know of a woman by the name of Fanny Hardrich? And she did, and he said—that's my grandmother—.

—Your grandmother was Fanny Hardrich?—she says.

—Yes Ma'm—

—She was one fine woman, Miss Fanny, worked as hard as a ol' mule and sent all those chilluns of hers to school, and which one of all those little pickinnies she had running in there was your daddy?—

But they wouldn't have known him because he was the son-in-law, not her own child, and came often to see Robbie and William in Lynchburg, but worked elsewhere.

—On the canal boats?—she asks.

—No Ma'm—says Robert—in the timber yards around Lexington—

And then, after a carefully calculated period of time, he said he really must be going on, and said (albeit reluctantly) good-bye, and yes, he'll be back in Boston in early June and see her at church.

He walked down Endicott Street and when he turned the corner onto Wilston, he looked up and down to see if anyone was watching and then executed one of the stage leaps he had seen at the Orpheum Theater. He arched off the ground, snapped his heels together, landed crouching, arms outspread, spun, and leapt again. Adjusted himself and marched on. Straight up.

—Stay calm Robert Gilbert—he said to himself.

Soon he's there every week. Rose likes him. He's dark-skinned, but he's a refined dresser, a gentleman, and he can play the piano beautifully.

—No cards?—her mother asked.—No, Mama, he does not play cards. And, yes, of course he can read. He reads poetry from a little red book, leather-bound, with engraved gold filigrees, Palgrave's *Golden Treasury,* and he reads me the saddest, most beautiful poems you ever heard, all about owls and tolling bells and fading evening lights. He reads. He plays the piano. Wears hand-sewn calfskin shoes and German cloth suits, and he walks with style. He knows how to walk, you just look at him, the way he moves, and you know he be a gentleman, and you should hear his stories about the theater and the people he's seen and the places he's been on that boat he works on. All kinds of things you see on those boats. He's seen a whale once.

Rose Scott was born a slave in northern Virginia, in a site unstated in the federal records. Her daughter, Anna, was born in 1872. Anna's father, according to the census, was unknown, although what that means is that, like so many thousands before him, he was only unknown to the official, if obscured, Virginia histories. To Rose he could have been fondly remembered, a husband even, fixed in ceremony of a Sunday afternoon during slavery time by the simple ritual of stepping over a broomstick. He subsequently wandered off somewhere to make money, perhaps to sea, perhaps to Oklahoma, and never returned, and since he couldn't write, never did write home, or if he did, she, Rose, may have changed addresses by then and the forwarding address never was communicated. He was presumably out there somewhere in the world, but Anna never knew him.

She was delicate, small, like Gilbert, trim with large eyes and flickering eyelids and she had a sweet smile and (this much is on record) a fine singing voice. And he, Gilbert, was hopelessly in love. He couldn't wait; he had imagined her for so long. Hips. He saw the female curve of her hips beneath the figured Sicilian cloth skirt, and even in church, even when he was supposed to be praying, he imagined her.

They were married in 1896 and moved over to 10 Winchester Street.

The change of address represented a move up, away from the squalor and the catfights around Sussex Street. The place was only a few blocks from the Boston Public Gardens and a short walk to the Boston Common, where, on Sunday afternoons when he was in port, they strolled, taking in the puppet shows, walking determinedly past the stalls selling liquor, but stopping at the lemonade stalls, and watching the bands of children with their black, southern-born nannies, and the handsome white ladies with their full bustled skirts and parasols, and the swan boats, passing to and fro on the lagoon. The elms and the maples flowered, the beds of daffodils bloomed, and the popular Gardner Brewer fountain spilled a fall of sparkling waters, and it was all green and golden and a new century rising over the horizon.

Although they did not see it, they walked on the great roll of North American history in that park, the hard-won Common, settled by William Blackstone in 1625, resettled and re-formed by the Puritan fathers who cleared the native trees from the hills, grazed their cattle here and fenced the narrow neck connecting Boston to the mainland to keep the wolves out. On the east side of the hill in the late seventeenth century lay the established, thriving quarter known as New Guinea, where native Africans, both bound and free, once lived and where folktales out of the old continent were whispered in the alleyways on summer nights. Africa had a long and proud history in the place the Puritan forefathers called Boston.

In 1894, Gilbert had quit his job on *The Star of the East* and had begun working part-time at various odd jobs and offering private piano lessons and teaching music in the colored schools on the back side of Beacon Hill. The couple stayed on at Winchester Street for the next four years. It was not a bad place; they had three furnished rooms; they had use of a kitchen, and they were allowed to use the clothesline in the back lot. Furthermore, there were white families living nearby, pleasant people, and if not exactly their friends socially, at least familiar and polite, and even helpful on occasion. It was a good neighborhood.

Of more concern to the young couple were the cotton-belt blacks who were now moving into the South End, whence they had fled. These newer types were giving the northern blacks a bad name with all their sporting, their rough, country accents, and their whooping and their hollering out in the street and lack of respect for law and order and peace. The great in-migration of illiterate southern field hands and tenant farmers had yet to reach full flood in the city, but they were coming. Northern blacks—a group to which Mr. Gilbert now felt he belonged, having jettisoned whatever remnant of the southern drawl he had brought north—were uncomfortable with these newcomers. Embarrassed by them. They gave black people a bad name.

These were good years in general for the established black families of Boston; you could find work; you were still appreciated by the rich Brahmins, tolerated by the Jews and the Italians, albeit less so by the Irish, whom the upper-middle-class blacks tended to look down upon in any case. The 1890s was an expansive period in the city. There was an emerging social conscience that held that the one great benefit for the struggling working classes, trapped as they were in their squalid tenements, was access to space, air, and light. Frederick Law Olmsted and his protégé Charles Eliot were finishing up the grand designs for the green park known as the Emerald Necklace that wound through the city and, as Olmsted had planned, would give access to fresh air to the working poor. Mr. and Mrs. Gilbert, as they addressed each other when others were about, often walked there, and walked also along the greening banks of the linear parks that stretched along the Charles River, past the newly fashionable Back Bay district.

On May 31st, 1897, Robert and Anna would have joined a large group of people, white and black alike, at the top of Beacon Hill to celebrate the unveiling of Augustus Saint-Gaudens' monument to honor the all-black Massachusetts 54th Regiment, which had acquitted itself so bravely in the attack on Fort Warren in South Carolina during the Civil War. Many dignitaries had gathered there that afternoon and there were many speeches by white men and black men, including one by the popular African American reformer Booker T. Washington. The crowd at the foot of the State House was large and respectful. Given the spirit of the times in the United States in the 1890s, this was something of a unique event in African American history.

Boston was still better than most northern cities when it came to treatment of its African American citizenry. The Massachusetts senator Henry Cabot Lodge annually introduced a bill aimed at reducing representation in those states that disenfranchised blacks. And Boston was home of William Monroe Trotter's radical African American newspaper the *Boston Guardian,* which was the primary voice of the black cause for equality in the United States and a precursor to W. E. B. Du Bois' popular NAACP journal *The Crisis.* Black officials and representatives were regularly elected to the state legislature, and as of 1854 the schools had been desegregated—at least in theory.

But generally speaking in the late 1890s in the United States, the climate of the nation was turning against the recently liberated slaves, and this was no less true in the so-called Negro Paradise that had once been Boston. Partly by choice, blacks tended to live together in various neighborhoods and so black students filled the schools in those sections and did not attend schools elsewhere in the city. Furthermore, although there were exceptions, as with the case of the Harvard-educated reformer Trotter, most African American adults were still mired in the serving classes.

Saint-Gaudens' monument offered a curious reversal of these attitudes. The monument was a complex statement for postwar America, even a catalyst. The 54th was the first black fighting unit in the United States military and was a landmark in the theoretical advancement of colored people. The bas-relief, with its troop of black soldiers leaning forward with the upright, horsed commander in their midst, eventually came to be recognized as one of the finest expressions of public art in America, a monument to the most honorable of causes. In the bronze bas-relief, the black soldiers of the 54th are not depicted as a mass of anonymous figures but are finely rendered as sympathetic individuals, marching off to fight for their brothers. Most of the soldiers in the 54th were freeborn, and when the United States government for whom they were fighting determined, in its frugal wisdom, to pay blacks less than the average white soldier, the regiment chose to fight on for no pay. Seven weeks later, most of them were dead—killed at the charge against Battery Warren in South Carolina and buried in a common grave along with their Brahmin commander, Robert Gould Shaw.

The monument was commissioned by the leading Boston-based abolitionists, one of whom was Sarah Shaw, the mother of the commander of the unit. Robert himself, although a supporter of the abolitionist cause, was not an entirely dedicated warrior for the rights of blacks. He had misspent part of his youth in Europe, but was, historians suggest, always under the sway of his mother and became more or less a sacrificial lamb to her cause. In spite of this, when he finally accepted the position, it is said that he discovered a strength of character he himself perhaps was not aware of and led his men unwaveringly into the almost certain death of the assault on the well-defended Confederate battery. In the end he was thrown into the common grave "to rot with his niggers," as the Confederate soldiers who threw him in the pit phrased it.

The sculptor, Augustus Saint-Gaudens, had a similar story. He lived a wild, dissolute life in the company of the likes of the talented but equally debauched architect Stanford White, and had never shown any particular interest in black causes. But for whatever reason, he had worked harder on this piece than on any other, and the result was a creation of a public monument that surpassed the mere expression of patriotism to attain the realm of high art. William James said in his talk that day that you could almost hear the bronze Negroes breathe.

There were many well-known speakers at the unveiling, including one of the veterans of the company, as well as William James, who in his remarks cited Emerson's lines "So nigh is grandeur to our dust / So near is God to man." The monument and the ceremony of dedication were a final expression, James argued in his speech, of the Emersonian ideal of the individual, the lonely kind of courage that induced Shaw to leave a comfortable post and take up the command of the 54th. The African American troops and Shaw represented, James said, the self-reliance necessary for a common people to work out their salvation together if left free to try.

Of all the conflicting messages that Gilbert was hearing in these times, this one may have had the most resonance. He was, in some ways, a member of that class of American blacks who believed in the educational doctrines of Booker T. Washington, which held that the newly emancipated colored people of the nation should take whatever work was available, even if it was menial, do it well, and slowly work their way up through society by the simple application of education and hard work. This basic idea would have appealed to Gilbert, but so too did the emerging theories of Washington's contemporary, W. E. B. Du Bois, who held that blacks should have immediate access to higher education and equal opportunities in the workplace. Gilbert was of neither camp exactly. He believed in Mr. Gilbert, and William James' Emersonian message that day may best have defined Gilbert's own personal philosophy.

As far back as 1882, when he left Lexington to go to high school in Lynchburg, Gilbert seems to have known what he wanted in life, and he must have believed that he could get it through his own intelligence and perseverance. I daresay that later, when he was associating with William Brewster and his friends, who were great readers of Emerson and Thoreau, he might even have picked up Emerson's seminal American essay, "Self Reliance," and found there an accurate expression of his own beliefs. Never mind that as a result of the vagaries of history, and place of birth, and the happenstance structure of his DNA, the wind and tide were against him all along his voyage; he beat on.

✠

William James was a well-known, somewhat controversial professor at Harvard who was at the time attempting to understand the origins of memory. His work was part of a general trend of study of the relationship between religion, science, and philosophy that was coming out of Paris and Vienna at the time. One of the other investigators of these fields was a Beacon Hill doctor by the name of James Chadbourne, who was studying memory by working with rats and mazes. Chadbourne had advertised for a laboratory assistant, basically someone who would take care of his rats. Gilbert read about the work, applied, and got the job. He worked there for less than a year and then, when things were slow, was "lent" as an assistant to a man who was setting up a bird museum over in Cambridge.

Gilbert crossed the river one day and walked up from Harvard Square along Brattle Street to number 145 to learn about the work. He was greeted at the door by a young blond woman in a maid's uniform who had a strange lilting accent. Gilbert must have marveled as he entered. The foyer was large and dark and airy, with a wide flight of stairs giving onto a landing with a stained glass window above, depicting Saint Michael armed with his flaming sword. There was a large fireplace on the left with a marble inlaid frieze showing Greeks fighting against wild-looking creatures whose lower bodies were those of horses and whose upper bodies had all the features of human beings. The blond woman with the accent showed Mr. Gilbert into a large drawing room in the east wing and told him to wait. Soon a tall bearded man with dark serious eyes wandered in and introduced himself as William Brewster and extended his hand.

—Chadbourne—he said—has told me about you, Mr. Gilbert, and has spoken highly of your work in his laboratory and I need an assistant here for a few weeks arranging things in my collection—.

And would he like to see it? And so they go up to the third floor, and here Gilbert sees row upon row and case after case of dead birds, smelling of mothballs and lying in state, side by side, with white cotton for eyes. In other glass cases are birds mounted in lifelike positions—perched on tree branches, hunting the ground among dried leaves brought in from the forest, or standing on real tree stumps, also brought in from the wilds.

—We are—says William Brewster—in the process of creating a small museum and we need some help documenting what we have, and moving these birds, and setting up the displays—.

This was new work for Gilbert, a world unknown to him, but just the sort of thing he seemed to like, given the fact that he had done a little of everything in the ten years that he had been in Boston. The pay was modest, but the work was interesting and he and Mr. Brewster agreed to terms. It was a casual arrangement from the beginning. No particular hours, really, so Gilbert could continue giving music lessons and picking up the odd jobs with which he was then supporting himself. All he had to do for Brewster was show up and help the man, who seemed to be one of those very rich whites whom Gilbert had seen occasionally around Beacon Hill but had never met personally.

After ten weeks, the work was completed and Gilbert went back to Chadbourne, and then later, when the rat experiments were completed, Mr. Brewster decided to hire this Gilbert fellow full-time. He would stay on with Brewster for the next twenty-four years, drawing closer and closer to this curiously formal, even aloof, gentleman who seemed not to make much of the fact that he was a white man out of a long and distinguished family, having its roots deep in English soils and English traditions, and that he, Gilbert, was a black man of obscured origins, with roots deep in West African village life.

Gilbert was twenty-seven years old when he was hired by Brewster. Although he had no higher education, he knew how to read and write well, he was good with his hands, he had a sharp mind for detail, was open-minded, and was, above all, bent on self-improvement. He does not appear to have accepted the prevailing conviction, accepted even by many African Americans of the era, that blacks were inherently inferior to whites. As a result of some long-buried, unsuccessfully repressed inner core passed on to him by the Old King, he seems to have lived with the private knowledge, unstated perhaps even to himself, that he was equal to this white man with his meticulous note taking and his tiny cramped handwriting and his obsessive attention to the documentation and classification of species of birds.

In contrast to Gilbert, William Brewster never had to work, his father having predetermined, it appears, that he was not cut out for the business world. The adult William Brewster's only efforts in this regard required him to cross the Charles River to Boston once a month and spend a few tedious hours in the stuffy offices of his accountants to see to the rents and incomes from properties left to him by his father.

One of the great burdens of having money is that it requires one to invent a life for oneself. Mr. Brewster did, after all, have to get up every morning and, having risen, had to do something with his day, and so he took up his childhood hobby involving the collection of birds' eggs, then birds' nests, and then, finally, birds themselves, which in later years he took to collecting by means of photography.

Some five years into my quest for Gilbert, I met a man named George Blackwell, who had known Gilbert and Brewster when he was a little boy. Blackwell's family had rented one of the Brewster properties near 145 Brattle and Blackwell remembered the bird museum when it was active and open to the public by appointment. It was a red brick, solidly built structure behind the main house at 145 Brattle and had an upper-storey gallery encircling an open room with display cases of birds' nests, bird skins, and row upon row of eggs, moose antlers, a full birch tree trunk with a large artist's fungus attached to it, stuffed mammals from the North Country, and mounted birds of many species. Blackwell and his gang of boys would sometimes attempt to visit, feigning a deep interest in birds, but in fact having no interest whatsoever save to penetrate this darkened inner sanctum.

"I remember them," Blackwell told me. "They used to hover over their collections, two formal old gentleman, wringing their hands, the Negro dressed all in black, with a starched white collared shirt, and ever watchful. The guardian angels of a bird cemetery."

Blackwell also remembered one particular occasion when his father let the date for the rent payment slip by. Brewster appeared after a few days asking about the money. There are also a few sporadic complaints in Brewster's journals concerning improvements requested by the Blackwells to the rented property. Brewster meticulously records the amount of money that would be needed for the renovations.

✠

Having spent years poring over the voluminous slave narratives, my intrepid guide Tre Williams had a lot of theories on the master-servant relationship that developed between Brewster and Gilbert. One of his theories was that they lived in a curious, inverse relationship. "It's an old theme," he said, "the wise slave and the incompetent, dawdling, somewhat confused master."

Dramas based on this theme began in the theater of ancient Rome, he said, reappear in Shakespeare, then in eighteenth-century France in the plays of Diderot, and occur even in twentieth-century England in the novels of P. G. Wodehouse, with bumbling Bertie Wooster and his wise valet, Jeeves.

"Even Harold Pinter used the plot—albeit darkly," Tre said. "But my favorite variation isn't even a fiction. There was a slave named Mark living somewhere in Virginia in the 1830s who was very light-skinned. He and his master had traveled widely in Europe, where Mark picked up a number of languages and learned a thing or two about European culture. When they came back to Richmond the master was forced to sell Mark and he was bought by an infamous, swarthy slave trader who carried him down to the market in New Orleans to be sold. En route, the trader decided to keep Mark for himself. Mark knew French and soon learned his way about the city and one day met a man who was looking to buy a strong field hand. 'I know just the man you want,' said Mark. 'He's strong as an ox and feisty. He'll fight you at first and even claim that he's a white man, but I'll sell him to you for a fair price.' Whereupon Mark takes the money and guides the buyer to his former master. He fought like hell, and of course claimed he was white and free, but was put in chains all the same."

As far as this little history is concerned, Tre's whole premise of the slow-witted master remains questionable. Brewster was a competent, independent man. But Tre once summed up the enduring connection between these two by turning a contemporary pop psychological term on its side. "Wherever he went," he says, "there he was"—meaning that Gilbert was more than the accomplice of Brewster. He was Brewster.

But all that was to come. Now, in 1896, the two of them were at the beginning of their journey.

Entr'acte

Gilbert moves to Boston, 1886

That year Henry James published *The Bostonians.* Robert Louis Stevenson published *The Strange Case of Dr. Jekyll and Mr. Hyde,* and Karl Marx's *Das Kapital* was translated into English. John Singer Sargent painted *Carnation, Lily, Lily, Rose* and, in France, Georges Seurat painted *Sunday Afternoon on the Grande Jatte.*

In 1890 U.S. troops massacred four hundred Native American children, women, and men at Wounded Knee in South Dakota. William McKinley was elected president in 1896, was assassinated in 1901 in Buffalo by an anarchist, and Teddy Roosevelt was sworn in as president. In 1897 Saint-Gaudens' monument to the all-black 54th Regiment was unveiled on Boston Common. That same year, Gilbert went to work for William Brewster.

The slave parody of white ballroom dances known as the cakewalk became the rage among fashionable whites in these years. Down in New Orleans, in 1895, the cornetist Buddy Bolden was leading a band that played a new kind of music known locally as "jass," purportedly named for the jasmine perfume worn by the prostitutes of Storeyville.

In 1896, *Plessy vs. Ferguson* established the separate but equal concept and Jim Crow laws were legally sanctioned. Booker T. Washington, who in 1895 had delivered his Atlanta Compromise speech stressing vocational training for blacks, was invited, in 1901, to dine with Teddy Roosevelt at the White House. Whites were outraged. Roosevelt less so. W. E. B. Du Bois, in protest to the ideology of Washington, put forth his idea of "the talented tenth," a population of literate, academic black leaders. In 1903 he published *The Souls of Black Folk,* and seven years later began publishing the NAACP magazine *The Crisis.* In 1909 a black man, Matthew Henson, was the first human being to reach the North Pole. There was a white man with him.

In 1900 Eastman Kodak introduced the box roll-film camera known as the Brownie, the first mass-marketed camera, and the snapshot came into being, named for a quick, ill-aimed rifle shot used by hunters. The photographs of Lewis Hine, particularly those of children working in mills, alerted the public to child labor exploitation at this time. Some 600,000 children aged 10 to 14 were then working at regular jobs in the United States. In 1890, Hine had published *How the Other Half Lives,* depicting tenement life in New York City. The earlier photographic work of Timothy O'Sullivan helped enlarge public awareness of the beauty of Western landscapes during this period.

Vast, wide-brimmed hats bedecked with feathers and plumes and sometimes whole birds were in vogue at the end of the nineteenth century, along with flaring, gored skirts that swept the streets. The hat fashion had the ancillary effect of decimating populations of herons and egrets, and in reaction, in 1896, in Boston, the first Audubon Society was organized and a boycott was instituted. William Brewster was chosen as first president. Bird-watching had become a fashionable weekend hobby for ladies and gentleman of a certain class.

The first moving picture to tell a story, *The Great Train Robbery,* was produced in 1903 by the Edison Company. The film was tinted —yellow for a dance hall scene, blue-green for a forest scene.

CHAPTER FIVE

Rare Birds

PHOTOGRAPHY DEALS EXQUISITELY WITH APPEARANCES, BUT NOTHING IS WHAT IT APPEARS TO BE.

Duane Michals

Brattle Street, Cambridge, Massachusetts, June 1898

Judging from the rise of the manes of the two horses you would say that the carriage is moving at a fast clip. The heads are blurred and straining forward, the hooves unfocused, clip-clopping straight on; you can almost hear the regular chop of the hoofbeats and the creak of the carriage and smell oiled leather and horse. The driver of the phaeton is heavyset. He has a fulsome white walrus mustache with waxed points and is dressed formally in livery, with a shiny top hat. He sits upright, hands relaxed on the reins, but intent on his work. There is a large brass carriage lantern at his left, and the sweep of a whip rises up behind him, flowing backward like a thin spray of water and adding to the overall sense of speed. It is a fine day besides, late morning, by the shadows beneath the carriage. Also June. This much I know because someone scratched the day, year, and place on the side of the glass plate negative in a small scrolling hand that looks a lot like Gilbert's: "Cambridge, June 18th, 1897."

The house behind the phaeton is a clapboard Georgian structure, shuttered in the upper windows, with diamond-patterned windows on the first floor. Huge elm trees obscure the place, and there is a clean, plain, white picket fence in front of the yard and a sidewalk with well-cut granite curbs. The street is still unpaved, and if you look carefully you can see that other carriages have passed that day, which means that the weather has been dry for a while.

I recognize this place, even though it's not identified on the plate. It is 145 Brattle Street, William Brewster's boyhood home, and the site of his famous bird museum and his (some would say) infamous, or at least eccentric, yard. Over the years, after he inherited the house, he planted many native trees and shrubs on the two-acre plot and then surrounded the whole with a twelve-foot wire-mesh fence—not to keep out human intruders, mind you, but to hold at bay his archenemies in Cambridge: cats. William Brewster was not fond of cats.

Number 145 Brattle Street is now owned by the Armenian

Apostolic Church, and although the interior has been altered, the exterior remains the same; you can even shade yourself under some of the trees planted by William Brewster. The house is one of the old grand mansions on the so-called Tory Row in Cambridge. Many of the larger houses here were built by successful merchants who fled the country when rumors of revolt began in the mid-eighteenth century. Two doors east, toward Harvard Square, is the Craigie Mansion, the former home of Henry Wadsworth Longfellow, a house also famous for the fact that George Washington lived here during the Boston campaign in 1775.

Although descended from William Brewster, the first minister at Plymouth Plantation, the Brewster family moved north to Wolfeboro, New Hampshire, in the third generation and lived there until the early nineteenth century, when the current William Brewster's father came south toward Boston. William the younger was born in Wakefield, in 1851, but the family soon moved to the big house on Brattle Street, where he grew up. Will, as he was known in his younger years, expressed an early interest in birds and used to go out every Saturday on egg-collecting and nest-collecting forays with his friends, one of the favorite pastimes of country boys in those years. Cambridge was essentially rural at the time. There were fields running down to the Charles River in this section of the town; there was an orchard behind Brewster's house, and there were pastures, a large vegetable garden, a plot of berry bushes, and a horse barn closer to the house.

Whoever made the photograph that day must have been preparing to take a picture of the house and had seen the phaeton coming. He inserted the glass plate, quickly focused on the house, and then waited.

The horses' heads entered the ground glass image. He waited.

They reached the east side of the dark porch; he waited, then squeezed the shutter bulb.

The heads of the horses are stopped just beyond the door, the carriage obscures the lower windows, the leaves of the trees no longer flutter, the arching carriage whip freezes in a spraylike curve, and, could we see inside the parlor, the hands of Caroline Brewster perhaps halt, mid bar, on the keyboard as the phaeton chops by.

There is no other traffic that day, no automobiles as yet on Brattle Street, even though there are automobiles elsewhere. In fact, the nearby town of Newton was well known for the manufacture of the new vehicles. All of these were private firms, operating out of carriage houses in back of the main houses by mechanically inclined tinkerers. The new machines, or "bubbles," as they were called, were popular with a certain class of rich, although not with Brewster. He would not deign to be so vainglorious. Mr. Brewster, although a bit of an outsider by choice, maintained the old Brahmin traditions of frugality. Why buy anything new when what you already owned was good enough for your grandparents. In Mr. Brewster's case, this thriftiness did not extend to cameras, but then cameras were an exception, even fashionable, among the Brahmins. Oliver Wendell Holmes himself—a neighbor of the Brewster family and the man who invented the term "Boston Brahmin"—owned one and even wrote essays on photography for the *Atlantic Monthly*.

Mr. Gilbert observed closely the behavior of the Brahmin class around him. He watched the studious attention to detail practiced by his employer, Mr. Brewster. He taught himself to type. He learned to develop and print the photographs taken by Brewster. He learned how to set up the camera. Then he learned how to take the pictures. By this time, he had also learned to play the piano well enough to teach young people and I suspect he halted at the living room door whenever he passed through the hallways of 145 Brattle when Caroline was at the piano. And I suspect that she noticed this. And I think she invited him to listen. And then, after he let it slip that he knew something of the keyboard, suggested that he sit, and that he run through a chord sequence and play a few melodies. Which he did, with consummate and surprising skill, playing in the classical style, his long fingers fluttering easily through the phrases. In certain quiet moments when he and Caroline were alone and Brewster was out tinkering in his bird museum, the two of them talked about music. William had no particular patience for music and Caroline perhaps enjoyed having someone around the house who appreciated her piano abilities. And in this manner, little by little, through shared interest, I believe that these two became fast friends. I say this because later, when Gilbert was hard-pressed financially because of family illnesses, it was Caroline who approached her husband to ask if he could not lend Mr. Gilbert some funds. He did, "... but I do not know when I shall be repaid," he confided to his diary, in an uncharacteristic personal aside.

Caroline was given to illnesses, was fond of dogs, music, reading. She was a full-bosomed woman with noticeable blue eyes, a sweep of auburn hair, and was close with a certain friend, identified in Brewster's diaries as ERS, which was code for Elizabeth R. Simmons. Caroline and ERS, not unlike William and Mr. Gilbert, were together often. They visited each other's houses regularly, and Caroline would periodically spend the night at the house of ERS, who was unmarried and lived alone. They went to the theater and to dinner. They traveled abroad together, sometimes starting out with William in tow, sometimes meeting up with him later, usually in England, although on several occasions on the Continent, where they traveled through Belgium and France. Periodically William and Caroline, accompanied by ERS and Gilbert, would voyage by train northward to Bethel, Maine, the jumping-off point for the then wilderness fastness of Lake Umbagog. In Bethel, they would visit an apparent family friend named "Doctor G"—code, I later learned, for Dr. John Gehring, a popular neurastheniologist of the period, who treated both Caroline and William.

This relationship between ERS and Caroline, which, in the common parlance of the era, came to be known as a "Boston marriage," was a curious phenomenon of the period, outlined most completely in Henry James' contemporary novel *The Bostonians.* The best known of these marriages, and the possible model for James' book, was the relationship between the novelist Sarah Orne Jewett and Annie Fields, the wife of the famous editor James T. Fields. The two friends, Jewett and Fields, were drawn together after the death of James Fields, and their relationship rapidly evolved into a long-term union of intense mutual affection. They were a recognized and accepted couple within Boston literary social circles.

Although the apparently lesbian involvement of the Boston marriage would be taken for granted in our time, in fact the sexual nature of these relationships has been the subject of continued discussion. Social historians—never a group normally known to shrink from controversy—have tended to deal more with the emotional needs of these unions, rather than sex. If nothing else, the marriage may have been a "romantic friendship," a relationship that is rare nowadays, closer to a sisterly or spiritual communion between two individuals. In any case, the nuances of interrelationships in that polite age were usually merely hinted at in print, although they may have been more freely discussed over brandy and cigars in the exclusive all-male clubs of Boston.

Whatever went on between Miss Simmons and Mrs. William Brewster can only be implied from the frequent references to some of the outings that these two went on in Brewster's diaries and journals. "ERS and C. to dinner," for example, or "C spent the night with ERS, returned with 'Larry' the next morning." (Larry was the Brewsters' beloved springer spaniel, a dog later replaced by an Irish terrier named Timmy, whom William and Caroline loved as they would a child.) William Brewster did not seem to resent in any way the "marriage" of these two. In fact he seems to have had a genuine fondness for ERS as well as a solicitous, caring relationship with Caroline. The three of them often dined together and would always join one another on holidays. From time to time in the diaries and journals, Brewster lets slip a little aside that opens a slight crack in the secret door of his relationship with Caroline, however: "Another long, sad talk with C this morning . . . ," he wrote at one point, or in another entry, "C feels she is unable to maintain the household any longer. . . ."

Generally, Brewster's diaries and journals concern the birds he had seen, and other natural history notes, along with a few details on his property management. He had constant problems with the Irish workers at October Farm, some of whom, on certain occasions, become surly, and some of whom he had to fire. His struggles over these decisions are hinted at. And so too is the involvement of his great ally in this ongoing struggle with the Irish workers, his factotum, Gilbert. Nowhere in these writings, however, are there any significant asides about ERS, save for his concern about her when she was sick—probably with pneumonia. She is referred to almost every day in this period, a thorough record of her convalescence. Furthermore, when Caroline was sick and in the hospital—this troop was often ill, it appears—Brewster spent a great deal of his time with ERS. It was one big happy family, with dogs supplanting children, ERS as sister, maiden aunty, or sometime husband, and Gilbert as some rare species of helpful younger sibling who was willing to do anything requested of him.

Married women of the Victorian era, generally speaking, were prisoners of the hearth. The Brahmin gentleman, unless he was a rebel (of whom there were a few in this group), always married a woman of his class. She was to manage the household and oversee the nurturing of the children (although she was not required to change their diapers, or put them to bed, or play horsy with them—that was Nursey's job). By day, she was permitted to go to her sewing circle and she was permitted to go to the Friday afternoon symphony, and to hold teas and even go on outings in the field. She was, however, expected to be home at night. Meanwhile the man, the hunter, was out in the wilderness of the banks and the clubs and the committee meetings. Elsewhere, in more degenerate American cities than Boston, he might even descend to the ninth circle of the brothels and the gambling houses. Young Bostonian males were repeatedly warned against such practices, however, and Harvard men were not to be seen (not supposed to be seen, at least) in the squalid West End, among the foreign element, where there were loose women and questionable card games. Nor were the students supposed to frequent the bars and taverns of Scolley Square, where sailors and prostitutes were known to congregate. They did anyway, of course. But it is difficult for me to imagine Mr. Brewster and his company of nature-loving companions slumming in the squalor of the West End on hot summer nights, or downing whiskeys with the whores of Scolley Square.

Given these social conditions, it is curious to note that in most of the photos of people taken by Brewster or Gilbert the separation of sexes is not apparent. Out in the wilds of the North Woods, there are women present. They are there in the lean-to hunting lodges, dressed in their heavy woolen riding skirts and straw hats; they are out in the forest with rough-bearded local guides, dressed in summer whites and backed by a tangle of the foreboding dark trees. You see women seated primly in the sterns of the handsome Adirondack-style pulling boats that Brewster and Gilbert rowed around on Lake Umbagog, in Maine. You see them along the banks of the more civil Concord River, in all their feather-bonneted finery. And of course you see them in the gardens of Cambridge, and in the pastures of Concord and on the porches of the summer houses in Lancaster, and in Dublin, New Hampshire, where they would retreat during the hot weeks of the Boston summer. My sense is that Brewster's group was atypical. Although he counted many Harvard professors in his circle, as opposed to paunchy clubmen and financiers, and even though he was friends with a few of the socially accepted Boston Ten painters, Frank Benson and Abbott Thayer, for example, and counted Daniel Chester French as one of his longest and deepest friends, he was not necessarily literary, or professorial, or artistic.

Brewster, ERS, Caroline, and their company of friends seem to have been able to mix with everyone to a certain degree. They were in some ways a unique species, endemic perhaps to Cambridge. Their sacred texts were Emerson and Thoreau, and they entertained one another with private dinners, traveled much, read Dickens by night to each other, and went out to the parks of the Emerald Necklace at dawn to look for songbirds. Brewster's "colored friend" (as he is often designated in contemporary diaries and articles about William Brewster), Mr. Robert A. Gilbert, went with them. As my earliest informant, the research librarian from Harvard, suggested, Gilbert appears to have been a favorite of the Brahmins, a pet, what we might now call their token Negro. But he was, withal, under the employ of Mr. William Brewster, and although he seems to have come and gone on his own, without scheduled hours, interweaving Brewster's world with his own private affairs and his family, he was, in the end, a paid employee.

✠

One evening at one of his favorite Cambridge watering holes, I told my guide, Tremont Williams, the long story of the relationship between Gilbert, Caroline Brewster, and her apparent Boston marriage with ERS. I could see his mind working before I even finished.

"What do you think?" I asked, once I had outlined the picture.

"What do *you* think?" he countered. "Pretty obvious."

"No it isn't and you know it. This is no *ménage à trois* if that's what you're thinking."

"How about a *ménage à quatre?*" he asked, winking.

"Forget it," I said. "This is cold roast Boston."

But as the evening wore on the possibilities continued to grow in his mind and by way of entertainment he began to outline a novel.

"Caroline and William have a sexless marriage, tied together by a mutual love for dogs," he began. "In comes Mr. Gilbert. Young. Twenty-seven, did you say when he first starts working for Brewster? He meets Caroline. Smooth white skin, coppery hair, ten years older, but well preserved. Plays the piano beautifully. Loves flowers. Dogs everywhere. Gilbert loves dogs too. Remembers them from his youth. The two of them talk. They find they have a lot in common in spite of the social and racial chasm between them. He plays the piano. She's sympathetic, is moved by his skill. More talk. These Brahmins loved their 'Negroes,' I can tell you that much. In the meantime, Brewster finds in Gilbert everything he lacks in himself, including a competency with machines, the craftsman's skill, a good companion, an excellent field observer. Brewster's got bad eyesight, no?"

"In his youth, yes."

"Gilbert is his bird spotter, begins to supply all the material for his field notes. Soon he begins to write up the notes in Brewster's hand. Then he commences to write the articles that Brewster is publishing. He's his secretary, his valet, his chauffeur, his gentleman's gentleman. Doltish Brewster plods on. His success increases, and it's all because of Gilbert. This is all more or less true, isn't it?"

"To an extent, yes," I said. "But very exaggerated. I see where you're going and it is totally outrageous."

"No, there's more. Who's this picky fellow at the museum you told me about?"

"Samuel Henshaw?"

"Right. Henshaw. One day, after hours at the museum Henshaw catches Gilbert doctoring Brewster's notes. He pretends not to notice. Begins snooping. Builds a case."

"And?"

"I'm thinking . . ."

He downed the last of his whiskey and looked off for the waiter.

"Did you say Gilbert made money in the shoe polish business? Went to Paris?"

"Yes, but it doesn't fit. The timing is wrong."

"When did Henshaw die?" he asked.

"I don't know. Long after Brewster though, the early thirties, I think. He stayed on at the museum until he was seventy-five, never took a day's vacation in thirty or more years."

"Gilbert couldn't have, you know, eased him out through intrigue?"

"No. But then shortly after Brewster died, Gilbert began working full-time at the museum. Not long after that the museum finally got rid of Henshaw."

"Plot thickens," he said.

"To what, though? No case, Tre. No story."

"There is a story. There's got to be. There's always a story. You just have to know how to find it. How about an affair between Caroline and Mr. Gilbert?"

"Never!" I said loudly, feigning indignation. "Never on this earth. Gilbert was a family man and a churchgoer. An upright citizen."

Tre rolled his eyes.

"I mean it."

"I know you do."

"Caroline, much as she may have loved Gilbert as a friend, would be horrified at anything physical. Would faint outright even at the suggestion. She was sensitive, a hothouse flower," I said.

"How do you know?" Tre asked.

"I just know. I know them. I know a little about the period."

"We don't know anything," he said, leaning forward and looking at me directly—which was rare for him. "We don't even know what we are supposed to know. You don't even know who really took all those old photos you cart around."

There was, as there is in all fictions, a certain amount of truth to his drunken ramblings. And he was spot on about one thing. We really only know the externalities.

✠

By this time in the quest to find Mr. Gilbert, whenever I had the chance, following the suggestions of Mr. Tremont Williams, I would run off to various libraries and search through federal records and the like, tracking down leads wherever they appeared. But I realized I would never find the man at the rate I was moving. Facing this reality, I managed to obtain some funding through a series of generous grants from organizations that were apparently intrigued by the fact that I may have discovered one of the few African American photographers to have engaged in landscape photography. Using the funds, I was able to hire a research assistant named Jill Brown to help chase down some of the intriguing clues I was finding concerning Mr. Gilbert's ventures.

Ms. Brown was an indefatigable researcher who had worked mainly in the field of art history and whose credentials included an award from Harvard University named for the African American painter Allan Crite, who is best known for his stylized scenes of black life in the Boston neighborhoods in the 1930s. If not an outright associate, he would have been known, at the very least, to Mr. Gilbert.

Jill Brown and I began following the leads for Gilbert and Brewster beyond the confines of Cambridge and Concord. One of these excursions took us to the town of Wolfeboro, New Hampshire, on the shores of Lake Winnipesaukee, the family home of William's line of Brewsters. Caroline and William, usually accompanied by Gilbert, would often visit the area to attend to family matters and dedications and social events that required their presence.

There is a well-endowed private school on the lakeshore, a collection of neoclassical buildings set on a rise, with rolling lawns that drop down to the banks from the east. The school was founded (resuscitated from an early institution, actually) by William's father, John Brewster. The institution was defunct in the 1830s, but old John Brewster, the elder, bailed it out on condition that the name be changed to Brewster Academy and that the school accept anyone, regardless of age, sex, and—interestingly enough—race. It was an early statement of the aborning New England fight for Negro equality.

John Brewster was a local farm boy with an eye to success. He worked first in a local dry-goods shop, and having tasted the possibility of more lucrative ventures, moved to Boston and, with his savings and a few loans, started his own business. After a few wise investments, coupled with good timing, he prospered, and by the time his only child, William, was born, in 1851, he had established a banking firm that, within a decade, was averaging half a million dollars a week. When he died, in 1886, he was a millionaire and left his son in good standing. Old John never forgot his country roots, though. He came back to Wolfeboro every summer and was more than generous to the town in his will.

Wolfeboro, which advertises itself as America's oldest summer resort, is now one of those small-town New England summer colonies whose population swells each season and declines every winter. There's a main street lined with generally useless shops and the usual assortment of small restaurants, historical sites, museums, and the main attraction, the wide lake. In fact the town is not that much different from how it was in the 1890s, when Wolfeboro was at its height as a summer retreat. Old photos of street scenes taken back then show crowds of revelers out on the main thoroughfare, pushing their bicycles and baby carriages, dressed in their straw hats and long skirts, and wandering the shops, scouting for tourist trinkets.

We first arrived in town on a hot July day, and set out to hunt the local libraries and town archives. John Brewster's magnanimity was everywhere evident: Brewster Academy, Brewster Beach, Brewster Street, Brewster this and Brewster that, all over the town. But no Gilbert. No trace anywhere except perhaps in a local oddball natural history museum in the town, established by a turn-of-the-century dentist named Doctor Libby, who was a contemporary of William Brewster and was an eclectic and energetic collector of artifacts. Along with cases displaying the dried, brown hands of Egyptian mummies, long curling Chinese fingernails, hideous nineteenth-century dental tools, one of Henry Thoreau's pencils, mouse skeletons, and cases of stuffed endemic mammals of the region, you will find there row upon row of bird skins, some of which were collected by Brewster and may have been stuffed for the museum by Robert Gilbert.

Shooting and stuffing the bodies of local birds as a means of maintaining records of the resident and migratory species of birds was the standard method of study in the nineteenth century, and both Brewster and Gilbert were skilled at taxidermy. You can find sorted and displayed skins probably prepared by Gilbert, but credited to William Brewster, in little natural history museums all over New England, everywhere from the Berkshires to the Harvard Museum of Natural History (the new name for Mr. Brewster's Museum of Comparative Zoology).

It was beastly hot that day and, rather than continue, we deserted our quest early and wandered down to an old dock opposite the museum, jumped in the lake, and swam out and drifted there for a while, cooling off. After our swim, we went for a drink at a local pub that had a terrace facing the lake, hoping to catch a breeze. While we were there we spotted a poster indicating that the Preservation Hall Jazz Band was to perform that night at (where else?) the Brewster Performance Tent and I suggested that we attend.

"We shouldn't go to this event now," Ms. Brown said. "Mr. Gilbert wouldn't like it."

This gave me pause. It is true that neither William, nor Caroline, nor Mr. Gilbert liked jazz. The closest the Brewsters ever came to letting loose were the Virginia reels they sometimes held in the front halls—Caroline at the piano, with the formal lines of high-buttoned Brahmins tramping up and down in stiff processions.

"This is our research," I said. "We have to understand what he so hated."

✠

Mr. Gilbert might have hated the music that night. But he would not have minded the audience. Here on this summer night there were only two black couples and they were cut in Mr. Gilbert's style, formal banker-type families up from Boston or Washington. Everyone else was white—and white-haired to boot—and dressed for the night in their finest L.L.Bean summer casuals.

The lead singer for the band was a Louis Armstrong look-alike with a gravelly voice who played a mean trumpet and was soon stomping and swinging through all the old numbers. The band tried its best to roust the New Englanders, but they just sat there and clapped weakly after each number, and there wasn't any shouting or jumping and nobody chopping the floor with their arms flinging akimbo in the Charleston, as there would have been back in the old days when the Charleston was in vogue and the Jazz Age was in full swing in America. Sensing this, the band worked harder, and the harder they worked, the more the old folks dug in, clapping politely, sometimes even enthusiastically at the familiar numbers, but no hooting or hollering. They sat, upright in their uncomfortable wooden chairs as if still bound in whalebone corsets, high-button collars, and starched boiled shirts of the late nineteenth century.

Finally the band took a break and disappeared backstage. There was a bar in the back of the tent and the polite Yankees lined up for their bottled spring water, Coke, and ginger ale in spite of the fact that champagne was being served as well.

"Let's have a toast," I said to Ms. Brown. "Let's drink to Old Mr. Gilbert and let the night be damned."

We had a couple of glasses, then another, and then the band picked up again.

It was a still night beyond the tent, a hot night; the lawns of Brewster Academy swept down to the dark shores of the lake, and above us the stars were sharp and the lights of the summer cottages were winking across the waters and a warm breeze was coming in, smelling of lake, rank vegetation, and ancient earth.

"Let's take a walk," I said, and we stood outside the lightened tent for a while, watching the performance from afar. One of the hot, jumping numbers ended. There was the usual round of polite applause, and then, quietly, the piano man struck a few introductory notes, ran through a sequence, and the banjo player stood up and took the mike.

We did not see it coming at first. He started to sing quietly, a warm honey-smooth voice, just the way Mr. Gilbert would have liked to hear it:

"Just a closer walk with thee . . ."

We didn't see it coming.

"Grant it, Jesus, is my plea . . ."

Trumpet moved in, thickly fluid, like wild honey.

". . . daily walking close to thee . . . ," he sang, *"Let it be, dear Lord, just let it be . . ."*

"Come on," I said, "let's dance."

She glanced heavenward. "Mr. Gilbert, forgive us," she said.

I gathered her up and we spun off slowly, the trumpet winding through, the clarinet player leaning into the music.

"—Guide me safely, gently o'er . . . ," the banjo man sang.

A riff from the clarinet . . .

"—to Thy kingdom shore, to thy shore."

An easy, slow statement from the trumpet, like an afterthought.

"Dear Lord, let it be."

And then before the last note faded, the trumpet cut in again and then the drum smacked and suddenly the whole band broke into a snarly jump and the players were all over the stage, dipping and bowing, and even the old New Englanders worked into it little by little, some began clapping rhythmically, then one or two got up and started to dance and then a few more, then they spilled out onto the lawns, and soon they're all over the place, skinny old geezers in narrow L.L.Bean trousers, throwing their arms every which way, clapping and swinging their lowered heads from side to side in replication of what they believe to be the style of those few Negroes whom they may have seen from time to time, and some of the old ladies in print shirtwaists back in the tent, swaying, and swinging their hips like sluts and singing along with their eyes shut tight, arms outspread, snapping their fingers and the lights seem to brighten, the music grows faster and louder.

We looked back at the tent and the whole white space seemed on fire, a brightly lit vision of feet and arms and undulating bodies, and then, abruptly, just before the music got too frenzied and the older ones started dropping from coronaries, it ended.

The crowd surged toward the stage, band members took their bows, holding up their instruments and thanking each other, extending their arms to one another to give credit where credit was due, the singer, the piano man, the clarinet, the trumpet, drums and bass.

"What was that all about?" I said once the applause had died down.

After that the group played a few of the old popular chestnuts, and then, at the end of the concert, tried to get a conga line going and broke into "When the Saints Go Marching In," and most of the old-timers got up again and grasped onto each other by the hips and more or less walked in a shuffling line around the hall without much spirit, as if spent, or perhaps embarrassed, by their earlier expression of feeling.

CHAPTER SIX

Negro Paradise

THE CAMERA CANNOT LIE,

BUT IT CAN BE AN ACCESSORY TO THE TRUTH.

Harold Evans

An early gathering of the Nuttall Club in William Brewster's bird museum, Cambridge, Massachusetts William Brewster is third from right, front row.

One Monday evening on Brattle Street Mr. Gilbert set up Brewster's Empire State bellows camera in the southeast corner of the bird museum. A group of his friends had gathered that Monday evening and, after much chatter and banter, the twelve men arranged themselves in a double row of chairs set at an angle in the northwest corner of the lower gallery, just beneath a shelf with a mounted otter and a stag white-tailed deer head. They composed themselves carefully while Gilbert tended to the details of preparing the plates. He shook a small pile of lycopodium powder onto the flash pan, twisted the rack-and-pinion brass knobs to bring the men into focus, and then, satisfied, began counting—one, two, three—and opened the shutter and sparked the powder.

The men are trapped, mid pose. Some have folded their hands carefully and stare to the right or left with a studied pensive look, some have self-consciously fixed their hands in their vest pockets, heads jutted forward as if ready to spring. This is a mixed group. There are some young men who look to be in their late twenties, and there are also some balding or gray-haired gentlemen among them. Many are bearded, and not one of them looks directly into the camera.

Just right of center is a carefully composed older man with a full gray trimmed beard, his legs are crossed, hands folded in a relaxed manner, and he is staring into space, stage left. This is the president of this little club of men, Mr. William Brewster.

The plate for this photograph is lost, but I discovered a print in the archives of the Museum of Comparative Zoology in a file of images marked "Brewster." It's undated, the men are unidentified, but scrawled on the back of the print there is a humorous indication of the site that states with familiar simplicity—"his lair"—which is to say, Brewster's famous bird museum behind his house on Brattle Street.

Even without the notation you could guess the venue. Behind

the seated men is a glass case with a kingfisher, an oriole, a towhee, and nine or ten other birds. More birds in a glass case on the right, below a set of snowshoes. Here, mounted forever on their perches are a screech owl, a willet, and several unidentifiable shorebirds.

Fascination with birds began early in Brewster's life. Every Monday evening, starting in 1871, when Brewster was 20 years old, he and a group of friends who were also interested in the subject used to meet in the attic of Brewster's parents' house on Brattle Street to discuss birdlife and peruse a rare treasure owned by the Brewster family, John James Audubon's five-volume *Ornithological Biography*. The group had no name or particular organization to it, the friends would simply get together to talk. But in 1873 they decided to expand and formalize their meetings and sent a letter around to half a dozen similarly minded men to form an ornithological society. The result was the creation of the Nutall Ornithological Club, and the group elected Brewster as their first president. Three years later, the organization began publishing a bulletin documenting some of the current scientific work in the field, illustrated with hand-colored plates of birds. Club membership was low, twenty or thirty men in the first years, but the journal was popular and the print run of these early editions was three or four hundred. Ultimately the club put the bulletin on sale through booksellers and began to actively seek subscribers—a dollar a year for four issues. Unintentionally, it seems, the little publication had gone national.

To assist with their creation, in 1876 they chose a professional ornithologist as associate editor, Joel Asaph Allen, who was head of the ornithological department at the Museum of Comparative Zoology and a distinguished figure in the field. The group changed the name of the bulletin to "The Auk," and the publication went on to become one of the outstanding journals in the field—still is in fact. Ten years later Brewster got the idea to establish another smaller, more intensive organization of even more dedicated bird men. The result was the creation of the American Ornithologists' Union, which is also still with us today and is an important scientific group that eventually took over publication of the journal.

These two groups were strictly scientific, there was no intention of forming an organization that would be at all political. But the times were working against such isolationism and Brewster recognized this. In October of 1884, he delivered a short talk at the annual meeting of the AOU at the American Museum of Natural History, in New York. He was concerned about the wholesale slaughter of birds along the coasts of North America for the millinery trade.

Fashions of the late nineteenth century required the addition of feathers on the large, wide-brimmed, and increasingly cumbersome decorative hats of women. This fad became ever more excessive, with sweeping plumes taken from the nuptial feathers of herons and egrets as well as the mounting of entire birds, generally terns, wings half open and sweeping across the forehead in apparent flight. Some of the early photographs of the outings of Brewster and his friends show—even among this enlightened group—women with feathered hats, albeit more subdued versions than some of the constructions of their more urban and urbane sisters.

The collection of these birds and feathers created a full-scale trade for hunters, especially in the marshes of the American South, where the herons and egrets gathered in huge noisy rookeries. The decline in bird populations was compounded by the fact that the hunters were seeking the ornate white plumes that these birds develop during the mating season. Hunters would go into a rookery, shoot the adults for their feathers, and leave whole nests of young to starve to death. Populations dropped dramatically, a fact that few noticed or perhaps even cared about, save for ornithologists. At the annual meeting that October day Brewster called for the formation of a committee to halt the indiscriminate and wanton destruction of North American birds. There was earnest support for the move, and after some debate a committee was formed to study the problem. It was only a committee, however, and no action was taken to do anything.

Bird watching, as opposed to bird hunting, or egg collecting, was beginning to evolve into a pastime among certain segments of society in this period. Men would go out in the field of a weekend morning to spot local birds through opera glasses. Those with more scientific interests, including Brewster and his friends, would actually shoot the birds they so loved, especially the rare ones, and take them home to stuff and preserve as a record. It was in this manner that Brewster began to assemble the collection of bird skins and birds' eggs that were eventually housed, along with a few other natural history objects, in his museum at Brattle Street.

The two Cambridge-based bird clubs were exclusively men's groups, but women would often accompany men into the field and sometimes went out by themselves. It was, among other small and conservative pleasures, a favored pastime among the Boston Brahmins. One of the popular birding spots was Hall's Pond, across the river from Brewster's house, in what is now Brookline. A single woman named Minna Hall lived at Hall's pond and she and a good friend, her cousin Harriet Hemenway, would walk around the shores of the pond looking for songbirds and noting their observations in diaries and journals. On one of these walks, Harriet Hemenway began telling her friend of a horrendous article she had read about the slaughter of birds in Florida. The article included graphic descriptions of the dead and dying young, including accounts of the horrific odor emanating from these devastated rookeries.

One of the characteristics of Boston women of means, particularly those involved in the Boston marriages, was a burning social and reformist attitude. Even after two hundred and fifty years, the old Puritan moralist streak endured in these people. And now these two women were about to give birth to another social cause, the American activist conservation movement.

There is a certain irony afoot in the life and times of the now lost world of the Boston Brahmins. It is a fact of history that they evolved out of the intolerant Puritan class and that many of them made their money in the Satanic Mills of the woolen industry and that many were involved in questionable trades, including the slave trade and the China trade, one aspect of which involved the introduction of opium to the already oppressed Chinese peasant classes. But it is also true that once they acquired their riches they had a strange tendency to pour bad money after good causes. Unlike the midcentury rich of New York, Pittsburgh, and Chicago, who gained their wealth through equally nefarious industries, once the Brahmins were rich, they tended to support settlement houses, institutions for the blind and the deaf, libraries, a symphony orchestra, and, in their finest hour, the financial (and moral) support for the abolition movement. And when the conflict finally came, they willingly sent their sons off to war, unlike the moneyed New York families who paid off impoverished Irish immigrants to take their sons, places in the military.

Given this lineage, Harriet and Minna, in 1896, determined to do something about the slaughter of the innocents that was taking place in the marshes of the Americas. They went home and ticked off the names of all their friends in the social register of Boston, the Blue Book, and then invited them to a tea party at Harriet Hemenway's house on Clarendon Street. Here over Lapsang souchong tea and petit fours they described the wanton slaughter and proposed, in effect, an early version of a boycott of hats bearing the feathers of wild birds. The tea party was a success, so they proposed forming an organization and, having done so, and understanding the nature of the political climate of the era—this was, after all, the period of the suffragettes—they wisely decided that if they were to have any clout they must have a gentleman as their leader, and who of these would be best suited but Sir William Brewster of Brattle Street, who was by then the veritable dean of American ornithology and a name that anyone in the field would recognize. Brewster, more than anyone else, would lend a mantle of authority to the group.

Then came the matter of a name. The women decided, following the lead of an earlier, albeit failed organization, to call the group the Audubon Society. The intention was not to limit the organization to one state. This was to be a national, even international, cause from the beginning, and by the third meeting the board resolved to use every effort to establish similar organizations in other parts of the country. Within the year, using seed money from the Boston group, five other states from New York to Colorado had joined the cause. By 1905, the group had increased its membership substantially and went on to create a national Audubon society. Their little war was fought on two fronts. Women eventually killed the market for plumes through social pressure, and in 1900 Congress passed a law that prohibited the interstate shipment of animals killed in violation of state laws. In 1916, Congress passed the Migratory Bird Treaty, which prohibited outright the trade in feathers.

As far as the Mr. Gilbert story is concerned, there is a curious twist in the choice of names for their newly formed bird group. Although years of research have tried to "clear" his name, there is fairly good evidence that John James Audubon, the father of so many white bird organizations, was in fact at least partly black. Audubon was a great self-promoter and illusionist and marketer and liked to boast that his mother, who died when he was young, was a lady of Spanish extraction and a great beauty. More accurate biographical work indicates that her name was Mademoiselle Rabin, and that she was an unmarried woman from Santo Domingo, and that she was black. Over the decades, with the changing attitudes toward race, the story has unfolded. A 1964 biography claims that she was white, a chambermaid from Les Touches parish in France, who had traveled to Santo Domingo. But further research revealed that John James' foster mother, his father's French wife,

Anée Moinet Audubon, in her will dated December 4, 1814, referred to her adopted son, Jean, as a *"créole de Saint-Dominque."*

None of this would be of particular concern in our time; in fact an illegitimately born black artist who painted birds with the skill of Audubon, in cynical hands, could likely be used as a marketing angle. But in the early nineteenth century, darkness was a blot on character, especially in the circles that Audubon traveled and among the people whom he solicited to buy his monumental and expensive work, *Birds of America.* He looked white enough to pass, as the expression has it, with long, straight dark hair and blue eyes, and it's no wonder, given the times, that he reinvented himself, at one point spreading the rumor, carried on by his descendants, that he was the lost dauphin of France. It was a good story, except that there were many lost dauphins in mid-nineteenth-century America. Mark Twain even gave one a role in *Huckleberry Finn.*

By 1896, when the Audubon Society was organized, Mr. Gilbert was under the employ of the egalitarian William Brewster, who in keeping with Brahmin tradition did not seem to care what color he was. The numerous encomiums, letters, book introductions, and remembrances of the man published after his death suggest that Brewster was a tolerant, likeable fellow who tried his best to get along with people of all classes. Old man Bensen told me at one point that his father used to deliver greens to the Brewsters' Cambridge house around Christmastime, and that since it was too long a wagon ride to return to Concord on the same day, he would be invited to spend the night. The old, rough-cut farmer, smelling of pitch and balsam, dressed in stained coveralls, would be invited to sit at the dining room table with the Brewsters for their candlelit dinner with silver service and Swedish maids.

There is a further irony in the fact that if it had somehow come out in 1896 that the namesake of the august Audubon group was a black man, it would not necessarily have been seen as a blot to the founders of the Audubon Society. As Dorothy West, the African American novelist, pointed out, Bostonians of the proper sort never did mind a few Negroes beside them on the trolley, provided they were well attired. Harriet Hemenway once hosted a dinner party for a black man, and even had him spend the night at her family home on Clarendon Street. Never mind that the man was the former slave Booker T. Washington; in the eyes of the lower-echelon whites of Boston, he was nothing more than an upstart darkie out of the southern fields. Harriet's father was a supporter and generous funder of the abolitionist movement, and there were even a few blacks mixing in with the white Beacon Hill Brahmins as early as the 1850s.

Living in book-lined apartments on Beacon Hill or in large brick mansions in the South End, there was an enclave of wealthy African Americans known as the Black Brahmins who had been brought over in the seventeenth century and had eventually bought their freedom and worked their way up through the social ranks. They sent their sons to Harvard, had second homes in Newport and in Oak Bluffs on Martha's Vineyard, and in the last decades of the century they would send their children to M. Papanti's fashionable dancing school and would attend the Friday afternoon symphony, just like the white Brahmins. This was a small group, no more than twenty or thirty families, but the mere fact of their existence and of the generally liberal atmosphere of the city of Boston spread throughout the South. In the minds and hearts of the oppressed peoples still living under the whip of slavery, the city became a version of an earthly promised land, "Negro Paradise" as it was known. If you could only make it to Boston you would come alive.

To their credit, the Puritans were not entirely comfortable with the peculiar institution known as slavery. They referred to their slaves as "servants," and considered them in some ways as part of the family. The Puritans taught their "servants" to read so that they too could enjoy the fruits of salvation. Local laws allowed the

Africans to acquire, hold, and to transfer property—which was more than was granted to the Indians of the region. They were permitted, as was any individual of the period, even an Indian, to a trial by jury, and they were even allowed to sue their masters, if the situation arose. The Puritans were guided in this by the biblical tenets of the Old Testament tradition that viewed servants as individuals divinely committed to their work.

By the mid-nineteenth century, among a certain class, this Puritan ethic, coupled with Quaker pacifism, hardened into downright moral repulsion for the practice of holding black people in bondage. Boston, more than any other northern city, supported the abolitionist movement. Although the movement began tentatively, pushed to the fore by a few firebrands such as William Lloyd Garrison, the cause was generally supported by the white upper classes, and finally by many of the residents of the city. In 1854, after the passage of the much hated Fugitive Slave Act, when an escaped slave named Anthony Burns was caught in Boston by federal authorities and sent back to his master in the South, some 50,000 Bostonians lined the streets in protest as he was marched from prison to the awaiting transport ship. The national guard had to be called out to make sure he was not liberated by the crowd.

Although they may have had political differences with the southern states, other cities in the North were not so certain about their support for the emancipation of Negroes. One New York paper editorialized that the attitudes of the Brahmins were such that it would not be long before the great founding families of Boston, the Lymans and the Endicotts and the Eliots, would soon be "amalgamated with the Sambos, the Catos, and the Pompeys. . . ."

During the antebellum period and after the war, groups of freeborn blacks began working their way north to Boston to work as porters, crewmen on the steamers, hotel clerks, bellboys, and washerwomen. This was a generally literate group who had had the benefit of some schooling. But they were an unrefined rough class of people in the eyes of the established black families, and they did not have the same special relationship with the Boston whites that the Black Brahmin families enjoyed.

Following this immigration, in the first decades of the twentieth century there was a second influx of southern blacks, a far less educated group who came to be known as "Homies" (presumably because they came from "down home"). These were the illiterate field hands and hardscrabble tenant farmers and sharecroppers who had been uprooted by the failure of the cotton crops as a result of the boll weevil infestations that swept through the South in the early years of the new century.

In response to these migrations, the Black Brahmins attempted, through the creation of elite social clubs not unlike the white-only Daughters of the American Revolution, to maintain their identity and status. The educated middle class, modeling itself on their white employers and to some extent on the Black Brahmins, endeavored to work their way upward through society and even managed to send a few of their own off to Harvard, Radcliffe, and, later, Boston University. Finally, the recently arrived energetic classes of refugees struggled along with menial jobs and were looked down upon by all groups, except the white, socially conscious Brahmins—who were so far removed as to be unaffected by this tribe of illiterate dirt farmers. One member of a proper Boston family was walking in the West End with a member of the Black Brahmin class talking of settlement houses and social issues when they spotted a band of recently arrived black children playing in the street. "And what is to become of them?" the white man asked. "Let them rot . . . ," said the black man.

There was also in Boston in these years a generally more liberal openness in the educational institutions, which tended to attract black activists such as William Monroe Trotter, who graduated magna cum laude from Harvard, and who was the son of a member of one of the black regiments that had been raised in Boston to fight in the Civil War. Trotter, along with many other Boston blacks who were raised in the climate of equality and possibility, rejected the approach of the popular Booker T. Washington, the educator who held that blacks should raise their position slowly, by demonstrating their competency in the lower-level jobs that were being created by the industrializing society. Washington had emerged from a different social climate. He was born a slave and had lived under the yoke and was not as yet so liberated as to believe that his people could attain equal status overnight. Trotter, by contrast, was associated with the group that came to be known of as the Boston radicals, which was later joined by W. E. B. Du Bois, a similarly educated New Englander who founded the National Association for the Advancement of Colored People.

Living within this social structure, keeping their heads low, working at their day jobs, attending black churches, forming black social clubs, living in a more or less reflection of the white world around them, but still maintaining, in their quiet way, the ambitions of the Boston radicals as well as the belief in the hard work of Washington and his group, was the God-fearing, self-improving equivalent of a silent black majority, a middle-class, middle-grade group of people who led their daily lives without praise or blame. It was to this group that Mr. Gilbert ultimately migrated.

CHAPTER SEVEN

Memento Mori

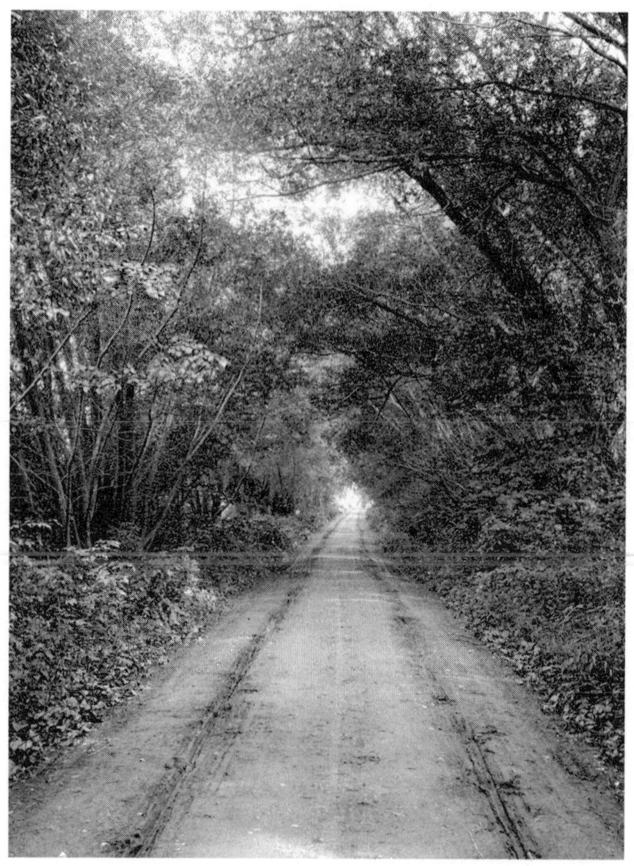

ALL PHOTOGRAPHS ARE ACCURATE.
NONE OF THEM IS THE TRUTH.
Richard Avedon

Circa 1910, Belmont, Massachusetts

On the morning of December 11th in 1901, William Brewster asked Gilbert to take the wagon over to the woods on Arlington Heights and cut some evergreens for Christmas decorations at the Brattle Street house. Gilbert dutifully went about the business of harnessing the horse, Frances, to the traces, a process that took him, when he was working quickly, all of twelve minutes. Then, with the wagon hitched, he set out, intending to return in the early afternoon.

He did not reappear at three o'clock, was not there by four, and had not returned by dark. Gilbert's arrangements with Brewster were never exacting; there were some days when he would not show up at the museum, called away, Brewster says in his journals, on personal affairs. But if ever Brewster asked him to be somewhere at some specific time, Gilbert would be there. Now Brewster began to worry.

Around midmorning Gilbert had come to the heights and began walking up the hill, cutting greens and stacking them as he climbed, but shortly after he reached the summit, in a hollow on the west side of the hill, he saw what would later come to be known in the black vernacular as "strange fruit"—a hanged man, strung up by his suspenders. Gilbert dropped his saw and ran down to grab the man, caught himself, and stood staring for a few seconds, thinking. When he was 15 in Lynchburg he and his friends had seen the body of a black man hanging from a railroad bridge over the James. But that was different, they actually had gone out of their way to look at it—not without a certain amount of *schadenfreude.* This was a white man, somehow more lonely and sad, as if white men don't hang.

Gilbert collected his thoughts, picked up his saw, left the woods, and took the wagon down the hill to the Arlington police station to report the find. The police accompanied him to the scene, then brought Gilbert back to the station and led him into a back room with officers Joseph White and Lieutenant Dooley, who instructed Mr. Gilbert to sit down at a wooden table.

Why was he in the woods, they wanted to know. Gilbert explained.

Who was this Brewster fellow he worked for, then? Gilbert explained.

He's a what? they ask.

—An ornithologist. He looks at birds—.

—Spell it—.

—So how well did you know the dead man—they ask.

—I did not know the dead man—.

—Well, then, how did you know where to find him?—they ask.

—I happened upon him. I did not "know" him as you say, nor where to find him—.

And so on and so on, and the day was creeping onward and Gilbert, being Gilbert, knew that Mr. Brewster, being Mr. Brewster, would begin to worry about his whereabouts. He tried to explain this, and finally after four hours of interrogation, they let Gilbert free.

It may have been shocking treatment for the quiet, well-dressed, and law-abiding Gilbert, but it was an average day for the Arlington police.

Earlier that same year on August 22nd, for example, a dead body dressed in a dark outing suit and a striped shirt with a white collar and cuffs had been found floating in Spy Pond. The man had laced shoes and a silver watch chain.

On September 5th a sick boy passed out on the street. Two suspicious men had offered him strong drink, the reports indicate.

Earlier in the year, on February 26th, Edward Barro, a laborer, broke into the room of Miss Helene Alderman by way of the piazza roof, whereupon Miss Alderman emptied the contents of a shotgun into Mr. Barro's stomach, near the "naval" *[sic]*.

And lesser incidents: Scarlet fever stalks the neighborhoods. The police are called out to tack quarantine cards to front doors. Boys throwing stones. A stray fox terrier with brown ears is captured. Mrs. Burns finds a bulldog. Miss Splain reports that she was chased by a man. A dead cat is buried by the police, dangerous dogs are shot. More scarlet fever cards posted, and Mrs. Mallaway reports that on October 13th, two overcoats, a pair of trousers, opera glasses, and a silver spoon were stolen from her house. That same day, the reports state, a colored man had been seen in the neighborhood. Miss Splain stops in to say that a man has been staring at her. The great sweep of time ticks on, carrying with it all the events of the era from second to second, minute by minute, day in day out, with only the stoptime of the stilled image of the camera to fix it.

The information concerning the events of that day in 1901 was not obtained as easily as some of the other records I had been searching during my quest. At the Arlington police station, I was stopped at a door by an indifferent dispatcher who directed me to a certain Officer Toms who wanted to know why I wanted to know what happened on December 11th, 1901, and what was my name again? And who was it I worked for, and how do you spell "ornithologist." And then I was ushered upstairs where a variety of dusty volumes were brought out and put at my disposal. But the year 1901, which I had requested, was not there. Much discussion, and then the archivists remembered that Lieutenant Delaney had taken away the 1901 records because there had been an incident that year in which a policeman was shot in the line of duty and the department wanted to erect a plaque in his honor. It took me two more tries to get the right ledger. At one point during this process I was placed in the hands of a muscular, red-haired officer in his mid-thirties who seemed to take offense at my quest. After the usual grilling and the careful explication of the orthography of "ornithologist" he watched me silently as I wrote down one of the telephone numbers he had given me.

"You got to write that down?" he asked.

I said I did, that I was bad with telephone numbers and couldn't remember them unless I wrote them down.

"You should be able to remember that. Smart guy like you."

I caught his drift and feigned stupidity.

"I am not very good with numbers, sir."

"You teach at Harvard, you don't know how to count?"

I explained that I did not teach at Harvard but that the man I was seeking had worked at Harvard.

"I thought you said you were looking for a black man."

"I did."

"You're looking for a black guy who taught at Harvard?" he snorted. "Shouldn't be too hard to find."

I let it go and after some more elaborate explanations on my part managed to escape.

I should add that the following week, I was passing through the sentry post of the dispatcher's office, ready now for the interrogations with my usual explanations. The officer in charge, who apparently had a personal interest in local history, immediately grew interested and began relating stories of past crimes in Arlington and how, in those times, if any unknown Italian or Negro appeared in town he would be immediately suspected of any of the various crimes that took place that week.

"Back then," he said, "you had to be light-haired and white-skinned to walk in this town without raising red flags. And God forbid that you're Irish Catholic," he added.

✠

On September 14th (the same day that, in 1901, the police noted that Miss Splain had seen an "Italian" man looking at her in a lewd fashion), I packed my camera and set out to take a little walkabout through Cambridge, following more or less the daily route taken by Mr. Gilbert from his home, to and from Mr. Brewster's house and the Harvard Museum of Comparative Zoology.

It was a Friday, a warm afternoon. Harvard had reopened, the beginning of its three hundred and sixty-fourth year, and the tree leaves in the yard were just taking on some color and the lawns were still green. Troops of intense students passed, leaning toward each other, gesticulating. Widener Library rose like a wall on my right as I walked through the yard, its wide steps flowing upward to the ornate doors. I had been in there recently, sniffing around for Mr. Gilbert, but all I smelled was that interior closeted library odor of moldering books and paper, a rainy day sort of smell that took me back to my own college years. There is a tablet in the pink marble vestibule of this famous architectural memorial honoring Harry Elkins Widener, a 27-year-old graduate of Harvard who died at sea on April 15, 1912, "upon the foundering of the steamship *Titanic.*" The library was erected in loving memory of Harry by his mother.

Beyond Harvard Yard, through the gates, is another architectural memento, Memorial Hall, which was constructed in 1874 to commemorate those Harvard students and graduates who died in the Civil War. I've been in there too, most recently to read the cenotaphs on the walls. Here, rank on rank, in a sad litany, are inscribed the names of the students along with the names of the battles in which they died: Antietam, Bull Run, Shiloh, Manassas, Gettysburg. For those who now have, or had, or even will have, children in college, this is a profoundly sad inventory.

It's dark and somber inside the hall, old stone and wood, and high, shadowed ceilings, but out in the street there is a burst of the light airs of bright September with life streaming by on all sides.

Here came a man dressed, for some odd reason, in plaid pajamas —he's lean, chiseled and bearded, and running along at a steady no-nonsense pace. A golden retriever trots effortlessly beside him with no leash.

No photo. They're moving too fast.

Three female students, arms linked, laughing and walking fast.

An old Asian man in Chinese slippers, shuffling along, smiling to himself.

On Oxford Street, I passed a long row of workers in jeans and white sweatshirts, sitting on a wall, eating lunch and eyeing the women who pass. Some are smoking, one is asleep on the grass, one is loudly proclaiming his views on the current political situation.

My final destination is east of here, a little less than a mile down Cambridge Street to Inman Square.

From 1916 until he died in 1942, Robert Gilbert lived at 66 Inman Street. He used to walk from his house to Brattle Street to Brewster's bird museum, and then later, after Brewster died and he began working at Harvard, he would turn right at Memorial Hall and walk down Oxford Street to the Museum of Comparative Zoology. For twenty-six years, with a few indeterminate breaks in between, this was his domain. On my way to his house, which still stands, I passed a crazy local hero named Juke, a white boy longing to be black. He hiphops down Broadway, bouncing and swaying, headphones holding down a wool knit cap even though this is September and warm. White, high-topped sneakers, half-shaven, black trousers. He lives in some other world, I'm told. Snaps his fingers, catches my eye and winks as he passes. "Hey Bro'," he growls in a smoky blues accent. I lift my head in greeting.

At the corner of Cambridge, Springfield, and Antrim lies the S&S Deli, locally famous. Also Rosie's Bakery, which serves, among other things, something called chocolate orgasms.

Two Asian women.

A white man in baggy clothes with a hangdog drug-beaten look. Rosev's Dairy truck, white against the red brick fire station. Royal White laundry truck. And then, ironically, a white dog, on its way home.

The Internacional Presbyterian Church: *"Onde milagre espera por voce . . ."* in Portuguese, for the Azorean and Brazilian population in this area.

Another sign: Coughlin's Insurance. Irish.

This was a mixed neighborhood in 1916, Irish, a few Yankees,

Jews, and four black families, the Allens and the Gilberts among them. There were three Jewish businesses, one of which, run by a man named Ben Weisman, delivered groceries in a horse-drawn wagon. When he was a boy, after school, Tom Allen, Mr. Gilbert's young neighbor, worked for the family. Fifty cents a week.

"Was a fine family," he told me once. "Trusted the little kids no matter what color you were."

A hundred yards down Inman Street on the left there is a framed duplex with a mansard roof, built sometime in the 1870s. Mr. Gilbert bought this house in 1916. In the American world in which he was forced to live, the purchase of this particular property amounted to something of a coup for Mr. Gilbert. His neighbors were white, and he was in a good neighborhood. He and Anna had four children by this time: a boy, Robbie, who was born in 1899, Mary, born in 1901, Emily, 1903, and Edyth, who was born in 1906.

Tom Allen, who is a stocky, energetic man, lives two doors down and remembers Gilbert's daughters.

"I was only a kid," he said, "but my mother was a good friend of Mr. Gilbert's daughter, Edyth. They went to Cambridge Rindge and Latin school together and stayed friends till Edyth died. That was in the late fifties. But they were a different people 'round here back then, when I was little. That family, the Gilberts, they always wore suits and ties, and the women put on white gloves on Sunday, dressed to the nines, and Mr. Gilbert—always in a starched, detachable collar. I didn't know him, really, just see him around the house. He would pass through the parlor while Mary was singing at the piano—she had a fine singing voice, and they was always playing music there. Mr. Gilbert was just an old gentleman, passing through. But sometimes he'd sit down and play and Mary would sing. And once or twice, I think I remember him singing too, a deep old voice. That was a formal household if ever there was one," he said, "it was 'Mr. Gilbert' this, and 'Miss Gilbert' that. You don't act up in that parlor. You just sit there and wait and you don't fidget either. We were just little kids, you know. Don't speak unless spoken to, better seen than heard. That kind of thing."

He paused here and looked back at the house.

"Should be like that today," he said, nodding to himself.

Tom Allen was young in comparison to some of the people I had been talking with in my quest. He was only 75. His grandfather, who was born in Halifax, Virginia, in 1869, the same year as Gilbert, came north to Boston in the same wave of postwar immigrants that Gilbert and his brother rode. He moved over to Cambridge in 1902 and settled on Inman Street at a time when there were no blacks in the neighborhood.

Gilbert and Anna followed a decade later and moved into the house at number 66, where Gilbert lived for the rest of his life. There were only three other black families in the district at the time, the Merrimans, the Steadmans, and the Allens.

I left Inman Street and walked back up Broadway, stopping here and there along the way, and then went into the Broadway Café and bought a sandwich, which I took out to one of the streetside tables with a cup of coffee. I lingered on for a while, watching the schoolchildren passing to and fro, the delivery men unloading groceries, basking cats, and Harvard students en route to classes.

If you live in the world of old photographs long enough, you come to appreciate the contemporary human comedy. Here they are, 20-year-olds, 30-year-olds, 40-year-olds. Young people, old people, babies, dogs, pigeons sweeping through, cats, and all of them, cats, dogs, pigeons, and people, alive. They walk, eat, meet each other, flirt, mate, raise children, walk some more, eat again—always eating, always walking—everything in motion: cars, trucks, people, bicycles, dogs, pigeons. Alive and in motion and not as yet stilled by the interference of a device that has the ability to stop all action in a singular sixtieth of a second.

Nowadays the dress around here is different. No one, save the lowliest, most downtrodden hod carrier, would dress in the manner of these twenty-first-century pedestrians, men and women alike in their baggy, bleached-out jeans and sweatshirts, carrying backpacks like North Country wilderness guides, and all of them coatless, skirtless, tieless, and hatless, and the women wearing—of all things—pants!

Short hair too.

Mr. Gilbert would have understood the short hair, having lived through the 1920s, when, by way of rebellion, women chopped off their long locks. But not the pants. In his time, *dishabille* consisted of a man in his shirtsleeves of the type that so offended the father of George Apley, in J. P. Marquand's novel. You look at the old movies from the 1940s and everyone, even the murderers, dressed in suits and ties.

I should take more pictures here. I should shoot as many rolls as I can afford. I should try to stop all this walking and talking and eating and preserve these poor, ill-fated mortals who in a few decades, perhaps a few years, will be lying in the cold earth with Mr. Gilbert and his generation.

✠

While I was daydreaming there on the ephemeral nature of the human parade, a pretty woman with reading glasses pushed up into a cloud of dark hair spotted me and came over and sat down.

"How've you been?" she asked.

"Not bad," I said, stuttering. "Still getting by . . ."

"Are you still working?"

"Sure, off and on."

"I so hate my work."

"I know it's tedious."

We carried on in this manner for a bit while I tried to figure out who she was. I have a bad head for names, and it often happens that people in this town have seen me somewhere, or have met me and expect that I am intelligent enough to recall our conversation. In point of fact, as soon as I'm introduced to someone, I tend to forget their name, but I rarely forget a face, and this woman did not look familiar. But I calculated that if I just kept talking, something would come up that would spark my memory. Not in this case, though. She started talking about the Rockies, and the canyons of Utah, then Santa Fe, none of which I count among my usual haunts. Then she started to talk about Bill, whoever he was, and had I heard that he and Mary had split up finally, and then she said she really had to push on and rose from the table.

Just before she left, she put her hand on my arm and looked me in the eye.

"You know, don't you, that I have always loved you."

She squeezed my arm, spun on her heels, and walked off quickly before I could even begin to explain my way out.

Maybe that was another life.

Still perplexed I decided to walk up to Mr. Brewer's house at the corner of Sparks and Brattle Streets. It was a pleasant day, everyone out, the happy throngs of students, sparrows chattering in the privet hedges, and at Harvard Square, just opposite the old Harvard bookstore, I saw a lanky black man dressed entirely in blue, with a blue beret slouching along with that relaxed, free-as-bird, studied gait that some blacks develop. I knew this man, though. His name is Brother Blue and he is a local storyteller and man-about-Cambridge. He plays the part of an eccentric street person, but in fact he graduated from Harvard in the 1940s and then went on to earn a master's degree in playwriting from Yale. After that he became an ordained minister and worked with prison inmates, which is where he learned the value of storytelling. More to the point as far as I'm concerned, though, is the fact that Brother Blue is married to Ruth Hill, who, when I first started on this quest for Mr. Gilbert, was the librarian at the Museum of Comparative Zoology. She directed me to some of the letters and journals that must have first inspired the man in the cowboy hat who led me into this morass of unknowns.

"Good day, Brother Blue," I said as I walked by.

Brother Blue doesn't know me, I don't think, but as he passed, he reached out and slapped my hand in a friendly way without breaking stride.

"All right my man, all right, good to see you again," he says.

The bees are busy in the Brattle Street flower markets. The tourists and shoppers are out, and everyone is happy, but the town, in my opinion, is in sad decline, little more than a shopping mall consisting of brand name shops and a far cry from Mr. Gilbert's time, when there were bookstores and open-stall groceries, free dogs, genuine eccentrics, and Harvard professors who pedaled along to their classes on bicycles, dressed in their tweeds. The whole world is richer now. Also a lot poorer. I can't walk through here at night anymore without spending three or four dollars on the homeless.

Down by Sparks Street, where Brewster's house is located, the crowd is gone. The people walk more slowly, sometimes nod to you as you pass. The friendly women at the Armenian church that is now housed in Brewster's former property know of my curious mission and usually permit me to enter to look around. Here, the interior structure and decorative elements that Caroline and William lived with are still visible. You can see the marble frieze over the foyer fireplace, the dark wood paneling, and the wide flight of mahogany-railed stairs with the powerful image of St. Michael with his flaming sword fixed in the stained glass window above the second-floor landing.

On this particular day in September, there was a crowd of people milling about between the house and the church next door. I asked a tall gray-haired gentleman and his wife what was happening.

"A priest has died. A favorite of this parish," he said. "And only forty years old. He was so popular. You see people here from all over. Worcester. Leominster, Watertown, of course. He was a beloved figure."

We talked on and I told him about my reasons for coming here, but at one point he halted me in midsentence.

"What did you say this white man's name was who lived here?"

"William Brewster," I said.

He looked at me wide-eyed, shaking his head slightly in disbelief.

"That's my name," he said.

No relation, it turned out. The man was a later immigrant whose name was changed for convenience of pronunciation at Ellis Island.

Gilbert's and Brewster's direct lines are all dead ends. Brewster never had children, and none of Gilbert's surviving daughters had children. Only ghostly images on glass plates live on to tell their stories.

✢

Later that same autumn, rummaging through the shoe boxes of the thousand-odd snapshots left behind by my parents after they died, I found a photograph of a tall man, leaning casually against a birdbath constructed of local New England stone. He was dressed in a white summer suit and tie, had a brush-cut mustache, straight black hair, straight eyebrows, and high cheekbones. His right hand was relaxed, the fingers curled, and he had a straight-stemmed pipe stuck at a rakish angle in his teeth. In the background was a wood-shingled New England outbuilding, and what appeared to be a young walnut tree. I have no idea who this man is, nor do my two older brothers. All my older relatives are dead, which means that this individual, whoever he was and whatever his relation to the family might have been, is lost.

What is significant about this photograph is the inscription on the back of the print, penned neatly in black ink:

"You may someday discover this in some out-of-the-way place and say to yourself—'the face is familiar; where have I met this fellow?' And then the horrible thought: 'Ye gods! I've never answered Roy's letter.'"

The print is dated: March 3rd, 1934.

We have indeed discovered the photograph in an out-of-the-way place, but the face is unfamiliar, we've never met the man, his letter will never be answered, and all that remains is the cast of late-morning shadows and the walnut tree, forever budding in the March sun.

CHAPTER EIGHT

World Enough and Time

THE VERY THINGS WHICH AN ARTIST WOULD LEAVE OUT,
OR RENDER IMPERFECTLY, THE PHOTOGRAPHER TAKES
INFINITE CARE WITH, AND SO MAKES ITS ILLUSION PERFECT.
Oliver Wendell Holmes

An outing on the Concord River, 1909

Given the fact that the trees are bare and the river is low, it was probably November.

A clear day, brisk, with harsh light, but warm enough to allow one of the women that day to strip off her jacket and sit in the sun in her shirtwaist. She is wearing a white blouse of taffeta silk with full flouncy upper arms and a black silk neck scarf, a long black crepon skirt, and a wide white beret that she has cocked down over her left eye. One hand is resting on the gunnel of the Old Town canoe, the other touching the bow with her fingertips, as if to balance herself. The other three women stand and sit in various positions ranged between the other two boats. One, dressed all in dark, holds a rough walking stick, and one is seated on the gunnel and has a rising bird feather in her cap. The third is dressed in a double-breasted cheviot jacket, a white shirtwaist, and a black neck scarf, and has one hand resting jauntily on her hip. The face is familiar; I have seen her before in other plates, sometimes in the forest, sometimes out on lakes, once on the porch of an unnamed house in an unnamed location. Although hard to distinguish at a distance of a hundred years or so, I believe this is the woman referred to in the Brewster diaries as ERS.

There are two men there that day as well: a younger one in shirtsleeves and a tie and a natty jockey's cap, seated on a picnic hamper on the bank beside the canoe, and then someone who looks a little like an older Mr. Brewster, leaning forward, his hand on the gunnel.

Gilbert is there too, the invisible man, as usual. He stands somewhere off stage, behind the lens and the tripod, and it appears that he has climbed up on a rock or small promontory to shoot this picture. The angle is downward, the river beyond, ruffled by a light wind, a woodland beyond the river, and on the dry banks in front of the group, you can see the spaniel, Larry, a constant companion on the Brewster outings. He is curled up, asleep on the dank shores—which serves to tell us something about this particular moment. This happy throng has just come back from the woods along the western bank of the Concord River, downstream from Ball's Hill, about a mile above the Carlisle bridge, I would say, judging from the lay of the land beyond the riverbanks. They had pulled the boats on the shore and then proceeded into the forest on the west bank, perhaps searching for a good picnic site. We know this because the shadows are still shortened, the light is morning light, the century is young, the walking stick is still in hand, and the dog is curled up on the bank, asleep in the sun. If they had just landed, in the manner of dogs he would have bounded off along the shore.

I know this place. I've poked up this section of the stream in my own boat, an antique craft from the same period in fact, a 1910 Old Town rowing canoe and a type—judging from other photos—favored by Mr. Brewster and company.

One early autumn day I rowed up the river in this section and when I was a few hundred yards upstream from Ball's Hill, I turned the boat and let the river carry me downstream, lounging in the stern, eyeing the passing hills and low swamps through my camera lens—the banks of black willow and buttonbush, the small streams that feed into the river, and, higher up, away from the shores, a few of the newly constructed mansions of the *arrivistes* of Concord, Massachusetts. These are huge neo-Georgian megastructures, of three, sometimes four storeys, containing room after room, and all of them, I would judge—given the fact that these people must work to maintain their manor houses—empty for most of the day.

From the bend in the Concord River at Ball's Hill, not far from the site where Gilbert took the photograph on the morning of April 6th, 1911, the land rises gently in a series of fields and patches of woodlands and flows into a large, somewhat ill-defined tract of land known ever since the early eighteenth century as Estabrook Woods. This section of the town of Concord contains some important historical sites, including, among other places, Punkatasset Hill, where the American colonials gathered on the morning of April 18th in

1775, just before they descended to the nearby bridge over the river to fire the first shots of the American war of rebellion.

The woodland was named for one of the early settlers in this section of the town, a certain Thomas Estabrook who built a homestead in the forest there in the late 1600s, after the so-called second division of Concord, when the children of the earliest settlers began occupying land holdings outside of the town center. The stone walls, the foundation, and some of the remains of the home lot of Thomas Estabrook can still be found along the so-called Carlisle road, an abandoned track that is now used by hikers, dog walkers, and cross-country skiers. Some of the original trees are still growing there too, and an old limestone quarry and the remains of a kiln can be found near the road. The few people who settled there in the nineteenth and twentieth centuries, Mr. Bensen included, I suppose, tended toward eccentricity. One old outlander, having heard that China lay directly below Concord on the other side of the globe, decided to dig a tunnel through the earth to get there. In Henry Thoreau's time, an old gentleman named Brooks Clark lived here. He rarely wore shoes and used to collect wild apples and dead birds in the forest for his dinner. Even into the late twentieth century bands of citizens of the community who were down on their luck maintained hobo camps in the northern end of the woods, near the town of Carlisle.

A little farther upstream on the east bank of the Concord River there is a federal wildlife sanctuary known since Thoreau's time as the Great Meadows. This wide floodplain of freshwater marsh, streams, and ponds was Brewster and Gilbert's hunting grounds. On spring and autumn days, they would often cross the river from Ball's Hill and go boating along the banks counting birds and eyeing the skies for incoming flights of ducks, geese, and swans. In their time, this was also a favored hunting spot; gunners from the region would descend in autumn, including William Brewster, who, perhaps ironically, was a great waterfowl hunter himself. One of Gilbert's best portraits of him shows Brewster in front of one of his lodges, his rudder-straight nose below his old slouch hat, shotgun crooked in his right arm, and a brace of unidentifiable ducks dangling from his left hand.

Brewster and company did not limit themselves to shooting birds for the pot. At the time, the common practice in establishing a bird's presence in a given location was to shoot them. John James Audubon himself killed virtually everything he painted so lovingly. Brewster, to his credit, was the one who altered this somewhat violent bird-watching technique. One of the things he is known for in the birding community is his use of field observation techniques as a means of establishing a record. He had a "glass" that he used to spot birds, and he was a great chronicler of bird behaviors, an early ethologist of sorts. For these collection trips, Gilbert, who was also handy with a gun, may have been his shooter, certainly his spotter, and I believe that it was out of this custom of going out together in the forests and fields of the northeast that the two of them came to field photography. They simply substituted the camera for the gun and began collecting landscapes as well as birds. (Interestingly enough, the mounted specimens of Gilbert and Brewster's birds, most of which are still in the collection of the Harvard museum, have sadly deteriorated. The photographic plates remain as sharp as the day they were made.)

On their expeditions along the Great Meadows, Brewster and Gilbert tended to go upriver, thence southwestward, under the North Bridge, and on to the spot known as Fairhaven Bay, where the river widens into a lakelike expanse that was thick with waterbirds. From here they would sail or row onward to the wide marshes below the section of the river known as Nine Acre Corner, also a great bird site and now protected under the federal wildlife refuge system.

This whole reach of the Concord, Sudbury, and Assabet Rivers ranks as one of the most significant natural history sites in the United States, not so much for its scenic qualities, or for the concentrations of wildlife, but mainly because it must be one of the most intensely studied parts of the American continent. Ever since the founding of Harvard College and the creation of a department of science, field researchers would come out to the river and the woodlands to the west of Cambridge to study wildlife. Extensive woodland tracts such as the Estabrook were rare, even as early as the time of the Revolution. Most of the forestlands had been cleared by the 1770s in eastern New England, and the biologists must have welcomed the opportunity to study the trees of the forest and such denizens of the woodlots as remained in the region.

Of all the naturalists who have spent time on the riverbanks and woodlands of the Estabrook, no doubt the best known, and probably the most thorough documenter of the natural history of the area, was Henry Thoreau. His father maintained a sawmill in the Estabrook tract in the 1820s where he used to mill cedars for his pencil factory, and Henry himself haunted this untrammeled section of the town, looking for adventure and new plants and animals. William Brewster settled at October Farm in 1883 and began scouring the region for birdlife, which he recorded religiously in his journals. He and Gilbert would make daily forays into the fields and woods when they weren't rowing and sailing the river looking for birds. Of the two thousand or so photographs they made, many glass plates, as yet unnumbered and unprinted, depict river scenes and tributaries, as well as fields, swamps, and extant woods in the Concord region.

Not long after I met old man Bensen, I too began haunting the Estabrook Woods. Along with their river expeditions, Brewster and Gilbert used to make regular excursions there, especially along the unpaved carriage track that stills runs north to Carlisle.

One day coming out of the forest onto this road, I saw a tall older man with close-cropped hair, carrying what looked like some sort of military radio device. He was accompanied by a younger woman, who also carried in a pack a variety of electronic devices. We fell into conversation about the equipment and this led to a discussion of animal communication, which turned out to be the field of study these two were engaged in. They were embarked on a project to learn more about the vocalizations of young beavers. They eavesdropped by lowering the microphones into active beaver lodges and then recording the mews and squeaks and snarls of the beaver family.

It was only after we said our good-byes that I learned that the man I was talking to was Donald Griffin, the scientist who had discovered echolocation in bats, and had gone on to a lifetime of study of animal communication at Cornell University. Now at age 80-plus, having associated himself with Harvard, he had started a study on beaver communication.

On another occasion, near this spot I met another old man with big ears and a German accent. We began talking about the forest and he became passionate about the advances of developers to the north and east and especially about the inroads of the Middlesex School, which was intending to build playing fields on the west side. "They have the perfect outdoor laboratory here," he said, chopping the air with his hand, "and what do they do but make sport fields."

This brought on a diatribe on the decline of field studies at Harvard and the fact that modern biologists were spending all their time in sterile brightly lit labs, looking through electronic microscopes.

I later learned that the man was the renowned Ernst Mayr himself, author of *Systematics and the Origin of Species* and the guru of modern evolutionary theory.

But what of Mr. Gilbert? I knew he was in here often, sometimes alone, sometimes with Brewster and his friends. The Brewster journals periodically refer to the fact that Gilbert returned from the Estabrook having seen some interesting species of bird or having collected for Brewster's Ball's Hill plantings a number of native azaleas.

Late in my quest, when I knew a little more about Gilbert's comings and goings, I began purposefully going into the Estabrook at odd times when I knew no one else would be there. I went in once during a snowstorm. I went in on March days when sleet was sweeping across the ponds and the trees were howling ominously in the wind. I went once in heavy summer rain and I also went in once or twice on moonlit nights. On these occasions I would select some likely site along the old Carlisle road and sit there waiting for the ghosts of the place, hoping some spirit would appear to guide me. All I managed to do was scare myself.

On one of these excursions, late on a summer evening, I was sitting on the wall at the ruins of the old Estabrook homestead when a man dressed all in white slowly materialized from the woods on the east side of the road. He wore cotton trousers cut off in midcalf, sandals, and a loose kahdi-cotton shirt and had long black hair that fell freely around his shoulders. On a colorful woven cloth strap, he carried, slung over his right shoulder, a long wooden flute.

Seeing this figure emerge in the gloaming I thought to myself that he was perhaps some manner of spirit traveler, so I purposefully put myself in harm's way and greeted him as he drew near.

I would like to say he bowed deeply upon my greeting, and asked how he could be of service to me, but in fact he merely pressed his fingertips together quickly, nodded coolly, and carried on without a word.

"Is that a Cherokee flute?" I asked as he moved off.

This served to stop him.

"Yes," he said. "But how did you know? Are you Cherokee?"

It was actually only a guess but the dark polished wood looked like Native American flutes I had seen.

Having broken the ice, the traveler, although deeply serious, became chatty, indeed, voluble, and happy to talk about his religion, although his responses to my questions tended to take on the form of sermons. He was, he explained, a student of Thoreau and Ashokan Buddhism, mixed in—as far as I could make out—with Emersonian transcendentalism. He was well-versed in the somewhat off-center religio-philosophic theories of nineteenth-century Concord and, like Bronson Alcott and Alexander Graham, the inventor of Graham crackers, he said he followed a prescribed diet and would feed only upon "aspiring" vegetables, that is to say plants such as beans, corn, and squash, which in their growing habits strive upward toward the heavens.

"I do not consume the lowly potato, or onions, or turnips, beets, or carrots," he explained.

"How about a bird?" I asked. "Would you eat, say, a wild goose? They fly very high during migration."

He looked at me in horror.

I regretted my little dig, and to cover myself began to explain my mission here in the woods and my attempts to locate the spirit of Mr. Gilbert. Since we were fairly deep into the territory of philosophies I tried to explain my perhaps bizarre theories of light: how any moment in history is illuminated by light and how, after the invention of the camera, it became possible to use existing light to halt the linear flow of time and pluck a discontinuity from an otherwise continuous flow of events.

"Only the image, of course," I explained. "The dimensions, the wholeness of the moment flies past."

None of this seemed at all odd to him.

"That's one way of looking at it," he said. "But there are also those who can freely move within the flux of things."

"Time travelers, you mean?"

"Yes, you might, in the common parlance, use that discredited term as a manner of speaking. Certain famous sanyatsi in India were said to be able to travel freely on the wheel of time."

"Not the river of time?" I asked (already knowing what his answer would be).

"No, the wheel. The great cycle of life and death. The sanyatsi were able to voyage along the course of the wheel, living in other life times, those to come, and those gone by."

"But given their theories of metempsychosis," I said, "would this not mean that they would be living for a while, perhaps, as a snake?"

"Yes, in some cases. They could know snakeness. They would never kill a cobra, for example."

"But would the cobra kill them?" I asked.

He was silent for a minute.

"This is a very good question," he said. "I have considered this question myself, when it comes to my own passage across the divide, and I believe, given the circumstances of the holy man and the snake, that there are in fact two responses to this proposition."

He folded his hands together, nodded gravely, and carried on.

"If the cobra struck, the sanyatsi would say it is a good thing that this cobra has bitten me at this time and this place. The lesson on this plane of existence, he would say, has been completed, and the wheel will now carry me onward. But it is also possible that the cobra would not strike, because the cobra would know that the sanyatsi knows that he, the snake, is only a cobra trapped, like any other soul, on the same wheel as the sanyatsi and that these two are fellow travelers in the realm of the great cycles. The cobra has no desire to eat the man, so he will not strike."

"You are a student of these things," I asked. "Could you possibly travel backward a few decades to, say, the year 1905?"

"No," he said quickly. "At least not yet. And probably never. I started too late. I was twenty-five when I became a seeker. And anyway I know what you're thinking. You are thinking that I could carry you back and you could talk to this man you seek and get to know him."

"Yes, that's the idea."

Suddenly he fell out of character.

"No way, man," he said with far less sanctimony. "You don't do that kind of thing, all right? This stuff is beyond that, you know what I'm saying? This is serious. It's the way to heaven."

"Sorry," I said.

"Right."

"I didn't understand," I said.

"Right. I know you don't."

"I've read Henry Thoreau too, the journals," I said. Given the context this was not a non sequitur and he took my drift.

"The man's been there," he said.

"He was a great traveler," I said.

"That he was," said my new ally, softening.

We ended amicably and he pushed on, while I resumed my daydreams on the rock wall by the ruins of linear time.

It occurred to me thinking about our encounter that somewhere, someday, I could perhaps contact a more willing seer who could go back to 1905 and tell me more. Such things were, after all, very much in vogue in the late nineteenth and early twentieth centuries when Gilbert and Brewster haunted these woods. In fact a gentleman of this vocation passed through the town of Medford not far from where Brewster lived, in the 1890s, offering séances and sessions with the dead. But then I remembered that in some ways I already had a blind seer in the form of Sanfred Bensen. So a few days after this encounter I went down Ball's Hill Road to pay a visit.

As usual I found him out puttering in his yard, dressed in his stained coveralls and a peaked cap.

"Any more thoughts about going in to see the grave of Mr. Brewster?" I asked. This was a perennial opener for me by this time, an excuse really to visit. His answer was always the same.

"Well, yes," he said. "Someday I should like to visit the gravesite but there's so much to do around here, and I'm worried about leaving Muffin. I will have to wait until Colburn comes down."

This was his perennial excuse to my perennial question. He was always waiting for his nephew Colburn, who was at the time living somewhere north of Concord and would periodically make visits to the farm to work on his Stanley Steamers. Colburn even had a pallet somewhere inside the cavernous dilapidated house and would sometimes spend the night there. He seemed a most loyal and attentive nephew. I had encountered him at the farm on several occasions before and he was very protective of his uncle and would say that I couldn't visit him that day because he was sleeping, or ill, whereupon old Sanfred would appear at the door and spend the next hour or two standing in the sun, telling me stories, while Colburn puttered around the yard, glancing over periodically to see if I had left yet.

I heard later, digging for rumors and stories in the dusty corners of the memories of old Concordians, that there had been some gossip that Colburn was not in fact Bensen's nephew, but his son, the unidentified mother having departed for other parts.

"There is really so much to do around here on the farm, ever since Father died," Mr. Bensen said.

I believe his father had died in 1928.

"Did Mr. Gilbert ever help out on the farm here?" I asked.

"No, but he would come down to visit with me and tell stories. He always had stories. He went to Washington sometimes to arrange his papers, as he used to say. One day there he saw the president of the United States out walking."

"Which president was it?" I asked.

"Well, I think it was Abraham Lincoln."

"Really?" I said. "I thought he died around the time that Gilbert was born."

"Did he? Well then it must have been someone else. Gilbert

said he was a very tall man. Lincoln, I have heard, was a very tall fellow. Father told me that."

"Maybe it was Woodrow Wilson."

"Yes, that sounds right. Woodrow Wilson."

"1914."

"Yes, I believe. That must have been the same year the chickens came down the river. I was walking one day, you see, and I heard chickens clucking out on the river. So I went to the banks and waited, and soon enough, around the bend came two canoes and they were filled to the gunnels with paddling Chinamen, stroking in rhythm. They were all talking in chicken, though, and I could not understand a word they said."

Up until the 1920s there had been a boathouse down the river toward Carlisle that would rent out canoes and rowboats to weekend day-trippers who would take the train out to Bedford on the east side of the river. I had read that the traffic began to disturb Brewster and in his latter years he tended to stay around the farmhouse, away from the river.

"Did Mr. Gilbert see the Chinese paddlers?" I asked.

"No, he wasn't there that day. He was too busy. You see he was the manager of the October Farm and there was always trouble up there. Mr. Brewster was such a kind man, the kindest man who ever walked the earth, he would never reprimand his people, and there were some low types who worked for him. One day, Mr. Gilbert told me, a man by the name of Charles was found to have stolen some tools from the barn. When Mr. Brewster confronted him about the theft, Charles became angry, and even raised his voice to Mr. Brewster and used strong language, I'm sorry to say. Mr. Brewster went home and did not sleep that night because, Gilbert said, he thought he would have to fire Charles the next day. So Gilbert came out to the farm and said to this Charles that he should quit first. Charles again became enraged, and made references to Mr. Gilbert's race and used strong words again. Mr. Gilbert told me he was afraid that Charles would strike him in the face. But he was more afraid that this fellow would come back and burn down the barn if Mr. Brewster fired him. 'It was better that he was angry with me,' Gilbert said. You see he was that kind of man. He took care of things quietly. Well, Mr. Brewster, he learned of all this, but he was such a kindly man he decided to give Charles a second chance. After that Charles became humbled and reformed himself and became a loyal servant to Mr. Brewster."

"He sounds like a forgiving man, Mr. Brewster," I said.

"Oh yes, ever so gentle with people. Now there was another man there named Patrick, an Irishman. Patrick was fond of whiskey and would sometimes disappear for days at a time and then return all full of tears and apologies and Mr. Brewster would always forgive him. One day Gilbert found Patrick sleeping on the floor of the woodshed and tried to rouse him. Patrick attempted to strike Mr. Gilbert with his fist upon awakening and, like Charles, said things about Gilbert's race. But then he began to cry and apologized. When Patrick was sober everyone loved him, he was a jolly, joking fellow who would do anything for you. He came down here once with Gilbert. He was a big ruddy-cheeked fellow with sandy hair who used to slap Mr. Gilbert on the back and call him his barber lad."

"His what?" I asked.

"A barber chap, but a good one."

"What did he mean, a barber?"

"A barber old chap, he would say, but a grand one at that."

"Barbarous maybe?"

"Yes, that's what I mean, a barber's chap and a good one at that. But all this was part of Mr. Gilbert's work, you see, keeping these Irish in line and, Mr. Brewster, he often knew nothing of it."

CHAPTER NINE

North Country

THERE ARE ALWAYS TWO PEOPLE IN EVERY PICTURE,
THE PHOTOGRAPHER AND THE VIEWER.
Ansel Adams

William Brewster photographing the landscape from Lake Umbagog, Maine, c. 1900

On Thursday March 16, 1898, Brewster and Gilbert spent the day packing photographic equipment, field glasses, clothing, and Brewster's personal items in two trunks and a portmanteau and the next day boarded the Grand Trunk rail line at North Station in company with Caroline and ERS. The four of them traveled north to Portland, Maine, and thence inland to the town of Bethel, in midstate, near the New Hampshire border and about thirty miles east of the White Mountains. Here they debarked and took a carriage up to an imposing yellow mansion with a wrap-around porch located at the southern end of the Bethel town common.

A medium-sized man with thick-lensed eyeglasses met them at the door and ushered them into a large sitting room on the west side of the house with windows overlooking orchards and pastures that dropped down to a stream and a lake, with a high band of ridges to the west.

Given the fact that he was living in a small town at the edge of a great wilderness, the man with the glasses was dressed rather formally. He wore a dark cheviot wool suit, a pressed white shirt with a starched collar, linen cuffs, and a silk neck scarf with a swirling Persian floral pattern. This attire was no accident; Doctor Gehring believed in proper dress.

John Gehring was a friend of William and Caroline Brewster, but he was also their personal physician and a specialist in diseases of the nerves. He concentrated his practice—and his unique cures—on those patients of the educated and moneyed classes who suffered from what was then known as neurasthenia.

No one in our time ever seems to suffer from neurasthenia—fortunately. It was one of those ill-defined diseases that struck those of a nervous temperament. Indications, according to contemporary medical literature, were characterized by an unspecified weakness of the nervous system, symptomized by a general feeling of malaise, combined with excitement or depression, flushings and sweats, unrefreshing sleep, headaches, noises or ringing in the ears, functional disturbances of the organs (whatever that means), muscular fatigue, and, among the many other symptoms, pseudo anginal attacks and—among men—loss of sexual power, "nocturnal pollutions," and premature ejaculations. Dr. Gehring, in his wisdom, claimed to be able to cure all of these symptoms through his therapeutic programs.

His therapies were quite simple, and given the number of bizarre cures then (as now) at large, they were actually quite rational. Although the term is never stated in his literature, he recognized the power of psychosomatic illnesses and attempted to cure the various afflictions of neurasthenia by simple behavioral modifications. The harried, world-weary "inmates," as they jokingly called themselves, were required to rise early in the morning, awakened by the sound of a gentle xylophone. They were to be at the breakfast table at 7:30, where they would dine on wholesome foods only. Following this they were offered a choice of outdoor activities, sawing or chopping wood for the fireplaces, tree trimming, nature walks, or, in the proper season, gardening, all to the aim of gained fresh air and exercise. There were lectures and discussion groups in the afternoons, and Dr. Gehring would meet with his patients privately for one hour a day to review their conditions. All patients were required to dress for dinner. The idea was that a properly maintained exterior would lead to a more balanced mental interior. With this in mind, no discussion of one's illness was permitted outside of the sessions with the good doctor, and patients were not permitted to carry their medicines to the table but must consume them in private, in their rooms. Good posture, a smile, a sprightly walk were encouraged at all times.

Oddly enough, given the simplicity of the cure, it seems to have worked. Between the early 1890s and the late 1920s, Dr. Gehring's institute was the rage among the rich and the intellectual community. It was, in the words of one contemporary article about the institute, a veritable spa for Harvard professors.

After Doctor Gehring's death the institute lingered on under the direction of his wife and, after she gave up the practice, the building languished. It was refurbished in the 1940s and outfitted as a new establishment known as the NTL Institute, the National Training Laboratory, whose purpose was to advance the field of "applied study of behavioral science" through group discussion and interchange. Courses at the institute were designed to help executives understand the dynamics of the human interactions within their organizations, a role not always understood by those whose primary mission in life was generally concerned with the acquisition of personal wealth. Managers and corporate officers were instructed through the art of group dialogues to open the closed minds of business leaders to the feelings of others. No small task.

As with Dr. Gehring's program, the institute made use of the natural surroundings and the isolation of the place to get the harried executives some perspective on themselves and their work, and their relationship to their employees—meaning, according to David Garrison, a local man who was associated with the local historical society, "get their acts together. . . ."

"NTLs," as the participants in the programs are known in the community, are not entirely popular with the shopkeepers and hotel and restaurant staffs in the town of Bethel, Garrison said.

The NTL program was the first by twenty years of a long line of similar encounter groups that arose in the late 1960s and still carry on today. I heard from a man who works in a similar field that it had actually enjoyed some success in humanizing powerhouse executives. Sometimes, he said, the program was too successful. Participants would return to their companies, work for a few months, then quit their jobs, divorce their wives, and fly off to the South Pacific, never to return.

✢

I went up to Bethel looking for Mr. Gilbert because he often accompanied Brewster to the area, although he himself did not live at the Gehring Institute. He was quartered off campus in one of the cabins the institute owned down by a nearby lake, and here, while Mr. and Mrs. Brewster spent their days walking in the woods, chopping wood, dressing for dinner, and listening to lectures by Mrs. Gehring on cultural matters such as the structure of the late Beethoven quartets, Gilbert was free to do as he liked.

He must have enjoyed these outings in the new country of the north. Although he no doubt missed Anna and his children, the sojourns in Bethel had the elements of a vacation for him, a tradition that did not come into currency for most people of his class until the labor reforms of 1910. He fished in the lake and the streams, slept late, and, in later years, wandered over the landscape taking photographs on his own. He had learned to identify northern birds by this time and would report his findings to Mr. Brewster, thereby adding species accounts to Brewster's growing annotated list that would be posthumously published as *Birds of the Lake Umbagog Region.*

I had presumed, when I first read of the Gehring Institute, back in Cambridge, that the old building housing the institute had been torn down. I had been in Bethel some years earlier—before I even knew Brewster was there—and had noticed the large yellow mansion at the end of town but had presumed it was someone's private estate.

One of the photographic plates I had found in the Lincoln attic happened to have been annotated, which is what brought me back to the area. The image shows the back of the Gehring Institute, looking to the northeast. It's not much of a picture to my eye: an old overgrown field of shrubs in March, bare limbs, no intriguing shadows, no definition anywhere, no singularity, just a brushy background, a light sky beyond. Just beyond the frame of the photograph is the house and an interesting, architecturally detailed railing at the edge of its surrounding porch. Not to criticize, but the inclusion of the carved wood human construction in contrast to the wildwood tangle just beyond, and beyond that the sky, might have improved the image. There are old trees just behind the photographer, which would have been there in Brewster's time, an ancient white pine that soars ever upward and is trimmed of branches lower down. Nearby is a long sweep of field that was probably there in Brewster's time too, and if the photographer had but turned the camera forty-five degrees, and waited, on any given evening there, he could see a low ridge of hills, the lighted sky beyond, images of sundown and the remains of the day. I don't know what anyone saw in the dull tangle, but it must have evoked in the photographer some feeling, some essence that he wanted to capture. It is possible, however, that whoever took the picture did not have much of an eye.

By this time, having reviewed so many of the various images, I had come to recognize two different styles at work. A few of the plates and prints I discovered were signed or credited to Gilbert, and pairing these with others in the collection, unsigned, but taken during periods when Gilbert was not with Brewster, I came to be able to guess who would have taken a given photograph. I suspect, knowing what I now know about the styles of the two men, that it was William Brewster who took the Bethel photograph. Gilbert seems to have concerned himself more with balance; he would have swung the camera right to add some contrast with the railing, or farther left to exclude the brushy nothingness and show the full sweep of the valley below and the flaring sky above.

Mr. Brewster began going up to Doctor Gehring's in the late nineteenth century, shortly after he hired Gilbert. At some point, while he was in the region, on his own, he began to explore the country to the north, along the western banks of Lake Umbagog. In the 1890s, this was still a wild region, wilderness even, and rarely visited. One of the earliest and best descriptions of the wild nature of the region appears in Brewster's *Birds of the Lake Umbagog Region,* which was published after his death by the Museum of Comparative Zoology. It is likely that Gilbert had a hand in preparing the final manuscript since he was working at the museum at the time, and in fact in one of Gilbert's obituaries he is listed as coauthor.

The book is primarily an annotated list of birds of the area, but there was a long introductory history of the town of Upton on the west bank of the lake, which the editors at the museum left out in the final publication. Here, along with accounts of the early white settlers of the region, are rich descriptions of the area before it was thoroughly logged over. Moose were common—as they are today—but interestingly enough, the white-tailed deer, which is not a deep-forest creature, was relatively rare. Forest-dwelling animals such as fisher, Canada lynx, and even woodland caribou occurred there, and otters were everywhere along the many rivers and streams of the region. Brewster and Gilbert describe huge rafts of ducks and geese out on the lake in the seasons of migration, and report that in early times the sun would be darkened for days at a time by the vast flocks of migrating passenger pigeons that flew over the area. By their time, however, most of these flocks had been decimated and the last passenger pigeon on earth died in the Cincinnati Zoo in 1914, at the age of 29.

Given the wildness of the region, this section of the Maine woods began to attract a few urban dwellers who had been swept up into the back-to-nature movement that became popular at this time, of which William Brewster and his company were in some ways the forerunners. The American conservation movement had been set in motion by groups like the Sierra Club, the Appalachian Mountain Club, and the burgeoning bird organizations fostered by Brewster's Massachusetts Audubon Society were gaining membership. There was throughout the United States an appreciation for wilderness and the presumed benefits of outdoor activities, such as hiking, hunting, fishing, and camping. In the East, the Adirondacks were the epicenter for this movement, but northern Maine also attracted visitors. Guiding these "sports," as the citybound hunters and fishermen were called, became an industry for the woodsmen who lived in the region around Umbagog.

By the turn of the twentieth century, more and more urban visitors were visiting. In time the road was improved from Bethel north to Upton, the town nearest the southern end of the lake, and within a decade the first noxious automobiles began appearing on the roads, spewing their poisonous fumes and spreading a coating of white dust over the roadside wildflowers.

Around Umbagog the earliest of the guides for the newcomers was a famous Indian named Metalluc, who is still talked about today. Metalluc had been a member of the St. Francis tribe in Canada, but for some reason had been banished by his tribesmen and had moved south. He lived for a while around the lower lakes of the Rangeley chain but also had an island sanctuary on Lake Umbagog that now bears his name. He was a great boon to the early settlers, and since he was a skilled hunter he would often bring them fish and game when they were hard-pressed. Eventually he began guiding whites through the forest on hunting expeditions, and soon became a well-loved forest character, just the sort of tamed "wild Indian" that Easterners so appreciated and Westerners loathed. Metalluc had a taste for drink, but he was reported to have been a friendly, tractable drunk and was often invited into the white people's cabins to share a dram. His one curious characteristic was that he had an almost pathological fear of dogs and would not enter a house until all the dogs were tied.

Backcountry guiding is still a thriving business in the region. Early one morning I saw a truck with empty dog cages pulled over beside a back road and got out of my car to listen. Not far back in the woods I could hear the baying of hounds—somebody off tracking raccoons or foxes, I thought. As I was listening a blond man with wide cheekbones and flat blue eyes emerged from the forest down the road and came up to his truck.

"Foxes?" I asked.

"No," he said. "Just a little bear problem at one of the camps in there. State boys called me out to take care of it."

We talked for a while about his business: How he much preferred the fishermen to the tough guys who think they want to hunt bears and then get drunk and piss in their pants when they finally see one, and how some of his "sports" tip very well at the end of an expedition and how some—usually the big bear hunters—drive off without so much as a thank-you. He told me about two men from the NTL Institute who asked him to take them out to have a "nature encounter." This involved an overnight at a place not far from the Androscoggin River, which runs through this region. His sports stayed up half the night, drinking beer and listening to owls hoot and coyotes yowl and then told the guide they wanted to go for a walk in the night woods by themselves.

"'Don't do it,' I says, 'you'll get lost and we'll have to call out the search parties.' But you know these guys, they do what they want, so off they go, and sure enough I'm up the rest of the night waiting for them to come back. They don't show up by dawn, so I begin to track 'em. It's easy at first, they're breaking branches off and stuff, then they come to Crooked Brook there, cross, and I don't see their tracks on the other side. They must have got it in their minds to walk in the water or something, or maybe they're thinking they got enough power by this time to walk on it. Anyways, three hours I'm looking for them and then I give up, go back to the camp. Here they are happy as larks, brewing up coffee, and talking about 'essence' and 'realization' and shit like that."

I told him about my own mission in this area, and he said there was an old guide in Upton named Buster Williamson who lived at the lower end of Umbagog and might be able to tell me something about the old days around the lake, since he was just about the oldest man alive in these parts.

I had heard of Buster from others and went up to see him that afternoon. He lived with his sprightly old wife at the mouth of the Dead Cambridge River, on the site of the Lake House, a boardinghouse where the Brewsters used to stay in the late 1800s. I had with me prints of the Lake House and the surrounding landscape that I had found at the Museum of Comparative Zoology. I showed these to the old couple and we were able to line up some of the same hills and points of land that appear in the images.

Buster was one of those chiseled old men you still can find in remote areas. Although he was weathered out from all his years living in camps in the woods, he had bright blue young eyes and a full head of thick white hair, and he was still trim. He had been hunting deer just the winter before and talked as if he was intending to go out again when the season rolled around, "maybe sooner," he mumbled under his breath. Deer were overrunning his property, he said. He was well known in the area, a counselor for the younger guides, but he was too young to have known Brewster and Gilbert—he was born the year after Brewster died, and in any case, Brewster had quit the area long before 1919; he was not happy about the increase in visitors and he was especially put off by the invasive automobiles.

For several seasons, whenever he was away from his getaway at Doctor Gehring's Brewster would live at the Lake House. But he so loved the area he decided to build a place of his own there. He constructed a cabin on a point of land, now known as Brewster's Island, and lived there for a while, but he decided to have a large houseboat built where he could sleep, but also move around the lakeshore to investigate the still lightly described region. I also had with me a photograph of this famous houseboat, which used to be anchored in a small bay just below Buster's property. Buster said the boat had endured long after Brewster deserted the region and that he had been on board many times when he was a boy.

The boat was a long bargelike craft with a narrow, open deck on which two sheds had been constructed, the foremost of which was roofed over with canvas. Slightly aft and attached to the first shed was a low cabin with a cambered roof, apparently a galley, since in the photograph there is a man standing in the doorway in a white apron, apparently a cook. On this day, the houseboat was lying in very shallow water among a congregation of kayaks and two lapstrake Rangeley Lake guide boats. There is a gangplank running from the houseboat to the muddy shore and, standing at its head, one hand on the galley shed, is an obscured figure dressed in a light suit and waistcoat, a high soft-collared shirt, buttoned to the neck, and a strange, light-colored derby, like a sun hat. This I believe is Robert A. Gilbert, one of the few images of the man that I was able to find, and even that one, suspect. There is an old woman in the front deck house and a rangy man in a tam-o'-shanter leaning against the wall next to her. The cook in his apron has appeared for the photograph from his stovehouse, and, standing askew on the gangplank, with an odd, gate-legged stance, is another man. Although his features are not clear, he looks to me to be Jim McLeod, Brewster's perennial guide on his birding expeditions in this curious unpeopled country.

Periodically, sometimes in company with Caroline (who appears with her husband in another photo from this period taken by Gilbert), Brewster would move the houseboat to the head of the lake and ascend the wild Magalloway River, which in their time was heavily populated with loons, moose, otters, muskrats, and even a few of the then rare beavers.

On one of these expeditions, in 1903, Brewster, Gilbert, and Jim McLeod packed one of the Rangeley Lake canoes and set out to explore the upper reaches of the Magalloway, recording the birds and wildlife as they ascended the river. As they slowly paddled and poled up the river they saw fleeting images of unidentifiable creatures appearing and disappearing in the shadowed forest and heard the splashes of waterbeasts such as otter or muskrats. About a mile upstream they passed a settlement—a low log cabin set on a rise on the east bank, standing among stumps and half-cleared brush piles. There was a tow-headed little boy standing by the riverbank as they approached. He took one look at them and fled to the darkened interior of the cabin. Slowly, one by one, adults emerged to stare. They collected in front of the cabin and watched in awe as the canoe and its crew slowly poled and paddled upstream. There were two men in flannel shirts, their braces hanging loose at their hips, a woman in gingham, and three or four ragamuffin children, wild-eyed. Mr. Brewster hallooed to them and waved, and as they passed one of the men raised his arm above his hip in a weak wave and dropped it—not a word exchanged, nor a greeting. They continued to stare blankly, mouths opened, as the boat slid by.

—What was that all about?—Brewster asked McLeod, once they were around the bend and out of sight.

—Ain't nothing—he said.—Just that they, ah, never seen the likes of him before—

He glanced at Mr. Gilbert.

✠

One day while I was poking around this part of the lake I set out to ascend the Magalloway myself, rowing and paddling upstream in my 1910 Old Town rowing canoe. I had been here before on the upper reaches and was disappointed to see, lining the banks, any number of summer cottages, each with a dock and a requisite outboard motorboat, many of them powered by enormous high-speed engines. For some reason, other than a few intrusions, the lower reaches of the Magalloway (and also the far, upper reaches) are less populated, and I set up a good stroke and slid forward through the smooth waters, the wake streaming out astern in a dark rippling V.

Where the river narrowed I put away the oars, switched to the stern, and began to paddle quietly, passing loons, headed downstream, who would dive at my approach and then reappear astern of me. I also saw a mother moose, who watched dumbly as I paddled by, while her calf fed indifferently, and there were periodic dives from kingfishers and still-as-a-statue great blue herons standing on the overhanging branches or rocks, eyeing the dark waters.

At a high point at a bend in the river, on the left bank I saw a large stocky man with shoulder-length black hair and dark eyes and pulled up to ask him (by way of openers only; I knew he wouldn't know) if he had ever heard of a birdman in these parts named William Brewster.

"Don't know the man," he said. "But I'm not from around here."

"Where are you from?" I asked.

"West of here—way west. I'm Sioux, come from the Pine Ridge, and I been living up the river a pace with a guy who runs a campground kind of place he calls the Tee Pee. He's a dumb son of a bitch, but he likes Indian stuff, and he keeps me around for the tourists. I sell moccasins, hides, stuff like that."

I curved the canoe toward the shore and held it in the current. The man seemed anxious to talk to someone.

"The stuff I sell," he said, "doesn't come from here. It's made in China. Got nothing to do with these woods, but the dumb bastards, they like it, and the guy that owns the place, he likes it that the tourists like it. I teach 'em stuff about the Maine woods, tell 'em stories about wolves and bears, even though I don't know squat. And they believe it. I just lie, you know, make stuff up and they say, ah, the guy's a real Indian, they live close to the land, they know all about animals and the Great Spirit. I don't tell I'm an Episcopalian. Don't believe in no Great Spirit."

I had been by this Tee Pee place the year before and even stopped in to talk. It was indeed a weird spot, with plywood teepees, a few cabins on the river, and a few camping and tenting sites. But the owner was nice enough, a talkative type who liked the country. I think he was a city boy himself, from Bangor or Portland maybe, or somewhere near the coast.

The Indian offered me a cigarette, and then asked me if I could take him across the river.

He didn't know anything about boats (why should he, after all?) and nearly swamped me when he got in. He was a big man and sat up in the bow and brought the head down so low that I could hardly paddle against the current, but I got him over and grounded him without much problem and he climbed up on the bank and started off upstream.

"Come up the camp later, I'll sell you some moccasins cheap," he said, joking.

"I will," I said.

As I was backing off, he called out again.

"Hey, you got any herb with you?"

"No," I said. "Sorry."

"I bet you do."

"No, none."

"I know guys like you. You smoke a lot of dope, then don't share it. The Indians, they always share, you know what I mean. You come up to the woods here, you got to share."

"Well, I would share if I had any. I'd give it all to you."

"I'd like a smoke. The boss—he's some kind of religious nut. Doesn't drink. Doesn't smoke. How you going to live that way?"

"I don't know," I said. "Never could figure it out myself. Anyway, good luck," I said, and began to push off.

"Yeah, sure, good luck. Come up anyway, though, and bring some herb. We'll have a talk. I'll even buy it if you won't give me any. I hate this place," he said. "Too many trees. I'm going back where you can see some sky. There's too many trees here. Can't see the horizon except out on the lake, and I hate boats. I'm scared of them."

"Get a horse," I said.

"You said it, Mack. I wished I had a horse again."

I left him grumbling on the shore and began thinking about what old Metalluc would have to say about this character.

✠

I was staying down in Bethel at this time at a restored house called something like the Bistro that had been turned into a bed and breakfast and restaurant. It was run by New Yorkers who had come up to the area to ski and liked the place so much they decided to stay. The concierge, a man named Allen, was a displaced Londoner with a strong East End accent who had made a lot of money rigging the sound systems for rock groups. He and his wife, who did all the cooking, had a couple of young children and, unlike so many of the overly precious New England bed and breakfasts, they ran the place somewhat haphazardly.

This custom had gotten them into some difficulty with the stray NTLers who would come to eat at the restaurant and take rooms there when the institute rooms were filled. The Bistro had no air-conditioning, no TVs in the rooms, no blow-dryers, no hookups or connections for the electronic devices carried by the harried NTL executive visitors. This begat many complaints from the guests who expected special services.

"I just shrug, don't I, when they say that," Allen told me. "What are we to do, run out and buy a TV?"

Allen had his own complaints about the NTLers.

"You get the troubled ones here, sometimes. You get these types who are sent by their companies because they don't have many people skills, as they like to say, and the NTL staff tries to get them to face up to the fact. Sometimes it works; they begin to look at themselves for the first time and you'll see people sitting here in a corner in the living room sobbing bitterly while the other guests are trying to enjoy a drink."

I had heard similar complaints about the NTLers voiced by

waitresses in some of the other Bethel restaurants. The NTLers come in, stare at the menu, drink some water, eat some of the rolls, stare at the menu again, and then get up and walk out. Or they demand things that are unavailable, or require special orders, or change their minds after the chef is halfway through preparation of their dish.

"They're all screwy in one way or another," a woman named Linda, who ran a little spot on the green, told me. "I'm telling you, they get some real weirdos up there. Late one night, I'm closing the place up, and I hear some scuffling and grunting out on the green there. Here's two naked guys, wrestling, right by the fountain, trying to 'work it out,' I suppose. People who live around the green sometimes hear yowling and singing at three in the morning. It's like these middle-aged dorks finally figured something out. They grew up too soon, like they never had childhoods. Hey," she said, "we all got problems. Get over it."

All this talk about the NTLers made me want to go there myself and attempt to become normal. I had talked with the staff already while I was looking around the grounds and the main building, and they told me that there was a new group of "trainees" coming in the next day, so I went up in the afternoon as they were arriving.

In contrast to what I was hearing, they seemed a friendly lot. I met a woman named Mary, from Cincinnati, a large-figured lady who was having trouble lugging in her baggage. I offered to carry her suitcases for her, and found why she was having so much trouble. They were incredibly heavy. I had to horse them up the wide stairs around a bend on the landing to her room, which was a large airy space on the west side of the building with maple furniture and a view to the ridges beyond.

A huge friendly man named Bill strode in while I was helping her and shook my hand, firmly, with a hardy, hail-fellow-well-met grip that almost broke my fingers.

"Great place, isn't it," he said. "Great place. Marvelous views from here, I mean this is it, right? Kind of place to get away from it all, kick back and relax, take in the scenery. Right, Mary?"

Then he turned back to me.

"What company are you with?"

"My company?" I said, haltingly. "Well, I'm actually here because—"

"I'm with the AKL, out of Detroit," he said, "we're a great group, mission-critical applications, up and coming, we're moving, a real operations-oriented group, got the staff, got the organizational charts worked through, and how about you, Mary, who're you with?"

This generated an equally incomprehensible (to me) explanation from Mary, who found herself on firmer ground than I was, and off they went talking about plug-ins and electronic devices identified with acronyms that I, in my nineteenth-century innocence, had never heard of.

Downstairs again I met another man named Bill (which got me wondering if you had to be named William to be associated with this building). This Bill was draped with electronic devices, a cell phone connection clapped to his ear, small black boxes hooked to his belt and looped to his pants pockets, and a laptop case clutched in his right hand. He was a much quieter sort, though, shy even, and seemed a little frightened to be so far from home in so wild a place and amid the formal calm of polished hardwood floors, stained glass windows, and Oriental rugs. Home for him was Texas, and he was with the DNC, as he explained earnestly.

Mary, I believe, was from ABD, Carlos, whom I met later, was from San Diego and worked for the OAL Corporation, and another woman I met worked for a company called Eunix, or Eunice, or something that sounded to me a lot like eunuch—at any rate, a company with which I personally would not wish to be associated.

At seven the next morning, a Sunday, there was to be an inspirational "encounter" in the green room, and I was told by staff that anyone from the village could attend, so I got up early and walked over to the big event.

I was a little late and couldn't find the right building, and when I finally arrived the encounter session was already in progress. Here, in a large circle, sat ten or fifteen men and women of various ages, holding papers and looking attentively at a huge African American man dressed entirely in black, with a halo of pure white hair and the white dog collar attached somehow to his black tee shirt. He sat overflowing his chair more like the Buddha than a Christian leader of sheep.

"Come in, come in," he said, spreading his arms and indicating a free chair. "Please. Have a seat, we're just introducing ourselves."

If there is one thing I hate, it is "introducing" myself. It appeared that I had burst in on an ecumenical religious service of the New Age sort, conducted with a decidedly Christian bent. One man said he was an Episcopal priest. Another told us at length how he had found the Truth of the Bible. Another explained that she was an OD consultant (whatever that is) who had recently returned to her Methodist church. And all the others were good churchgoers of one faith or another. No Hindus, though, no Jews, no Muslims, and as far as I could tell not one good old-fashioned heathen—save myself. When my turn came, I didn't dare explicate my pagan worship of the sun and nature and said I had been raised a Christian but had fallen by the wayside.

The Great Father pastor smiled and smiled and accepted my explanations.

"We all fall from time to time, do we not?" he said.

He himself, as he explained, was a worldly sort. He had worked with street kids in the Bronx—in fact he had a tough white man's New York accent—and he still ran a little storefront church in the city most of the year and would come up here every summer to serve those few NTLers who still had a faith.

Most of the trainees I met at the NTL Institute, it must be said, appeared to be more comfortable with the religion of the god Mammon than with traditional religion, and even this devoted morning encounter crowd managed to use their Christian faith to either excuse or guide their work. Part of the program that morning was an analysis of Ezekiel 37:1-14, the passage in which a traveler comes upon a valley of dry bones, and the Lord commands that the traveler prophesy to the bones the Word of the Lord, whereupon the bones rattle and come together, bone by bone, assume flesh, and come alive. The bones, the Lord says to the traveler, are the whole house of Israel.

Having read the passage to us, the Great Father asked us for our personal explanations.

First to speak was the born-again Christian. He said the story of the bones was God's way of breaking down and putting back together, and that that is what he was doing with his leadership group at the SoftData Corporation.

"I don't always attempt to reveal the Truth in this group—there are three Hindus in my unit and a practicing Jew. But I apply the teachings of the Bible. The answers are all there and it works."

The explication from the Episcopal priest I think was lost on most of the crowd. He proceeded to analyze the passage using arcane theological language, basically explaining the scene (I think) as a metaphor for the pilgrimage of the spirit from birth to grave to salvation.

A French Canadian woman with thin lips and tiny steel-rimmed glasses said she was a practicing Catholic but that the teachings of the church were not always conducive to good business practices ("Hear, Hear!" I said to myself silently), and that she was having a problem balancing her faith with her work; somehow she saw the dry bones as relevant to her work, but I couldn't follow her logic.

The instructions and discussion carried on in this manner, with the participants revealing more and more of their personal problems and their faults and their attempts to improve themselves and work ethically in a basically unethical environment. Toward the end, there were actually a few emotional expressions of their faith, and then came the moment I was dreading.

"Let us pray together," said the Great Father. "Let us join hands in prayer and seek in silence the proper path . . ."

Whereupon he took up the hands of the parishioners on either side of him and waited for the circle to close. The French Canadian woman snatched my hand and held me firmly in her dry claw, and a skinny fellow with thinning hair who hadn't said a word tentatively took up my right hand. Poor fellow, his palm was cold and sweaty.

"We ask you, Oh Lord, to grant us a moment of silent reflection," the Great Father said.

I don't know what the prayers of the other participants were. Mine was for this affair to end as soon as possible.

On my way out I saw Carlos, the business executive from San Diego.

"You missed the religious encounter group," I said.

He shrugged and blew out his cheeks.

"Did I? Well ain't that a crying shame," he said.

Carlos smoked a lot of cigarettes and didn't seem happy from the start. I suspect his presence here was a command performance.

The Great Father announced that there would be coffee and pastries following the encounter, in the main dining hall. As I was passing by I ducked in to have a look and saw poor, shy Bill, he of the myriad electronic devices, eating alone in a corner. (Most of the new trainees had formed little cliques by this time.) I went over and asked him how he was getting by.

"I think I am learning," he said, nodding. "Mainly, I think, I am learning that I still have a lot to learn."

He looked down into his coffee cup. I touched his shoulder and said farewell and good luck.

Entr'acte

In 1916, Gilbert moves to Inman Street in Cambridge

In 1902 a volcanic eruption and fire destroyed the entire town of St. Pierre on Martinique.The first successful airplane flight was accomplished in December 1903. Headlines declared emphatically that there was no balloon attached to the aereoplane.

In 1913, Congress authorized the Hetch Hetchy Valley Dam, a major defeat for the Sierra Club and the aging John Muir.

In 1914 Archduke Franny Ferdinand and his wife were assassinated in Sarajevo, setting in motion a great world war. Germany declared war on France and Russia and invaded Belgium. Britain declared war on Germany. Austria declared war on Russia and France. Britain and Russia declared war on Turkey. British troops landed in France.

Charlie Chaplin began making films in 1914. In 1915, D. W. Griffith's produced *Birth of a Nation.* Blacks in Boston boycotted the screenings and demonstrated in the streets. Robert Frost published "North of Boston," and George Washington Carver began popularizing alternative crops for the depleted soils of the American South—peanuts and sweet potatoes.

By the 1920s there were more than 100,000,000 people in the Unites States, of whom more that 2,000,000 were unemployed. Ku Klux Klan membership was at 4,000,000. Life expectancy was 53 years for males, 54 for females. The illiteracy rate was estimated at six percent, a new low. There were 400,000 miles of paved roads in the United States and it took about thirteen days to reach California from New York. Trouser legs widened during this period, knickers came into vogue, white linen suits were the rage in summer, and by 1925 the Flapper style was in full force: short skirts, no bosom, no waistline, clipped hair hidden beneath rounded cloche hats, and the sin of cosmetics was loosed on the land—powder, rouge, eye shadow, and painted nails.

In 1919 William Brewster dies.

The black photographer James Van Der Zee and his wife opened the Guaranteed Photo Studio in Harlem in 1918. Thirteen days of violence raged across the nation during the "Red Summer" of 1919, with twenty-three blacks dead, fifteen whites, 537 people injured, and 1,000 black families left homeless. Marcus Garvey led a parade of 50,000 blacks in Harlem in 1920, and A'lelia Walker, the daughter of Madame C. J. Walker, the hairdresser queen, maintained a salon of black writers and artists of the Harlem Renaissance. Louis Armstrong left New Orleans and joined the King Oliver Creole Jazz Band in Chicago in 1920.

Gilbert began working at Harvard's Museum of Comparative Zoology in 1919, the same year as the Treaty of Versailles. Claude Monet painted the late Impressionist masterpiece *Les Nymphéas.* Renoir died, and in 1921, in Paris, Man Ray began making "rayograms" by placing objects on photographic paper. James Joyce published *Ulysses* in Paris in 1922.

That year in the United States, the Supreme Court established a woman's right to vote. Plumed hats were out of vogue by this time, women smoked cigarettes, and the loathsome music known as jazz was sweeping the country. The consumption of alcoholic beverages was illegal in the United States—which is not to say that no one drank.

CHAPTER TEN

After They've Gone

WHERE THERE IS PERHAPS A PROVINCE IN WHICH THE PHOTOGRAPH CAN TELL US NOTHING MORE THAN WHAT WE SEE WITH OUR OWN EYES, THERE IS ANOTHER IN WHICH IT PROVES TO US HOW LITTLE OUR EYES PERMIT US TO SEE.

Dorothea Lange

Old road, Ball's Hill, Concord, Massachusetss, undated

On December 7, 1909, when he was 58 years old, Mr. William Brewster, at the urging of Caroline, had himself baptized at St. John's Episcopal Church in Cambridge. He makes a short note of the event in his journals, a passing one-line statement. Previous to this service, in earlier years, he would rarely attend church, except at Christmas and again at Easter, and even then mainly to keep Caroline happy. Curiously, on many occasions it appears, he seems to have taken ill on Christmas or Easter and would be unable to attend, and sometimes the two of them would simply retreat to the Hotel Abbottsford on holidays, dine, and then read in their room by night.

Brewster was approaching 60 and aging fast, his multiple symptoms of neurasthenia catching up with him. He may have sensed somehow that the end was in sight, perhaps, and believed that it was necessary to prepare to meet his Maker. Although he never openly writes about the subject in his journals, I believe that his was a transcendental persuasion. If he experienced God at all, he saw him in the form of birds: God was a wingèd thing with feathers and Emerson and Thoreau were his prophets.

Mr. Gilbert, by contrast, always had a strong Christian faith, and increased his devotions as he aged. Around 1905, he and Anna switched from the Baptist church on Massachusetts Avenue to Saint Bartholomew's Episcopal Church, which was closer to home. The change also represented a move upward socially. Gilbert was becoming uncomfortable with the shouting and hollering of the southern blacks who were crowding into the pews at the Union Baptist Church—jumping to their feet to bark "Amen" with every other word the preacher shouted and clapping and swaying from side to side whenever they sang. The Episcopal service at Saint Bartholomew's in Cambridge could be lively too on occasion, but here was a deeper, more intellectual faith, driven more by the book and a deep history than by the pure emotion of the spirit. Besides, he liked the music. The old traditional English hymns: "Nearer My

God to Thee" and "Come! Oh Come! Emanuel" with its slow scythelike pace. The music suited his character.

In the first decades of the new century, he found he needed that old world order. There was a nasty sort of popular Negroid music moving uncomfortably close to the world of the Brahmins—white and black alike. Down in New Orleans, the likes of Buddy Bolden, Louis Armstrong, and someone with the off-color name of Jelly Roll Morton had taken the old minstrel songs, combined them with gospel shouts and the brassy rhythms of marching bands, and come up with a music known as "jass," later transformed to "jazz."

Upper-class whites and the white churches were, understandably, suspicious of this new music. By 1913, there were editorials in local newspapers and sermons suggesting that all of America (read all of young America) was falling prey to the collective soul of the Negro. Jazz and its evil sister, ragtime, were sweeping the country, and everywhere the primitive jungle morality of Africa was surfacing. For the white populace, the white poet Vachel Lindsay summed it all up with his rhythmic, pre-rap verses of his popular contemporary poem "The Congo," with which he used to crowd the halls for his public readings:

"Fat black bucks in a wine-barrel room, barrel-house kings with feet unstable, sagged and reeled and pounded on the table. Pounded the table with handle of a broom . . . boomlay, boomlay, boomlay, BOOM."

Nearly all middle-class homes in this period were in possession of a piano and at least one person in the family could generally play reasonably well. Sales of sheet music of new popular songs would skyrocket around the country as soon as they were published, with new tunes coming out furiously from the squalid little offices clustered around Times Square known as Tin Pan Alley. Even worse, the new music encouraged questionable, suggestive dances such as the turkey trot, the bunny hug, Bango Bingo, the shim sham shimmy, and, worst of all, the grizzly bear, a clasping syncopated embrace, body to body and cheek to cheek, "a vertical expression of a horizontal act" in the words of the old-school Brahmins.

All this was just as upsetting to middle-class blacks as it was to whites. It flew in the face of the image that all the reformers were trying to avoid. New York's Adam Clayton Powell, the popular preacher, said that the new music and dances were suggesting that the blacks were a frivolous people, that all they wanted to do was have a good time. Like the minstrel shows from which jazz evolved, the music perpetuated the image of the free spirit, the happy slave, who, when he was troubled, just went out and danced and sang. Or worse, had illicit sex.

There was in fact through all of this music the deep, throbbing undertone of sex, a suggestion of primitive fertility dances and unspeakable tribal practices. It was an exact reversal of the cold roast Brahmin, the unemotional, intellectual, orderly world of Mr. William Brewster and his wife Caroline and ERS. Whatever these people did, they did privately and with grace and civility. They read Emerson as their liturgy, sang stately hymns in the King's English, and danced the Virginia reel—no hotjump barrel-house kings here, no Congos creeping through the black, with tattooed cannibals dancing in files, as Vachel Lindsay suggested.

The popular metaphor for this decline into the hot music, perverse dancing, petting parties, and all the other perceived vices of the age was the sinking of the great ship *Titanic.* Down with the old canoe, as the expression had it, went a whole culture. But the real end began in June of 1914, with the assassination of Archduke Franny Ferdinand in Sarajevo, and finished in the mud of Flanders Field and Verdun.

Jazz was not the only offense in the years that followed the end of the Great War. Women began chopping off their long hair and skirts began to rise. First they advanced slightly beyond the ankle, then beyond the requisite six inches, then to seven and a half, eventually above the knees themselves. Wilder women rolled their stockings below their knees to reveal the actual flesh of their smooth legs. Necklines began descending even as the hemlines rose. But by then a flat boylike chest had come into vogue rather than the full bosom of Mrs. William Brewster and her tribe. It was the decline and fall of Olde England in America, and in the view of some concerned proper citizens it represented the triumph of the Negro.

After the war was over, homecoming soldiers were crowding the streets of port cities as the troop ships unloaded. There were so many victory parades that you sometimes had to plan your route through the city to avoid the great phalanx of tired soldiers, who had left the country as boys and returned as men, and broken men at that, men educated in the course of a single night in some cases, in the mud and filth of the trenches, with the Angel of Death sparking overhead in the form of bursting shells.

Although it was prohibited, the American soldiers had enjoyed the loose morals of France while they were between battles. When they came home they were supposed to board the trains and head back to Kansas to settle down into the tedious routine of the American way of life, which by 1919 prohibited, by mandate of federal law, the consumption of alcohol, and which held suspect any woman who wore too much makeup, or dressed in a manner that even vaguely suggested the existence of sex. What could they do but bring up the hemlines and bring down the house?

The malaise was worse, of course, if you were black. Following on the groundbreaking work of Robert Gould Shaw and the 54th Regiment, black soldiers had been—reluctantly—allowed into the American military. There were some thirty African Americans on board the USS *Maine* when it sank in 1898 in Havana harbor, and the all-black 9th and 10th Cavalries, the Buffalo Soldiers, were the first to charge up the hill at San Juan in advance of Teddy Roosevelt's Rough Riders. Full companies of black soldiers packed off with the Doughboys to Europe in 1918 and won their share of medals for bravery (although more of them were awarded by the French than by the Americans).

Bringing the African American soldiers over to Europe en masse, as they did, had the effect of engendering a little social problem not considered by American political and military officials. The Germans, having some experience in these matters, knew all about racism and began distributing flyers through the black fighting units, asking whether they enjoyed the same rights as white people did in America. But more of a problem were the French. The French citizenry seemed to have a particular liking for the black Americans, especially after the jazzband leader of the 39th Regimental Band, James R. Europe, entered Paris and marched down the Champs Élysées playing a hipped-up version of the "Marseillaise" with such a strange counterbeat rhythm and with so many wild and ranging improvisations and musical asides that the French hardly recognized the tune. They stood in confusion at first, then caught the idea, and after that, all across France, they began dancing and strutting in the streets. The long French *affaire* with American blacks had begun.

The French were not unfamiliar with Negro soldiers. They had Senegalese troops of their own in the field, who were wild and brave fighters and were often employed as shock troops in battle. When the non-French-speaking black Americans arrived and were quartered in the small rural villages, knowing the wildness of the Senegalese, the local peasantry was at first suspicious. They had already had their problems with white American soldiers. But American black people proved to be different. Little children liked them, of course, they liked all the soldiers, but they especially seemed to love these dark ones; you'd see the children riding piggyback with them around the villages and kissing their chocolate cheeks. Adults found the new recruits to be polite and friendly and noticed that, for some reason, they seemed especially grateful for the smallest kindnesses and seemed to genuinely appreciate French people. There was, of course, good reason for that. If a black person came into a café or a restaurant, the white waiter would point to a table and bring over a bottle. If you were on leave and needed a hotel room, the concierge would look over the guest book, select a room, and give you the key. A young white bellhop might even carry your bags up in the better hotels. And best of all were the women. Pretty village women with red lips, coiffed hair, and rosy cheeks were not opposed to dancing with a Negro. If she got to know you and you were polite, she might take you home to meet her parents, who would show you to a seldom-used front parlor and give you a tiny glass of fiery brandy and a little sweetcake and with the help of sign language and dictionaries attempt to hold a conversation. For an African American, such open-minded social treatment could not have been dreamed of back home.

White American officials saw the danger in all this. They segregated the troops; they issued proclamations to the French citizenry instructing them to avoid socialization with Negroes, which, with a Gallic shrug, the French commanders and the village mayors tore up. Besides, the French generals needed soldiers and were indifferent to color. In one instance they trained the American blacks with the French troops instead of segregating them.

There were two black divisions in France by 1918, the 92nd and 93rd New York, later joined by the 370th U.S. regiment of the all-black Illinois National Guard, which arrived to fight under French command. After one horrendous assault that lasted for 191 days, the French government awarded a black unit known as the Hell Fighters a record number of citations and medals.

None of this went unnoticed by W. E. B. Du Bois, who was in France at the time and reporting for his journal *The Crisis.* Word began to spread, stories of fraternization abounded, and there was a widely publicized letter circulating in the American black community from a French village woman who, among other words of praise for the black troops, said that villagers were honored to have a black person at table. She ended her evocation of village life with an unforgettable line: "Soldiers . . . you will always live in our hearts."

News of all this had gotten out even before the war was over. Those who read *The Crisis*—mostly an intellectual, more elevated crowd—became curious, and after the war black writers and painters began to flock to Paris. The musicians, especially the jazz musicians, were already there; some had never gone home after the war.

When it was over the black regiments sailed home along with the other soldiers and, with James Europe leading them, black troops marched down Fifth Avenue to tremendous cheering. That event turned out to be an anomaly, however. All through the eastern United States the Great Migration had begun. The boll weevil devastation of the cotton crop, the failure of the old tenant system, the poverty, the poor, worn-out red soils, all were conspiring to evict the former slave families from the only American earth they had ever known. The Dixie Flyer and similar rail lines were jammed with people headed for Chicago, Detroit, St. Louis, and, to a lesser extent, Boston. Earlier, African Americans had been able to find work producing war supplies in the northern factories, but when the war was over, blacks were the first to be laid off. Race riots and lynchings began. In July of 1917 in a race riot in St. Louis, forty blacks and eight whites were killed and entire black neighborhoods were burned to the ground. This was followed by the famous Silent March down Fifth Avenue, organized by W. E. B. Du Bois' group, the NAACP. In a strangely surreal and peaceful demonstration, thousands of men, women, and children marched silently through the city to the sound of muffled drums.

As the layoffs in the factories grew after the war, the tensions increased, the lynchings mounted, black soldiers were hanged wearing their uniforms, and by 1919 there had been more than twenty-five race riots across the country, ranging from Tennessee all the way west to Nebraska. And all the while, brewing in the mind of those blacks who had been overseas, was the lure of France. Paris began to replace Boston as the Negro paradise.

Back home in Cambridge, Gilbert knew of all this, of course, although he did not join the huge crowd of Boston blacks who flocked to the streets in 1915 to protest the Boston screening of D. W. Griffith's blatantly racist *Birth of a Nation.* He did boycott the movie, however—not that he was much of a moviegoer. He knew all about the freedom American blacks had experienced abroad; he knew also about the lynchings, and the race riots, and the restrictive controls of the Black Codes. What he did not know was that he too might need Paris someday.

✠

It was a custom of the children of Cambridge to go out caroling in the neighborhoods of Brattle Street in the early part of the century. On Christmas Eve in 1915, a group of them crossed the lawn at 145 Brattle Street, collected themselves below the front door, and sang "God Rest Ye Merry Gentlemen." The French doors of the upper balcony opened slowly and, according to an account of the night written up by one of the participants, a beautiful old couple emerged, dressed in white bedclothes, their white hair glowing in the backlight, and their faces dimmed in the sad spirit of the age, as if in remembrance of youth and wild nature. With the clear, hard stars shining above, and the jingle of bells from one of the passing sleighs cracking the night air somewhere on the hill behind the house, the carolers struck up "Silent Night."

Mr. Gilbert, who was a religious man, might well have burst into tears had he stepped out of the bird museum that night to listen. It was the beginning of a dark season for him.

Two months earlier, in October, his 16-year-old son Robbie, his firstborn, had came down with a serious chest cold. Gilbert was away with Brewster the following evening, and on October 8th, quite suddenly, Robbie died of acute lobar pneumonia. There was a brief personal notation in the journal of Mr. William Brewster marking the occasion:

"Oct 8th: Rain. Dull. Gilbert motored to Cambridge to find that his only son, Robbie, had died just before he got there after a brief illness of which he [ie Gilbert] first learned last night."

For some years during this period, Gilbert's wife, Anna, had been suffering from Graves' disease, a malfunction of the thyroid that left her fatigued and nervous. As a result, she was generally debilitated much of the time, and when the symptoms increased, she was sent to a specialist and diagnosed with Addison's disease, which is an illness of the kidneys indicated by some of the same symptoms. This was in 1918, and although Boston was a major medical community then, as it is now, it is possible that, since she was black, she did not have the best of care. She grew progressively worse, and was in and out of the hospital on several occasions, at great expense to Mr. Gilbert. It was during this period that he came, hat in hand, to Caroline and explained the situation of his finances and his wife's condition, and received, via her intervention and perhaps her explanations, possibly even her pleas, the funds from Mr. Brewster to cover her medical expenses.

It was all to no avail. On June 5th in 1919, after prolonged illness, she died at the age of 48, leaving Mr. Gilbert alone with his three teenaged daughters, Mary, Emily, and the youngest, Edyth, who was only 13.

By the middle of that month, though, perhaps seeking forgetfulness, Gilbert was back at work. He went out to October Farm and collected strawberries and brought them back to the ailing Mr. Brewster, who seems by this time to have been spending most of his days in his bedroom above his junglelike yard.

One of the most useful characteristics of Robert Gilbert as an employee was that you never had to tell him what to do once he knew what was needed. He fixed the cars without being asked, he would run into Boston to purchase his own choices of Victrola records for Mr. Brewster and Caroline without being told specifically which records to purchase. He came home with recordings of Enrico Caruso, Amelita Galli, and Antonio Pini-Corsi, the perfect choices for the old couple. He also managed the staff at October Farm, quelling the riotous drunks, and was so essential as an assistant that he would be present at interviews of prospective employees and was asked to pass judgment on them. He would work alone in the museum on little chores, without Brewster's knowledge. He taught himself to type; he ordered photographic supplies before they ran out; he prepared the skins of birds he or Brewster had collected in the field, and he was often out in the field on his own, recording birds, especially in Brewster's later years. He would return to report sightings, many of which were entered in the Brewster journals, which were later culled for publication in Brewster's three posthumous books.

From what I can determine from the minimal entries, 1919 ushered in a fine and flowering spring. The migratory birds had returned early that year, the jungle was flourishing with birdsong and fruit, and the apple trees at October Farm were flowering well and promising a rich crop for the end of summer.

In cruel contrast, in the human community, Mr. Brewster's world was slipping. He was "suffering terribly"—much nausea—all through the winter of 1919. His political ally and sometime acquaintance, Teddy Roosevelt, died in early January. His family friend "Lizzy," whose last name never appears in the diaries or journals, had an attack of heart failure; several old friends had succumbed; Caroline's nephew, Robert Jefferson, was killed on Hill 47 along the Dardanelles, and Caroline herself was ill and temporarily living separately from Brewster. He had moved out to October Farm that spring and saw more of ERS than he did his wife. In the evenings, ERS sat by his bedside reading to him from *David Copper-*

field, and he slept alone at night in the old creaking ghost house, served by a Mrs. Burbank who brought him his paltry meals.

Beyond the meadow and the apple orchards, on the other side of the river in these years, the new noisome devices known as "aereoplanes" had begun appearing like vulturous omens, circling over the Great Meadows near his former sanctuary at Ball's Hill. Earlier that year a marauder had broken into two of the cabins by smashing the padlocks on Gilbert's cookhouse door and forcing open a window. Whoever it was stole Brewster's old Smith & Wesson revolver and all the bed pillows, and then went around battering the locks on the log cabin, attempting to break in. The act had soured the place. What's more, the boathouse downstream in Carlisle, the same one that brought the canoes of chattering Asians up the river to Mr. Bensen, had introduced motorboats, which made a racket on the river and disturbed Mr. Brewster's peace whenever he was at the cabins. He was even forced to fight an early version of the typical environmental battles that now so commonly flare up in the town of Concord. In this case it was the development of a pig farm on the opposite shore of the river. Brewster was rich enough to have solved the problem by buying the land outright if necessary, but for some unrecorded reason the farmer gave up on the idea and pulled out.

Slowly, Brewster's journal entries become shorter and more sporadic. On certain days in 1919 they consisted of mere notes:

"May 2nd. Hermit thrush singing near Pulpit Rock."

"May 5th. One of my mean days. Spent most in bed."

"May 12th. Not feeling well."

"May 29th. I see nobody save Gilbert and members of my family."

That winter, Mr. Brewster had recorded one of the longest entries in the twenty-five years of his journal keeping. His Irish terrier "Timmy" had come to his sickroom on the evening of March 11th, jumped up on the bed and cuddled close to his thigh, licking his hand. Brewster covered him, as was his custom, with a red blanket, "and thus we lay together, as we have so often done before, until Nurse came back and took him away in her arms. That was the last I saw, or shall ever see, of him on this earth."

The entry that followed the next day gives the details. A small boy brought word to Gilbert that a brown dog had been run over by a "motor truck" on Craigie Street. The boy thought the dog might belong to the house. Gilbert went out and found Timmy lying by the curb. He was still alive, but did not seem to know Gilbert, and soon died.

Then came the troublesome business of informing the old man, who lay in his sickbed on the second floor. Gilbert told Caroline, who broke the news to Mr. Brewster.

"Thus perished the very dearest dog I have ever had," Brewster wrote in his diary.

Read all this as metaphor—the unexpressed love that passeth all understanding. His was not a class that permitted the outward display of emotions. And yet, for all his meticulous note keeping, his separate bedroom from his wife, his punctuality, his concern for his rents, his exact notations of the arrivals and departures of trains to Concord, and, most especially, his detailed observations of the behavior of birds in the wild, there beat within him a warm, humane heart that would permit expression of an abiding love for the silent, unquestioning loyalty of dogs.

A few nights after Timmy's death Brewster had an intensely realistic dream, also revealed in uniquely personal detail in his diary.

He dreamt that Charon was ferrying him across the River Styx and that as they approached the dark shore, he saw Timmy there, waiting to greet him: "he was wagging his tail and smiling, loving eyed, and when I landed, he whirled around and around many times just as he always would do when eager to pass or nose his way through a door or gate. . . . All this seemed very real."

It was to be real indeed.

On June 14th, back on Brattle Street, he wrote a short entry about the strawberries Gilbert had brought back from the farm. The next day, a Sunday, he slept most of the morning and only got up and dressed in the afternoon, sitting by the chamber window looking out over his "Jungle" of native plants that he had personally transplanted to the yard from the wilds beyond. It was the last entry in his journal.

A month later, in his upstairs room, on the night of July 11th, with Caroline and Nurse in attendance, leaving behind the works of his time—his books, his bird museum, his voluminous journals, houses, servants, accounts, stocks, rentals, as well as his wife, ERS, and his many male friends and his loyal valet—he went down to the dark shores of the underworld. In the dimmed light, he saw Charon's ferry ahead of him, waiting by the banks. Mr. Brewster climbed on board and sat grimly in the stern sheets, staring back at the fading banks, watching his past recede as Charon poled slowly across the river.

One hopes that if the gods were just, he found Timmy on the other side.

Mr. Gilbert went home alone that night. His son was long in his grave. His wife was dead. His employer was dead. His daughters were living elsewhere at the time and his house was large and empty. And now, suddenly, it was no longer necessary for him to rush off to tend to anyone but himself.

CHAPTER ELEVEN

A Journey Through the Memory House

THE CAMERA IS A MIRROR WITH MEMORY.

Anon.

Concord River, undated

It was late winter in New England, 1920, and a warming trend had melted the ice of the Concord River so that the dark stream filled and flooded over the riverbanks. Below a seamless sky, the river flowed northward between the bankside red maples, leafless now, their branches and trunks black with rain. It was *nature morte,* as the French term a still life painting, only worse: no flowers or fruits, no dead game birds and rabbits, no color. No birds, and the trees skeletal, the sky a uniform pearl and paled to white, sunsets and sunrises mere slashes of dull light, the outline of a structure with no color.

He may have taken the train out with Caroline and ERS that winter day, then left them to putter in the house above the river while he went out for a walk. He trod over the hill, through Mr. Brewster's beloved birch field, where the two of them so often spotted the bluebirds, then down through the cow pastures where, in spring, the meadowlarks boasted their presence with their two-note whistles, and then onward, dropping always downhill, through the dark pines, where the two of them once photographed the nest of young great horned owls, all whited out in their immature plumage. Farther along still, to the place where they once saw a fox making off with a grouse in its mouth, and finally to the old cabins where the two of them had spent so many days. The doors were secured, the lack of human footprints in the snow indicated to him that no one had been here for months; he had to break through the crust and force his way to the doors—a small black figure in a vast white woods, all bundled in scarves and his fedora pulled down low, his tricot box coat, the collar drawn up high and tight on his neck.

He carried with him this day his Maximar roll-film camera with its Zeiss Tessar f:4.5 lens and double-extension bellows—easily portable and folded now in its leather case. Gilbert tended to work in the pictorialist style, soft focus, warm, favoring patterns, the broken reflections of tree limbs in meltwater, gray tones shading from black to a filtered blurry white of new-fallen snow, the light softened and even kind in an otherwise heartlessly cold season. I wonder if, alone by the river, away from Caroline and ERS, far removed from the scurrying of his attentive daughters, who without a mother grew up quickly and watched after him; I wonder if, alone there by the river, a lump did not rise in his throat and a short sob escape.

He snapped open the camera, raised it and squinted through the viewfinder, adjusted the bellows with the focusing lever, and then turned away, a tear blurring the landscape.

I only wonder, but the images are sad and long. Cold. The quiet beauty of the frozen world. Time and death, and the river flowing.

A scream overhead, and he looked up to see a rough-legged hawk circle once and stream off to the southeast.

Mr. Brewster would want to know about that. It was not common in 1920 to see the rough-legged hawk in winter, so many having been shot out of the sky by vindictive farmers and sportsmen practicing their aim. It was in these same years that gunners would collect at high points along the migratory flyways, and, for no particularly good reason, slaughter thousands of hawks and eagles as they passed along the ridges, riding the thermals southward on their migratory routes. By this year, the Lacey Act, which made it a federal crime to shoot anything but game birds, had passed, Mr. Brewster and his Audubon Society having been instrumental in its passage. But nevertheless the practice continued, causing a precipitous decline in the populations of predatory birds.

Kind-eyed William Brewster was now dead and buried, and the river ran on without him. At his many memorials and subsequent encomiums, Brewster had been recognized as the very dean of American ornithology, the father of field studies of bird behavior, the founder of two professional organizations dealing with ornithology, writer and conservationist, and also a gentleman. Brewster's childhood friend, the American sculptor Daniel Chester French, who later would design the Lincoln Memorial, had made a short expedition to Concord earlier that year. He and Gilbert had scoured the fields around October Farm in search of a suitable memorial to the naturalist. Gilbert thought he remembered that somewhere on one of the sharp ridges above the river he had seen a particularly beautiful granite boulder, so he and French had tramped the ridge looking for it. It was not in the place that Gilbert recalled, so they walked on farther southward, and then found it, a large pink granite stone, about three feet high, leaning out of the autumn leaves. They dug it out, and French eyed it, studying the shapes, the grain, the subtle colors.

—Perfect—he said—but I won't touch it—

—Don't—Gilbert said—he would have liked it the way it lies—

—You have a man to haul this?—French asked.

He did. Patrick and company, the Irish and Swedish workers who had helped around the farm. Gilbert said he would arrange to have the boulder hauled up to the farm where it could be loaded on a motor truck and carried to Mount Auburn Cemetery.

French came to the cemetery the day it was put in place, once again eyeing the placement, requesting to have the boulder moved a foot this way, twisted upward a half a foot that way, and then changing his mind and shifting it again, and then turning it to set the flat face forward. They had the wording of the inscription ready, a passage from The Song of Solomon:

"For lo, the winter is past, the flowers appear on the earth; the time of the singing of birds is come."

Caroline had turned over the funeral arrangements to William's lifelong friend R. H. Dana, who set the date for July 14th and retained the Concord minister Dexter Smith, who was an avid birdman and a friend of Brewster's, to conduct the service. There was a big crowd at the funeral, and all the dignitaries, the Harvard men, the members of the American Ornithologists' Union, members of the Nuttall Club, Miss Minna Hall, one of the two founders of the

Audubon Society, along with her cousin and cofounder, Harriet Hemenway, and the company of associated friends and relatives and all of them dressed in black.

The Reverend Mr. Smith spoke in darkly religious terms of the great man (knowing full well that William Brewster was not a religious man) and it was all ashes to ashes and dust to dust and all to the earth return, and they stood there in their black hats and veils, and one or two tears slipped from the squinty Brahmin eyes, from the women mostly, and even Mr. Gilbert remained dry-eyed, holding his emotions in for the time being, here in the presence of all the powerful whites, and he the only black man there that day. Men did not weep openly in 1919—except for Patrick. They could all hear him back there sobbing and blubbering and blowing his nose loudly with a great waterfall of tears rolling down his ruddy old cheeks. Sanfred's father, Lars Bensen, who stood near Patrick in Nordic fortitude, must have been uncomfortable. But the black-clad rows of Brahmins standing in front would have understood—"He's an Irishman; they're so emotional, so childlike, can't help themselves" —whereas in fact a great number of them would have loved to wail that day, such was the depth of their feeling.

Gilbert may have choked back a tear himself; but it was more in lament for the exigencies of life; this was a dark and clouded summer for him. He had cried freely at Anna's funeral a month earlier, burying his face in his big white handkerchief, his shoulders hunched and shuddering and his daughters weeping beside him, and the old preacher strutting and jabbing the air and singing loud that here was a daughter of God lying in her casket, gone now to meet Jesus in that bright and shining Kingdom where now there was no separation, no differentiation by color, or by creed, or by class, no distinction—white or black, or even Irish, and wasn't sister Anna entering now into that lustrous Heaven.

And inasmuch as this was a musical family, the full choir was there that day, all fixed in clean black silken robes with white vestments over the gowns, and the girls choir, hair straightened, all lined up and accompanied that afternoon by two violinists and a man with clarinet, Mr. Baldwin, whom the Gilberts knew from Robert's Washington Street days, and the preacher sang out then—swing low now, sweet chariot, swing low and carry your sister upward—and the tears by this time were rolling freely down Mr. Gilbert's cheeks and he just can't help himself, sobbing bitterly, and his daughters—especially little Edyth, the youngest—wailing, although Mary, the female head of the family now at age 18, was handling herself well, it was said. And then the organ and violins pitched in and the clarinet whined sadly, hitting here and there a flatted third and seventh, and all the choir starts: Sway right. Sway left, dipping with each oscillation, and then a step forward, "Swing Low," step backward, "sweet chariot," and they begin to clap, a slow workaday hammer, singing and swaying and even though he doesn't do that normally, there he is, rocking along with the rest of them—hard to the east and hard to the west, rolling and dipping and singing out in that great, darkened baritone of his, "A band of angels coming . . . for to carry me home."

It was even worse for him at the gravesite, when they lowered Anna into that brown earth on Montbretia Path in the Cambridge Cemetery by the river Charles, where their only son, Robbie, lay buried. It was July. Hot. The winds were off the river, the sun flattening the light and making everything a yellow white and ugly. The black community of Inman Square was there that day, all gathered together for yet another funeral (there had been many in the past year because of the 1918 pandemic, the plague of the Spanish Lady); all the church people were there, as well as Mr. and Mrs. Allen, their neighbors, and Anna's cousins, and a few people from across the river in Boston.

When Gilbert and his daughters got home to Inman Street

after the funeral there was a big bouquet of flowers waiting, and a little card, signed by the Brewsters (arranged by Caroline and ERS, not by William) "with deepest regrets."

He and his daughters and Anna's cousins drank iced lemonade in the parlor, and later, after everyone had left, Mr. Gilbert sat down at his upright Estey piano and he and Mary and Emma and Edyth sang a few of the old hymns that Anna had loved.

"It's what they did in that household," Gilbert's old neighbor, Tom Allen, told me. "They sang together, you could hear them even on a weekday night, they sang together."

But after the girls went up to bed Mr. Gilbert stopped singing, he could still hear them sobbing through the floors and, hearing this, he broke down again and then he got down on his knees all by himself and folded his hands together and alone there on the first floor of the big house, he prayed.

✠

Also in attendance at William Brewster's funeral were a few members of the staff of the Museum of Comparative Zoology, where Mr. Brewster had served as curator of birds, among them the director, Samuel Henshaw, who, it should be noted, was probably there because he felt that in his position it was important to be seen in the company of the august figures of the world of natural history. Samuel was the brother of William Brewster's very good friend Henry Henshaw, an avid birdman who shared correspondence with Brewster and who recently had published a book about his bird adventures. Frank Chapman, who was by then with the American Museum of Natural History, in New York, was also there. Although younger, he too was a good friend of Brewster's, and, along with Daniel Chester French and a younger man from the Harvard museum named Thomas Barbour, would write one of the biographical introductions for Brewster's four posthumously published books.

This Thomas Barbour was a rising star at the museum. He was a Harvard graduate, but was not, as were so many of the Brewster crowd, a native Bostonian, and was not an ornithologist, but concentrated primarily on reptiles and amphibians. He was a large, heavyset man with a mass of curly hair, and had great jowly cheeks, and a profound curiosity about the living things of the world. He and his wife Rosamond, who was a star in the Brahmin constellation and well off (as was Barbour's family), ranged the world every year hunting new specimens for the museum's growing collection.

Everybody liked Thomas Barbour. He was a shambling hail-fellow-well-met type who would slap you on the back and invite you out for a drink, and if you professed even a passing interest would invite you to come hunt obscure lizards with him on remote islands of the South China Sea. On more than one occasion he had been known to leap over café tables in exotic places and go crashing after the fleeting shadow of some rare lizard he thought he had seen. His wife was no slouch either. She was a bluestocking low-heeler, as the Boston Brahmin females were categorized, and hardly knew the difference between a reptile and an amphibian before she married Barbour, but she went everywhere with her world-rambling husband, and on a few occasions even personally helped capture strange snakes for his collections.

Barbour had met Robert Gilbert through Brewster and came to know him better after Brewster's death, instructed by undocumented orders from Brewster that arranged to have Gilbert come over and carry on the work he was doing at the Brattle Street bird museum at the Harvard museum, funded, I believe, by the legacy of William Brewster.

Brewster had left most of his estate to Caroline: all the furniture, most of the books in his extensive library, silverware, his watch, his automobile, plus fifty thousand dollars, and the house and land at 145 Brattle Street, along with additional properties to the north and east. His collection of mounted birds and bird skins, nests, and eggs, along with their cases and cabinets, his manuscript catalogues, and his collecting pistols, he gave to the Museum of Comparative Zoology. To his loyal assistant, Robert A. Gilbert, he willed a thousand dollars.

The will also instructed that on the death of Caroline the sum of $60,000 should be conveyed to the museum, three quarters of which should go to the payment or part payment of the salary of a competent ornithologist, who would take charge of the collection, the remaining one quarter to be used at the discretion of the director. It was funds out of this one quarter, I think, plus perhaps a little from the larger fund, that financed Gilbert's position at the museum, a post that he held, off and on, for the rest of his life.

Barbour was not technically the curator of the museum at the time of Brewster's death. Officially Samuel Henshaw was still curator, but for some years the staff and board had been plotting how to get rid of him. He was a very good accountant; his books, his desk, his management of the collections and matériel were precise. But he was rigid, humorless, unimaginative, and antisocial, and not liked by any of the people who were associated with the museum He reigned from his window desk in a large upstairs room at the museum, surrounded by his terror-struck female staff who, following his minute instructions and attentive oversight, did virtually all the work as precisely dictated by Henshaw. There is an undated photograph of him, caught unawares, staring out the window with his round Lenin-like bald head, shadowed by natural light. He kept on his person all the keys to the museum cabinets and doors and closets; you had to request permission from him to open a cabinet, and he required that his secretaries request paper clips from him rather than help themselves. He was an entomologist by training and had been hired in 1892 to oversee the management of the place and did such a good job at his menial tasks that he thoroughly impressed the equally controversial Alexander Agassiz, who had no interest in petty details. Henshaw had insisted, with constant wheedling, to have his title advanced from "assistant in charge" to "curator." This was essentially the same title held earlier by the world-famous naturalists Alexander and his father, Louis Agassiz, and it gave Henshaw, in effect, control of the whole museum, including the management of the generally independent-minded staff. Alexander Agassiz, who was arguably as skilled a naturalist as his father, and a world authority on coral reefs as well as embryology, tired of the details of the management and resigned in 1898, which catapulted Henshaw ever upward in the hierarchy.

Barbour had first visited the museum when he was 15 years old, and loved the place at first sight. He was such a sharp naturalist even at his young age that he recognized an error in the labeling on one of the exhibits and privately vowed that he would someday return to Harvard and become director of the museum. He was a New Yorker, from a rich family, and normally would have been bound for Princeton, but he came to Harvard instead to be near the collections and the renowned biologists associated with the research the museum was then carrying out. He somehow managed to have himself posted to Cuba during the First World War, the equivalent of the brier patch for him, given the number of as yet unidentified lizards and snakes on the island. He had rich friends; he was a crack biologist; he himself contributed funding to the museum through his family; he got along with people; and he had that insatiable curiosity and energy that often drive the likes of great naturalists such as Brewster and company. Furthermore, unlike anyone else at the museum, he got along with Samuel Henshaw, an art in itself.

When Barbour came back to the museum after the war, he was 25 years old, Henshaw was then 67. Everyone, from the president of Harvard College, A. Lawrence Lowell, on down to the secretaries, and probably Mr. Gilbert himself (although he wouldn't have mentioned it, even if asked), felt that the Henshaw regime had lasted long enough and that Barbour should assume the role of director. In fact he already was, de facto. Henshaw would never answer people's letters, would not respond to requests, and cloistered himself away from personal encounters so that staff members had to go through Barbour to negotiate their requests. Finally, in exasperation, Lowell came to Barbour to help him convince the little tyrant to retire. Barbour, incredibly, was sympathetic to Henshaw. He was a precise little old man, he said, who had no life other than the museum—in all of his thirty odd years there he had never taken a day of vacation. Barbour convinced Lowell to let him ride, and Henshaw held on for another ten years, supported by his ebullient, outgoing subaltern. When, in 1927, he was finally ordered to retire—he was by then 75 years old—he flew into one of his rages, turned on Barbour, his sole protector, spit his cobra venom, and walked out the door and (to no one's regret) never returned. He took with him stacks of documents from the museum and made a cold fire of them in his home. Reportedly the fire burned for two nights straight.

Gilbert came into the museum in the midst of all this and was taken under the vast protective wing—the bulk, actually—of Thomas Barbour, who was his junior by twenty-five years. There is a certain cosmic justice in the fact of Mr. Gilbert's employment there in these years. He was the first black person to work at the museum and the environment there was not particularly favorable to blacks, or for that matter anyone who was not Caucasian, or in fact, male. Harvard scientists, along with the staff of most other American institutions, had been deeply engrossed in the classification of races, an obsession that lasted well into the 1940s. There were still some American textbooks in the mid-twentieth century that placed Africans between Caucasians and gorillas on the evolutionary scale. In fact Gilbert's presence at the museum, not to mention his popularity there among students and staff, would have turned the gorge of the founder, Louis Agassiz.

Agassiz was one of those all-round naturalists favored by natural history museums of the time. He had come to Harvard to deliver the Lowell lectures in 1846 from his native Switzerland, where he had made a name in the scientific community for his studies in both geology and ichthyology, his primary field. He is considered, even today, the founder of the field of glacial geology, and he was one of the most respected, innovative scientists working in Europe at the time. He stayed on at Harvard after the lectures, established himself in the department of science, and in time founded the Museum of Comparative Zoology. When he died, in 1873, his son Alexander took over as curator.

Louis Agassiz did his most insightful work abroad while he was still young, but as he aged, he seemed to have become stuck in his opinions. He was notorious for his rejection of Darwin's theories on evolution, and he stubbornly maintained his position even after the scientific community came to embrace the theories. Furthermore, for all his good science, Agassiz was an abject racist who was repulsed by Negroes.

Stephen Jay Gould, another controversial Harvard professor who worked at the museum in the late twentieth century and who was a strident critic of the inherent racism of the early anti-evolutionists as well as contemporary creationists, unearthed and published in his 1981 book *The Mismeasure of Man* a damning passage from Agassiz, describing an early encounter with a perfectly innocent, probably gentlemanly, black waiter in Philadelphia:

> *. . . it is impossible for me to repress the feeling that they are not of the same blood as us. In seeing their black faces with their thick lips and grimacing teeth, the wool on their head, their bent knees, their elongated hands, I could not take my eyes off their face* [sic] *in order to tell them to stay far away. And when they advanced that hideous hand towards my plate in order to serve me, I wished I were able to depart in order to eat a piece of bread elsewhere, rather than dine with such service. What unhappiness for the white race to have tied their existence so closely with that of Negroes in certain countries! God preserve us from such a contact.*

This would be standard fare were it to appear in some Ku Klux Klan screed, but the fact that it was written by a man considered to be the father of American science is worrisome.

Agassiz carried his racism through his life, but although not on record that I know of, Alexander, who was widely traveled, was probably a little more tolerant. Henshaw was at least polite and tried to be fair, but he probably did not accept blacks as social equals. Barbour himself may have carried all the contemporary prejudices too, but he was far more worldly than any of the previous curators, having spent weeks in the field with people of various colors, hunting his lizards.

✠

I stepped into this somewhat cloistered world of the Museum of Comparative Zoology early on in my hunt for Gilbert. Shortly after my photographic land use project was completed, I took a job as research assistant for a man named Wayne Hanley, who worked at the Massachusetts Audubon Society and was writing a book to be called *Natural History in America.* My job was to scout out the artwork that would appear in his forthcoming book, and this begat many trips to the library of the MCZ, as the museum was called. It was during this time when I came to know Ruth Hill and an assistant named Ann Blum, who, among other useful contributions, discovered a Brewster photo album of a trip he had taken without Gilbert through the American South, down to Key West and on to Cuba. We were looking through this album one afternoon when I noticed a photograph of an ivory-billed woodpecker, a species that is now believed to be extinct. We also found the extensive diaries and journals of William Brewster with their meticulous accountings of bird arrivals, train schedules, and the daily comings and goings of Mr. Brewster and his associates.

It was in this collection that I also found one of the most reprinted photographs of William Brewster, a portrait by Gilbert of Brewster standing in front of one of the lodges somewhere in Maine, with his Belgian Back Action collecting gun crooked in his elbow and his rudder-straight nose poking out from a slouch hat with its brim folded back. He's in tweeds that day, and high boots, staring off at the forest beyond, and has a brace of ducks dangling from his left hand.

While I was working in the library looking for artwork to illustrate Hanley's book, it was my custom to take periodic breaks and go wandering through the inner sanctum of the back halls of the display rooms, where the offices of the biologists who worked at the museum were located. I was interested to note there, in the shadowed warren of narrow hallways, the tiny offices of some of the most famous names in American science: Stephen Jay Gould, E. O. Wilson, Ernst Mayr, and the ornithologist Richard Paynter. I asked Ruth Hill about the older biologists to see if I could find anyone who might remember Gilbert, but even though the museum tends to maintain its hold on employees, there weren't many left. Ernst Mayr had come to the museum in 1953, after Gilbert's death. Paynter, who arrived in the 1940s, had heard a lot about Gilbert, but never knew him. There was at the time an old entomologist, age 90, who still came to the museum every day to study his insect collections, but he had no memory of Mr. Gilbert—possibly not much accurate memory of anything, save insect genera.

During this time, through the auspices of a fellow researcher, I came to know a few of the scientists who used to inhabit the caves of the museum and was invited to join them at their regular midday meals in the Department of Malacology. These lunches were the remnants of midday meals established at the museum in the 1930s by Thomas Barbour and were held in what came to be known as the "Eateria," a wide, airy room set at the end of the museum and lined with Barbour's collected volumes on natural history.

In Barbour's time, these repasts were elaborate, prolonged Roman feasts, consisting of delicacies such as elephant's-foot stew, the meat of exotic snails, the sweetmeats of bush babies, and white grubs. Barbour himself was a prodigious eater and gourmand who would commonly down a quart of rum a day, and he presided over these meals with Rabelaisian gusto. The lunches began modestly enough with the installation of an electric stove and sink and refrigerator in the museum, but having discovered the culinary talents of Mr. Gilbert, Barbour soon expanded the festivities. Gilbert began preparing more and more inventive dishes, using first the meats from some of Barbour's local hunting expeditions—ducks, geese, medallions of venison, terrapin soup, and the like. News of the quality of the presentation began to spread and soon visitors from outside the department began to attend, and as the popularity of these lunches increased, Rosamond brought a parchment guest book to the Eateria and attendees began signing in with the dates. President Lowell was a regular there and would often bring important visiting dignitaries from around the globe to the lunches—world-renowned biologists from Western Europe, Japan, and China. In time the guest book accumulated the signatures of visitors from more than forty countries. At the same time, the exoticism of the dishes began to increase as foreign biologists imported delicacies from their own countries and as the wide-ranging Harvard botany staff began bringing home tropical fruits such as mangoes, white sapotes, agles, and canistels and other exotic fare as yet unknown in New England, or even North America. Each of these new ingredients represented a challenge to the resourceful Gilbert, who, using his own devices and recipes, managed to present savory new dishes.

One of his lunches was even written up in *Life* magazine in the 1940s. Photographs show Barbour at table—a vast Roman emperor with full cheeks and a mass of marble-gray curls, holding forth, no doubt, on the virtues of rum and Chinese frog stew with diced pig's ears and white grubs.

Gilbert, of course, was always there in the background, the invisible man as usual, but also as usual, the driver of the machine. He was versatile, able to switch menus or expand the quantities when it was announced to him that there would be ten more guests than expected that day. The few mentions of him in museum publications are couched in the race-tinged language of the period, "the loyal colored servant" with his "old fashioned courtly manners" and such like. He shadowed through the gatherings in his starched collars and his black suits, the silent presence, a mere adjunct as far as the collected dignitaries were concerned. As Gilbert himself used to tell people, with subtle self-mockery—he had been willed to the museum with Brewster's collection of birds skins.

No one took especial notice while he was there. But they noticed when he wasn't. After he died, the Eateria declined and eventually devolved to the old lunch hour of sandwiches and milk brought in from home.

The time I spent there was a period of upheaval in biological sciences. Up until the middle of the twentieth century, biologists based their work on field studies and were generally well-rounded, versed in botany, or mammalogy, as well as geology and herpetology and other fields unrelated to their own particular subject. But in the latter part of the century, as a result of the decoding of DNA and the subsequent advances in molecular biology, computers, new biometric tools, and quantitative methods began overtaking the adventurous world of field studies that had dominated the development of natural science in the past. It was no longer necessary to send bearded and bedraggled ornithologists and herpetologists out into the unexplored tributaries of the upper Amazon to collect original specimens to build museum collections; computers and molecular biologists could reveal yet undiscovered connections among life-forms by studying genetic codes in the sterile comfort of university laboratories—at less expense besides.

The old guard among the field staff of the Museum of Comparative Zoology, such as the ant specialist E. O. Wilson and the even more famous evolutionary scientist Ernst Mayr, who started the whole reexamination via genetics, were saddened by this decline. The lunchtime crew I was familiar with spent at least part of every meal peppering their dishes with laments for the decline of these expeditions to exotic, unexplored territories and the rise of a race of biochemical monks who now labored in laboratories filled with electronic devices. This decline was often contrasted with animated accounts of the grand museum expeditions of the past and the larger-than-life naturalists who were contemporaries of William Brewster. These included ichthyologists who scoured remote South Sea beaches and deep seas in search of unidentified species, malacologists who specialized in the parasites of extinct shellfish, famous bird collectors who were lost in the Amazonian tributaries, presumably eaten by cannibals, as well as authorities on the sex life of tamarin monkeys and on the deep-forest canopy flora of the Ituri forest in West Africa, and even students of psychoactive plants who, under the guidance of jaguar shamans and shape-shifters, had consumed all manner of bizarre mind-altering drugs. The consummate master of this latter group was Richard Schultes, a balding old man in steel-rimmed glasses whom I sometimes saw puttering around the museum's famous glass flowers collection. It was said that by the time he quit his field studies he had partaken of most of the known psychedelic drugs of Amazonia.

But the ultimate hero of the contemporary Eateria was the wandering naturalist Thomas Barbour.

In the autumn of 1906, Barbour married Rosamond Putnam, who was a child of one of the old Brahmin families and a woman more accustomed to the social subtleties of *thé dansants* than the fetid forests of Borneo. And yet, the day after their wedding Barbour announced to Rosamond that by way of honeymoon they would embark on an expedition to the Dutch East Indies, a journey that had surprised but not deterred the fair Rosamond. This singular expedition began a lifelong voyaging. On this first trip, Barbour was charged and nearly slashed to death by a wild boar in the Sundarbans, and brave Rosamond had risked her life prodding a cobra for an action photograph taken by her husband near Lucknow. Later on, in China, while he and Rosamond were ascending the Si-kiang River, a local warlord had offered to have two recently captured pirates released from their cages and brought down to the steamer to be beheaded for the entertainment of the visiting foreigners. Rosamond politely refused that particular offer.

On all of these voyages, through the West Indies, through South America, Africa, and the then no less exotic swamps of Florida, Barbour collected his frogs and salamanders and snakes and lizards. He was indefatigable, and Rosamond seems always to have been in on the action. Barbour took many photographs on these various voyages, mostly of his newly captured specimens, but included among the albums in the museum collections were a few photographs of his wife. You see her there, ever straight up, dressed in her ankle-length crepon cloth skirts and white cotton shirtwaist with her flat, wide-brimmed straw hat fixed firmly over her brow. She stands there on the island of Amboina, squinting in the sun, thigh to thigh with bare-breasted women and half-naked warriors with penis sheaths and huge curving boar tusks fitted through their noses—and she, a banker's daughter from Clarendon Street, more familiar with the delicacies of Lapsang souchong tea in Limoges cups than stews of still-paddling, fresh-caught frogs and roasted white grubs served with the meat of unidentifiable venomous snakes. At Japen Island, in the Dutch East Indies, one of their guides, Ah Woo, refused to go ashore inasmuch as too many Chinamen had been eaten there. At Wiak Island, as they approached the shore in their pulling boat, Ah Woo noticed that all the females of the tribe fled to their perched quarters and turned to stare back at them. Bad sign, he said, unfriendly males here, preparing for attack. No sooner had he spoken than a band of shouting, mop-headed natives, their nose tusks gleaming in the midday sun, appeared on the beach and began threatening them with spears.

✠

One of the presiding judges of these last days of Barbour's Eateria was a man named Richard Johnson who worked at the museum as an associate researcher in the malacology department. He was a 1951 graduate of the university who, not unlike Barbour, had started working for the department as a volunteer when he was 16 years old in the 1930s. He was subsequently drafted and sent overseas during the Second World War and then returned after the war to enter the college as a freshman. He was said to be a gentleman scholar of the old school who had produced more than fifty papers on malacology, most of which were published in scholarly journals of limited circulation devoted entirely to obscure species of bivalves, chitons, and snails and of no interest whatsoever to the general public. In the relatively cloistered world of shells, Johnson was a well-known character who smoked good cigars, had enjoyed a number of marriages, and even at age 70 liked to range through the New England countryside on his motorcycle. I was told by some of the other museum staff members that he was probably the only man left at the museum who might remember Mr. Gilbert. So I went to see him.

Johnson's office was located behind a steel door in the upstairs gallery in the hall of mammals, just off the right fin of a vast skeleton of a sperm whale, which is suspended below the ceiling and floats above the lower galleries wherein lie the mounted displays of okapis, guanacos, klipspringers, and, in a large glass corner case of its own, a huge mountain gorilla with its fangs bared, beating its chest. All of these beasts were tended to and even stuffed for display by the versatile Mr. Gilbert in his latter years at the museum.

Having gained entry into the halls of the cosseted mollusk department, and having negotiated a narrow labyrinth of halls, I came finally to a door marked "R. Johnson." There was a little ditty posted on the door that advised me that "if Johnson respondeth not, perhaps he is on a journey, or peradventure he sleepeth . . ."

I took a chance on awakening the sleeping scholar and knocked.

There was a scraping of chairs from inside the office and a rangy man with a shock of gray hair and horn-rimmed glasses, perched low on his nose, opened the door—very much awake.

Following my usual introductory method, I described my mission while Johnson eyed me cautiously, as if I were slightly mad. He was at first nonplussed by my quest and stood twisting a pen in his long fingers.

"A black man who was assistant to Barbour?" he asked. "Here, in this museum?"

"Yes," I said, "he is cited in papers and in his obituaries as assistant to the curator from the '30s up to 1941. That would be Barbour, no?"

"Yes, but a black man? A Negro curator in the 1930s? I doubt it. This is a natural history museum, you understand. Maybe he worked at the Peabody."

He was referring to the anthropology museum that is housed in the same building.

"No, it was here," I said. "He worked first for William Brewster, then came here after Brewster died. He must have been here off and on, because he appears to have also been in Europe after the war."

"Which war?"

"First."

"This man is old," he said. "I will confess to being long of tooth myself, but I'm not that old."

I explained that Gilbert had returned to the museum in the thirties.

He thought some more, rambling through the names of various workers he had known and then he nodded vaguely.

"Come to think of it," he said, "I do remember a black man here. But it's not the same person, I don't think. This man was a shuffling old Negro, like a porter on a train. He used to cook for Barbour and the distinguished guests of the Eateria, I think he was the one who was famous for his elephant's-foot stew, which was a favorite of the regulars there. I think he also cleaned the exhibits and built shelves, that sort of thing, but he wasn't a biologist, he wasn't trained, just an old loyal servant. He was a shadow figure here. You'd see him in the halls . . ."

So be it. But there were one or two things the white staff of the museum did not know about the quiet old serving man who cooked their exotic stews, puttered around the exhibits of mounted bongos, tree possums, and civet cats who still live on today, forever frozen in their cases, their dusty glass eyes fixed on some feral past.

CHAPTER TWELVE

Gilbert's Ghosts

PHOTOGRAPHS FURNISH EVIDENCE.

Susan Sontag

Lancaster, Massachusetts, in the early 1900s

By 1914, when the war began in Europe, Gilbert had become indispensable to the aging Brewsters. He had access to Brewster's Ford touring car at this time and made very good use of it. He's everywhere, doing everything. He drives out to Concord and to locate the wayward Patrick whenever he would disappear on a binge. He makes peace with the nasty Charles. He drives the dog Larry here and there, visits with ERS when she is sick, visits with Caroline when she is in the hospital. He brings Larry to her, leading him, his nails clicking, down the polished wood hallways of the hospital, and lifts him onto the bed to lick Caroline's cheeks. Then he's off to Wolfeboro for a time. Then he sees to Brewster's luggage for a sojourn at Doctor Gehring's, and while he's there he hikes along the shore, recording bird sightings for addition to Brewster's lists. Then he's off to Warren, New Hampshire, with his camera. He seems to have been in England at one point, when the Brewsters went over to see Caroline's brother and nephew, who were living in Surrey. He was with Caroline back in Cambridge when news came that her nephew was killed at Hill 47. He's in Belgium, toting bags. He's often in Washington "on private business," according to Brewster's journals. And time and time again he goes off to Lancaster, Massachusetts, in the Ford motor car to the estate of the Thayer family, who were very good friends of the Brewsters. Sometimes he drives the Brewsters there, sometimes he goes out on his own to deliver packages or to leave Larry off for care when the Brewsters are traveling or too scattered or too sick to take care of him.

The Brewsters and the Thayers would always spend Christmas together and sometimes even travel together. They were a wealthy New York family, distantly related to the American Impressionist painter Abbott Thayer. Their large estate was set on a hill to the northwest of the town and is now the headquarters for a center devoted to ayurvedic medicine—the once fashionable health guru Deepak Chopra had his offices there in the 1990s. Nowadays the place has a somewhat portentous cast; the grounds, although maintained, do not flourish with the same opulence as they did in Gilbert's time when the flowerbeds were extensive, the hedges neatly trimmed, and the trees and flowering shrubs were fresh and young.

In those decades, on arrival in the Ford car, Gilbert would pass through well-pointed stone gates, slowly putter upward, curving along the gravel drives, and pull to a stop with Larry, or the Irish terrier Timmy, release him and allow him to scamper over the grounds for an airing before reattaching him to his leash and conducting him up to the front door. On occasion here, Gilbert was greeted by a new white servant, who would instruct him to go around to the back to make his delivery, whereupon Mr. John Thayer, if he happened to be passing, would cancel the new servant's order and usher Gilbert in warmly. Like Brewster, like Harriet Hemenway, Thayer understood that you should not discriminate against black people. What they thought, of course, was one thing, but what they did was another.

One Sunday afternoon in early autumn, I drove out to the grand estate to pay a call, knowing full well that there was only one Thayer left in the town and that she lived down the hill, below the main house in the former horse stable and in fact preferred horses to people, I had heard. I had taken back roads out from Concord, following an old map someone had made for Gilbert, and once in the town I stopped to ask the locals for directions and collect gossip about the old estate. One of these informants was a long-haired man with a pudgy face who was sitting by a pond just on the outskirts of town. He told me the Thayer estate had now been taken over by immigrants and then proceeded to lecture me on U.S. immigration policy. Following this, he switched to the subject of turtles, which, he allowed, was his primary interest, following immigration issues. Then he launched into a diatribe against the local police, who, he said, had been trying to oust him from his housing unit.

I managed to extricate myself and drove on, and then, since I happened to be passing the police station, pulled in to ask more directions and see if they knew anything about the locally famous Thayer family. The dispatcher, an indifferent woman with bulging blue eyes and lacquered blond hair, wasn't able to help, but she did know the turtle man.

"That's just Kenny," she explained. "He's harmless, lives here on the dole and takes up half the town meetings trying to get the town to do something about immigrants."

"You have a lot of immigrants here?" I asked. Lancaster is a small rural town located in rolling, wooded foothills and did not seem to me to be a major center for immigration.

"No, but there are a lot of Africans and people from the Caribbean here at the school."

The town is also the home of the Atlantic Union College, which apparently has a high number of foreign students.

"Kenny, he doesn't seem to like the blacks," the dispatcher said matter-of-factly.

I was glad I had not explained my mission more fully to this Kenny.

I found my way up to the Thayer estate, turned in the gates and wound up the old drive to a somewhat bare, empty terrace. As is often the case with grand mansions that have been taken over by institutions, the welcoming and highly ornate main door, no doubt the pièce de résistance of the architect, was tightly sealed, and I had to wander around knocking on various nondescript side doors until I was finally admitted by a well-attired man of indeterminate Middle Eastern roots with impeccable manners and a loose wave of black hair falling over his left eye. I explained my purpose and was invited to review the books in an extensive library off the main foyer, but my guide explained that he knew nothing of the estate itself, or the family, having been there only a matter of months. He said I would be welcome to come back and review the books on the history of the building, but he believed that most of the records they had dealt more with the construction of the house and gardens than with people.

This was the second of my attempts to chase down the remnant Thayers. When I first uncovered the name in Brewster's journals, I had presumed that the better-known Abbott Thayer, who was associated with the Harvard museum, was Brewster's associate. Abbott was a member of the American Impressionist group of painters known as the "Boston Ten," some of whom, such as the painter Frank Benson, were friends with William Brewster. Abbott was also connected to the Boston-based art colony at Dublin, New Hampshire, which included a few renegades from the Brahmin class, such as the poet Amy Lowell.

The summer houses around the lake in Dublin are modest affairs generally, hardly the grand estates of the New York money, and in fact nothing like the Thayer mansion in Lancaster. Some of the Dublin houses are set back from the shores under ancient pines and maples, some lie on the low rises at the end of open pastures and have modest, curving drives.

Making my usual rounds one summer afternoon, after having brazenly wandered up to one or two of these summer houses asking about the Thayers, and once again having unsatisfactory results, I decided to go for a swim. I set out in a slow, four-beat crawl to the middle of the lake and then turned to look back at the great shark-fin rise of Mount Monadnock, which looms over the lake just to the southeast.

This was in late June, and the great green sweep of forest that rises up the northern slopes of the mountain was cool and brooding. Back on shore, I lingered for a while as evening approached and the surrounding woods began to ring out with the haunting, descending song of the veery and the fluted trilling of the wood thrush. I saw a spotted sandpiper teetering along the banks; earlier in the day, up in the woods, I had heard the "teacher" call of the ovenbird, had seen a Louisiana waterthrush, and had heard the slow, lazy song of the red-eyed vireo. It was all somber greens and browns in the woods, with bubbling streams heading downward toward the lake, large mossy boulders strewn about, and in some sheltered sections immense boles of craggy sugar maples. No wonder painters such as Rockwell Kent and Abbott Thayer were attracted to this place.

Thoreau visited Monadnock many times. Emerson came up here, and so did William Brewster. So did Mr. Gilbert, but except for a few references in the Brewster journals, the records of his sojourns here can only be determined by images: A running stream in nearby Jaffrey. The ground nest with eggs of a ruffed grouse. A close-up of a tame chipmunk, its paws raised to its mouth. More birds' nests with eggs. The massive trunk of an oak. The dark interior of the forest. Jack-in-the-pulpit in bloom. Bloodroot in bloom. Trout lily in bloom. It's late spring in the images and the forest murmurs, the green mosses glister, there are dripping springs with banks of Lilliputian forests of thuidium, wolf's claw, princess pine, and sphagnum, and all of it full and welling and rank with metaphor.

What did they see there? you have to wonder. Why did Brewster and Gilbert feel it necessary to record again and again the dense greenwood tangle of life? Why did these two so concentrate on running rivers and streams as subject matter? Was it all sad metaphor for the passage of time and a life, or was it perhaps some unrecognized attempt to halt the age and return to an older order of things, some prelapsarian world populated by innocent birds and chipmunks, where there were no debilitating bouts of diseases and, for Gilbert, no iron ceilings of racism pressing down on your every move.

This green world was not necessarily a transcendental paradise for them, I don't think. Brewster was indifferent to God, and Gilbert was a good Episcopalian, where man was at the top of the great earthly chain of being and was created in the very image of the

Father. No gods of nature in his philosophy, no paganism. But there had to have been something else that sucked the two of them down into this wild world, so far from Boston, so close to chaos.

The attraction may have been the very act of capturing the image, the art of seeing. This idea of "capturing" or "taking" a photograph, which these two so involved themselves with, is charged with overtones. Capture suggests the hunt, and hunting suggests a union or mergence with the subject. We "shoot" photographs. Even the popular term "snapshot," which arrived with the invention of George Eastman's mobile and facile Brownie camera in 1900, evolved from the hunt. In the end the photographer captures the prey, kills the subject, immobilizes it, and carries it home to the camp. The immortalized, frozen image can serve as a portal into another world, a threshold to transformation. All this puts the photographer in the position of shaman as well as hunter, the individual in a tribal group who is capable of altering realities and who can manipulate, through magical intervention, the basic elements of time and place, or even personality.

Gilbert and Brewster must have had something of the hunter and the shaman in them, even though they did not recognize it. They went out into the land and captured things. I believe that for Brewster, who was also a skilled bird hunter, the act of photographing represented the kill, the union with the beloved object, be it bird nest or running stream. But for Gilbert, it was perhaps something more, something ineffable, a matter of control or mastery of his environment, which, given the social conditions in which he was forced to live, he was unable to effect in everyday life. The photograph offered freedom. Furthermore, it was Gilbert who carried out what was, at the turn of the last century, the real art of the photograph, the development of the film and the printing. His was the art of shaping the final image. He was alchemist, magician, and shaman all in one. He set the aperture, flicked the shutter, flashed the prepared glass plate negative with the natural light of the sun, and carried home his prey, whereupon he entered into a dark cave of shadows, a half-lit *sanctus sanctorum,* where, through his alchemy, he reestablished (or reinvented) a world. And now, even though he is gone, and even though the world in which he lived has transformed itself into something that would be perhaps unrecognizable to Mr. Gilbert, we who have since appeared in this same environment can stand where he stood. It is the only way we can know him.

✠

After Brewster died in 1919, Gilbert took up teaching piano again. But all along while he worked for Mr. Brewster he had had ventures of his own. There are hints of this in the Brewster journals, one-line suggestions, three-word clues: "Gilbert's business venture not going well." "Gilbert is off to Washington." "Gilbert is in Boston on business." "Gilbert did not show up today." And, finally, at one point, the curious, suggestive line in a personal letter to a friend: "Gilbert seems to have left his ghosts in Washington."

What could that mean? I called Tremont Williams and we met for our ritual drink to analyze the facts, such as they were. I spelled out what I knew so far: That Gilbert had worked at the museum after Brewster died. That he played at being the cook, reverted to the role of servant, developed a step-'n-fetch-it shuffle, for all I know, and learned to say "Yessir" and "Nosir."

"I doubt that much," Tre said.

"Well just listen. Before Brewster died he used to run out to Lancaster all the time, taking the dogs back and forth and that sort of thing. That's a long drive around 1915; I even know the route. I found a little hand-drawn map made by one of the Thayers to help Gilbert find the place. He would follow Route 117 all the way west, went through Still River, Bolton, and Sterling. It must have been an all-day journey out and back."

"So he stopped along the way?"

"Yes."

"May have had car trouble?"

"Maybe."

"Maybe got to know some businesses out that way. Perhaps stopped at roadhouses?"

"Yes."

"He's got a good dog in the car, a classy breed. He's driving a good car. And he's a fine dresser?"

"Yes, all true."

"Black man with a high-breed dog, driving a regular route through the New England countryside in 1915. He was probably a known character out that way, maybe he set up his business around there. Go check related businesses, shoe polish manufacturers, that sort of thing. Go look in the Boston Library. Business directories, 1914 to 1920. You'll find something."

So we did that. Six more months of digging with the help of Ms. Brown—winter afternoons in the surrounds of bookshelves at the museum, library archives, blinding ourselves, turning over page after page of Brewster's tiny scrawlings—rainy mornings in the bureaucratic offices of the census bureau—cool autumnal afternoons at the Harvard Business School, reading over lists from business directories. We found a leather-dressing company in Leominster, which was close by and which was on a route Gilbert might have taken on his way to and from Lancaster. But the company manufactured a dressing for the leather car tops, not shoes. No shoe polish companies except for an obscure business that started up in Stow in the 1930s—too late for Mr. Gilbert. We made photocopies of the material we discovered. Filed them, began carrying around a fat notebook, jammed with disparate documents. And all the while we were both hunting down old people in Cambridge who might have known the man.

Gilbert's three daughters were remembered in Cambridge. One

went into the real estate business, one moved away to New York to teach, and the oldest, Mary, was still alive in 1992 and had married her third husband late in life, after her first two husbands died. His name was George Alexander and the two of them were members of a singing group known as The Silvertones that was organized by the local Salvation Army.

One day at the Salvation Army headquarters on Massachusetts Avenue, in Cambridge, I met with Major Susan, a tough-talking officer with short-cropped blond hair and full cheeks. She remembered Mary and knew that George had outlived her. After Mary died, he had moved away from Cambridge, she said, but she had no idea where he was.

As we were talking, a skinny black man in an oversized vest came out of an interior door, greeted Major Susan with a nod, and carried on.

"Randolph," Major Susan commanded. "You remember old George Alexander. Where'd he go to, do you know?"

The old man stopped in midstep and thought for a minute.

"George? He left town. But I don't hear he's dead. Not yet anyway."

Major Susan turned to me.

"He says George has left town but since he hasn't heard or read any news, he's probably still alive."

"How old would he be, do you know?" I asked, directing my question to the old man.

"George?" he said. "He's old now. He must be 110 years old if he's a day." He chuckled to himself.

"He says he's very old, could be a hundred," Major Susan said.

The old man dared to break in and offer information, directing himself to me now.

"He had a stepdaughter from the islands. Madeleine somebody, but I don't know her last name. Wilson maybe?"

Major Susan glared. "That's right," she said. "Madeleine Wilson."

Out from the same door there now appeared another old man, who touched the first man lightly on the back as he passed and said good-bye.

"Henry, whatever happened to old George Alexander? He move away? Or did he just up and die?" Randolph asked.

"George? George Alexander? He in't dead, should be, though; he must be two hundred year old by now. He's living over in Roxbury somewhere. Lives with his daughter Madelon somebody."

"Wilson?" I asked.

"Yes," he said, then corrected himself. "No. Winston. Like Churchill."

"This man here is looking for him," Major Susan said. "He knew Mary's father."

He looked me over careful and nodded cynically.

"Uh-huh, sure enough," he said incredulously.

Anyone with lucid memories of Mr. Gilbert would have to be at least eighty years old by that time. I didn't fit the bill.

I corrected the misunderstanding and asked some more detailed questions, and all the while, having been shuffled to the sidelines, Major Susan stood by, overseeing the conversation.

In the end I located George Alexander and on a snowy February afternoon went to see him. I brought my camera along.

The first image—shot quickly through the rain- and sleet-speckled window of the car—shows a dark rain of snow and sleet, cars sloshing by, narrow streets, and narrow yards with hurricane fencing and the dead stalks of marigolds making inverted V's over crusted snow.

Then a dog nosing a fire hydrant. He has a white body and a brown saddle on his back. Lifts his leg. Moves on.

Two black girls approaching in puffy winter coats, scarves

twisted around their necks. Tight jeans. One is laughing so hard she has doubled over and has to hold onto the arm of her friend. When they see me they straighten up and walk on by, glance back after they've passed.

Another: A huge sheeting spray of slush hitting the window of my car as a delivery truck slashes by at what the police would term "a high rate of speed."

The path was concrete, cleared of snow, the house had a glassed-in front porch, and inside there were shovels and a flat broom, neatly stacked in one corner. Old Christmas decorations placed there with the intention of storing them somewhere else. A small, island-dark woman in a gray suit answered the bell. This was Madelon Winston, aged 72, the stepdaughter of George Alexander. Behind her, nodding expectantly, was a frail, cocoa-colored man dressed in a tan shirt, a gaily decorated necktie, and wire-rimmed glasses, low on his nose. This was George Alexander, 99 years of age, third husband of Gilbert's third daughter.

Inside, the room was warm: the smell of chicken soup and sweetened pork. The dining room table was set for an apparent dinner party to come, or one that had passed, or was, perhaps, a permanent installation—flatware, an old tea urn in the middle of the table, stacked plates with blue floral circular trim, and old Christmas cards scattered on the white damask tablecloth. On the walls, framed photographs: Madelon at graduation, obscure family members, Gilbert's daughter, Mary, a print of Jesus, and a scene of an all-white New England rural winter, complete with steepled white church. The couch where I was instructed to sit was old and well broken in. We were close to one another, his sharp elbows leaning into my arms, his knees and upper thigh sometimes pressed against mine, as if for warmth. He had a fresh, salty smell of something I couldn't place, something familiar from my childhood. I had been in these rooms before with my father, who used to make rounds, visiting with black families. We would sit on striped couches, the arms covered with crocheted antimacassars, and the adults would sit upright with good posture and speak formally to one another about matters that I could not comprehend except that I would know, having been forewarned by my father, that someone in the family had recently died, or that somewhere in an upstairs room someone was gravely ill.

Madelon gave us tea, sweet cakes, and cookies. She was from the Caribbean and was once a ward of the state before she was adopted by George and his first wife. She was businesslike and indifferent to intimacies—this was not her family, after all, and she had turned fifty by the time her adoptive father married Mary. Nonetheless, it was she who was the final guardian of the family papers.

Finally, after all the small talk and the preludes and the explication of my mission, the point of my visit. Did he remember Mr. Gilbert, and what was he like?

Mr. Alexander began verifying little facts we had been accumulating all along the way: that Mr. Gilbert was a perfect gentleman of the old school type, that he was of small stature, that he was always well attired, soft-spoken and well spoken, a pianist and a photographer, and that, in his time with Mr. Brewster, he had traveled widely.

"Was he ever in Paris, do you think?" I asked, following up on Sanfred Bensen's anecdotal biography of Gilbert.

"He was," Mr. Alexander said definitively. "He often went abroad. He traveled a great deal with his employer, who was a professor at Harvard University. Mary told me he went everywhere with the professor. He had been in the north and seen many wild animals—moose, even bears."

I pressed on. "But he was in Paris, too?" I asked.

"Oh yes, he used to tell us about it," he said. "He traveled everywhere. He would go away, I don't why, and then he would come back and tell us about his travels and his adventures."

"Did he ever go to Stockholm?" I asked.

"I imagine so. Paris, London. He could even speak French; he used to teach French words to the children, and he had many adventures on his travels."

"What kind of adventures, do you know?"

But here he hit a dead end.

"Oh, I don't remember, do I? He had so many in his life. It was in Norwell, mostly, I would see him. We used to meet in Norwell, on the beach, and I worked at the dairy in those days. I filled the milk cans. This, you see, was a very long time ago. I am ninety-nine years old and will be one hundred in June and before I married Mary we knew each other as children, but we lost our partners and so we knew each other again. She was a singer and beautiful lady, and she moved like a dancer when she walked. At least when she was young. I remember the way she walked on the beach. Later, she had that cane, you know."

All the while Madelon had been shuffling around the room, pulling out drawers and carrying manila folders to the couch where we sat. Periodically she would select a photograph or an obituary from one of the folders and pass it over to us.

There was one in particular she was hunting for, a snapshot of Mr. Gilbert on a beach, dressed as usual in his formal dark suit.

"You remember that one?" she said to her stepfather.

"That one on the beach?"

"Yeah, with his hat pushed back," she said.

They both began to laugh.

"Why was that one funny?" I asked.

"He was dancing," Madelon said.

"You never did see that man dance," said Mr. Alexander, laughing again. "And he's cutting up for the camera. Only time in his life, I s'pect."

They brought out a photograph of Mary taken by Gilbert in Warren, New Hampshire, when she was two years old, and then another of Mary, some eighty years later, on her wedding day with George. She's in a shiny pink rose dress, emerging from a limousine, supported by the driver, a natty slim man who seems to be enjoying the honor of his work. She holds his arm, bending slightly forward and laughing broadly. Silvery gray hair curls, wide cheekbones. It is summer in Cambridge. Mr. Alexander, the groom, is offstage. The event is such that it warrants a news story in the *Cambridge Chronicle*. Both celebrants were in their eighties and well known in the black community.

"She was proud that day," Mr. Alexander said. "She walked to the altar without her cane, straight, shoulders back."

"Mary always could sing," Madelon said.

"She had the sweetest voice," Mr. Alexander said. "We met through the Silvertones."

Outside it was now snowing hard, but I was reluctant to leave. It was warm indoors, the tea and sweet cakes had made me sleepy, and the afternoon rolled slowly along and no one seemed in a hurry. Madelon passed over more news clippings, documents, Gilbert's obituaries, many of which I had seen. Then she handed me a Xeroxed page with another obituary, which I had also seen before. Just as I was about to pass it back, she pointed to a label at the top of the page that she had also photocopied.

"You see this one?" she asked.

It was the label from a shoe polish can: "Gilbert's Shoe Dressing: Lightning speed . . ."

The label showed a rising sun trademark with the lettering beneath. Directions for use were printed below with detailed instructions.

"So he made shoe polish?" I asked rhetorically.

"That was his business once," George said. "He made all kinds of money on that shoe polish, then he went and lost it all."

✠

Snow was falling all across Boston now, snow upon snow. It had covered the cars in the driveway, the plows had yet to pass on the side streets beyond the steamy windows, and the world had shocked out to a blurry white, interrupted with the dark structured angles, horizontals, verticals, and solid squares of buildings. We three were suspended briefly in a frozen image in the tea-baked odor of the moment, cut off from the silenced city beyond.

CHAPTER THIRTEEN

Ain't We Got Fun

A PHOTOGRAPH IS NEITHER TAKEN NOR SEIZED BY FORCE. IT OFFERS ITSELF UP. IT IS THE PHOTO THAT TAKES YOU.

Henri Cartier-Bresson

Coppiced willows, undated and unidentified, but probably Great Meadows, Concord, Massachusetts

One winter I lived in a one-room cabin without running water or electricity. It was set in a hickory grove about three hundred yards back from a paved road and when the first snows fell, as they did early that year, I would sometimes become encased in the cabin. Not that I minded, I had gathered about me there a large number of eclectic books, and I spent most of the winter reading—everything from the collected works of Lafcadio Hearn, to natural history volumes dealing with moths and butterflies, to obscure travel diaries.

Along with these books, I found myself rereading many of the old classics that I was supposed to have studied in college. One of these was F. Scott Fitzgerald's *Tender Is the Night,* which made especially pleasant reading on sleety afternoons, with its evocation of the hot light of Antibes and the Cote d'Azure and the degenerate, hedonistic life of the collection of expatriates who gathered at La Garoupe beach in the late 1920s. I remembered, probably from college days, that Fitzgerald tended to rework his own life into his fiction and that most of the characters in his novels could be identified. The central character of Dick Diver and his wife, Nicole, for example, are a combination of the famous expatriate couple Gerald and Sarah Murphy and Scott and his wife Zelda. The drunken Abe North is supposedly based on Fitzgerald's friend, the sportswriter Ring Lardner.

Things go well for this group of characters as long as they are in the south. But in the second half of the novel, after they all move up to Paris, the action begins to spiral down, with drunken forays, pointless shopping sprees, eventual madness on the part of Nicole, and a descent into drunkenness by Dr. Diver, who started the whole group rolling.

I was in the midst of one of the Paris scenes one Sunday afternoon and came across a passage that snapped me out of my winter dreams and set me on a more intensive hunt for Mr. Gilbert.

The episode concerned a dispute in a café in Montparnasse. In the narrative, Nicole Diver was awakened in her hotel room by a handsome Paris police official who questioned her concerning the whereabouts of her friend Abe North. It seems that North had been robbed the night before and had filed a complaint and the policeman said they had arrested the miscreant and wanted North to come down to the station and file the charges. Later in the morning, North appeared at the hotel, accompanied by a black man from Stockholm named Jules Peterson. North explained that Peterson was in trouble and that he, North, was the cause of it all and needed help. It seems that North was in a bar in Montparnasse, drunk as usual, and a Negro had snatched a thousand-franc note from his hand and disappeared. North went to the police, accompanied by Peterson, who had witnessed the incident. They returned to the bar with the police agent and too hastily identified the perpetrator as a man who had only entered the bar after North left. A dispute began, there were accusations, and then the police complicated the situation by arresting a prominent black bistro owner named Freeman. In fact, the crowd at the bar insisted, the thousand-franc note had only been taken from North to pay for the drinks he had already consumed. With the black clients now up in arms against him, and Freeman hauled off to jail, North fled the scene accompanied by Jules Peterson, who had assumed the role, Fitzgerald writes, of the friendly Indian who had helped a white man. Now the raucous blacks were more out to get Peterson than to get North.

In the hotel scene, North ushers Peterson into the room to meet Dick Diver and Nicole. Peterson is described as "a small respectable Negro on the suave model that heels the Republican party in the border States . . . ," which is to say, a literate, ambitious, middle-class black man with aspirations of equality.

The next line gave me a jolt.

"Up in Stockholm," Fitzgerald writes, "Peterson had failed as a small manufacturer of shoe polish, and now possessed only his formula and sufficient trade tools to fill a small box. . . ."

I stopped reading, went to the window, and watched the sleet hammer down. It rattled on the roof of the cabin, and beyond a little pasture, the wall of the sleet-patterned forest assumed a dense, stippled look. How many American blacks in 1927 failed as manufacturers of shoe polish in Stockholm and ended up in Paris?

Peterson must have been based on Mr. Gilbert.

It seems that my first and singular account of the life and times of Mr. Robert A. Gilbert, delivered to me by an old hermitlike farmer who could stand in one place and tell stories one after the other for two hours without tiring, was proving true in almost every detail. Sanfred Bensen had told me that Gilbert was the jack-of-all-trades for Mr. William Brewster, that he ran October Farm, and that he went everywhere the great white man went. Then I found the evidence of this in the form of Brewster's journals, which chronicled, day after day, year after year, for twenty years, the comings and goings of Gilbert. He was, as Bensen said, everywhere.

Mr. Bensen told me that Gilbert had graduated from Harvard. He didn't actually graduate, I learned, but he was very much associated with Harvard. He knew, among other dignitaries, the president of the university. He knew Thomas Barbour, and the former curator, Samuel Henshaw, and the head of the ornithology department, Joel Asaph Allen. Bensen said that Gilbert was a favorite of the Brahmins and their associates. Gilbert knew Daniel Chester French, and R. H. Dana, Harriet Hemenway, and the ornithologist Frank Chapman of the American Museum of Natural History. He met Rudyard Kipling, who was an acquaintance of Brewster's. He was with Brewster the day Brewster met President Teddy Roosevelt and probably had a few words with him about wildlife. In short, as Bensen had told me, "He knew many world famous people. . . ."

And now, just as Bensen said, here he was in Paris, having failed as a shoe polish manufacturer, and having fallen in with a low group of "musicianers."

Long before there was a Jules Peterson character, Fitzgerald had wanted to have a murder at the core of *Tender Is the Night.* He decided to use the Peterson scene to create one.

The young movie star Rosemary Hoyte, as well as the Divers and North, were all staying in the hotel together. In the hotel room, with Peterson now present, Diver tried to straighten out the matter. He encouraged Abe North to go sleep it off first and attend to the problem later, but North argued, saying that there were innocent Negroes now in jail. Seeing the complicated situation (and true to Gilbert form), Jules Peterson politely excused himself and said he would wait in the hall while they decided what to do. When North finally departed, still garbled and drunk, Peterson was no longer in the hall. Later Rosemary Hoyte burst in and made Dick return to her room with her. There, stretched out on the bed, was Jules Peterson, dead. Apparently, as North had predicted, he had been tracked and killed by one of the irate blacks of Montparnasse.

It's a bit of an outrageous scene—after all, how many murders occur in upscale Paris hotels—but the event marks a turning point in the novel and, in the seventy-odd years since *Tender Is the Night* was published, scholars and critics have analyzed the scene meticulously and have come up with a variety of imaginative interpretations, everything from a reversal of the Emancipation Proclamation to an interracial psycho-sexual drama—a dead black man on the bed of a white vedette. The whole of *Tender Is the Night* is a confusion of events, national identities, races, and all of it played against the background of the hot, jazz-driven, champagne-fueled age.

The portrait of Robert A. Gilbert delivered to us at the hands of Mr. F. Scott Fitzgerald is hardly a favorable one, nor is it a particularly egalitarian portrait of black people in general, but the scene has to be viewed from the perspective of Scott Fitzgerald, the context of the novel, and the period of history in which it was written. Inasmuch as he gave the matter any thought at all Fitzgerald seems to have accepted, without examination, all the engrained stereotypes of deeply seated American racism—spelled out in the extreme by the beloved scientist of an earlier era, Louis Agassiz. This was, unfortunately, the norm in the United States. Those who were not racist, or at least tried not to be, as with, perhaps, some of the Boston Brahmins, were the anomalies.

To be kind about the matter, you could say that Fitzgerald used black people as a metaphor. According to critics, the presence of Negroes in a scene tended to indicate a crack in the thin cover of civilization. They represented an older, more chaotic order. Ironically, he did the same thing in reverse with very white people. All the social climbing newcomers at La Garoupe beach, for example, the destroyers of the civilized, cultured, and spirited world of Dick Diver, are pale and pasty, whereas the fashionable crowd in the novel are all tanned and colored by the sun. Rosemary Hoyte, happening upon this group in the opening scenes of the story, immediately gets a sunburn; she joins the crowd in other words. (She also knows how to swim. Those in the inside group all know how to swim. The *arrivistes* don't.)

✠

The long party in Paris of which Fitzgerald and company were so much a part began on a hushed November day in 1918. Edith Wharton was living in Paris at the time, in a quiet quarter on the Rue de Varennes. By 1918, she and the other members in her floating salon had become accustomed to the dull thud of cannonades and the deep-throated roar of the Germans' huge, distant cannon, Big Bertha, whose deathly trajectory permitted shells to fall on Paris. But on this particular day, from the open windows of her flat, Wharton heard an altogether different sound. It was the familiar bell of the nearby Sainte Clotilde, ringing at an odd hour. She went out on the balcony and listened. The cannon throb and the roar of Big Bertha had stilled, and all across the city she could hear, one after another, the bells of Paris starting up—first Saint Louis, then, more distant, Saint Sulpice, then Saint Etienne du Mont, and, farther off, Sacré Coeur, the Madeleine, and finally, joining the chorus, the deep solemn voice of Notre Dame itself. The bells began tentatively, one following the other until all of Paris consisted of bells—a huge, joyous chorale that rang like rain from the skies.

The people of the city had lived for four years for this moment. The chorus of church bells could mean only one thing; the war was over. From that date forward, for the next ten years, it was a madcap joyride in a fast Bugati.

✠

You can find evidence of the decade-long party in old photographic prints in the bookstalls along the Left Bank of the Seine:

Here's a dark-haired woman in a bar with her right arm draped around the shoulder of an effeminate dandy with painted lips, manicured nails, and a monocle. He leans forward, kissing her cheek. She's just lifting a glass of champagne to her lips: Montmartre, 1928.

Another shows two pretty women in cloche hats at an indoor table at the Coupole, also dated—Montparnasse, 1926. There is a man with the two women, dressed in a wide-brimmed slouch hat with a leather band and a square watch that looks like a Bulova. On the table in front of them is an open bottle of champagne in an ice bucket. One of the women is lifting her glass seductively to the cameraman.

Here's the bar at the Rotonde, also in Montparnasse. Crowded that night: three women, one with a drawn-back Spanish-style hair-do, the other two in cloche hats, their arms draped around a man with owlish black-rimmed glasses and straight bangs, his hat pushed to the back of his head. Behind him a man in his cups, eyes half-closed, barely able to stay on his feet. Sugar shakers on the polished wood bar. Empty glasses, spilled beer on the counter, everyone drunk. Later, perhaps, on a lark, this group will descend to one of the so-called "interchange" clubs, Le Monocle maybe, a famous lesbian nightclub with an all-woman band and tough-guy singers who pretend to beat up their female partners—who, in this case, could just as well be some man in drag—or was it a woman, playing a man, playing a woman. Nobody cared.

Maybe the group would go up to Pigalle, or the Rue St. Denis and hire a whole troop of *putains* to make a *quadro,* all of them naked and piled together, performing despicable acts with one another, and maybe one of the crowd spills red wine down his shirtfront and someone else is sick, and there is some shouting and the madame comes in and chases everyone out and it's night again in the streets, or is that light in the east the dawn and has yet another night in Paris in 1927 come to an end. Nobody gave a damn, nobody cared; the war was over and what could be worse than that war, with all the pretty young boys dying with the mud of Verdun in their mouths, and gas, and people without legs coming home, sons dead, millions of sons dead, and then, thank God, the sun goes down and here comes another night and it's off to the Rotonde to have a drink and get started all over again.

The party seemed unstoppable. It was the short, sweet decade that the French came to call *"les Années Folles."* Even their president was crazy, would act a bit odd at times, was overly theatrical in his speeches, played to an approving crowd, and was once found near some railroad tracks wandering around in his pajamas. His claim was that he had fallen off a train. Nobody cared. And so it was off to the Beaumont Ball—1927—prancing horses, demimondaines, transvestites, *artistes* of all sexual persuasions, and champagne, of course, always champagne, every night champagne. Or they'd go off to the silly bourgeois Bal des Loufoques in Montmartre, or over to La Baker's club or go looking for the white Russians and the cocked-hat accordion players and violinists making people weep with their renditions of "Dark Eyes" and "Little Snowbell." Or they'd go up to Montmartre again to the Hot Club or the Jazz Hot, or go slumming with the apache dancers, or maybe go over to the really sick club where the abortionist and Irish tenor homosexual Dr. Maloney held his nightly parties. Nobody cared. They could find something. On almost any night in Paris between the wars there would be a fancy dress ball, Egyptian pharaohs, bare-bosomed harem girls, many Mandarins, African medicine men, Cleopatras with real vipers, powerful mustachioed men in drag, jungle men and clowns and overweight ballerinas, Red Indians, and Roman warriors and gorillas in checked suits, dancing up a storm.

These were the American years in Paris, the era of the Lost Generation and its followers, of whom, it should be said, there were many. The American expatriates felt that anything was possible in Paris. They were away from the restrictions of home. They learned about free love and nightclubs where men dressed up like women, and what's more, you could drink anything you wanted in Paris, even absinthe if you could find it. Back home, after 1919, it was against federal law to have a drink. In Paris it was de rigueur. The Americans were tolerated by the French—generally—but they were not a particularly civilized lot. The rowdy, would-be artists fought with each other, they beat up bartenders, they got themselves arrested and abused by the French police. They pissed so often in the streets that the police slang of the period had a code for them—yet another *pisseur américain,* they would write in their record books. One of the worst behaved of this group was F. Scott Fitzgerald, who was so rude when he was drunk that it was said he had been punched in the nose by every taxi driver in Paris. The nightclub owners knew all the cutups, and on occasion, when they saw trouble brewing from a particular American client, they would have the waiters serve up a Mickey Finn for his next drink.

The visiting Americans may have relaxed many of their old inhibitions on arriving in the night world of Paris, but there was one taboo that was perhaps so deeply rooted that it was difficult for even the most liberated of them to let go of entirely, one social stricture that still lingered and about which the French, in their decadence, did nothing. Drunks and spitting clochards the Americans could handle, opium, cocaine, homosexuals, and lesbian whores, petty criminals, filthy pictures, men in gorilla suits, they became accustomed to. But they had a problem with the large company of free-wheeling, uppity, seemingly enfranchised American Negroes who had been loosed on the streets of Paris in these years. If you wanted to be bad, really bad, you could associate with them. Scott Fitzgerald's wife, Zelda, who was from the South (and happened also to be crazy), danced with one once at a nightclub, causing a scandal among the visiting tourists.

The French, with typical laissez-faire, allowed the resident American blacks to attend the same dance clubs as the whites; they ate in the best restaurants, and they sat table to table with trim little families from Illinois and Georgia as if—well—as if it were their right to be there. What was worse, what really must have galled the Americans, is that the French, with their infamous degeneracy, actually enjoyed them. Some had even married Negroes after the war, an act that was illegal in most of the United States until 1967.

One night in the mid-twenties, the Théatre des Champs Élysées staged a show called *le Revue Nègre.* It was a short performance, no more than an hour or so, and it had an all-black, mostly American cast. The show was attended by a number of influential painters and writers and was risqué, of course, they all were, but something happened that night that had not so far occurred in the other revues in town, something that struck a chord. The crowd wouldn't stop clapping after the show, and those who didn't clap shouted with outrage, and there was a curiously loud and sustained applause and many bravos for one performer in particular, a 19-year-old bright-eyed black girl from St. Louis with a crazy dance style named Josephine Baker. After that night, Paris never could get enough of "La Baker." France could not get enough of "La Baker." She was so popular that shops actually sold little black dolls named "Josephine," and fifty years later in Paris you could bring tears to the eyes of old men with long memories by simply asking questions about her. She reminded them of their youth and les Années Folles.

For all their popularity with the French, the American blacks in Paris were no better behaved than the white revelers, maybe even a little worse. They too stuck together in their own district, mainly around Montmartre, a quarter that housed many artists and writers but was also plagued by racketeers and petty gangsters, and was one of the hangouts for many American black jazz musicians. All these lowlife types were armed with one manner of weapon or another. The underworld thugs of Paris used to carry knives to do their work, but by the twenties pistols, a Chicago import, began to be the weapon of choice, with, of course, much deadlier consequences. Many of the American jazzmen packed heat, as the American expression had it, and sometimes used their weapons. The popular clarinetist Sidney Bechet got eleven months in jail for a little shooting spree he participated in after an all-nighter at a club where he was playing. And then, perhaps reluctantly, the authorities exiled him. He came back, though, in the 1950s. Who wouldn't have?

A contemporary African American minister named Henry Hugh White, who visited France after the war to observe the situation of blacks abroad, wrote a book called *Between White and Black* about the American Negroes in France. He believed that the French and the African Americans had somehow found in each other a kindred spirit and that there was an almost spiritual connection between the French of that period and American blacks, an affinity of some sort that affected both cultures during this period of history. "They are both emotional, artistic, musical, fun-loving, and religious," he wrote. None of which was necessarily true, but the statement sums up the zeitgeist of Paris in the 1920s (except perhaps for the religious part).

✠

It is not likely that you could find two cities as disparate as Paris and Boston in these years. Back in Gilbert and Brewster's world the ever-vigilant Watch and Ward Society, which was founded to protect family life in New England, or more accurately to keep Puritans pure, was censuring movies, plays, and literature. The Society was founded in 1878 and, among other works, promptly suppressed Whitman's *Leaves of Grass.* 1927 was a banner year for the group, no less than sixty-eight volumes were skewered, including the Paris authors John Dos Passos and Ernest Hemingway. Drinking of even so refined a beverage as a good claret was against federal law by 1919, and the speakeasies were subtle in Boston and well-obscured.

In Paris the party was still going on, ever increasing in degeneracy and frenzy as the end drew near. And now, into this tumultuous scene, in 1927 there comes a small well-tailored Boston black man, dressed in old-fashioned starched shirts and a high collar, with a little suitcase of goods and a ramrod-straight walk. He's 56 years old now and wears steel-rimmed glasses and has a high, balding forehead. And here he comes down the Boulevard des Italiens. He passes the Café de la Paix, looking over the happy throngs of white, recently arrived tourists. He has heard that if he sits there long enough he will eventually see someone he knows. But he knows also, having spent some time by now in Paris, that whomever he recognizes there will be someone from Boston, from the Brahmin world of Brewster. He pauses, thinking to take a citronade, and then proceeds down l'Avenue de l'Opéra and along the river, which he crosses eventually on the Pont du Carousel.

It was near here, on a February evening, earlier in the year when Gilbert first arrived, that he came upon a bizarre scene, as strange as anything he had yet encountered in this strange and otherworldly city. He was stopped by a procession of young people in a variety of spangled costumes and outrageous hats and wigs. They were led by a bare-breasted woman riding on an elephant and wearing a long blue wig. Ahead of her was a blackfaced white man dressed as an African chieftain in leopard skins, waving a threatening spear at the curious passersby, and behind the elephant stretched a long dragon-like float and behind the dragon, bowing to the sidewalks, was a man wearing a collar of dead pigeons, carrying a bag of living snakes. He was followed by shocking lines of costumed dancers and chanting faux priests, nuns, and monks, more bare-breasted women dressed as Algerian harem girls, a few pharaohs striding regally along, and finally files of marching dogs, leashed and dressed for the occasion in flaring ruffled circus collars and pointy hats.

Gilbert watched as the troop passed, singing, hammering cymbals, and pounding drums.

"Qu'est-ce que c'est?" Gilbert asked a passerby in his halting French. *"Qu'est-ce qui se passe?"*

"Ce n'est rien," the pedestrian said. *"C'est le Bal des Artistes."*

Once he's over on the Left Bank, Mr. Gilbert cuts through the Rue Jacob where, he has heard, an odd, very rich American woman named Natalie Barney lives. She is (so Gilbert has heard) a woman who attracts to her person a number of artists and writers and he has heard that she prefers women to men. He walks slowly up the Rue de Rennes, glancing to left and right. It's March, and all through the Latin Quarter the tables are strewn all over the sidewalks and the shock-haired students and poseurs are all there, drinking coffees and *demis* of beer—most of them white. At the Rue de Fleurus he pauses again. There is another odd American woman living down there someplace. She cuts her hair short like a man and lives intimately with another woman and inside her flat, or so he has heard, there are some very strange paintings—broken, jagged images, and distorted people with African eyes, three noses and four eyes, going every which way. Americans gather here as well, white ones from the Midwest mostly (so he has heard).

He carries on, and at the Boulevard Raspail comes upon a collection of crowded cafés. Here they are again, an older crowd of Americans, English, Italians, and French, more weathered out than the students, and slightly more wasted from drink and too many all-night parties, only this time there are also a few black faces. He looks over the crowd at the Rotonde—all sorts there too, the noisy Americans all sitting together at one side of the café. A few blacks, also noisy. He does not like their loud, braying laughter. While he's standing there a man in a wide-checked suit and a big gorilla mask stumbles out onto the street accompanied by a woman with loose hair. They're laughing and dipping and grabbing each other indecently. Gilbert averts his eyes, turns down the Rue Delambre, and goes into a place he knows called the Dingo Bar and, speaking in English, orders his citronade.

The bar man there is friendly, Gilbert has been here before and he even recognizes some of the faces. There's a big barrel-chested white man with a brush moustache he sometimes sees, who seems to be respected by the other whites. There is a French woman with black bangs who is apparently attached to a narrow-faced American man who is (so he has heard) some kind of photographer who creates pictures that are as strange as the paintings in the short-haired woman's apartment. Someone told him that for three francs his woman friend, whose name is Kiki, would reveal her breasts to anyone in Paris. Sometimes in here Gilbert has seen a friendly drunken American man with strawberry blond hair who seems to be slightly richer than the others, but is loud, makes a fool of himself, and demands club sandwiches from the barman any time of the day or night.

Among this same crowd he has also encountered American Negroes. Back home he would avoid this type. They're loud, they drink a lot, and talk about books and jazz, and some are from the northern cities in the Midwest, and there are also some low types there from the cotton belt. But they all speak his language, and he falls into conversation with them, asks questions. He is looking for work, needs money.—What you do?—they ask—I am a pianist—he says in his straight-shot broad A'd northern accent, and they name a few spots, none of which appeals to the classically trained Mr. Gilbert. But then another man comes in. He's a light-skinned fellow with a pencil-thin moustache, well-attired in a houndstooth sport coat. He and Gilbert start to talk and Gilbert can hear his refined accent, no trace of the giveaway southern drawl. He is, unlike the others in the bar that day, an educated man, and it turns out he went to Harvard, where he had earned a master's degree in English. He's a lot younger than Gilbert, but he knows Cambridge, and even though he doesn't know anything about the museum and has never heard of Brewster or even Barbour, he has met President Lowell, and so has Gilbert (sort of), having served him elephant's-foot stews (except that he doesn't make clear). The two of them have a lot to talk about. This man is not the low type of barfly that Gilbert has been meeting in Paris. He tells Mr. Gilbert that he has come to the bar only because there are a few American literati there whom he knows. He's modest, a published poet, and he's refined and knows another side of Paris. His name, he says, is Countee Cullen and he knows (sort of) the man with the strawberry blond hair (but tries to avoid him) and also Langston Hughes, the poet, and what's more, he is married to the daughter of W. E. B. Du Bois. He gives Gilbert some leads. And in time, Gilbert was able to move from his squalid three-franc-a-night closet in Montmartre to a long-term Right Bank hotel, where other blacks were then living. Not far away is the fancy upscale hotel where that silly young cutup Josephine Baker lives.

While he was living in the cheap Montmartre hotel room, there were, perhaps, some regretful memories of his early days in Boston and the dark little room on Sussex Street in the South End that he shared with his brother, and perhaps he experienced a certain amount of reexamination of his days, his successes, and his current spate of bad luck. But he carries on. He avoids the lowlifes, goes to bed early when he can, and must have found some employment. He stayed on in Paris for two years. Maybe more.

In the Cambridge, Massachusetts, phone directory, after 1926, you will not find his name until 1930.

CHAPTER FOURTEEN

A Night at the Dingo Bar

UNLIKE ANY OTHER VISUAL IMAGE, A PHOTOGRAPH IS NOT A RENDERING, AN IMITATION OR AN INTERPRETATION OF ITS SUBJECT, BUT ACTUALLY A TRACE OF IT.

John Berger

Unidentified trail, probably Ball's Hill, Concord, Massachusetts

It rains often in Paris in April. It can be cold then too, and those dark northern sea-run skies can hang over the city for days on end, casting the infamous Paris *grisaille* over the city, the monotonous, depressing, flat light of a black-and-white photograph that would beget, one would guess, an existential outlook on life, introspection, and a preference for warm cafés, steamed milk, and the rattle of newspapers. Or perhaps the opposite. A brightly lit nightlife, extravagant, coloratura singing in the gaslit concert halls, or smoky voices in below-ground clubs, riotous processions, parties, and *bals des nuits.* It is said that Parisians, the real ones, favor the gloomy light of their city. The true dwellers of the revolutionary cafés of the Belle Epoque were said to have hated the sun. By contrast, the good bourgeoisie and the young mothers of Paris come out in the sun whenever it shines, you see them there in the parks, their faces turned to the light, not unlike those basking lemurs of Madagascar that have to warm themselves each morning to get started.

The cast of Paris light lent itself to the black-and-white art of Brassaï, Atget, and the other Paris-based photographers—the night glow of the lamplights on the bridges of the Seine, the cobbled, wet streets, a subdued, implied substance of old night and fog.

Through the lens, in the last days of the twentieth century, the streets of Montparnasse still had the usual dreary gleam, a black-and-white foggy dampness that made it impossible to warm oneself. It had rained earlier that day, the rains of Paris in April, and I had purposefully lowered my expectations and sauntered through the district, coat collar turned up, turned right off the Boulevard Montparnasse, and walked halfway down the Rue Delambre, crossed over to the north side and positioned myself opposite a restaurant called l'Auberge de Venise, a small Italian trattoria, which has now replaced the old Dingo Bar. Here I waited for something to happen. I raised the camera and eyed the entrance through the lens, then saw to my left a long-legged woman in a pea jacket and high-topped boots approaching with an eager, wire-haired dachshund straining forward enthusiastically on its lead, legs spinning. There was a torn concert poster just to the left of the café. I raised the camera again, focused, waited, and when the woman and the dog entered the view field, released the shutter.

In the resulting image, the dog's tail blurs hard right. The woman's left leg reaches forward in midstride, her head, a mass of shoulder-length dark hair, dark glasses pushed up above her brows, is backed by the white underbase of the concert poster. Just to the right is the door to l'Auberge de Venise.

The *patron* here, whom I had met before, was a friendly round-faced man with the burr of an Italian accent and a brush-cut moustache. This was late afternoon—I went in and asked him some more questions.

"Yes, yes, yes, it was here," he said. "Right here." He pounded a small polished wood bar to the left of the dining area with the flat of his hand. "This is the very bar. People come here from all over the world to see this bar. Even from Japan." He slapped the bar again.

✠

Scott and Zelda had stumbled into the Dingo Bar that August evening in 1929, already drunk, and had ordered a round. While he was drinking there, chatting up his acquaintances, a company of American blacks pushed in and joined their friends and began carousing in loud voices, throwing back their heads and laughing freely, as they often did in the liberated, undiscriminating milieu of Paris.

In the typical blaze of double-ended candles that characterized their madcap years in Paris and Antibes, Zelda and Scott elected to move on to another bar, but as they made to leave, Scott took out his wallet and something happened—either he paid, or he didn't pay, and left his wallet on the bar, or he paid and then dropped the wallet and was too drunk to remember to pick it up and walked out.

Whatever happened, he somehow lost his wallet and at some point later that night, discovered this fact and decided that it had been stolen by the blacks at the Dingo Bar and summoned the police. Accompanied by the gendarmes the little troop came back to the bar and Scott saw the culprit, a well-known local American black named Louis Mitchell, who ran a club in Montmartre, and charged him with the theft. Despite the accused's protests of innocence, the police began to haul him off. There followed a great uproar from the other blacks in the bar, since Mitchell had not come into the Dingo until after the Fitzgeralds had left. Surrounded by angry blacks, Scott and Zelda fled to their flat on the Right Bank, maintaining the charges. Police continued to arrive and depart through the night, questioning Scott. Later the next morning, the young Canadian novelist Morley Callagan arrived with his wife to pay a visit and found Fitzgerald still awake and having a massage in a back room. When he learned of the disturbances of the night before, Callagan paid his respects and made to leave, but Scott called him back, miraculously revived, and insisted they go out to a café. He was clear-headed by this time and lucid. By midafternoon he was drunk again.

That chaotic night, with the perceived danger of a surround of angry American blacks, police reports, and half-remembered, alcohol-hazed events, slowly cooked and simmered and was finally served as the hotel scene with Jules Peterson.

There is no record of this either way, but I'm guessing that Gilbert was not actually at the Dingo Bar that night. He was older, for one thing, and was not a drinking man. Once he had finished performing for whatever tearoom he was working, he would probably have gone home to bed. What this means—guessing again—is that Fitzgerald may have encountered him somewhere else, perhaps at the Dingo in company of Countee Cullen, one of the few black literati with whom Gilbert would have deigned to associate. Countee's father was a minister, a well-born New Yorker, and Countee himself was a popular figure and a rising young star of the Harlem Renaissance and was known to Fitzgerald. I had discovered a photograph of young Cullen from this period; he was a dashing, well-dressed chap, much younger than Gilbert.

Everyone in Paris who was not a passing tourist knew everyone else, in those years. You had but to go over to the Brasserie Lip or the Closerie des Lilas, or Harry's Bar if you had the money, or the Rotonde, and you could find someone you knew. You'd see them all there, Kiki of Montparnasse, with her black bangs and her chronicler and lover Man Ray. And here's big bull Hemingway all puffed up with assurance, and Scott and Zelda, poppy-eyed John Dos Passos, the one writer that the French adored, and all the now anonymous faces in makeup and fancy dress, and harem clothes and Indian headdresses, image after image, snapped during the decade-long party.

On a later trip to Paris, I once met a very pleasant American expatriate woman who had gone to school with the Fitzgeralds' daughter, Scotty.

What was she like? I asked.

"Oh, normal," she said. "Very normal, very nice, kind of tame."

Who wouldn't have been with a childhood such as hers.

Zelda had that kind of crazy spirit that would let her do almost anything—a literal madness in her case, as it turned out. Earlier that summer she had scandalized the staid Americans by dancing at a club with the black man; she also danced with women, also by herself, often by herself, in fact—in the summer of 1929, she was obsessively studying to be a ballerina even though she was far too old to dance anything but some obscure passage with the corps de ballet. Zelda (who was actually a distant cousin of mine on my mother's side) was finally committed to a series of mental institutions, one of which my mother once worked at as recreational director—she used to take the crazy ladies out to the opera. Scott used Zelda's earliest sojourns in Swiss sanatoriums as a basis for the trajectory of the life of his heroine, Nicole Diver, in *Tender Is the Night,* and his own alcoholic downslide as a model for Dick Diver.

Zelda's one sane refuge at that time was expressed in her letters to Scott, in which she moved into nostalgic reminiscences of her youth with the dashing young writer. The letters are filled with the poetry of achromatic sun and hot flowers and moonlight. The fragrance of the Riviera wafts through them—"the long citroneuse beams of five o'clock sun on the plage at Juan-les-Pins and the sound of the drum and piano being scooped out to sea by the waves."

Reading these entries under the dark umbrella of the Paris sky, I suddenly was seized with an urge to be there—my own sentimental journey, I suppose. I had lived in Nice once, when I was young, and I remember the same hot light on the sand beach at Juan-les-Pins and the sea-spiced, open-air restaurants filled from eleven in the morning 'til two at night with tanned people in minimalist bathing costumes, and well-oiled older gentlemen in white ducks and houndstooth jackets escorting tanned women my own age along the promenades. It was, in contrast to Atget and Brassaï and company, a brightly keyed world, best documented by the hedonistic playboy photographer Jacques-Henri Lartigue.

Jill Brown had joined me by this time. "I think we should go south," I said to her, rationalizing that Mr. Gilbert might have been there, following the musicians who, after the first jazzed-up frenzy of the early twenties, drifted down to play in the big civilized hotels. So we took the night train from Paris and walked down to the Promenade des Anglais from the station in Nice, through the filtered scent of flowers, knowing in rational moments that I would find no clues, but irrationally determined to leave no stone unturned.

At least the light changed. Somewhere south of Lyon the grays of Paris *grisaille* that so oppress sun lovers gave way to a blue-green mountain dawn light that faded to blue and white as we reached the coast.

Later in the day down in the big square in the old quarter of Nice, some crazy artists had rolled out a piano and it sat there alone, asking to be played, so I wandered over, sat down, and picked out, for old times' sake, Mr. Gilbert's "Just a Closer Walk." Magical thinking—maybe I could summon him forth from the dead.

I sat there alone in the square, lost myself in the music and played on, and slipped into a few improvisations. Ms. Brown retreated to a café—pretending not to know me—but unbeknownst to me a few people gathered. I looked up at one point and saw them, apologized, recused myself, thanked them, and then skulked over to the bar.

No Gilbert.

So we went down to Antibes and found a place in the sun. When I lived in Nice, friends of mine and I used to take the bus down the coast to the sand beaches of Juan les Pins and spend the day. I hadn't been back since, and of course things had changed for the worse. The whole coast was unrecognizable, thick with new establishments, but we poked around anyway and even found the site of the old Gausse Hotel from *Tender Is the Night,* now rebuilt, renamed, and tending to favor proper Dutch clients in slippers and bathrobes rather than reprobate Americans.

Over at the Hotel America in Juan les Pins, where Scott and Zelda had spent a summer, we found a plaque honoring the famous *écrivain américain* and even fell in with an older man who had worked at the nearby Eden Roc for decades. He was too late to have known the Fitzgeralds or Hemingway, but after some questioning he said he did remember an American black man who used to stay there.

"He was my good friend," the concierge said.

"What was his name?" I asked.

"Jimmi. He was a delicate man, not fond I do not believe of America."

It turned out he was talking about James Baldwin.

Back in Paris, we began café crawling again, looking for Mr. Gilbert. The polished wood bar at the Closerie du Lilas has little brass plaques indicating where the well-known American writers and poets of the American colony at Montparnasse used to sit. Quite by accident we found ourselves at the far end of the bar on the left, a favorite spot of Hemingway's. Then we went over to the Rotonde, a place that, by the late twenties, had fallen from favor with all but the literary tourists because of a change in management. We went to La Coupole, and the Sélect, the Metropole, and the Café du Monde. And then, having been sufficiently lubricated, we decided to eat.

It was late, ten in the evening, the restaurants were jammed, with long waiting lines and what appeared to me to be generally dull, unimaginative menus. So we poked along the boulevard, reading the cartes of other restaurants. Near the corner of the Rue Delambre, as I was so engaged, rocking on my heels and leaning forward, squinting at the type, a woman came around the corner and nearly bumped into me. She drew back and apologized and glanced up at the restaurant.

"Not here," she said, wagging her finger. "Whatever you do, wherever you go, do not eat here."

"Why not?"

"Criminals. They are known criminals. Even that would be all right, but the food . . ." She waved her left hand in a dismissive gesture.

She was about 60, dressed in a short black cape, and she had amassed silver jewelry about her person and cut her thick black-dyed hair in bangs that covered entirely her forehead. She had masked her eyes like a vamp and wore white makeup to cover her age. In fact she looked not unlike an aging Kiki of Montparnasse.

"I could tell you a thing or two about Montparnasse if you like. I could tell you about the criminals and the whores and famous clochards who would expose themselves to the gendarmes as a joke. I grew up here, and I am writing my biography, and it will be filled with the abuses wrought by the criminals of Montparnasse."

"I am searching for criminals myself," I told her. "Criminals from the 1920s."

She threw out her hand again dismissively.

"They were innocents. Babes in the woods. Back then they did not know what were criminals."

Ms. Brown appeared at this point from checking other restaurant menus and I went to introduce her to my new friend—who beat me to it and kissed her cheeks, four times, in the Parisian fashion. These two began an animated conversation on the glorious days of the art community at Montparnasse, before the "criminals" moved in, and in time we went off with her to a restaurant of her choice, an excellent Ethiopian spot, not far from Raspail.

Among other interesting facts, we learned that she had been married to "a criminal," had once had money in her family, had spent her life between Montparnasse and Cannes, and had been born too late to have known any of the players who would appear in my history. Her parents, she said, might have known them, but they were bourgeoisies of good standing who spent their Sunday afternoons out at Argenteuil and would not, in an case, have ever associated with the likes of artists and writers—let alone *les américains,* whom, she explained, somewhat apologetically, they held in very low esteem, only slightly more elevated on the evolutionary scale than baboons. (Or buffoons—I missed the word.) But she did know Montparnasse well and since she seemed to have had a number of interactions with known criminals, she was also familiar with the police.

"You know many police, then?" I asked. "We're trying to dig out the records for a crime that took place here in August of 1929."

"To find that," she said, "you go to the archives on the Rue de

Montagne. There is a police museum there, and in the back there are the records. You will ask for Armand. He is nice. Not a criminal, like most of the others."

She agreed to meet us there the next day at eleven and introduce us to Armand. We appeared, waited till eleven thirty, and when she didn't show up went inside on our own, and went looking for Armand.

We were directed to a large second-floor room with many desks, and three or four police bureaucrats lounging around, some with their feet on the desks. Armand was a small, tough-looking type from Normandy, who listened to our story and then went off to get some record books for us. There was an older police archivist there with gold-rimmed glasses and a sharp nose who, having overheard the discussion, came over and asked us some more questions about the event and made a few suggestions. He was soon joined by a fat man with an ugly necktie, whose lower shirt button was undone, and by the time Armand returned with an armful of books, there were four or five middle-aged officers surrounding us and offering all manner of helpful suggestions and asking questions about where we lived and why we were so interested in a black man who had lived in the nineteen twenties and was he rich and had we checked the passport offices and the steamship passenger lists and did he perhaps live with a family here. And then they offered us some coffee, and said that maybe while he was here, he had changed his name, and that people did that when they came to Paris to live, especially if they were musicians, and on and on with a great outpouring of enthusiasm for our quest. It was a far different scene from the suspicious grilling I had experienced back home in the Arlington, Massachusetts, police department. Part of their eagerness, I'm afraid, may have had something to do with my research assistant, who is small and blond, speaks French with an upper-class Parisian accent, and knows how to bat her eyelashes.

Finally they sat us down at a long polished wood table with a whole stack of record books inscribed with all the crimes of the season in 1929. As with the police logs back in Arlington, these made very interesting reading. If nothing else they gave us a flavor of the era: arrests for disorderly behavior, arrests for politicizing, arrests for knifings, for poisonings, for brandishing a weapon. It was while I was there reviewing all these that I came across the crimes of Mr. Sidney Bechet for his little shooting match. But as far as Mr. Gilbert is concerned, it was a dead end. The crimes for mid-August in Paris were few, everyone had fled south to the sun, and in the end we learned nothing save that on the night of 14 August, when I thought the incident had taken place, a few *pisseurs américains* were arrested, a gentleman had disrobed in the lobby of the Hotel des Jardins, three more *putains* were arrested on the Boulevard Saint Michele, where they weren't supposed to be, and a man with a knife stood in the middle of the intersection of Boulevard Montparnasse and Raspail, alternately shouting insults at God, dancing the Charleston furiously, spinning his knife on his forefinger like a circus performer (which he was believed perhaps to be), and singing arias from *La Traviata*—off-key, as the records point out. The performer was taken in for a rest period.

We thanked the gentlemen gendarmes for their kind assistance and made to leave.

"By the way," I asked as we parted company. "Do any of you know of a woman of about sixty named Celeste?"

"Mais oui!" they said as a body. "Celeste d'Arquino. Of course we know her. Everyone around here knows her . . ."

Armand rolled his eyes and spun his index finger up the right side of his temple.

"Pazza," he said in Italian. "Did she tell you that she is the daughter of Modigliani?"

"No, many other things she told us, but not that."

"You must have caught her on a good day."

✠

One of the centers of the English-speaking literary world of Paris in the twenties was Sylvia Beach's bookstore Shakespeare & Company, which still exists. Some years earlier in Paris before I knew very much about Mr. Gilbert, and was flying blind, I stopped in to ask a few questions, not realizing at the time that the current shop had moved from its original location and was now under the direction of a decidedly un-Sylvia Beach-like character named George Whitman. I had presumed back then (wrongly it turned out) that Mr. Gilbert would have fallen in with the English-speaking literary crowd that frequented the first Shakespeare & Company.

The current bookstore is located on the Left Bank opposite Notre Dame, and is as much an atelier for wandering writers as a purveyor of books. There are three floors of musty book-lined rooms, many cats prowling here and there and perched on upper shelves, and there are even a few apartments where wandering troubadours can spend a few days. The front room of the store is devoted to books by writers of the Lost Generation. Here, in both first and second and even new editions, are the works of Fitzgerald, Hemingway, Kay Boyle, and the like. Deeper into the gloom of the interior are the books of the postwar beats and their crew. Farther inward and upward are tables and shelves of books strewn in much disorder, in many languages, some torn and worthless, some in fine condition. Here were old translations of *The Tibetan Book of the Dead,* an illustrated catalogue of Egyptian tomb contents, the collected works of Lafcadio Hearn in French, H. G. Wells, in English, and, of course, the works of Sartre, Camus, Malraux, and Gide in a variety of editions. Milling about were a few starry-eyed American and English students of literature, and in the back there was a small goateed man, much ravaged by cigarettes, dressed in a moth-eaten blue cardigan. This was the owner, an American expatriate named

George Whitman who, as he explained, had moved the store from its original location.

After the Second World War he had stayed in France and went to the Sorbonne courtesy of the G.I. Bill. He fell in with the literary crowd in Paris, including Eugène Ionesco, the then unknown Samuel Becket, and Jean Genet, and in 1951 opened a bookstore called The Mistral and began holding readings for the new writers. One day Sylvia Beach herself came to one of the events and the two became friends. After she died in 1964, he renamed his store Shakespeare & Company in her honor (he also named his daughter after her).

Whitman was about 75 when I met him and still had a fine leonine head of thick gray hair clipped above his ears and combed back in the style of an R.A.F. fighter pilot. He had done a bit of wandering before he settled in Paris, having walked all the way through Mexico from the United States until he stacked up at the Panama Canal and turned around and went home. He was an avid reader who could consume three or four books at a time and was a collector of people as well as old volumes. No wonder. The world, or the world he cared about at least, would eventually come to him. He, of course, had never heard of Gilbert—no one has—but he did know some of the characters I used to see around the streets of this section of Paris when I lived there, and I tried to catch up on the local gossip. Most, he said, with a decidedly French shrug, were either dead or *disparu.*

Since I knew by then that Gilbert was an accomplished pianist I theorized that he perhaps kept himself solvent by playing the nightspots around Paris (I didn't know yet that he did not like jazz). I thought maybe Whitman might know of some older person in town who might have heard of a piano player named Gilbert who hung around the old store. While we were talking, I heard the lilt of an American southern accent speaking in fluent but ungrammatical

French and noticed an older black man in a gray vest and a red beret.

"Go ask him," Whitman said. "That's Billy Broadway. He claims to know every black in Paris. He's a cornet player."

After the proper introductions I slipped the perennial question to Mr. Broadway, who answered in English in the hipspeak of the nineteen fifties. While he talked, which he did—volubly—he hunched his shoulders and slouched slightly forward, fingers snapping and his hands flying off in every direction, like frightened sparrows.

"Cat named Gilbert from Boston?" he asked, repeating my question.

"Yes, an accomplished piano player, as far as I know. He might have played in the bistros around Montparnasse."

"American spade. Plays piano," he said to himself, as if rifling through his files.

"Played . . ."

"Long time back?"

"Right, last time he was here was maybe in the early thirties."

"Now, man, you're talking back there, you're talking history, Jack, you're talking ancient history. But let me cogitate on the matter for a minute. There was an American gentleman of color played piano at one of the *boites* down on the Rue Mouffetarde but he got hisself shived by an Algerian dude and died that very night. And anyway that was twenty-five years ago. His name was Alex something, not Gilbert."

"This man's middle name was Alexander," I said. "But the time's wrong."

"Lemme think a little minute—all right, you got Wing Ding, he was American, played piano at the Hot Club, you got Petey. You got an old cat named William, used to do bass all around town, he dead too, though, then you get way back there, you get Bricktop and Sidney and all the hep cats what diddled Josephine. But you talking before my time, Jack, long before my time—I do not know. I cannot help you, my man."

"Where'd you get that tie?" I asked out of the blue.

He looked down at his tie and lifted it to inspect it, as if he had never seen it before. It was a garish black thing, handpainted, with yellow and purple palm trees.

"Oh now if this tie could talk. If this tie could talk you would hear some tales, my man. I got this tie on Broadway, 1946, July, just after the war. See, after the war I made the grievous error of returning to the United States of America, Land of the Free and the Home of the Brave, and I land in New York City, mustered out with a cornet and a strong hankering to get my black ass back to this here City of Light. I played the strip joints on Forty-second Street, played the Metropole and I knew everybody, and all that time, what do I do? I think about Paris. And then one day"—he snapped his fingers—"I count my *fric,* figure I've got enough for passage on a freighter, and so I *fous le camp,* as the Frenchies say."

"But you never heard a word about a well-dressed piano player who once made a fortune in the shoe polish business in Stockholm?"

"Not a word, Jack, not a word do I hear."

On another occasion on this same trip, still generally uninformed, I tried another gambit. Fitzgerald and Zelda were sometime inhabitants of Harry's Bar at the Ritz. There is a scene in *Tender Is the Night,* reset in Antibes, in which Abe North and the drunken crew capture a waiter and threaten to saw him in half. The event actually took place at the Ritz, and Fitzgerald and, of course, Hemingway and company also habituated the bar when they could afford to. Gilbert, in the guise of Jules Peterson, also makes a cameo appearance there. One morning, with nothing else in mind, I went over and dared to enter into these august halls. The Civil Guard, in the form of an old, arrogant concierge, held the citadel against me at first. But through persistence, and (I think) the proper expression of humility, I managed to disarm him with Gilbert's story and I was guided to the office of no less a figure than the vice president of the hotel, a civil gentleman named Bernard who dressed in striped trousers and a cutaway, and who had written a history of the luminaries of the Ritz.

French hotels used to commonly maintain what was known as the Golden Book, the registry of guests. I asked if by any chance they still had the registry from 1929. He smiled sympathetically and, with his hands held together, nodded weakly. He spoke a refined, European English. "Ah, but you see, in those times, it was, how shall I say, perhaps better to leave certain things unrecorded. Even left unsaid." He tipped his open palm from side to side and smiled apologetically.

He was intrigued by the story, though, and invited me into a plush inner office where he drew out the book he had published and skimmed through the index. Along with the Aga Khan and many other dignitaries, he did find Scott and Zelda Fitzgerald, who, unlike so many of the other writers and artists who flocked to Paris after the war, actually had money. Fitzgerald's first book, *This Side of Paradise,* had been a great success, the emblematic story of the Jazz Age.

"I must ask you," I said to my guide, "in the 1920s, would a black person have been allowed to drink at the bar here? Or even stay here."

I asked this because in one scene in *Tender Is the Night,* the Gilbert character comes to the bar asking for Abe North and there is some question as to whether he would be allowed in.

He laughed, knowingly. "But yes, of course, as far as we French are concerned. But in these times then, you understand, we had great numbers of Americans who stayed here. Rich Americans, I say, very rich indeed, in certain cases. They were regular guests, although difficult—they would demand breakfast, cereal with milk and weak, watered-down coffee, and sandwiches with American white bread for their dinner. The management, to its credit, tolerated them. But you see, these people, as you probably know, did not like the Negro, even the Africans, and this created a problem for us. We had very rich Senegalese and other blacks from the French colonies staying here back then, kings and diplomats no less. But the presence of the American whites, you see. It was difficult, very complicated. I remember my predecessor. He used to say that it was as if these were fighting dogs, you had to keep them apart. I'm glad I was not the manager back then. Now it is not a problem. Black, white, no one cares, not even the Americans."

The vice president began offering other possible documents that would shed some light on Gilbert's sojourn in Paris, some of which I had already run down. One of these was the police identity cards that had to be filled out by any visitors from foreign countries. This search had involved many phone calls and a journey to the records department in Versailles, where I learned that because of the reforms engendered by the 1968 student revolts, entire files of identity cards dating back to the 1870s had been destroyed.

According to Sanfred Bensen, with corroborating circumstantial evidence from *Tender Is the Night,* Gilbert had come down to Paris from Stockholm, where he had made money with his formula. Through American friends, I had a contact in Sweden named Birgitta Tolson who as a favor had been running through the various state archives, bank registries, and country administrative board lists and the like, looking for Mr. Gilbert. I had learned that she would be passing through Paris that spring and arranged to have dinner with her while she was there, to meet her in person and pick up whatever new information she might have found.

We met at a small Left Bank restaurant and spent the evening discussing Sweden in the 1920s and the reluctance of Swedish culture to fall in with the zeitgeist of the years between the wars. "As now, if you were serious, and wanted to be in the center of things," she said, "you had to come to Paris."

In spite of her research, Birgitta said, she could find no evidence of a Robert A. Gilbert, but she said that did not mean he wasn't there. "We Swedish people are all registered with our birth numbers, which means, among other things, that the state knows absolutely all about us. But a foreigner with a rather ordinary name like Gilbert, that is just a man in the street with no registration at all. I checked the old police records of foreigners living in Sweden in the 1920s, but they were sporadic, whole months were missing, and I know that some were not registered. So there's no absolute proof, I am afraid to say."

I told her about the police archivists and their theory that he may have assumed a different name while he was abroad.

"That, too, is possible," she said. "Also, I think, in time of peace, many countries did not require, absolutely, a passport, and if he had been in Sweden, living under a different name, he could perhaps have moved around more freely."

"Could he have called himself Jules Peterson?" I asked.

"Why not," she said.

✠

The big question surrounding Gilbert's European sojourn was why he went at all. What would cause Gilbert, who had so many connections among the rich whites in Boston and Cambridge, who had family ties, who was a believer in the American dream of possibility, and had laid a course in life that required him to beat on for years against the tide of white restrictions, steering by ingenuity and wit, why would a man of this sort give it all up and go to Europe?

One argument is that he may have tasted, through association with Brewster, the freedom that he knew American blacks in Europe were experiencing. But he was, as far as I could tell, not unhappy in Cambridge, rather satisfied in fact, a homeowner, a known, albeit minor, figure in the halls of Harvard, but a respected upper-middle-class citizen in the black community. He lived door to door with white people, no small feat in the American landscape in those years, even in Boston. Furthermore, by whatever means, either his shoe polish ventures or his thousand dollar inheritance from Brewster, he had managed to send his three daughters to college. And not just any college. Mary had gone to Boston University, Edyth went to Radcliffe, and Emma to a teacher's college in New York. So why did he leave?

Back in Cambridge, carrying my usual baggage of letters, photographs, newspaper clippings, and assorted documents, I went to see Tre at the Café Algiers and tried to sum up what my research assistant and I had learned. There was still no absolute proof of anything except Gilbert's years at Harvard and his time with Mr. Brewster.

Tre spread out some of our material on one of the coffeetables and began casually leafing through various documents, pondering, sipping his coffee, without lifting his eyes from his readings. I remained silent while the master detective went to work. Like a card player, he began setting aside certain documents, shuffling them to and fro, and pairing them up. One of the papers was the label from Gilbert's shoe dressing canisters that I had been given at Mr. Alexander's house, some of the others were Xeroxed labels from the U.S. Secretary of Commerce, which he had suggested we look into.

"I have to ask you something," Tre said. "Does the name Jan Matzeliger mean anything to you?"

The name actually did sound familiar to me but I couldn't remember why.

"Shoe business," Tre said. "He was a black from Suriname, came up to the shoe factories in Lynn where, of course, he met the usual prejudices of Americans. But he was a tinkerer and a genius, along the lines of Edison and that sort, only no education. He taught himself mechanical drawing, and physics, and he used to invent machines on paper, one of which was a machine of some sort for making shoes. No money, of course, not even for a patent, but he believed in his invention and kept pushing. Finally two white guys from Lynn backed him up, and the thing revolutionized shoemaking. His machine could turn out something like six or seven hundred pairs of shoes a day, instead of the usual ten."

"Interesting, but what's the point?" I asked.

"Black people were part of the Industrial Revolution in America, if you look behind the scenes."

"Maybe so, but what's the point, what does it have to do with Mr. Gilbert?"

"Matzeliger got the backing. Gilbert might have done a similar thing, I think. Shoes were a major part of the fashion world back then, no one wore these . . . whatever you call them that black kids love today. The shoes were all leather. You had to take care of the leather. Scuffed, dirty shoes were looked down upon. You had to have dressing. Same with any leather. Same with cartops of the convertibles of the era. Hard-topped cars didn't come in until much later. Twenties and early thirties, I think . . ."

He ordered another espresso. Shifted his card deck of papers, lined two of them up and told me to look.

There were four labels on the second page, selected from a 1926 business directory, which was the year of the copyright on Gilbert's shoe dressing: Clearwater Laundry with a big waterfall trademark plus something called the World Receiver Radio Corporation with jagged electric lines spreading out from double globes, a label called Sun Lac lacquer, Auto Top Dressing, and then the label for Gilbert's shoe dressing.

I inspected the labels dumbly.

"What?" I asked.

"Look."

"I am looking."

He tapped the Sun Lac label.

"All right?" he asked.

"No, not all right, just tell me, Tre."

Tre could be very smug when he had made a discovery or was about to reveal a great truth unto me. He would never just come out and say what he had found.

He tapped the Sun Lac label again, and then tapped Gilbert's shoe dressing. Both labels feature a rising sun as their trademark.

"I see. But what does it mean? What's your point?"

He tapped the bottom of the cartop dressing label.

"Look at the manufacturing city," he said.

It was Leominster, Massachusetts.

"Lay it on Tre. Let me hear what you've come up with now."

He began with his typical review of the known facts. Gilbert would drive regularly to Lancaster, often return by way of Leominster. Gilbert liked mechanical things, liked automobiles. He stops sometimes to pick up a canister of the Sun Lac cartop dressing for Brewster's Ford. Later, he has his own car to care for. He takes care of things. He falls into a jocular friendship with someone at Sun Lac, perhaps even the boss or one of the chemists. He learns the formula, goes home, and using his knowledge of chemistry, garnered from his familiarity with photographic materials, creates his own cartop dressing, which he then tries on shoes. It's basically a waterproofing paste, and works well on shoes.

"And so," Tre said, "he decides to try to market it. All this may be early on, around 1915 or so, before Brewster dies. Gilbert is back and forth, as you say, to Washington around this time. And did you not tell me that at some point Brewster said something about his business ventures failing?"

"Yes," I said. "There are several notes. At one point Brewster writes that Gilbert seemed to have left his 'ghosts' in Washington. Whatever that means."

"I know what it means," Tre said.

He lifted his coffee, sipped, and looked at me squarely.

"Will you be telling me?" I asked.

"I suppose I shall have to," he said. "So your man, he goes down to Washington to the trademark office and tries for a patent, or a copyright. And he finds—and I'm not sure exactly how or why—that he can't get what he wants. But apparently he needs whatever it was to expand his business. It could have been even worse, though. He could have been manufacturing this stuff and gotten caught up in a trademark or patent issue, maybe even a court case, a lawsuit. Anyway, he's in trouble. But then he calculates that if he takes his business out of the country, he can do what he wants. So it's off to Stockholm."

"Why not Paris? He must have known that blacks were accepted there."

"I don't know. Are you sure it was Stockholm?"

"That's what the old man told me."

"Well, what did that old man know? How about Copenhagen? There were shoe industries there in the twenties."

"I thought Bensen said Stockholm, but I noticed Fitzgerald uses Copenhagen once in the hotel scene instead of Stockholm. It's in a quote though, he could have just used that to show how disinterested his characters were in the life of this man Peterson."

"How did he spell Peterson, with an 'e' or an 'o' at the end?"

"With an 'o,' I think that's the Swedish spelling? Danish is Petersen. But Fitzgerald wouldn't have known that sort of thing, I don't think, or cared, and anyway I read that the character Peterson was originally called Headstrum or something in an earlier manuscript."

He drank more coffee and pondered.

"There is one other possibility," he said. "Remote, but here it is. Did you not tell me that at some point the Brewsters had two Swedish maids?"

I had forgotten this fact. They were two young scullery maids who cleaned and took care of Caroline and served the Brewsters at table. At Christmas, as the Brewsters aged, they used to dress up in their traditional costumes and sing Swedish carols for the old couple. But I told Tre that I had no idea what the relationship between these two and Gilbert may have been. They were a lot younger than he.

"Well, Gilbert would have had access, in all likelihood, to both worlds, would he not? By then he was somewhere between servant and old friend of the family, no?"

"True, but he would go home for dinner when he was in Cambridge. No reason not to. He had nothing to do with cooking except when they were in the camps, and then later, at the museum."

"Well, just put the case that he's in the kitchen a lot in Cambridge. Maybe he even fancies one of them. They sound like a friendly lot, without the inherent American racism. They may even have enjoyed him."

"Possibly," I said, "but he was not the type to fool around. Didn't joke much, I don't think."

"So be it. But he may have talked with them seriously. Did they miss their home? Did they like America? Why had they come? What was it like in Stockholm? That sort of thing. I don't know. And maybe from them he senses something about Sweden, the liberal attitudes, the old city of Stockholm, the Bostonian sense of place, who knows? But maybe he thought from what he learned from the maids that it would be a good place to start, and then, years later with Brewster dead and he at the end of his tether, and his girls taken care of, he sails off to make his fortune."

"Sounds good," I said. "But we've checked the business directories, the police logs and the like in Stockholm. No records. I just don't know."

"Maybe we'll never know, will we?" Tre said. "He's gone. They're all gone now."

He seemed to be visibly softening, as if he himself was getting old and had had a glimmer of mortality.

I shrugged. He drank his coffee and stared at the film of

grounds on the bottom of the cup. His father had died a few months earlier and he had carried on as if nothing had happened. It occurred to me that now the past was catching up with him.

"Maybe you go around looking to make something of this guy, trying to place him up on some kind of pedestal, invent some new African American hero, unsung and unrecognized. But in the end, maybe this is just another form of racism. You have to prove that this Gilbert was some kind of talented photographer. But who cares, really? What's the big deal? If he were a white man—no story, right?"

It was a good point, I suppose. But if I didn't find him who would?

"That's reality, though, isn't it?" Tre said, softly. "That's life; it's what history is, a fiction. The supporting cast just dies in anonymity."

"That," I said, "is exactly why I want to find him."

CHAPTER FIFTEEN

Gone Are the Days

THE CHARM, ONE MIGHT EVEN SAY THE GENIUS, OF MEMORY IS THAT IT IS CHOOSY, CHANCY AND TEMPERAMENTAL; IT REJECTS THE EDIFYING CATHEDRAL AND INDELIBLY PHOTOGRAPHS THE SMALL BOY OUTSIDE, CHEWING A HUNK OF MELON IN THE DUST.

Elizabeth Bowen

Mary Gilbert, Warren, New Hampshire, 1907

On my last visit to George Alexander, Madelon Winston gave me the print of Gilbert's daughter, Mary, taken in 1907, when she was two years old somewhere in Warren, New Hampshire. Judging from the shadows, the image was made a little after midday in summer. Mary is seated on the doorstep of an old farmhouse, dressed all in white, in a high-collared cambric dress that reaches to her ankles and a wide-brimmed white summer hat topped with a pompom. She has a pudgy-round rabbit face and is looking sideways, her head angled to the camera, and fidgeting. Her father, Mr. Gilbert, has positioned the camera low to the ground; he must be sitting in front of her, cross-legged, attempting to get the camera low enough to shoot upward so as to show the rise of the narrow, dark screen of the farmhouse door above her, contrasting the white of the pompomed hat that is balanced, top right, by a tiny white porcelain door pull. It's an old place, wherever it is. Cracks on the sill, unpainted clapboards and uneven steps. Somewhere out there, behind Mr. Gilbert, the sun is shining, casting a short midday shadow. It was summer, also hot, judging from Mary's clothes and the gleam of her rounded cheeks.

Later that same year, in summer, during one of my customary rambles, I met a white man in Warren who cut timber for a living. I showed him a copy of the photograph, but even though he knew the landscape of Warren, having grown up there, he couldn't name the place. How could he; the photograph was a door frame like any other rural door frame in a thousand New England towns, dated only by the presence of screens, which did not come into use until the end of the nineteenth century. What was anomalous was the dark child in the white dress in rural New England.

"There weren't many black people in this town in 1907, I can tell you that," he said, scuffing the dust with his boot. "Weren't many people even. It's a dead end up here, all woods, abandoned farms, hills, a few ponds and the lake. But who'd want to spend a life here. I should have got out myself."

I was in the region looking around to fit a wooded saddle of hills I had seen in other unidentified Brewster or Gilbert photographs taken in Warren in this same period, and had driven up through southeastern New Hampshire, passing through small, idle towns, some with deep green lakes beset with summer cottages. Village centers in the area were unremarkable, characterized mainly by musty convenience stores, a depot for snowplows and service trucks, and a vast surround of forests that have taken over the landscape since Mr. Brewster's time. It's a lonely, empty quarter now, the farms, or what there were of them, long since worn out, the farmgirls gone to the mills, the men to the anonymity of the West, those who stayed behind long since gone to their graves, and the houses gone to ground. Walking through the woods in this part of the world you come across the remains of their lives—sunken foundations, miles of stones walls running through wooded hills, a few errant apple trees back in the woods, and, saddest of all somehow, stands of daffodils still blooming in the long deserted dooryards where farm wives once spun their wool and linen.

Mr. Brewster used to come up to Warren periodically to visit Mr. Grover Allen, who had a farm nearby, a summer place where he would retire to watch birds. Gilbert must have come with him, perhaps on an extended visit, bringing his whole family with him this time, or perhaps traveling alone with Mary. Brewster, of course, favored backwaters of this sort, and retreated ever woodward when the motors came. He complained in his diary that aereoplanes were sometimes appearing in the sky over Cambridge. He quit going down to his riverside cabins when the motor-powered boats from the downstream boathouse began coming up the river, and quit Umbagog when the new visitors arrived with their motorcars and began driving over the summer roads, spewing dust everywhere. "Noxious beasts," he called them.

✠

The last time I saw old George Alexander the snow was long gone and the time of singing birds had come and the little flocks of English sparrows were squabbling in the hot dust below the privets. Mr. Alexander was more frail, but only slightly, and I spent only a short time with him before thanking him and then making my excuses. He had turned 100 that year, and I had sent him a little birthday gift and had promised to stop by to see him.

I was on another mission on that particular day to retrace a route periodically taken by both Gilbert and, less often, William Brewster from Cambridge over to Boston, via the Harvard Bridge, and on to Inman Square.

I began where, in the larger sense, Gilbert's story also began, on the north slope of Beacon Hill. It was here that the first African Meeting House in the United States was established, built by freeborn blacks of Boston. It was also here, in these halls, where the first African American voices of liberation thundered, including that of the firebrand speaker Frederick Douglass, who recruited for the all-black 54th Regiment in the main hall.

This part of old Boston is one of the last places where you can still glimpse the lost world that characterized the city in the stiff years when Brewster and his Brahmin friends still held sway. The streets here are narrow and winding, some are still cobblestoned, and most of the buildings date from the eighteenth and early nineteenth centuries and have well-maintained front doors and lush, hidden gardens in private inner courtyards. With only a slight suspension of disbelief, you could be in Europe.

On the north side of the hill, where the Black Brahmins used to live, the streets drop riverward in a winding pattern, like a single-coursed labyrinth. On the south slope, from time to time, you can still see some of the old-fashioned proper Bostonians making some way along, dressed for their outings in tweeds, or summer whites and blue cambric shirts, bowties, and, in a bow to pragmatism, running shoes. There are many proper little English-styled shops in this district, with their wares exhibited neatly in front windows (too many little shops according to the Old Guard, and too many infiltrators as well). But they mix. They adapt to one another, as they always have.

This had been old home month for me in some ways. A few weeks before I went to see Mr. Alexander, I had gone down Ball's Hill Road again to see if I could get Sanfred Bensen interested in coming to Brewster's grave with me. I had been trying to get a good picture of the camera-shy Bensen and his nephew Colburn, but these two seemed impossible to photograph. They would formally compose themselves for each photo, glaring suspiciously at the lens, as if they truly believed, along with much of the preliterate world community, that the camera eye would penetrate their bodies and draw out some critical element of themselves. They were never comfortable; the light was always wrong; the background was too charged with the details of ramshackled sheds and the accumulated artifacts of their recent histories.

Sanfred was looking no less frail than he did when I first had met him. He must have been pushing 90 at least by that time. His old taped-up glasses had completely clouded over by this time, which made me think that he indeed must have been at least half-blind all along, since the tape didn't seem to concern him. The difference that day was that he was sitting down on a rickety kitchen chair he had hauled out to the yard. I don't remember ever having seen him sitting. I noticed that, like an old cat, he had found a good place in the sun.

"Good day to rest," I said, when I saw him off his feet.

"Yes, well, at my age, one must rest now and again."

Muffin the dog was curled up at his feet, licking one of her paws. To get Sanfred loosened up I offered to take some more pictures of her.

Sanfred liked the idea very much and, in the end, he hauled over an old wheelbarrow and got her to jump in. She wasn't quite sure of the situation at first and began licking her chops and looking over at him, instead of me.

"Look at the camera, now, Muffin," he said.

She sat, I squeaked, she cocked her head.

I snapped the shutter.

Bensen went back to his chair after that and since there was an upturned log nearby, I took the liberty of sitting down, and we chatted for a while. It was, as far as I can recall, the first time I had ever had the privilege of sitting down with this man.

As was his custom, he began talking about the old days with Mr. Brewster, and then he told me that he thought he was seeing a lot of birds that he did not remember seeing in Gilbert and Brewster's time.

"There's that big long-tailed one with the white wing bands. And the red one, the cardinal, we never used to see him back then. Never did see those little crested grays, as I call them . . ."

"The titmouse?"

"Yes, that one. He was never here. There are ever so many new things. But I think it was a livelier place in the days when Robert Gilbert was here, and when Dr. Brewster would come by and there were ladies in long skirts and big hats and everybody went out rowing on the river. He was a fine rower, Robert Gilbert—all the ladies asked to be taken in his boat, as I recall."

"You've seen a lot, haven't you, just from this one spot?"

"Oh yes, I think. It seems all the world is here. Or was. But then I still haven't been to Mr. Brewster's grave."

"Well, the offer still holds," I said. "I'll take you over any time you like. The dog can come too."

"Well, that would be very nice. Perhaps next week I could get free . . ."

He seemed to be a little sleepy—something I had never observed in this man—so I prepared to leave, telling him I would bring back the prints of Muffin and that we could arrange a time to go to Brewster's grave.

The next week I printed the photos. Here was Muffin at her finest, looking loyally over at her master in one print, and in another her head cocked at the camera. In every print, though, there was a shadow of Bensen falling over the scene, something I hadn't noticed in my rush to get the proper expression from the dog. It was a dark rounded streak that loomed in from the right and, as it turned out, it was portentous.

Many of the cultures that hold the camera in suspicion also revere the shadow of a person. It is believed to be a vital part of the individual, the visible image of the soul. If you step on someone's shadow, or worse, somehow detach it from the body, that person will be injured or will die. Some ancient tribes even maintained special magicians who had the ability to make people ill by hacking at their shadows with a sword after they have passed. None of these traditions say anything about detaching a shadow from a person by means of a photograph. But a few days before I was planning to take the prints down to Ball's Hill, I read in the local paper that Sanfred Bensen had died in his sleep.

✠

As I passed down Joy Street on Beacon Hill a man dressed in a seersucker suit, straw boater, and beaten-up topsiders waved me over and asked how I'm doing. I'd never seen him before, I don't think, but I chatted with him, waiting for some clue to figure out who he was and how he knew me, then spotted a telltale reddened nose and a few streaky veins in his cheeks. Just an old Brahmin—a bit down on his luck.

Shortly thereafter, I passed a troop of mixed-race schoolchildren, headed for the Museum of Afro-American History, girls mostly, from some local private school. They were dressed in navy blue skirts and white blouses and they chattered intimately as they hurried along. The museum they were headed for is a national historic site now, managed by the U.S. Park Service. The personnel there dress in Smokey the Bear Park Service hats and wear police-like pressed gray uniforms. Somehow the accoutrements don't match the venue.

It was here, in this place, that the ground was prepared for the continuing struggle for African American liberation. The original work was done by the second and third generations of transported Africans whose families had managed, by the grace of Puritan guilt, to have stayed together longer than any of the slaves on the big southern plantations. These people, along with the New England–based white abolitionists, were the creators of the myth of Boston as Negro Paradise, a legend so strong as to have reached the small remote valleys of western Virginia.

At the base of Beacon Hill, on the west side, you will come to another defining characteristic of this coastal town, the great artery that is the river Charles. There are two bridges over the Charles near Beacon Hill, the Longfellow Bridge, which has an unfortunate swirl of overpasses and traffic circles on its Boston side, and the slightly more sane Harvard Bridge, which lies upstream at the end of Charles Bank Park, which is part of a riverlong linear green space with promenades and walkways that originally extended for nine miles along both banks. In the middle of the bridge I stopped and looked back at the modern city with all its seething, twenty-first-century squalor and traffic and shining towers. From this vantage point, you can still see the works of the old Puritan idealism, the celebrated city on a hill—the green Esplanade, the gold dome of Bullfinch's State House, the square towers of MIT on the left bank, the spired towers of Harvard farther upstream, the crew shells skimming below, the rocking sails of the oldest sailing school in the country at the yacht basin, and somewhere back on the Cambridge side, Memorial Hall and the old Victorian redbrick pile known as the Museum of Comparative Zoology, where Mr. Gilbert ended his days.

✠

The Paris sojourn came to an end for Gilbert sometime in 1930. By 1931 he was back in Cambridge at his house at 66 Inman Street living with Mary and her current husband and also back at his post at the museum, painting the exhibits, combing out the fur on the lioness, and remounting the ferrets and the meerkats and the pangolins.

A *Boston Herald* reporter named Travis Ingham somehow got word of his work there and did a story on Gilbert for the August 23rd, 1931, edition. The story focuses on the ingenuity of Gilbert, who is identified with the slightly elevated title of assistant to the curator, Thomas Barbour. Gilbert is also cited in the story as an associate of William Brewster and is mentioned as coauthor of Brewster's published study of birds of the Rangeley Lakes region, of which Umbagog is a part. There is even a photograph of him at work on one of the museum's llamas, dressed casually on this occasion in a soft-collared white shirt and necktie and dark suit trousers. Other than this there is not much about Gilbert the man. The piece focuses primarily on Gilbert's versatile techniques in caring for the exhibits—his use of coloration and, interestingly enough, the chemical formulas he devised for cleaning the fur of the mammals. There is nothing in the story about Robert A. Gilbert, the pianist and photographer, nothing about an inventive shoe polish mogul, who, for unrecorded reasons, fled to Europe and lived for a brief period as an ordinary human being rather than a "Negro." But then it is likely the reporter did not ask.

Gilbert had resumed his role in the world drama on his return to America and was replaying his part, successfully disguised to the ruling white-skinned class of Cro-Magnons as "colored man." This role is evident in the text of the news story. Gilbert is, in the racially tinted language of the period, touted as a brave hunter who stalks among the lions and the gorillas, a "fearless negro" who dares to touch the hairy arm of "Tarzan," the huge five-foot-eight-inch gorilla.

Ever since I heard from the aging malacologist Richard Johnson that the Mr. Gilbert he remembered was little more than an old porter who shuffled around the museum touching up the exhibits, I had been intrigued by this apparent double life of Robert A. Gilbert. References to him in Brewster's time invariably describe a versatile and competent well-attired "colored man" with good carriage and an aristocratic demeanor. What had happened to change the image? (If indeed it had changed. My primary white source on these last years was the memory of Richard Johnson alone. According to African Americans who remember him, he maintained his dignity to the end.)

Part of the change might simply have been old age; Gilbert had turned 70 when Johnson first met him. But Mr. Gilbert was a consummate actor. His first role, played out on the stage of the white world, was written by the dictates of the time and place in which he had to live. Whenever he appears in print, for example, Mr. Gilbert is identified, for all his talents, ambitions, intellect, and ingenuity, as a "colored" man. (Although to his great credit, in the many thousands of words in the writings of William Brewster, with all its hundreds of references to "Gilbert," there is no way that a reader happening upon these documents without prior knowledge would know that Gilbert was black.) When he was around whites, Gilbert, knowing all this, played his role on the white man's stage, and then exited left, to Inman Square, where he assumed another part.

We do not know what subtle mental or psychological changes took place in the psyche of this man at five in the evening, when he turned down Massachusetts Avenue, walked over to Broadway, straightened his shoulders, developed a slower and more regal pace, and entered onto Inman Street, as if crowned with laurels. Here he became Robert A. Gilbert, deacon of Saint Bartholomew's Church, respected for his business ventures, known for his knowledge of birdlife, his travels, his photography, his association with the well-loved, well-known egalitarian white man William Brewster, and perhaps best known (and in the white world almost unknown to all but Caroline Brewster) for his piano virtuosity. Through his ingenuity, he had sent his children off to good colleges, in the case of his middle daughter, Emma, to Radcliffe, one of the finest educational institutions in the country.

In 1931 when he returned from Paris, Gilbert was 62 years old. His high forehead was balding by this time, he wore spectacles, and he would sometimes go about town wearing the new soft-collared shirts instead of his starched detachable collars. Gilbert still dressed in dark suits, though, and favored bow ties, and walked more slowly, straighter, and was up sometimes at night, when he would descend to the parlor and sit alone in the quiet house, thinking. For the next ten years Gilbert lived on his comfortable double role—now puttering around the museum, preparing his inventive dishes for Harvard's visiting biologists, touching up the exhibits he himself had created back in the 1920s, and then by night and on weekends reassuming his true persona as pillar of the Cambridge black community. The world swirled around him. The Depression was worsening when he returned from Paris, bread lines had lengthened, black unemployment had soared. Back in Europe, in Germany, a nasty form of racial discrimination, vaguely similar to the current Jim Crow laws governing southern blacks in America, was surfacing. But Gilbert forged on, the invisible man, improving his Chopin, tending to church matters, and singing old hymns with his family on Sunday afternoons on Inman Street.

Then came the news of the German invasion of Poland. European racism spread. And then one Sunday afternoon in December of 1941, while he and his family were at home in the parlor, news of the attack on Pearl Harbor broke in over the radio. Gilbert was old. There was nothing he could do.

By this time his daughters had learned a thing or two about the world from their father and their schooling and were respected women in the colored social circles of Cambridge. Often in his last years, the whole family would sing together on Sunday afternoons, and little children such as Tom Allen and his friends, as well as adults, were invited in to sit and listen. His daughters eventually started the equivalent of a local finishing school at 66 Inman Street for the children of the neighborhood. The black children learned how to serve tea, speak a few words of French, and dance the waltz, and even learned the fox-trot, which by 1930 had been around long enough to become acceptable, having been replaced by a wilder and more suggestive style of music and dance.

In these years, Mr. Gilbert would customarily leave the house at eight o' clock in the morning, after his normal breakfast of toast, cornflakes, and coffee. He could be seen proceeding down Inman Street toward Broadway, where he would turn left, and, still straight-backed, make his way westward toward Harvard Square and Memorial Hall, where he would turn right and head for the staff doors of the museum on Oxford Street. Periodically, when the weather was fine, he would continue on through Harvard Square and walk down Brattle Street. He would rest in the park opposite the Longfellow House, enjoying the view of the river, and then wander up the street and make a circuit around his old haunts at 145 Brattle on the corner of Sparks Street.

Elizabeth Simmons, aka ERS, had died by this time, and Caroline had sold the house after her husband's death and had moved in with a niece in Boston. Gilbert would get Christmas cards from her, but her handwriting grew wavy and, in March of 1924, Mr. Gilbert read that she had died. He attended her funeral at Saint John's Episcopal Church, and assumed a seat in the back. He was recognized and greeted by several of the parishioners, who, knowing of Caroline's fondness for this small, formal man, shook his hand warmly and claimed to understand that this must be a blow to him as well, and how much Caroline would have appreciated his attendance. But the conversation churned mainly among the white women, and the only other people he knew there were the two Swedish maids who had once worked for the Brewsters, and who wept quietly in the back of the church during the service.

Gilbert lived in a past of his own invention by this time, based mostly on his memories of the outings at Concord, the wide-ranging journeys into the wilderness of the rivers above Lake Umbagog, Paris, sojourns in England to see Caroline's nephew, and to northern France, where someone with a camera eye very much in the style of Robert Gilbert took an extant print of La Verne Castle.

Sometimes, after-hours in winter, Gilbert would linger in the museum halls, lulled by the new steam-heating system and the smell of mothballs and formaldehyde. He paced the halls, reviewing the half-lit cases, flicking off the lights one by one as he passed, his leather shoes creaking and the polished wood floors groaning beneath his step. Down the halls of African mammals he went, blackening the lights on the lions, the zebra, the giraffe, and the great mountain gorilla in its corner case, its hairy arms forever beating its chest, teeth forever bared, all animation halted on the forested slopes of Zaire on a day in 1926. Gilbert moved on to the halls of marsupials wherein lay the platypus, the tree possums, the kangaroos, also frozen in attitudes of a life once lived. And then, finally, the bird halls and the memories of Brewster himself, each mounted specimen, each thrush and vireo, each Lapland longspur, a memory, a story, a whole history of himself—hundreds of birds, long dead and now affixed with small, oaktag labels inscribed with his own hand, indicating the species, the sex, the date of capture, and the conditions under which the bird was found.

Maybe he stayed on some nights after all the lights were flicked off, allowing other reveries to drift in as he paced the dark halls; maybe he heard some old echoes there of Caroline at the keyboard, or the voice of Mr. Brewster. And perhaps, on such nights, alone in the empty halls surrounded by the afterlife of African beasts and American songbirds, some buried memory of his father, the Old King, and Grandma Fanny surfaced, and there came to him the smell of honeysuckle and persimmons and the scented mountains of the valley of Broad Creek.

✠

On the Cambridge side of the Harvard Bridge I clipped off the main thoroughfare of Massachusetts Avenue and laid a course for the museum through the warren of little streets between the river and Cambridge Common. The route passes the A. J. Spears Funeral Home on Western Avenue, which is black-owned and one of the oldest gossip centers in this part of Cambridge. Ardis Spears, who took over the business from her father some years ago, had offered a wealth of information on the past, since most of Gilbert's generation ultimately had utilized the services of the business. The funeral home has, perforce, excellent records—who was married to who, the number of children the couples had, and who died when, and where they are buried.

Ardis Spears is a large, smooth-skinned warm woman whom we had talked to periodically, and after a little doorstoop chat she ushered me into her inner office. It was a hot day, about ninety degrees, but all the Venetian blinds were down, the slats half-lifted so that there was a brownish yellow summer light infusing the room with an almost artificial glow. On the walls were a painting of Jesus at prayer, kneeling in shafts of light, and another of him receiving a poor lamb to his bosom, and there were photographs of old Mr. Spears, and group portraits of other relatives. We talked, as usual, about the old days around Cambridge. Like most of our informants, Ardis was too young, at 75, to know the players in this story, but she knew all the people who remembered the main characters, in fact it was she who supplied us with most of their names.

One of my great regrets in this quest was that for a while I lived not far from one of the most literate chroniclers of the world of Gilbert's generation in Boston, the novelist Dorothy West. She was the youngest member of the Harlem Renaissance and, along with a number of highly respected short stories, wrote a book called *The Living Is Easy*, all about the struggles and familial complications of members of the rising black middle class in the city. She ended her days in Oak Bluffs on Martha's Vineyard, where I lived for a short time, and although we never met, she and I shared a number of acquaintances, mainly through the *Vineyard Gazette*, for which she wrote a society column. I never met Mary Gilbert either, who was still alive in the 1990s while I was beginning to get serious about finding her father. I also missed by only a few years some of the participants in the Eateria who would certainly have known Thomas Barbour and would have remembered Gilbert.

Other than Sanfred Bensen, my closest call to meeting an adult associate of William Brewster came through the great-grandson of the famous abolitionist William Lloyd Garrison. He lived in Lincoln, Massachusetts, not far from the headquarters of the Massachusetts Audubon Society, and just down the hill from the famous environmentalist Paul Brooks, who first published the most popular version of the Brewster methods of field observation, Roger Tory Peterson's *Field Guide to the Birds*. I had learned that Garrison, the younger, who was about 95 when I met him, had joined the Nuttall Club as a very young man and would have known Mr. Brewster. So I arranged to pay him a visit.

He was a small, frail old man with watery blue eyes and a weak handshake, but he seemed perfectly lucid and we talked about birds by way of introduction. Then he mentioned the famous Peterson Field Guides, edited by Brooks, and said he owned a signed first edition of the book and went to get it from the shelf. It wasn't where he thought it was, so he went looking on another shelf. Then he rummaged through his desk, and then a table by a south-facing window that was littered with books, and then he went into the kitchen and began looking for it in the cupboards, among the dishes, and when he didn't find it there, he looked under the sink. Then he informed me that Roger Tory Peterson had been to visit just this morning, which was curious, since Peterson had died four or five years earlier. Then Mr. Garrison said the book was on a shelf in the study and went to get it in the same place where he had begun. After that his nurse came in and said that it was time for him to take his medicines and have his lunch, indicating to me that he needed a rest.

"This was one of his good days," she said as she led me to the door.

✠

Outside the Spears Funeral Home the sun was blasting down and I put in for a break at a strange Ethiopian café that sold, among other choices, espresso, American tuna fish sandwiches, hamburgers, sushi, and a wide selection of East African dishes. I ordered an Italian soda and sat at an outdoor table, watching the street pass.

All the world seemed to cross here in our time. Along with students of various Asian and European nationalities, there were people from Central and South America, as well as Russians, Middle Easterners, black women of undetermined African nations in long white robes and head scarves, and even a few of the remnant of Irish, the original inhabitants of this old neighborhood. These latter were all older and looked stolid and very white in the hot July sun.

While I was sitting there, on the other side of the street a man in a gorilla suit emerged from the back door of a church, unlocked his bicycle from an iron rail, and pedaled off toward Central Square.

No one even watched him pedal by.

On the other side of the street, an older Asian man in black Chinese slippers stopped two young black boys and asked them something. After they answered they trotted off, their heads together, glancing back at the old gentleman. He must have asked a senile question. He asked the next person, an older white man who held the Asian man's elbow as he answered and pointed westward, making zigzags with his right arm. Then the Asian gentleman asked a third person, a middle-aged black woman, who enfolded his right hand in hers while she stood talking with him.

While I was watching this interchange, the Queen of Sheba strode by. She was an exquisitely beautiful Ethiopian woman with smooth dark skin, high cheekbones, long dreadlocked hair fixed with white cowry shells, and large golden hooped earrings. She was wearing a light shift that revealed the power of her muscled legs and she walked with graceful long strides, her shoulders squared and her chin uptilted. In contrast to the gorilla man, everyone turned to look after she passed—women, young men, old men, and even the doddering Asian man.

Ardis Spears would probably know who she was.

On my route again, I saw a modest black limousine turn onto Cottage Street and recognized the driver from a photograph George Alexander had shown me. He was the son of Ardis Spears. In the photograph of Mary Gilbert's wedding he is the one escorting the 80-year-old bride from this same vehicle. He was older now and heavier, and I may not have recognized him except that I was recently introduced to him by his mother. He works for the funeral home and attends many of the services. So does Tom Allen, Mr. Gilbert's old neighbor, who took up the work after he retired from the postal service.

At the Broadway intersection, I decided to change course. It was late by now, the museum would be closing up, so I turned right and went down to Gilbert's old homestead instead. On Inman Street Tom Allen was out in his side yard poking at something with a rake.

By this time I did not have to reintroduce myself and we chatted on about the heat, and the changes in the neighborhood—one of his favorite subjects—and then the old days, and then, finally, the Gilbert family.

Tom Allen still rides his bicycle at least twelve miles a day, and chops the air energetically when he talks. He and George Alexander were the last living individuals I met who have any memory of Robert A. Gilbert, and virtually every one of them agrees to the word with the written descriptions of this man: including the attempted disparaging characterization of Gilbert at the hands of Mr. F. Scott Fitzgerald. He was, in sum, the last gentleman.

✠

January 7th of 1942 was a bitterly chill day in Boston. Extreme cold had been gripping New England for almost a week, and on the seventh the thermometer plummeted to the lowest point in six years. The Charles River froze over, ice appeared in the inner harbor, and strange flights of Iceland gulls appeared on the outer islands, according to the records of the Massachusetts Audubon Society. Photos of Boston Harbor taken during this cold spell show fishing vessels, in from Georges Bank, their rigging and deckhouses iced over with salt spray so that they look for all the world like ghost ships or messengers from some unearthly world of ice spirits.

Things had changed in Gilbert's Inman Square neighborhood by 1942. The young men had disappeared from the streets and were overseas fighting in another war. At the museum, Thomas Barbour was personally questioning in his journals the ultimate meaning of his obsession with the study of obscure species of frogs and snails while men were slaughtering each other around the world. There were some new faces working at the museum, including a new

Russian lepidopterist named Vladimir Nabokov, who would periodically attend the luncheons at the Eateria. (No mention of Gilbert in his journals, however.)

Back in Gilbert's old haunts in Paris, in 1942, Nazi officers crowded into the Montmartre bistros and clubs, calling for the best champagnes and the wildest shows. By 1929, with Wall Street spiraling, the American party had started to break up in Paris, the would-be writers had given up and gone home, the successful ones went off looking for other adventures. Although the American black musicians had stayed on after the Depression hit France in 1931, they all fled the city with the coming of the Germans. Jazz had been banned as degenerate music by the Nazis, and blacks were subjected to some of the same regulations that attempted to control French Jews. In spite of restrictions forbidding Negroes from performing in nightclubs and theaters, or moving between zones, some stayed on in other parts of France or went south through Vichy and then took ship for the repressive but relatively safe sanctuary of America. A few simply went underground in Paris. One older black expatriate actually stayed on at his old job at the transport offices, working under the nose of the German officers.

As 1942 opened, the Japanese were undertaking terrorist raids throughout the Pacific. In the Philippines, their machine gunners had leveled seven defenseless villages, and on January 7th Franklin Roosevelt called for fifty-six billion dollars for the war effort, and the Office of Price Management was predicting a twenty-five percent increase in the income tax. Most Americans were willing to support whatever it took to smash the enemy.

That morning, huddled in his robe and a muffler, Mr. Gilbert took a breakfast of buttered toast and coddled eggs, but feeling tired, and unwilling to face the cold, decided not to walk to work. He spent the day puttering around his darkroom, playing the piano, reading *A Farewell to Arms,* written by the burly man he believed he had once encountered in the Dingo Bar. But he took two naps that day and was still tired at dinner. In fact he told Mary he did not feel well, and did not eat much. He knew the symptoms of flu, he said, and calculated that he had something gnawing at his ankles, as he used to say, and retired early.

As was his custom, before he got into bed he knelt at the bedside, folded his hands, and said, as a matter of rote, his customary prayer—"If I should die before I wake," he concluded, "I pray the Lord my soul to take."

When the paganistic William Brewster was languishing and near his end, his prophetic dreams were based on pre-Christian imagery: He dreamed of the River Styx, the dark shore beyond, with his companion dog awaiting his arrival.

We do not know what dreams or visions Mr. Gilbert experienced in the last, tired days of his life. Perhaps, as with so many older displaced southern blacks, as he dozed in his chair he was dully aware of a vague, sweet scent of flowering trees and shrubs, filtering down from the green hills above the valley of Broad Creek, and perhaps he heard again the trill of the cardinal, the Carolina wren, and the warbling nightsong of the mockingbird. Gilbert died alone, in his sleep, and since he never woke, we, of course, have no way of knowing what hallucinatory reveries passed before his dimmed eyes. But given the hymns, the prayers, legends, and painted images of his deep Christian faith, we might imagine what he would have expected. You can see images of his final hour on the walls of Ardis Spears' funeral home, in religious leaflets and illustrated editions of the Bible.

Sometime late in that last night, when all was quiet in the house, when the delivery wagons of Mr. Weisman did not pass, and the city slept, perhaps he opened his eyes and saw that the sky over Cambridge had parted; the overcast pall of winter clouds had pulled back like a curtain to reveal a clear golden light, brighter than the desert sun. Out from the goldleafed clouds, in a glistering chariot drawn by white steeds, he would have seen a company of angels, all in white, passing through a cerulean sky. The driver is a woman with loosed hair, and as the chariot heaves across the heavens, she glances down, sees Mr. Gilbert in his bed, and turns the heads of the white horses earthward. The chariot arcs across the firmament, slows, and swings low, crossing over the Harbor Islands, over the spiky towers of Boston, over the Charles, and as it passes over Inman Street, the angels bend and hoist the fragile dark frame of Robert Alexander Gilbert aboard, comforting him in their arms. The thrashing horses, held in check by the charioteer, snort and throw back their heads, anxious to be off. Then, urged by the angel at the reins, they bunch into a full gallop and mount higher and higher into the blue rift and disappear into the light.

The winter clouds of New England filtered and spun after the chariot passed, the curtain drew closed, and night returned to Cambridge.

Mary found the shell of his soul in the morning when he did not appear for breakfast.

✠

The death of Mr. Gilbert did not go unnoticed in the white community. Students who worked at the museum knew Gilbert well and remembered him in an obituary in the student paper, the *Harvard Crimson.* In particular, a 1932 graduate named William Harrison felt compelled to announce his passing to "Harvard men of several generations." He used, as did so many of the encomiums, the language of the day—praising "this ingenious Negro's skill" and his "courtly manners and instinctive courtesy."

The *Boston Herald* lauded his work at the museum and his long association with Brewster, and also made it quite clear in the lead sentence that this talented man was "a Negro." Interestingly, two of Gilbert's obituaries compare him to the unnamed black man who taught Charles Darwin the art of taxidermy. Only one of the papers, the black-owned *Boston Chronicle,* made no mention of his race.

Services for Mr. Gilbert were held on Saturday, January 19th, at the A. E. Long Memorial Chapel in North Cambridge. As he would have wished, the ceremony was subdued, a display of flowers, Episcopal hymns, and a reading from The Book of Common Prayer. But there were tears at the end of the service. With the organ backing her in slow cadences, Mary sang his old favorite, "Just a Closer Walk with Thee," and no one present refrained from taking out their handkerchiefs.

He was interred at Cambridge Cemetery beneath the stone where his wife and son and Anna's aunt lay buried. There were many friends and family members there that day, and although there is no record of this, it is my guess that no white people were in attendance, inasmuch as there were none left alive who remembered Gilbert in his finest years when he tramped the fields and forest paths with the likes of William Brewster and his company of sharp-eyed ornithologists.

After her father died, Mary stayed on in the house with her current husband, Carl Williams, and lived there for the next fifty years. None of Mr. Gilbert's daughters ever had children, but the sisters would continue to meet at the house on Inman Street over the years and became, as was their father, a part of the black middle-class community of Cambridge. The Gilbert sisters were known throughout the town, even into North Cambridge, which had a growing population of island people and had developed a separate cultural and social system of its own, with different churches and different community leaders.

Many of the young black men of Cambridge had joined the military and gone off to the fight by the time Gilbert died. But the struggle for black equality was hardly over in these years. On the same front page of the *Boston Chronicle* announcing the passing of the "Famed Harvard Zoologist" Robert A. Gilbert, there was a news piece about an order from the War Department calling for the death penalty for white and "colored" males and females who engaged in sexual relations, whether voluntary or not. After a vociferous protest from the NAACP, the order was withdrawn, the article said.

✠

I asked Tom Allen again about his mother and her friendship with Mary Gilbert and about the Sunday afternoons at the house after her father died.

"Oh, they carried on all right," he said. "But it wasn't the same. The old man, you know, he was like some old preacher. You see him coming, you straighten up. Got looser in there, I think, after he died. My mother and Mary used to laugh a lot. Then Mama died, then old Mr. Williams, Mary's husband died. And then along comes George Alexander. I didn't know him very well, though, just read about them getting married in the papers. Eighty years old. There was a picture of them kissing. That was good times. Then Mary dies. She wasn't even that old either. Only eighty-two."

"That's young, isn't it?" I said. I had Tom in mind, he was closing in on eighty himself.

"These days, yeah. Me, I figure I'm just going to live until I die."

After Mary's death, George Alexander, who was too old to live alone by then, sold the house and moved in with his foster daughter, Madelon Winston. Mary's sisters had predeceased her, and when Mary died, in 1992, the Robert Gilbert genetic line, nurtured for a thousand generations through the rise and decline of the great kingdoms of Dahomey, the slave raids, the squalid holding pens on the beaches of Ouida, the Middle Passage, five generations of American slavery, and on up into the relative freedom of Boston, where the line could have established an American identity for itself, after all this, that singular genetic code passed from existence.

"After old George moved out an antique man from somewhere

in New Hampshire came down here and bought the entire contents of the house," Tom said. "Mr. Gilbert's old piano, dining room table. Chairs. You name it, he bought it. Now they're who knows where. Then one day I see a dumpster out in front of the house. They thrown everything that was left in that thing," he said.

"His personal photographs?"

"Yeah, probably. Photos. Books, files, letters about I don't know what. I seen them. Everything what was left—all went in that dumpster."

"You mean all his letters, his pictures too?" I asked.

"Everything. Truck come the next day and hauled it all off and that was the end."

He paused and looked down the street to the former Gilbert mansard-roofed house. A spotted dog at the end of a long leash emerged from a driveway a few doors down from the Gilbert place followed by a tall white woman in jeans and dark glasses. They turned left and moved down the street away from us, then disappeared around the corner of Cambridge Street.

"I guess that's the way it goes," Tom said.

"A whole life," I said.

"Hey. A whole generation," he said.

EPILOGUE

The River

IN ORDER TO DESIGNATE REALITY, BUDDHISM SAYS SUNYA,

THE VOID; BUT BETTER STILL: TATHATA . . .

THE FACT OF BEING THIS, OF BEING THUS, OF BEING SO . . .

Roland Barthes

Unidentified, undated. Great Meadows?

The school of photographers known as the pictorialists would have appreciated the river Charles in autumn. On certain days there, mists and clouds roll down from the upper reaches of the watershed, softening the arches of the bridges and blurring the hard edges of the buildings of Boston, muting all color to a few monochrome shades that range from off-white to dark gray to absolute black.

The shutter snaps and the water turns to marble. Dark leaves hang on the old sycamores that line Memorial Drive, and out on the river the shells of the college students are halted, the rowers leaning forward on their oars, caught eternally in midstroke.

On November 3rd, 2001, small nervous flocks of wild ducks had settled on the wide expanses at the southwestern curve of the river, just upstream from the Eliot Bridge. Close by the banks, in Longfellow Park, white-throated sparrows were sounding out their plaintive little descending whistles, and back from the river, in the shaded islands of Mount Auburn Cemetery, I could hear the chips of savannah sparrows, the checks and clicks of passing myrtle warblers, and the hollow, popping call of the resident chipmunks. At a turning in one of the paths, a vast company of blackbirds rolled through in a chattering flock and settled on the bare branches of the oaks and the tulip trees, squawking and rasping among themselves. As I watched, for no apparent reason, they suddenly rose up in a body and spirited through the trees and shrubs, banked once, and then flowed out over the treetops to the river in a shifting dark stream.

The sometime photographer Oliver Wendell Holmes is buried at Mount Auburn Cemetery. So is the Atlantic Monthly founder, James T. Fields, as well as his associate, George Ticknor, and Henry Wadsworth Longfellow, the poet James Russell Lowell, the novelist William Dean Howells, and many of the other literary and intellectual lights of nineteenth-century America.

William Brewster is also buried here. My first frame, shot from a low angle, shows the rough landscape of his gravestone, the pink granite boulder unshaped by human hands, with wind-stripped oak branches above, a few late-clinging leaves suspended from the bare limbs like sleeping bats.

The second frame is a close-up with the name: William Brewster. Also his epitaph:

"For lo, the winter is past, the flowers appear on the earth; the time of the singing of birds is come . . ."

The next frame is a wide shot of the Mount Auburn Cemetery landscape, with a narrow, curving pathway winding under the skeletal beeches, the glowing white of the monumental tombs incised with twining vines, fluted pilasters and architraves, and many of the stones surmounted with ornamental urns. We see the dark islands of rhododendrons, a marble angel, half-hidden in the shrubbery, her wings spread backward, and in the distance, near a straight-trunked oak, a high marble pillar with a figure on top.

The fourth frame, taken from a rise, shows a foreground of trees and shrubs, the gray river with the silver cliff dwellings of Boston beyond, and above that a misty white nothingness, where all things are possible.

Although it too has its share of honored dead, Henry and William James, for example, the Cambridge Cemetery, which lies closer to the river, on the south side of Coolidge Avenue, is less prestigious; you will see, along with the old New England inscriptions, the names of Germans, Poles, Italians, and Swedes. Also a few Irish Protestants. And although death has equalized the races and the names are the same as those of the old English families, you will also find buried here a number of African Americans.

Inside the gates, two or three hundred yards to the south, is an unadorned tombstone with three family names inscribed on its plain marble face. Any stranger passing idly through this graveyard and happening upon this particular grave, reading the inscribed names, would not know that there are in fact four people buried beneath that stone. Three of them are listed, but the name of the fourth individual is unmarked. As with so many of the facts of the life of this invisible man, you have to search to find his identity. You'll find him listed in the cemetery offices, in a thick record book with the inventory of burials for January, 1942:

"Robert A. Gilbert, Plot 12, Lot 4. Monbretia Path. January 13th, 1942."

My last frame shows the Gilbert family grave. It is a squared-off, plain gravestone with a twining daisy chain running up the right and left sides and arching over to meet at the top. You see a few flecks of lichens, the unambitious sans serif lettering, and above, viewed through the lens from a low angle, a flare of branches rising upward like a fountain.

Beyond the gravestone, beyond the cemetery, a few hundred yards to the south, the dark river of grackles and redwings shifts, curves in a lazy bend, turns, and heads back for the Cambridge shore.

Below them, the Charles rolls down to the sea.

Postscript

William Brewster's personal diaries, field journals, letters, books, and an extensive collection of his own photo albums are located in the Ernst Mayr Library at the Harvard Museum of Natural History, the former Museum of Comparative Zoology.

In 1998, the Brewster and Gilbert glass plate negatives were removed from the attic in Lincoln and placed in a climate-controlled art storage facility at the Massachusetts Audubon Society's Visual Art Center, in Canton, Massachusetts.

In 2002, George Alexander, the last relative (by marriage) of Robert Gilbert, died at home at the age of 101.

October Farm is still privately owned, but the lands are being restored, and many of Brewster's artifacts, including his old Rushton canoe, have been preserved.

In the mid-1990s, after Sanfred Bensen's death, Colburn Bensen put the property up for sale. After much negotiation and many offers and counteroffers, the town of Concord purchased most of the riverfront land for conservation. The old house, which was determined to be an early eighteenth-century structure with a gunstock stud wall, was carefully dismantled piece by piece and now languishes in storage in two truck containers, waiting to be reborn.

In the autumn of 2001, carrying my old camera, I went down to the former house site. The tangle of bittersweet, arborvitae, maples, and blackberries that once threatened to overwhelm the homestead had been cleared away, along with the house, and the grounds had been regraded and planted to grass. All that was left to photograph in place of Sanfred Bensen and his dog was the wind and the empty sky.

Acknowledgments

Research Assistant: Jill G. Brown

Informants: Frank Adams, George Alexander, Thomas Allen, Jim Baird, Reinier and Nancy Beeuwkes, Ellie Bemis, Sanfred Bensen, John Blackwell, Ann Blum, Billy Bunting, "Cappy" (in the Tuileries Gardens), Adelaide Cromwell, Celeste d'Arquin, Franklin Dorman, Father Nelson Fox, Roland Gibson, Frank Golhke, Ulysses Gore, Suzanne Greene, Donald Griffin, Wayne Hanley, Ruth Hill, Della Hardman, Richard Johnson, Joan Kaufman (Mount Auburn Cemetery archivist), Judy and Jonathan Keyes, Lillian Kiner, David Lakari, Merloyd Lawrence, Ivan Masser, Ernst Mayr, Lawrence Millman, James Archibald Mitchell, Hugh Morgan and family, Lansing Old, "Pierre" (in Juan-les-Pins), "Priscilla" (Inman Square), Ardis Spears, "Spiff" (in Paris), Mario Valdez, Kathleen Walcott with the Ethnic Foundation, George Whitman, Tremont W. Williams, Buster and Marge Williamson, Deborah Willis, Lieutenant Johnny Wilson, Madelon Winston, Gwendolyn Wood. Dana Fisher and Robert Young at the Museum of Comparative Zoology archives, Jayne Gordon, Martine and Julian Crandall-Hollick, Amy Montague, Emily Walden, and Steve Landry at the Visual Art Center. Aurore Eaton at the Cambridge Historical Society, Anita Israel at the Longfellow House, Kit Rawlins at the Cambridge Historical Commission, Richard Newman at the Du Bois Center, Leslie Wilson (Concord Library archivist), Marilyn Richardson

Generous grants from: The Nathaniel and Elizabeth P. Stevens Foundation, The Claneil Foundation, and The Charles Engelhardt Foundation. Brewster/Gilbert photographs courtesy of the Massachusetts Audubon Society's Visual Art Center, Canton, MA.